THE YOUNG
STUDENT'S DICTIONARY

THE YOUNG
STUDENT'S
DICTIONARY

WHEATON *of* EXETER

PREFACE

BOOKS are among man's most treasured possessions. They provide an unfailing source of pleasure and information and it is never too early to start building up a personal library of well-loved stories and reliable reference books. Some of these will be read again and again and give a life-time of enjoyment, while others will be discarded to make room for better, more grown-up books.

But suppose your personal library had to consist of only a single book. Which book should it be?

There can be only one answer. A dictionary!

You will naturally want to own many of your favourite books, but you will probably read a great many more books than you can ever buy and there is scarcely a village or hamlet that does not nowadays have its public library.

But your dictionary is the indispensable tool that will enable you to prise out the treasure from our great gold-mine of literature. If you cultivate the habit of using it regularly there is no knowledge that need not be yours. Even the most difficult books can be made to give up their secrets.

This dictionary contains over 9,000 words—far more than the average person ever uses in ordinary speech or writing—and it will give you all the help you need for a very long time. Some day you will want a more grown-up dictionary, but, until you do, may this little book share with you many happy hours.

USING THE DICTIONARY

When you are reading a book and come across a word you do not understand it is unwise to just skip the word and go on reading. Sometimes, the sentence in which the word is used will help you to guess its meaning, but more often than not you will miss some important point in the story. What is even worse is that you will miss an opportunity to add a new word to your vocabulary—your personal stock of words.

If you take the trouble to look up the word in your dictionary you will enjoy your book much more, and next time you write a composition you may be able to make your work more interesting by using that very word.

"The contraband was found in the crypt of the old church."

Suppose that you have just read that sentence in your book and you are not sure what the word *contraband* means.

Open your dictionary and find the section containing words beginning with **C**. Now turn your attention to the words printed in bold capitals at the top of each page. You will see that these are the first and last words to be found on that page.

One of the pages has **CONTAIN** and **CONTRACT,** and, as the words are arranged in alphabetical order, the word *contraband* must be on that page. Run your eye down the side of the page and you will find the word you want near the bottom.

Immediately after the word **contraband** you will see (*con'-tra-band*). From the way this word in brackets is divided you can tell that it has three syllables. In other words, it must be said in three parts. The little mark after the first syllable (*con'*) tells you that this is the syllable that must be emphasized.

You might have to look up the word *crypt* as well, but this time you will find that there is no word in brackets after it.

This is because the word *crypt* has only one syllable and it is impossible to divide such words into smaller parts.

Very often a word has several different meanings and you will have to read the sentence very carefully to find which meaning is intended.

"Joan was delighted when her arithmetic book came back covered with ticks."

"The few cattle that grazed on the scant grass were covered with ticks."

All the time you spend learning new words is time very well spent. The more words you know, the better able you will be to express yourself and the more easily you will be able to understand what you read in books and newspapers and what you hear on the radio or on television. Indeed, some people say that the whole business of education consists of learning a lot of new words. There is a great deal of truth in that, too, for if you knew the meaning of every word in the dictionary, what a well-educated person you would be!

THE YOUNG
STUDENT'S DICTIONARY

A

aback *(a-back')*. When someone is taken aback, he is surprised.

abandon *(a-ban'-don)*. To give up; to desert. When sailors leave a sinking ship, they are said to abandon it.

abate *(a-bate')*. To grow less; to make less. We speak of floods abating when the water level falls.

abattoir *(ab-at-toir' or ab'-at-toir)*. A building where butchers may kill cattle.

abbey *(ab'-bey)*. A monastery or convent in which monks or nuns live. The church belonging to such a monastery is, itself, often spoken of as an abbey.

abbot *(ab'-bot)*. The leader or chief person in a monastery. The feminine form is **abbess,** the head of a convent.

abbreviate *(ab-bre'-vi-ate)*. To shorten. We usually speak of abbreviating words, and the short form of the word is called the **abbreviation** *(ab-bre-vi-a'-tion)*. Fri. is the abbreviation for Friday, and lb. is the abbreviation for pound.

abdicate *(ab'-di-cate)*. To give up; most often used of a monarch's giving up his throne. King Edward VIII abdicated his throne in 1936.

abdomen *(ab-do'-men or ab'-do-men)*. 1. The lower part of the body, which contains the organs of digestion. 2. An insect's body consists of three parts: the head, the thorax, or middle section, and the abdomen.

abduct *(ab-duct')*. To lead away unlawfully; to kidnap. The act of abducting someone is called **abduction.**

abhor *(ab-hor')*. To dislike very much; to detest.

abide *(a-bide')*. 1. To stay with; remain. 2. "I cannot abide" means "I cannot put up with".

ability *(a-bil'-i-ty)*. The power or skill needed to do something. A clever pupil has ability in many subjects, and he will do well if he works well.

ablaze *(a-blaze')*. On fire. "The building was ablaze when the firemen arrived."

3

able *(a'-ble)*. To be able is to have the power. People are able to walk but they are unable to fly as a bird can fly.

ablution *(ab-lu'-tion)*. The act of washing.

abnormal *(ab-nor'-mal)*. Not normal or ordinary.

aboard *(a-board')*. On board. "The passengers climbed aboard the train."

abode *(a-bode')*. The place where a person lives. Your house is your abode.

abolish *(a-bol'-ish)*. To do away with.

abound *(a-bound')*. To be plentiful. Fish abound in the sea.

above *(a-bove')*. Over.

abridge *(a-bridge')*. To shorten. Thus a pocket dictionary is made by abridging a large dictionary.

abroad *(a-broad')*. 1. Overseas; to or in a foreign country, such as America or France. "His journey abroad took him to France." 2. Far and wide, as in "The news of the St. Lawrence Seaway spread abroad". 3. Out of doors, as in "He walked abroad every morning".

abrupt *(ab-rupt')*. Anything that comes suddenly is abrupt. A steep hill is abrupt. When someone speaks **abruptly** to you, you may feel hurt.

abscess *(ab'-scess)*. A collection of pus in the body.

abscond *(ab-scond')*. To go away hurriedly and secretly.

absence *(ab'-sence)*. Being away. "Her absence from school was caused by sickness."

absentee *(ab-sen-tee')*. A person who should be present but who is away.

absolutely *(ab'-so-lute-ly)*. Entirely or completely. A broken light bulb is absolutely useless.

absolve *(ab-solve')*. To free a person from blame is to absolve him of blame.

absorb *(ab-sorb')*. To suck up. A sponge absorbs water and blotting paper absorbs ink.

abstain *(ab-stain')*. To refrain from doing a thing.

abstract. 1. *(ab-stract')*. To remove, perhaps secretly. "A thief abstracted the money from her purse." 2. *(ab'-stract)*. An idea is abstract. You cannot touch it, hear it, smell it, see it or taste it; it exists only in the mind. Goodness, justice and love are all abstract ideas.

absurd *(ab-surd')*. Silly or ridiculous.

abundant *(a-bun'-dant)*. Plentiful. A plentiful supply of something is an **abundance**.

abuse *(a-buse')*. 1. To make bad use of. 2. To speak unkindly of someone.

abut *(a-but')*. To put two things end to end so that they touch. When a house is built to touch another house, the two abut against each other.

abyss *(a-byss')*. A hole or cavity of great size.

academy *(a-cad'-e-my)*. 1. A school; a private school or a school where special subjects may be studied, such as a military academy. 2. A society of authors, artists, etc.

accede *(ac-cede')*. If someone accedes to your wishes, he gives in to or agrees with them.

accelerate *(ac-cel'-er-ate)*. To go faster and faster; to increase speed.

accent *(ac'-cent)*. 1. A mark placed over one or more letters in a word to show emphasis. If the word ac'-cent be taken as an example, it will be seen that the mark follows the ac'; thus the word must be pronounced AC-cent and not ac-CENT. 2. A local way of speaking. The accent used in the south of England is different from the accent used in the north.

accentuate *(ac-cen'-tu-ate)*. To emphasize or stress; to do what the accent on a word tells you to do. (See **accent**.)

acceptable *(ac-cept'-a-ble)*. To accept is to take what is offered you, and a thing is acceptable when it is worth taking.

accessible *(ac-ces'-si-ble)*. Easy to reach; easy to obtain.

accessory *(ac-ces'-so-ry)*. 1. Helping or contributing in a small way. 2. Something which helps or contributes in such a way. A light, for example, is an accessory to a bicycle. 3. A person who helps another to commit a crime, but takes no actual part in it himself, is called an accessory to the crime.

accident *(ac'-ci-dent)*. 1. Something that happens unexpectedly or by chance. 2. A mishap or disaster.

acclaim *(ac-claim')*. 1. To clap or cheer. 2. To hail someone as king, conqueror, etc., with cheers. 3. Applause (see **applaud**).

acclimatize *(ac-cli'-ma-tize)*. To cause to become used to the climate. "When he first came to England from the Congo he found the winter very cold, but he has now become acclimatized and doesn't mind the cold."

accommodate *(ac-com'-mo-date)*. 1. To provide a person with the things he wants. 2. To provide lodgings or make room for.

accommodation *(ac-com-mo-da'-tion)*. Lodgings or other necessities. (See **accommodate**.)

accompany *(ac-com'-pa-ny)*. 1. To escort, as "The man accompanied his wife to the opera". 2. In music, to play or sing with, as "Mrs. Hughes accompanied the violinist by playing the piece on the piano".

accomplice *(ac-com'-plice)*. One who helps another to commit a crime.

accomplish *(ac-com'-plish)*. To complete or do something; to succeed in doing something.

accord *(ac-cord')*. 1. To agree. 2. To give a person something, as "They accorded the tribute to the victor". 3. If people are said to be in accord, they are in agreement.

accordion *(ac-cor'-di-on)*. 1. A musical instrument which has a bellows, reeds and a keyboard. It is usually held over the chest when being played and shoulder straps hold it to the body. 2. Having folds like a bellows of an accordion, as accordion pleats in a skirt.

accost *(ac-cost')*. To stop a person and speak to him.

account *(ac-count')*. 1. In "He gave an account of his travels", account means description. 2. In "The baker handed in his account", account means bill or charge for bread. 3. In "He accounted for his absence", accounted for means explained.

accumulate *(ac-cu'-mu-late)*. To collect or gather together.

accumulator *(ac-cu'-mu-la-tor)*. 1. Anything that gathers together. 2. A battery for storing electricity.

accuracy *(ac'-cu-ra-cy)*. Correctness or exactness.

accurate *(ac'-cu-rate)*. Correct; without mistake.

accuse *(ac-cuse')*. To blame; to tell a person he has done something wrong.

accustom *(ac-cus'-tom)*. To cause to get used to a thing.

ace. 1. A playing card, of high value in most games, marked by a single spot. 2. An expert. 3. A skilled fighter pilot.

ache. A pain which continues, such as a toothache.

achieve *(a-chieve')*. To reach a goal; to succeed in doing something, usually something difficult.

acid *(ac'-id)*. 1. Sour. 2. In chemistry, a substance having a sharp or sour taste. Vinegar, for example, is an acid. Strong acids have the power to eat away metal.

acknowledge *(ac-knowl'-edge)*. 1. To admit. 2. To recognize. 3. To say "thank you" for something.

acorn *(a'-corn)*. The fruit, seed or nut of the oak tree.

acoustics *(a-cous'-tics)*. The science dealing with sounds and hearing.

acquaint *(ac-quaint')*. To make aware of or familiar with.

acquaintance *(ac-quaint'-ance)*. Someone known to you.

acquiesce *(ac-qui-esce')*. To agree to or agree with.

acquiescence *(ac-qui-es'-cence)*. The act of agreeing, as "The head teacher gave his acquiescence to our new plan".

acquire *(ac-quire')*. To obtain.

acquit *(ac-quit')*. To acquit someone of a crime is to declare that he is not guilty of it.

acre *(a'-cre)*. A piece of land measuring 160 square rods or 4,840 square yards.

acrid *(ac'-rid)*. Having a bitter or sharp taste or smell.

acrimonious *(ac-ri-mo'-ni-ous)*. Bitter in feeling.

acrobat *(ac'-ro-bat)*. A person who performs tricks that require agile limbs. A tight-rope walker is an acrobat.

action *(ac'-tion)*. 1. The doing of something. 2. Going into action means beginning something. Often it means going into battle.

active *(ac'-tive)*. Showing a busy, brisk or quick nature.

actor *(ac'-tor)*. A man who plays a part, usually on a stage. The feminine form is **actress**.

actual *(ac'-tu-al)*. Real.

actually *(ac'-tu-al-ly)*. Really; in fact.

actuary *(act'-u-ar-y)*. A person who has the necessary training to be able to deal with the tables of figures used by insurance companies.

actuate *(act'-u-ate)*. To make active. Thus the balance wheel of a watch is actuated by the mainspring.

acute *(a-cute')*. 1. Sharp or pointed. Any angle measuring less than 90 degrees is an acute angle. 2. Severe; thus one might complain if one had an acute pain in the chest.

adage *(ad'-age)*. A maxim, proverb or well-known saying. "It takes two to make a quarrel" is an adage.

adamant *(ad'-a-mant)*. 1. A substance that is hard; thus a diamond is adamant. 2. A person is adamant when nothing can make him change his mind.

adapt *(a-dapt')*. To alter a thing so that it serves some new use. This word must not be confused with **adept** or **adopt.**

addend *(ad'-dend)*. A number that is to be added to another.

adder *(ad'-der)*. 1. A poisonous viper of Europe. 2. A small, harmless snake of North America.

addict *(ad'-dict)*. A person who is devoted to some habit so strongly that he is unable to give it up. We say he is **addicted** *(ad-dict'-ed)* to the habit.

addition *(ad-di'-tion)*. 1. 2 + 2 = 4 is an exercise in addition. In addition two or more things are added together. 2. Something added, as "The family found the house too small; so they made it bigger by the addition of several rooms".

addle *(ad'-dle)*. 1. To make a thing go wrong or bad. 2. To muddle.

address *(ad-dress')*. 1. The location of a house; in the town it usually consists of the name and number of the street. 2. When you address a letter you write on the outside of the envelope the name of the person to whom it is being sent and where he lives. 3. To address a person is to speak to him. 4. A speech.

adenoids *(ad'-e-noids)*. Growths of spongy tissue in the throat behind the nose. They may interfere with talking or breathing.

adept. 1. *(ad'-ept)*. A person who is clever at doing a certain thing. 2. *(a-dept')*. Skilful.

adequate *(ad'-e-quate)*. Sufficient; enough.

adhere *(ad-here')*. 1. To stick. Glue and paste, for example, adhere to paper and are **adhesives.** They have the power of **adhesion.** 2. A person who follows some party, or holds some belief, is called an **adherent** to that party or belief.

adjacent *(ad-ja'-cent)*. Next to or touching.

adjective *(ad'-jec-tive)*. A word that tells something about a noun. Thus in "black cat", the word black is an adjective because it helps us to know a little more about the noun, cat.

adjourn *(ad-journ')*. To put off to another time; to postpone. "The meeting was adjourned" means the meeting ended for the time being but was to begin again at another time.

adjudicate *(ad-ju'-di-cate)*. To judge.

adjunct *(ad'-junct)*. A thing joined to another or added to it.

adjust *(ad-just')*. To set a thing right or make it correct.

administer *(ad-min'-is-ter)*. 1. To manage or direct the way something is carried out or looked after. 2. To administer justice is to see that justice is done. 3. To administer a remedy is to apply a remedy.

administration *(ad-min-is-tra'-tion)*. 1. The act of administering. 2. A group of people who administer; usually used of those in charge of a business or a government.

admirable *(ad'-mi-ra-ble)*. Worth admiring; excellent or very good.

admiral *(ad'-mir-al)*. The highest officer of a navy or a fleet of ships.

admiration *(ad-mi-ra'-tion)*. A feeling of respect, wonder or delight caused by the excellence of something or someone.

admire *(ad-mire')*. To regard with respect.

admission *(ad-mis'-sion)*. 1. The act of admitting or allowing to enter. 2. A confession.

admit *(ad-mit')*. 1. To allow to enter. 2. To accept as true, as in "I admit that the sky is usually blue". 3. To confess.

admittance *(ad-mit'-tance)*. The right to enter. You cannot gain admittance to a cinema if you have no money.

admonish *(ad-mon'-ish)*. 1. To scold. 2. To warn.

adobe *(a-do'-be)*. 1. Brick which has been dried in the sun. 2. A house made of sun-dried brick which is common in Mexico.

adolescence *(ad-o-les'-cence)*. Youth; the period of growth that comes directly after childhood.

adopt *(a-dopt')*. To take and look after. When a person adopts a child, he looks after the child as a parent would.

adore *(a-dore')*. To admire greatly; to love.

adorn *(a-dorn')*. To make beautiful; to decorate.

adrift *(a-drift')*. Floating or moving about without control.

adulation *(ad-u-la'-tion)*. Flattery; praise that is more than is reasonable.

adult *(a-dult'* or *a'-dult)*. 1. Fully grown up. 2. A fully grown up person.

adulterate *(a-dul'-ter-ate)*. To make some article impure by mixing another article with it, usually for dishonest purposes. For example, if a farmer mixed water in his milk in order to make the milk go further, he would be adulterating the milk.

advance *(ad-vance')*. 1. To go forward. 2. In the case of money, an advance is a payment made before the proper time.

advantage *(ad-van'-tage)*. 1. A condition favourable to success, as in "John has an advantage over the other boys in the basketball team because he is tall". 2. A benefit or gain.

adventure *(ad-ven'-ture)*. An experience of a thrilling kind; a bold undertaking.

adverb *(ad'-verb)*. A word that modifies a verb. In "He ran quickly", quickly is an adverb because it tells how he ran.

adversary *(ad'-ver-sa-ry)*. An enemy; an opponent; one who is not on your side.

adverse *(ad'-verse)*. 1. Opposite to what is wanted. 2. Unfriendly or hostile.

adversity *(ad-ver'-si-ty)*. Misfortune.

advertise *(ad'-ver-tise)*. To make known by public notice. The notice is an **advertisement** *(ad-ver'-tise-ment)*; the person who gives the notice is an **advertiser** *(ad'-ver-tis-er)*, and his action is that of **advertising** *(ad'-ver-tis-ing)*.

advice *(ad-vice')*. To make a suggestion or to offer an opinion is to give advice.

advise *(ad-vise')*. When a person gives advice, he advises.

adze. A tool formed like an axe used for chipping wood, etc. Its sharp edge is at right angles to the handle.

aerate *(aer'-ate)*. To cause air or gas to enter. When you loosen the earth in your garden you aerate it. Aerated soft drinks are filled with tiny bubbles of gas.

aerial *(aer'-i-al)*. 1. Belonging to the air. 2. A wire or rod connected to a radio or television set which picks up radio waves from the air. Sounds and pictures are sent through the air by means of these radio waves.

aerodrome *(aer'-o-drome)*. A piece of open, level ground where aircraft may take off or land.

aeroplane *(aer'-o-plane)*. A flying machine which carries passengers or freight from one place to another.

affable *(af'-fa-ble)*. To be affable is to speak and behave in a pleasant way.

affair *(af-fair')*. 1. Business; something to be done. "The manager has many affairs to attend to." 2. In "Tom's birthday party was a happy affair," affair means happening. 3. "That is my affair" means that is nobody's business but mine.

affect *(af-fect')*. To influence or have an effect upon. Disease affects the body.

affectation *(af-fec-ta'-tion)*. A manner or habit which is not natural but is deliberately put on. A person who has affectations is said to be **affected** *(af-fect'-ed)*. When we say that someone puts on airs and graces, we mean that that person is affected.

affection *(af-fec'-tion)*. Fondness, love. Anyone showing affection is **affectionate**.

affiliate *(af-fil'-i-ate)*. To unite a small body of people with a much larger, central body. Many local football clubs affiliate with certain leagues.

affirm *(af-firm')*. 1. To say strongly and definitely. 2. To make a formal declaration.

affirmative *(af-firm'-a-tive)*. That which agrees. An answer in the affirmative is "Yes". The opposite to affirmative is negative, when the answer is "No".

affix *(af-fix')*. To fasten or fix on.

afflict *(af-flict')*. To cause harm to. The person who suffers is **afflicted** and what he suffers from is an **affliction**.

affluence *(af'-flu-ence)*. Considerable wealth or riches.

afford *(af-ford')*. 1. In "He can afford to buy the car", afford means spare the money. 2. "She cannot afford to annoy the teacher again" means she cannot annoy the teacher again without being punished.

affray *(af-fray')*. A violent quarrel or fight.

affront *(af-front')*. 1. To insult. 2. An insult.

afloat *(a-float')*. Floating. A ship at sea is afloat.

afoot *(a-foot')*. 1. On foot or walking. 2. When it is said that mischief is afoot, the suggestion is that mischief is planned.

afraid *(a-fraid')*. Frightened; feeling fear.

afresh *(a-fresh')*. Again; anew.

aft. Towards the back part or stern of a ship.

afternoon *(af-ter-noon')*. The part of the day after the noon hour and before evening.

afterward *(af'-ter-ward)*. Later.

against *(a-gainst')*. 1. From an opposite direction to, or in an opposite direction to. "The aeroplane takes off against the wind." 2. Close or touching. "Place the chair against the wall." 3. Upon. "The rain beat against the window." 4. "She went out against my orders" means she went out even though I had ordered her to stay inside.

age. 1. In "His age was five years", age means the length of time he had lived. 2. Age also means a long period of time in the past, such as the Great Ice Age. 3. To come of age is to become 21 years old.

agent *(a'-gent)*. A person who does business for another person or company. A travel agent will book a sea passage or a hotel room for you.

aggravate *(ag'-gra-vate)*. 1. To make worse. In "The boy aggravated his misdeeds by telling lies", aggravated means made worse. 2. To annoy or exasperate.

aggregate *(ag'-gre-gate)*. 1. The sum total. 2. To collect together.

aggressor *(ag-gres'-sor)*. One who starts a quarrel is an aggressor; his actions show that he is **aggressive** and takes part in **aggression.**

aggrieve *(ag-grieve')*. To cause grief to or to injure.

aghast *(a-ghast')*. Amazed or struck with horror.

agile *(ag'-ile)*. Able to move quickly. An agile person has **agility** *(a-gil'-i-ty)*.

agitate *(ag'-i-tate)*. 1. To stir up; to set in motion, as "The wind agitated the surface of the pond". 2. To agitate for something is to attempt to obtain something by stirring up public feeling or interest.

agony *(ag'-o-ny)*. Intense pain. Anything that causes agony is **agonizing.**

agree *(a-gree')*. To consent; to be of one mind about something, as "They agreed to be friends again". They had an **agreement.**

agriculture *(ag'-ri-cul-ture)*. Farming; the cultivation of land for growing crops and rearing livestock.

aground *(a-ground')*. On the ground, as "The ship ran aground", meaning that the ship became caught in the bed of the sea or river and could not move.

ail. To be ill.

aileron *(ail'-er-on)*. A movable flap on the wing of an aeroplane by means of which the pilot can make the aeroplane bank to the right or left.

aim. 1. To point or direct, as "He aimed the rifle at the target". 2. Purpose, as "The boy's aim was to become a doctor".

aircraft *(air'-craft)*. A flying machine of any kind.

airily *(air'-i-ly)*. In a gay, light-hearted manner.

airport *(air'-port)*. A landing place for aeroplanes.

aisle. A path between two rows of seats or along a wall.

ajar *(a-jar')*. Not quite shut; open a little. A door is often said to be ajar when it is not properly shut.

akin *(a-kin')*. Related to; belonging to the same family. Things are said to be akin when they are alike.

alacrity *(a-lac'-ri-ty)*. Liveliness; briskness. A person who does a thing with alacrity does it quickly and cheerfully.

alarm *(a-larm')*. 1. To alarm is to cause sudden fear. 2. An alarm is a sudden warning. An alarm is **alarming**.

albeit *(al-be'-it)*. Although; even though; in spite of.

album *(al'-bum)*. A book in which to place a collection of photographs, stamps, autographs, etc.

alcohol *(al'-co-hol)*. The spirit in such liquids as brandy, wine and beer. Without alcohol, no drink is intoxicating.

alcove *(al'-cove)*. A space in a room set back into a wall; a niche.

alderman *(al'-der-man)*. A senior person elected to the council of a town or city by the councillors.

alert *(a-lert')*. 1. Watchful, wide-awake. 2. On the alert means ready for anything that may happen.

alga *(al'ga)*. Any plant in a large group of water plants which includes seaweeds. The plural form, **algae** is used more commonly than the singular.

algebra *(al'-ge-bra)*. An advanced form of arithmetic in which letters as well as numbers are used.

alias *(a'-li-as)*. The name by which a person is known but which is not his correct name. Thus, if a man calls himself Jones and his real name is Smith, the name Jones is an alias.

alibi *(al'-i-bi)*. If a person claims that he was somewhere else when a crime was committed he is presenting an alibi.

alien *(a'-li-en)*. Any person who does not belong to the country in which he happens to be; thus a Belgian or a Turk becomes an alien on entering this country and we become aliens when we go to Belgium or Turkey.

alienate *(a'-li-en-ate)*. To destroy the friendship of two people and cause them to be enemies.

alight *(a-light')*. 1. In "The house is alight", alight means on fire or lighted up. 2. In "Passengers must not alight while the train is in motion", alight means get down.

alive *(a-live')*. Not dead, as "My aunt is alive but my uncle is dead".

alkali *(al'-ka-li)*. A substance such as potash, soda or ammonia which is opposite in character to an acid. When placed with an acid, the alkali will neutralise the acid and form a salt.

allay *(al-lay')*. 1. To make less. 2. To relieve; to calm, as in "Her fears were allayed when she heard he was safe and sound".

allege *(al-lege')*. To declare; thus a person who declares something alleges it, and what he declares is an **allegation** *(al-le-ga'-tion)*.

allegiance *(al-le'-giance)*. The loyalty a person has for his country or for a cause.

allegory *(al'-le-go-ry)*. A story in which the characters and happenings stand for deeper ideas than those apparently presented. Aesop's fables are simple allegories, and some stories in the Bible, such as the story of the Prodigal Son, are allegories.

allergy *(al'-ler-gy)*. An unusual or serious sensitivity of the body to some substance, as "The boy developed a rash because he had an allergy to strawberries".

alleviate *(al-le'-vi-ate)*. To relieve, in the sense that food relieves hunger and medicine relieves pain.

alley *(al'-ley)*. 1. A narrow passage-way. 2. A place for bowling. 3. A ball-shaped piece of marble or glass used to play certain games.

alliance *(al-li'-ance)*. A union or joining together of things. A marriage is an alliance.

alligator *(al'-li-ga-tor)*. A large reptile like a crocodile that lives in the warm, swampy regions of America.

alliteration *(al-lit-er-a'-tion)*. Repetition of the same initial letter or sound at the beginning of two or more consecutive words. An example of alliteration is "An Austrian army, awfully arrayed, boldly by battery besieged Belgrade".

allocate *(al'-lo-cate)*. To allot; to distribute.

allot *(al-lot')*. 1. To distribute to several people, in portions. 2. To set aside as the portion intended for a special purpose, as in "The money was allotted for the building of a hospital". An **allotment** is a small portion of land.

allowance *(al-low'-ance)*. 1. In "The father made his son an allowance of 6d. per week", the allowance is the sum that the father allowed or gave his son. 2. In "We must make allowance for his weakness", the meaning is that we must not be too hard on him because of his weakness.

alloy *(al'-loy)*. A mixture of two or more metals. Because a shilling is made of silver with other metals added, it is not pure silver but an alloy.

allude *(al-lude')*. To refer to.

allure *(al-lure')*. To tempt or attract by offering some kind of reward.

allusion *(al-lu'-sion)*. A reference made to something in an indirect way.

ally *(al-ly'* or *al'-ly)*. A person or country which joins with another for a common cause.

almanac *(al'-ma-nac)*. A book which gives information about the days of the week, the months of the year and the weather.

almond *(al'-mond)*. 1. A small tree with beautiful white or pink blossoms. 2. The fruit of the almond tree, which contains a white nut oval in shape and very good to eat.

almost *(al'-most)*. Nearly.

alms. Charitable gifts. The word is never used in the singular.

alone *(a-lone')*. Without anyone or anything else.

alongside *(a-long-side')*. By the side of; side by side with.

aloof *(a-loof')*. Apart. Thus "He keeps aloof from his friends" means that he keeps apart or away from them.

aloud *(a-loud')*. In a loud voice; not in a whisper.

alpha *(al'-pha)*. The name of the first letter in the Greek alphabet. From this, alpha has become a term for the first or beginning of anything.

alphabet *(al'-pha-bet)*. The twenty-six letters used in writing and spelling. Any list of words arranged in the order of these letters is said to be in **alphabetical** *(al-pha-bet'-i-cal)* order.

already *(al-read'-y)*. By this time; even now, as "The house is already empty". Do not confuse **already** with **all ready** in such sentences as "The people were all ready to begin", which means all the people were ready to begin.

altar *(al'-tar)*. 1. The communion table in the most sacred part of a church. 2. A table on which sacrifices were made in early times.

alter *(al'-ter)*. To change.

altercation *(al-ter-ca'-tion)*. An angry quarrel.

alternate *(al'-ter-nate)*. To follow by turns; thus odd and even numbers alternate in 1, 2, 3, 4, 5, 6, 7 and 8.

alternative *(al-ter'-na-tive)*. 1. An opportunity to choose between two things, as in "He gave the boy only one alternative to cleaning up the ink he had spilled, and that was to stay in after school". 2. Something which may be chosen instead of something else. Thus, if Mother says, "Will you have a jam tart or apple pie?" apple pie is an alternative to jam tart.

although *(al-though')*. Though or despite the fact that, as "He came although he was ill".

altitude *(al'-ti-tude)*. Height.

alto *(al'-to)*. The lowest female voice or the highest male voice.

altogether *(al-to-geth'-er)*. 1. Entirely, as "The girl's answer was altogether wrong". 2. In a complete set, as "The whole class went altogether in one large bus to the concert".

aluminium *(al-u-min'-i-um)*. A silver-coloured metal useful for parts of aircraft because it is light in weight, strong, and does not rust.

always *(al'-ways)*. Continually or at all times, as "Good music is always enjoyable".

a.m. 1. Before noon. 2. The part of the day between midnight and noon.

amalgamation *(a-mal-gam-a'-tion)*. A mixture or union.

amass *(a-mass')*. To collect together in large quantities; to heap up. A miser who collects large quantities of money is said to amass a fortune.

amateur *(am'-a-teur)*. 1. A person who works at something for pleasure, not for a living. 2. Rough; inexperienced, as "The girl's performance seemed amateurish in comparison to that of the concert pianist".

amaze *(a-maze')*. To surprise; to astonish.

amazement *(a-maze'-ment)*. Great surprise.

Amazon *(Am'-a-zon)*. 1. One of a race of tall, strong women warriors mentioned in the old Greek stories. 2. Thus, any woman who is tall and has the strength of a man may be referred to as an amazon. 3. A river in South America, emptying into the Atlantic Ocean on the coast of Brazil. It is the longest river in the world.

ambassador *(am-bas'-sa-dor)*. The representative of a government in a foreign country.

amber *(am'-ber)*. A pale yellow resin produced by pine trees that grew thousands of years ago. It is extremely hard and is used for such articles as the mouth-pieces of pipes and for jewellery.

ambiguous *(am-big'-u-ous)*. Having two different meanings, so that nobody can tell which is intended. To say that a child is *trying* is ambiguous because it may mean that he is doing his best or that he makes himself a nuisance.

ambition *(am-bi'-tion)*. A great wish to get on in the world.

ambitious *(am-bi'-tious)*. An ambitious person is one who aims high in whatever he is doing.

amble *(am'-ble)*. To go along at a gentle pace.

ambulance *(am'-bu-lance)*. A car or vehicle used in moving an ill or wounded person from one place to another.

ambush *(am'-bush)*. 1. To ambush someone is to lie in wait for him and then to jump out and surprise him. 2. The act or state of lying in wait and then attacking in this manner. 3. Troops lying in wait in order to surprise an enemy.

amen *(a-men')*. So be it, said at the end of a prayer.

amenable *(a-me'-na-ble)*. A person is amenable when he is ready to listen to reason or do what he is told.

amend *(a-mend')*. To change, alter, improve or correct.

amendment *(a-mend'-ment)*. An alteration or correction.

amends *(a-mends')*. Compensation for a wrong done. When a person makes amends for an injury he has caused, he gives something to the injured person.

amenity *(a-men'-i-ty)*. 1. Pleasantness; pleasing ways. 2. A thing or act which makes life more pleasant, as "the amenities of civilization".

amethyst *(am'-e-thyst)*. 1. A purple or violet quartz used for jewellery. 2. The colour of purple or violet.

amiable *(a'-mi-a-ble)*. Friendly and pleasant.

amicable *(am'-i-ca-ble)*. Friendly.

amiss *(a-miss')*. 1. Astray; wrongly. 2. Wrong. When we say something has gone amiss, we mean it has not happened as it should have done.

ammonia *(am-mo'-nia)*. A strong-smelling, colourless gas. Ammonia gas dissolved in water is very useful for cleaning.

ammunition *(am-mu-ni'-tion)*. 1. Bullets, shells, gunpowder, etc., which are used in shooting. 2. Anything which is shot or thrown.

amorous *(am'-o-rous)*. Loving.

amount *(a-mount')*. The sum of something; how much there is of it.

amphibian *(am-phib'-i-an)*. 1. An animal which can live on land and in water. A frog is an amphibian. 2. A type of aeroplane which can operate from land or water.

amphibious *(am-phib'-i-ous)*. Able to live on land and in water.

amphitheatre *(am'-phi-the-a-tre)*. 1. An oval or circular building with rows of seats around a central, open space. 2. Any open place arranged as a theatre.

ample *(am'-ple)*. Enough; sufficient; plenty.

amplify *(am'-pli-fy)*. To make larger or more.

amputate *(am'-pu-tate)*. To cut off a limb. Thus a man with one arm has probably had the other one amputated.

amuck *(a-muck')*. To run amuck (or amok) is to run about wildly causing damage or even killing people.

amusement *(a-muse'-ment)*. Anything which amuses, entertains or helps leisure time to pass pleasantly.

anaesthetic *(an-aes-thet'-ic)*. A drug which deadens the senses so that the person to whom it is given cannot feel pain. Ether, which makes you fall asleep, and the "freezing" which the dentist puts in your gums are both anaesthetics.

anagram *(an'-a-gram)*. A word made by changing the position of the letters of another word, such as "live" and "evil".

analysis *(a-nal'-y-sis)*. To separate a thing into its several parts and study them is to make an analysis of it or **analyze** *(an'-a-lyze)* it. In grammar lessons, when a pupil divides a sentence into subject and predicate, etc., he does an analysis of it. When a chemist speaks of the analysis of water, he means the separation of water into oxygen and hydrogen, the two elements forming it.

anarchist *(an'-arch-ist)*. A person who tries to overthrow the government of a country because he does not want *any* form of government.

anatomy *(a-nat'-o-my)*. The study of the build or structure of a person, animal or plant. A person's body is his anatomy.

ancestor *(an'-ces-tor)*. Your ancestors are the people from whom you have descended. Thus, your father (mother), grandfather (-mother), great-grandfather (-mother) and so on are your ancestors.

anchor *(an'-chor)*. 1. A heavy piece of iron at the end of a long cable, which is dropped over the side of a ship to hold the ship in one spot on the sea. 2. Something used to hold a thing in place. 3. To hold something in place.

anchovy *(an-cho'-vy* or *an'-cho-vy)*. A small sea-fish, like the herring in appearance. It has a very salty taste.

ancient *(an'-cient)*. Belonging to the distant past; existing many centuries ago.

anecdote *(an'-ec-dote)*. A story of one single happening. Often an anecdote is amusing.

angel *(an'-gel)*. 1. A messenger of God. 2. A spirit.

angle *(an'-gle)*. 1. When two straight lines meet each other at a point they form an angle. A square, for example, has four angles. 2. To try to catch fish. Sometimes we speak of a person angling for things other than fish. Then we mean that the person is trying to obtain those things by scheming.

angry *(an'-gry)*. Furious; very upset.

anguish *(an'-guish)*. Great pain; but the word usually means mental pain rather than bodily pain.

animal *(an'-i-mal)*. A living thing which is not a plant.

animate *(an'-i-mate)*. Having life. A living person is animate, and so are a tree and a fly, but a house and a brick wall are not animate.

animosity *(an-i-mos'-i-ty)*. Great hatred.

ankle *(an'-kle)*. The joint which connects the foot to the leg.

annex. 1. *(an'-nex)*. A part of a building in addition to the main portion, though not necessarily attached, as "The hotel annex is three doors down the street". 2. *(an-nex')*. To join to a larger thing, as "Our city may annex the suburbs".

annihilate *(an-ni'-hi-late)*. To destroy absolutely.

anniversary *(an-ni-ver'-sa-ry)*. A day on which a happening is celebrated year after year. Your birthday is an anniversary and so is Christmas.

annotate *(an'-no-tate)*. To supply with notes. There is an annotated version of the Bible. It has columns of notes which explain the text.

announce *(an-nounce')*. To make something known in a public way, as when a headmaster announces that the next day will be a holiday. What he says is an **announcement.**

announcer *(an-nounc'-er)*. A person who announces on radio and television.

annoy *(an-noy')*. To vex a person, to tease or trouble him. Anything that annoys is an **annoyance.**

annual *(an'-nu-al)*. 1. Yearly; happening once a year. 2. A book published once a year is an annual. 3. Plants which normally live one year are called annuals.

annuity *(an-nu'-i-ty)*. A sum of money paid yearly. Many pensions are annuities.

anoint *(a-noint')*. To pour on oil or ointment, usually for medical reasons or as a religious act.

anon *(a-non')*. 1. Soon; later on. 2. With a full stop after it, this word is the abbreviation for **anonymous.**

anonymous *(a-non'-y-mous)*. Without a name. If I write a letter to you and do not sign my name to it, I am sending you an anonymous letter.

answer *(an'-swer)*. 1. If someone asks you what time it is and you say "One o'clock" "One o'clock" is your answer. 2. When you say "One o'clock" you answer the question.

ant. A small insect well-known for being a hard worker. Ants live together in colonies, usually in underground tunnels called **ant-hills.**

antagonist *(an-tag'-o-nist)*. A person who is against another; a rival.

antarctic *(ant-arc'-tic)*. To do with the region around the South Pole.

antelope *(an'-te-lope)*. A deer-like animal.

antenna *(an-ten'-na)*. 1. A feeler on the head of an insect. 2. A radio or television aerial. The plural is **antennae.**

anthem *(an'-them)*. A song or hymn with words usually taken from the Scriptures and music written for several voices.

anther *(an'-ther)*. The part of the flower which bears the pollen.

anthology *(an-thol'-o-gy)*. A book containing a collection of writings by different authors.

anthracite *(an'-thra-cite)*. A kind of hard coal which burns with very little smoke.

antic *(an'-tic)*. A silly trick; an odd and ridiculous action.

anticipate *(an-ti'-ci-pate)*. To look forward to something and expect it to happen.

antidote *(an'-ti-dote)*. 1. A remedy; thus, if a person swallows a poison, the doctor gives him an antidote. 2. A remedy for evil is also an antidote.

antipathy *(an-tip'-a-thy)*. A strong dislike; a great objection; thus, if you hate and detest a thing, you have an antipathy for it.

antipodes *(an-tip'-o-des)*. A place on the opposite side of the world. Every place has its antipodes. When people in England speak of the antipodes they mean Australia and New Zealand.

antiquated *(an'-ti-quat-ed)*. Old-fashioned; out of date; thus blunderbusses, warming-pans, horse trams and bows and arrows are antiquated things.

antique *(an-tique')*. 1. Of old times; old-fashioned. 2. Something which has existed since old times. A table made in 1860 would to-day be called an antique.

antiseptic *(an-ti-sep'-tic)*. A substance used to prevent infection. Iodine, for example, is an antiseptic.

antler *(ant'-ler)*. The branch-like horn of a deer.

antonym *(an'-to-nym)*. A word which is opposite in meaning to a given word. Hot and cold are antonyms.

anvil *(an'-vil)*. The iron on which a blacksmith places his work and hammers it into shape.

anxiety *(anx-i'-e-ty)*. An uneasy feeling that something will go wrong. A person who suffers anxiety is one who worries and fears the worst.

anxious *(anx'-ious)*. One who is anxious is worried and fearful.

anybody *(an'-y-bod-y)*. Any person, as "Has anybody been here before?"

apace *(a-pace')*. Quickly.

apart *(a-part')*. 1. When you take a thing apart, you separate it into all the pieces that it is made of. 2. Away from each other, as "Boys and matches should be kept apart". 3. Off to one side, as "He stood apart and listened".

apartment *(a-part'-ment)*. An apartment may be a group of rooms or a single room in which people live. Often one sees a large building which is divided into apartments.

apathy *(ap'-a-thy)*. Lack of feeling or lack of interest. If someone told you a terrible tale of woe and at the end you merely said "Well, what about it?" you would be showing apathy.

ape. 1. An animal of the monkey family. 2. To mimic or imitate. Thus, in "He aped the antics of the clown", aped means imitated.

aperture *(ap'er-ture)*. An opening.

apex *(a'-pex)*. The point at the top, especially of a triangle; the tip of a thing.

aphides *(a'-phides)*. Plant lice which live by sucking juice from plants. The singular is **aphis.**

apiary *(a'-pi-ar-y)*. A place for housing bees.

apiece *(a-piece')*. Each; for each one.

aplomb *(a-plomb')*. Self-assurance; poise; confidence. One who has aplomb is sure of himself and, as a result, is calm and not easily embarrassed.

apology *(a-pol'-o-gy)*. A statement spoken or written, expressing regret for something you have done. The person making the apology shows he is **apologetic** *(a-pol-o-get'-ic)*. He **apologizes** *(a-pol'-o-giz-es)*.

apoplexy *(ap'-o-plex-y)*. A sudden paralysis, and often fainting, caused by the breaking of a blood vessel in the brain.

apostle *(a-pos'-tle)*. 1. One of the twelve men chosen by Christ to preach the gospel. 2. A Christian missionary or leader. 3. A leader of a reform movement.

apostrophe *(a-pos'-tro-phe)*. A comma placed above the line to show that something has been left out, or to show that a word is possessive.

apothecary *(a-poth'-e-car-y)*. A druggist; one who prepares medicines and sells them.

appal *(ap-pal')*. To fill with horror or dread.

apparatus *(ap-pa-ra'-tus)*. Things needed for doing certain work. Thus photographic apparatus consists of cameras, developing dishes, chemicals, dark-room lamps, etc.

apparel *(ap-par'-el)*. Clothes; the things people wear.

apparent *(ap-par'-ent)*. 1. Visible; plainly seen, as "The moon was apparent at 9.45 p.m.". 2. Obvious; thus "It was apparent that the boy had touched the wet paint".

apparition *(ap-pa-ri'-tion)*. A ghost.

appeal *(ap-peal')*. 1. An earnest request; a plea for something. 2. To make an earnest request or plea.

appear *(ap-pear')*. 1. To become visible; to be seen, as in "He appeared at the window". 2. To seem, as "He appeared to be very ill".

appearance *(ap-pear'-ance)*. The way a person, place or thing looks to you, as "The appearance of the dog, as it lay still on the road, made one think it was dead".

appease *(ap-pease')*. To calm or to pacify.

append *(ap-pend')*. To add to, as "He appended his signature to the note".

appendage *(ap-pend'-age)*. A thing joined to another; the part of a thing that hangs from another part; thus "The horse's tail is a useful appendage for flicking away flies".

appendix *(ap-pen'-dix)*. 1. Something added to the end of a book to describe more fully certain passages in the book. 2. That part of the intestines that sometimes becomes inflamed and causes the illness known as **appendicitis** *(ap-pen-di-ci'-tis)*.

appertain *(ap-per-tain')*. To relate to; to be connected with.

appetite *(ap'-pe-tite)*. A desire or longing for something. It is usually used in reference to the desire for food, as in "The sick boy lost his appetite; therefore, he was not interested in food".

applaud *(ap-plaud')*. To show pleasure or satisfaction, usually by clapping the hands or by shouting suitably. Such clapping, etc., is **applause.**

application *(ap-pli-ca'-tion)*. 1. In "The boy shows much application in his studies", application means close attention. 2. In "One application of paint is enough", application means putting on. 3. In "He sent an application for a driving licence", application means request.

appoint *(ap-point')*. To choose, as "They appointed a time for the meeting", or "He was appointed to be their captain". We call such a choice an **appointment.**

apportion *(ap-por'-tion)*. To distribute according to some plan; to give out in portions, as "In his will the old man apportioned his fortune equally among his four sons".

appraise *(ap-praise')*. To set a value, price or worth on something, as "Before selling his bicycle, the boy asked a bicycle repairer to appraise it so that it could be sold at a fair price".

appreciate *(ap-pre'-ci-ate)*. 1. To value properly, as "The girl fully appreciated her mother's kindness". 2. To rise in value. It is the opposite word to **depreciate**.

appreciation *(ap-pre-ci-a'-tion)*. 1. Approval, as "The audience showed its appreciation by clapping". 2. Understanding. Some people have an appreciation for fine music because they understand it and enjoy it. 3. An increase in value.

apprehensive *(ap-pre-hen'-sive)*. To be anxious, worried or frightened about something that may happen is to be apprehensive.

apprentice *(ap-pren'-tice)*. One who receives instruction in a craft or trade. The apprentice usually agrees to serve his employer for a definite period of time, as "The young man was an apprentice to a carpenter for four years".

approach *(ap-proach')*. To come near.

appropriate *(ap-pro'-pri-ate)*. 1. Suitable, as "He recited a poem about Santa Claus because it was appropriate for the Christmas Concert". 2. To take for oneself, as "He appropriated his brother's hockey stick". 3. Set apart for special use, as "He appropriated money for taxes".

approve *(ap-prove')*. To be satisfied with; to think a thing is suitable.

approximately *(ap-prox'-i-mate-ly)*. Roughly; nearly; almost. Thus, 999 is approximately equal to 1,000.

apricot *(a'-pri-cot)*. A small fruit which is shaped like a peach and is a pale orange colour.

April *(A'-pril)*. The fourth month of the year. There are 30 days in April and the first day is called April Fool's Day.

apron *(a'-pron)*. A piece of cloth worn over the clothes for protection, as "Mother wears an apron while cooking dinner".

apt. 1. Suitable; correct, as "He has a way of saying apt things". 2. Likely, as "He is apt to contradict people".

aptitude *(apt'-i-tude)*. A natural power of being able to do a thing well.

aquarium *(a-qua'-ri-um)*. A glass tank filled with water in which are kept fish, water-plants, water-snails, etc.

aquatic *(a-quat'-ic)*. Belonging to water. Thus a fish is an aquatic animal.

aqueduct *(aq'-ue-duct)*. 1. A man-made channel or a large pipe for carrying water over a distance. 2. A structure that supports the channel or pipe.

aqueous *(a'-que-ous)*. Watery.

arable *(ar'-a-ble)*. Capable of being ploughed. We speak of arable land.

arbour *(ar'-bour)*. A shady place among trees, usually with a seat provided.

arc. A part of a circle; therefore a curve.

arcade *(ar-cade')*. A walk or passage-way with a covered roof.

arch. A structure designed to support a roof or a bridge, and built in the shape of a curve.

archipelago *(ar-chi-pel'-a-go)*. A group of islands, or a sea with many islands in it.

architect *(ar'-chi-tect)*. A person who designs or plans a building and then sees that his plan is followed.

architecture *(ar'-chi-tec-ture)*. The science of building and the styles of building, such as Saxon, Norman, Gothic, etc.

arctic *(arc'-tic)*. To do with the region around the North Pole.

ardent *(ar'dent)*. 1. Hot; fiery. 2. Burning; eager. An ardent desire is a burning, or very great, desire.

ardour *(ar'-dour)*. Eagerness, zeal.

arduous *(ar'-du-ous)*. Hard to do; thus a climb up a steep mountain side could be arduous.

area *(a'-re-a)*. The surface of a thing; its total space found by multiplying the length by the width.

arena *(a-re'-na)*. 1. A place where games or contests are held, such as a hockey arena. 2. An open space in which contests took place in ancient times.

argue *(ar'-gue)*. 1. To fight verbally over a matter to try to convince a person that his opinion is wrong and yours is right. 2. To give reasons for disagreeing; to state your opinion.

argument *(ar'-gu-ment)*. 1. Discussion; debate. 2. Reason given.

arid *(ar'-id)*. Dry. Deserts are arid.

arise *(a-rise')*. To rise up. If you have a sound sleep, you will arise fresh and bright.

arithmetic *(a-rith'-me-tic)*. The study of numbers.

ark. 1. The ship in which Noah escaped from the Flood. 2. The chest into which Moses put the stone tablets on which he had written the Ten Commandments. A copy of the ark is kept in every Jewish church.

armada *(ar-ma'-da)*. A huge fleet of warships.

armaments *(ar'-ma-ments)*. The arms and supplies of ammunition needed in warfare.

B

armistice *(ar'-mis-tice)*. A truce; an agreement to stop fighting for a while.

armour *(ar'-mour)*. A protective covering over the body. King Arthur's knights wore armour.

army *(ar'-my)*. A large group of people joined together to fight for a cause.

aroma *(a-ro'-ma)*. Pleasant smell or odour.

arouse *(a-rouse')*. 1. To wake up, as "His alarm clock aroused him at 7 a.m.". 2. To stir up, as "The man's remarks aroused his temper".

arrangement *(ar-range'-ment)*. When parts of something are placed in order, the result is an arrangement; thus we speak of musical arrangements and floral arrangements.

array *(ar-ray')*. 1. In "She was arrayed in her best clothes", arrayed means dressed. 2. In "The soldiers were lined up in battle-array", array means order. 3. In "The merchant arrayed his goods so that they made a splendid show", arrayed means arranged.

arrears *(ar-rears')*. Debts that have not been paid. To be in arrears means to be behind with work, money, etc.

arrest *(ar-rest')*. To stop, seize or detain.

arrive *(ar-rive')*. 1. To come to a place, as "He arrived at the station in time to meet the train". 2. To arrive at a decision is to reach a decision, as "Once he arrived at a decision about the problem, he stopped worrying and took action".

arrogant *(ar'-ro-gant)*. Haughty; boastful; exceedingly proud.

arrow *(ar'-row)*. 1. A slender pointed missile shot from a bow. 2. A sign which points the direction.

arsenal *(ar'-se-nal)*. A place where weapons or war materials are either stored or made.

arsenic *(ar'-sen-ic)*. A very poisonous chemical.

arson *(ar'-son)*. Setting fire to a building or other property on purpose and with wicked intentions.

art. 1. Skill, as in "the art of cooking". 2. Learning; a branch of learning. 3. The use of skill, imagination and judgment to produce a work such as a painting, a poem or a musical composition. Such productions are called works of art.

artery *(ar'-ter-y)*. One of the tubes which carry blood from the heart to all parts of the body. Main roads are often called **arteries**.

artesian well *(ar-te'-sian well)*. A well which goes deep in the ground and from which water spouts.

artful *(art'-ful)*. Cunning; crafty.

article *(ar'-ti-cle)*. 1. A separate thing. 2. An account in a newspaper or magazine. 3. In grammar, the words "a", "an" and "the" are called articles.

articulate *(ar-tic'-u-late)*. To utter sounds distinctly when speaking, as "The B.B.C. announcer has to articulate his words clearly".

artifice *(ar'-ti-fice)*. A cunning trick; skill.

artificial *(ar-ti-fi'-cial)*. Not natural but made by man. Artificial flowers, for instance, are not those grown in a garden or elsewhere; they are those made by the art of man.

artillery *(ar-til'-ler-y)*. 1. The part of the army which handles the big guns or cannons. 2. The weapons of war.

artisan *(ar-ti-san')*. A workman who is skilled in his particular trade; a mechanic.

artist *(art'-ist)*. A person who is very skilled in music, painting, writing, etc.

artistic *(ar-tis'-tic)*. Belonging to art or an artist; made or arranged with skill, imagination and judgment.

artless *(art'-less)*. The opposite of artful; without trickery; unskilled.

asbestos *(as-bes'-tos)*. A mineral that will not burn. It forms naturally in long fibres, which can be woven into cloth that will not burn.

ascend *(as-cend')*. To move upward.

ascension *(as-cen'-sion)*. 1. The act of ascending or going up. 2. A steep slope upwards is an **ascent.**

ascertain *(as-cer-tain')*. To find out.

aside *(a-side')*. 1. To or at one side. 2. Words spoken on the stage which are not supposed to be heard by the other players.

askance *(a-skance')*. To look askance is to look with suspicion or in a questioning manner.

askew *(a-skew')*. To one side or on the tilt. Thus "He wore his cap askew" means that he wore it tilted on one side.

aspect *(as'-pect)*. Look; outlook.

asperity *(as-per'-i-ty)*. Harshness; roughness.

asphalt *(as'-phalt)*. The tarry substance often used for the surface of roads and pavements.

asphyxiation *(as-phyx-i-a'-tion)*. Suffocation.

aspirate *(as'-pi-rate)*. 1. A letter pronounced by breathing outwards, such as H. 2. To pronounce by breathing outwards.

aspiration *(as-pi-ra'-tion)*. 1. Act of breathing. 2. Desire; ambition.

aspire *(as-pire')*. To have a great wish to do a thing.

assail *(as-sail')*. To attack. The person who makes the attack is an **assailant**.

assassin *(as-sas'-sin)*. A murderer.

assault *(as-sault')*. 1. An attack. 2. To attack.

assemble *(as-sem'-ble)*. To come together or to bring together. When people assemble they form an **assembly**. A meeting is often called an assembly.

assent *(as-sent')*. 1. Agreement. 2. When a person agrees to a thing, he gives his permission for it to be done; he assents or gives his assent.

assert *(as-sert')*. To say very positively or definitely.

assess *(as-sess')*. To fix the amount of money; to decide how much it shall be. The Income Tax authorities assess the amount of income tax a man must pay.

asset *(as'-set)*. 1. Something of value, as "His biggest asset was his sense of humour". 2. Something which is owned and which can be used to pay debts.

assiduous *(as-sid'-u-ous)*. Hard-working; diligent; the opposite to lazy.

assign *(as-sign')*. To appoint; to allot; to give, as in "The father assigned half his fortune to his son".

assimilate *(as-sim'-i-late)*. To absorb; to digest; to take in, as "The pupil could not assimilate all the facts he was told".

assist *(as-sist')*. To help. A person who helps or assists is an **assistant**, and the help he gives is **assistance**.

associate *(as-so'-ci-ate)*. 1. To join with, as "He associated with bad company". 2. To connect in one's mind, as "He always associated the cross-roads with the accident he once saw there". 3. A companion or partner, as "his business associate named Smith".

association *(as-so-ci-a'-tion)*. Usually a group of people joined together to carry on a business ,or tofollow a common interest.

assorted *(as-sort'-ed)*. Mixed; of more than one kind. A pocketful of red marbles would not be of assorted colours; but if they were red, blue, green, etc., they would be assorted as far as colour was concerned.

assortment *(as-sort'-ment)*. A mixture; a collection of things of different kinds. (See **assorted**.)

assuage *(as-suage')*. To ease; to soften.

assume *(as-sume')*. 1. In "The man assumed the responsibility", assumed means took upon himself. 2. In "The man assumed that you would not be coming", assumed means took for granted.

assure *(as-sure')*. To make certain, as "She assured herself that all was safe".

assuredly *(as-sur'-ed-ly)*. Surely; certainly.

aster *(as'-ter)*. A flower with little petals arranged around a yellow centre.

asterisk *(as'-ter-isk)*. A mark like this *.

astern *(a-stern')*. 1. At the back of a ship. 2. Backwards. In "The captain set his ship full speed astern", astern means backwards.

asthma *(asth'-ma)*. An illness which causes difficulty in breathing. Someone who suffers from asthma is **asthmatic** *(asth-mat'-ic)*.

astonish *(as-ton'-ish)*. To surprise very much.

astray *(a-stray')*. Out of the right way, as "The path through the woods is so dark and winding that it is easy to go astray".

astride *(a-stride')*. With one leg on each side as when riding horseback, etc.

astringent *(as-trin'-gent)*. A drug or chemical which makes things contract slightly. Thus an astringent placed on a wound that is bleeding helps to stop the flow of blood, because it contracts or tightens up the blood vessels.

astronomy *(as-tron'-o-my)*. The science that deals with the stars and other heavenly bodies.

astute *(as-tute')*. Clever; shrewd; cunning.

asunder *(a-sun'-der)*. Apart; in pieces, as "Buffeted by the waves, the wreck split asunder".

asylum *(a-sy'-lum)*. A place of refuge or shelter. An asylum is a place in which those who are mentally ill are cared for, or a shelter for orphans.

ate. The past tense of eat, as "He ate slowly and chewed his food well".

athlete *(ath'-lete)*. A person who takes part in sports that require strength, skill, speed, etc.

athletic *(ath-let'-ic)*. Suited to **athletics** or sports, as "He had an athletic build".

athwart *(a-thwart')*. Across.

Atlantic *(At-lan'-tic)*. An ocean which lies east of North and South America and west of Europe and Africa.

atlas *(at'-las)*. A book containing maps. An atlas is used in studying geography.

atmosphere *(at'-mos-phere)*. 1. The air surrounding the earth. 2. "He lived in an atmosphere of strife" means he lived among people who quarrelled.

atom *(at'-om)*. Smallest possible piece of matter or material.

atone *(a-tone')*. To make amends; to do something good to make up for something evil already done.

atrocious *(a-tro'-cious)*. Very wicked; very horrible. A thing that is atrocious is an **atrocity** *(a-troc'-i-ty)*.

attach *(at-tach')*. To fix or fasten.

attack *(at-tack')*. 1. To set upon with words or weapons. An army attacks its enemy but a newspaper might attack somebody by printing unpleasant facts about him. 2. The act of assailing.

attain *(at-tain')*. To reach or gain, as "He attained the top position of his class".

attempt *(at-tempt')*. When you attempt something, you try to do it.

attend *(at-tend')*. 1. To be present. 2. To take notice or to pay attention. 3. To look after, take care of, or wait upon.

attention *(at-ten'-tion)*. 1. In "The pupils gave their attention to the teacher", gave their attention means listened carefully. 2. Courtesy; consideration; politeness, as "It is polite to show attention to older people". 3. To stand to attention is to stand perfectly straight and still as soldiers do on a parade ground.

attest *(at-test')*. To bear witness; to give evidence.

attic *(at'-tic)*. A room at the top of the house, usually the one just under the roof.

attire *(at-tire')*. Dress.

attitude *(at'-ti-tude)*. 1. The way a person stands, as "He had a slovenly attitude". 2. The way a person thinks, as "His attitude towards work was not what it should have been".

attorney *(at-tor'-ney)*. A lawyer.

attract *(at-tract')*. Something which draws other things to it is said to attract them. Thus, a magnet attracts objects made of steel, and a candle attracts moths. A person who draws other people's attention to himself and pleases other people is said to be **attractive.**

attribute. 1. *(at'-tri-bute)*. A characteristic, as "Understanding is the attribute of a good teacher", or "Mercy is an attribute of God". 2. *(at-trib'-ute)*. "We attribute the success of good students to intelligence and industry" means we think that the success of good students is due to their intelligence and industry. "That play is attributed to Shakespeare" means that play is generally considered to have been written by Shakespeare.

attune *(at-tune')*. 1. To put in tune musically. 2. To put in sympathy with.

auburn *(au'-burn)*. Reddish-brown.

auction *(auc'-tion)*. A sale at which things are sold to the people who offer the highest prices for them. The person who conducts the auction is an **auctioneer** *(auc-tion-eer')*.

audacious *(au-da'-cious)*. Bold and impudent. An audacious person has **audacity.**

audible *(au'-di-ble)*. Loud enough to be heard.

audience *(au'-di-ence)*. 1. A number of people who have come together to hear or see something. In a theatre, for example, all the people who are sitting in front of the stage or orchestra are the audience. 2. A formal interview.

auditor *(au'-di-tor)*. 1. A person who examines the accounts for a group or company. 2. One who listens.

auditorium *(au-di-to'-ri-um)*. A large room in which people gather to hear concerts, etc. The people are called an **audience.**

aught. Anything.

augment *(aug-ment')*. To increase or make more.

august *(au-gust')*. Grand; majestic; worthy of reverence.

August *(Au'-gust)*. The eighth month of the year.

aunt. A sister of one's father or mother; the wife of an uncle.

auspices *(aus'-pi-ces)*. In "The flower show was held under the auspices of the town council", auspices means leadership.

auspicious *(aus-pi'-cious)*. Favourable; indicating success. We say that bright sunshine on a wedding day is auspicious. It is a sign that a happy life is in store for the newly-weds.

austere *(aus-tere')*. 1. Harsh; stern; frowning. 2. Extremely plain and simple.

Australia *(Aus-tral'-ia)*. A continent in the eastern hemisphere, south of Asia.

authentic *(au-then'-tic)*. Reliable, genuine, real.

author *(au'-thor)*. 1. A person who writes books, articles for newspapers, etc., as Dickens or Bernard Shaw. 2. A person who is the first to do a thing.

authority *(au-thor'-i-ty)*. Legal power or right, such as the authority of a policeman.

authorize *(au'-thor-ize)*. To give someone the necessary power to do a certain thing; thus if Smith has a horse and he authorizes Brown to drive it to market, he gives Brown authority to drive it to market.

autobiography *(au-to-bi-og'-ra-phy)*. A **biography** is the story of a person's life, and an autobiography is the story written by the person himself. There is only one person who could write your autobiography, and that person is yourself.

autocrat *(au'-to-crat)*. 1. A king, queen, or ruler of a country who has absolute power to rule exactly as he or she likes. 2. A person who will not listen to others and who always expects others to do as he wishes.

autograph *(au'-to-graph)*. A person's own handwriting. Collectors sometimes ask a noted person for his autograph, meaning his signature.

automatic *(au-to-mat'-ic)*. 1. Acting without the help of man, as in the case of an automatic machine. 2. Acting without will power. Breathing, for instance, is done without any effort of will power, and is therefore automatic.

automobile *(au-to-mo-bile')*. Another name for a motor-car.

autopsy *(au'-top-sy)*. A medical examination of a dead body which is made in order to find the cause of death.

autumn *(au'-tumn)*. The season of the year between summer and winter; the fall.

autumnal *(au-tum'-nal)*. Having to do with the autumn season.

auxiliary *(aux-il'-ia-ry)*. A thing that helps or assists another. When a train has to climb a long, steep hill an auxiliary engine is sometimes put on to help.

avail *(a-vail')*. 1. To be of help or value, as in "How does that avail?" 2. To avail oneself of something is to take advantage of it, as "Every child should avail himself of the opportunity of education". 3. When used as a noun, avail means advantage or use. "Of little avail" means of little use; "of no avail" means of no use.

available *(a-vail'-a-ble)*. At hand; capable of being used.

avalanche *(av'-a-lanche)*. A huge mass of snow, ice or earth that slides down the steep side of a mountain.

avarice *(av'-a-rice)*. Greed, such as a miser has for money.

avenge *(a-venge')*. To take revenge for.

avenue *(av'-e-nue)*. 1. A wide street. The abbreviation is ave. 2. A way of approach, as in "Regular habits are the avenue to good health".

average *(av'-er-age)*. The average of 2, 4, 6, 8 is 5. The average speed of a car during a day's run is found by dividing the total mileage by the time spent on the run. A man's average weekly wage can be found by adding what he earns each week and dividing by the number of weeks. Thus an average is a middle quantity.

averse *(a-verse')*. Not liking; having an objection to.

avert *(a-vert')*. To turn aside; to prevent.

aviary *(a'-vi-a-ry)*. A place for keeping birds.

aviation *(a-vi-a'-tion)*. The science of flying aircraft.

aviator *(a'-vi-a-tor)*. The pilot of an aircraft.

avid *(av'-id)*. Eager.

avoid *(a-void')*. To escape; to get out of the way.

avow *(a-vow')*. To admit frankly, without hiding anything.

awake *(a-wake')*. 1. To arouse; to wake up. 2. Not asleep.

award *(a-ward')*. 1. In "He received the first award", award means prize. 2. In "The judge awarded the man £50 damages", awarded means decided he should have.

aware *(a-ware')*. Conscious of; knowing. Thus in "Are you aware of what people think of you?" "Are you aware of" means "Do you know".

awe. Fear and reverence.

awful *(aw'-ful)*. 1. Dreadful; terrible. 2. Anything causing fear and reverence is awful.

awkward *(awk'-ward)*. Clumsy.

awl. A small tool for putting holes in leather or wood. An awl is used by shoemakers and carpenters.

awning *(awn'-ing)*. A covering placed over a door, window, etc., to keep out the sun or rain.

awry *(a-wry')*. 1. Twisted or crooked, as in "She knocked her hat awry as she passed through the low doorway". 2. Amiss, or wrong, as in "Our best plans often go awry".

axe. A tool used for chopping, usually with a wooden handle and an iron head.

axis *(ax'-is)*. An imaginary line running through the middle of a body from end to end. If the body spins or turns over and over it is said to be turning about its axis. The axis of the earth, for example, is an imaginary line drawn from the North Pole to the South Pole through the centre of the earth. The earth turns about this axis once every twenty-four hours.

axle *(ax'-le)*. The rod or bar on which two wheels of a cart or motor-car turn.

azure *(az'-ure)*. Blue; the colour of the sky.

B

babble *(bab'-ble)*. Silly talk; the sounds a baby makes when trying to talk.

baboon *(ba-boon')*. A kind of monkey which has a short tail and a face like a dog's. It lives in southern Asia and Africa.

baby *(ba'-by)*. An infant child, usually under one year old.

bachelor *(bach'-e-lor)*. 1. A man who has never married. 2. A person who has taken a degree at a university, such as a B.A. or B.Sc.

background *(back'-ground)*. 1. The part at the back. In a picture the house may be in the foreground and the mountains in the background. 2. One's early training or experience. A person with a rural background is one who has spent his early life on a farm.

backward *(back'-ward)*. 1. With the back first. 2. Slow; stupid. 3. Shy. 4. Late; behind time.

bacon *(ba'-con)*. A kind of meat which comes from the back and sides of a pig.

bacteria *(bac-te'-ri-a)*. Very small, single-celled plants found almost everywhere. Some cause illnesses.

badge. A sign or mark worn on the clothing which shows that its owner is a member of some group or has some special authority. Badges are worn by policemen.

badger *(badg'-er).* 1. A small, four-legged animal which lives in burrows. 2. To badger means to worry or annoy.

baffle *(baf'-fle).* To puzzle; frustrate the efforts of. A thief whom the police cannot find is said to baffle them. He frustrates their efforts to find him.

baggage *(bag'-gage).* Luggage or suit-cases; the belongings of a person which he needs when moving about from place to place.

bail. 1. When a person is waiting to be tried in court, he is kept in prison unless someone puts up bail for him. The bail is a sum of money which is given as security that the accused person will appear in court at the time of his trial. If he does not appear, the bail is not returned. 2. To bail out a boat is to scoop out the water that has leaked into it. 3. To bail out of an aeroplane is to jump out of it in order to make a parachute landing.

bait. 1. Material with which traps, fish-hooks, etc., are made tempting. 2. To torment.

baker *(bak'-er).* One who makes and sells baked goods such as bread, pies, cakes, etc.

balance *(bal'-ance).* 1. A delicate pair of scales. 2. To balance two things is to make them equal, as "His good qualities balanced his bad ones". 3. To balance something is to cause it to remain in a steady position without falling. 4. A balance-sheet is an account of how the money of a business was received and spent.

balcony *(bal'-co-ny).* 1. A small platform outside an upstair window, on which people can stand. 2. A part of a theatre, raised above the ground floor.

bald. Lacking hair or feathers where these should be.

bale. A large bundle of merchandise which is tied with cord or metal wire to secure it for shipment.

balk. 1. To baffle or disappoint. 2. To be stubborn or refuse to move. When a mule sits and refuses to move, he is balking.

ballad *(bal'-lad).* 1. A simple popular song. 2. A short poem written in four-line verses that tells a sad or exciting story.

ballast *(bal'-last).* Heavy material, such as sand, placed in the lower parts of a ship to steady it and to prevent rolling in high seas.

ballet *(bal'-let)*. 1. A kind of dancing. 2. A stage perform-ance in which ballet dancing is the chief feature.

balloon *(bal-loon')*. 1. An air-tight container which is filled with a gas lighter than air so that it will rise. 2. A bag-like rubber toy that can be filled with air or gas.

ballot *(bal'-lot)*. 1. A slip of paper used in voting. The voter marks his choice on the ballot, which is then folded and put into a ballot-box. Thus the vote is kept secret. 2. The method of taking a secret vote.

balsam *(bal'-sam)*. A kind of fir tree.

balmy *(balm'-y)*. 1. Fragrant. 2. Soft and soothing.

bamboo *(bam-boo')*. A tall, thick tropical grass with hollow stems. Bamboo is used for making canes, furniture and houses.

ban. 1. To forbid a thing. 2. A prohibition, as in "There is a ban on talking in the corridors".

banana *(ba-na'-na)*. A tropical fruit which grows in clusters called hands. It is shaped like a finger and grows 4 to 6 inches in length.

bandage *(band'-age)*. A narrow strip of material used for dressing a wound.

bandit *(ban'-dit)*. A robber, highwayman, or any kind of thief who uses violence.

bane. Something causing death, harm or grief.

baneful *(bane'-ful)*. Harmful; worrying; destructive.

bangle *(ban'-gle)*. A thin bracelet worn on the wrist.

banish *(ban'-ish)*. To force someone to go away and not return, at least not for a long time. To send into exile.

banister *(ban'-is-ter)*. One of the posts supporting the handrail of a staircase Also spelled **bannister.**

banjo *(ban'-jo)*. A stringed musical instrument belonging to the same class as the guitar. The strings are plucked with a finger or a metal pick.

bank. 1. The side of a river. 2. A place where one can take one's money for safe keeping. 3. A shallow area in the sea or in a river. 4. To bank up a fire means to heap small coals on it in order to make it burn slowly. 5. An aeroplane banks when it dips one wing as it makes a turn in the air.

bankrupt *(bank'-rupt)*. A person who cannot pay his debts and who goes to one of the law courts and makes a full statement as to what he owes and what money he possesses.

banner *(ban'-ner)*. A kind of flag.

banns. A notice given out three times in church before two people marry.

banquet *(ban'-quet)*. A grand dinner, usually followed by speeches.

bantam *(ban'-tam)*. 1. A small fowl. 2. Small competitors in boxing matches are spoken of as bantam-weights.

banter *(ban'-ter)*. Talk in which people jokingly make fun of the others present.

baptism *(bap'-tism)*. The admission of a person, usually a baby, into the Christian Church by the act of sprinkling him with holy water. In some cases, the person is dipped completely in the water.

barbarian *(bar-bar'-i-an)*. 1. A person belonging to an uncivilized race. 2. A rude or savage person.

barbarous *(bar'-ba-rous)*. 1. Uncivilized. 2. Savage and cruel.

barbecue *(bar'-be-cue)*. 1. Food which is cooked over an open fire. 2. Device on which food is cooked. 3. To cook in a flavoured sauce.

barber *(bar'-ber)*. A person who cuts hair, shaves, or trims beards for money.

bard. A poet.

bare. 1. Without clothes or covering; naked. 2. Without furniture; empty.

bareback *(bare'-back)*. On a horse without a saddle, as "Mary was in such a hurry that she did not wait to saddle the pony but rode him bareback to the next farm".

barefaced *(bare'-faced)*. Impudent; shameless.

barely *(bare'-ly)*. Scarcely.

bargain *(bar'-gain)*. 1. To agree to exchange something for something else is to bargain, or to make a bargain. To bargain also means to argue over the price of an article. 2. Something bought cheaply.

barge. A flat-bottomed boat for carrying goods, usually on rivers or canals.

baritone *(bar'-i-tone)*. A man who sings, his voice coming between that of a tenor (high) and a bass (low).

bark. 1. The outer covering of tree trunks. 2. The noise made by dogs, etc.

barley *(bar'-ley)*. A kind of grass, the seeds of which are used as a cereal and in making malt.

barn. A farm building, used for storing grain and housing animals.

barometer *(ba-rom'-e-ter)*. A scientific instrument for measuring the pressure of air and thus indicating changes of weather.

baron *(bar'-on)*. A man belonging to the lowest class of the nobility.

barracks *(bar'-racks)*. A building for housing soldiers.

barrage *(bar'-rage)*. 1. A dam. 2. A barrage of gun-fire is a heavy shelling in one direction to prevent the advance of the enemy.

barrel *(bar'-rel)*. 1. A cask. 2. The tube of a gun or rifle. 3. A measure of liquids.

barren *(bar'-ren)*. 1. Not bearing fruit, children, etc. 2. A tract of waste land.

barrier *(bar'-ri-er)*. A thing put up to stop people and animals from passing.

barter *(bar'-ter)*. The exchange of goods.

base. 1. The bottom part of a thing, such as the base of a triangle. 2. The headquarters of an army is known as its base. 3. Base also means selfish, mean, or worthless.

basement *(base'-ment)*. The bottom floor of a building, usually below ground level.

bashful *(bash'-ful)*. Shy; uneasy.

basin *(ba'-sin)*. 1. A bowl used to hold water. A basin may be found in the bathroom or the kitchen. 2. The land which is drained by a river and its tributaries.

bask. To warm oneself comfortably by sitting in the sun, before the fire, etc.

basket *(bas'-ket)*. 1. A container made from wood. 2. The amount which it holds. "We ate a basket of apples." 3. A goal scored in basketball.

basketball *(bas'-ket-ball)*. 1. A game played by two teams of five players. The object of the game is to throw a large ball through a basket-shaped device which is suspended above the floor. 2. The ball which is used in basketball.

bass. 1. The lowest male voice. 2. A kind of fish with prickly fins.

baste. 1. To stitch together loosely before putting in the finishing stitches. 2. To moisten roasting meat with fat or butter.

bastion *(bas'-tion)*. A part jutting out from the wall of a castle or fort. It enabled defenders to shoot at the backs of the enemy attacking the castle.

bat. 1. A winged animal resembling a mouse. 2. The striking instrument used in baseball, table-tennis, cricket, etc.

batch. Several things considered together, all being in some way alike.

bate. 1. To hold back, as "With bated breath—he was holding his breath—he watched the door open slowly". 2. To lower, as, for example, the price of a thing.

bath. 1. The complete washing of the body. 2. The tub of water in which the bath is taken. 3. To put into a bath and wash.

bathe. 1. To go swimming. 2. To place in water as "He bathed his sore finger in a bowl of warm water". 3. To bathe also means to cover, as in "The fields were bathed in sunlight".

baton *(ba-ton'* or *bat'-on)*. 1. The stick used by the conductor of an orchestra for beating time. 2. The stick carried by field-marshals and others as a symbol of their rank.

battalion *(bat-tal'-ion)*. A portion of an army of soldiers; usually about a thousand men.

batten *(bat'-ten)*. 1. To secure with battens. 2. A wooden board like a plank. 3. A bar of wood used to clamp other boards.

batter *(bat'-ter)*. 1. The mixture used for making pancakes, certain puddings, etc., which consists largely of flour and water. 2. To hit or beat with many blows.

battery *(bat'-ter-y)*. 1. Cells which produce a current of electricity. 2. A group of similar things, such as a battery of tests all made to test a person's education. 3. A term used in the army to refer to a number of large guns and to the men who operate them.

battle *(bat'-tle)*. 1. A fight, usually between armies. 2. A contest: "The angry boys had a battle of words".

battlements *(bat'-tle-ments)*. A wall at the top of a tower, etc., which has regular cut-out parts all the way along.

bawl. To cry out in a loud way. A sergeant may bawl commands to the soldiers.

bay. 1. A portion of a large body of water which makes a curve into the land. 2. The colour brownish-chestnut. 3. An evergreen bush of the laurel family the leaves of which are used as a spice. 4. A part of a wall that stands out from the rest, thus allowing extra space in the room inside. A window is often set out from a wall in this way and such a window is called a bay-window. 5. To bark, said usually of a hunting dog when it is chasing some animal. 6. When the dog has caught up with the animal, and the animal turns to face its pursuers, it is said to be at bay.

bayonet *(bay'-o-net)*. A knife-like weapon with a sharp point, attached to the end of a rifle.

bazaar *(ba-zaar')*. 1. The shopping centre in oriental towns. 2. A sale of work held in a church hall, etc., to collect money for charitable purposes.

beach. 1. The fringe of sand on the edge of the sea. 2. To beach a boat is to run it up on the shore.

beacon *(bea'-con)*. The light at the top of a lighthouse, or any other light serving as a warning.

bead. Small shapes of attractive material threaded on a string and worn for ornamental and religious purposes.

beagle *(bea'-gle)*. A small dog used in hunting hares.

beak. The bill of a bird, consisting of its mouth and nostrils.

beaker *(beak'-er)*. A large cup.

beam. 1. A piece of timber such as is used for the framework of houses. 2. A ray of light. 3. A pleasant smile.

bean. 1. A kidney-shaped seed which is eaten as a vegetable. 2. A green or yellow pod containing such seeds and eaten as a vegetable.

bear. 1. To carry. 2. To endure; put up with. "He bears his misfortune well" means that he shows courage and patience in putting up with his misfortune. 3. A very large, clumsy, four-legged animal with shaggy fur.

beard. Hair on the lower part of the face.

bearer *(bear'-er)*. A person who carries or brings something.

bearing *(bear'-ing)*. 1. In "He had a fine bearing", bearing refers to his way of moving, standing and dealing with his fellow-men. 2. In "We soon lost our bearings", bearings means way or direction. 3. In "He was bearing a load", bearing means carrying.

beast. Any large four-footed animal.

beat. 1. To strike or hit. 2. In cookery, to stir quickly. 3. To get the better of. 4. In music, the time or the rhythm. 5. A regular journey, as a policeman's beat.

beautify *(beau'-ti-fy)*. To make **beautiful**; to adorn.

beaver *(bea'-ver)*. 1. An amphibious, thick-furred animal of the rat family with a large flat tail. It cuts down trees to build dams and lodges. 2. A man's top hat made of beaver-fur or some imitation of it. 3. The lower part of a knight's helmet, which protected the mouth.

becalmed *(be-calmed')*. When a sailing ship is becalmed, it is unable to move because there is no wind to fill the sails.

beckon *(beck'-on)*. To make a sign with the hand or head, in order to ask someone to come to you.

becoming *(be-com'-ing)*. Appropriate and fitting.

bedeck *(be-deck')*. To adorn or make beautiful with fine clothes.

bedlam *(bed'-lam)*. A great noisy uproar.

bedraggled *(be-drag'-gled)*. Dirty and untidy, as though dragged through dust and mud.

bedridden *(bed'-rid'-den)*. Forced to stay in bed.

bee. 1. The insect that gives honey. 2. A spelling-bee is a contest between two sides. Each side asks the other side to spell difficult words. 3. A gathering for getting work done, as a sewing bee.

beech. A large tree with a smooth greyish bark.

beef. The flesh of oxen, bulls, cows, etc.

beehive *(bee'-hive)*. 1. A home for bees. 2. A busy place.

beet. A plant having a fleshy root. Red beetroot is eaten in salads, etc., and white beetroot is grown for beet sugar.

beetle *(bee'-tle)*. 1. An insect with hard, shiny wings. 2. A wooden mallet or hammer. 3. To overhang. People sometimes refer to beetled eyebrows, meaning eyebrows that stick out.

befalls *(be-falls')*. Happens; comes to pass.

befitting *(be-fit'-ting)*. Suitable; becoming.

beforehand *(be-fore'-hand)*. Some time in advance. In "She bought a ticket for Europe beforehand", the word "beforehand" tells that the ticket was bought some time before the journey was made.

befriend *(be-friend')*. To be friendly to.

beggar *(beg'-gar)*. 1. A person who lives by asking others to give to him. 2. A very poor person.

beggary *(beg'-gar-y)*. A state of poverty.

beginner *(be-gin'-ner)*. A person who is doing something for the first time.

begone *(be-gone')*. Usually a command, this word means "Go away!"

begrudge *(be-grudge')*. To envy a person because he has something you want.

beguile *(be-guile')*. 1. To cheat. 2. To let the time slip away pleasantly. 3. To amuse.

behalf *(be-half')*. Usually found in sentences such as "He went there on my behalf", meaning for me, in my interest or in my favour.

behave *(be-have')*. 1. To conduct oneself; to act. 2. When a mother says to her child, "Now, behave yourself!" she means "Now, act properly!"

behold *(be-hold')*. To look at or to see.

beholden *(be-hol'-den)*. In your debt. In "I am much beholden to you for all you have done", beholden shows you have done me a favour and I am in your debt.

belated *(be-lat'-ed)*. Late; delayed; out-of-date.

belfry *(bel'-fry)*. A tower in which a bell is hung.

belie *(be-lie')*. To represent falsely; to give a wrong idea of. Thus, if a person has a pleasing nature but a fierce look, it might be said that his looks belie his nature.

belief *(be-lief')*. 1. An idea or teaching in which one has trust, as in "Christian beliefs". 2. An opinion or a view.

believe *(be-lieve')*. To trust; to think; to have faith in.

belligerent *(bel-lig'-er-ent)*. 1. The opposing sides in a battle or a war are called belligerents. 2. Fierce; warlike.

bellow *(bel'-low)*. To roar like a bull.

bellows *(bel'-lows)*. An instrument which, when quickly opened and closed, produces a wind. This wind may be used for blowing up a fire, making sounds in organ pipes, separating chaff from grain, etc.

belt. 1. A piece of material worn around the body to hold clothing or weapons in place. 2. A strap in the shape of a loop which connects a moving wheel with another one, so that both turn. Sometimes such a moving strap is used to convey objects from one place to another. It is then called a **conveyor belt**. 3. A particular strip or zone of territory such as the cotton belt of the U.S.A.

bemoan *(be-moan')*. To wail or moan about something.

bench. 1. A long seat. 2. A carpenter's work-table. 3. A group of judges or magistrates.

bend. 1. To apply pressure to something straight so as to curve it. "The strong man was able to bend the bar." 2. A curve or turning. We speak of bends in rivers and roads. 3. To bend to someone's will is to give in to him.

benediction *(ben-e-dic'-tion)*. A blessing.

benefaction *(ben-e-fac'-tion)*. An act of kindness.

benefactor *(ben'-e-fac-tor)*. A person who benefits others, usually by giving them money.

beneficence *(be-nef'-i-cence)*. The act of doing good.

beneficial *(ben-e-fi'-cial)*. Advantageous; favourable; helpful.

benefit *(ben'-e-fit)*. Anything that is an advantage or produces good effects.

benevolent *(be-nev'-o-lent)*. Kind; charitable; anxious to make others happy.

benign *(be-nign')*. Kind; gentle; harmless.

bequeath *(be-queath')*. To give by will (see **will**, No. 2). Gifts so left are called **bequests.**

bereaved *(be-reaved')*. A person who is bereaved is one who has lost a relation or friend through death.

beret *(be'-ret)*. A flat woollen cap.

berry *(ber'-ry)*. Any small, roundish fruit without a stone.

berth. 1. A sleeping place on a train or ship. 2. The side of a dock or quay where a vessel is tied.

beseech *(be-seech')*. To beg and implore.

beset *(be-set')*. Hemmed in on all sides.

besiege *(be-siege')*. To lay siege to; to attack.

bespattered *(be-spat'-tered)*. In "He went along the road and was bespattered with mud", bespattered means splashed.

bespeak *(be-speak')*. 1. To ask for a thing in advance. 2. To be evidence of, as in "A bright smile bespeaks a happy person".

bestial *(bes'-tial)*. Beastly; like a beast; vile.

bestir *(be-stir')*. To rouse; to stir up.

bestow *(be-stow')*. To give.

bet. 1. To promise payment to another person if a certain event does not turn out as you predict. If it does turn out as you predict, the other person will make the payment to you. 2. The payment which is promised, as "The bet was sixpence".

betide *(be-tide')*. To happen. Thus "Whatever betides" means "Whatever happens".

betray *(be-tray')*. 1. To deliver someone who trusts you over to an enemy is to betray him. 2. To betray someone's hopes is to disappoint him after you have led him to believe that you would not disappoint him.

betrothal *(be-troth'-al)*. The engagement of two people to be married.

better *(bet'-ter)*. 1. More than good, but not the best (**good, better, best**). 2. When a person has been ill, and is recovering, he is said to be better. 3. A person who bets is a better. 4. To get the better of someone is to beat him at some game or contest.

bevel *(bev'-el)*. A sloping or slanting edge. Looking glasses often have bevelled edges.

beverage *(bev'-er-age)*. A drink such as tea, cocoa or beer.

bevy *(bev'-y)*. A flock (of birds) or a gathering (of women).

bewail *(be-wail')*. To cry over; weep for; show great sorrow for.

beware *(be-ware')*. Take care; thus a notice saying "Beware— High Tension Wires", calls your attention to the fact that you must take care because of the electric current.

bewilder *(be-wil'-der)*. To make a person feel puzzled and anxious about what may happen.

bewitch *(be-witch')*. To charm somebody by magic, or as if by magic.

beyond *(be-yond')*. 1. Further than; in the distance. "The aircraft climbed beyond the clouds." 2. More than, as in "The price of the suit was beyond his means".

bias *(bi'-as)*. 1. A line that slants. **On the bias** means diagonally. 2. A prejudice. A person who has prejudices is said to be **biased.**

biceps *(bi'-ceps)*. The muscles of the upper arm.

bicker *(bick'-er)*. To quarrel; to nag.

bicycle *(bi'-cy-cle)*. A vehicle having two wheels, a cross-bar and handle-bars, on which a person sits and moves forward by using foot pedals.

bid. 1. To offer to pay, as in "He bid two pounds for the chair at the auction sale". 2. The amount which is offered. 3. To say, as in "I bid you farewell". 4. To command, as in "The leader bids his men to rest".

bide. To wait. To bide one's time is to wait patiently.

biennial *(bi-en'-ni-al)*. 1. Happening once every two years; lasting for two years. 2. A plant that normally lives two years.

bier. A carriage or stretcher for taking a dead body in a coffin from one place to another.

bigamy *(big'-a-my)*. A man who takes a second wife while he is still married to his first has committed bigamy. A married woman who takes a second husband while married to the first also commits bigamy.

bigot *(big'-ot)*. A person who holds a strong opinion without having any real knowledge of the matter.

bilious *(bil'-ious)*. Suffering from ill-health because the liver is not working properly.

bill. 1. A public notice serving as an advertisement, stuck on a hoarding, etc. 2. The horny mouth and nose of a bird. 3. An account of purchases made in a store, or of work done, for which payment must be made. When payment is made, a receipt is given. 4. A draft of a law before it is passed and made official by the Royal signature.

billet *(bil'-let)*. 1. A place where soldiers are lodged. 2. To assign to lodgings.

billion *(bil'-lion)*. In Great Britain, a million millions. In North America and some continental countries, a thousand millions.

billow *(bil'-low)*. 1. A wave on the sea. 2. To swell out in the shape of a wave. Thus, "Her skirt billowed in the breeze".

bin. A box in which goods are stored; there are corn bins, bread bins, coal bins, dust bins.

bind. 1. To fasten with a cord; tie up, as in "Bind the package before shipping so that it will not break open". 2. To bind yourself to do something is to promise to do it. 3. To bind a book is to sew the pages together and put on a cover. The cover is called the **binding.** 4. To bind the edge of a piece of material is to fold another strip of material lengthwise over the edge and sew it down on either side. The strip of material is called the **binding.**

binder *(bind'-er)*. 1. A machine which is used to tie things together. 2. A loose-leaf note-book cover which holds sheets of paper in place.

binoculars *(bin-oc'-u-lars)*. Field glasses or opera glasses which make distant things seem nearer than they are.

biography *(bi-og'-ra-phy)*. The story of a person's life. (See **autobiography.**)

biology *(bi-ol'-o-gy)*. The study of living things.

biped *(bi'-ped)*. An animal with two feet. You are a biped.

biplane *(bi'-plane)*. An aeroplane with two sets of wings, one over the other. A plane with only one set of wings is called a **monoplane.**

birch. A tree with a silvery bark.

birth. 1. Being born. The day you were born was your day of birth, or **birthday.** 2. The beginning, as in "the birth of the idea". 3. Family, in such expressions as "He was of noble birth".

biscuit *(bis'cuit)*. A small crisp cake.

bisect *(bi-sect')*. To divide into two equal parts.

bishop *(bish'-op)*. 1. The chief clergyman in a district or diocese. Often his church is a cathedral. 2. One of the pieces used in a game of chess.

bison *(bi'-son)*. A kind of buffalo or ox.

bit. 1. A small piece, as "a bit of cake". 2. A steel bar which fits inside a horse's mouth, to which the reins are attached. 3. In a small way, as "He is a bit stupid".

bitch. A female dog.

bite. 1. To injure with the teeth. 2. A mouthful, as "Give me a bite, please". 3. The wound made by teeth.

biting *(bit'-ing)*. 1. Sharp or cutting, as "A biting wind will sting the face", or "A biting remark will hurt the feelings of the person to whom you address it".

bitter *(bit'-ter)*. 1. The opposite of sweet. 2. Anything causing grief or great discomfort is bitter.

bitumen *(bit'-u-men)*. Black minerals of the asphalt group used for surfacing roads, etc.

bivalve *(bi'-valve)*. 1. Having two shells joined together by a hinge. 2. Creatures that have such shells, such as cockles, oysters, etc., are called bivalves.

bivouac *(biv'-ou-ac)*. To camp without a tent, usually for a short time.

bizarre *(bi-zarre')*. Odd; unusual; curious.

blackberry *(black'-ber-ry)*. A small black or purple fruit which grows on bushes and which may be eaten.

blackboard *(black'-board)*. A large wooden board painted a dark colour on which one writes with chalk.

blackmail *(black'-mail)*. 1. To threaten a person that unless he agrees to pay a sum of money something which he wants kept secret will be revealed. 2. The crime of obtaining money in this manner.

blacksmith *(black'-smith)*. A man who makes things of iron, such as horseshoes.

bladder *(blad'-der)*. 1. Any organ in the body which serves as a bag to hold air or liquids. 2. Any container for air or liquid with a thin outer skin.

blade. 1. A long, thin, flat piece of steel with one or more cutting edges. 2. The leaf of a piece of grass. 3. The flat, wide part of an oar.

blame. 1. To say that someone has done wrong is to blame him. 2. When one accepts the responsibility for a wrong deed, he accepts the blame.

blameless *(blame'-less)*. One who does no wrong is blameless. Innocent.

blank. 1. Empty. 2. Something which is empty, as "His mind was a blank". 3. A blank cartridge is a cartridge without a bullet.

blanket *(blan'-ket)*. 1. A woollen covering. 2. Anything which covers a large area or a number of things, such as a blanket of fog or a blanket law to cover many things.

blare. To make a sound like that of a trumpet.

blasphemy *(blas'-phe-my)*. Speaking disrespectfully of sacred things. To do so is to **blaspheme** *(blas-pheme')* and what is said is **blasphemous** *(blas'-phe-mous)*.

blast. 1. To blow up rocks with explosives. 2. A rush of wind or air. 3. A harsh noise made by a bugle, etc. 4. To shrivel up and die.

blaze. 1. A rush of flame. 2. To burn with a flame. 3. To spread (news) about. 4. A white mark made by stripping bark from or cutting a mark into a tree trunk. 5. A white mark on the face of a horse or ox.

bleach. To bleach something is to take the colour out of it.

bleak. 1. The weather is bleak when it is cold and windy. 2. A place is bleak when it is bare and dreary.

bleat. The cry of sheep, etc.

bleed. 1. To lose blood. 2. Plants bleed when they lose sap. 3. To feel sorry for someone, as "My heart bled for the little boy when I saw the car hit his dog".

blemish *(blem'-ish)*. A mark or defect which makes a thing imperfect.

blend. To mix together two or more things so that they cannot be separated again. Blended tea is made from several kinds of tea leaves mixed together to give the required quality.

bless. 1. To ask God's favour for someone or on something. We bless our food before eating. What is said is a **blessing.** 2. To praise, as in "We bless Thee, Our Father".

blew. The past tense of blow, as in "The wind blew for three days".

blight. 1. A disease of plants which makes them wither. 2. Anything causing misfortune.

blind. 1. Unable to see; without sight. 2. Closed at one end, as a blind alley. 3. To blind someone is to take away his ability to see. You might blind a bear by shining a bright light in his eyes. 4. An inside covering for a window, which can be pulled down to shut out the light.

blink. To open and shut the eyes rapidly.

bliss. Great happiness.

blister *(blis'-ter)*. A swelling on the skin, filled with a watery fluid. An ill-fitting shoe often causes a blister on the heel.

blithe. Jolly; cheery; happy.

blizzard *(bliz'-zard)*. A blinding snowstorm with a raging wind.

bloated *(bloat'-ed)*. Puffed and swollen.

block. 1. A solid mass, as a block of ice. 2. An obstacle, such as a block in the traffic. 3. A piece of wood or iron for supporting a pulley-wheel. 4. A piece of land with buildings on it, enclosed by streets. 5. To obstruct; to stand in the way of.

blockade *(block-ade')*. When an army or navy, in time of war, prevents people or goods from entering or leaving a place, we say that they are imposing a blockade.

blockhead *(block'-head)*. A person with no sense.

blonde. A person with light hair, a fair complexion and, usually, blue eyes.

blood. 1. The red liquid which flows through the veins. 2. The expression "bad blood" refers to ill feeling or animosity between two people.

bloodhound *(blood'-hound)*. A kind of dog used for hunting. The bloodhound has a keen sense of smell.

bloodshot *(blood'-shot)*. When eyes are bloodshot, they are red or inflamed.

bloodsucker *(blood'-suck-er)*. 1. A leech or animal which sucks blood. 2. A person who does his best to take advantage of others by unfair means.

bloodthirsty *(blood'-thirst-y)*. Cruel; eager to kill.

bloom. 1. A flower. 2. The dusty covering seen on such fruits as grapes, peaches, etc.

blossom *(blos'-som)*. A flower; a bloom.

blot. 1. A spot of ink, etc., dropped on paper. 2. To blot writing is to dry the ink by pressing a kind of paper on it which will absorb ink. Such paper is called **blotting paper.** 3. To blot out means to rub out, cross out, or cover up so that it cannot be seen.

blotch. A spot with uneven edges. We speak of blotches on the skin or of a blotch forming when ink is spilled on tissue paper.

blouse. A garment worn by women on the upper half of the body.

blow. 1. In "The wind blows sharply", blows sharply means moves along quickly. 2. In "The whistles at the factory blow at noon", blow means sound. 3. In "He gave the boy a sharp blow", blow means a slap or hit. 4. In "His death was a blow to the family", blow means a surprise that caused great sorrow. 5. When one blows up a balloon, one fills it with air.

blubber *(blub'-ber).* 1. The oily part of a whale. 2. To cry noisily.

bludgeon *(bludg'-eon).* 1. A stick or club heavy at one end and used in fighting. 2. To hit many times with a heavy object.

blue. 1. A colour, as in "blue sky". 2. Sad: "He felt blue when he lost the race".

blueprint *(blue'-print).* A drawing or a plan which shows white lines on a blue background. When men are building a house, they follow a blueprint or a plan.

bluff. 1. A steep hill or cliff. 2. Kindly, in a rough sort of way. 3. A man who speaks bluffly says what he thinks, without worrying about being polite. 4. To act as though you could do something you cannot do, in the hope of deceiving others.

blunder *(blun'-der).* 1. To make a careless mistake. 2. To stumble and perhaps fall over something.

blunt. 1. Having a cutting edge that is not sharp. 2. Outspoken; saying just what you think.

blur. Smear.

blush. To turn red in the face through shame, fear, or through feeling awkward.

bluster *(blus'-ter).* 1. To talk in a boasting way. 2. When the wind blows boisterously we say it is a blustery wind.

board. 1. A flat and fairly thin piece of wood. 2. The meals provided for a lodger. 3. A gathering of people who meet to control some society or business, such as a Board of Directors. 4. The edge of certain things, as the seaboard.

boarder *(board'-er).* One who pays to be provided with a room and meals in a house he does not own.

boast. 1. To brag; to speak with too much pride about yourself, about what you have done or about what you are able to do. 2. An arrogant claim. "I'm the cleverest boy in the class" is a boast.

bob. To move up and down quickly, as "The cork bobbed up and down on the water".

bobbin *(bob'-bin).* A spool or pin on which thread, cotton, etc., is wound.

bobsleigh *(bob'-sleigh).* A long board attached to two short sleighs. It is sometimes called a **bobsled.**

bodkin *(bod'-kin).* A blunt needle, used for threading cord, elastic, etc., through holes.

body *(bod'-y).* 1. The whole of a person or animal, as when speaking of a dead body. 2. That part of a person which does not include the head, arms or legs. 3. A group of people, as "The main body of soldiers advanced". 4. In the sentence, "The moon is a heavenly body", body means object.

bodyguard *(bod'-y-guard).* Men whose duty it is to guard some important person.

bog. A piece of wet, spongy ground.

bogus *(bo'-gus).* Sham; imitation; not real.

boil. 1. To heat liquids, etc., until they reach a temperature at which they turn into steam. To froth and bubble. 2. To be furious, as when a person boils with rage. 3. A painful swelling filled with pus.

boiler *(boil'-er).* 1. A container for heating water or other liquids. 2. A tank in which hot water is kept.

boisterous *(bois'-ter-ous).* Stormy; rough and noisy.

bold. 1. Daring and fearless. 2. Lacking in manners; cheeky.

bollard *(bol'-lard).* A stout wooden or iron post to which ropes are secured on a ship, dock or quay.

bolster *(bol'-ster).* 1. A long pillow placed at the head of a bed. 2. To bolster up means to support.

bolt. 1. A sliding bar used to fasten a door. 2. A rod of steel or iron, used to fasten something in place. It has a head at one end and at the other a nut screws on to tighten the bolt. 3. To run away suddenly. A horse often bolts when it is frightened. 4. To bolt food is to swallow it quickly without chewing it enough. 5. A **thunderbolt** is a flash of lightning with a crash of thunder.

bomb. 1. Any article filled with an explosive that explodes and blows things to pieces. 2. To place or throw a bomb so that it will explode.

bombard *(bom-bard')*. To attack an enemy with bombs or other explosives.

bombast *(bom'-bast)*. Pompous or boastful talk. Such talk is **bombastic** *(bom-bas'-tic)*.

bona fide *(bo'-na fi'-de)*. In good faith.

bond. 1. Anything that binds people. 2. Most governments issue bonds, which are certificates for money lent them. 3. An arrangement in writing between two people by which one of them promises to pay a sum of money in return for which the other agrees to do something. 4. Goods are said to be in bond while they are being stored, awaiting the duty to be paid on them. 5. The way bricks are placed together by a bricklayer when building a wall or the side of a house.

bondage *(bond'-age)*. Slavery.

bondsman *(bonds'-man)*. A slave.

bone. 1. The hard parts in the body or the skeleton of a person or animal. When you break your leg, you break the bone in your leg. 2. To cut out the bone. The butcher bones meat when he prepares some kinds of joints.

bonfire *(bon'-fire)*. A fire which is made out of doors.

bonnet *(bon'-net)*. 1. A hat worn by children and ladies which pulls over the ears and fastens under the chin. 2. A lady's hat. 3. A covering for machinery such as the engine of a motor-car.

bonny *(bon'-ny)*. Handsome; happy and contented looking; looking in the pink of health; plump.

bonus *(bo'-nus)*. Money or goods given in addition to what is owing. A bonus payment is money paid in addition to wages.

bony *(bo'-ny)*. Thin; with very little flesh covering the bones.

booby *(boo'-by)*. A dunce; a silly person.

book. 1. A set of printed pages put in a cover. This dictionary is a book. 2. To book means to reserve or engage, as "He booked three seats at the Opera".

bookworm *(book'-worm)*. 1. A person who spends most of his time in reading and studying books. 2. An insect that chews the leaves and bindings of books.

boomerang *(boom'-er-ang)*. 1. A weapon made of a curved piece of wood which can be thrown in such a way that it goes forward, then curves round and comes back. 2. A plan or action that boomerangs has an unexpected bad effect on the person who made or did it.

boon. 1. A blessing. 2. A favour.

boor. A coarse, ill-mannered person.

booth. 1. A small building used as a store. You may buy sweets at one of the booths you find at a fair. 2. A small public building in which you may make a telephone call.

boot. Shoe that covers the ankles.

booty *(boo'-ty)*. 1. Plunder or things stolen by pirates, robbers, etc. 2. The things that are left behind when an enemy has to retreat in warfare.

border *(bor'-der)*. The edge, limit or boundary of something. We speak of the border between England and Scotland. You may draw a border around a picture.

bore. 1. To drill a hole in something is to bore a hole in it. 2. The hollow part of a tube, such as the bore of a rifle. 3. When you are tired out by something that is not interesting, you are bored with it. 4. A person or thing that is boring or uninteresting is a bore. 5. Bore is the past tense of **bear.**

born. 1. Brought into existence, as "A baby was born at our house". 2. Having certain characteristics from birth, as "He was a born cricketer".

borough *(bor'ough)*. A town of some size having its own mayor and corporation.

borrow *(bor'-row)*. To have the use of another person's money or goods for a time.

bosom *(bos'-om)*. 1. Breast; the upper front part of the body. 2. Trusted or close, as in "a bosom friend".

boss. 1. Master. 2. To tell what to do.

botany *(bot'-a-ny)*. The study of plants. A person who studies plants is a **botanist.**

botch. To spoil a thing by not taking pains when making it.

bother *(both'-er)*. 1. A worry or trouble; a nuisance. 2. To worry or trouble; to cause a nuisance.

bottle *(bot'-tle)*. A container made of glass which holds liquids.

bottom *(bot'-tom)*. 1. The lowest part. "He did not drink all his milk; he left some in the bottom of the glass." 2. The land under water, as in "the river bottom". 3. Cause, as in "The police will get to the bottom of the mystery".

bough. A branch of a tree.

bought. The past tense of **buy.** "You may not buy a book to-day because you bought one yesterday."

boulder *(boul'-der)*. A large rock worn smooth by water or weather.

boulevard *(bou'-le-vard)*. A French word meaning a wide street or road, usually lined with trees.

bounce. 1. To rebound; to hit something and then fly back, as a rubber ball does when it hits the ground. To bounce into a room is to burst in noisily or energetically. 2. A bouncing baby is a lively, healthy baby.

bound. 1. In "With one bound he cleared the fence", bound means jump or leap. 2. In "The ship was bound for Australia", bound means going to. 3. In "The book was bound in leather", bound means covered. 4. In "You are bound to stay", bound means forced. 5. In "They bound him hand and foot", bound means tied.

boundary *(bound'-a-ry)*. A line showing where one place ends and another begins. A border or limit.

bounteous *(boun'-te-ous)*. Generous.

bounty *(boun'-ty)*. A gift or reward.

bouquet *(bou-quet')*. A bunch of flowers carefully arranged.

bout. 1. A fight or contest. 2. A stage or round in a fight or contest. 3. A spell or turn, as a "bout of 'flu", meaning an attack of 'flu.

bow. 1. To bend, kneel or nod the head in greeting. 2. The front of a boat or ship. 3. A weapon for shooting arrows, made of a curved stick and a string. 4. An instrument used to play the violin, consisting of a wooden stick along which strands of horsehair are stretched. The horsehairs are pulled back and forth across the violin strings. 5. A slip-knot with one or two loops.

bower *(bow'-er)*. A leafy shelter provided by trees, vines and bushes, etc., whose branches form the roof and walls. Usually a seat is set in the bower.

bowl. 1. A container with curved sides that will hold liquids as well as dry things. 2. To toss the ball at the stumps in cricket. 3. One of the wooden balls which are rolled along the ground in the game of bowls. 4. To bowl along is to roll along smoothly like a bowling ball.

box. 1. A six-sided case of cardboard, wood or metal for packing or storing things. 2. A private enclosure with seats at the theatre. 3. A smack on the side of the head. 4. To box is to slap with the hand or to fight with the fists.

boxwood *(box'-wood)*. 1. An evergreen shrub used for hedges and borders. 2. The wood of the box tree.

boyhood *(boy'-hood)*. The state of being a boy; the time of life when a man is a boy.

brace. 1. Two of anything, such as a brace of pigeons. 2. A rod used to strengthen or hold two parts of a building together. 3. A tool used for holding a drill; this machine altogether is called a **brace and bit.** 4. To support; to strengthen with a brace. 5. A leather strap across the shoulder used to support trousers. In this sense the word is usually found in the plural.

bracelet *(brace'-let)*. An ornament worn on the wrist.

bracing *(bra'-cing)*. Usually said of air when it refreshes or makes one feel full of life.

bracket *(brack'-et)*. 1. Something fastened to a wall on which one end of a shelf rests. 2. Marks used to enclose words: [ ] ( ).

brackish *(brack'-ish)*. Having a slightly salty taste.

brag. To speak boastfully about the things you have done or could do. A person who brags is a **braggart.**

braid. 1. To weave or to plait strands of material together. 2. The material thus made.

braille. A system of writing in which letters are represented by raised dots. By touching these dots blind people can read. (Named after Louis Braille, a Frenchman who invented the system.)

brain. The organ inside the top of the head by which thinking and feeling are done and action is controlled.

brake. A thing used to slow down or stop a moving object.

bramble *(bram'-ble)*. A blackberry bush.

bran. The outsides, or husks, of grains of wheat.

branch. 1. A smaller part of a larger thing such as the branch of a tree; an arm; a tributary, such as the branch of a river. 2. A business may have a main office or store and several branches. The branches are smaller offices or stores which are all owned by the same business.

brandish *(bran'-dish)*. To wave or shake a thing such as a stick or a sword.

brass. A metal which is an alloy or mixture of copper and zinc.

bravado *(bra-va'-do)*. Pretended bravery.

brave. If a person faces danger without giving way we say that he is brave and that he displays **bravery.**

brawl. A noisy quarrel.

brawn. Muscular strength; a person with much brawn is **brawny.**

bray. The noise of an ass or a donkey.

brazen *(bra'-zen)*. 1. Made of brass. 2. Shameless; anyone who is so thick-skinned that nothing shames him is brazen.

breach. 1. A hole or gap made in something. 2. A breach of promise is a breaking of a promise.

bread. An article of food made from flour and baked in an oven. Bread and butter are eaten by most people every day.

break. 1. If you drop a glass on stone, the glass will break. 2. Sometimes prisoners break out of jail. 3. Farmers plant rows of trees to break the wind so that it will not blow soil away.

breaker *(break'-er)*. A large wave that rolls over on the beach and bounds upwards with a huge splash.

breakfast *(break'-fast)*. The first meal of the day.

breakwater *(break'-wa-ter)*. A wall built to protect a shore-line from the force of waves.

breast. 1. The front part of the body, just below the neck. 2. To make a clean breast of something is to own up to it or confess it.

breath. The air which comes from the mouth or nose.

breathe. 1. To take air into the lungs and expel it. 2. To whisper, as in "The baby's mother breathed sweet words into his ear."

breeches *(breech'-es)*. Trousers ending at the calf.

breeding *(breed'-ing)*. 1. The rearing of animals, as when farmers speak of cattle breeding. 2. The training or up-bringing that gives people good manners.

breeze. A slight wind.

breezy *(breez'-y)*. 1. The weather is breezy when there is a light wind blowing. 2. A man is said to be breezy when he is lively, happy, and never seems to have any troubles or cares or to be aware of those of others.

brevity *(brev'-i-ty)*. Shortness; briefness.

brew. 1. To make certain drinks, such as tea, by soaking, boiling or infusing. 2. To plot; plan, as "to brew up trouble". 3. "A storm is brewing" means a storm is gathering.

briar *(bri'-ar)*. 1. The wild rose plant. 2. A low shrub that grows in Southern Europe, from the roots of which pipes are made. 3. A pipe made of briar. Also spelled **brier**.

bribe. To give money or valuables to a person in order to make him do something that you both know to be wrong.

brick. 1. A block of clay which is baked in an oven. Bricks are used to make the outer walls of a house. 2. Anything shaped like a brick, such as a brick of ice-cream.

bride. A woman on the day she is married.

bridegroom *(bride'-groom)*. A man on the day he is married.

bridge. 1. A structure which is built to carry a road over a river. 2. The upper part of the nose. 3. A game played with cards. 4. A device to which false teeth are fixed to keep them in place.

bridle *(bri'-dle)*. 1. A piece of harness made to fit over the head of a horse, to which a bit and reins are attached. 2. Something that controls, holds back or checks.

brief. Short.

brigade *(bri-gade')*. 1. A large number of soldiers, usually about three battalions. 2. A group of people working for one object, as a fire brigade.

brigand *(brig'-and)*. A robber who robs people in lonely places.

bright. 1. Giving out or reflecting light. Sunshine is bright and new coins are bright. 2. A clever person is said to be bright.

brilliant *(bril'-liant)*. Shining; sparkling; also used when speaking of a very clever person.

brim. The upper edge of a cup. The edge of many things, as of a hat, etc.

brine. Salt water.

brink. The edge of a steep place such as a cliff, deep water, etc.

brisk. Lively; quick.

bristle *(bris'-tle)*. 1. Short stiff hairs. Brushes are made of bristles. 2. When hairs bristle they stand up on end. When an animal is angry, its hairs stand up on end and the animal is said to bristle. When used of people, to bristle means to take on an aggressive attitude. We sometimes say, "He was bristling with anger".

brittle *(brit'-tle)*. Easily breakable; fragile.

broach. 1. To bring up a topic for conversation. "After Jim had been speaking for a while, he broached the subject of honesty." 2. To open by making a hole. "He broached a keg of cider."

broad. Wide, not limited. We speak of a broad river. A person with broad views is one who sees a thing in many ways instead of one or two.

broadcast *(broad'-cast)*. The original meaning was to scatter over a wide area, as when a farmer sows seed by throwing it here and there by hand. The newer meaning, to send out information over the radio, may still be looked upon as "scattering over a wide area".

brocade *(bro-cade')*. Heavy, rich silk material with a raised, embroidered pattern.

broccoli *(broc'-co-li)*. A plant of the cabbage family with an edible flower.

brogue. 1. Speech that is marked by a special accent, particularly that of the Irish. 2. A heavy leather shoe.

broil. 1. To cook meat over an open fire. 2. To sit in the sun and become very hot.

broke. The past tense of break. "She broke her doll yesterday."

broker *(bro'-ker)*. A person who buys and sells things for someone else, charging a fee for his work.

bronchitis *(bron-chi'-tis)*. Inflammation of the bronchial tubes or **bronchi,** the two tubes which connect the lungs to the windpipe.

bronco *(bron'-co)*. A wild or half-tamed horse or a type of pony.

bronze. A metal composed of copper and tin. Thus, bronze is an alloy.

brooch. An ornament fastened by a pin and worn on the clothing.

c

brood. 1. The young birds hatched in a nest at the same time. 2. To worry a great deal over some trouble.

brook. A small stream.

broom. A brush on a long handle, used for sweeping the floor.

broth. A kind of soup made by boiling meat in water.

brother *(broth'-er).* 1. When one of two children in a family is a boy, he is a brother to the other child. 2. Fellow members of a religious group are said to be brothers.

brought. Past tense of bring. "Last Christmas Santa Claus brought many toys."

brow. 1. In "His brow is wet with honest sweat", brow means forehead. 2. In "We sat on the brow of the hill", brow means the top edge.

browbeat *(brow'-beat).* To bully a person.

brown. A colour like that of coffee or toast.

browse. 1. To feed upon trees, bushes, etc. 2. To move leisurely or easily, as when browsing through a store, or browsing through a book.

bruise. 1. An injury to the skin, caused by pressure. The skin turns black and blue but does not break. 2. To give such an injury to. 3. When we say that meat or fruits are to be bruised, we mean that they are to be crushed or pounded.

brunette *(bru-nette').* A person with brown or black hair and dark skin.

brush. 1. A tool used for painting, cleaning or dusting. It is made of hair, wire or bristles, which are attached to a handle. Some examples of brushes are a paint-brush, hair-brush, tooth-brush, etc. 2. To rub with a brush, as in "Brush your shoes". 3. To move past in such a way as to touch or rub against very gently while passing, as "Fortunately the car just brushed the child and did not hit him".

brusque. The opposite to gentle; rude; abrupt.

brutality *(bru-tal'-i-ty).* Cruelty; brutal behaviour.

brute. 1. A low, stupid animal. 2. Anyone who acts like an animal rather than a human being. Such a person is **brutal** or **brutish**.

bubble *(bub'-ble).* Air or gas enclosed in a very thin film of liquid. Bubbles in glass are air caught up in the glass when the glass was a liquid.

buccaneer *(buc-ca-neer').* A pirate, or one who robs ships.

buck. 1. A male goat, rabbit, deer, etc. 2. The action of an animal when it jumps with its back arched, its legs down and held stiff, as a bucking bronco.

bucket *(buck'-et)*. A wooden or metal vessel for holding and carrying water, coal, etc. A pail.

buckle *(buck'-le)*. 1. A metal frame with a hinged rod for securing a belt. 2. To bend.

bud. The part of a plant that grows into a flower, leaf or branch.

budge. To move.

budget *(budg'-et)*. 1. To budget is to decide how much money will be needed for certain purposes. 2. An estimate or plan of the amount of money that will be received and spent.

buff. 1. The colour light yellow-brown. 2. To polish anything by holding it against a wheel that is turning round quickly.

buffalo *(buf'-fa-lo)*. A wild ox; a bison.

buffet. 1. *(buf'-fet)*. A blow with the fist; to hit continually. Thus, we speak of a ship's being "buffeted about by the wind and waves". 2. *(buf-fet')*. A sideboard or counter where food and drink may be laid out. 3. A buffet dinner is a dinner party at which the guests do not sit down at the table but come and help themselves to the food that is laid out.

buffoon *(buf-foon')*. A fellow who acts like a clown.

bugle *(bu'-gle)*. A hunting horn or small trumpet.

build. To erect or make by putting things together. Builders build houses. When the materials have been put together we call the result a **building.**

bulb. 1. The roundish root of certain plants such as tulips and onions. 2. A lamp used in electric lighting.

bulge. To swell out, as "Her bag was so full of things that it bulged".

bulk. 1. Great size. 2. The greater part of anything.

bulkhead *(bulk'-head)*. A division separating one part (often watertight) from another in the interior of a ship.

bull. The male of the ox family.

bullet *(bul'-let)*. The lead pellet which is shot from a gun.

bulletin *(bul'-le-tin)*. An official statement of news, or of a sick person's progress.

bullion *(bul'-li-on)*. Gold or silver in bars.

bull's-eye *(bull's'-eye)*. 1. The middle circle of a target. 2. A half-sphere of glass placed in front of a lamp to make the light more powerful. 3. A kind of hard sweet.

bully *(bul'-ly)*. A person who, knowing that he is stronger than another, orders the other about rudely and perhaps treats him roughly.

bulwark *(bul'-wark)*. 1. That part of a ship's side which is higher than the level of the deck. 2. A place made strong for defence purposes by a bank of earth, a wall, a pile of sandbags, etc.

bumblebee *(bum'-ble-bee)*. A type of large bee which is thick and hairy and has yellow stripes around its body. It makes a loud buzzing sound.

bumper *(bump'-er)*. 1. Something to protect something else from bumps, such as the bars of metal at the front and back of a car. 2. Unusually large, abundant or successful, as "a bumper crop".

bumpkin *(bump'-kin)*. A rough, uneducated country fellow.

bunch. Several things of the same kind together. Either they grow together, as a bunch of grapes, or are arranged together, as a bunch of flowers.

bundle *(bun'-dle)*. 1. Several things tied up together, as a bundle of old clothes. 2. To send off quickly, as when a bad child is bundled out of the room.

bung. A stopper, often made of cork or wood, which is placed in the hole of a cask or barrel to prevent the contents running out.

bungalow *(bun'-ga-low)*. A house with no second storey.

bungle *(bun'-gle)*. To do a thing clumsily.

bunk. A type of narrow bed. Usually we speak of bunk beds when we refer to narrow beds built one above the other.

bunker *(bunk'-er)*. The place on board ship where such things as coal are kept.

buoy. A marker floating on a body of water and anchored to the bottom, put there to warn of some danger. Some buoys have lights.

buoyant *(buoy'-ant)*. 1. Able to float; having a strong tendency to rise to the top of water and float there. A cork is buoyant. 2. Cheerful; not easily discouraged or saddened.

burden *(bur'-den)*. A load that is too heavy to carry comfortably.

bureau *(bu'-reau)*. 1. An office, such as a travel bureau. 2. A chest of drawers. 3. A writing desk with drawers for papers.

burglar *(bur'-glar)*. A thief who enters a house at night to steal.

burial *(bur'-i-al)*. The act of placing a dead body in the earth.

burly *(bur'-ly)*. Big and strong.

burn. 1. To destroy with fire. 2. To be destroyed with fire. 3. To injure with fire or heat. 4. An injury caused by fire or heat. 5. A brook.

burnish *(bur'-nish)*. To polish and make bright.

burrow *(bur'-row)*. 1. A hole in the ground serving as the home of some animal, such as a rabbit or a fox. 2. To dig a hole with the hands or paws, as "The dog burrowed into the lawn to find his bone".

burst. To break open suddenly; to explode. If you blow too much air into a balloon, it will burst.

bury *(bur'-y)*. To put into a hole in the ground and cover with earth; to cover with a pile of something, as "The book has become buried under these papers".

bus. A large motor vehicle, capable of carrying many people.

bushel *(bush'-el)*. A dry measure for fruit or grain. A bushel will hold 4 pecks.

bushy *(bush'-y)*. 1. Overgrown or covered with bushes. 2. When it is said that a man has bushy eyebrows, the eyebrows are very thick.

business *(busi'-ness)*. 1. The activity of buying and selling goods and services. A man who owns and operates a store is said to be in business, and his business is buying and selling. 2. The thing at which a person works. Your business is to succeed in school.

bustle *(bus'-tle)*. 1. To be noisily excited and in a hurry. 2. A frame worn under a skirt to make the back of the skirt stand out.

busy *(bus'-y)*. Active or working. When in school, a pupil should be busy with his studies.

busybody *(bus'-y-bod-y)*. A meddler; a person who does not mind his own business but interferes in everybody else's.

butcher *(butch'-er)*. One who kills animals for meat, cuts them up and sells the meat.

butler *(but'-ler)*. A manservant in a large house.

butt. 1. The end of a gun or rifle which is held to the shoulder. 2. In "Goats often butt children who tease them", butt means charge at them with their horns. 3. In "The soldiers went to the rifle butt", butt means the place where they practise shooting. 4. A butt is also a large barrel or cask.

butter *(but'-ter).* A solid yellow fat which is usually made by churning milk or cream.

buttercup *(but'-ter-cup).* A plant which has yellow cup-shaped flowers.

butterfly *(but'-ter-fly).* An insect with large wings. The wings are usually brightly coloured.

button *(but'-ton).* 1. A round piece of material used to fasten clothes together. 2. To fasten the clothes with buttons.

buttress *(but'-tress).* A support placed against a wall or a building to prop it up and keep it from falling.

buxom *(bux'-om).* Cheerful; plump and in good health. Usually said of women, not of men.

buy. To purchase. To pay money for something. Most children like to buy ice-cream.

buzzard *(buz'-zard).* A bird of prey, a kind of falcon.

by. 1. At the side of. 2. By and by means later on.

bygone *(by'-gone).* Gone by; past; belonging to the past.

bystander *(by'-stand-er).* Somebody who is standing near.

C

cab. The covered part of an engine or a lorry in which the driver sits.

cabbage *(cab'-bage).* A round, green, leafy vegetable.

cabin *(cab'-in).* 1. A room on board ship. 2. A house or hut made of rough materials.

cabinet *(cab'-i-net).* 1. A piece of furniture in which books, china, etc., are kept. 2. **Cabinet.** A small body of people who, with the Prime Minister at their head, decide all the most important matters of government.

cable *(ca'-ble).* 1. A thick, wire rope which is very strong. The rope is made of many smaller wires twisted together. Cables are used to support television towers, bridges, etc. 2. An electric telegraph line placed underground or on the sea-bed.

cablegram *(ca'-ble-gram).* A message sent by cable. (See **cable**.)

cackle *(cack'-le)*. 1. The noise a hen makes. 2. To make the kind of noise a hen makes; particularly, to laugh with that kind of sound.

cactus *(cac'-tus)*. A plant which has sharp spines and which usually grows in desert regions.

caddie *(cad'-die)*. A boy who carries a golfer's clubs.

caddy *(cad'-dy)*. A small box for holding tea.

cadet *(ca-det')*. 1. A student in a naval or military college. 2. A member of a school military corps.

café *(ca-fé')*. 1. The French word for coffee. 2. A restaurant where only coffee is sold. 3. A small restaurant.

cafeteria *(caf-e-te'-ri-a)*. A restaurant where the customers serve themselves.

cage. A movable prison of wires or bars, especially for birds or animals.

cairn. A pile of stones to mark a boundary, the spot where someone is buried, etc.

cake. 1. Sweet bread. 2. A small, flat form, as a "cake of soap".

calamity *(ca-lam'-i-ty)*. Something that causes tremendous misery and upset, such as a railway accident in which many people are killed.

calcium *(cal'-ci-um)*. A chemical element which is almost white in colour. Calcium is found in milk and in bones.

calculate *(cal'-cu-late)*. To reckon or find out by arithmetic.

calendar *(cal'-en-dar)*. An almanac; a table that sets out the days, weeks and months of the year.

calf. 1. The young of the ox, elephant, whale, etc. 2. The fleshy back part of the leg, below the knee. The plural is **calves.**

calico *(cal'-i-co)*. Coarse cotton cloth.

callous *(cal'-lous)*. A person is callous when he does not mind how much other people and animals may suffer.

callow *(cal'low)*. Young and inexperienced.

calm. Quiet, unruffled. "When the wind ceased blowing, the lake became calm."

calorie *(cal'-o-rie)*. A unit of measurement of heat or energy. The amount of energy provided by food can be measured in calories.

calumny *(cal'-um-ny)*. Slander; things said of someone which are not true and which are said purposely to do him harm.

calyx *(ca'-lyx)*. The sepals, usually green, that enclose a flower when it is in bud.

camber *(cam'-ber)*. The state of being slightly arched in the middle. Most road surfaces are cambered, and the curve of an aeroplane wing is called the camber.

camel *(cam'-el)*. An animal found in eastern Mediterranean countries and in Asia. A camel with one hump is found in Arabia and is called the Arabian camel or dromedary, while a camel with two humps, called the Bactrian camel, is found in southern Asia.

cameo *(cam'-e-o)*. A precious stone on which is carved a design that stands out from the background.

camera *(cam'-er-a)*. An apparatus for taking photographs.

camouflage *(ca'-mou-flage)*. To disguise a thing so that it cannot be easily seen, by making it look like its surroundings. Guns and buildings are camouflaged in warfare. Animals are often camouflaged naturally.

camp. 1. A group of tents, cabins, or trailers where people live, usually for a short time. 2. When you sleep out of doors in a rough shelter you are said to be camping.

campaign *(cam-paign')*. To make a special effort to get a certain thing done. Thus, a manufacturer may start a sales campaign by advertising, to make people know of his products; a town may start a campaign to stop people throwing litter in the street, by putting up notices. A government may send an army to some place to carry out military operations; that, also, is a campaign.

camp-fire *(camp'-fire)*. A fire built by campers for cooking.

canal *(ca-nal')*. 1. A man-made, navigable channel which enables ships to sail to inland towns or across land from one ocean to another. The Manchester Ship Canal is a famous example. 2. A tube or passage-way in the body.

canary *(ca-nar'-y)*. A small, yellow songbird. Some canaries are wild and some are kept as pets in cages.

cancel *(can'-cel)*. To cross out or mark over. Thus a postage-stamp, when postmarked or cancelled, cannot be used again; the mark is a **cancellation** *(can-cel-la'-tion)*.

cancer *(can'-cer)*. 1. A harmful and abnormal growth of cells in a living body. 2. Something evil that eats away slowly and fatally.

Cancer *(Can'-cer)*. The Tropic of Cancer, an imaginary line running around the earth north of the equator and parallel to it. (See **tropics.**)

candid *(can'-did)*. Frank. A candid person says just what he thinks.

candidate *(can'-di-date)*. One who offers himself, or is offered by others, as a suitable person to hold a certain position or honour. A candidate in an election is one who is running in the election. A candidate at examinations is one who presents himself to take the examinations.

candied *(can'-died)*. Treated with sugar and preserved.

candle *(can'-dle)*. A stick made of wax, through the centre of which runs a wick. When the wick is lighted the candle burns, giving off light.

candour *(can'-dour)*. When a person speaks with candour, he speaks with frankness and says what he honestly thinks is true.

candy *(can'-dy)*. 1. Crystallized sugar. 2. A kind of sweet.

cane. A jointed stem, such as sugar cane or bamboo.

canine *(ca'-nine)*. To do with dogs.

canister *(can'-is-ter)*. A tin box in which such things as tea are stored.

cannibal *(can'-ni-bal)*. 1. A person who eats human flesh. 2. Said of an animal that eats its own kind. Cannibal fish, for example, are fish that eat other fish of the same kind.

cannon *(can'-non)*. A large gun which fires big shells.

canny *(can'-ny)*. Wise; careful; thrifty.

canoe *(ca-noe')*. A small boat made of light material and moved by paddles.

canopy *(can'-o-py)*. A raised covering placed over a seat, a bed, a doorway, etc.

cant. 1. Conventionally pious talk which the speaker says merely in order to make a good impression, not because he really believes what he is saying. Thus **canting** means speaking cant. 2. To cant a thing is to turn it sideways. Note the difference between **cant** and **can't**. **Can't** is a short form of **cannot.**

cantankerous *(can-tan'-ker-ous)*. Said of a person who is always ready to quarrel and find fault with others.

canteen *(can-teen')*. 1. A place in a barracks, factory, etc., where food can be bought. 2. A water-bottle carried by soldiers, travellers or explorers.

canter *(can'-ter)*. To gallop on horseback at a moderate speed.

canvas *(can'-vas)*. 1. A tough, rather coarse material which is used to make tents and sails. 2. The backing with its frame on which the artist does his oil painting.

canvass *(can'-vass)*. To go from door to door, or place to place, asking people to vote in a certain way, or asking them to buy certain goods.

canyon *(can'-yon)*. A very deep valley with high, steep sides and a stream along the bottom; a gorge.

cap. 1. A hat having a peak and worn by men and boys. 2. A bit of gunpowder sealed in paper which is fired in toy pistols.

capable *(ca'-pa-ble)*. Skilful; having the knowledge to do certain things well.

capacious *(ca-pa'-cious)*. Having plenty of room; able to hold a great deal. Thus a capacious bag is one in which you can put many things.

capacity *(ca-pac'-ity)*. 1. The amount of room or space inside a thing. Thus, the capacity of some milk bottles is one pint. 2. A person has the capacity for doing something when he is able to do it well.

cape. 1. A piece of material which is sleeveless and is worn over the shoulders and fastened round the neck. 2. A part of land which extends into the water, such as the Cape of Good Hope.

caper *(ca'-per)*. To jump or hop about in a playful way.

capillary *(cap-il'-la-ry)*. Long and slender like a hair. The word is usually used in reference to the smallest blood vessels in the body, or the fine tubes through which the sap of a plant flows.

capital *(cap'-i-tal)*. 1. The chief city of a country or a province. 2. The amount of money a company or a person owns. 3. Letters used in writing or printing which are not small letters. The letter **A** is a capital but **a** is a small letter. 4. Capital punishment is punishment by death. 5. To make capital of a thing is to take advantage of it.

capitulate *(ca-pit'-u-late)*. To give in.

capricious *(ca-pri'-cious)*. Changeable. A person who is capricious cannot be relied upon because he always acts as he fancies.

Capricorn *(Cap'-ri-corn)*. The Tropic of Capricorn, an imaginary line running around the earth south of the equator and parallel to it. (See **tropics.**)

capsize *(cap-size')*. To turn upside down.

capsule *(cap'-sule)*. A small container, often used for medicine. The capsule is usually made of gelatin so that it will dissolve in the stomach.

captain *(cap'-tain)*. The man in charge of other men; the leader or chief. We speak of the captain of a ship, a plane, a team, or a group of soldiers.

captivate *(cap'-ti-vate)*. To capture by using one's charms.

captive *(cap'-tive)*. A person who is held prisoner. He is held in **captivity** *(cap-tiv'-i-ty)*.

capture *(cap'-ture)*. To seize or take by force or trickery.

caramel *(car'-a-mel)*. 1. Burnt sugar used as a flavouring. 2. A kind of sweet.

carat *(car'-at)*. 1. A measure of weight for precious stones. 2. The term carat, when said of gold, refers to its purity. In "My watch chain is made of 9 carat gold", the meaning is that the metal consists of 9 parts of pure gold and 15 parts of some other metal mixed with it, 24 parts in all.

caravan *(car'-a-van)*. 1. Merchants or pilgrims travelling together. 2. A covered cart or wagon.

carbine *(car'-bine)*. A rifle with a short barrel.

carbohydrate *(car-bo-hy'-drate)*. Sugar and starch are carbohydrates and they produce energy for the body.

carbon *(car'-bon)*. A non-metallic element found as diamonds, graphite and charcoal.

carburettor *(car'-bu-ret-tor)*. A piece of machinery which mixes air with petrol in engines.

carcass *(car'-cass)*. The dead body of an animal.

card. 1. A piece of stiff paper. 2. Cards are used in playing games.

cardigan *(car'-di-gan)*. A knitted woollen sweater, which buttons down the front.

cardinal *(car'-di-nal)*. 1. A high official in the Roman Catholic Church. 2. Cardinal means chief in "His cardinal fault is greediness". 3. The cardinal numbers are 1, 2, 3, 4, etc., as opposed to the ordinal numbers, 1st, 2nd, 3rd, 4th, etc. 4. Cardinal red is the colour bright red.

care. 1. To give attention, as "We care for sick people by bathing them and carrying meals to them". 2. A worry, as "Few people are free from care".

career *(ca-reer')*. 1. When a person plans what he hopes to become in life, he plans his career. 2. To rush along madly, as "The car went careering downhill at break-neck speed".

careful *(care'-ful)*. Cautious, as "You must be careful when crossing the street".

caress *(ca-ress')*. To stroke or pat in fondness.

cargo *(car'-go)*. The load of goods carried by a ship.

caribou *(car'-i-bou)*. A North American reindeer.

caricature *(car'-i-ca-ture)*. Usually a picture or sketch which exaggerates and makes fun of whatever it shows.

carnage *(car'-nage)*. Great killing; great slaughter.

carnation *(car-na'-tion)*. A red, white or pink flower.

carnival *(car'-ni-val)*. Merrymaking in which a number of people take part.

carnivorous *(car-niv'-o-rous)*. Feeding on flesh.

carol *(car'-ol)*. A joyous song sung at Christmas.

carpenter *(car'-pen-ter)*. A person whose trade is making things with wood.

carpet *(car'-pet)*. A rug.

carriage *(car'-riage)*. 1. A vehicle used to carry people, usually pulled by horses. 2. We speak of a person's bearing as his carriage.

carrier *(car'-ri-er)*. 1. A device which is used to carry things, such as a bicycle carrier. 2. A person who carries things, such as a paper carrier.

carrion *(car'-ri-on)*. Decayed flesh which certain creatures such as vultures eat.

carrot *(car'-rot)*. A tapered root, orange in colour, which is eaten as a vegetable.

cartographer *(cart-o'-graph-er)*. One who makes maps or charts.

carton *(car'-ton)*. A lightly-made cardboard box suitable for packing cereals, sugar, soap and a host of other everyday things.

cartoon *(car-toon')*. A sketch which pokes fun at some person or thing mentioned in the news of the day.

cartridge *(car'-tridge)*. The case which holds the explosive powder and the bullet or shot to be fired from a gun.

carve. 1. To cut into shapes, as "The man carved the statue out of a piece of wood". 2. To cut into slices or parts. The roast is carved for dinner.

cascade *(cas-cade')*. A waterfall.

case. 1. A container used for carrying something. 2. Doctors and nurses may speak of their patients' illnesses as cases. 3. Lawyers may speak of a legal or court action as a case, as "The case of Jones against Smith was brought to court". 4. "In case" means if.

casement *(case'-ment)*. A window which opens on hinges in the same way that a door does.

cash. Money.

cashier *(cash-ier')*. 1. A person whose work it is to take charge of the money belonging to a business. There is a cashier at the theatre who takes your money and gives you tickets. 2. When an army officer has disgraced himself he may be cashiered, that is paid off and dismissed from his regiment.

casino *(ca-si'-no)*. A building in which amusements such as dancing and gambling take place.

cask. A wooden barrel bound with metal hoops.

casket *(cas'-ket)*. A small box specially fitted for storing jewels and other treasures.

casserole *(cas'-ser-ole)*. A kind of dish in which food may be both baked and brought to the table.

cast. 1. To cast a thing is to throw it. 2. When things are made in a mould from molten metal they are cast. 3. The actors in a play are called the cast. 4. A man may run his mind over certain things that have happened; he casts his mind over them.

castaway *(cast'-a-way)*. A person cast adrift at sea in an open boat or on a raft—a thing that often happened in the days of pirates. A shipwrecked person.

caster *(cast'-er)*. Small wheels fitted to the legs of tables, chairs, etc., are called casters.

castle *(cas'-tle)*. A large fortified house, in which people usually of noble or royal rank live. The Queen often stays in Balmoral Castle.

casual *(cas'-u-al)*. 1. Happening by chance or accident. 2. Careless, as in "He acted in a casual way". 3. Casual clothes are informal clothes, the sort that you might wear on a beach or in your garden, but not the sort you would wear out to dinner. 4. "He was a casual labourer" means "He worked only now and then at no particular job".

catalogue *(cat'-a-logue)*. A book in which things are listed. This may be a list of articles with their prices. 2. To catalogue things is to arrange them in order in a list.

catapult *(cat'-a-pult)*. 1. A machine for launching an aeroplane from the deck of a ship. 2. An ancient war machine for hurling large stones at the enemy. 3. A weapon made from elastic and a forked stick, used for shooting stones, etc.

cataract *(cat'-a-ract)*. 1. A waterfall. 2. A growth on the eye-ball which affects the sight.

catarrh *(ca-tarrh')*. A chronic cold in the nose and throat.

catastrophe *(ca-tas'-tro-phe)*. An unexpected misfortune which causes misery and ruin.

catch. 1. To take hold of something, as when you catch a ball. 2. You catch a person when you play hide-and-seek. 3. Dry grass will catch fire, or become lighted, very easily.

catechism *(cat'-e-chism)*. 1. A book which contains questions and answers about religion. 2. A book of questions and answers about any subject.

cater *(ca'-ter)*. To provide food or supplies for others. The person who carries or manages the delivery of the food is a **caterer.**

caterpillar *(ca'-ter-pil-lar)*. A hairy, worm-like form of the butterfly or moth. While in this stage, the caterpillar eats a large amount of leaves.

cathedral *(ca-the'-dral)*. A large or important church.

catholic *(cath'-o-lic)*. 1. Covering or including everything or all people; broad; general. A person who enjoys eating all kinds of food is said to have a catholic taste. 2. **Catholic.** Belonging to the Roman Catholic Church. 3. A person who belongs to that church.

catkin *(cat'-kin)*. The long, drooping flowers of the willow, the hazel and certain other trees.

catmint *(cat'-mint)*. A kind of plant which cats enjoy.

cattle *(cat'-tle)*. Cows, bulls and oxen. The livestock used on a farm for meat and for milk.

caught. The past tense of **catch.** When someone catches you, you are caught.

cauliflower *(cau'-li-flow-er)*. A large round vegetable which has a white head covered with green leaves. It is a kind of cabbage.

cause. 1. Something which makes something else happen. 2. To make something happen. A carelessly thrown match might cause a forest fire. If it did, it would be the cause of the fire.

causeway *(cause'-way)*. 1. A path or roadway raised above ground-level, so that when the surrounding land is flooded people can cross. 2. A kind of bridge made over a body of shallow water by piling up earth, rock, etc.

cautious *(cau'-tious)*. A person who takes care is cautious. He exercises **caution.**

cavalcade *(cav-al-cade')*. A parade; a procession; a pageant.

cavalry *(cav'-al-ry)*. Troops mounted on horseback.

cave. 1. A hollow place in the side of a hill or mountain or underground. Some caves stretch for miles underground. 2. To cave in means to fall in.

cavern *(cav'-ern)*. A cave.

cavity *(cav'-i-ty)*. A hollow. If the dentist says you have a cavity in a tooth, he means there is a hole or hollow in it.

cease. To stop.

ceaseless *(cease'-less)*. Never-stopping.

cedar *(ce'-dar)*. An evergreen tree with wide flat branches.

cede. To give up a thing to another person when you would prefer to keep it.

ceiling *(ceil'-ing)*. 1. The surface opposite the floor of a room. 2. The highest altitude at which a plane can fly. 3. The distance between the ground and the lowest cloud. On a foggy night the ceiling is zero because the fog is a cloud floating on the ground.

celebrated *(cel'-e-brat-ed)*. Noted; famous. Horatio Nelson was a celebrated sailor. A celebrated man is often called a **celebrity** *(ce-leb'-ri-ty)*.

celery *(cel'-er-y)*. A vegetable, the stalks of which are green or white in colour. Celery is usually eaten raw.

celestial *(ce-les'-tial)*. 1. To do with the sky. The stars are celestial bodies. 2. Heavenly.

celibacy *(cel'-i-ba-cy)*. State of being unmarried or single. An unmarried grown-up person is a **celibate.**

cell. 1. A small room, such as a prison cell. 2. The tiny parts or units that, taken together in millions, form a plant or animal body. 3. The sections which make up an electric battery and which create the electric current. 4. The small spaces in a honeycomb.

cellar *(cel'-lar)*. The basement of a house.

cellophane *(cel'-lo-phane)*. A substance as thin as paper which is as transparent as glass and which is used for wrapping packets of sweets, etc. (This is a trade name.)

celluloid *(cel'-lu-loid)*. A plastic material that is tough and hard, which can be given an attractive colour and is used for making thin toys, hair combs, knife handles, table-tennis balls, etc. It catches fire very easily.

cement *(ce-ment')*. 1. A grey powder which is mixed with sand and water to make paths or to hold bricks together. 2. To fasten things together is to cement them.

cemetery *(cem'-e-ter-y)*. A plot of ground in which the dead are buried. A graveyard is a cemetery.

censor *(cen'-sor)*. 1. A person who reads books or looks at plays and films before they reach the public, in order to make sure they are suitable. If he does not think they are, he may cut out parts of them, to prevent their being published or shown. 2. To censor something is to cut out part of it or to prevent it from reaching the public, as a censor does.

censure *(cen'-sure)*. Blame.

census *(cen'-sus)*. 1. The counting of anything. 2. An official numbering of the population. In Britain this is done every ten years.

centenarian *(cen-te-nar'-i-an)*. One hundred years old; a person one hundred years old.

centenary *(cen'-te-nar-y* or *cen-te'-na-ry)*. 1. A period of one hundred years. 2. A one-hundredth anniversary.

centennial *(cen-ten'-ni-al)*. 1. Having to do with a period of one-hundred years or its completion. 2. A one-hundredth anniversary or its celebration.

centigrade *(cen'-ti-grade)*. A centigrade thermometer is one which measures one hundred degrees between the boiling and the freezing point of water. The abbreviation is C.

centimetre *(cen'-ti-me-tre)*. A hundredth part of a metre. (A metre is roughly 39 inches.)

centipede *(cen'-ti-pede)*. A small insect supposed to have one hundred feet.

centre *(cen'-tre).* The middle part, or point, or place. The centre of a target is the bull's-eye. A shopping centre is a central or middle place to which people go to shop.

century *(cen'-tu-ry).* A period of one hundred years. The twentieth century began in 1901 and will end in the year 2000.

cereal *(ce'-re-al).* Any kind of grain used for food. The oatmeal that many of us have for breakfast is a cereal.

ceremony *(cer'-e-mo-ny).* A sacred rite; a formal and stately occasion, as a coronation. A wedding is sometimes called a marriage ceremony.

certainty *(cer'-tain-ty).* Something about which there is no doubt. It is a certainty that night will follow day because there is no doubt about it.

certificate *(cer-tif'-i-cate).* Something written or printed to prove a fact. Many pupils have cards which say that the holder can swim one hundred yards. Such cards are certificates. The wording often starts "This is to certify". **Certify** means to state, declare or prove.

chafe. 1. To rub, as "Her new shoes chafed her heel". 2. To fret, as "John chafed while his teacher scolded him".

chaff. 1. The husks or horny covering of wheat. 2. Hay and straw used for feeding horses, etc. 3. To make fun of.

chagrin *(cha-grin').* Vexation; disappointment; embarrassment.

chairman *(chair'-man).* The person who is given charge of a meeting and who decides how it shall be conducted.

chalet *(cha-let').* A wooden house or cottage in Switzerland, sometimes used for holiday purposes.

chalice *(chal'-ice).* The cup used in the Communion service at churches.

chalk. A soft, white limestone used in schools to mark a blackboard or in tailors' shops to mark material for cutting.

challenge *(chal'-lenge).* 1. An invitation to engage in a contest or a fight. 2. To challenge someone is to invite him to compete with you or fight you. To challenge a thing is to call it into question. 3. When a sentry challenges someone, he asks him to tell who he is.

chamber *(cham'-ber).* 1. A room or office. 2. A number of people working together for a special purpose, as a Chamber of Commerce.

chambermaid *(cham'-ber-maid).* A woman servant whose duty it is to look after the bedrooms.

chameleon *(cha-me'-le-on)*. An animal of the lizard family which can change colour at will. It can turn from a darkish brown to a bright green, but not to red, blue, pink, etc., as many people think.

chamois *(cham'-ois)*. 1. A kind of mountain antelope, about the size of a goat. 2. A very soft yellowish leather made from the skin of goats, sheep and deer, etc.

champ. 1. To chew food noisily. 2. When a horse fidgets with the bit in its mouth, it champs on the bit. 3. To be champing at the bit is to be very eager to get started.

champion *(cham'-pi-on)*. 1. A person who stands up for another. 2. A person who is better than all others at something.

chance. 1. Opportunity, as in "He had the chance to do better at another job, so he changed jobs". 2. Possibility, as in "There is a chance that he may arrive late for dinner". 3. Risk, as in "He took a chance and jumped the wide river, but his foot slipped and he fell into the water".

chancellor *(chan'-cel-lor)*. 1. A high official in a government. 2. The head of a university.

chandler *(chand'-ler)*. Formerly, one who made or sold candles. Nowadays, one who sells supplies of all kinds. Thus, a ship's chandler might sell stores and provisions to be carried on board ship.

change. 1. To alter; to make different to what it was before. If I write "three" and you change it to "four", you have changed the number I wrote. When a person changes, he becomes different to what he was before. 2. Money given back to a customer who has given a larger coin or note than was necessary in paying for something. 3. To change a note is to give for it coins equal in value to it.

changeable *(change'-a-ble)*. Fickle; altering often; not the same for any length of time. The announcer says, "Weather changeable", meaning that it is likely to alter several times during the day.

channel *(chan'-nel)*. 1. The course of a river. 2. A strip of water joining two seas, as the English Channel does. 3. When you change channels on radio or television, you change stations. 4. To direct, as when a person wishes to channel or direct the thinking of others to another or a special topic.

chant. 1. A song. 2. To sing. 3. To recite musically, often on a single note.

chaos *(cha'-os)*. A state of muddle or disorder. When things are in a state of chaos they are **chaotic** *(cha-ot'-ic)*.

chapel *(chap'-el)*. A small church or a part of the church which will not seat as many people as the nave.

chaplain *(chap'-lain)*. A clergyman who conducts Divine Service for some special body of people, rather than for the people of a parish. Thus, he holds services in barracks, on ships, in school halls, etc.

chapter *(chap'-ter)*. 1. A section or division of a book. 2. A general meeting of the monks in a monastery.

character *(char'-ac-ter)*. 1. The qualities of a person or thing that make him or it different from others, as "We all admire Mary's character, because she is so kind and considerate". 2. A person in a play, who is supposed to be real but is not. 3. Any letter, figure, or sign used in printing or writing.

characteristic *(char-ac-ter-is'-tic)*. 1. Anything that distinguishes a thing from others. 2. Distinctive; typical; as "One of the characteristic features of the lemon is its sour taste".

charade *(cha-rade')*. A game in which one group of people acts out the meaning of a word and another group tries to guess the word.

charcoal *(char'-coal)*. The black, porous cinders left after burning wood or bone in a furnace which allows very little air to enter.

charge. 1. To load or fill. To charge a gun is to load it and what it is loaded with is the charge. 2. Act of rushing at an enemy. To charge the enemy is to rush at him. 3. To set as the price of something. 4. To put someone in charge of something is to make him responsible for it. Thus "in charge of" means "responsible for" and your charges are the people or things for which you are responsible. 5. To order; command, as "The judge charged him to appear before the court". 6. To charge someone with something is to accuse him of it, as "He was charged with murder".

charger *(charg'-er)*. A war horse.

charitable *(char'-i-ta-ble)*. 1. Generous to the poor. 2. Not anxious to note faults in others.

charm. 1. To delight and please others by one's actions. 2. A thing having supposed magic powers, such as the charms which people carry about for luck.

CHART 76 **CHERISH**

chart. 1. A map specially drawn for use at sea. 2. A set of pictures or diagrams drawn to explain something.

charter *(char'-ter)*. 1. To hire. 2. A paper signed by a king or queen on which it is stated that certain rights belong to certain people. To charter something is to give it a charter. 3. A document given to a learned society or a professional body as a mark of distinction.

chase. 1. To race after and try to catch. 2. Hunting.

chasm. A deep opening or crack in the earth.

chassis *(chas'-sis)*. The frame, with the wheels and engine, on which a motor-car is built.

chasten *(chas'-ten)*. 1. To correct by punishing. 2. To refine.

chastise *(chas-tise')*. To punish.

chat. 1. To gossip or talk. 2. Gossip or talk.

chatter *(chat'-ter)*. To talk a great deal about things that do not matter much.

chauffeur *(chauf'-feur)*. The paid driver of a private motor-car.

cheap. Inexpensive; of poor quality.

cheat. 1. To deceive is to cheat. 2. A person who cheats.

check. 1. To stop or hold back, as "He checked the horse before it dashed into the fence". 2. To go over something in order to make sure it is correct or in order. 3. A pattern made of squares on material, as "I do not like this check suit".

cheek. The part of the face beside the nose and under the eyes.

cheer. 1. Joy; happiness; good spirits. 2. To cheer someone is to make him cheerful. 3. A shout of encouragement. 4. To cheer someone on is to shout encouragement to him.

cheese. A type of food made from curds of milk.

chemical *(chem'-i-cal)*. 1. Substance used in chemistry. 2. Having to do with chemistry.

chemistry *(chem'-is-try)*. The study of the basic elements and the ways in which elements combine. When you study chemistry you will learn that water is made of the elements hydrogen and oxygen.

cheque. A written order to a bank requiring payment of a stated sum of money to a person or persons.

cherish *(cher'-ish)*. 1. To treat with kindness; to show love for somebody. 2. To cling to something is to cherish it, as "The boy cherished the watch which his father had given him".

cherub *(cher'-ub)*. 1. An angel of high rank. 2. An angel in the form of a child. **Cherub** is sometimes written **cherubin**. The plural is either **cherubs** or **cherubim**.

chest. 1. The front of the body, between the neck and the waist. 2. A large wooden box.

chestnut *(chest'-nut)*. A kind of tree which bears nuts in prickly shells: The tree is a chestnut tree, and the nuts are chestnuts.

chew. To grind with the teeth.

chick. A baby chicken or bird.

chicken *(chick'-en)*. A rooster or hen which may be eaten.

chide. To scold without being very angry.

chief. 1. A leader; the most important person in a group or tribe. 2. First; most important.

chieftain *(chief'-tain)*. The leader of a clan or a tribe.

chilblain *(chil'-blain)*. A painful, inflamed swelling of the hand or foot caused by exposure to cold. It feels hot and itchy and is sometimes ulcerated.

childhood *(child'-hood)*. The years of a person's life while he or she is still a child.

childish *(child'-ish)*. Like a child; foolish, silly.

children *(chil'-dren)*. The plural of child; said when there is more than one child.

chill. 1. Coldness. 2. Catching a chill is another way of saying catching a cold. 3. To make very cold, but not quite freezing. 4. To take the chill off a thing is to warm it slightly.

chime. 1. A set of bells that are tuned so as to be capable of producing a melody. 2. To ring, as "The grandfather clock chimes the hour".

chimney *(chim'-ney)*. 1. A chimney is a pipe that extends up through the roof to allow smoke to escape from a furnace or a fireplace. It also creates a draft which helps the fire to burn. 2. The glass shield around a candle or the wick of an oil lamp is a chimney.

chimpanzee *(chim-pan-zee')*. An African ape which is smaller than a gorilla.

china *(chi'-na)*. 1. Cups, saucers, plates and all sorts of ornaments made of white clay, often called porcelain. 2. **China**. A country in East Asia, bordering on the Pacific Ocean.

Chinese *(Chi-nese')*. The people who live in China are Chinese.

chintz. Cotton cloth with a pattern printed on it in colours.

chip. 1. A cup with a small piece knocked off is said to have been chipped. 2. If, when chopping wood or smashing stones, a small piece flies off the larger piece, the small piece is a chip.

chisel *(chis'-el)*. A tool with a sharp tip used by carpenters for shaping wood

chivalry *(chiv'-al-ry)*. 1. The order of knighthood. 2. The system of rules for the behaviour of knights. A knight was expected to be brave, honourable, generous, merciful, gentle to women and pious. 3. Chivalry nowadays means consideration for women, or the showing of good manners to women.

chlorine *(chlo'-rine)*. A chemical used for purifying water.

chocolate *(choc'-o-late)*. 1. A preparation made by grinding and roasting cocoa beans. 2. Some sweets and drinks are made with chocolate. 3. A brownish colour.

choice. 1. Of good quality, as when a shopkeeper writes on a ticket "Choice, 10d. lb." 2. The thing or things chosen, as when someone says, "I do not like Henry's choice of ties". 3. A selection of things, as "You haven't much choice in this shop".

choir. A group of singers, often in a church or school.

choke. To plug a narrow passage. The passage may be a person's throat, or a river, etc.

choose. To select the one preferred.

chop. 1. To cut a thing with many repeated blows. 2. To chop up usually suggests to cut up into small pieces. 3. A small cut of meat, usually including part of a rib.

choppy *(chop'-py)*. Rough; jerky. When the sea is choppy it has many short, tumbling waves.

chord. 1. Three or more notes of music played together. 2. A straight line joining two points on the circumference of a circle.

chorister *(chor'-is-ter)*. A member of a choir.

chorus *(cho'-rus)*. 1. The part of a song which is repeated after each verse. 2. A choir. 3. A piece of music that is sung by a chorus. 4. In "'Yes, yes!' they chorused", "chorused" means shouted all together.

chose. The past tense of **choose.** "Yesterday he chose a ride on the pony and to-day he chooses to ride on the merry-go-round."

chosen *(cho'-sen)*. 1. The past participle of **choose**; "Have you chosen the work you want to do when you grow up?" 2. "The chosen" are the people who have been chosen or favoured.

Christ. Jesus is Christ, the founder of the Christian religion.

christen *(chris'-ten)*. To admit into a Christian church; to baptize with holy water and then give a name to. The name given is a Christian name.

Christian *(Chris'-tian)*. A person who follows the teachings of Jesus is a Christian.

Christianity *(Chris-ti-an'-i-ty)*. The religion of Christians, of Christ and His followers.

Christmas *(Christ'-mas)*. A holiday on which we celebrate the birth of Jesus. Christmas falls on the 25th of December.

chronic *(chron'-ic)*. Diseases that last for a very long time are called by doctors chronic diseases. Chronic is often used as slang to mean unpleasant or severe.

chronicle *(chron'-i-cle)*. A story of things that have happened, told in the order in which they happened.

chronometer *(chron-om'-et-er)*. A clock or watch that keeps time very accurately.

chrysalis *(chrys'-a-lis)*. Pupa of insects, especially butterflies. (See **pupa**.)

chubby *(chub'-by)*. Plump.

chuckle *(chuck'-le)*. To laugh to yourself.

chum. A close friend is a chum.

church. 1. A building used for public worship. 2. (Usually with a capital.) The body of people who believe in one religion. 3. (Usually with a capital.) The religious authorities, as "The Church forbids us to do that".

churchman *(church'-man)*. 1. A minister or a priest. 2. A member of the Church.

churchwarden *(church'-war'-den)*. A member of a church who is not a clergyman. He has certain duties connected with the money belonging to the church.

churn. 1. The container in which butter is made from milk or cream. 2. To beat or stir violently.

chute. A slide. In many factories, goods are moved from one department to another by means of a chute. The things are set on the chute and they slide down to wherever they are wanted. In some houses there are coal chutes, and chutes down which people slide are seen at fairs.

cider *(ci'-der)*. A drink made by pressing juice out of apples.

cigar *(ci-gar')*. A tight roll of tobacco leaves for smoking.

cigarette *(cig-a-rette')*. Tobacco leaves finely ground and rolled in a thin paper for smoking.

cinder *(cin'-der)*. A piece of wood or coal which has been burned and is black in colour and light in weight.

cinema *(cin'-e-ma)*. A machine for projecting moving pictures. Now also the hall in which films are shown.

cinnamon *(cin'-na-mon)*. A spice made from the inner bark of the cinnamon tree. It is a yellowish-brown colour.

cipher *(ci'-pher)*. 1. The figure 0. 2. A person or thing of no importance. 3. A code or secret writing.

circle *(cir'-cle)*. A flat figure enclosed by a line drawn around a centre, which is curved in such a way that every point on the line is the same distance from the centre.

circulation *(cir-cu-la'-tion)*. 1. The motion of going round in a circle or going from a place and returning to it. The blood in our bodies does this. Thus we speak of the circulation of the blood. 2. The number of copies a newspaper or magazine sells each time it is issued.

circumference *(cir-cum'-fer-ence)*. The line around the outside of a circle.

circumstance *(cir'-cum-stance)*. 1. A state of things, a fact or a happening accompanying another fact, or a condition upon which a fact depends (see **condition,** No. 1). "It was the best he could do in the circumstances" means it was the best he could do with things the way they were. "Under no circumstances will the prisoner be released" means the prisoner will remain in jail no matter what occurs. 2. "He is in bad circumstances" means he has little money or wealth; and "He is in good circumstances" means he has much money or wealth. 3. "Pomp and circumstance" means show and ceremony.

circus *(cir'-cus)*. A travelling show in which there are acrobats, tight-rope walkers, tame and wild animals and usually a band. The circus is held in a huge tent.

cistern *(cis'-tern)*. A well or a tank used for storing water.

citadel *(cit'-a-del)*. A fortress.

citizen *(cit'-i-zen)*. A person who lives in a certain country and gives his allegiance to that country.

citron *(cit'-ron)*. A fruit like a large lemon.

citrus *(cit'-rus)*. A citrus tree is one that bears some kind of citrus fruit. Citrus fruits are citrons, lemons, limes, oranges and grapefruits.

city *(cit'-y)*. A very large town. London and Manchester are two of the largest **cities** in England.

civic *(civ'-ic)*. Belonging to a city, a citizen or citizens. In "A man has many civic duties, one of which is to pay his taxes promptly", civic refers to his duties as a citizen or his duties to the city in which he lives.

civil *(civ'-il)*. 1. Polite and obliging, as "The shop assistant was very civil". 2. Having to do with the life and government of ordinary people. Thus, Civil Law is the law that governs the people, while Military Law is that which governs the armed forces.

civilian *(ci-vil'-ian)*. Any person not in the Navy, Army or Air Force.

civility *(ci-vil'-i-ty)*. People who are obliging, amiable and polite show civility.

civilization *(civ-i-li-za'-tion)*. 1. The condition of being civilized. 2. The making civilized, or the state of becoming civilized, as "The civilization of the head-hunting tribe could not be accomplished overnight".

civilize *(civ'-i-lize)*. 1. To bring out of a primitive state. 2. To refine and educate.

clad. Clothed; dressed.

claim. To ask for a thing because you have a right to it; thus "Harry saw a girl with his note-book; he went up to her and claimed it".

claimant *(claim'-ant)*. A person who claims something, especially one who makes his claim in a law court.

clam. An oyster-like shell-fish which lives in a hinged shell. Clams are found in sand along the shores of rivers, lakes and oceans. Many types of clams are eaten.

clamber *(clam'-ber)*. To climb with difficulty.

clammy *(clam'-my)*. Moist or damp and sticky.

clamour *(clam'-our)*. A great noise. To clamour for a thing is to ask for it time after time and to do it noisily. A person who clamours for a thing is **clamorous.**

clamp. 1. To fasten things together. 2. A tool for holding things together. It has two jaws which are screwed together to tighten it.

clan. A group of people who are related, or a group of people having the same social and political interests.

clandestine *(clan-des'-tine)*. Secret; underhand.

clap. 1. An unexpected noise, as a clap of thunder. 2. To smack the hands together and make a noise, as people do in the theatre; to applaud.

clarify *(clar'-i-fy)*. To make clear.

clarinet *(clar-i-net')*. A wooden tube-shaped musical instrument with a single reed which produces a mellow, high-pitched sound. It is played by blowing into one end and pressing keys along its length.

clarion *(clar'-i-on)*. A long trumpet with a narrow tube which, when blown, makes a shrill, harsh sound.

clash. 1. To hit two things together; the sound made when two things are hit together. 2. When two things happen at the same time and interfere with each other, they are said to clash, as "Mary could not go both to the dance and to the concert because they happened on the same evening. As they clashed, she decided to go to the dance".

clasp. 1. To hold tightly. 2. A thing like a buckle which grips something and keeps it in its place.

class. 1. A group of people or things alike in some way. Thus, children of the same age at school form a class. 2. "First-class" means "excellent; the very best"; "second-class" means "good but not the best"; "third-class" means "rather poor"; and so on. If you travel first-class on a railway you pay more money but you obtain the best service and accommodation.

classic *(clas'-sic)*. 1. Excellent; of the very first class. 2. A work of art, especially a book, which is excellent. 3. A fine work of art from some historical period of great excellence. 4. A writer known for his excellence.

classical *(clas'-si-cal)*. Belonging to ancient Greece and Rome; like something belonging to ancient Greece and Rome.

classify *(clas'-si-fy)*. To sort out into groups or classes.

clatter *(clat'-ter)*. A noise like that made when a tray loaded with dishes is dropped.

clause. A part of a sentence. In the sentence, "He came when he was called", "He came" is the main or principal clause and "when he was called" is a subordinate clause.

claw. 1. The sharp nail on the foot of an animal. Most birds have claws. 2. To scratch.

clay. Earth which, when wet, is very sticky and, when dry, very hard. Bricks are made of clay.

clean. 1. Without dirt or stain. 2. To remove dirt.

clear. 1. Transparent, which means that you can see through it. When water in a river is clear, you can see to the bottom, because the water is not muddy. Thus a clear sky is one that allows the stars to be seen, because there are no clouds in the way. 2. To clear a room, cupboard, etc., is to empty it or make it tidy.

clearance *(clear'-ance)*. The act of clearing things away; getting rid of them and leaving the space that they used empty or clear. Merchants have clearance sales, meaning sales to empty their stores in readiness for new goods.

cleave. To split open.

cleft. An opening; a crevice.

clemency *(clem'-en-cy)*. Mercy.

clench. To close the teeth or the fists tightly.

clergyman *(cler'-gy-man)*. A minister, pastor, or priest.

clerk. An office worker.

clever *(clev'-er)*. Bright, intelligent. A person with a quick mind is said to be clever.

click. To make a small, sharp noise. A key turning in a lock produces a clicking noise.

client *(cli'ent)*. 1. A customer. 2. A person who seeks the help of a lawyer.

cliff. A steep face of rock.

climate *(cli'-mate)*. The climate of a place is the kind of weather it usually has. The climate of England is fairly moist, with a temperature neither too hot nor too cold.

climax *(cli'-max)*. A thing reaches its climax when it arrives at its highest or most important point. Thus, the climax of a story is the part where the interest is greatest; the climax of an illness is the moment when it is most serious.

climb. To ascend or go up. A person climbs a ladder.

clinch. 1. To make fast; to settle. 2. A tight hold in wrestling.

cling. To hold on tightly.

clinic *(clin'-ic)*. 1. A place where sick or injured people are given treatment. 2. A place where practical instruction is given. Thus in a medical clinic, doctors in training receive practical instruction in treating illness because patients are present who have illnesses of many kinds.

clip. 1. To cut with scissors or shears, as long as the cutting is done in little snips. A barber clips hair and a gardener clips a hedge; but a dressmaker, when cutting cloth with the aid of a pattern, does not clip. 2. To fasten things together, such as a number of sheets of writing paper. 3. The metal things used for fastening such papers.

clipper *(clip'-per)*. A fast sailing ship.

cloak. 1. A garment to wear over all other garments. It has no sleeves. 2. To hide a thing or cover it up.

clock. A device for showing time in minutes, hours and often in seconds.

clod. 1. A hard lump of earth, or a lump of earth sticking to something, as "If you walk over a muddy field your shoes will be covered with clods". 2. A stupid, slow-witted person.

clog. 1. To choke up. If you drop putty into a sink, you clog the drain. 2. A wooden shoe worn in Holland, or a wooden-soled shoe.

close. 1. To stop, shut or bring together. You may close a book or close a meeting. Soldiers close ranks by moving closer together. 2. Near. A close race is one in which there is little space between the runners.

clot. A lump of some substance that is neither hard nor soft. Doctors often speak of a clot of blood, and dairymen sell clotted cream.

cloth. The material used for making shirts, dresses, suits, etc. It is made from cotton, silk, etc.

clothe. To cover with wearing apparel. You may be clothed in a suit or a dress.

clothier *(cloth'-ier)*. One who makes or sells clothes.

clothing *(cloth'-ing)*. Clothes. Dresses and shirts are articles of clothing.

cloud. When droplets of moisture gather in the sky, they form a cloud which may be white, grey or almost black in colour.

clout. 1. A hit or a blow. 2. To hit.

cloven *(clo'-ven)*. Split in two. For that reason, we say that a cow has a cloven hoof, meaning that the hoof is split into two portions.

clover *(clo'-ver)*. A plant grown by farmers for cattle food, etc. Each leaf is divided into three equal parts. Very rarely, a leaf has four such parts and, if you find one of these plants, people say you will have good luck.

clown. A man with a painted face and a cone-shaped hat, who earns his living by doing and saying funny things.

cloy. To fill to overflowing; to cause loss of appetite or a feeling of sickness by eating, drinking, smelling, etc. too much of something. For example, if you ate so much chocotate that you became sick of it, your taste for chocolate would be cloyed. Cloying perfume is perfume so sweet and strong that it is sickening.

club. 1. A heavy stick, used as a weapon, etc. 2. Sticks used in sports and athletics, as golf clubs and Indian clubs. 3. A society or group of people who have joined together for a purpose that interests them, as tennis clubs. 4. One of the black suits in a pack of playing cards.

clue. Some little piece of information which helps to solve a mystery. If a thief escaped from the scene of the crime without being seen, but dropped his handkerchief, the initials on it might be a useful clue in tracking him.

clump. 1. A number of plants, etc., growing together, as a clump of pansies or a clump of ferns. 2. To clump means to bang your feet down while walking.

clumsy *(clum'-sy)*. Awkward in movement.

cluster *(clus'-ter)*. Many things of the same kind growing together or joined together, as a cluster of grapes. The word can be a noun or a verb.

clutch. 1. To grasp tightly, as "A drowning man will clutch a straw". 2. A tight grasp, as "The monkey held its youngster in its clutch". 3. A brood of chickens or the eggs from which they are hatched. 4. An arrangement for throwing working parts of a machine into or out of action; such as the clutch in a motor-car.

coach. 1. A large, closed-in, four-wheel carriage; a stage-coach. 2. A motor bus. 3. A private teacher; a tutor. 4. A trainer in sports. 5. To teach privately.

coagulate *(co-ag'-u-late)*. To curdle or become thick.

coal. A fuel which is burned in a fireplace. It is black in colour and is mined.

coarse. 1. Rough and rude. 2. Vulgar.

coast. 1. The edge of the land where it touches the sea. 2. To coast down a hill in some vehicle is to let yourself be carried down by the force of gravity.

coat. An outer garment or covering. In winter you wear a coat. A cat has a coat of fur. When painting a house, you apply a coat of paint.

coating *(coat'-ing)*. A layer or covering, such as a coating of paint.

coax. To wheedle; to persuade by gentle words and flattery.

cob. 1. A sturdy, short-legged riding horse. 2. The hard stem in an ear of maize on which the kernels grow in rows.

cobble *(cob'-ble)*. 1. To make or mend a thing clumsily. 2. A stone, often called a **cobblestone,** which serves as a rough kind of paving.

cobbler *(cob'-bler)*. A man who mends boots and shoes.

cobra *(co'-bra)*. A very poisonous snake of Africa and Asia which when excited puffs up its neck.

cobweb *(cob'-web)*. A spider's web.

cock. 1. The male of any bird, especially of a chicken. 2. A weathercock is a weather vane. Examples may be seen on the tops of high buildings; they show the direction in which the wind is blowing.

cockroach *(cock'-roach)*. A dark brown insect like a beetle.

cocoa *(co'-coa)*. The powder made from the nibs or nuts of the cacao tree.

coconut *(co'-co-nut)*. The fruit of the coconut palm. It is large, brown and oval, with a hard, hairy shell. Inside, it contains edible white flesh and, in the centre, a watery liquid called milk.

cocoon *(co-coon')*. The silky case which many insects spin around themselves just before entering the pupa stage (see **pupa**). They then pass the pupa stage in the cocoon.

cod. A large sea-fish found in the North Atlantic.

coddle *(cod'-dle)*. 1. To cook gently. 2. To make too much fuss over.

code. 1. A set of rules or laws. 2. A system of symbols used to represent words. 3. The Morse Code is an arrangement of dots and dashes to simplify signalling from one person to another.

coffee *(cof'-fee)*. The drink which is made from crushed coffee beans. It is medium to dark brown in colour and has a noticeable aroma.

coffer *(cof'-fer)*. A chest, trunk or box in which valuable articles are kept, usually money.

coffin *(cof'-fin)*. The box in which a dead person is buried.

cog. One of the teeth on the edge of certain wheels, such as on the gear-wheel of a bicycle.

cogitate *(cog'-i-tate)*. To think over; ponder.

cognate *(cog'-nate)*. Related to; to do with.

cohesion *(co-he'-sion)*. Holding together. A stone, for instance, is made of millions of crystals, and they all hold together. The force keeping them together is cohesion.

coiffure *(coif-fure')*. Hair style; the way a person's hair is done.

coil. 1. To wind anything into a ring. 2. Anything that has been wound in this way is said to be in a coil. 3. A spiral wire carrying an electric current is called a coil.

coin. A piece of money stamped out of metal.

coincide *(co-in-cide')*. 1. To happen at the same time. 2. To agree. If your plans coincide with mine we shall do the same thing at the same time.

coincidence *(co-in'-ci-dence)*. An accidental and remarkable occurrence of two or more ideas or events at the same time.

colander *(col'-an-der)*. A strainer used in the kitchen. It is a kind of bowl with many holes in it through which water drains.

collapse *(col-lapse')*. 1. To fall to pieces or break up suddenly. 2. To sink to the ground.

collar *(col'-lar)*. 1. The strip of linen worn by men and boys round the neck; also the turned-over part of the coat. Horses wear leather collars and so do dogs. 2. If plumbers want to join two pipes, they fit a metal collar over the two ends.

colleague *(col'-league)*. A friend; a person who works with you and helps you with your job.

collect *(col-lect')*. To gather, to bring together. Perhaps you collect stamps or pictures; if so, you are a **collector** and the things you collect make a **collection.**

college *(col'-lege)*. 1. A school of higher learning. 2. A society of scholars forming part of a university.

collide *(col-lide')*. When things knock against each other they collide. If two cars collide, there is a **collision.**

collie *(col'-lie)*. A large sheep-dog with a pointed nose, sharp ears and long brown and white, or black and white fur.

colliery *(col'-lier-y)*. A coal mine, including all the buildings and machinery above ground. A man who works down in the mine is a **collier**. Another meaning of **collier** is a ship that carries coal.

colon *(co'-lon)*. A punctuation mark (:). This is a semi-colon (;).

colonel *(colo'-nel)*. An officer in the army who usually commands a regiment.

colonial *(co-lo'-ni-al)*. Anything to do with a colony.

colonnade *(col-on-nade')*. A number of columns or pillars set out in a row and forming part of a building.

colony *(col'-o-ny)*. 1. A number of people living together in a country that is not their native country but is ruled by their native country. 2. The place where they live is also called a colony. 3. A colony of insects is a group of the same kind of insects living together.

colossal *(co-los'-sal)*. Very large or huge.

colour *(col'-our)*. 1. Red, blue, yellow, green, etc., are colours. 2. The flags of an infantry regiment are called colours. 3. To say that a person has coloured the facts means that he has altered them and he is not speaking the truth.

colt. A young horse.

columbine *(col'-um-bine)*. A garden flower, shaped something like a snapdragon.

column *(col'-umn)*. 1. A pillar forming part of a building. 2. Soldiers moving along one behind the other are in a column. 3. Many things that are long and narrow are called columns; there are columns of print in the newspaper, and the backbone is the spinal column. Lists of figures set one under the other are spoken of as columns of figures.

coma *(co'-ma)*. A heavy, unnatural sleep caused by sickness or injury; a state of unconsciousness.

comb. 1. A toothed instrument used for smoothing the hair. 2. The fleshy part that stands up on the head of a rooster. 3. To search through thoroughly. "They combed the district for him," means they searched thoroughly for him.

combat *(com'-bat)*. 1. To fight. 2. A fight. Those who take part are **combatants.**

combination *(com-bi-na'-tion)*. 1. A joining together of persons or things for a common purpose. A number of football clubs may combine to form a league. 2. An arrangement of two or more things. A motor-cycle with a side-car is called a combination. 3. One of a number of ways in which a group of things might be arranged.

combine *(com-bine')*. 1. To join together or to put together. *(com'-bine)*. 2. A number of firms in business together. A number of firms making soap, for example, may join together and form one large soap combine.

combustion *(com-bus'-tion)*. Burning either by fire or by chemical action. Things that burn easily are said to be **combustible.** Thus petrol is highly combustible.

comedian *(co-me'-di-an)*. 1. An actor who is seen at his best when playing in comedies. A **comedy** is a funny play that makes people laugh. 2. A comedian may be a man who amuses people by telling funny stories and using funny actions.

comely *(come'-ly)*. Pleasing to look at; neat and good-looking.

comet *(com'-et)*. A heavenly body, like a shooting star, often with a fiery tail.

comfort *(com'-fort)*. 1. Saying or doing things to ease a person's pain or sorrow. Anyone who does so is a **comforter** and he tries to make the person **comfortable.** 2. Relief; ease.

comical *(com'-i-cal)*. Funny.

comma *(com'-ma)*. This is a comma (,). It is used in writing to mark a pause, but not such a long pause as is marked by a full stop.

command *(com-mand')*. 1. To order a thing to be done; to tell a person to do a thing. A person who is in a position to tell others what to do is a **commander.** 2. An order.

commandant *(com-man-dant')*. The officer in charge of a military base. Usually used in connection with the Army.

commemorate *(com-mem'-o-rate)*. To honour the memory of somebody or something, often by some form of rejoicing.

commence *(com-mence')*. To begin.

commend *(com-mend')*. To praise; to say pleasing things about the good a person has done.

comment *(com'-ment)*. 1. To say what you think of a thing; thus if I say I think you ought to take longer over your home-work, I am commenting on the way you do your home-work. 2. A remark so made.

commerce *(com'-merce)*. The buying and selling of goods; trade.

D

commercial *(com-mer'-cial)*. 1. A word used to refer to anything which has to do with commerce or trading. 2. The advertising part of a television programme is called the commercial.

commission *(com-mis'-sion)*. 1. To give a person the power to do something for you, as "I commissioned my brother to buy me a new hockey stick". 2. A number of people who meet to decide important matters to do with government business, as a Trade Commission. 3. The money paid to a person who buys or sells goods for you, the amount being set on the value of the goods. Thus, if a person buys shoes for you to the value of £100 and he charges 3 per cent. for his services, his commission would be £3.

commit *(com-mit')*. 1. To hand over, as when a magistrate commits a person to be tried by a judge and jury. The magistrate hands over the person to the police, who keep him in jail until the trial. 2. To do something bad, as to commit a crime. 3. To commit yourself to do something is to promise to do it.

committee *(com-mit'-tee)*. A group of people which is elected or appointed to act for a special purpose. Thus, a food committee may be appointed to arrange for food at a meeting.

commodious *(com-mo'-di-ous)*. Spacious; having plenty of room.

commodity *(com-mod'-i-ty)*. An article having a real use; an article of trade. Wool is a commodity and so is butter, but snow is not.

common *(com'-mon)*. 1. Not unusual. Thus, apples are common in the autumn but scarce in spring. 2. Of all; belonging to all. When something is done for the common good, it is done for the good of all.

commonplace *(com'-mon-place)*. So ordinary as to be worth nothing or next to nothing.

common sense *(com'-mon sense)*. The good sense that comes to a person through keeping his eyes open and noting how things are done.

commonwealth *(com'-mon-wealth)*. 1. The body of people making up a state. 2. A group of states that are associated in some way. 3. A state or country.

commotion *(com-mo'-tion)*. Noisy disorder.

commune *(com-mune')*. If several people talk things over together, they are communing.

communicate *(com-mu'-ni-cate)*. 1. To impart; convey, as to communicate a disease. 2. To give or exchange ideas or opinions, by speaking, writing, etc. "We communicated by long-distance telephone."

communion *(com-mun'-ion)*. 1. Conversation, or act of sharing thoughts or feelings, usually with a close friend. When you hold communion with someone, you are in communion with him. 2. In the Christian Church, a special service is held at which the members of the Church share the Lord's Supper together. This is called the Communion.

community *(com-mu'-ni-ty)*. 1. The people living together in a place. The place may be a town, village, university, etc. 2. To do with such a group of people, as "community singing".

commute *(com-mute')*. 1. To change one thing for another. 2. To change a court sentence for a much lighter one.

compact. 1. *(com'-pact)*. An agreement, as in "The two friends made a solemn compact", meaning that they came to a solemn agreement. 2. *(com-pact')*. Solid; closely-packed. A room would be compact if it was small but had a great many things fitted neatly into it.

companion *(com-pan'-ion)*. 1. A friend. 2. One who goes somewhere with you.

company *(com'-pa-ny)*. 1. When people gather together they are called a company of people. 2. Guests are sometimes referred to as "the company". 3. A business firm may be known as a company. When you speak of more than one company, you speak of **companies.**

compare *(com-pare')*. To find the ways in which two or more things are alike or different.

comparison *(com-par'-i-son)*. To make a comparison is to compare one thing with others.

compartment *(com-part'-ment)*. A division, as "In my mother's purse there is a compartment for coins, another for a mirror, and a third for notes".

compass *(com'-pass)*. 1. An instrument for finding direction, often having a magnetized needle or disk. 2. An instrument for drawing circles, usually in the plural, **compasses.**

compassion *(com-pas'-sion)*. Pity; fellow-feeling; sympathy.

compatriot *(com-pa'-tri-ot)*. A compatriot of yours is a person who belongs to the same country as you do.

compel *(com-pel')*. To make something happen; to force some-one to do something.

compensate *(com'-pen-sate)*. To make up for; to make an equal return to. Thus, if you lend me a book and I lose it, I would compensate you for the loss of the book by giving you the price of a new one.

compensation *(com-pen-sa'-tion)*. Whatever is given in order to **compensate.** In the example above, the money given is the compensation.

compete *(com-pete')*. To take part in a test of skill or strength. You compete when you run in a race.

competition *(com-pe-ti'-tion)*. An affair in which a number of people try their best to do something better than one another. Those taking part are **competitors** *(com-pet'-i-tors)*.

complain *(com-plain')*. 1. To find fault; to say that something is wrong and it ought not to be. When a person finds fault he is making a **complaint.** 2. Complaint also means illness.

complete *(com-plete')*. A thing is complete when it is whole or finished. If you tore a page out of this dictionary it would be complete no longer.

complex *(com'-plex)*. Being made of many parts; therefore a complex thing is difficult to understand. A watch is a complex thing and very few people understand how it works.

complexion *(com-plex'-ion)*. The colour and condition of the skin of a person's face.

complicate *(com'-pli-cate)*. To twist together; to entangle; to mix up; to make difficult. "Tom complicated the arrange-ments by bringing two of his friends unexpectedly."

compliment *(com'-pli-ment)*. Polite words of praise; to praise someone in this way is to compliment him or pay him a compliment. Be careful to notice the difference between this word and the word **complement,** meaning something which makes another thing complete.

comply *(com-ply')*. To do what you are asked to do.

compose *(com-pose')*. 1. To make up; thus "Water is composed or made up of hydrogen and oxygen", and "He composed or made up a detective story". 2. To pull oneself together and become calm, as "At first he was very worried, but when the telegram arrived he became more composed".

composition *(com-po-si'-tion)*. Something which is made of parts. Thus, a piece of music is a composition because it is made of notes. You write a composition when you put words and sentences together to express your ideas.

compound *(com'-pound)*. A thing made of parts. Cowboy is a compound word.

comprehend *(com-pre-hend')*. To understand.

compress. 1. *(com-press')*. To squeeze into a smaller space. 2. *(com'-press)*. A wet cloth which is placed on a part of the body.

comprise *(com-prise')*. Consist of, as "The dictation comprised or consisted of six lines taken from today's paper".

compromise *(com'-pro-mise)*. When two people settle an argument by each giving up some demands, they compromise. For example, if Tom and Mary both wanted to use the same bicycle all day but wanted to settle their argument about it, each might agree to use it for only part of the day. They would be compromising, and their agreement would be a compromise.

compulsion *(com-pul'-sion)*. Anything a person is forced to do or compelled to do is done under compulsion.

compute *(com-pute')*. To count; to reckon.

comrade *(com'-rade)*. A friend; a companion.

concave *(con'-cave)*. Hollowed out or curved like the inside of a ball; that is, the curve goes inwards. When curved like the outside of a ball a thing is said to be **convex.**

conceal *(con-ceal')*. To hide.

concede *(con-cede')*. To admit; to grant, as "Of course, you will concede (admit) that there are 24 hours in a day".

conceit *(con-ceit')*. A good opinion of oneself. People who have conceit think that they are much better than they really are. We say that they are **conceited.**

concentrate *(con'-cen-trate)*. 1. If an army concentrates its forces at a spot, it brings them together at that place. 2. If you concentrate your mind on some work, you gather all your wits together and think hard about it. 3. A concentrated solution is one that is strong, and in many cases it needs water with it before it can be used.

concern *(con-cern')*. 1. Anxiety, as "She looked so pale that Tom's concern for her was great". 2. To have to do with, as "The quarrel between the two boys is no concern of yours", that is, it has nothing to do with you.

concert. 1. *(con'-cert)*. 1. A musical entertainment. 2. *(concert')*. To plan together; to agree; to combine. "Let us concert our plans" means let us make our plans together so that they agree.

concession *(con-ces'-sion)*. 1. Something given up, conceded or yielded to another person. 2. In "As a concession for the good work they had done, the teacher dismissed the class early", concession means reward.

conciliate *(con-cil'-i-ate)*. 1. To win over. 2. To set a person's mind at rest by soothing him.

concise *(con-cise')*. Brief; saying a great deal in a few words.

conclude *(con-clude')*. 1. To end, as "He concluded or ended his speech with the hope that we should all meet again soon". 2. To come to the conclusion or to have the idea of, as "From your excuses I conclude you don't want to come with me".

conclusion *(con-clu'-sion)*. 1. The last part of anything, the end. 2. An opinion arrived at after some thought.

conclusive *(con-clu'-sive)*. 1. Without any doubt. 2. Final.

concoct *(con-coct')*. To make up, as "He put water, treacle and oil in soapsuds and concocted a most weird mixture".

concord *(con'-cord)*. Agreement; peace.

concrete *(con'-crete)*. 1. The opposite to abstract (see **abstract,** No. 2). A book and a table are concrete objects; you can see them, touch them, and weigh them. Ghosts and greediness, on the other hand, are not concrete. 2. A mixture of cement, sand and stones used in building.

concussion *(con-cus'-sion)*. 1. A blow on the head or spine that injures the brain causes concussion. 2. A severe shaking, or a violent shock.

condemn *(con-demn')*. 1. A person is condemned when it is decided he has done a wrong. 2. A thing is condemned when it is decided it is no longer fit for its purpose.

condense *(con-dense')*. To make a thing take up less space; to change into a denser form, as steam into water.

condiment *(con'-di-ment)*. A seasoning for food. Mustard and pepper are two condiments.

condition *(con-di'-tion)*. 1. A necessary requirement before something else can be done. If your mother told you you could have ice-cream for dessert but only if you ate all your cabbage, she would be making a condition. The condition would be that you eat all your cabbage. 2. The state of a thing; when your dictionary is new it is in good condition, but if you throw it about and treat it roughly it will be in bad condition.

condole *(con-dole')*. To show your sorrow for.

condone *(con-done')*. To forgive; to pass over.

conduct. 1. *(con'-duct)*. Behaviour, as in the remark "Good conduct" or "Bad conduct" on a report card. 2. *(con-duct')*. To lead or guide, as "The blind man asked to be conducted across the road". 3. To direct an orchestra.

conductor *(con-duc'-tor)*. 1. A person who guides or leads, as a conductor of an orchestra. 2. A thing which carries heat or electricity is a conductor.

cone. 1. Ice-cream is served in a cone. Anything so shaped is known as a cone. 2. Cones are, also, the fruits of the evergreen tree.

confection *(con-fec'-tion)*. A sweet is a confection. One who sells sweets or sugared fruit is called a **confectioner.**

confederate *(con-fed'-er-ate)*. Ally; accomplice.

confederation *(con-fed-er-a'-tion)*. A group of people, states, etc., who join together for a special purpose.

confer *(con-fer')*. To talk together; to decide together what is best to do. When people confer they hold a **conference** *(con'-fer-ence)*.

confess *(con-fess')*. To own up; to admit you have done something. When a person confesses, he makes a **confession.** A person who confesses is called a **confessor.** In certain churches the confessor is the person to whom you confess.

confidant *(con-fi-dant')*. A close friend, to whom you tell your secrets; a person in whom you confide.

confide *(con-fide')*. 1. To tell a secret. 2. To trust.

confident *(con'-fi-dent)*. A person is confident of something when sure of it, as "I am confident that it will rain soon".

confidential *(con-fi-den'-tial)*. A thing is confidential when it is told to you in secret.

confine *(con-fine')*. To keep within as, "The soldier was confined to barracks", meaning he was not allowed to go out, as a punishment.

confirm *(con-firm')*. To make sure about; to make certain by saying the facts a second time. Thus a man orders some goods over the telephone; then he sits down and writes a letter confirming his order.

confiscate *(con'-fis-cate)*. To seize something and take it away from the owner.

conflict. 1. *(con'-flict)*. A battle; a struggle. 2. *(con-flict')*. To fight; to clash; to be contradictory, as in "The evidence given by the two witnesses was conflicting".

conform *(con-form')*. 1. To make like or be like, as "The finished article must conform to the pattern", meaning that it must be like the pattern. 2. To act in agreement with, as "You must conform to the rules of the game", meaning that you must behave in the way required by the rules.

confound *(con-found')*. To astonish; to put somebody in such an awkward position that he does not know what to do.

confront *(con-front')*. To bring face to face.

confuse *(con-fuse')*. To throw into a muddle.

confusion *(con-fu'-sion)*. A muddle; a state of disorder.

congenial *(con-gen'-ial)*. People are congenial when they have the same likes and dislikes, and therefore are able to get on well together.

congestion *(con-ges'-tion)*. A condition of being overcrowded; when there are too many things crowded into the same space there is congestion.

congratulate *(con-grat'-u-late)*. To tell a person that you are pleased that such and such a thing has happened to him.

congregate *(con'-gre-gate)*. To gather in a crowd, mass, heap, etc. When you attend church you are part of the **congregation** *(con-gre-ga'-tion)*.

congress *(con'-gress)*. A group of delegates meeting for discussion. In the United States, Congress is the body of the government that makes laws.

conical *(con'-i-cal)*. Having the shape of a cone. (See **cone.**)

conjecture *(con-jec'-ture)*. Guess.

conjunction *(con-junc'-tion)*. 1. A union; a coming together. 2. In grammar, a word used to connect clauses, phrases or words.

conjurer *(con'-jur-er)*. A magician; a person who amuses people by seeming to do things which are impossible, such as snatching money out of the air.

connect *(con-nect')*. To join things together.

connive *(con-nive')*. To help a person to do wrong, or to pretend not to see the wrong he is doing.

connoisseur *(con-nois-seur')*. An expert; a person who knows a great deal more than the average person does about a certain kind of art or about things people collect, such as old furniture, old pictures, silverware, etc.

conquer *(con'-quer)*. To get the better of by force. A person who conquers is a **conqueror**, and what he gains by conquering is called his **conquest.**

conscience *(con'-science)*. The natural feeling everyone has that some things are right and others wrong.

conscientious *(con-sci-en'-tious)*. Anxious to do what is right.

conscious *(con'-scious)*. Awake; aware.

consecrate *(con'-se-crate)*. 1. When something is consecrated it is usually blessed and then set aside for sacred purposes only. 2. To devote; dedicate, as "He consecrated his life to music".

consecutive *(con-sec'-u-tive)*. Following in a regular order; thus 1, 2, 3, 4 are consecutive figures, and so are 4, 3, 2, 1; but 1, 3, 4, 9 are not. January, February and March are consecutive months, and Monday, Tuesday and Wednesday are consecutive days.

consent *(con-sent')*. To agree; agreement.

consequence *(con'-se-quence)*. Result; something that follows naturally on something else. "When he got his feet wet, he did not trouble to change his shoes. As a consequence, he caught a bad cold."

conserve *(con-serve')*. To keep in good condition; to keep from harm.

consider *(con-sid'-er)*. 1. To think about very carefully, as "I will consider whether you can go to the football game when I know that you are no longer ill". 2. To think or imagine, as "I consider you have been very lazy".

considerate *(con-sid'-er-ate)*. Kind to others.

considering *(con-sid'-er-ing)*. Taking something into account. In "Considering what they cost, your shoes have worn out too quickly", the word "considering" may be replaced by the words "taking into account".

consign *(con-sign')*. To hand to another person; to place in somebody's care.

consist *(con-sist')*. To be made up of.

consistent *(con-sist'-ent)*. 1. Agreeing; in accord, as "Socrates taught that men should love wisdom and his actions were consistent with his teachings, for he always conducted himself wisely". 2. Always the same; holding to the same practice. If you change your mind rapidly and are very unpredictable in your actions, you are not consistent.

consistency *(con-sist'-en-cy)*. 1. State of being consistent. 2. Degree of thickness, softness, stickiness, etc., of substances, especially of thick liquids, as "What is the consistency of glue? It is thick and sticky".

console. 1. *(con-sole')*. To comfort; and the comfort given is a **consolation** *(con-so-la'-tion)*. *(con'-sole)*. 2. Part of an organ: the keyboard, stops and pedals. 3. A radio or television set which stands on the floor.

consolidate *(con-sol'-i-date)*. To bring together and make into one whole thing; thus, if your school and another one were joined together, it could be said that the two schools were consolidated.

consonant *(con'-so-nant)*. All the letters of the alphabet except the vowels. (The vowels are a, e, i, o, u.)

conspicuous *(con-spic'-u-ous)*. Easily seen.

conspire *(con-spire')*. To plot. The plot itself is a **conspiracy.**

constant *(con'-stant)*. Unchanging; faithful.

constellation *(con-stel-la'-tion)*. A group of stars. The Plough is a constellation.

consternation *(con-ster-na'-tion)*. Surprised dismay.

constitute *(con,-sti-tute)*. To make up. "Twenty shillings constitute a pound" and "Twenty shillings make up a pound" both have the same meaning.

constitution *(con-sti-tu'-tion)*. 1. In speaking of the constitution we refer to the way in which the government of a country is made up, or organized. 2. When speaking of a person's constitution we mean the amount of life and strength he has within him to help him ward off disease.

construct *(con-struct')*. To build.

construction *(con-struc'-tion)*. 1. The putting together or building of something. 2. The object built.

consult *(con-sult')*. If you consult a person, such as a doctor, you go to him for advice.

consume *(con-sume')*. To use up; to eat up.

contact *(con'-tact)*. Two or more things are in contact when they touch.

contagious *(con-ta'-gious)*. Passing on by contact. A contagious disease is one that can be passed from one person to another by contact. Scarlet fever and chicken pox are examples of contagious diseases.

contain *(con-tain')*. 1. To hold within. 2. To check.

contaminate *(con-tam'-i-nate)*. To make dirty, poisonous or unfit by touching. If mice ran over your food you would not care to eat it because you would know the mice had contaminated it with their dirty feet.

contemplate *(con'-tem-plate)*. 1. To think about something for a long while. 2. To look at attentively.

contemporary *(con-tem'-po-rar-y)*. 1. Living or existing at the same time. 2. A person or thing that lives or exists at the same time. You are a contemporary of your classmates.

contempt *(con-tempt')*. Scorn; feeling of looking down on something.

content *(con-tent')*. Happy; pleased.

contents *(con'-tents)*. That which a thing holds within it; what it contains.

contest. 1. *(con'-test)*. A fight; a struggle; anything in which two or more people try to get the better of each other. 2. *(con-test')*. To strive for.

contestant *(con-test'-ant)*. A person who takes part in a contest.

continent *(con'-tin-ent)*. A very large mass of land usually comprised of several countries. Europe is a continent, but England is not a continent.

continual *(con-tin'-u-al)*. Not stopping.

continue *(con-tin'-ue)*. To go on with.

contort *(con-tort')*. To twist and turn, as when a person makes an ugly face by twisting it. Making ugly faces is making **contortions.**

contour *(con'-tour)*. Outline; shape; form. In geography, contour lines are the lines drawn on a map through places that are at the same height above sea level.

contraband *(con'-tra-band)*. Goods smuggled into a country to avoid the payment of customs duty on them.

contract *(con-tract')*. 1. To bring closer together; to shrink; to cause to become smaller, shorter, etc. 2. To grow smaller, shorter, etc. *(con'-tract)*. 3. A legal agreement. There might be a contract between a worker and the man he works for. 4. To make a contract; to agree by contract, as "He contracted with the coal merchant to buy a ton of coal every month".

contractor *(con-trac'-tor)*. A person who agrees to do certain jobs, such as the plumbing, in a new building.

contradict *(con-tra-dict')*. To deny or to tell a person that what he says is wrong.

contrary *(con'-tra-ry)*. Being opposite to. Thus if you want to go in one direction and your friend wants to go in the opposite direction, not only are your wishes contrary, but the ways the two of you want to go are also contrary.

contrast. 1. *(con-trast')*. To compare two things so as to show their striking differences. 2. *(con'-trast)*. A noticeable difference between things.

contribution *(con-tri-bu'-tion)*. 1. Something that you give to a common cause, to which other people also give things. For example, you might send a contribution of money to the hospital. 2. An article or story sent into a newspaper or magazine. A person who sends a contribution is a **contributor** *(con-trib'-u-tor)* and to make a contribution is to **contribute** *(con-trib'-ute)*.

contrite *(con'-trite)*. Feeling deeply sorry for having done something wrong.

control *(con-trol')*. 1. To keep in check; thus "We must control our tempers". 2. The instruments in a plane or car which help the driver or pilot to operate it are called the **controls.**

contusion *(con-tu'-sion)*. A bruise.

convalescent *(con-va-les'-cent)*. Getting better after an illness.

convenient *(con-ven'-ient)*. Handy; suitable; not causing trouble; saving time or work.

convent *(con'-vent)*. A building in which nuns live.

convention *(con-ven'-tion)*. 1. A large formal meeting. 2. A rule, way of behaving, etc. which is customary or in common use. It is a social convention that men should walk on the outside of the pavement and let women walk on the inside. Something which is done according to convention is **conventional.**

converge *(con-verge')*. Two things are said to converge when they move towards each other, until they perhaps meet. Two sides of a triangle converge and so do two motor-cars that collide.

conversation *(con-ver-sa'-tion)*. Talk.

convert *(con-vert')*. To change from one thing to another. Thus a person who changes his religion is a convert *(con'-vert)*, and so is a person who changes from bad to good habits.

convex *(con'-vex)*. When curved like the outside of a ball, a thing is said to be convex. When curved like the inside of a ball it is **concave.**

convey *(con-vey')*. To carry; to take something somewhere.

convict. 1. *(con-vict')*. To find a person guilty of having done wrong. 2. *(con'-vict)*. A person who is serving a long prison term.

convince *(con-vince')*. To convince someone is to bring him to your way of thinking by giving strong arguments and proofs. To be convinced means to be sure; to be certain; to believe strongly.

convoy. 1. *(con-voy')*. To accompany and protect. *(con'-voy)*. 2. Whatever accompanies and protects. 3. A fleet of ships under escort.

convulse *(con-vulse')*. To shake considerably. A person is said to be convulsed with rage when he is in such an angry mood that he shakes; he is convulsed with laughter when the laughing makes him rock from side to side. A child in **convulsions** loses his senses and shakes all over.

cook. 1. A person whose business it is to prepare food. 2. To prepare food for eating.

cool. Rather cold, but not very much so. A breeze on a hot day feels cool.

coolie *(coo'-lie)*. A hired labourer or porter in China and other eastern countries.

coop. A small cage for chickens, etc.

cooper *(coo'-per)*. A man who makes wooden barrels.

co-operate *(co-op'-er-ate)*. To act together with another person or persons; to make a united effort. If you co-operate with others, you give your **co-operation** *(co-op-er-a'-tion)*.

co-operation *(co-op-er-a'-tion)*. A united effort. If every member of a family would co-operate in clearing the table and dishes after dinner, then, through co-operation, the task would be finished quickly.

co-pilot *(co'-pi-lot)*. The second or assistant pilot in an aeroplane.

copious *(co'-pi-ous)*. Abundant; plentiful.

copper *(cop'-per)*. 1. A soft, reddish metal. 2. A penny or halfpenny.

coppice *(cop'-pice)*. A small wood or thicket. A copse.

copy *(cop'-y)*. 1. To imitate or make one thing like another. 2. One of a number of books, magazines, newspapers, etc., when hundreds have been printed alike. You are now using a copy of a dictionary.

coral *(cor'-al)*. 1. A stony substance formed in the ocean by the piling up of skeletons of certain small sea animals. 2. A deep pinkish-orange colour.

cord. 1. A strong kind of string. 2. To cord means to tie up. 3. A measure of wood (128 cu. ft.).

cordial *(cor'-dial)*. 1. Hearty and warm; thus cordial greetings are hearty and warm greetings. 2. A sweet non-alcoholic beverage.

corduroy *(cor'-du-roy)*. A cloth which has a piled or napped surface like that of velvet, raised in cords or ridges.

core. The centre or middle. You find the seeds in the core of an apple.

cork. The light, outer bark of a tree, which is used as bottle-stoppers, floats for fishing, etc.

corn. 1. A general name for wheat, barley, oats, rye, etc. 2. A growth of hard skin on the feet or hands.

corner *(cor'-ner)*. 1. The place where two converging walls meet. 2. The place where two streets meet.

cornet *(cor'-net)*. A musical instrument which is shaped like a trumpet and is played by blowing into one end.

cornice *(cor'-nice)*. An ornamental edging fixed along the upper line of the wall of a room, the side of a building, etc.

coronation *(cor-o-na'-tion)*. The crowning of a king or queen.

coroner *(cor'-o-ner)*. An official whose duty it is to find out the cause of a person's death when the death may not have been from natural causes.

coronet *(cor'-o-net)*. A kind of crown worn by princes, noblemen, etc.

corporation *(cor-po-ra'-tion)*. 1. A body of persons united usually for business purposes. 2. The mayor, aldermen and councillors of a borough or city.

corps. A body of troops or trained people.

corpse. A dead body.

corpulent *(cor'-pu-lent)*. Stout; bulky; fat.

corral *(cor-ral')*. An enclosure for horses and cattle.

correct *(cor-rect')*. 1. Accurate; right; without a mistake. 2. To correct is to look for mistakes and to put right any that are found.

correspond *(cor-re-spond')*. 1. To exchange letters with. 2. To agree with, as "What he said corresponds with all you have told me".

correspondent *(cor-re-spond'-ent)*. 1. A person employed by a newspaper to live in a distant place and report on the news there. 2. One who writes letters.

corridor *(cor'-ri-dor)*. A passage from which rooms open.

corrode *(cor-rode')*. To eat away, a little at a time, by chemical action. Rust, for example, is the result of the **corrosion** of iron by the action of the air.

corrugate *(cor'-ru-gate)*. To wrinkle; to mark in folds; to bend into ridges, as corrugated iron.

corrupt *(cor-rupt')*. The real meaning of the word is decayed, but as a rule it is used to speak of a person who is ready to take money for doing things he should not do.

cosmetics *(cos-met'-ics)*. Preparations used by women to beautify their faces. Lipstick and face creams are cosmetics.

cost. The price paid for a thing.

costly *(cost'-ty)*. Things are costly for which a high price is charged.

costume *(cos'-tume)*. Dress; clothing.

cosy *(co'-sy)*. 1. Snug and comfortable. 2. A tea-cosy is a covering for a tea-pot to keep the tea warm.

cot. A small bed, suitable for little children.

cottage *(cot'-tage)*. A small or humble dwelling-house.

cotton *(cot'-ton)*. 1. A plant grown in warm climates. Its seeds are attached to long, white fibres, from which cotton thread is made. 2. Cloth made from cotton thread.

cough. To force air from the lungs quickly and noisily. When you have a cold, you usually have a cough.

council *(coun'-cil)*. Several people grouped together to decide matters to do with their work. The local council of your district looks after such things as the repair of the roads, the lighting of the streets and the sanitation of the houses, etc. The people who form the council are named **councillors.**

counsel *(coun'-sel)*. To advise; advice. If someone counsels you to look both ways before crossing a road, he advises you to look both ways. He gives you good counsel or good advice.

count. 1. In "When you count the sheep, do not frighten them", count means add up the number. 2. In "The little girl can count up to fifty", count means that she can say the figures one after the other. 3. In "I count on your helping me", count means depend. 4. In "The Count lives in a fine castle", Count is a title of a nobleman.

countenance *(coun'-te-nance)*. 1. The expression on a person's face. 2. The person's face. 3. To approve of, as "Her mother won't countenance that sort of behaviour".

counter *(coun'-ter)*. 1. A kind of table in a shop at which customers stand while being served. 2. A metal disc made to look like a coin, which people use instead of money when playing cards. 3. Counter means in opposition to, thus "He acted counter to my wishes", means that he did just the opposite to what I wanted.

counterfeit *(coun'-ter-feit)*. 1. An imitation of the real thing, especially made to make people believe it is real. Thus, if somebody draws a pound note to look like a real one, the drawing is a counterfeit. 2. To counterfeit something is to imitate it, or make a sham copy of it in order to deceive.

countermand *(coun-ter-mand')*. When someone orders a thing to be done, and then another order is given to say it is not to be done, the second order countermands the first.

countless *(count'-less)*. So many that it is impossible to count them.

country *(coun'-try)*. 1. Land where there are far more things growing, such as crops, plants and trees, than there are houses and buildings. 2. The land, whether made up of towns, fields, forests, etc., which forms a nation.

county *(coun'-ty)*. A division of a country. England is divided into counties.

couple *(cou'-ple)*. Two of something, as a couple of people, a couple of books, a couple of days, etc.

coupon *(cou'-pon)*. A ticket which shows that the owner is entitled to goods, money, services, some privilege, etc.

courage *(cour'-age)*. Bravery.

course. 1. A track where races are run. 2. Direction, as "The captain steered his ship on a northerly course". 3. A part of a meal; dinner often consists of several courses. 4. A series; a series of lessons or medical treatments. If someone says he is taking a course in mathematics, he means he is taking a series of lessons in mathematics. 5. "Of course" means naturally.

court. 1. A place where justice is decided by a judge and jury, a magistrate or a person appointed to make the decision. 2. An open place surrounded by buildings. 3. A play area such as a tennis court. 4. The followers of a king make up the king's court. 5. A royal home or palace.

courteous *(cour'-te-ous)*. Polite and well-mannered.

cousin *(cous'-in)*. The son or daughter of your uncle or aunt.

cover *(cov'-er)*. 1. To spread over with a cloth or lid. 2. The thing that covers. 3. The binding of a book.

covet *(cov'-et)*. To want very much a thing belonging to somebody else.

covetous *(cov'-et-ous)*. Greedy; envious. A person who wants the things others have is a covetous person.

coward *(cow'-ard)*. A person who is often afraid; one who has very little courage. Such a person is **cowardly** and suffers from **cowardice.**

coxswain *(cox'-swain)*. A man who steers or directs the steering of a boat.

coy. Shy; bashful.

coyote *(coy-ote')*. A North American prairie wolf.

crab. A shell-fish with a hard body-covering and a pair of pincers.

crack. A long, narrow opening. You may have seen cracks in the earth when there has been a long dry season.

cracker *(crack'-er)*. A thin biscuit.

cradle *(cra'-dle)*. 1. A small bed used for a baby. It is usually on rockers. 2. A frame which supports a very heavy object such as a boat.

craft. 1. Skill. 2. A trade. 3. A boat.

crag. A steep, rugged rock; a rough, rocky cliff; a large rock jutting out of a cliff.

cram. To fill overfull by forcing, as "He crammed his mouth so full of food that he could not swallow".

cramp. 1. To cramp things into a small space is to huddle them together. 2. A cramp is a tool which grips two things and holds them together. 3. To have cramp is to suffer the pain brought on by muscles in the leg, foot, etc., tightening or twisting.

crane. 1. A machine able to lift heavy weights. 2. A bird with long legs. 3. When a person cranes his neck, he stretches it so as to be able to see over something that is in the way.

crank. 1. An eccentric person. 2. The part of a machine that, when turned, sets the motor running.

crash. 1. To fall to earth, as in "The aeroplane crashed, killing seventy people". 2. A loud noise, such as is made by breaking dishes.

crass. Stupid and coarse.

crate. A kind of packing-case, usually made of light strips of wood.

crater *(cra'-ter).* A bowl-shaped hole in the earth, caused by an explosion, or by the impact of a large falling object, such as a meteor, or by the eruption of a volcano.

crave. To wish for intensely.

crawl. 1. To move on hands and feet as a baby does. 2. To move at very slow speed. 3. To feel **crawly** is to feel as though something were crawling on you.

crayon *(cray'-on).* A piece of wax or chalk used for colouring or drawing.

crazy *(cra'-zy).* 1. Insane. 2. Full of cracks or flaws.

creak. To make a kind of squeaking noise.

cream. 1. The thick yellow part of milk, which is rich in butter fat. 2. Anything that resembles cream, such as furniture cream, shaving cream, face cream and chocolate cream. 3. Cream is also a colour, yellow-white.

creamery *(cream'-er-y).* 1. A place where butter and cheese are made. 2. A place where you can buy butter, cream, milk, cheese and eggs.

create *(cre-ate').* To make a thing; but there is, in addition, the idea that the thing has not been made before, as in the case of the **creation** of the world.

creature *(crea'-ture).* A live thing; usually used when speaking of animals.

credible *(cred'-i-ble).* Believable.

credit *(cred'-it).* 1. To believe, as "I could hardly credit his story". 2. To buy on credit means to buy now and pay later on. 3. Anything that is to a person's credit is something in his favour.

creditor *(cred'-i-tor).* A person to whom you owe money is your creditor.

credulous *(cred'-u-lous).* Said of a person who believes all he is told and is too simple to know when someone tells him an untruth.

creed. 1. A system of beliefs; especially religious beliefs. 2. The Christian Creed is a summary of the main things which a Christian should believe.

creek. A narrow inlet of the sea.

creep. 1. To move on hands and knees or with the body close to the ground. 2. To move at a slow speed.

cremate *(cre-mate').* To burn, usually a corpse. Sometimes, instead of being buried a dead body is cremated.

cremation *(cre-ma'-tion).* An act of burning.

crêpe. 1. A crinkled cloth of wool, cotton or silk. 2. There is a kind of stretchy paper used for decorating which is called crêpe paper. 3. Black crêpe is often worn by a person who has lost a relative through death.

crescent *(cres'-cent).* 1. Shaped like the moon when less than half of it can be seen. 2. Anything shaped like the crescent moon. Thus, a curving street that does not form a complete circle is often called a crescent.

crest. 1. A tuft or comb on the head of a bird. 2. The top of anything which juts out over the rest, such as the crest of a hill. 3. The plume on a helmet. 4. A coat of arms. 5. The top part of a wave; the white foam as it curls over.

crestfallen *(crest'-fall-en).* Sad and discouraged.

crevasse *(cre-vasse').* A chasm in the ice forming a glacier, a glacier being a river of ice.

crevice *(crev-'ice).* A crack, cleft or fissure.

crew. A group of people working together, as the crew of a ship.

crib. 1. A baby's cot. 2. The rack in a stable. 3. To cheat by dishonestly using the knowledge of another person.

cricket *(crick'-et).* 1. A small black insect of the grasshopper family. Male crickets make a loud chirping noise in summer.

crime. A dishonest act which is against the law and punishable by a fine or a prison sentence.

criminal *(crim'-i-nal).* A person who commits a crime. (See **crime.**)

crimson *(crim'-son).* A deep red colour.

cringe. 1. To wince; to shrink away in fear; to crouch as if you were caught doing something wrong. 2. To show too much admiration or fear of someone; to let someone see that you think he is much better than you are.

crinkle *(crin'-kle)*. To fold something so that it has a wavy surface. Crêpe paper is crinkled; so are sheets of corrugated iron.

cripple *(crip'-ple)*. 1. A lame person. 2. To lame someone is to cripple him.

crisis *(cri'-sis)*. The point of time when some danger reaches its highest pitch. The danger may be a serious illness, a clash in the desires of nations, etc. .

crisp. Brittle and easily snapped.

critic *(crit'-ic)*. A person who gives his opinions on a thing. Newspapers employ critics to say what they think of new books, new plays, new films, etc. But the word is also used to describe people who are always finding fault.

critical *(crit'-i-cal)*. 1. A thing is reaching a critical condition when the crisis (see **crisis**) is due. 2. The work of a critic (see **critic**) is critical work. 3. A person who is critical is one who finds fault too often.

criticize *(crit'-i-cize)*. To give your opinion of something; to say why you think it is good or bad.

croak. To make a noise like the sound which a frog makes.

crochet *(cro-chet')*. 1. A kind of knitting done with a hooked needle. 2. To do such knitting.

crockery *(crock'-er-y)*. Things made of earthenware, as pots, basins, kitchen cups and saucers, etc.

crocodile *(croc'-o-dile)*. A large lizard-like member of the reptile family which lives on land and in water. It has a long head, a long mouth and powerful jaws.

crocus *(cro'-cus)*. A small early spring flower.

crook. 1. Anything which is bent, hooked or is not straight. A shepherd's crook has a hook at one end. The crooked man of the nursery rhyme had a bend in his back. 2. A crook is, also, a dishonest man. He is not straight in his dealings.

crop. 1. The plants which a farmer grows in his fields. 2. The food-bag inside a fowl, etc. 3. To cut short, as when a barber crops your hair. 4. A horseman's whip.

croquet *(cro'-quet)*. An outdoor game played by knocking wooden balls through wire hoops with wooden hammers or mallets.

cross. 1. Anything having the shape produced by placing one piece of material across another. Usually, crosses have one upright strip and one horizontal strip, making four arms; but it must be remembered that the cross of St. Andrew is an **X**. 2. To be cross is to be angry or bad tempered. 3. To cross a road, a river, or even a room is to go from one side to the other. 4. An animal is said to be a cross when its parents are of different breeds.

crossbow *(cross'-bow).* A kind of bow used as a weapon in the Middle Ages.

crouch. To stoop down by bending the knees.

crow. 1. A large black bird. 2. The sound made by cocks. 3. To boast, as when a bragging person crows or boasts about the wonderful things he has done.

crowd. 1. Very many people collected together. 2. To put many things in a space hardly large enough for them.

crown. 1. An ornament worn on the head by kings and queens to show their high rank. 2. The top, as the crown of the head.

crucify *(cru'-ci-fy).* To put to death by nailing to a cross.

crude. 1. Raw; unfinished; not refined. Things in their natural condition are in a crude state. Thus we speak of crude oil and crude rubber, meaning the natural products before they have been prepared for use. 2. Rude; vulgar.

cruel *(cru'-el).* Unkind; without mercy. Any cruel action is one of **cruelty.**

cruise. A voyage at sea taken for pleasure, health and sight-seeing rather than for business.

crumb. A very small piece broken off bread, cake, etc. If you place a piece of bread on the table, you may find crumbs on the table when you lift the bread.

crumble *(crum'-ble).* To break into little pieces.

crumple *(crum'-ple).* To crush so as to spoil the shape.

crunch. To crush noisily with the teeth or foot.

crusade *(cru-sade').* 1. A war fought in the cause of religion. 2. Any action taken to fight some evil, as a crusade against poverty. A **crusader** is a person taking part in a crusade.

crush. 1. To squeeze, break, or bruise a thing by pressing. 2. To crush an enemy is to overwhelm him. 3. A crowd.

crust. The hard outside of many substances, not only of bread, but of the earth and many other things as well.

cry. 1. To weep; to make a loud sound such as babies make when hungry or small children when hurt or unhappy. 2. To exclaim; speak loudly; shout. 3. The sounds that some animals make are called cries.

crypt. An underground vault or chamber, especially one beneath a church, used as a chapel or burial place.

crystal *(crys'-tal)*. 1. A transparent mineral resembling glass. 2. Clear or transparent like glass. 3. Certain substances, when they turn solid, form naturally into tiny shapes called **crystals.** You are familiar with snow crystals.

cub. The young of a lion, fox, etc.

cube. 1. A solid shape having six square faces. Each die of a pair of dice is a cube. 2. In arithmetic, a cube is the result of multiplying a number by itself twice; thus 8 is the cube of 2.

cubic *(cu'-bic)*. 1. Shaped like a cube. 2. Cubic measurement is three-dimensional measurement (see **dimension**), or measurement of volume. If you wished to find the volume or capacity of a box 2 feet long, 2 feet high and 2 feet wide, you would multiply $2 \times 2 \times 2 = 8$. The result is 8 cubic feet.

cud. A mouthful of food. Some animals, such as cattle, have more than one stomach. When they graze, the food, such as grass, passes first into the first stomach. Here it is held until the animal is ready to chew it thoroughly. Then it is brought back up. The food that is brought back up from the first stomach is called the cud. After the animal has chewed the cud thoroughly, the food passes into a second stomach, where it is digested.

cudgel *(cudg'el)*. A heavy stick or club suitable for a weapon.

cue. A signal which tells you what to do or how to act. Actors learn to follow cues which tell them when to come on stage, when to speak, etc.

cuff. 1. The end of a sleeve, as a coat cuff or a shirt cuff. 2. To give someone a short, sharp blow or hit.

culinary *(cu'-li-nar-y)*. To do with the kitchen or cooking.

cull. 1. To sort out; to select. 2. To pluck (flowers, etc.).

culprit *(cul'-prit)*. A person who is guilty of some fault or crime.

cultivate *(cul'-ti-vate)*. To prepare land for crops by digging, ploughing and manuring.

cultured *(cul'-tured)*. A person who is polite and educated is cultured.

culvert *(cul'-vert)*. A channel built under roads and railways to allow water to flow.

cunning *(cun'-ning)*. Sly; clever in dishonesty.

cupboard *(cup'-board)*. A small room for storing things; a cabinet with shelves.

cupful *(cup'-ful)*. As much as a cup holds. When you want to refer to more than one cupful you say **cupfuls.**

cupidity *(cu-pid'-i-ty)*. Greed.

cur. 1. A worthless, miserable-looking mongrel dog. 2. A nasty, mean-tempered person.

curator *(cu-ra'-tor)*. A person whose work is to take care of something. Usually, a curator is put in charge of a museum.

curb. 1. To check; restrain, as in "You must curb your appetite for sweets".

curd. When milk turns sour, it separates into two parts, one lumpy and thick, the other watery. The thick part is the curd, and it is from this that cheese is made.

curdle *(cur'-dle)*. To turn lumpy and thick. (See **curd.**)

cure. 1. To make a sick person well again. 2. To dry meat, fish, bacon, etc., and to preserve it by a system of smoking. 3. A remedy.

curious *(cu'-ri-ous)*. 1. Anxious to know or learn; inquiring; inquisitive. 2. Strange; odd; unusual. Anything that is curious is a **curiosity** *(cu-ri-os'-i-ty)*.

curl. 1. To twist into rings. 2. A spiral of something, as a curl of hair, a curl of paper, a curl of wood shaving.

currant *(cur'-rant)*. 1. A fruit which grows on bushes and has small red, black or white fruits, which are soft. 2. The dried currants sold by grocers; they are really small grapes.

current *(cur'-rent)*. 1. A flowing or moving; a stream. The current of a river is its motion in one certain direction. There are also air currents and electric currents. The electric current flows through electric wires. 2. Belonging to the present time. The latest issue of a magazine is called the current issue.

curse. 1. To use bad words. 2. To wish a person harm.

cursory *(cur'-so-ry)*. Hasty; not thorough.

curt. Short; so short as to be rude; thus, if someone asked you a question and you replied "No" in a rude way, your answer would be curt.

curtail *(cur-tail')*. To cut short.

curtain *(cur'-tain)*. A piece of material placed over windows. A curtain is used to cover or hide something.

curvature *(cur'-va-ture)*. The curve of anything. Thus, the surface of a ball is an example of curvature.

curve. A line bent into the shape of a round arch.

cushion *(cush'-ion)*. A small pillow used for sitting or kneeling.

custard *(cus'-tard)*. A baked mixture of eggs and milk served as a dessert.

custody *(cus'-to-dy)*. 1. A keeping or guarding. 2. The state of being guarded. Something that is given into your custody is given to you to guard or look after. When we speak of people being taken into custody we mean arrested.

custom *(cus'-tom)*. 1. A habit, as "It was his custom to take a walk after dinner". 2. Something that is done by most people; a rule of behaviour which most people follow. Thus, "The Indians had the custom of painting their faces with war-paint before going into battle". Something which is done by custom is **customary.**

customer *(cus'-tom-er)*. 1. A person who buys at a certain store is a customer of that store. 2. A shopper.

cute. Clever and sharp-witted.

cutlass *(cut'-lass)*. A short, curved sword.

cutler *(cut'-ler)*. One who makes or deals in knives, swords, shears and other cutting implements.

cutlery *(cut'-ler-y)*. Articles such as knives, scissors, razors, etc.

cycle *(cy'-cle)*. A period of time in which a round of events is completed. These are events that always follow each other in a certain order. Thus, a complete cycle of the seasons is the period of time in which winter is followed by spring; spring by summer, and so on, back to winter again.

cyclone *(cy'-clone)*. A terrible wind storm that travels round in a circle.

cygnet *(cyg'-net)*. A young swan.

cylinder *(cyl'-in-der)*. A tube, or solid, tube-shaped form. A cylinder is long and straight, and the surface of both ends is circular. A stick of chalk has the form of a cylinder.

cynic *(cyn'-ic)*. A person who has the habit of sneering at things.

czar. 1. Before 1917, the King of Russia was called the Czar. The feminine is **czarina.** 2. A person having great power is sometimes called a czar.

D

dab. To touch lightly.

dabble *(dab'-ble)*. 1. To do something without real interest. 2. To make a thing wet by dabbing. 3. To paddle.

daffodil *(daf'-fo-dil)*. A yellow spring flower with a long stem and a trumpet-shaped blossom.

dagger *(dag'-ger)*. A short weapon, like a sword, but with a pointed tip. It is used for stabbing rather than cutting.

dahlia *(dahl'-ia)*. A plant of the aster family which flowers in autumn.

daily *(dai'-ly)*. Happening every day.

dainty *(dain'-ty)*. 1. Delicate; fresh. 2. Having delicate tastes. 3. Delicious.

dairy *(dai'-ry)*. A place where milk is stored, sold or made into butter and cheese.

dais *(da'-is)*. A platform placed in a room so that people on it can be seen easily by the audience.

daisy *(dai'-sy)*. A plant with white or pink petals around a yellow centre.

dale. A valley.

dally *(dal'-ly)*. To play; to waste time by trifling or by being idle.

dam. 1. A bank or wall built across a stream to keep the water from flowing away. 2. The mother of an animal.

damage *(dam'-age)*. To harm, hurt or injure a thing and make it less perfect or useful than it was before.

dame. The title of a lady equal in rank to a knight or baronet.

damsel *(dam'-sel)*. A maiden or young woman.

damson *(dam'-son)*. A small, bluish-black plum. The word refers either to the fruit or to the tree.

dance. 1. To move the feet with measured steps to music. 2. The occasion when a number of people come together in order to dance. 3. To lead someone a dance is to put him to much trouble or bother. 4. To dance attendance upon someone is to wait on him hand and foot.

dandelion *(dan'-de-li-on)*. A weed with a bright yellow flower and notched leaves.

dandy *(dan'-dy)*. 1. Someone who thinks too much about dress and appearance. 2. Smart; fine.

danger *(dan'-ger)*. When there is a chance that harm may befall you, there is danger; a peril.

dangerous *(dan'-ger-ous)*. A thing is dangerous when it may cause harm. Swimming too soon after lunch is dangerous because you might develop cramp.

dangle *(dan'-gle)*. 1. To sway from side to side while hanging down. 2. To hang loosely.

dank. Moist and damp.

dapper *(dap'-per)*. Smart and brisk. When a man is said to be dapper, there is also the idea that he is not very tall.

dapple *(dap'-ple)*. To mark with spots; thus a horse is dappled when it is of one general colour with spots of another colour.

dare. To have the courage to do something that needs a certain amount of pluck. A person who dares is **daring.**

dark. Not light; having little colour; almost black.

darkness *(dark'-ness)*. The opposite to light; when there is no light there is darkness.

darn. To mend holes in garments, etc., by making stitches that cross over each other.

dart. 1. A sharp-pointed object thrown by the hand and intended to stick into the target at which it is thrown. 2. To dart somewhere is to move there quickly. 3. To dart a glance at somebody is to turn the eyes on him and look away again immediately.

dash. 1. To throw something with a quick jerk, as "We dashed water over the burning rug". 2. To dash off somewhere is to go there very quickly. 3. To dash a thing to bits is to smash it by throwing it against something.

dashing *(dash'-ing)*. 1. Smart; showy. 2. Full of energy or spirit.

date. 1. January 1, 1950 is a date. 2. The fruit of the date palm, which is sweet, brownish and contains a long, hard stone.

daub. 1. To smear or plaster with something soft and sticky. 2. To smear on in patches or spots. Thus, an unskilled painter is sometimes called a **dauber.**

daughter *(daugh'-ter)*. A girl in a family is a daughter of the parents.

daunt. To frighten or make a person lose pluck. A **dauntless** person is one whom you cannot frighten.

dawdle *(daw'-dle)*. To do a thing or go somewhere too slowly and thus waste time.

dawn. 1. The beginning of day; the point of time in early morning when the sun rises. 2. Since dawn means the beginning of the day, it has grown to mean also the beginning of many other things, as the dawn of a new age, meaning the beginning of a fresh period of time. 3. If a thing dawns on you, it flashes across your mind for the first time.

daybreak *(day'-break)*. The time in the morning when light first appears; dawn.

day-dream *(day'-dream)*. 1. A reverie. 2. To let your thoughts wander; to be lost in your imaginings.

daylight *(day'-light)*. The light of day.

daytime *(day'-time)*. The time when it is day.

daze. 1. To stun someone; to do something to someone which prevents him from thinking or seeing clearly. 2. A state of being confused in your mind or muddled.

dazzle *(daz'-zle)*. 1. To make it difficult for the eyes to see, because something set before them is remarkably bright or unexpected. 2. To surprise by beauty or cleverness.

dead. 1. Lifeless; said of plants or animals that were once living. 2. In "Are you dead sure?" dead means absolutely. 3. The dead of night is the part of the night when everything is most quiet. 4. To **deaden** means to lessen, as "The patient was given drugs to deaden his pain".

deaf. 1. A deaf person is one who cannot hear as well as ordinary people, or one who cannot hear at all. 2. Deaf is also used for people who do not want to hear; thus, "He turned a deaf ear to all I said" means that he did not want to listen to my words.

deal. 1. To give in portions; to distribute, as in "Deal the cards—seven to each person". 2. "He deals in Indian cloth" means he buys Indian cloth and sells it. 3. A great deal means a large amount. 4. The timber of the fir tree; a deal table is made of fir wood.

dearth. Scarcity.

death. The end of life.

debate *(de-bate')*. 1. To argue; to discuss. 2. A discussion.

3. A thing that is **debatable** is one about which you cannot be sure.

debris *(de'-bris).* Wreckage; ruins; rubbish; things scattered about in disorder.

debt. Something which one person owes another. Usually what is owing is money, but it may be something else. You may owe a person a debt of kindness, because he has been kind to you. A person who owes something is a **debtor.**

decade *(dec'-ade).* Any period of ten years; thus, from 1940 to 1950 is a decade.

decadent *(de'-ca-dent).* Decaying; growing less satisfactory.

decalogue *(dec'-a-logue).* The Ten Commandments.

decamp *(de-camp').* To go away in a hurry.

decapitate *(de-cap'-i-tate).* To cut off the head.

decay *(de-cay').* 1. To become rotten. 2. To decline, as "The strength of the country decayed".

decease *(de-cease').* Death.

deceit *(de-ceit').* The act of deceiving; cheating; treachery; underhandedness. Anyone guilty of deceit is **deceitful.**

deceive *(de-ceive').* To mislead; to cheat; to make someone believe something that is not true. One who deceives others is a **deceiver** and practises **deception** *(de-cep'-tion).*

December *(De-cem'-ber).* The twelfth month of the year.

decent *(de'-cent).* Proper, modest and respectable.

decide *(de-cide').* To make up one's mind.

decidedly *(de-cid'-ed-ly).* Without any doubt, or considerably, as "His chances have improved decidedly".

deciduous *(de-cid'-u-ous).* Said of trees whose leaves fall every year. Thus, an evergreen tree is not deciduous.

decimate *(de'-ci-mate).* 1. In ancient history, to put to death one man in every ten. 2. Nowadays, to destroy a large part of anything.

decipher *(de-ci'-pher).* To decode; to translate from secret marks into ordinary language; to make out the meaning of words badly written or partly blotted out. Thus, if you turned a message in Morse code into ordinary language, you would be deciphering it. Also, if you made out the letters of a badly written signature you would be deciphering the signature.

decision *(de-ci'-sion).* 1. The act of making up your mind. 2. What you make up your mind to do.

deck. 1. The floor of a ship, where people can walk about. 2. To adorn or dress yourself. Usually this is applied to women and girls.

declare *(de-clare')*. To say something about a thing and to say it positively, not in any half-hearted way. What a person declares is a **declaration**.

decline *(de-cline')*. To refuse, as "He declined the invitation to come to dinner". 2. To grow less, as "The membership of our football club has declined", meaning that now there are fewer members. 3. To become weak in body.

decompose *(de-com-pose')*. To decay.

decorate *(dec'-o-rate)*. 1. To adorn; to make beautiful. A plate might be decorated with a pattern of roses. When you decorate a room, you paint or paper the walls, hang curtains, etc. A person who decorates a room is called a **decorator** *(dec'-o-ra-tor)*. To **redecorate** is to decorate again. 2. To decorate someone is to pin a medal on him. Thus, "He has been decorated twice for bravery".

decoration *(dec-o-ra'-tion)*. 1. Something used to decorate with; an ornament. 2. A medal.

decoy *(de-coy')*. To lure into; to trap.

decrease *(de-crease')*. To become less; the opposite to increase.

decree *(de-cree')*. A kind of law decided upon by people in power. Such people may be the King, Parliament, a court of law, etc.

decrepit *(de-crep'-it)*. A person or animal is said to be decrepit when he is old and tottering.

decry *(de-cry')*. To blame or to speak badly of a thing; to run it down.

dedicate *(ded'-i-cate)*. To set apart; to consecrate; to give up to, as in "The nurse dedicated her life to nursing".

deduce *(de-duce')*. To draw a conclusion; to arrive at some knowledge by reasoning from the facts. Thus, if you were picking apples and it took you two hours to pick 200 apples, you might deduce that in one hour you could pick 100 apples.

deduct *(de-duct')*. To subtract.

deed. 1. A thing that is done. Any action is a deed. 2. Deeds are the legal papers which show who owns a certain house or other property.

deem. To think; believe; suppose; judge.

deep. Not shallow.

deer. An animal with four legs, brown hair and the ability to run very fast. The male deer has antlers.

deface *(de-face')*. To spoil the appearance of; thus when somebody tears a poster on a wall or sign-board, he defaces it.

defame *(de-fame')*. To say things which injure a person's character.

default *(de-fault')*. To neglect to do what is required.

defeat *(de-feat')*. To conquer an enemy or to win a victory of any kind over somebody; thus "Miss Jones defeated Miss Brown at tennis".

defect *(de-fect')*. A fault in something; thus an explosion might be caused by a defect in a gas-pipe. "Her slovenly way of speaking is a defect she should try to overcome".

defend *(de-fend')*. To ward off danger; to protect from harm. That which stops the harm is a **defence.**

defer *(de-fer')*. 1. To put off to another time. 2. To show respect.

deference *(def'-er-ence)*. 1. Respect. 2. Giving in to the wishes of others, as "In deference to your wishes, I will stay at home".

defiance *(de-fi'-ance)*. Determination not to submit to the will of another.

deficiency *(de-fi'-cien-cy)*. A lack; a shortage. If there is a deficiency of fresh air in the room you will have trouble breathing. If a company discovered a deficiency in its accounts, it would know that some money had been lost or stolen. A man who has a deficiency of good manners is **deficient** in good manners.

defile *(de-file')*. 1. To spoil by making a thing impure; thus, if a man threw a dead animal into a reservoir, the water would be defiled. 2. To march in single line or file. 3. A narrow way between rocks or mountains wide enough for only one person to pass.

define *(de-fine')*. To describe something accurately and in full. In writing these words we have defined the word "define". The words are a **definition** *(de-fin-i'-tion)* of "define".

definite *(def'-i-nite)*. Having fixed limits; exact; precise.

deflect *(de-flect')*. To turn something aside or carry it out of its proper direction, as "The arrow was deflected by the shield".

deform *(de-form')*. To spoil the shape of; to make ugly.

deformity *(de-form'-i-ty)*. An unnatural shape.

defraud *(de-fraud')*. To take or get something from another person by cheating him.

defray *(de-fray')*. To pay the cost of something, as "The society sent the poor woman to the country and defrayed all her expenses".

defy *(de-fy')*. 1. To challenge; to dare. 2. To resist openly; to show that you care nothing for something, as "His father told him to stay indoors but he defied him by walking out immediately". Someone who defies others is **defiant** *(de-fi'-ant)*.

degenerate *(de-gen'-er-ate)*. Having become worse; sunk to a lower level of behaviour.

degrade *(de-grade')*. 1. To reduce a person from one position to a lower position; thus if a captain in the Army were reduced to a private, he would be degraded. 2. Anyone who lowers himself by his actions degrades himself.

degree *(de-gree')*. 1. A step or point in a series, as "We advanced by slow degrees". 2. A unit of measurement of heat, as in "36 degrees F.". 3. Rank; "He was a man of high degree" means he was a man of high rank or noble birth. 4. A university degree is a rank or position to which scholars are admitted in recognition of their achievements. 5. Any circle may be divided into 360 degrees; that is, its circumference (see **circumference)** may be divided into 360 equal lengths. 6. The unit of measurement in longitude and latitude.

deign. A person who deigns to do a thing does it in a haughty way. By his actions he shows that he thinks himself an important person and that he feels he is lowering himself to do what he is doing.

dejected *(de-ject'-ed)*. Downcast; sad; in the mood to think that everything has gone wrong.

delay *(de-lay')*. 1. To put off, as "We will delay the dinner until she arrives". 2. To make late, as "The train was delayed five minutes".

delegate *(del'-e-gate)*. 1. A representative; a person elected or appointed to attend a meeting. 2. To assign power to another. The head of a school may delegate power to one of the teachers to be in charge of morning prayers.

delete *(de-lete')*. To cross out; to rub out; to blot out.

deliberately *(de-lib'-er-ate-ly)*. Purposely; intentionally.

delicate *(del'-i-cate)*. 1. A person who often falls ill is delicate. 2. Anything very fragile and easily broken is delicate. 3. Very soft colours are said to be delicate. 4. To ask a lady her age is to ask a delicate question.

delicious *(de-li'-cious)*. Pleasing in taste.

delight *(de-light')*. Great joy.

delinquent *(de-lin'-quent)*. A person who fails to do what he should.

deliver *(de-liv'-er)*. 1. To give up; to set free. 2. To carry and give out as "The postman delivers letters". 3. To speak, as "The jury delivered the verdict".

delivery *(de-liv'-er-y)*. The handing over of something to another.

dell. A little sheltered valley.

delta *(del'-ta)*. The triangular piece of land sometimes formed at a river mouth by the depositing of sand and mud. The Nile delta offers a good example.

delude *(de-lude')*. To deceive; to mislead.

deluge *(del'-uge)*. 1. A name given to the Flood mentioned in in the Bible. 2. The word is now used to describe any great flood, not only of water, but of other things as well, as "The post office had a deluge of parcels at Christmas", meaning that it received a great many parcels.

delve. To turn over with a spade. To dig. This word is often used figuratively, as "I do not want to delve too deeply into your affairs".

demand *(de-mand')*. 1. To ask for a thing and show you mean to have it. 2. A determined request.

demeanour *(de-mean'-our)*. Behaviour. The way a person acts is his demeanour.

demise *(de-mise')*. Death.

democracy *(de-moc'-ra-cy)*. 1. Government by the people. 2. A country governed by the people. Such a country has a **democratic** *(dem-o-crat'-ic)* government. England is a democracy.

demolish *(de-mol'-ish)*. To destroy.

demonstrate *(dem'-on-strate)*. To show and explain; thus "We demonstrated a method of finding the average price of biscuits by taking as examples three different kinds of biscuit at three different prices".

demur *(de-mur')*. 1. To hesitate; to stop and think and not be too sure. 2. To object or take exception to.

demure *(de-mure')*. Prim; grave; proper and without a trace of boldness.

den. 1. A cave. 2. A hovel. 3. A study.

denial *(de-ni'-al)*. 1. A contradiction; thus if you say I did a thing and I say I did not, my remark is a denial of what you say. 2. A refusal.

denizen *(den'-i-zen)*. One who dwells in a certain place. Now used also of animals, etc., as "He waited quietly for the denizens of the wood to appear".

denominator *(de-nom'-i-na-tor)*. The number below the line in a fraction. Thus, in $\frac{3}{4}$ 4 is the denominator.

denounce *(de-nounce')*. To accuse; to tell the bad things you know about someone, as "He denounced the boy because he was cheating".

dense. 1. Thick; close-packed. Thus we speak of a dense cloud and a dense jungle. 2. Stupid.

dent. A slight dip inwards on the surface of something, caused by a blow of some kind. If you struck a tin of sardines with a hammer, you would make a dent in the tin.

dental *(den'-tal)*. To do with teeth: thus a dental hospital is one where teeth are attended to, and a dental mechanic is a man who makes false teeth.

dentist *(den'-tist)*. A man who is trained to repair, clean or extract teeth, and to make false teeth.

denude *(de-nude')*. To strip; to make naked; to lay bare.

deny *(de-ny')*. 1. To contradict something. If a person said to you, "You broke the jug", you might deny this by saying "I did not break the jug". Deny means you contradict what the person says. 2. Deny also means refuse, as "When she was ill there was nothing her mother denied her".

depart *(de-part')*. To leave.

department *(de-part'-ment)*. 1. A separate part; the housing department is a part of city government. 2. A department store is a store which sells many different kinds of things which are arranged in separate places.

departure *(de-par'-ture)*. The act of going away. At some railway stations there are notice boards showing the arrival and departure times of the trains. The arrival times are those at which trains will arrive at the station, and the departure times are those at which they will leave from the station.

E

depend *(de-pend')*. 1. To rely on, as "You can depend on me to do it". 2. To be conditional upon (see **condition,** No. 1); as, "Whether I can buy the cricket bat or not depends on whether my father gives me the money".

dependant *(de-pend'-ant)*. Someone who relies on someone else.

dependent *(de-pend'-ent)*. Relying on or depending on something. A child is dependent on his parents for food, shelter and clothing.

deplete *(de-plete')*. To empty; to exhaust.

deplore *(de-plore')*. To regret or show sorrow for, as "He deplored the loss of his dog".

deposit *(de-pos'-it)*. 1. To put down; to put, as "He deposited his money in the bank". 2. A deposit is something that has been put down, as "There is a deposit of gravel in the driveway". 3. An amount of money paid towards the cost of a thing, but not the whole price. If you wanted to buy a bicycle that cost £15 but had only £5, you might pay the £5 as a deposit on the bicycle.

depot *(de'-pot)*. 1. A place where things are stored. 2. A bus station is known as a depot.

depraved *(de-praved')*. Said of a person who has lost his self-respect and has become bad or wicked.

depreciate *(de-pre'-ci-ate)*. 1. A thing depreciates when it loses some of its value. If a motor-car is not looked after, it depreciates. 2. To speak of in a slighting way.

depress *(de-press')*. 1. To press down. 2. To cast gloom over. The weather is **depressing** when it is wet and cold.

deprive *(de-prive')*. To take away from.

depth. The distance downward from the surface of something. Deepness is depth.

deputy *(dep'-u-ty)*. Someone who is appointed to do the duties of another. When a headmaster is away another master, who is his deputy, will carry out his duties.

derange *(de-range')*. To upset; to put everything in a muddle.

derelict *(der'-e-lict)*. 1. Given up by its owner; abandoned. 2. Something that has been given up, particularly a ship left to drift about until it is wrecked. 3. A useless vagabond.

deride *(de-ride')*. To laugh at; to make fun of.

derive *(de-rive')*. To get from; to obtain from. Thus if you get enjoyment from listening to music, you derive enjoyment from it.

derrick *(der'-rick)*. A powerful machine with a long arm used for lifting heavy girders, etc.

descendant *(de-scend'-ant)*. You are a descendant of your parents; thus a descendant is one who belongs to a family. Queen Elizabeth II is a descendant of Queen Victoria because she belongs to the same family.

descent *(de-scent')*. 1. A going down. 2. A downward slope. 3. In such sentences as "He is of royal descent", descent means family or birth.

describe *(de-scribe')*. 1. To give an account of. 2. To trace out or draw, as "He described a circle".

description *(de-scrip'-tion)*. The act of describing something. In "He gave a description of his journey to Europe", description means an account.

desecrate *(des'-e-crate)*. To treat in a shameful way something which is sacred.

desert. 1. *(des'-ert)*. A region where there is not enough water to support plant life; a wilderness. 2. *(de-sert')*. To leave; to forsake; to go away from, as "The cowardly soldier deserted the army and fled". 3. **deserts** *(de-serts')* means what a person deserves. Thus, "The cruel man who set traps for dogs in his garden was given his deserts when he stepped into one of his own traps". Do not confuse the word **desert** with **dessert.**

deserve *(de-serve')*. To be worthy of; to be suitable for; to merit.

design *(de-sign')*. 1. To draw; to plan; to intend. 2. A drawing or plan; a scheme; a plot; an intention.

desire *(de-sire')*. A wish. A person who wishes for something desires it or is **desirous** of it.

desist *(de-sist')*. To stop doing something.

desk A piece of furniture with a flat top and drawers or an opening for books and papers. You sit at a desk at school.

desolate *(des'-o-late)*. 1. Lonely; gloomy. A place is desolate when there is no one about, or when it looks neglected. 2. Unhappy and not able to be comforted. A person is desolate when thoroughly miserable.

despair *(de-spair')*. To lose all hope.

desperado *(des-per-a'-do)*. A desperate person; one who does not care about danger; a wild ruffian.

desperate *(des'-per-ate)*. 1. Reckless because hope has gone, as "The desperate man jumped into the roaring stream to get away from those who where chasing him". 2. A desperate illness is one in which the invalid has little hope of getting better.

despicable *(des'-pi-ca-ble)*. Mean and vile.

despise *(de-spise')*. To look down on; to scorn.

despite *(de-spite')*. In spite of.

despondent *(de-spond'-ent)*. Having lost heart and hope. A despondent person suffers from **despondency.**

despot *(des'-pot)*. A tyrant; a ruler who makes everybody do as he wishes.

dessert *(des-sert')*. The last course of a meal, at which something sweet is usually served, such as fruit.

destination *(des-ti-na'-tion)*. The end of a journey. The place to which you are going.

destiny *(des'-ti-ny)*. What is bound to happen; fate.

destitute *(des'-ti-tute)*. Not having the money to buy what is necessary; thus a starving man is destitute.

destroy *(de-stroy')*. To smash; to ruin or spoil a thing.

destruction *(de-struc'-tion)*. Ruin; the act of destroying.

detach *(de-tach')*. To separate; unfasten; undo. If you pull the buttons off your coat, you detach them, because they are then separated from the coat. A detached house is one that stands alone and is separated from other houses.

detail *(de'-tail)*. A small part.

detain *(de-tain')*. To keep back or hold back against the will of somebody. Thus, if a person stops you in the street and talks for a long time, and all the time you want to be going, the person detains you.

detect *(de-tect')*. To discover; to find out. A **detective** is a policeman who "finds out" about a crime.

detention *(de-ten'-tion)*. 1. A holding back. 2. Keeping in school as punishment.

deter *(de-ter')*. To prevent.

deteriorate *(de-te'-ri-o-rate)*. To decrease in value or quality; to become worse.

determine *(de-ter'-mine)*. To make up one's mind, as "She determined to have a better report card next time". When you have made up your mind, you are **determined.**

detest *(de-test')*. To hate or dislike very much.

detour *(de'-tour)*. A way around an obstacle. When travelling by car it is often necessary to take a detour or to go around when the main road is blocked.

detrimental *(det-ri-men'-tal)*. Causing harm or damage, as "It is detrimental to a car to drive it at excessive speed".

devastate *(dev'-as-tate)*. To lay waste; to spoil a place so as to make it of no use.

develop *(de-vel'-op)*. 1. In "The photographer developed his films", developed means brought out the pictures. 2. In "The man developed a bad cold", developed means that he caught a cold. 3. In "The rosebuds developed into beautiful blooms", developed means grew.

development *(de-vel'-op-ment)*. 1. Growth, as "At what stage in its development does a butterfly grow wings?" 2. Something that happens as a result of something that happened before; a turn of events. Thus, "He listened to news of the latest developments in South Africa".

device *(de-vice')*. 1. Something designed to do a certain piece of work, as "A lawn-mower is a device for cutting grass". 2. A badge, emblem or picture with a motto.

devil *(dev'-il)*. 1. An evil spirit or a demon. Satan is the devil in the Bible. 2. A fearless and reckless person is called a devil.

devise *(de-vise')*. To plan something in your mind; to invent. Thus, if you think out a new way of, say, peeling potatoes, you devise a new way.

devoid *(de-void')*. Empty; not in possession. If someone is devoid of shame he is without shame.

devote *(de-vote')*. To give up; to give over, as "He devoted a day's pay every week to helping the poor". "He devoted himself to science" means he gave all his time and attention to scientific work. "The girl was devoted to her dog" means the girl was very fond of her dog.

devotion *(de-vo'-tion)*. 1. Great affection; state of being **devoted**. 2. Devotions are prayers or religious worship.

devour *(de-vour')*. If referring to animals the word means to eat; but if referring to people the meaning is to eat in a greedy way or to take in greedily, as "He devoured two thrilling story-books yesterday", i.e., he read them hurriedly and greedily.

devout *(de-vout')*. Devoted to religion; pious; deeply religious.

dew. The moisture deposited on the ground and on plants during the night.

diagonal *(di-ag'-o-nal)*. A line running from one corner to an opposite corner in such figures as a square or a rectangle.

diagram *(di'-a-gram)*. A drawing made specially to explain something. Many books contain diagrams to make it easier for the reader to understand the printed words.

dial *(di'-al)*. Most dials consist of flat, circular faces which are regularly marked in some way. A clock-face is the most common example of a dial, but there are dozens of other examples. Most gas-meters are provided with dials, and automatic telephones have dials with letters and figures on them.

dialect *(di'-a-lect)*. A regional form of speech. Some people in London speak the Cockney dialect.

dialogue *(di'-a-logue)*. A conversation between people who speak one after the other. Really, the talk should be between two persons, but the word has grown to mean two or more persons.

diameter *(di-am'-e-ter)*. Any straight line drawn through the centre of a circle which begins and ends on the circumference.

diamond *(di'-a-mond)*. 1. A very hard and very precious mineral. It can be cut and polished so that it sparkles a great deal. 2. A flat figure bounded by four equal straight lines which come together in points at the bottom, the top and the sides.

diary *(di'-a-ry)*. 1. A book giving spaces in which the owner may write notes for every day of the year. 2. A daily account of things that have happened similar to that which Pepys wrote.

dice. 1. Small cubes with dots marked on each surface used for playing a game of chance. 2. When your mother dices vegetables, she cuts them into cubes.

dictation *(dic-ta'-tion)*. When a teacher speaks words aloud which students are to write, he gives dictation.

dictionary *(dic'-tion-ar-y)*. A book which describes the words of a language, as this book does.

die. 1. To finish with life, as when death comes to a person. 2. To stop gradually, as "The noise died away". 3. A metal stamp, such as the dies used by the Mint to stamp pennies. 4. A small cube with the numbers 1 to 6 on its faces.

died. The past tense of die, as in "He died yesterday".

diet *(di'-et)*. The food a person eats.

differ *(dif'-fer)*. To be unlike; thus red differs from black; the two colours are **different.**

difference *(dif'-fer-ence)*. The way or amount in which one thing is different from another. The difference between five and seven is two.

difficult *(dif'-fi-cult)*. 1. Hard to understand, or do. Thus, it is difficult to understand a person who seems to enjoy being cruel to animals. 2. Hard to please.

diffident *(dif'-fi-dent)*. Shy; retiring; unable to make up one's mind; not eager.

dig. To make a hole in the ground is to dig in the ground.

digest. 1. *(di-gest')*. To dissolve food in the stomach. 2. To think over something. 3. *(di'-gest)*. A summary of a book or of a newspaper article.

digestion *(di-ges'-tion)*. The dissolving of food in the stomach.

digit *(dig'-it)*. 1. Any finger or toe. 2. Any of the figures from 1 to 9.

dignitary *(dig'-ni-tar-y)*. One holding high rank, especially in the Church.

dignity *(dig'-ni-ty)*. Nobleness of mind; what there is about a person which makes others respect him.

digress *(di-gress')*. Not to keep to the point while talking or writing. To wander away from the subject.

dike. A mound of earth built along a river, lake or ocean to prevent flooding. Also spelled **dyke.**

dilapidated *(di-lap'-i-dat-ed)*. Going to ruin; falling to pieces.

dilate *(di-late')*. 1. To talk about something very fully. 2. To become wider or larger.

dilatory *(dil'-a-to-ry)*. Slow in doing things.

dilemma *(di-lem'-ma)*. When a person has to choose between two things and he finds it difficult to decide which to choose, he is in a dilemma.

diligent *(dil'-i-gent)*. Industrious; hard-working. A diligent person shows **diligence.**

dilute *(di-lute')*. A liquid is diluted when some other liquid is added to it to make it thinner or less strong. You might dilute orange juice with water, or paint with turpentine.

dim. Not bright, not clear. Difficult to see because the shapes are blurred.

dimension *(di-men'-sion)*. 1. An extent which can be measured, such as length, breadth, width, height, depth, etc. A line has one dimension, length. A piece of paper has two

dimensions, length and width. A figure with only two dimensions is called a plane figure. A box has three dimensions,
length, width and height. 2. "Dimensions" often means size
or measurements, as "He was a man of huge dimensions".

diminish *(di-min'-ish)*. To make less.

diminutive *(di-min'-u-tive)*. Tiny; very small.

dimple *(dim'-ple)*. A slight hollow or depression on the surface
usually in the cheek or chin of a person.

din. A loud noise.

dine. To eat.

dingy *(din'-gy)*. Soiled; dirty; not fresh and bright.

dining *(din'-ing)*. The act of eating dinner.

dinner *(din'-ner)*. The main meal, often consisting of meat and
vegetables, which is eaten at the end of the day or at noon.

dinosaur *(di'-no-saur)*. A kind of huge reptile which lived
many thousands of years ago and is now extinct.

diocese *(di'-o-cese)*. The churches and the people attending them
in an area under a bishop.

dip. 1. To place a thing in water and then to take it out almost
at once. 2. To dip a flag is to lower it for some seconds and
then raise it. 3. A dip in the hills, a dip in the road, etc., is
a downward slope followed by an upward rise.

diphtheria *(diph-the'-ri-a)*. A very dangerous and infectious
disease of the throat.

diphthong *(diph'-thong)*. Two vowels coming together and
pronounced together, such as the **oi** in **oil.**

diploma *(di-plo'-ma)*. A certificate stating that someone has
completed a certain course of studies or has graduated from
a school.

diplomacy *(di-plo'-ma-cy)*. 1. Tact; skill in obtaining advan-
tages for yourself without making enemies. "Using great
diplomacy, Tom was able to persuade the other boys to
appoint him captain of their football team." 2. The art or
skill of conducting dealings between countries, such as arrang-
ing treaties, etc.

diplomat *(dip'-lo-mat)*. An important person who arranges the
business affairs of his country with other countries.

dipper *(dip'-per)*. 1. A drinking utensil with a long handle.
2. A bird which dips or dives in water.

direct *(di-rect')*. 1. When a man orders a person to do certain
things, he directs him to do them. 2. If a man directs a

motorist to a town, he tells him the way. 3. If you go in a direct line from here to X, you go in a straight line. 4. If you direct an envelope, you address it. 5. If a man directs a factory or store, he manages it.

direction *(di-rec'-tion)*. 1. The way along which a person or thing is moving. 2. The directions on a packet are the instructions. 3. Direction means management in such sentences as "The business is under the direction of Mr. Brown".

directory *(di-rec'-to-ry)*. 1. A book of names and addresses and, in some cases, telephone numbers. 2. A book of instructions.

dirge. A song or tune played or sung at a funeral.

dirigible *(dir'-i-gi-ble)*. A large balloon which can be steered.

dirt. Unclean matter such as mud or soot. Anything covered with dirt is **dirty.**

disabled *(dis-a'-bled)*. No longer able to do things.

disagree *(dis-a-gree')*. When two or more people disagree, they have different ideas or opinions about certain things.

disagreeable *(dis-a-gree'-a-ble)*. A disagreeable person is one who is bad-tempered. A thing is disagreeable when it is unpleasant.

disappear *(dis-ap-pear')*. Go out of sight.

disappoint *(dis-ap-point')*. To fail to fulfil the hopes or expectations of someone is to disappoint him. When you hope that something will happen and it does not happen, you feel
• **disappointed.** Something that disappoints is a **disappointment.**

disapprove *(dis-ap-prove')*. To find fault with someone or something.

disarrange *(dis-ar-range')*. To make untidy; to throw into disorder.

disaster *(dis-as'-ter)*. A very terrible event.

discard *(dis-card'-)*. To throw aside.

discharge *(dis-charge')*. 1. To unload a ship or a train. 2. To fire (a gun). 3. To set a prisoner free. 4. To perform or fulfil, as "He discharged his duties". 5. To dismiss from employment.

disciple *(dis-ci'-ple)*. A follower of a noted person; a scholar.

discipline *(dis'-ci-pline)*. 1. Training of a person's character; thus in "Discipline is good for us because it causes us to understand the value of law and order", discipline stands for training. 2. Control of others by demanding strict obedience.

disclaim *(dis-claim')*. To refuse to agree that a certain thing is your own. To refuse responsibility for something.

disclose *(dis-close')*. To make known something that was secret.

discomfort *(dis-com'-fort)*. Uneasiness; annoyance.

disconnect *(dis-con-nect')*. To undo; unfasten; separate.

disconsolate *(dis-con'-so-late)*. Unhappy; without hope or comfort.

discontent *(dis-con-tent')*. Unhappiness; state of not being satisfied.

discord *(dis'-cord)*. 1. Disagreement; quarrel. 2. Harsh noise.

discount. 1. *(dis'-count)*. A reduction in price. 2. *(dis-count')*. To deduct some money. 3. To leave out of account; to disregard.

discourage *(dis-cour'-age)*. To make a person lose courage; to make him lose hope; to persuade a person to stop doing something.

discover *(dis-cov'-er)*. To find for the first time.

discredit *(dis-cred'-it)*. 1. Anything which lowers a person in the eyes of others. 2. To disbelieve.

discreet *(dis-creet')*. Prudent; careful to say and do things that will not hurt others. A discreet person is one who has **discretion** *(dis-cre'-tion)*.

discriminate *(dis-crim'-i-nate)*. To distinguish; to note the difference between; to judge; to discriminate against is to be prejudiced against.

discuss *(dis-cuss')*. To talk about.

disdain *(dis-dain')*. Scorn. A **disdainful** person is one who looks down on others.

disease *(dis-ease')*. An illness.

disembark *(dis-em-bark')*. To leave a ship and go on land.

disfigure *(dis-fig'-ure)*. To spoil the appearance of.

disgrace *(dis-grace')*. Shame; a loss of honour.

disguise *(dis-guise')*. 1. To alter the appearance of a person or thing, so that he or it will not look like himself or itself. 2. A disguise is clothing, a wig, a false nose, etc., used to disguise someone's appearance. To be in disguise means to be wearing a disguise.

disgust *(dis-gust')*. 1. Strong dislike for something that is sickening or offensive. 2. To cause the feeling of disgust. A thing which causes disgust is **disgusting.**

dishearten *(dis-heart'-en)*. To discourage; to make a person wonder what is the good of trying.

dishonest *(dis-hon'-est)*. Not honest. If a person steals or lies he is dishonest.

disinfect *(dis-in-fect')*. To destroy harmful germs.

disinterested *(dis-in'-ter-est-ed)*. Impartial. Usually, a person is said to be disinterested when he is not expected to make some profit out of a thing for himself.

disk. A round, flat, thin object. A gramophone record is a disk. This word is also spelled **disc.**

dislike *(dis-like')*. If you don't like something, you dislike it.

dislocate *(dis'-lo-cate)*. To put out of joint.

dislodge *(dis-lodge')*. To drive or force out.

disloyal *(dis-loy'-al)*. Not loyal; unfaithful.

dismal *(dis'-mal)*. Gloomy; unhappy.

dismantle *(dis-man'-tle)*. To take to pieces. To dismantle a room is to take out all its furniture, carpets, pictures, etc. To dismantle a fort is to unmount its guns and send away its soldiers and equipment.

dismay *(dis-may')*. Dread; fear; dejection.

dismiss *(dis-miss')*. 1. To send away, as when pupils are dismissed at the end of a day. 2. To discharge from work, as when workmen are dismissed from their jobs.

disobedient *(dis-o-be'-di-ent)*. When you refuse to do as you are told, you are disobedient, and you **disobey** the person who gave the orders.

disown *(dis-own')*. To refuse to accept as belonging to you. To cast off. A person disowns one of his relations when he decides to have no more to do with him.

disparage *(dis-par'-age)*. To speak ill of a person or thing; to belittle. If you disparaged someone you would say that that he is not as good as he really is.

disparity *(dis-par'-i-ty)*. Inequality. When two people or things are so different that they cannot be compared, there is a disparity between them.

dispatch *(dis-patch')*. 1. In "He dispatched the letter", dispatched means sent. 2. In "Take this letter to the post office with all dispatch", dispatch means speed. 3. In "He dispatched the wounded rabbit", dispatched means killed. 4. In "He received a new dispatch", dispatch means message. Also written **despatch.**

dispel *(dis-pel')*. To disperse or scatter. Mostly used in the case of abstract nouns; thus we speak of dispelling evil thoughts, doubts, misery, etc., when we mean driving them away.

dispensary *(dis-pen'-sa-ry)*. A place where medicines are prepared.

dispense *(dis-pense')*. 1. To distribute; to give out. 2. To dispense with also means to do without or go without.

disperse *(dis-perse')*. To scatter; to drive off in various directions.

dispirited *(dis-pir'-it-ed)*. Disheartened; having lost courage.

displace *(dis-place')*. To cause to lose its place; to crowd out and take the place of. When you get into the bathtub you displace some of the water.

display *(dis-play')*. 1. To make a show of a thing. 2. A performance or exhibition, such as a school display or a scouts' display.

displease *(dis-please')*. To annoy; to make angry.

dispose *(dis-pose')*. To get rid of; to part with; to sell.

disposition *(dis-po-si'-tion)*. The word is most often used to refer to a person's nature, as "He had a kindly disposition".

disrespect *(dis-re-spect')*. Lack of respect; rudeness. To speak with disrespect is to speak **disrespectfully.**

dissect *(dis-sect')*. To cut into pieces.

dissipate *(dis'-si-pate)*. To throw away; to waste. A man who dissipates his money wastes it.

dissolute *(dis'-so-lute)*. Living a bad life.

dissolve *(dis-solve')*. 1. To melt, as sugar melts in water. 2. To separate or break up.

dissuade *(dis-suade')*. To coax a person not to do what he was intending to do. The exact opposite to dissuade is persuade.

distance *(dis'-tance)*. The space between things.

distant *(dis'-tant)*. 1. A long way off or a long time ago. 2. When a person is distant, he is not friendly.

distasteful *(dis-taste'-ful)*. Unpleasant. Medicine which has an unpleasant taste is distasteful. Unpleasant work is also distasteful.

distinct *(dis-tinct')*. Separate; clear.

distinguish *(dis-tin'-guish)*. To tell the difference between.

distinguished *(dis-tin'-guished)*. Notable; famous; handsome and dignified in appearance.

distort *(dis-tort')*. To twist out of shape. You may distort facts and make them untrue; you may distort your face and make yourself ugly; you may draw a funny picture of a person in which you distort his face and body.

distract *(dis-tract')*. 1. To take the attention off, as "You talk so much that it distracts me while I am reading". 2. To have one's mind upset, as "He was distracted when he heard the sad news".

distress *(dis-tress')*. 1. Misery; worry. 2. To cause pain or worry.

distribute *(dis-trib'-ute)*. To give out to a number of people; to spread out.

district *(dis'-trict)*. A part of a city, county, or province.

disturb *(dis-turb')*. 1. To throw into disorder or confusion, as "He disturbed the bees and they came swarming out of their hive". 2. To agitate; to stir up, as "He threw a pebble into the water and disturbed the smooth surface". 3. To cause trouble, annoyance or worry to someone, as "We were disturbed when we heard that a forest fire had broken out a mile away". Something that disturbs causes a **disturbance.**

ditch. A trench or long narrow opening dug in the earth.

divan *(di-van')*. A couch or sofa.

dive. 1. To plunge head first into the water. An aircraft dives when it moves quickly, nose first, towards the earth. 2. A headlong pitch into something.

diverse *(di-verse')*. Very varied or mixed.

divert *(di-vert')*. 1. To turn something aside as when the road is being repaired and a policeman diverts the traffic by sending it down a side street. 2. To entertain and amuse, as "The comedian diverted his audience with funny jokes".

divide *(di-vide')*. 1. To break into parts. A fence divides one yard from another. 2. In arithmetic, divide means to divide into equal parts. If you break a chocolate bar into six pieces and divide it among three boys, each boy will receive two pieces.

dividend *(div'-i-dend)*. 1. The number which is divided. In the example above (see **divide**) the dividend is six. 2. Some people own part of a business and when that business makes a profit, it often pays a dividend, or sum of money, to its owners.

divine *(di-vine')*. 1. Godly; heavenly. 2. To guess or foretell.

division *(di-vi'-sion)*. 1. The act of breaking into parts. When you are finding the number of threes in six, you are doing division. 2. A part of something is a division; as a division in the army is part of the whole army.

divorce *(di-vorce')*. To separate. Mostly used when speaking of the legal separating of a husband and wife.

divulge *(di-vulge')*. To tell a secret or give away news that most people do not know.

dizzy *(diz'-zy)*. Having a feeling that everything is turning round; giddy.

docile *(doc'-ile)*. Obedient; easy to teach; not difficult to manage.

dock. 1. A place where ships are loaded and unloaded. 2. A coarse weed believed to cure the sting of a nettle. 3. The place set apart those who are being tried in a law court is a prisoner's dock. 4. To dock is to cut off a part, as when a horse's tail is docked, or when a man's wages are docked. 5. To dock is to bring a boat to shore.

dockyard *(dock'-yard)*. A place where ships are built, repaired, fitted out, etc.

doctor *(doc'-tor)*. A learned man, especially one learned in medicine; a physician.

document *(doc'-u-ment)*. Printed or written papers, usually of a legal kind describing something of importance, are documents.

dodge. 1. A quick movement, made to get out of the way of something. 2. Some kind of trick intended to cheat, as "The cunning fellow is always up to one dodge or another".

doe. The female of a deer, hare or rabbit.

dogged *(dog'-ged)*. A person is dogged who will not give in easily, but who goes on trying, even though the chances of success are few.

doleful *(dole'-ful)*. Sad; sorrowful; dismal.

dolphin *(dol'-phin)*. A sea animal that looks like a porpoise and is about 8 to 10 feet long. It is found in warm waters.

dome. 1. A roof built in the shape of a half sphere, or nearly so. An observatory has a large dome. 2. Anything shaped in the form of a half sphere is said to be domed.

domestic *(do-mes'-tic)*. 1. Having to do with the house or home. 2. Domestic animals are those which are raised by man. 3. A domestic is a household servant. 4. A domesticated person is one skilled in and fond of housework.

domicile *(dom'-i-cile)*. A place in which people live.

dominate *(dom'-i-nate)*. To rule over.

domineer *(dom-i-neer')*. To be tyrannical; to be overbearing; to rule over others and order them about aggressively.

dominion *(do-min'-ion)*. 1. The territory under one government. Canada is a dominion. 2. To have dominion over something is to have control over it.

dominoes *(dom'-i-noes)*. A game played with flat, rectangular pieces which have dots marked on one side.

don. To put on (clothes).

donation *(do-na'-tion)*. A gift; something given.

donkey *(don'-key)*. An animal which looks like a horse, but is smaller and has long ears.

doom. 1. Dreadful fate; death; destruction. 2. A person is said to be doomed when it is obvious that he is going to die or that something dreadful is going to happen to him.

doorway *(door'-way)*. An opening in a wall through which one may pass.

dormitory *(dor'-mi-to-ry)*. A place in which many people sleep. In some boarding schools, the pupils sleep in dormitories.

dose. The quantity of medicine to be taken at one time.

dot. A small point or spot. A full stop is sometimes called a dot, and the letter i, when not a capital letter, has a dot over it.

dote. To love somebody or something to excess.

double *(dou'-ble)*. 1. Twice as great, as "4 is double 2". 2. To make twice as great; to multiply by two, as "Double the amount of flour in this recipe". 3. Being in pairs, as double beds, double doors, etc. 4. Twofold; thus, "The boy was trying" has a double meaning or two different possible meanings; you cannot tell whether the boy was doing his best or being troublesome. 5. Double talk is speech that seems to make sense but is actually a mixture of sense and nonsense. 6. A person or thing exactly like another person or thing is said to be that person or thing's double. Your double would be someone who looked exactly like you.

doubt. 1. To be uncertain; to hesitate to believe; to be unsure whether something is true, etc.; to question. 2. Lack of certainty; unsettled state of opinion about whether something is real or true, etc. Thus, "There is a great doubt in my mind whether he is an honest man".

dough. A soft, thick mixture of wet, uncooked flour or meal.

dove. A kind of pigeon.

downright *(down'-right)*. Complete; not half and half, but absolutely, as "He is a downright bully", meaning that he is a perfect, complete or thorough bully.

downtrodden *(down'-trod-den)*. A downtrodden person is one who is made to suffer or one who is badly treated.

dowry *(dow-ry)*. 1. A marriage portion given with a wife. 2. A gift given to or for a bride.

dozen *(doz'-en)*. A group of twelve. A dozen eggs is a group of twelve eggs. A "baker's dozen" is a group of thirteen.

drab. 1. Light brown in colour. 2. Dull, dingy.

draft. (Sometimes spelled **draught**.) 1. A rough copy; first writing of. A writer makes a first draft of a book and then corrects it, before making a final draft. 2. To draft is to make a draft; thus, "He drafted the radio programme". 3. To draft money is to order someone to pay someone. The order itself is called a draft. 4. To draft soldiers is to select men to be soldiers.

drag. 1. To pull something without lifting it. 2. To move slowly.

dragon *(drag'-on)*. A huge, fierce mythical animal that spouts fire.

drain. 1. To allow liquid to flow or leak out of by degrees; thus, when you drain vegetables, you stand them somewhere to allow the water to run off them. 2. To flow or leak out by degrees, as "The water drained slowly out of the bathtub". 3. Rivers are said to drain the country through which they pass. 4. A drain is a pipe which carries water away.

drake. A male duck.

drama *(dra'-ma)*. A play.

drape. 1. To arrange in folds. 2. A curtain.

drastic *(dras'-tic)*. Violent; serious.

draught. 1. A current of air. 2. A quantity of liquid drunk all at once, as "He drained his glass in three draughts". 3. A rough drawing; a plan or outline. 4. To draw; a person who draws is a **draughtsman.**

draw. 1. To pull, as a horse draws a cart. 2. To take money from your account at the bank is to draw money. 3. To make a picture is to draw a picture. 4. To take out, as a cowboy draws a gun. 5. To draw near is to come near, or approach.

drawer *(draw'-er)*. A box-shaped container which fits into a chest or cupboard.

drawbridge *(draw'-bridge)*. A bridge that can be raised at one end to prevent people from crossing or to allow boats to go through. Such bridges were often placed before the gates of castles and fortresses.

dread. 1. To have great fear of what may happen. 2. Great fear.

dreadful *(dread'-ful)*. Something which causes dread.

dream. 1. To have visions while asleep. 2. A vision, thought, etc., that one has while asleep.

dreary *(drear'-y)*. Dull and dismal; not cheerful.

dredge. 1. A large net on an iron frame, which is dragged over the bottom of the sea in order to catch shell-fish. 2. A machine for scooping mud or wreckage, etc., from the bottom of a body of water. 3. To dredge is to drag a dredge, or to scoop out mud with a dredge. 4. To dredge, in cooking, means to sprinkle with flour or sugar, etc.

dregs. 1. The small particles in some liquids which settle at the bottom and cause a sediment. 2. The useless part of things.

drench. To wet or soak thoroughly.

dress. 1. An outer garment worn by women. 2. To dress is to put clothes on. 3. Clothing generally.

dresser *(dress'-er)*. A kitchen table or sideboard on which food is, or was, dressed.

dribble *(drib'-ble)*. To trickle; to let fall drop by drop.

drift. 1. To be carried along aimlessly; to float along with the tide. 2. A drift is a mass of something that has been piled up by the wind, such as a drift of snow.

drill. 1. A tool for boring holes, as a wood drill used to bore holes in wood. 2. To put holes in a thing is to drill holes in it. 3. Physical or gymnastic exercises. 4. To teach by making pupils do a thing over and over again. Most pupils have drill lessons in multiplication tables. 5. A machine used to plant seeds in rows.

drink. 1. To swallow a liquid is to drink. 2. A drink is a beverage.

drip. To fall in drops.

drive. 1. To drive a horse is to make it go where you want it to go. 2. To drive away your cares is to put them out of your mind. 3. To drive a bargain is to buy or sell something at a price to your own advantage. 4. To go for a drive is to go for a short trip in some vehicle. 5. A drive is a path in front of a house leading to the front door, wide enough for a car to drive along it. The way leading from the street to the garage beside or behind a house is also called a drive.

driver *(driv'-er)*. 1. A person who steers and causes a car or vehicle to move. 2. A person who forces others to work strenuously.

drizzle *(driz'-zle)*. Fine rain.

droll. Funny; comical.

drone. 1. The male honey-bee. 2. A person who idles his time away is a drone. 3. A deep humming sound.

droop. To hang over through weakness.

drought. A long period without rain.

drove. A herd of cattle or sheep being driven along. The man who does the driving is a **drover.**

drown. To die by being suffocated in water.

drowsy *(drow'-sy)*. Sleepy, but not enough to make you fall off to sleep.

drudgery *(drudg'-er-y)*. Work that is hard, never ending and not pleasant. A person who has a great deal of drudgery is a **drudge.**

drug. A liquid, powder or pill which when taken into the body may cause harm or may overcome pain and disease, depending on the dose.

druggist *(drug'-gist)*. One who deals in drugs.

dual *(du'-al)*. Twofold; double; made of two parts.

dubious *(du'-bi-ous)*. Doubtful.

duck. 1. A water bird with a fat body, short neck and webbed feet. Some ducks are tame and some are wild. 2. To push another person under water is to duck him. 3. A strong cloth used for sails, tents, etc.

duct. A tube or pipe for carrying liquid, air or wires.

due. 1. Money due is money owing. 2. Due to means caused by, in such sentences as "Our lateness was due to the storm".

3. The time when a train is due is the time when it is scheduled to arrive. 4. Dues are fees.

duel *(du'-el).* A fight between two people conducted according to rules decided beforehand. Duels are illegal in England.

duet *(du-et').* A piece of music played or sung by two people.

duke. A man whose rank is next below a prince.

dumb. Not having the power to speak.

dumbfounded *(dumb-found'-ed).* Made dumb, or not able to speak; surprised.

dummy *(dum'-my).* 1. A model of a person, such as can be seen in shop windows. 2. In card-playing, when there is one person short of the correct number, cards are some-times dealt to a dummy hand, i.e., to a person who really does not exist. 3. When things are imitated, the imitation is often called a dummy; thus in the windows of tobacconists, the packets set out are usually dummy packets, without cigarettes or tobacco in them.

dune. A mound or ridge of sand formed by the wind.

dungeon *(dun'-geon).* A place in which prisoners are kept in underground cells.

dupe. 1. A person who is easily misled; one who can be made to believe anything he is told. 2. To be duped is to be misled.

duplicate *(du'-pli-cate).* An exact copy of an original document, letter, etc.

durable *(du'-ra-ble).* Hard; hard-wearing; lasting.

duration *(du-ra'-tion).* The time taken by an event from start to finish. The duration of a war is the time it lasts.

dusk. The time between sundown and complete darkness.

dusky *(dusk'-y).* Darkish; dark-coloured.

duty *(du'-ty).* 1. The way a person ought to act towards his parents, superiors, country, etc. It is your duty to obey the law and to treat your parents with respect. 2. What a person's work requires him to do; thus, the duties of a stable boy include feeding the horses, cleaning out the stable, etc. 3. A tax on certain goods.

dwarf. An animal or plant very much smaller than ordinary.

dwell. To live in a certain place. One who lives in a certain place is a **dweller**. A house in which one lives is called a **dwelling**.

dwindle *(dwin'-dle)*. To become smaller and smaller, or fewer and fewer; thus if you make repeated trips to a chocolate box and take one out each time, the chocolates dwindle.

dye. 1. Colouring matter used to colour cloth, paper, plastic and many other things. 2. To colour something with dye.

dynamite *(dy'-na-mite)*. A powerful explosive used to blast trees, earth, rocks, etc.

E

eager *(ea'-ger)*. Keen; very anxious to have or do something.

eagle *(ea'-gle)*. A large bird of prey with a hooked bill, sharp claws or talons, and powerful wings.

ear. The organ of the body which permits hearing. It is located in the head. The ear that you see on a person's head is the outer ear.

early *(ear'-ly)*. 1. Before the usual time. If you arrive at the station at three-thirty to board the four o'clock train, you are early. 2. Early is used to refer to something which happened many years ago as in "early English history".

earn. 1. To receive money or honour by working for it, as when a man works to earn his wages. 2. To deserve, as when pupils at school earn their holiday because they have worked hard during the term.

earnest *(ear'-nest)*. Sincere; serious. A person who speaks in earnest speaks seriously, not jokingly. A person who settles down to work in earnest settles down to work hard.

earshot *(ear'-shot)*. A sound made within earshot is near enough to be heard.

earth. 1. The world we live on is the planet Earth. 2. The ground or soil. Seeds are planted in the earth.

earthenware *(earth'-en-ware)*. Cups, saucers, plates, flower pots and other utensils made of a coarse clay that has been baked.

earthquake *(earth'-quake)*. A shaking or trembling of the ground, due to violent movements within the earth.

earthworm *(earth'-worm)*. A reddish-brown worm which burrows in the earth and is often used as bait for fishing.

ease. 1. In "The patient is now more at ease", at ease means free from pain. 2. In "He can do it with ease", with ease means without trying hard. 3. In "He was able to ease the screw", ease means move it a little. 4. In "Can you ease this shoe?" ease means stretch it to make it fit better.

easel *(ea'-sel)*. A frame for holding a picture, blackboard, etc., while someone is working on it.

east. A direction on the compass opposite to west. The sun appears to rise in the east and set in the west.

Easter *(East'-er)*. A religious holiday on which we celebrate Christ's rising from the dead.

eastern *(east'-ern)*. Used when speaking of the east. "The eastern sky was cloudy."

easy *(eas'-y)*. 1. In "He found the question easy", easy means not hard. 2. In "We like his easy manners", easy means friendly, unaffected or natural. 3. "He bought the encyclopædia on easy terms" means that he paid for it a little at a time, not all at once. 4. In "He is an easy-going father", easy-going means not strict.

eat. You eat food, that is, you chew and swallow it.

eatable *(eat'-a-ble)*. Fit to eat. **eatables** means food.

eaves. The lowest edge of the sloping part of a roof.

ebb. The tide on the sea-shore goes out and comes in twice in every 24 hours. Ebb refers to its going out and flow to its coming in. Ebb is used for the going out of many other things; thus we say a person's life is ebbing when he is dying, when his life is going out.

ebony *(eb'-on-y)*. A black, hard wood which is used for the black keys of a piano, fancy woodwork, etc.

eccentric *(ec-cen'-tric)*. 1. Not in the centre of a circle; for example, a wheel with its hub not in the centre is eccentric. When such a wheel turns it does so in an odd way. It is said to have an eccentric motion. 2. Odd; peculiar. An eccentric old gentleman is one who has odd, peculiar ways.

ecclesiastical *(ec-cle-si-as'-ti-cal)*. To do with the church or the clergy.

echo *(ech'-o)*. The repeating of a sound due to the reflection of sound waves by some distant object.

eclipse *(e-clipse')*. 1. The darkening of the sun (**solar eclipse**) caused by the moon's passing between it and the earth; or the darkening of the moon (**lunar eclipse**) caused by the earth's passing between it and the sun. 2. To darken or hide; to outshine or surpass.

economy *(e-con'-o-my)*. 1. The management of money. When speaking of the economy of the country, we mean the management of its finances. 2. The prevention of all waste and getting the most for one's money. The thrifty housewife who never wastes anything practises economy.

ecstasy *(ec'-sta-sy)*. A state of great joy.

eddy *(ed'-dy)*. Water or air moving round in a circle; something like a whirlpool or a whirlwind, but on a much smaller scale.

edge. 1. The lines that give a thing its shape. 2. The cutting side of a knife, a razor blade, etc. 3. To edge away is to move off sideways.

edible *(ed'-i-ble)*. Fit to be eaten.

edict *(e'-dict)*. An order made by a body of people in authority, such as the church.

edifice *(ed'-i-fice)*. A large building.

edition *(e-di'-tion)*. All the copies of a book or newspaper that are printed at the same time.

editor *(ed'-i-tor)*. 1. One who runs a newspaper or magazine and decides what kind of articles will be printed. 2. One who arranges and corrects books and articles before they are printed.

educate *(ed'-u-cate)*. To train or develop in skill, ability or knowledge.

education *(ed-u-ca'-tion)*. 1. Training. 2. The knowledge which a person gains through learning.

eel. A long, snake-shaped fish.

effect *(ef-fect')*. 1. In "The doctor hoped the medicine would effect a great improvement in the patient's health", effect means bring about. 2. In "The effect of the punishment was soon noticed", effect means result. 3. In wills and other legal papers, people write of their effects, meaning belongings. 4. In "The new time-table does not take effect until Monday", take effect means come into use.

effective *(ef-fec'-tive)*. A thing or action which brings about the desired effect is said to be effective.

effeminate *(ef-fem'-i-nate)*. Though this word means womanish or feminine, it is seldom applied to women and girls. It is usually said of men and boys who have not the proper masculine ways. It is, therefore, used in a slighting way and anyone effeminate is looked down on.

effervesce *(ef-fer-vesce')*. To bubble. Soda water effervesces.

efficiency *(ef-fi'-cien-cy)*. The power to do things in a capable manner.

effort *(ef'-fort)*. An earnest attempt; to try hard is to make an effort.

effrontery *(ef-fron'-ter-y)*. Impudence; the conduct of a person who cannot be shamed.

effrontery *(ef-fron'-ter-y)*. Impudence; the action of a person who cannot be shamed.

effusive *(ef-fu'-sive)*. Gushing; too anxious to appear interested in others.

egg. An oval-shaped object covered by a thin brittle shell which is laid by female chickens and birds. The egg contains the young bird, or offspring. Female reptiles and fishes also lay eggs, as do frogs and insects. Even animals which are born, not hatched out, begin as very small eggs in their mothers' bodies. This type of egg is called an **ovum.**

egotism *(e'-go-tism)*. Thinking too much about yourself. People who are often saying "I did this and I did that" are **egotists.**

egress *(e'-gress)*. A way out; an exit.

eight. The number between seven and nine.

either *(ei'-ther)*. In "You may choose either apple", either means one or the other of the two apples.

ejaculate *(e-jac'-u-late)*. To say something suddenly and in a jerky manner.

eject *(e-ject')*. To throw out; turn out; cast out, as "The man was ejected from the house", meaning that he was turned out.

elaborate *(e-lab'-o-rate)*. 1. A thing is elaborate when it has many details or small parts; thus, an elaborate dress is one with much trimming—the exact opposite to a plain dress. 2. To elaborate a thing is to work out each detail of it fully and carefully.

elapse *(e-lapse')*. To pass; run away; run out. "How much time elapsed?" means "How much time passed?"

elastic *(e-las'-tic)*. Springy; stretchy; able to stretch out of shape and then spring back into shape. Anything which is elastic has the quality of **elasticity** *(e-las-tic'-i-ty)*.

elated *(e-lat'-ed)*. Very happy; in a jolly mood.

elbow *(el'-bow)*. 1. The joint between the shoulder and the wrist. 2. Anything that has the shape of a bent elbow is called an elbow.

elder *(eld'-er)*. 1. Older. 2. A tree with small, black, juicy berries.

elect *(e-lect')*. To choose, usually by voting. An **election** is the time when people vote. An **elector** is a person having the right to vote, and an **electorate** is the body of people who are allowed to vote.

electricity *(e-lec-tric'-i-ty)*. A form of energy which produces light, heat and magnetism. We use electricity in homes to give light at night, to give heat to stoves. We call the lights electric lights because they give a light which comes from a form of energy known as electricity.

elegant *(el'-e-gant)*. Refined; polished; having good taste.

elegy *(el'-e-gy)*. A sad poem, often in memory of someone who has died.

element *(el'-e-ment)*. A substance that cannot be split into other substances. Water can be split into hydrogen and oxygen and is, therefore, not an element; but hydrogen cannot be split into other things and is an element. As an element is a simple substance, the word is, also, used to mean the beginning of things or things in their simplest form; thus we speak of the elements of grammar, meaning the beginnings of grammar.

elementary *(el-e-men'-ta-ry)*. Having to do with the elements. Thus, a book on elementary algebra will deal with the first steps or elements.

elephant *(el'-e-phant)*. A large, powerful beast with a long trunk. Elephants are the largest living animal on land and they are found in Asia and Africa.

elephantine *(el-e-phan'-tine)*. Large, like an elephant.

elevate *(el'-e-vate)*. To lift up.

elevator *(el'-e-va-tor)*. A machine used for lifting things or people.

eleven *(e-lev'-en)*. The number between ten and twelve.

elf. A tiny fairy.

elfish *(elf'-ish)*. Like a fairy. Usually, a child is said to be elfish when he is mischievous in a good-natured way.

elicit *(e-lic'-it)*. To find out by asking questions.

eligible *(el'-i-gi-ble)*. Suitable; fit to be chosen; qualified. Thus, only peers of the realm are eligible to sit in the House of Lords.

eliminate *(e-lim'-i-nate)*. To remove; to get rid of; to throw out; to weed out.

elk. A large deer possessing great antlers.

ellipse *(el-lipse')*. An oval. Anything oval is **elliptical**.

elm. A large shady tree which has hard, heavy wood.

elocution *(el-o-cu'-tion)*. The art of speaking clearly and distinctly.

eloquent *(el'-o-quent)*. Able to speak well and never being at a loss for the right word to say.

elucidate *(e-lu'-ci-date)*. To explain clearly.

elude *(e-lude')*. To escape from; to avoid.

elusive *(e-lu'-sive)*. Hard to discover; not easily found.

emaciated *(e-ma'-ci-at-ed)*. Thin; wasting away.

emanate *(em'-a-nate)*. To come from, as "The cold winds emanate from the north". To issue.

emancipate *(e-man'-ci-pate)*. To give freedom; to set slaves free.

embalm *(em-balm')*. To preserve a dead body and prevent its decaying.

embankment *(em-bank'-ment)*. Earth piled up to keep water in its course and prevent it flowing over the land. Any piling up of earth or the building of a wall for purposes of levelling a road, railway track, etc.

embargo *(em-bar'-go)*. 1. A government order stopping ships entering or leaving certain ports. 2. An order to stop some particular thing.

embark *(em-bark')*. 1. To go on board ship. 2. To start doing something; to engage in.

embarrass *(em-bar'-rass)*. To embarrass someone is to cause him to feel upset, confused or ashamed. If you were caught telling a lie, you would probably feel embarrassed.

embellish *(em-bel'-lish)*. To decorate or to add details either real or imaginary. To elaborate.

embers *(em'-bers)*. The remains of a fire in which some pieces of coal or wood are still glowing.

embezzle *(em-bez'-zle)*. To take possession of people's money or property, which has been entrusted to you; to steal.

emblem *(em'-blem)*. A figure, sign, shape, etc., that has some special meaning given to it. Thus, a rose is the emblem of England, a thistle is an emblem of Scotland, etc.

embossed *(em-bossed')*. Any article with a raised pattern on it is embossed. A penny is embossed as the pattern on it stands up from the general surface.

embrace *(em-brace')*. 1. To hug; to clasp with the arms; to hold in the arms and kiss. 2. To take in; to include, as "Great Britain embraces three countries". 3. "He embraced the opportunity" means "He accepted the opportunity gladly and quickly".

embroidery *(em-broi'-der-y)*. Needlework consisting of ornamental or fancy stitches.

embryo *(em'-bry-o)*. A very young animal or plant before it has been born, been hatched out of the egg, or sprouted from the seed.

emerald *(em'-er-ald)*. A bright green precious stone.

emerge *(e-merge')*. To come out from. In "She emerged from the dark room and blinked her eyes", emerged means came out.

emergency *(e-mer'-gen-cy)*. A sudden necessity. Thus, in some buildings and in some buses, signs are shown saying "Emergency Exit". Such exits are to be used only when a sudden need arises such as a fire or an accident.

emetic *(e-met'-ic)*. Something given to make a person vomit.

emigrate *(em'-i-grate)*. To leave home and settle in a different place, usually in a different country. A person who emigrates is an **emigrant.**

eminence *(em'-i-nence)*. 1. A high place, such as the top of a hill. 2. Marked superiority; fame. 3. "Your Eminence" is a respectful form of address used when speaking to a cardinal of the Roman Catholic Church.

eminent *(em'-i-nent)*. Noted.

emit *(e-mit')*. To send out; to voice or utter. Thus we say, "The owl emits a weird, spine-tingling call".

emotion *(e-mo'-tion)*. Any exciting feelings of joy, fear, grief, hate, etc.

emperor *(em'-per-or)*. The ruler or king of an empire.

emphasis *(em'-pha-sis)*. Certain words or syllables are said with more force than others in order to bring out the proper sense. Take the word "emphasis" as an example. At the beginning of this paragraph, there is a word in brackets, which is divided into three syllables. One of the syllables is followed by a stress mark like this '. This mark shows how the word should be said. It should be said EM-pha-sis, not em-PHA-sis or em-pha-SIS. You put more force into saying the part with the stress mark than in saying the other parts.

emphatic *(em-phat'-ic)*. With emphasis. Forcible.

empire *(em'-pire)*. A group of countries under one king or queen.

employ *(em-ploy')*. To occupy the time of; to use; to give work to. A person who employs people is an **employer;** the people who are employed are **employees** and they are given **employment.**

empower *(em-pow'-er)*. To give someone the power to do a thing.

empty *(emp'-ty)*. The opposite of full. If you fill a cup with water, then pour the water from the cup, the cup is then empty. When you pour the water from the cup, you empty it.

emulate *(em'-u-late)*. To do as somebody else does and to try to do it as well or better than he.

enable *(en-a'-ble)*. 1. To make someone able to do something. "The money you gave me will enable me to buy a bicycle". 2. To give authority to.

enamel *(e-nam'-el)*. 1. A paint which dries to a smooth, hard, glossy surface. 2. The smooth hard outer surface which is put on stoves, refrigerators, etc. 3. The hard white coating on your teeth.

encamp *(en-camp')*. To put up tents and make them ready to be lived in. To go and settle at a place.

enchant *(en-chant')*. To delight or charm.

encircle *(en-cir'-cle)*. To put a circle round. To hedge in all round.

enclose *(en-close')*. To shut in. A field may be enclosed by a fence; a letter may be enclosed in an envelope, etc.

encompass *(en-com'-pass)*. To surround on all sides.

encore. 1. *(en-core')*. The French word meaning again. When an audience shouts "Encore!" to a performer, it wants the performer to perform again. 2. *(en'-core)*. A song, piece of music, etc., not on the programme of a concert, which is performed when the audience wishes something more to be played or sung.

encounter *(en-coun'-ter)*. 1. To meet face to face. 2. A meeting face to face; a meeting in battle, etc.

encourage *(en-cour'-age)*. To give courage to; to urge someone to do something.

encroach *(en-croach')*. To trespass on; to go where you have no right to go; to do something which interferes with the rights of another person.

encumber *(en-cum'-ber)*. To litter a place or fill it up so that one cannot move freely.

encumbrance *(en-cum'-brance)*. A burden or load; anything that is in the way and is an annoyance. Adults sometimes speak of children as encumbrances when they want to pretend that children are a trouble.

encyclopædia *(en-cy-clo-pæ'-di-a)*. A book which gives information about all subjects.

endear *(en-dear')*. To make dear, as "She endeared herself to us all by her happy nature".

endeavour *(en-deav'-our)*. 1. To try; to attempt. 2. An attempt.

endorse *(en-dorse')*. 1. To write on the back of something. 2. To give support or approval.

endow *(en-dow')*. 1. To give somebody money or property is to endow them with money. The money which is given is an **endowment**. 2. To give as a gift; to be born with, as "He was endowed with great courage and intelligence".

endurance *(en-dur'-ance)*. Strength or power to hold out to the end, as "The strong man's endurance enabled him to win the fight".

endure *(en-dure')*. To last; to put up with; to undergo.

enemy *(en'-e-my)*. 1. A person or group of people who try to harm another person or group of people. Thus, in a time of war, one nation rises against another nation and each is the enemy of the other. 2. Anything harmful, as in "Germs are the enemy of health".

energetic *(en-er-get'-ic)*. Active; having much energy.

energy *(en'-er-gy)*. 1. The ability to do a great deal of hard work without getting tired. 2. Power; force.

nforce *(en-force')*. 1. To make stronger. 2. To use force on; to force. 3. To put into force, as "The police enforce the laws". The police force people to do as the law says they must.

ngage *(en-gage')*. 1. In "He engaged three men to help him with his work", engaged means employed. 2. In "We engage to do the work in three days", engage means promise or bind ourselves. 3. In "The wheel engages the ratchet which turns the machine", engages means interlocks with. 4. In "He is engaged to Miss Brown", engaged means he has promised to marry Miss Brown.

ngaging *(en-gag'-ing)*. Attractive and pleasant.

ngine *(en'-gine)*. 1. A machine that causes other parts to move. 2. A machine that pulls a train.

ngineer *(en-gi-neer')*. A man who has been trained in some form of practical science, such as road- or bridge-building, mining, etc.

English *(En'-glish)*. Of or from England; the people of England; the language.

ngrave *(en-grave')*. To cut letters or designs in any hard material, as metal, wood or stone.

ngulf *(en-gulf')*. To swallow up.

nhance *(en-hance')*. To add to the value or beauty of.

nigma *(e-nig'-ma)*. Anything in the nature of a puzzle which is difficult to understand.

njoy *(en-joy')*. When something is making you happy, you enjoy it.

nlighten *(en-light'-en)*. To instruct; inform; throw light on something, so that it becomes clear to those present.

nlist *(en-list')*. 1. To join the Navy, Army or Air Force. 2. To enlist a person's sympathy is to ask for and to receive his sympathy.

normous *(e-nor'-mous)*. Very large; much larger than ordinary.

nough *(e-nough')*. Adequate; sufficient.

nquire *(en-quire')*. Ask. Attempt to find out. Also spelled **inquire**.

nrage *(en-rage')*. To make very angry; to put in a rage.

nrapture *(en-rap'-ture)*. To please somebody very much and delight him.

nrol *(en-rol')*. Sometimes spelled **enroll**. 1. To write in a list. 2. To enrol a person in something is to make him a member of it, as "He was enrolled in the Boy Scouts".

ensign *(en'-sign)*. A flag. There are white, red and blue ensigns.

ensnare *(en-snare')*. To catch in a snare or trap.

ensue *(en-sue')*. To follow; to happen as a result of.

entangle *(en-tan'-gle)*. 1. To make something tangled, as when a kitten plays with a ball of wool and entangles it. 2. To get someone into difficulties.

enter *(en'-ter)*. To go into. To enter a room means to go into it.

enterprising *(en'-ter-pris-ing)*. Said of a person who has courage and energy in attempting new things.

entertain *(en-ter-tain')*. 1. To interest and amuse people. Something which is amusing is **entertaining.** 2. To consider; to keep in mind, as "I will entertain the idea of getting my new car from you". 3. To invite people into your home and to give them a good time there, as "He entertains a great deal". Someone who entertains provides **entertainment.**

enthusiasm *(en-thu'-si-asm)*. When someone shows a great deal of interest and eagerness, he shows enthusiasm. A person showing keenness and excitement about something is said to be **enthusiastic** *(en-thu-si-as'-tic)*. If someone suggested a trip to the zoo you would probably be enthusiastic about going and you would show enthusiasm.

entice *(en-tice')*. To tempt; to persuade someone, perhaps against his will, to do something.

entire *(en-tire')*. All of something; the whole. When the entire class is present, every pupil is present.

entitle *(en-ti'-tle)*. 1. To give a title to someone or something. You should entitle your compositions. 2. To give a claim or a right to something. When you reach the age of 21 you will be entitled to vote.

entomology *(en-to-mol'-o-gy)*. The study of insects.

entrance *(en'-trance)*. 1. A going in or entering. An actor makes his entrance when he goes on the stage. 2. A doorway or gate, through which one enters.

entrance *(en-trance')*. To throw into a trance; to fill with great joy; to cast a spell over.

entreat *(en-treat')*. To beg someone to do something. To ask earnestly.

entry *(en'-try)*. 1. Entrance. 2. An entry in a book is something written in it.

enumerate *(e-nu'-mer-ate)*. 1. To count. 2. To name a number of things one after the other.

enunciate *(e-nun'-ci-ate)*. To speak or pronounce clearly. A person who mumbles does not enunciate properly.

envelop *(en-vel'-op)*. To cover over completely.

envelope *(en'-ve-lope)*. A folded piece of paper with glue-covered flaps, in which you seal letters or cards.

envious *(en'-vi-ous)*. Full of envy.

environment *(en-vi'-ron-ment)*. Surroundings; the place where you live; the things that are around you.

envoy *(en'-voy)*. A messenger sent on business by one government to another.

envy *(en'-vy)*. 1. To feel bitter toward someone because he has something you want; to feel jealous. 2. The feeling you have towards someone you envy; jealousy.

epic *(ep'-ic)*. A poem that tells a story about a hero.

epidemic *(ep-i-dem'-ic)*. A disease which spreads rapidly to many people in the same district at the same time.

epidermis *(ep-i-der'-mis)*. The outer layer of skin.

epigram *(ep'-i-gram)*. A short poem or short remark in which the thought is put smartly or funnily. Here is an epigram: "Greedy people live to eat, not eat to live".

epilogue *(ep'-i-logue)*. 1. A speech made by an actor at the end of a play to sum up what has happened in the play. 2. A final chapter or section at the end of some books.

episode *(ep'-i-sode)*. 1. A part of a story that is a complete story in itself. 2. A part of a person's life or a period of history that contains a complete sequence of events.

epistle *(e-pis'-tle)*. A letter; usually used with reference to the letters written by the apostles and found in the New Testament.

epitaph *(ep'-i-taph)*. The words written on a tombstone which refer to the dead person's character.

epoch *(ep'-och)*. An age or era; a long period of time.

equable *(eq'-ua-ble)*. Uniform; not changing much; thus "England has an equable climate", meaning that the weather does not change much.

equal *(e'-qual)*. 1. Exactly the same in amount, number, size, value, etc. 2. To be exactly the same. Thus, twelve inches equal one foot; three feet equal one yard.

equanimity *(e-qua-nim'-i-ty)*. Calm temperament. A person who has equanimity is one who never flares up in a temper, but is always calm.

equator *(e-qua'-tor)*. An imaginary line around the earth which divides the northern hemisphere (or half) from the southern hemisphere. England is north of the equator and Australia is south of the equator.

equilateral *(e-qui-lat'-er-al)*. Having all the sides equal in length.

equilibrium *(e-qui-lib'-ri-um)*. Balance; two things are in equilibirium when they balance each other, that is, when they weigh exactly the same. If a pound weight is put on one side of a scale and a pound of tea on the other, the weight and the tea will be in equilibrium.

equinox *(e'-qui-nox)*. The time when the sun's centre crosses the equator and day and night everywhere in the world are of equal length. That happens twice a year, around March 21 and September 21.

equip *(e-quip')*. To fit out.

equipment *(e-quip'-ment)*. The things which are used to equip or fit out something are called equipment.

equity *(eq'-ui-ty)*. Justice; fairness.

equivalent *(e-quiv'-a-lent)*. 1. Equal; equal in value, weight, etc. 2. Something which is equal to something else, as sixteen ounces are equivalent to one pound.

era *(e'-ra)*. A period of time; an age.

eradicate *(e-rad'-i-cate)*. The real meaning is to tear up by the roots; but the word is most often used to mean to get rid of completely; to wipe out.

erase *(e-rase')*. To rub out. An ink **eraser** is a rubber used to rub out ink marks.

erect *(e-rect')*. 1. To stand straight is to stand erect. 2. When workmen build a house, they erect a house.

ermine *(er'-mine)*. 1. The fur of the stoat, an animal of northern areas whose coat is brown in summer but changes to white in winter. The white fur is used for trimming women's coats, etc. 2. The animal itself.

erosion *(e-ro'-sion)*. The slow eating or wearing away of something. For example, when an ocean or a lake wears away the edge of a cliff, erosion is taking place.

err. To make a mistake. The mistake is an **error** and anything containing a mistake is **erroneous.**

errand *(er'-rand)*. A trip made to do something. Most children do errands for their parents.

errant *(er'-rant)*. Wandering.

erratic *(er-rat'-ic)*. Uncertain. A person is erratic when you cannot be sure what he will do next.

error *(er'-ror)*. A mistake.

erudite *(er'-u-dite)*. Learned. An erudite person is one who has a great deal of knowledge.

eruption *(e-rup'-tion)*. A bursting out; a breaking out. When a volcano becomes active, there is an eruption of smoke, steam, etc., and when a person has measles, he has an eruption on his skin consisting of tiny red spots.

escalator *(es'-ca-la-tor)*. A moving staircase which takes you up or down without any effort on your part.

escapade *(es-ca-pade')*. A mad prank; a foolish thing done for fun without any thought about what may result.

escape *(es-cape')*. To break free from something or someone is to escape. A prisoner may try to escape from prison and you may try to escape from your work.

escort. 1. *(es'-cort)*. A body of men or a single person accompanying someone else for his protection. 2. *(es-cort')*. To attend; to guard.

Eskimo *(Es'-ki-mo)*. A member of the race of people who live in the Canadian Far North.

especially *(es-pe'-cial-ly)*. 1. Unusually; exceptionally. When you see something exceptionally beautiful, you say that it is especially beautiful. 2. Particularly.

espionage *(es'-pi-o-nage)*. Spying.

esplanade *(es-pla-nade')*. A level road or path, usually along the sea-front.

espouse *(es-pouse')*. To marry. A **spouse** is a husband or a wife.

esquire *(es-quire')*. A title of respect seldom used except when addressing a letter or an envelope to a man. Usually, it is abbreviated and is written Esq., as John Brown, Esq.

essence *(es'-sence)*. 1. That which gives something its character, as "The essence of Christianity is love". 2. A concentrated or very strong liquid, as essence of vanilla, a few drops of which are enough to flavour a gallon of ice-cream.

essential *(es-sen'-tial)*. Necessary.

establish *(es-tab'-lish)*. 1. To prove beyond doubt, as "In spite of all they said, he established his point". 2. To open

F

or begin a business; thus we see on a shop, "Established 1907".
3. To set up a home permanently, as "He established his home in Devon".

estate *(es-tate')*. 1. In law, all that a person owns is his estate.
2. Ordinarily, an estate is a large piece of land with perhaps houses, trees, gardens and fields on it.

esteem *(es-teem')*. To think very highly of.

estimable *(es'-ti-ma-ble)*. Highly thought of.

estimate *(es'-ti-mate)*. 1. To form an idea or opinion of the size, weight, value, etc. If you look at a heap of bricks and say to yourself "I think there are 500 bricks in that pile", you estimate the number of bricks. 2. When a person wishes repairs done to his house, he may call a builder to give him an estimate of the cost; that is, the builder tells him about how much it will cost.

estuary *(es'-tu-a-ry)*. The tidal mouth of a river.

eternal *(e-ter'-nal)*. Without beginning or end. **eternity** means time or existence without a beginning and going on for ever.

ether *(e'-ther)*. 1. A colourless, strong-smelling liquid which is used in hospitals to deaden pain. 2. The medium through which light and radio waves are carried.

etiquette *(et'-i-quette)*. The rules of good manners. When a man raises his hat to a lady, he is following one of the rules of etiquette.

etymology *(et-y-mol'-o-gy)*. The science which deals with the history and uses of words. Be careful not to confuse the word with **entomology,** the study of insects.

evacuate *(e-vac'-u-ate)*. To go away from; to leave empty.

evade *(e-vade')*. To avoid, especially by being artful; to escape.

evangelist *(e-van'-ge-list)*. A preacher of the Gospels. St. Matthew, St. Mark, St. Luke and St. John were evangelists.

evaporate *(e-vap'-o-rate)*. 1. To drive off the water from, usually by means of heat. 2. To turn into vapour (steam).

eve. 1. The evening. 2. The day before a holiday such as Christmas Eve.

even *(e'-ven)*. 1. Level, smooth, flat, like the surface of a pane of glass. 2. An even number is a number which can be divided by two without leaving a remainder.

evening *(eve'-ning)*. The part of the day between sunset and bedtime. The last part of the day.

event *(e-vent')*. A happening.

eventually *(e-ven'-tu-al-ly)*. In the end; finally.

evergreen *(ev'-er-green)*. A tree or plant having green leaves all the year round. Pine, spruce and cedar are evergreens.

evermore *(ev-er-more')*. Always; forever.

everywhere *(ev'-er-y-where)*. In every place; in each and all places.

evict *(e-vict')*. To turn a person out of the house in which he lives or to turn him off the land he cultivates.

evidence *(ev'-i-dence)*. Facts stated by a person to prove some point that is doubtful; proof; information in a law case.

evident *(ev'-i-dent)*. A thing is evident when it is plain or easy for anyone to see or understand.

evil *(e'-vil)*. Wrong; bad; sinful; wicked.

evoke *(e-voke')*. To call forth. In "His answer evoked the master's anger", evoked means called forth or aroused.

evolve *(e-volve')*. To build up; to think out; to unroll; as "After much thought he evolved a plan for a machine which would save much labour".

ewe. A female sheep.

exact *(ex-act')*. 1. Accurate or correct, as "His counting of the apples was exact". 2. To demand something and get it, as "The landlord exacted a high rent from the poor woman".

exaggerate *(ex-ag'-ger-ate)*. To say that things are better, worse, quicker, slower, etc., than they really are. A boy who sees a dozen aeroplanes, and then tells his mother that he saw fifty, exaggerates.

examination *(ex-am-i-na'-tion)*. 1. A test of knowledge. You may have an examination in school. 2. A thorough inspection. Your doctor may give you a medical examination.

examine *(ex-am'-ine)*. To look at closely; to ask questions; to make tests to find a person's knowledge, skill, strength, information, health, etc.

example *(ex-am'-ple)*. A pattern; a sample; a thing that may be taken to be a specimen of many others.

exasperate *(ex-as'-per-ate)*. To annoy very much.

excavate *(ex'-ca-vate)*. To hollow out; to dig up something from the ground.

exceed *(ex-ceed')*. To go beyond the limit of something, as "You have exceeded your allowance".

exceedingly *(ex-ceed'-ing-ly)*. Very much.

excel *(ex-cel')*. To be better than others.

excellent *(ex'-cel-lent)*. Better than others. In "This is an excellent picture", excellent means that it is better than others and you choose it because of its **excellence.**

except *(ex-cept')*. 1. Leave out or take out. 2. In "All of the children went to the picnic except John", except shows that John did not go; he was left out.

exception *(ex-cep'-tion)*. 1. One that is left out. 2. An objection.

excess *(ex-cess')*. Something that is too much; something in addition to. If a man smokes to excess, he smokes too much.

exchange *(ex-change')*. To give a thing and to have something given back in return.

excise *(ex'-cise)*. A tax placed on certain goods that are made in this country before they are sold to the people of this country.

excite *(ex-cite')*. To stir up or arouse. When something pleasant is about to happen, you become excited. At Christmas we find young children excited about the things which they would like to receive.

excitement *(ex-cite'-ment)*. When people are excited, there is excitement in the air such as on Christmas morning.

exclaim *(ex-claim')*. To shout or speak as if surprised.

exclude *(ex-clude')*. To shut out; to keep out.

excruciating *(ex-cru'-ci-a-ting)*. Agonizing; very painful.

excursion *(ex-cur'-sion)*. An expedition; a journey to some place and back again.

excuse *(ex-cuse')*. 1. An attempt at a reasonable explanation. 2. To excuse is to give excuses for, as, for example, "He tried to excuse his lateness". 3. To pardon or forgive.

execute *(ex'-e-cute)*. 1. To do something, as "The soldier executes his orders promptly", that is, he carries them out without wasting time. 2. To put to death, as "The murderer was executed".

executive *(ex-ec'-u-tive)*. 1. A man in charge of a large shop, factory or business. 2. The people who are officers of an organization, as in "A new executive was elected each year in the Junior Red Cross".

exemplary *(ex-em'-pla-ry)*. 1. Worth imitating, as "His manner was exemplary". 2. Acting as a warning to others, as "His exemplary punishment will persuade others to obey the law".

exempt *(ex-empt')*. Free from some duty, danger or unpleasantness that other people are not free from, as "All boys with over 60 marks are exempt from home-work tonight", meaning they are excused from their home-work.

exercise *(ex'-er-cise)*. A practice to gain improvement. Thus you do exercises in arithmetic, spelling and in physical education.

exert *(ex-ert')*. To make an effort.

exertion *(ex-er'-tion)*. A great effort.

exhale *(ex-hale')*. To breathe outwards; the opposite to inhale.

exhaust *(ex-haust')*. 1. To use up and leave nothing. A person who uses all his energy is **exhausted** and he suffers from **exhaustion.** 2. Waste gases from an engine.

exhibit *(ex-hib'-it)*. 1. To show or display in public. 2. A collection of things put on show. An **exhibition** *(ex-hi-bi'-tion)* is a showing. There might be an exhibition of hand-made ash-trays; a small child might give an exhibition of bad temper. People who show things are called **exhibitors** *(ex-hib'-i-tors)*.

exhort *(ex-hort')*. To beg or urge a person to do something.

exhume *(ex-hume')*. To dig up from beneath the ground.

exile *(ex'-ile)*. 1. A person who is banished or sent away from his own country. 2. The banished person goes to live in exile. 3. To banish.

exist *(ex-ist')*. 1. To be alive, as "You cannot exist without food and water", meaning that without them you would not be able to continue living. 2. To be, as "How many rivers exist in the world?"

existence *(ex-ist'-ence)*. 1. The life a person leads, as "He had a miserable existence", meaning that the life he led was an unhappy one. 2. Anything that exists. 3. Being, as "The existence of sea-serpents is not proved".

exit *(ex'-it)*. The way out.

exonerate *(ex-on'-er-ate)*. To free a person from blame.

exorbitant *(ex-or'-bi-tant)*. Excessive; unreasonable.

exotic *(ex-ot'-ic)*. Coming from a foreign country; strange or rare; often said of plants that come from a foreign country.

expand *(ex-pand')*. To open out or spread out; to grow larger.

expect *(ex-pect')*. To look forward to; to feel sure of; to hope. You expect others to do unto you as you do unto them.

expedient *(ex-pe'-di-ent)*.   Suitable for the time being or for the occasion.

expedite *(ex'-pe-dite)*.   To hasten; to hurry.

expedition *(ex-pe-di'-tion)*.   1. A journey or voyage made for some definite reason.   2. Anything done quickly and smartly is said to be done with expedition.

expel *(ex-pel')*.   To force out or drive out.

expend *(ex-pend')*.   To spend.   Anything on which a great deal has been spent is **expensive.**

expense *(ex-pense')*.   Outlay; cost.   "The battle was won at the expense of the lives of many soldiers."

experiment *(ex-per'-i-ment)*.   1. A test or a trial in order to find out; thus, "After many experiments a way was found to make the material fire-proof".   2. To test or to try in order to find out; thus, "Astronauts experiment to find what men can do in space".

expert.   1. *(ex'-pert)*.   Someone with a great deal of knowledge about a certain matter; thus a man who knows a great deal about gas is a gas expert.   One who knows much about stamps is a stamp expert, etc.   2. *(ex-pert')*.   Skilful.

expire *(ex-pire')*.   1. To die, as "He expired early to-day".   2. To go out of effect, as "My season ticket expired yesterday".

explain *(ex-plain')*.   To make something clear; to describe the meaning of.

explode *(ex-plode')*.   To burst or blow up with a great noise.

explore *(ex-plore')*.   1. To travel to unknown places with the idea of finding out about them.   2. To examine or look into thoroughly.

explorer *(ex-plor'-er)*.   A person who explores is an explorer.

export.   1. *(ex-port')*.   To ship goods out of the country for sale in another country.   2. *(ex'-port)*.   Goods sent for sale to another country.

expose *(ex-pose')*.   1. To show, as "He exposed the book so that all might see it".   2. To uncover, as "He exposed the whole of the film", i.e., the lens was uncovered to make the exposures.   3. To leave without proper protection, as "The sheep were exposed to the full force of the gale as they had no shelter".

express *(ex-press')*.   1. To say in words, as "He expressed himself very badly".   2. Rapid or quick, as "The express train is due now".

expression *(ex-pres'-sion)*. 1. A look on a person's face which shows what he is thinking, as "The man's fury was seen in his expression". 2. A group of words which have a special meaning, such as "put up with". 3. The expressing of something (see **express,** No. 1), as, "His note was an expression of sympathy".

expulsion *(ex-pul'-sion)*. Driving out; banishment; the **expelling** of a person is an expulsion.

exquisite *(ex'-qui-site)*. Very attractive; beautiful; lovely.

extend *(ex-tend')*. To stretch out.

extension *(ex-ten'-sion)*. 1. A stretching out. 2. Something added to another thing to make it longer, larger, etc.

exterior *(ex-te'-ri-or)*. The outside; the opposite of **interior. external** has almost the same meaning; we see, for instance, on bottles, "For external use only", meaning that the contents are not to be drunk; they are for putting on the outside or exterior of a person's body.

extinct *(ex-tinct')*. Dead; existing no longer.

extol *(ex-tol')*. To praise highly.

extort *(ex-tort')*. To get something from a person by threats or force.

extra *(ex'-tra)*. In addition to; more; more than what is needed. Most children like an extra ice-cream.

extract *(ex-tract')*. 1. To draw out, as "He had a tooth extracted". 2. *(ex'-tract)*. Something taken from another thing, as "Vanilla extract is the flavour drawn from the vanilla bean".

extravagant *(ex-trav'-a-gant)*. 1. Spending too much money in foolish ways. 2. Beyond reason, as "He told an extravagant story", meaning a story so wild or exaggerated that it could not be believed.

extreme *(ex-treme')*. Much more than usual. In "He suffered extreme pain", extreme means more than was usual under the conditions.

extremely *(ex-treme'-ly)*. Very much; exceedingly.

extricate *(ex'-tri-cate)*. To free something, as "The hunter extricated his dog from the bear trap".

exude *(ex-ude')*. 1. To squeeze out. 2. To ooze out, as perspiration out of the pores of the skin.

eye. The organ of the body which is used for seeing.

eyebrow *(eye'-brow)*. The line of hairs on the ridge of bone above the eyes.

eyelid *(eye'-lid)*. One of the folds of skin which cover the eye when it is closed. Each eye has an upper and a lower lid.

eyewitness *(eye'-wit'-ness)*. A person who sees something happen.

F

fable *(fa'-ble)*. A tale that teaches a lesson.

fabric *(fab'-ric)*. Cloth or any woven material like cloth.

fabricate *(fab'-ri-cate)*. 1. To manufacture; make; construct. To invent or make up. 2. A remark that is untrue is often called a **fabrication** *(fab-ri-ca'-tion)*.

fabulous *(fab'-u-lous)*. 1. Imagined. A thing that has never existed, but which people pretend has existed, is a fabulous thing. Ghosts, Jack the Giant Killer and Cinderella are all fabulous. 2. A fabulous price is a very high price.

façade *(fa-cade')*. The front of a house or building.

face. 1. The front part of the head. The nose, eyes and mouth are located on the face. 2. The front part or surface such as the face of a clock. 3. The front part of a building is called the face. 4. When you face something you look toward it.

facetious *(fa-ce'-tious)*. 1. A person is facetious who always says funny things. 2. We often say that a person is facetious when he tries to be funny. 3. Humorous, comic.

facility *(fa-cil'-i-ty)*. An action is done with facility when it is done easily.

facsimile *(fac-sim'-i-le)*. An exact copy.

fact. A piece of information that is true.

factor *(fac'-tor)*. 1. A fact contributing to a result. 2. The factors of any number are the numbers which will divide into that number without leaving a remainder. 2, 3, 4 and 6 are all factors of 12. 3. An agent; one who buys or sells for another.

factory *(fac'-tor-y)*. One or more buildings in which articles are made. Bicycles are made in a bicycle factory.

fad. Something in which people are interested for a short time. For a while children may want to wear a hat similar to one worn by a famous cowboy; then children want to wear a badge similar to one worn by a space explorer. The hat is worn for a short time and suddenly it is forgotten and the badge is worn until something new catches the interest. These are fads.

fade. To wither; to lose colour.

faggot *(fagg'-ot)*. Also spelled **fagot.** A bundle of twigs or sticks gathered together for burning as firewood.

Fahrenheit *(Fahr'-en-heit)*. A Fahrenheit thermometer is one which measures 212 degrees between the freezing and the boiling points of water. The abbreviation is F. (The Fahrenheit thermometer is named after the German scientist G. D. Fahrenheit.)

fail. 1. Not to succeed. 2. To break down. 3. To die away.

failure *(fail'-ure)*. 1. Lack of success. 2. A person who has not succeeded in his ambition is sometimes called a failure.

faint. 1. Weak; fading; not bright. 2. To become weak; to swoon.

fair. 1. Light, as "She has a fair complexion". 2. Just, in such sentences as "The teacher is always fair". 3. A place where one may see displays of handiwork, livestock, factory-made goods (cars, etc.), and where he may find amusements. 4. Average. When a person receives a fair mark it is neither high nor low.

fairy *(fair'-y)*. A tiny, beautiful, dainty make-believe being which has a magic power.

faith. Belief; trust. A person who is always loyal and "keeps faith" is **faithful.**

fake. 1. To counterfeit or falsify. 2. Something which is false.

falcon *(fal'-con)*. A swift bird like a hawk which is trained to hunt and kill birds and small animals.

fall. 1. To tumble; drop. 2. A tumble; a drop, as "He had a nasty fall". 3. We speak of the amount of rain that falls as the fall of rain.

fallen *(fall'-en)*. Dropped.

fallible *(fal'-li-ble)*. Liable to make mistakes. Everybody, in fact, is fallible and no one is **infallible.**

fallow *(fal'-low)*. Ploughed land that is being left for a time to rest.

false. Not true.

falsehood *(false'-hood)*. A lie; an untruth.

falsify *(fal'-si-fy)*. To make a thing wrong purposely with the idea of cheating in some way.

falter *(fal'-ter)*. To hesitate either in walking or speaking.

fame. Reputation; renown. A person who seeks fame wishes to be known and admired by a great number of people.

familiar *(fa-mil'-iar)*. 1. Well known, as "He saw his mother's familiar face in the crowd." 2. To be familiar with something is to know it well.

family *(fam'-i-ly)*. 1. The father, mother and their children are one family. 2. A group of related persons such as the parents, children, aunts, uncles, cousins, etc.

famine *(fam'-ine)*. 1. A time when food is scarce and people die of starvation. 2. A shortage of anything may be spoken of as a famine.

famished *(fam'-ished)*. If a person says he is famished, he means he is very hungry, and is longing for something to eat.

famous *(fa'-mous)*. Very well known. Shakespeare is famous. The pyramids are famous.

fan. 1. A small wedge-shaped piece of paper or wood which is waved close to a person to cool him. 2. An electrical appliance with revolving blades which create a cooling breeze. 3. To fan is to wave a fan or something like a fan so as to create a breeze. 4. To fan out is to spread out in the shape of a fan.

fanatic *(fa-nat'-ic)*. A person who believes in something so strongly that he is unreasonable about it.

fancy *(fan'-cy)*. To imagine, as "She fancied the boat was going to sink". 2. To like, as "She fancies a cup of tea after lunch". 3. In "fancy dress", the word "fancy" suggests decorated, more beautiful than useful. 4. In "He paid a fancy price for it", fancy means unreasonable. 5. Your fancy is your imagination.

fanciful *(fan'-ci-ful)*. Imaginative; odd or quaint.

fang. A long, sharp, curved tooth, such as is found in the mouth of a wolf or dog.

fantastic *(fan-tas'-tic)*. Very unusual; wild or strange.

farce. A comic play in which fun is the chief thing.

fare. 1. The price paid for riding in a train, etc. 2. Food, as "We always enjoy eating the good fare at that restaurant". 3. To travel, as "He fared across the sea".

farewell *(fare-well')*. A good-bye.

farm. 1. An area of land which is used to raise crops, trees, animals or all three. 2. To till the ground; to manage a farm.

farrier *(far'-ri-er)*. A man who shoes horses or treats them when they are ill.

farther *(far'-ther)*. More distant. A tree appears smaller when it is farther away. **Further** is often used in the same way.

fascinate *(fas'-cin-ate)*. To charm. Those who can fascinate, do it by **fascination** *(fas-ci-na'-tion)*, or by their **fascinating** *(fas'-ci-na-ting)* ways.

fashion *(fash'-ion)*. 1. The style in which a thing is made or done, which may be popular to-day but quite unpopular in a year's time. 2. To make, as "He fashioned a walking-stick out of an old piece of wood". 3. The way something is done; manner, as "She eats in a disgraceful fashion".

fast. 1. When a thing is fast, it goes quickly. 2. When you fast, you go without food. 3. When a person is fast, he is too free and easy in his behaviour. 4. When a watch is fast, it is ahead of the proper time. 5. Firmly fixed.

fasten *(fas'-ten)*. To fix; close; tie; shut.

fastidious *(fas-tid'-i-ous)*. Difficult to please. A person is fastidious who needs everything done in a way to please his special wishes.

fat. 1. A yellow or white greasy substance that forms a layer under the skin of most animals. You often see fat on steak. 2. A person is fat when he weighs too much.

fatal *(fa'-tal)*. Deadly.

fate. 1. A force which is supposed to exist, and which decides ahead of time what is going to happen to everyone and everything. 2. Something that is fated is bound to happen; nothing can prevent or change it.

father *(fa'-ther)*. The male parent in a family.

fatherland *(fa'-ther-land)*. The country to which a person belongs by birth. We call England "The mother country" but Germans refer to Germany as the fatherland.

fathom *(fath'-om)*. 1. A nautical measure (6 feet). 2. To find the depth of. 3. To get to the bottom of; to find out.

fatigue *(fa-tigue')*. Tiredness; weariness; weakness.

fault. A mistake; an error.

fauna *(fau'-na)*. The animals living naturally in a country; thus the fauna of England includes rabbits, foxes, etc., but not lions and tigers, which belong to the fauna of other countries.

favourable *(fa'-vour-a-ble)*. Helpful; suitable; satisfactory.

favourite *(fa'-vour-ite)*. 1. Most liked. Thus, if you have more than one hobby, the one you like most is your favourite hobby. 2. The one liked most, as "Sir Francis Drake was for a time Queen Elizabeth I's favourite".

fawn. 1. A young deer. 2. A light-brown colour.

fear. 1. When you are afraid of something you fear it. You usually fear something dangerous or evil. 2. The feeling of being afraid; terror; fright.

fearful *(fear'-ful)*. 1. Dreadful; frightful; terrible. 2. Full of fear.

feast. 1. A religious festival, as the Feast of the Passover. 2. A dinner at which there is rejoicing and celebrations. 3. Any specially good meal.

feat. An act which can be done only by skill, pluck, strength, hard work, etc.

feather *(feath'-er)*. A bird's body is covered with feathers.

feature *(fea'-ture)*. A feature is the main or most noticeable part of something. Thus the nose, mouth, and chin are features of the face. Usually there is a feature or main picture at the theatre, and one or more short pictures.

February *(Feb'-ru-ar-y)*. The second month of the year. It is the shortest month of the year with only 28 days, except in leap years when it has 29 days.

federal *(fed'-er-al)*. Having to do with the central government of a federation. The federal government of Canada meets in Ottawa.

federate *(fed'-er-ate)*. 1. To join together by making a treaty. 2. To form a **federation.**

federation *(fed-er-a'-tion)*. 1. The joining together of states or countries by treaty. 2. A country which has been formed by the joining together of several states or provinces. Canada and the United States are federations. In a federation, there is a central government which rules the whole country, as well as state or provincial governments for each of the states or provinces.

fee. Price charged for work done, as the money paid to a lawyer.

feeble *(fee'-ble)*. Weak.

feed. 1. To feed someone is to give him food. 2. Food which is given to animals is called feed. 3. When you put more wood on a fire you feed the fire.

feel. 1. To touch something is to feel it. If you touch a piece of wool and a piece of silk you will find that they feel quite different. 2. When you say "I feel a cool breeze", you mean that you are aware of a cool breeze.

feelingly *(feel'-ing-ly)*. With feeling or emotion. If someone spoke to you feelingly about the misfortunes of poor, starving people in Africa, you would know from his tone of voice that he felt great pity for them.

feet. The plural of **foot**; more than one foot.

feign. Pretend, as "The pupil feigned illness to evade the examination".

feint. A pretended attack. A boxer might feint with his left hand and hit his opponent with his right.

felicity *(fe-lic'-i-ty)*. Bliss; happiness; gladness.

feline *(fe'-line)*. Having to do with the cat tribe.

fell. 1. Past tense of the verb to fall, as "He fell down in the road". 2. To cut down, as "The farmer is going to fell the tree".

fellow *(fel'-low)*. A friend; a comrade.

felon *(fel'-on)*. A criminal.

felony *(fel'-o-ny)*. A crime.

felt. 1. Cloth that is not woven but is pressed together. 2. Past tense of the verb **to feel**.

female *(fe'-male)*. 1. An animal of the sex which bears young ones, or lays eggs; the opposite to **male**. 2. A woman or girl.

feminine *(fem'-i-nine)*. Belonging to women or girls, such as "feminine clothes".

fen. Low, marshy land.

fence. A barrier built around fields and property. Fences are usually made of wire or wood.

fencing *(fen'-cing)*. 1. The art of using the sword and other similar weapons. 2. Fences surrounding land.

fend. 1. To keep off or ward off such things as a blow or a slash with a sword. 2. In "Now he is living alone, he has to fend for himself", fend means provide.

fender *(fend'-er)*. 1. A metal frame placed before a fire to prevent hot coals rolling into the room. 2. A large knot of old rope hanging from the side of a boat to protect it from damage. 3. Anything fitted to another object as a protection.

ferment *(fer-ment')*. 1. When something ferments it becomes sour or alcoholic and gives off bubbles. 2. *(fer'-ment)*. Agitation; uproar; excitement.

fern. A plant, often with feather-like leaves, which does not have flowers.

ferocious *(fe-ro'-cious)*. Savage; cruel.

ferret *(fer'-ret)*. 1. A half-tame animal of the polecat family used for unearthing rabbits. 2. To search out or hunt for as "He ferreted about among the papers on his desk".

ferrule *(fer'-rule)*. The metal cap at the end of a walking-stick or umbrella.

ferry *(fer'-ry)*. 1. A ferry is a boat which regularly goes to and fro across a river, etc., carrying people and goods. A ferry serves the same purpose as a bridge. 2. To carry people and goods by ferry.

fertile *(fer'-tile)*. Fruitful; producing abundantly. Trees and plants which bear large quantities of fruits, seeds, etc., are fertile.

fertilization *(fer-ti-li-za'-tion)*. 1. Treating the soil with fertilizer. 2. The act or process of joining a male with a female cell so as to produce fruit or offspring.

fertilizer *(fer'-ti-liz-er)*. Manure, chemicals or some other substance which is dug into soil in order to make the soil bear better crops, grass, flowers, etc.

fervent *(fer'-vent)*. Ardent; whole-hearted; earnest; warm in feeling.

fester *(fes'-ter)*. A wound which festers becomes infected and full of pus.

festival *(fes'-ti-val)*. A time of special rejoicing, merry-making or entertainment.

festoon *(fes-toon')*. 1. A chain or garland of flowers, coloured paper, etc., fixed at the ends and hanging down in the middle. 2. To decorate with festoons.

fetch. To go for and bring back.

fête. A feast; a festival; an outdoor gathering at which amusements and refreshments are to be had.

fetid *(fe'-tid)*. Nasty smelling.

feud. A quarrel that goes on for a long time. History describes many feuds that were carried on by sons when their fathers became too old to fight.

feudal *(feu'-dal)*. Said of the system by which land and property were lent by lords in mediæval times to men who, in return, had to serve the lords.

fever *(fe'-ver)*. A rise in the temperature of a person's body.

few. Not many; a small number.

fez. A Turk's cap, shaped like the lower half of a cone and provided with a tassel.

fibre *(fi'-bre)*. Any thread-like filament. Cloth is made from woven fibres or threads. You can see fibres on the shell of a coconut and in the roots of many plants.

fickle *(fick'-le)*. Said of a person who often changes his mind without a good reason.

fiction *(fic'-tion)*. A story that is not a true one.

fictitious *(fic-ti'-cious)*. Not true; not real; false.

fiddle *(fid'-dle)*. 1. A violin; usually said of a violin played at country dances. 2. To play a fiddle.

fidget *(fidg'-et)*. 1. To move in a restless way; to be nervous or uneasy. 2. A person who moves in a restless manner.

field. 1. A large piece of ground which is usually used for growing crops, and on which are very few trees. 2. We also speak of fields on which battles are fought, and fields on which games are played.

fiend. An evil spirit or a person who is evil.

fierce. Savage; wild; furious.

fiery *(fi'-er-y)*. 1. Like fire, or consisting of flame. 2. A person who is quick to anger is said to have a fiery temper.

fife. A musical instrument held sideways across the mouth. The notes are sounded by blowing.

fifteen *(fif'-teen')*. The number which is five more than ten.

fifth. The last in a group of five.

fifty *(fif'-ty)*. A number ten more than forty or five times ten.

fig. A small, soft, sweet fruit that grows in warm climates.

fight. 1. A struggle; a battle. A fight usually involves bodily contact. 2. To engage in conflict or in battle.

figure *(fig'-ure)*. 1. Here are some figures—7, 8, 9 and 3. 2. Geometrical figures are shapes such as squares, triangles, etc. 3. Figure means person in such cases as "Tennyson was a noted figure in the world of poetry". 4. Figure means a person's outline in such sentences as "In our dress shop, we stock the latest models for slim figures". 5. In books, the diagrams or pictures are often marked Figure 1, Figure 2, etc. In this use, figure means diagram.

filament *(fil'-a-ment)*. A very fine thread. A spider's web is made of filaments and the source of light in an electric bulb is a hot filament.

file. 1. A tool with a rough face. A file is used to rub over surfaces to make them smooth, or to make things into particular shapes. 2. A row of soldiers in line is a file. 3. A box for keeping papers, letters, etc., in order.

filial *(fil'-i-al)*. Pertaining to the relation of a person to his or her father or mother.

fill. 1. To put or pour into until no more can be held. 2. To occupy the whole of, as "This jelly fills the bowl". 3. To fill a position is to hold a position.

filly *(fil'-ly)*. A young mare or female horse.

film. 1. A very thin skin or coating of one substance resting on something else, as "A film of mist coated the window-pane". 2. The material on which photographers take snap-shots. 3. A moving picture.

filter *(fil'-ter)*. A strainer that allows water, air, etc., to pass through, leaving the impurities behind.

filth. Dirt.

fin. 1. The fan-like parts of its body by which a fish swims. 2. A part, similar in shape to the fin of a fish, projecting from a machine, aircraft, etc.

final *(fi'-nal)*. Last. The final edition of a newspaper is the last edition of the day.

finance *(fi-nance')*. 1. The science of managing money; the proper care of money. 2. To supply the money for, as "How will you finance the trip?" A **financier** *(fin-an'-cier)* is one who studies money matters or one who finances something. A man in **financial** *(fin-an'-cial)* difficulties is one experiencing problems with his money.

fine. 1. A thread is fine when it is very thin. 2. A fine day is a day when the weather is good. 3. When a motorist is caught speeding he pays a fine, or a penalty.

finger *(fin'-ger)*. One of the long slender parts of the hand. You have four fingers and a thumb on each hand.

finish *(fin'-ish)*. 1. The end or close. 2. When you stop work, you finish work. 3. The finish on something is the condition of the surface of it after it is made.

finite *(fi'-nite)*. Having an end or a boundary. Most things are finite because most things come to an end; but space and time are two examples of things that are not finite. They are **infinite**.

fiord. A long, narrow arm of the sea between high cliffs such as are found in Norway. Fiord is sometimes spelled **fjord**.

fir. A type of tree which has cones; an evergreen tree.

fire. 1. When something burns, it makes a fire. A fire gives off heat and light. 2. When you pull the trigger on a gun, you fire the gun.

fire-proof *(fire'-proof)*. Very difficult to set alight or to burn.

firm. 1. Strong and not easily shaken. 2. Not easily pressed into another shape, as firm flesh. 3. A business in which many people are employed.

firmament *(fir'-ma-ment)*. The sky.

first. Before anything or any-one.

fiscal *(fis'-cal)*. Fiscal matters are those having to do with the public revenue.

fish. A cold-blooded animal having gills and fins and living in any body of water.

fishing *(fish'-ing)*. The act of trying to catch fish. Some people engage in fishing to make a living, and others enjoy fishing as a sport.

fissure *(fis'-sure)*. A deep cleft in a rock or in the ground.

fist. When you close your hand you make a fist.

fit. 1. When you are fit, you enjoy good health, and you are fit or ready for anything. 2. The way in which one thing joins with another is called a fit. You fit the parts together in a jig-saw puzzle, thus joining them. 3. A sudden attack of disease is sometimes called a fit, e.g. epileptic fit. 4. A sudden burst of anger is called a fit of anger.

five. One more than four.

fix. 1. To fasten firmly, as when you fix a post in the ground. 2. When you gaze long and hard at something, you fix your eyes on it. When you concentrate on something, you fix your attention on it.

fixture *(fix'-ture)*. Something that is firmly attached is called a fixture. Electric light bulbs are placed in electrical fixtures.

flabby *(flab'-by)*. Soft and limp and hanging loosely.

flag. 1. A plant known as the iris. 2. A national or other banner. 3. A flat paving-stone. 4. To droop.

flagon *(flag'-on)*. A large bottle, often having a narrow neck and a handle.

flagrant *(fla'-grant)*. Scandalous; glaringly obvious.

flair. A talent or special ability which a person has. Some pupils have a flair for drawing pictures.

flake. A fleecy, thin, feathery particle, as a flake of snow.

flame. A tongue of fire. Usually, when you look at a fire you see flames and smoke.

flange. A projecting ridge or rim. The wheels of a railway train are flanged so that the wheels will not come off the rails.

flank. 1. The side of an animal, close to the thigh. 2. The side or edge of an army.

flannel *(flan'-nel)*. A soft material made of wool.

flannelette *(flan-nel-ette')*. A material made of cotton which has been fluffed up to feel like wool.

flap. 1. Something broad and flat which is joined by one edge to something else, as the flap of a table. 2. The motion and noise of something broad and flat being hit lightly against something else. For example, "With a flap of his tail, the beaver slid into the water". 3. To make such a motion and noise with something flat. A flag flaps in the wind.

flare. 1. A bright light which burns for a short time. Flares are used for signalling on railways, highways, at sea, etc. 2. To spread outwards gradually. Some girls wear flared skirts. 3. To burst into a sudden blaze, as "The flame flared up, and then went out". 4. To burst into sudden anger is to flare up with anger.

flash. 1. A sudden burst of light. 2. Anything showy and vulgar is **flashy.**

flashlight *(flash'-light)*. 1. A portable, battery-powered light. 2. Any light which flashes on and off.

flask. A bottle, often one to be carried in the pocket. Vacuum flasks are bottles which keep hot liquids hot and cold liquids cold for a long time.

flat. 1. Smooth; even; level; without lumps. 2. A self-contained dwelling which forms only part of a larger building. 3. Dull; uninteresting; without variety or excitement.

flatten *(flat'-ten)*. To make level.

flatter *(flat'-ter)*.   1. To praise someone too much or insincerely.
2. To show as more attractive than it is.   For example,
"This photograph flatters John" means "This photograph
makes John look more handsome than he really is".

flavour *(fla'-vour)*.   1. The taste.   2. To put the taste into something.

flaw.   A defect or fault in something is a flaw.

flax.   A small plant, the fibres of which are spun into linen thread.
The seeds are used to make linseed oil.

flea.   A small jumping insect which lives on animals by sucking
their blood.

flee.   To run away with all one's might.

fleece.   1. The wool of a sheep.   2. To cut the wool from a
sheep.   3. To fleece someone is to cheat him into giving you
a great deal of money.

fleet.   1. A number of ships under one leader or command.   2. A
number of other things working together, such as a fleet of
aeroplanes, taxis or buses, etc.   3. To move very fast is to be
fleet.

flesh.   The soft substances, such as muscle and fat, between the
bones and the skin of animals and people.

flexible *(flex'-i-ble)*.   Easily bent or twisted without cracking or
breaking.   Rubber, for instance, is flexible.

flew.   The past tense of fly, as "A jet plane flew over my house
yesterday".

flicker *(flick'-er)*.   1. To burn or shine unsteadily.   2. A brief
flame or light.

flight.   1. A trip in an aeroplane is a flight.   2. The manner in
which flying objects move across the sky.   We speak of the
bird's flight.   3. The steps between two levels are called a
flight of steps.   4. The act of running away is called flight.

flimsy *(flim'-sy)*.   Thin and easily destroyed.

flinch.   1. To shrink from danger.   2. To make a sudden movement of the body, something like a shiver.

fling.   1. To rush out violently.   2. To throw.   3. A violent
movement.

flint.   A hard stone.   Early man used flint for arrow-heads.
When struck with steel, flint will spark.

flippant *(flip'-pant)*.   Thoughtless; quick and pert in speech.   A
person who treats serious matters lightly is flippant.

flirt.   1. To throw with a jerk.   2. To pretend to make love to.

float. 1. To stay on top of water. A cork will float when thrown into the water. 2. Any flat vehicle or car used to carry something big and heavy. Thus we speak of floats which carry big, heavy decorations in a parade.

flock. 1. A group of animals, as a flock of sheep. 2. In "The people flocked into the park to see the fireworks", flocked means went in great numbers.

flog. To beat with a stick or whip.

flood. 1. A deluge; a great amount of water that has spread over the land. 2. Almost anything in large quantities may be called a flood, as "In response to his advertisement, he received a flood of applications".

floor. 1. The bottom surface in a room. You walk on the floor. 2. The bottom of an ocean is called an ocean floor.

flop. 1. To move about in a clumsy way. A seal flops about on land. 2. To throw oneself down awkwardly.

flora *(flor'-a)*. The plants which grow naturally in a country; thus the flora of England include daisies, dandelions, birch trees, etc., but not banana trees and orange trees which belong to the flora of other countries.

floral *(flo'-ral)*. Of flowers; thus a floral wreath is a wreath of flowers.

florid *(flor'-id)*. High-coloured; rosy. A person with a florid complexion is one whose face is redder than the faces of most people.

florist *(flo'-rist)*. A person who buys, sells and grows flowers.

flotilla *(flo-til'-la)*. A small fleet of ships.

flotsam *(flot'-sam)*. Wreckage of a ship or its cargo found floating on the sea.

flounce. 1. To throw oneself about in a bad-tempered way. 2. A frill sewn to something such as a dress.

flounder *(floun'-der)*. 1. To struggle in an awkward way. You will flounder when you try to walk in deep snow. 2. To act or to speak in a confused manner. 3. A flat fish with a large mouth.

flour. A fine, soft powder made by grinding wheat or other grain.

flourish *(flour'-ish)*. 1. To thrive; get rich; grow better. 2. To wave something about, as "He flourished his stick at the boys". 3. Curls, loops and curves unnecessarily added to handwriting are flourishes.

flout. To mock; to take no notice of.

flow. To go along as water does.

flower *(flow'-er)*. The part of a plant which blooms and produces seed.

fluctuate *(fluc'-tu-ate)*. To rise and fall; to waver. Thus when the cost of things varies from day to day the price is said to fluctuate.

flue. A pipe through which smoke may escape from a fireplace, furnace, etc.

fluent *(flu'-ent)*. 1. Flowing easily, like water. 2. Speaking or writing easily and smoothly.

fluffy *(fluff'-y)*. Soft and downy. Baby chickens are fluffy.

fluid *(flu'-id)*. Anything that is liquid is a fluid.

flurry *(flur'-ry)*. A gust or squall, as a snow flurry.

flush. 1. To blush or get red in the face. 2. To wash out by a rush of water. 3. Two things are flush one with the other when they touch each other along one side.

flustered *(flus'-tered)*. Muddled and confused through being excited.

flute. A wooden musical instrument shaped like a long pipe, which is played by blowing into a hole at one end as the remaining holes along its length are fingered.

flutter *(flut'-ter)*. 1. When a bird is trapped in a room, it flutters about, trying to escape. Flutter describes the rapid movement and sound of its wings. 2. A person is said to flutter about when he moves quickly and in an excited way.

fly. 1. A winged insect, such as a house-fly. 2. To move through the air as a bird or an aeroplane. 3. To escape or get away quickly.

foal. The young of a horse or donkey.

foam. Froth; millions of bubbles in a mass.

focus *(fo'-cus)*. A point where rays of light meet.

fodder *(fod'-der)*. Dry food for cattle, etc.

foe. An enemy.

fog. A cloud of fine mist which makes it very difficult to see.

foil. 1. A light sword with a pointed tip, used in fencing. 2. A thin sheet of metal, as tin-foil or gold-foil. 3. To prevent someone from doing something.

fold. 1. To bend so as to make a double thickness. 2. To draw close to the body, as a bird folds its wings, or a person folds his arms. 3. A place in which sheep are kept.

foliage *(fo'-li-age)*. The leaves of trees and plants.

folio *(fo'-li-o)*. 1. When a large sheet of paper is doubled so that it resembles two leaves in a book, it is a folio. 2. A large book. 3. A page in a book.

folk. 1. People. 2. Referring to common people, or their customs, etc.

follow *(fol'-low)*. 1. If you walk behind another person, you follow that person. 2. When you obey instructions, you follow those instructions.

folly *(fol'-ly)*. Foolishness; something silly.

foment *(fo-ment')*. 1. To bathe with hot water in order to relieve pain. 2. To rouse or stir up, as "That man is always fomenting trouble".

fond. To be fond of anything is to like it very much.

fondle *(fon'-dle)*. To pet; to caress or pat gently.

font. 1. The stone basin in a church containing the water used for baptism. 2. A fountain or source of water.

food. A substance which is taken in by plants and animals to enable them to live and grow. What you eat is food.

fool. A silly person.

foolish *(fool'-ish)*. Silly.

foot. 1. One of the two parts of your body on which you stand, which are attached to the bottom of your legs. 2. The bottom or base of a thing is the foot. 3. Twelve inches make one foot.

football *(foot'-ball)*. 1. A large leather-covered ball. 2. The game played with such a ball.

foot-hill *(foot'-hill)*. The low hill at the base of a mountain.

foothold *(foot'-hold)*. A place where you can put your foot and so gain a footing.

foot-note *(foot'-note)*. A note printed at the bottom of a page referring to or explaining something on the page.

footprint *(foot'-print)*. A mark on the ground made by a person's shoe, boot or foot.

forage *(for'-age)*. 1. Food given to cattle, horses, etc., as hay, oats, etc. 2. To forage is to search for something.

foray *(fo'-ray)*. A raid; an attack in search of plunder.

forbear *(for-bear')*. 1. To be patient; to put up with a thing without saying or doing anything about it. 2. To hold back from doing something.

forbid *(for-bid')*. If a person forbids something, he refuses to allow it.

force. 1. Strength or power. In a storm the force of the wind may topple trees. 2. To compel. Sometimes you may not feel well but you force yourself to smile. 3. To break into or through. A criminal may force his way into a shop after it has closed for the day. 4. A group of people who are organized for some purpose, such as a police force.

ford. A place in a stream where the water is shallow enough to allow a crossing on foot.

fore. In front or near the front.

foreboding *(fore-bod'-ing)*. A feeling that something unpleasant is about to happen.

forecast *(fore'-cast)*. To say what you think is going to happen before it does happen. Most daily newspapers forecast the weather.

forecastle *(fore'-cas-tle)*. The front part of a ship.

forefathers *(fore'-fa-thers)*. Ancestors; the generations of people in your family who lived before you.

forego *(fore-go')*. 1. To go before. 2. To do without.

forehead *(fore'-head)*. The front of the head above the eyes.

foreign *(for'-eign)*. Belonging to another country.

foreland *(fore'-land)*. A piece of high ground reaching out into the sea.

foreman *(fore'-man)*. A man in charge of other men, or a man in charge of a department.

foremost *(fore'-most)*. Most important.

foreshore *(fore'-shore)*. The beach between high-tide and low-tide marks.

foresight *(fore'-sight)*. 1. The ability to see what is likely to happen before it does. 2. The sight on the muzzle of a gun.

forest *(for'-est)*. A large number of trees growing close together; a thick, large wood.

forestall *(fore-stall')*. To do something before another person does it and thus get the better of him.

forfeit *(for'-feit)*. To give up or to do without through some fault of your own.

forge. 1. The workshop where a blacksmith melts and shapes metal. 2. To shape metal by first heating it and then hammering it. 3. To forge ahead is to go strongly ahead of others. 4. To make or imitate falsely; to counterfeit (see **forgery**).

forgery *(for'-ger-y)*. The crime of imitating something and pretending it is real; thus, a person who imitates a signature on a cheque or on a document commits a forgery, and he is a **forger.**

forget *(for-get')*. When you forget something, you do not remember it.

forgive *(for-give')*. To pardon or excuse is to forgive.

forgo *(for-go')*. To go without. Also spelled **forego.**

fork. 1. An instrument with a handle and two or more pointed tines of metal or wood which is used for cooking and eating. A larger size is used for digging. 2. The place where a river, road or path divides into two or more directions.

forlorn *(for-lorn')*. Miserable; wretched; deserted.

form. 1. A shape, such as a square or triangle, or a mould. The shape of anything is its form. 2. A class at school. 3. In "The team's form has improved", form means style. 4. In "It is good form for a man to raise his hat to a lady", form means manners. 5. A form is also a rule that it is customary to follow or a customary way of acting. The forms of address are the rules for addressing people. 6. In "He completed his income tax form", form means an official paper.

formal *(for'-mal)*. Done according to form, that is, to rules or conventions. When a person attends a formal dinner he must dress and behave according to certain rules.

former *(form'-er)*. The first of two things.

formidable *(for'-mi-da-ble)*. Causing fear or alarm. Likely to be difficult to deal with, as "They knew that it would be a most formidable task to rescue the shipwrecked sailors in the teeth of the gale".

formula *(for'-mu-la)*. 1. A formula for a bottle of medicine or a chemical solution is a list of all the different things, with their quantities, that have to be put together to make it. 2. A formula for a chemical is the combination of letters and figures that stand for a chemical; thus H_2O is the formula for water. 3. A formula in arithmetic is an expression which helps to solve a problem; $A = l \times b$ is a formula for finding area.

forsake *(for-sake')*. To leave; to give up.

fort. A strong building built or converted for defence.

forth. Out. In "He went forth", forth means out.

forthwith *(forth-with')*. Without delay; immediately.

fortify *(for'-ti-fy)*. To make strong. A person can fortify himself against the cold and an army can fortify a town against an enemy.

fortitude *(for'-ti-tude)*. Courage in the face of danger or trouble.

fortnight *(fort'-night)*. A period of two weeks.

fortress *(for'-tress)*. A strong place; a fortified place.

fortunately *(for'-tu-nate-ly)*. Luckily.

fortune *(for'-tune)*. 1. The wealth a person has. 2. The luck, good or bad, a person has.

forty *(for'-ty)*. A number ten more than thirty or four times ten.

forward *(for'-ward)*. 1. Towards the front. To go forward is to advance. 2. In front of others. To be forward is to be in front of others in position or in achievement.

fossil *(fos'-sil)*. The remains of a plant or animal that have turned very hard as a result of being buried in the ground for centuries.

foster *(fos'-ter)*. 1. To nurse; rear; bring up. 2. A foster-mother is a woman who brings up some other person's child. 3. To foster also means to help or encourage.

fought. The past tense of fight. "Yesterday he fought with John and to-day he fights with Jim."

foul. 1. To make dirty. 2. Dirty or very unpleasant, as "Rotten eggs have a foul odour". 3. Unfair. 4. In "His foul action surprised us all", foul means wicked. 5. In "the foul weather", foul means bad or nasty. 6. An act committed contrary to the rule of some game.

found. 1. Past tense of find. 2. To establish or build. In "The company was founded forty years ago", founded means started or established.

foundation *(foun-da'-tion)*. The support or base of something. The foundation of a building is built first and it supports the upper storeys.

founder *(foun'-der)*. 1. To fill with water and sink. 2. The person who founds or begins a business.

foundry *(found'-ry)*. A workshop where metal is melted and cast into shapes.

fountain *(foun'-tain)*. 1. A stream of water which shoots into the air. 2. A drinking fountain is a device at which one can obtain a drink of water.

four. The number between three and five.

fourteen *(four'-teen)*. The number which is four more than ten.

fourth. Last in a group of four.

fowl. 1. A bird. 2. A domestic cock or hen.

fox. A wild animal which is much like a dog in appearance.

fraction *(frac'-tion)*. 1. When a thing is divided into a certain number of equal parts, each part is a fraction. 2. A small piece or scrap.

fracture *(frac'-ture)*. 1. To break. 2. A break.

fragile *(frag'-ile)*. Delicate; weak; easily broken.

fragment *(frag'-ment)*. A piece of something; a piece broken off the whole thing.

fragrant *(fra'-grant)*. Having a sweet odour. The sweet odour is called **fragrance.**

frail. Weak, as "the frail old lady".

frame. 1. To form or shape. 2. To plan. 3. The edging around a picture or a window. 4. The internal structure which gives strength to a piece of furniture, a machine, an animal's body, etc.

framework *(frame'-work)*. A structure made up of component parts fastened together, as the steel framework round which a modern building is erected.

franchise *(fran'-chise)*. The right to vote at an election.

frank. A person is frank who says what he thinks.

frankincense *(frank'-in-cense)*. A gum which is burned to give off a sweet odour. Frankincense is resin from certain Asiatic and African trees.

frantic *(fran'-tic)*. Very excited; wild with rage, pain, etc.

fraternal *(fra-ter'-nal)*. Brotherly.

fraternize *(frat'-er-nize)*. To act together like brothers; to be good friends.

fraud. Any form of cheating is a fraud and so is the person who does the cheating. A dishonest action is **fraudulent.**

fraught. Filled with, as "When they saw the rapids they knew their journey down the river would be fraught with danger".

fray. 1. A quarrel in which there is fighting. 2. To wear out by rubbing.

freak. 1. Something of unnatural shape. 2. An odd thing.

freckle *(freck'-le)*. A brownish mark on the skin, usually found on the skin of a fair-haired person.

free. 1. Not costing anything. 2. In "He is now free from infection", free from means cleared of. 3. To set at liberty, as

"He freed the bird that lived in a cage".   4. In "He freed the pipes and then the water flowed through them", freed means cleared or unclogged.

freedom *(free'-dom)*.   State of being free or having liberty.

freeze.   1. To turn into ice.   2. When you freeze in a position, you remain perfectly still.

freight.   1. Goods carried in a train or ship.   2. The cost of such carriage.

French.   Of France or its people and customs.

frenzy *(fren'-zy)*.   A state of mad violence.

frequent.   1. *(fre'-quent)*.   Happening often.   2. *(fre-quent')* To go often to a place.

fresh.   1. New; not stale.   2. Fresh butter is unsalted butter.   3. A fresh complexion is one that is clear and healthy.

fret.   To worry; to be vexed.

friar *(fri'ar)*.   A monk. Usually a member of one of the orders of monks who are not confined to monasteries.

friction *(fric'-tion)*.   1. A rubbing together of things that causes them to wear out, or to get hot.   2. Disagreement or petty squabbling; quarrelling.

Friday *(Fri'-day)*.   The sixth day of the week.

friend.   A person with whom you associate because you and he like each other.

friendship *(friend'-ship)*.   The friendly feeling which exists between or among friends.

fright.   When you become afraid suddenly you suffer a fright.

frighten *(fright'-en)*.   If you frighten someone, you scare him.

frigid *(fri'-gid)*.   1. Stiff with cold.   2. A person is frigid who does not want to be friendly and who is quiet and keeps to himself.   3. The Frigid Zone is one of two areas on the earth's surface. The North Frigid Zone is the area around the North Pole, north of the Arctic Circle. The South Frigid Zone is the area around the South Pole, south of the Antarctic Circle.

frill.   The fancy edging to something, as a dress.

frisk.   To hop or leap about playfully.

frivolous *(friv'-o-lous)*.   Silly; not serious.

frock.   1. A loose outer coat.   2. A dress or gown.

frog.   1. A small, four-legged, jumping animal, usually green in colour, that lives near water.   2. A decorative fastening on a coat.

frolic *(frol'-ic)*. 1. To play noisily. 2. Merry-making. To be **frolicsome** is to be full of playfulness.

frontier *(fron-tier')*. 1. The line that marks the edge of a country; the place where two countries meet. 2. The edge of a settled area bordering on the wilderness.

frontispiece *(fron'-tis-piece)*. A picture placed at the front of a book to face the page with the title.

frost. 1. A temperature below the freezing point of water. 2. Frozen dew or moisture which may kill plants.

froth. Foam on liquids caused by boiling, stirring or shaking.

frown. To show anger or to show deep thought by creasing the forehead and lowering the eyebrows.

frowzy *(frowz'-y)*. Untidy; dirty; not properly clean.

frozen *(fro'-zen)*. When water turns to ice, the water has become so cold that it has frozen.

frugal *(fru'-gal)*. Careful and economical; a frugal person spends as little as possible.

fruit. 1. Seeds, or the part of a tree or plant which contains the seeds. Some fruits are good to eat. 2. Result; product.

fruitless *(fruit'-less)*. 1. Without fruit. 2. Useless, as "He went on a fruitless errand".

frustrate *(frus'-trate)*. To defeat; to cause to come to nothing; to stop the plans of.

fry. 1. To cook food in fat. 2. Tiny young fish.

fuel *(fu'-el)*. Material, as coke, coal, wood, oil, etc., which is burned to supply power or heat.

fugitive *(fu'-gi-tive)*. Any person or thing that flees.

fulcrum *(ful'-crum)*. The point at which a lever is supported. A see-saw is a kind of lever, and the fulcrum is the support placed under the middle of the plank.

fulfil *(ful-fil')*. To do something completely; to carry out.

full. 1. Complete, as in "a full moon". 2. When you pour water into a cup until it can hold no more, it is full.

fumble *(fum'-ble)*. To handle things in an awkward, clumsy way.

fumigate *(fu'-mi-gate)*. To disinfect things with chemical fumes or smoke.

fun. Amusement.

fund. 1. A sum of money. 2. An amount of anything, such as a fund of information, meaning a great deal of information.

funeral *(fu'-ner-al)*. The ceremony held when a body is buried.

fungus *(fun'-gus)*. A plant which has no flowers, leaves, or green colour, such as the mushroom or toadstool. **fungi** is the plural of fungus.

funnel *(fun'-nel)*. 1. A cone-shaped device with a pipe attached to the small end. A funnel is used for transferring a liquid or a powder from one container into another with a smaller opening. 2. The funnel of a ship is the column through which the smoke from the engines escapes. 3. To pour a liquid from one container into another which has a smaller opening.

funny *(fun'-ny)*. Amusing.

fur. The hairy coat of an animal.

furious *(ju'-ri-ous)*. Angry; violent; fierce.

furl. To roll up.

furlough *(fur'-lough)*. Leave of absence given to a soldier, or to someone working in a foreign country.

furnace *(fur'-nace)*. An enclosed chamber which contains fire.

furnish *(fur'-nish)*. 1. To furnish a home is to obtain the furniture needed for it and to arrange it in the rooms. 2. To furnish also means to provide, equip or supply; thus "Boys applying for the post must furnish a character reference from their teachers".

furniture *(fur'-ni-ture)*. All the things needed in a house to make it comfortable, such as tables, chairs, bedsteads, bookcases, etc.

furrier *(fur'-ri-er)*. A dealer or worker in furs.

furrow *(fur'-row)*. 1. A trench in a field made by a plough during ploughing. 2. A wrinkle on the face.

furry *(fur'-ry)*. Appearing like or feeling like fur; covered with fur.

further *(fur'-ther)*. 1. In "He went further than you", further means a longer distance. 2. In "He furthered my application", furthered means helped.

furtive *(fur'-tive)*. Sly.

fury *(fu'-ry)*. Rage; great anger.

furze. A prickly evergreen shrub with yellow flowers; gorse.

fuse. 1. To melt when heated. 2. The fuse in an electric meter is a soft piece of metal which will melt before the wires on either side of it can become red hot. 3. The mechanism for exploding shells and mines. 4. To unite or blend.

fuselage *(fu'-se-lage).* The body of an aeroplane, or the part which holds the crew, the passengers and the cargo.

fuss. 1. To make a bother about something. 2. Unnecessary and confused activity.

fussy *(fuss'-y).* A fussy person is one who must have everything done according to his liking or he is very much put out.

futile *(fu'-tile).* Useless.

future *(fu'-ture).* The time that has not yet come.

fuzzy *(fuzz'-y).* 1. If a boy has a very short haircut, his head feels fuzzy. 2. Something which is not clear is fuzzy, such as the appearance of a light in a fog.

G

gabble *(gab'-ble).* To talk so quickly that the words are not properly pronounced.

gable *(ga'-ble).* The triangular end of a house formed by the roof.

gadabout *(gad'-a-bout).* A person who is always out and about looking for amusement.

gag. 1. Something placed between the teeth to keep the mouth open, or to stop the person from talking. 2. A joke.

gaiety *(gai'-e-ty).* Merriment.

gain. 1. To obtain, as "He gained his object". 2. To profit, as "He gained a shilling when he sold for two shillings a pen for which he had paid one shilling". 3. To win, as "The British soldiers gained the day". 4. To reach, as "The ship-wrecked sailors gained the land".

gainsay *(gain-say').* To contradict or deny.

gait. The way a person walks.

gaiter *(gai'-ter).* A covering for the ankle or lower leg. Soldiers often wear gaiters.

gala *(ga'-la).* A festive show made attractive by the use of flags, streamers, etc., as decorations.

gale. A strong wind.

gallant *(gal'-lant).* 1. Grand; stately, as "a gallant ship". 2. Noble; brave, as a "a gallant knight". 3. A gallant man is one who is polite and attentive to women.

gallery *(gal'-le-ry)*.   1. An upper floor or hall, so arranged that a person in the gallery can look down into the main part of the hall.   2. A place where pictures are on show, such as the National Gallery.

galley *(gal'-ley)*.   1. A large boat needing several pairs of oars to drive it through the water.   In olden times, each oar was worked by four or more slaves, who had to pull with all their might.   To-day, people say they worked like galley-slaves when they want to say they worked very hard.   2. A place where cooking is done aboard ship.   3. A flat tray in which printers set up type.

gallon *(gal'-lon)*.   A liquid measure equal to four quarts.

gallop *(gal'-lop)*.   1. The fastest pace of a horse or other four-legged animal.   2. To run at a gallop.

gallows *(gal'-lows)*.   A vertical wooden frame with a crosspiece, on which criminals are hanged.

galore *(ga-lore')*.   In plenty; thus, "It was a good harvest and we picked apples galore".

galoshes *(ga-losh'-es)*.   Rubber shoes to slip over ordinary shoes in wet weather.

gamble *(gam'-ble)*.   1. To play games that depend largely or wholly on luck and bet money on the outcome.   2. To take unnecessary risks, as "He crossed the road reading a book. If ever anyone gambled with his life, he did".

gambol *(gam'-bol)*.   To run and skip about playfully.

game.   1. A contest of strength, knowledge, skill, or all three. Football is a game.   2. Wild animals or birds which men hunt are called game.

gander *(gan'-der)*.   The male goose.

gang.   1. A number of people working together.   2. A group of rowdy people.

gangster *(gang'-ster)*.   A man belonging to a gang of robbers, thieves or murderers.

gangway *(gang'-way)*.   1. A passage-way formed by planks with a hand-rail on either side.   People boarding a vessel do so by using a gangway.   2. Any passageway.

gaol.   (Often spelled **jail.**)   A prison.   A member of the prison staff who watches over the prisoners is a **gaoler,** or **jailer**.

gap.   A space or opening.   It may be a gap between two floorboards or a gap between two mountains.

gape. To open the mouth wide; to yawn.   To stare in wonder.

garage *(ga'-rage)*.   A place where motor-cars are housed, or where they are serviced.

garb. 1. The way in which a person is dressed.   2. The outward appearance of something.

garden *(gar'-den)*.   The plot of ground in which flowers and vegetables are grown.

gargle *(gar'-gle)*.   1. An antiseptic liquid used for washing the mouth or throat.   2. To gargle is to employ such a wash, moving it about in the mouth or throat with a gurgling sound.

gargoyle *(gar'-goyle)*.   An ornamental spout by which rain-water from the roof of a building is thrown clear of the walls.

garland *(gar'-land)*.   A wreath of flowers and foliage, usually for wearing on the head.

garment *(gar'-ment)*.   Any piece of clothing, as a skirt or vest.

garner *(gar'-ner)*.   1. A storehouse for corn; a granary.   2. To gather in the harvest into the store.

garnish *(gar'-nish)*.   1. To decorate something.   2. Something used to decorate with.

garret *(gar'-ret)*.   The space or the room just under the roof of a house.

garrison *(gar'-ri-son)*.   1. A building in which soldiers live.   2. The troops occupying such a building.

garrulous *(gar'-ru-lous)*.   Said of a person who is everlastingly talking in a noisy way.

garter *(gar'-ter)*.   An elastic band used to keep a stocking up.

gas. A substance which is neither liquid nor solid.   At times, doctors use a kind of gas to put people to sleep before operating on them.   Some kinds of gas are used as fuel.

gash. A long deep cut.

gasometer *(gas-om'-e-ter)*.   A large, round tank in which gas is stored at the gas-works.

gasp. To open the mouth wide and catch the breath.

gate. 1. An opening in a wall or fence with a movable barrier for closing it.   2. The barrier itself.   3. The number of people attending an open-air sporting event.

gather *(gath'-er)*.   1. To collect and put together.   2. To arrange in folds, as when a dress is gathered.

gathering *(gath'-er-ing)*. Many people who have come together, as "A large gathering waited at the church to welcome the bride".

gaudy *(gaud'-y)*. Showy; coloured with bright colours which do not go well together.

gauge. 1. To measure or estimate. 2. An instrument for measuring, as a rain gauge. 3. The width between two railway tracks.

gaunt. Lean; thin; bony; in a starved state.

gauntlet *(gaunt'-let)*. The long glove with steel plates worn by mediæval knights. Nowadays, any long, protective glove.

gauze. A very thin material in which the mesh is easily seen. Cotton gauze is used by doctors to dress wounds; wire gauze is used when doing scientific experiments.

gay. Happy; brightly-coloured.

gaze. To look steadily at something for a while.

gazelle *(ga-zelle')*. A kind of small, swift antelope.

gazette *(gaz-ette')*. 1. A newspaper. 2. To publish in a gazette. Thus, appointments made by the Crown are published in the *London Gazette* and the people appointed are then said to be **gazetted.**

gazetteer *(gaz-et-teer')*. A geographical dictionary.

gear. 1. A set of tools, etc., needed for doing a special job. 2. A set of toothed wheels which fit into each other. The gear wheels of a bicycle are a good example of this.

geese. More than one goose.

gelatine *(gel'-a-tine)*. Animal jelly; a gluey substance which is extracted by boiling the bones and other waste parts of animals. Also spelled **gelatin.**

gem. A precious stone. A diamond is a gem.

gender *(gen'-der)*. In grammar the sex (masculine, feminine or neuter) of a noun or pronoun. The noun actor is masculine gender; the noun actress is feminine gender. Gender is far less important in English than in many other languages.

general *(gen'-er-al)*. 1. What is ordinary or usual is general; thus "As a general rule, he goes to bed at ten". 2. A general is one of the highest officers in the Army.

generate *(gen'-er-ate)*. To produce; to make.

generation *(gen-er-a'-tion)*. 1. In "The people living in Queen Victoria's generation", generation means times. 2. Generation also refers to a whole group of people born at about the same

G

time. 3. Generation also means the making of, as the generation of heat and the generation of electricity.

generator *(gen'-er-a-tor)*. A machine used to produce heat, electricity, etc.

generous *(gen'-er-ous)*. Ready to give things away; unselfish; not mean and stingy.

genesis *(gen'-e-sis)*. The very beginning of a thing. The Bible begins with the Book of Genesis.

genial *(gen'-ial)*. Kindly and pleasant.

genius *(gen'-ius)*. A person who is outstandingly clever or intelligent; thus Mozart was a genius.

genteel *(gen-teel')*. Polite; well-mannered.

gentile *(gen'-tile)*. In the Bible, the Gentiles were the people who were not Jewish.

gentle *(gen'-tle)*. 1. A gentle person is one who is good, kind, mild and courteous. 2. A gentle wind is a soft, slight wind.

gentleman *(gen'-tle-man)*. A man who has been well educated and who has good manners. A **gentlewoman** has the same good qualities.

genuine *(gen'-u-ine)*. Real; not an imitation.

genus *(ge'-nus)*. A class of things; all the things of one kind. Thus a cat belongs to the genus of mammals.

geography *(ge-og'-ra-phy)*. The science which deals with the things on the earth's surface, as mountains, seas, countries, towns, etc.

geology *(ge-ol'-o-gy)*. The science which deals with the history and development of the earth's crust.

geometry *(ge-om'-e-try)*. The science that deals with the nature and measurements of lines, angles, surfaces, solids, etc., and with their relationships.

geranium *(ge-ra'-ni-um)*. A plant with clusters of bright-red flowers and sweet-smelling leaves.

germ. 1. A living thing so small that it cannot be seen with the naked eye. Many, but by no means all, are harmful. 2. The very beginning of a thing is often said to be the germ of it.

germicide *(ger'-mi-cide)*. A substance that is useful for killing harmful germs, such as tincture of iodine.

germinate *(ger'-min-ate)*. To sprout and send out shoots, as a seed does when it first begins to grow.

gesticulate *(ges-tic'-u-late)*. To wave your hands and arms about. Usually, the idea is to attract attention in order to express your views.

gesture *(ges'-ture)*. 1. A sign given by movements of the hands. 2. A friendly action, as "When they said we could have free use of their playing-field we thought it a very pleasant gesture".

get. 1. To obtain, as when you go to the shop to get a loaf of bread. 2. To catch, as when you get a cold. 3. To receive, as when you get permission to do something. 4. To become, as when you get lost.

geyser *(gey'-ser)*. A spring which sends hot water up out of the earth.

ghastly *(ghast'-ly)*. Dreadful; fearful.

ghost. The spirit of a dead person that is supposed to appear after death.

ghostly *(ghost'-ly)*. Like a ghost.

giant *(gi'-ant)*. Anything or any person that is huge or of great size.

gibe. 1. To sneer. 2. A sneer; a taunt.

gift. 1. When you give something to someone, you are making a gift. 2. A great talent, such as a gift for music.

gifted *(gift'-ed)*. A gifted person is one who is very clever, who has great ability.

gigantic *(gi-gan'-tic)*. Of great size.

giggle *(gig'-gle)*. To laugh in a silly sort of way.

gild. To cover with a thin coating of gold.

gill. 1. The breathing organ used by fish and other animals that live in water. 2. A measure of liquid, equal to a quarter of a pint.

gimlet *(gim'-let)*. A tool with a sharp tip and a twisted stem, used for boring holes in wood, etc.

gin. 1. A machine that separates cotton seed husks from the cotton. 2. A liquor or drink. 3. A snare or trap.

ginger *(gin'-ger)*. The root of a plant growing in hot countries, used as a flavouring and as spice. It gives the warm taste to ginger-beer, ginger cake, etc.

gingerbread *(gin'-ger-bread)*. A cake or biscuit flavoured with ginger and treacle.

gingerly *(gin'-ger-ly)*. Cautiously.

gingham *(ging'-ham)*. A cotton cloth, usually with a woven striped or checked pattern.

giraffe *(gi-raffe')*. A spotted animal with a very long neck and four thin legs. The giraffe is an African animal.

girder *(gird'-er)*. A beam of wood or a long bar of steel or iron, used in constructing the framework of houses and other buildings.

girdle *(gir'-dle)*. A belt or garment used to enclose or encircle.

girth. 1. The all-round measurement of something. The girth of a man is his waist measurement. 2. Girth is also the band that goes round a horse to hold the saddle in place.

gist. The chief points; thus, the gist of a talk is what the speaker said, put in a few words with all the unnecessary words left out.

gizzard *(giz'-zard)*. The part of a bird's stomach which contains stones to help in the digestion of food.

glacier *(gla'-ci-er)*. A river of ice.

glade. An open space in a wood or forest.

gladiolus *(glad-i-o'-lus)*. A plant with bright flowers and spiked leaves which belongs to the iris family.

glamour *(glam'-our)*. A magic spell, but the word has grown to mean dazzling beauty or charm.

glance. 1. A quick look. 2. To strike and glide off an object; to graze.

gland. An organ in the body which secretes or lets out certain substances. You will be familiar with sweat glands.

glare. 1. Light so bright as to be dazzling, as "The glare of the sun on the wind-screen almost blinded the motorist". 2. To stare fiercely.

glaring *(glar'-ing)*. Staring in an angry way.

glaze. 1. To make glossy. 2. Some substance used for making things glossy. 3. To glaze a window is to fit panes of glass to it. A man whose work it is to do this is a **glazier** *(gla'-zier)*.

gleam. 1. A small beam of light. 2. To shine.

glean. To gather little by little. Glean was first used to mean the gathering of the grain left after the reapers had finished the field.

glee. 1. Joy; happiness. 2. A part-song, sung by several people who sing different parts.

glen. A narrow valley.

glib. A person is glib who talks in a smooth, easy manner, but not sincerely.

glide. 1. To move along smoothly. 2. To fly in a glider. (See **glider.**)

glider *(glid'-er).* An engineless aeroplane that moves by the aid of wind.

gliding *(glid'-ing).* Moving along smoothly.

glimmer *(glim'-mer).* 1. To shine faintly, or off and on. 2. A feeble light.

glimpse. A quick, hasty glance or look.

glisten *(glis'-ten).* To shine.

glitter *(glit'-ter).* To sparkle.

gloaming *(gloam'-ing).* Dusk; twilight.

gloat. To stare at or think about with pleasure, as "The greedy old man gloated over his money".

globe. A ball; a sphere; a round body; the earth.

gloomy *(gloom'-y).* 1. A gloomy person is one who is miserable. 2. Gloomy weather is dark and cloudy. 3. A gloomy outlook is one that offers little hope.

glorious *(glo'-ri-ous).* 1. Magnificent; honourable.

glory *(glo'-ry).* 1. In "She glories in playing with the baby", glories means revels or rejoices. 2. In "He covered himself with glory", glory means honour. 3. In "The glory of the morning suddenly ended in a fierce storm", glory means brightness or splendour.

glossary *(gloss'-a-ry).* A list of words that require special explanation; usually found at the end of a book.

glossy *(gloss'-y).* Smooth and shiny.

glove. A covering for the hand, usually having a separate sheath for each finger.

glow. 1. The light made by something that is red hot, such as a cinder in the fire. 2. A bright reddish colour, as "The glow on her cheeks".

glower *(glow'-er).* To scowl.

glucose *(glu'-cose).* A form of sugar.

glue. A material used for sticking things together. It is made by boiling the skins and hooves of animals to a jelly.

glum. Dismal; gloomy.

glut. 1. More of a thing than can be used or more than is needed. A glut of herrings means more herrings than people want to buy. 2. To eat too much.

glutton *(glut'-ton)*. A person who eats more than is good for him.

gnarled. Said of trees which are twisted and bent in the trunk and branches.

gnash. To strike the teeth together in anger.

gnat. A small winged insect often found in marshy districts. The female lives on the blood of animals.

gnaw. To bite away bit by bit.

goad. 1. To force a person or animal into action. 2. A stick with a sharp point, used for driving animals.

goal. 1. The place where players of hockey, soccer, etc. try to place the ball in order to score. The goal-keeper tries to prevent players from scoring, or placing the ball in the goal. 2. A goal is also an object or aim in life which a person has, as "His goal in life was to be a famous musician".

goat. A horned, stiff-haired, four-legged animal something like a sheep.

gobble *(gob'-ble)*. 1. To eat quickly and greedily. 2. The noise made by a turkey-cock.

goblet *(gob'-let)*. A kind of drinking glass.

goblin *(gob'-lin)*. A mischievous elf.

God. The creator and ruler of all existing things, according to religious belief.

god. A person or thing which is worshipped.

goddess *(god'-dess)*. A female god.

godly *(god'-ly)*. Righteous; devout; religious.

godsend *(god'-send)*. A gift that comes as a very welcome surprise.

goggle *(gog'-gle)*. To roll the eyes.

goggles *(gog'-gles)*. Spectacles for motor-cyclists, etc., used as a protection against the wind.

gold. A shiny, yellow precious metal which is used to make coins and ornaments.

golden *(gold'-en)*. Anything which is gold, contains gold or is the colour of gold, is golden.

goldfinch *(gold'-finch)*. A small, yellow songbird.

golf. A game played by striking a small ball with one of a number of club-shaped sticks. Players try to use the fewest possible strokes to hit the ball into nine or eighteen small holes in different places on a piece of land called a golf course.

gondola *(gon'-do-la)*. A boat used on the canals of Venice, propelled by one oar at the stern.

gong. A saucer-shaped bell.

good-bye *(good-bye')*. Farewell.

goods. Possessions; things; wares. All the articles for sale in a store are goods. Your personal belongings are goods.

goose. A web-footed water bird which is larger than a duck but has the same shape.

gore. 1. To injure with horns or tusks, as "The bull tossed the man and then gored him". 2. Gore means blood, as "The battle-field was covered with gore".

gorge. 1. A narrow gap in the land between high mountains. 2. To eat greedily in a coarse way.

gorgeous *(gor'-geous)*. Magnificent; brilliantly coloured; splendid.

gorilla *(go-ril'-la)*. A large, man-like ape.

gosling *(gos'-ling)*. A young goose.

gospel *(gos'-pel)*. 1. That portion of the Bible which gives the history of Jesus Christ. 2. Gospel means good news. 3. People often say "That is the gospel truth"; gospel then means real.

gossamer *(gos'-sa-mer)*. The fine threads that make a cobweb; any thin material.

gossip *(gos'-sip)*. 1. Silly talk about other people's business. 2. A gossip is a person who talks in this way.

Gothic *(Goth'-ic)*. A style of building, marked by pointed windows, doorways and arches.

gouge. 1. A chisel with a hollow blade for cutting grooves. 2. To scoop out.

gourmand *(gour'-mand)*. 1. A person who is so fond of his food that he thinks too much about eating and is greedy. 2. See **gourmet**.

gourmet *(gour'-met)*. A person who is an expert at choosing good things to eat and drink.

govern *(gov'-ern)*. 1. To rule; to direct. 2. To hold in check or to restrain. **government** means the group of people who direct the affairs of a community. There are city governments, provincial governments, national governments, etc. A **governor** is a person elected or appointed to rule, represent a ruler, or direct. A **governess** is a woman teacher, or a woman in charge of little children.

gown. 1. A woman's dress. 2. A loose outer garment worn on certain occasions by certain people. A judge wears a gown in court.

grace. 1. A prayer of thanks offered before eating. 2. Charm or beauty, especially of form or movement, as "The man diving from the high board moves through the air with grace". 3. God's favour for all men is called grace. 4. You are allowed two or three days of grace for paying some bills, which means that you have an extra day or so in which to pay.

graceful *(grace'-ful)*. A graceful person is one who is neat and who moves about easily and without fuss; not clumsy.

gracious *(gra'-cious)*. Kindly and charming.

grade. 1. A step or degree in rank or quality. 2. To sort things into groups according to quality.

gradually *(grad'-u-al-ly)*. Happening little by little; not all at once.

graduate *(grad'-u-ate)*. 1. A person who has successfully completed a course at a university. 2. To receive a degree or certificate, from a university college, which shows that you have successfully completed your studies there.

grain. 1. The seeds of such plants as wheat, barley, oats, etc. 2. A very small bit of something, such as a grain of sand. 3. A measure of weight. There are 7,000 grains in a pound. 4. The markings in wood.

grammar *(gram'-mar)*. The science dealing with the forms and classifications of words and their uses in sentences.

granary *(gran'-a-ry)*. A place where grain is kept.

grand. Splendid; imposing; lofty; dignified.

grandeur *(gran'-deur)*. Splendour; magnificence.

grandfather *(grand'-fa-ther)*. Your father's father and your mother's father are your grandfathers.

grandmother *(grand'-mother)*. Your father's mother and your mother's mother are your grandmothers.

grandstand *(grand'-stand)*. The structure on which people sit at an athletic field, race-course, etc.

granite *(gran'-ite)*. A hard stone, often reddish or bluish, used in building and road making.

granivorous *(gran-iv'-o-rous)*. Living chiefly on grain or seeds.

grant. 1. To give; to allow. 2. The thing given.

granulated *(gran'-u-lat-ed)*. Made into grains. Sugar is often granulated.

grape. A small, round, sweet fruit which grows in bunches on vines.

grape-fruit *(grape'-fruit)*. A round, yellow citrus fruit which grows in warm climates.

graph. A chart which shows changes or growth.

graphic *(graph'-ic)*. Graphic means pictorial and refers to anything explained by means of pictures. But if a thing is so well described that the listener can almost picture the events in his mind's eye, the description is said to be a graphic description.

grapple *(grap'-ple)*. 1. To seize hold. 2. To fight to keep the hold. 3. A grappling iron is a kind of anchor with several hooks at the end which catch on rocks, etc., when let down in the sea, or on enemy ships in wartime.

grasp. 1. To catch at something. 2. To seize and hold by gripping with the hands. 3. To understand.

grasping *(grasp'-ing)*. Greedy; said of a person who wants all he can get.

grasshopper *(grass'-hop-per)*. A jumping insect with strong legs and wings.

grate. 1. The place where a fire is lit; a fireplace. 2. To rub a thing so as to wear it into small pieces. 3. To make a harsh sound. 4. To have an annoying effect on, as "Whenever he does that, it grates on my nerves".

grateful *(grate'-ful)*. Thankful for something.

gratify *(grat'-i-fy)*. To please; to satisfy.

gratis *(gra'-tis)*. A thing is gratis when it is given to you for nothing. Without payment.

gratitude *(grat'-i-tude)*. Thankfulness.

grave. 1. A hole in the ground in which a corpse is buried. 2. Serious, as "The announcement of the declaration of war was grave news".

gravel *(grav'-el)*. Sand mixed with small stones.

graveyard *(grave'-yard)*. A cemetery; a place for burying the dead.

gravity *(grav'-i-ty)*. 1. A force that draws or pulls objects towards the centre of the earth. Thus, if you throw a stone up in the air, it will always fall back, because the force of gravity pulls it towards the earth. The sun, the moon and other heavenly bodies all exert this force. 2. Weight. It is on account of the existence of the force of gravity that objects have weight. 3. Seriousness, as "When the boy broke the desk, the headmaster explained the gravity of his action to him".

gravy *(gra'-vy)*. A sauce which is made from the juice of meat.

graze. 1. To feed on grass. 2. To rub the skin off, as "The boy stumbled and grazed his knee". 3. To touch slightly when passing, as "The side of the bus grazed the shoulder of a man who was standing too close to the kerb".

grease. An oily substance; fat.

great. Large; important; very good.

greedy *(greed'-y)*. Grasping; selfish; never satisfied but always wanting more.

greet. To salute or hail someone, as when you say to a person, "Good morning, how do you do?"

grenadier *(gren-a-dier')*. A soldier of former days who was trained to fight with grenades. The name is retained as the title of the first regiment of foot guards, the Grenadier Guards.

griddle *(grid'-dle)*. A hot metal frame of parallel bars on which cooking is done.

grievance *(griev'-ance)*. Anything that causes grief. A person with a grievance is one who feels he has been wronged.

grievous *(griev'-ous)*. A thing is grievous when it is hard to bear.

grill. To cook.

grim. Harsh; stern; fierce.

grimace *(gri-mace')*. An ugly look made by pulling the face out of shape. Grimaces are made by people who want to be funny, impudent, or who are showing some special feeling, as pain.

grime. Dirt. **grimy** means dirty.

grin. A smile that shows the teeth.

grind. 1. To make into a powder by rubbing or rolling. 2. To sharpen by rubbing. 3. In "He loved to grind the poor", grind means crush or make it hard for.

grinder *(grin'-der)*. A machine used to grind something.

grip. To hold a thing tightly.

grisly *(gris'-ly)*. Ghastly; dreadful; horrible.

gristle *(gris'-tle)*. The tough, elastic part of meat, which is difficult to chew.

grit. 1. Very fine sand, as "When walking along the beach, I worked some grit into my shoe". 2. Pluck, as "That boy won't be beaten; he has a great deal of grit".

grizzly *(griz'-zly)*. 1. Greyish, as "The old man has a grizzly beard". 2. A grizzly bear is a large, fierce, grey or brownish-grey bear.

groan. A noise made by a person in pain. It is usually a low-pitched sound and rather long.

grocer *(gro'-cer)*. A man who sells food and supplies known as **groceries.**

groove. A furrow or long hollow; thus the wheels of a cart on a muddy road make grooves; a chisel drawn along a piece of wood makes a groove.

grope. To feel your way about with your hands.

gross. 1. A dozen dozen, or 144. 2. A person is gross who is too fat and coarse featured. 3. A person has gross manners when he is vulgar. 4. Gross receipts are the takings of a business before subtracting the expenses of running the business. When these expenses are deducted, the net receipts are found.

grotesque *(gro-tesque')*. Anything which has an odd or un-natural appearance is grotesque.

grotto *(grot'-to)*. A cave or cavern. A room made to look like a cave, decorated with shells, etc.

ground. 1. The soil or earth. The land around your house is the **grounds** of your house. 2. The past tense of **grind.** 3. A reason for believing something.

group. A number of persons or things.

grouse. 1. A kind of game bird. 2. To complain or grumble.

grove. A small orchard or cluster of trees.

grovel *(grov'-el)*. To crawl on the ground in fear or as a mark of respect for somebody, in the way a disobedient dog does when his master scolds him.

grow. 1. To produce, as "The farmer grows food". 2. To become larger, as "The baby seems to grow each day". 3. To become, as "It grows colder at night".

growl. The noise made by an animal when it shows anger and is preparing to snap at somebody.

growth. When something is growing, we speak of its growth. When a man does not shave, you can see his growth of beard.

groyne. A breakwater. A wall of wood or stone built on a beach to prevent the sand from being washed away.

grub. 1. The larva of an insect. 2. Food; provisions.

grudge. If a boy harms you and you make up your mind to pay him back, you have a grudge against him.

gruff. Stern; rude and speaking in a harsh, commanding way.

grumble *(grum'-ble)*. 1. To complain or find fault. 2. To growl faintly.

grunt. A low, gruff sound, such as that made by pigs.

guarantee *(guar-an-tee')*. To promise that you will be responsible for replacing something or repaying its cost if the thing is not satisfactory. If you bought a bicycle with a guarantee, the guarantee would be the promise that the bicycle was sound. If you found out later that it had a faulty wheel, the man who guaranteed the bicycle would have to replace the wheel free of charge, give you a new bicycle, or give you your money back.

guard. 1. To protect; to take care of. 2. The hilt of a sword. 3. A watch chain. 4. A position of defence in boxing or fencing. 5. A number of soldiers detailed for guard duty. 6. Anything that protects, such as a fire-guard, etc.

guardian *(guard'-i-an)*. A person who has the legal care of another person.

guess. To come to some opinion without knowing all the facts.

guest. A visitor; a person who is staying with you as a friend.

guide. 1. To show the way. 2. A person who shows the way. A person who does this gives you **guidance.**

guide-book *(guide'-book)*. A book which gives a number of facts and directions for travellers.

guild. A mediæval society or union of merchants or tradesmen. Each trade had its own guild; there was, for example, the weavers' guild, the tanners' guild, the carpenters' guild, etc. To-day, a guild is any kind of society that exists to help some cause.

guile. Fraud; cunning; deceit.

guilt. The fact of having done a wrong.

guinea *(guin'-ea)*. A coin that was in use many years ago; a sum of money equal to 21 shillings.

guinea-pig *(guin'-ea-pig)*. A rat-like animal without a tail, which scientists sometimes use for experiments.

guitar *(gui-tar')*. A musical instrument with strings which are plucked by the fingers.

gulf. A large bay or inlet on a sea coast.

gull. 1. A web-footed sea-bird. 2. To cheat or deceive.

gullet *(gul'-let)*. The throat or the passage between the throat and the stomach.

gullible *(gul'-li-ble)*. Said of a person who is easily deceived or cheated.

gully *(gul'-ly)*. A channel worn by water; a ravine.

gulp. To swallow hurriedly; to choke.

gum. 1. A sticky liquid which is used in making medicines and glue. Gum is taken from certain trees and plants. 2. You are familiar with chewing-gum which people chew. 3. The flesh about the base of the teeth.

gunwale *(gun'-wale)*. The edge or rim running round the side of a boat.

gurgle *(gur'-gle)*. Water flows with a gurgling sound when it bubbles and ripples over stones. Water may gurgle when poured from a bottle.

gush. 1. When water or any liquid rushes out quickly, it is said to gush out. 2. People gush when they say that everything is much better or nicer than it really is and when they describe things in terms that are far too rosy.

gust. A sudden blast of wind or air.

gutter *(gut'-ter)*. A narrow open passage-way for waste water. Most streets have gutters running along the kerb.

guy. A wire, rope, etc., attached to something to steady it. You will find a guy wire attached to the telephone pole which stands last in a row.

gymnasium *(gym-na'-si-um)*. A place fitted up for the practice of athletic exercises.

gymnast *(gym'-nast)*. An expert in performing athletic exercises. Athletic or physical exercises are sometimes called **gymnastics** *(gym-nas'-tics)*.

gypsy *(gyp'-sy)*. A person who belongs to a race of people who wander about the world. Sometimes spelled **gipsy.**

H

haberdasher *(hab'-er-dash-er)*. A person who sells such things as needles, pins, etc.

habit *(hab'-it)*. 1. When you do something continually you have acquired a habit. Many children make a habit of brushing their teeth. 2. Habit also refers to the clothes worn by people who belong to a religious order.

habitable *(hab'-it-a-ble)*. Fit to live in.

habitation *(hab-i-ta'-tion)*. A place in which to live.

habitual *(ha-bit'-u-al)*. Usual; done by habit.

hack. 1. To cut or chop something badly, so as to spoil it. 2. To cough in short, dry coughs. 3. A horse let out for hire.

hag. An ugly, bad-tempered old woman.

haggard *(hag'-gard)*. A haggard person is one whose face is drawn and lined with worry or hard work.

haggle *(hag'-gle)*. To bargain over the price of a thing.

hail. 1. Drops of rain that have frozen. 2. To greet someone, as "They hailed the boy on his return". 3. To call, as "He hailed a taxi".

hair. The fine strands which grow on top of a person's head.

hale. A person is hale when he is in good health.

half. When something is divided into two equal parts, each part is a half. When you share an apple with a friend, you give him half. When you divide a thing into two equal parts there are two **halves.**

halibut *(hal'-i-but)*. A large flat-fish which is used for food.

hall. 1. A passage-way or corridor in a building. Perhaps you walk along a hall to enter your classroom. 2. A large room in which meetings or banquets are held. 3. A public building, such as a city hall.

hallow *(hal'-low)*. To make holy.

Hallowe'en *(Hal-low-e'en')*. October 31, the day before or eve of All Saints' Day. In the evening of this day, witches, ghosts, goblins and other evil spirits are supposed to walk abroad.

halo *(ha'-lo)*. 1. A ring of light around the sun or moon. 2. A circle of light around the head of a holy person, shown in a painting.

halt. 1. To stop. 2. Lame, as "He gave to the halt and the blind".

hamlet *(ham'-let)*. A small village.

hammer *(ham'-mer)*. A tool used to strike nails and beat metal. A carpenter uses a hammer in building houses.

hammock *(ham'-mock)*. A kind of bed, made of cord or canvas, slung by the corners so that no part of it touches the ground.

hamper *(ham'-per)*. 1. To make it difficult for a person to do what he wants to do. 2. A basket made of wicker, having a lid.

hand. 1. The palm, fingers and thumb. 2. In "Please hand me that book", hand means pass to me with your hand. 3. In "The factory hands are working overtime", hands means working people. 4. In "On my right hand is the Tower of London", hand means side. 5. In "He only played one hand of cards", hand means round.

handbook *(hand'-book)*. A small book devoted to one subject, as a handbook on stamp-collecting.

handicap *(hand'-i-cap)*. 1. In a contest or game, a disadvantage given to a better contestant or player, or an advantage given to a poorer contestant or player, in order to make the chances of winning equal. 2. Handicap sometimes means a disadvantage, especially a physical disadvantage such as a speech defect or a club-foot.

handicraft *(hand'-i-craft)*. A trade or hobby that requires skill with the hands.

handkerchief *(hand'-ker-chief)*. A piece of linen or cotton cloth which is used to wipe the nose or face.

handle *(han'-dle)*. 1. The part of a thing that is supposed to be held. There is a handle on most pots and pans in a kitchen. 2. When you touch or feel a thing you handle it.

handsome *(hand'-some)*. Good-looking.

handwriting *(hand'-writ-ing)*. When you have written a composition, you should notice your handwriting, or the writing that you did by hand.

handy *(hand'-y)*. Convenient.

hang. 1. When you put your coat on a hook, you hang your coat. 2. When a man is put to death by having a rope tied around his neck, he is hanged. 3. When you paper the walls of a room you hang the paper.

hangar *(hang'-ar)*. A building for housing aeroplanes.

hanger *(hang'-er)*. Something on which objects are hung, such as a coat hanger.

haphazard *(hap-haz'-ard)*. Happening by chance.

happen *(hap'-pen)*. 1. To take place. 2. To take place by chance, as an accident does.

happening *(hap'-pen-ing)*. An event or thing which takes place.

happiness *(hap'-pi-ness)*. A state of joy.

harangue *(ha-rangue')*. 1. A speech made by someone in a noisy, forceful way. 2. To make such a speech.

harass *(har'-ass)*. To annoy by one attack after another. In "The soldiers harassed the retreating enemy", harassed tells that the enemy was constantly attacked while retreating.

harbour *(har'-bour)*. 1. A place where ships go for safety, and may load or unload. 2. To harbour means to shelter, as "The woman harboured the soldier in her house while the enemy was searching for him".

hard. 1. In "Stone is hard", hard means not soft. 2. In "The question is hard", hard means difficult. 3. In "The man is hard-hearted", hard-hearted means unfeeling. 4. In "It is raining hard", hard means heavily. 5. In "The house is hard by the stream", hard by means close to. 6. In "The water is hard", hard means containing minerals which interfere with the action of the soap. 7. In "He is hard of hearing", hard of hearing means partly deaf.

hardly *(hard'-ly)*. Scarcely; barely.

hardship *(hard'-ship)*. Anything that gives trouble or is hard to put up with.

hardware *(hard'-ware)*. Things made of metal such as nails, locks, hinges, etc.

hardy *(har'-dy)*. 1. Daring; brave; confident. 2. Able to bear hardships.

hare. An animal much like a large rabbit.

hark. To listen.

harmful *(harm'-ful)*. Causing harm; injurious.

harmless *(harm'-less)*. Causing no harm; not injurious.

harmonica *(har-mon'-i-ca)*. A small, long musical instrument played by holding it against the mouth and blowing into it. It is also called a mouth-organ.

harness *(har'-ness)*. 1. The leather straps and chains which hold a horse to the shafts of a cart. 2. To put on harness.

harp. A musical stringed instrument which is played by plucking the strings.

harpoon *(har-poon')*. A barbed spear attached to a rope and used for catching whales, seals, etc.

harrow *(har'-row)*. 1. A heavy frame with iron teeth or disks, pulled by a tractor and used to break ground or plant seeds. 2. **harrowing** means distressing, as "The soldier's escape from the enemy was a harrowing experience".

harry *(har'-ry)*. 1. To make raids against; to lay waste. 2. To worry with constant attacks.

harsh. 1. Rough. 2. Cruel.

hart. A male deer or stag.

harvest *(har'-vest)*. 1. To gather the crops, usually in autumn. 2. The crops gathered at this time.

hash. 1. Food consisting of meat and vegetables, cut small and cooked together in water. 2. In "The boy made a hash of his home-work", hash means a muddle.

haste. Quickness or speed as, "He ran in haste to tell his parents".

hasten *(has'-ten)*. To hurry.

hatch. 1. To bring young birds to life from eggs. 2. A trap door, especially one in the deck of a ship. 3. To hatch a plot is to make plans secretly.

hatchet *(hatch'-et)*. A small axe.

hate. To dislike very much.

haughty *(haugh'-ty)*. Looking down on people and considering yourself much better than they are. Proud.

haul. 1. To pull with great effort, as fishermen haul nets. 2. The amount won or caught, as "The fishermen made a large haul which filled the boat".

haunch. That part of the body between the ribs and the thigh.

haunt. 1. To go often to, as "He haunted the docks in the hope of hearing news of his sailor son". 2. A place often visited, as "This rocky shore is one of my favourite haunts".

haunted *(haunt'-ed)*. Said of places where ghosts are supposed to be.

haven *(ha'-ven)*. 1. A harbour. 2. A place of safety.

havoc *(hav'-oc)*. A great deal of destruction.

haw. A red berry of the hawthorn tree.

hawk. 1. A bird of prey with a hooked beak. 2. To sell goods from door to door. A person who peddles goods in this way is a **hawker.**

hawser *(haw'-ser)*. A thick, strong rope or cable.

hay. Grass and clover which is cut, dried and used to feed cattle, etc.

hayloft *(hay'-loft)*. A storage place in a barn for hay.

haystack *(hay'-stack)*. A large pile or stack of hay.

hazard *(haz'-ard)*. 1. A risk. 2. A man who hazards his life risks his life.

haze. A fine mist.

hazel *(ha'-zel)*. 1. A tree which bears hazel nuts in autumn. 2. A light brown colour.

head. 1. The top part of the body, where the eyes, ears, nose and mouth are located. 2. The top part of anything, such as the head of a nail. 3. The foremost or chief person, such as the head of a family. 4. To head something is to be the chief person in it.

headache *(head'-ache)*. A pain in the head.

headland *(head'-land)*. A piece of high land running out into the sea.

headlong *(head'-long)*. Going forward, head first, out of control.

headquarters *(head'-quar-ters)*. When a business or any other organization carries on its work from a number of places, it probably has a central office where its chief people and its chief work are to be found. This place is the headquarters of the business or organization.

headstrong *(head'-strong)*. A headstrong person is one who will not listen to the advice of others and always wants his own way.

heal. To cure a disease or a wound.

health. When you are free from sickness you enjoy health.

healthful *(health'-ful)*. Producing or maintaining health.

healthy *(health'-y)*. Full of, or enjoying, good health.

heap. A pile of things thrown together.

hear. When a sound reaches your ear, you hear it. To listen.

heard. The past tense of **hear**. "When the pupils heard the bell, they entered school".

hearken *(heark'-en)*. To listen. Also spelled **harken.**

hearsay *(hear'-say)*. Gossip.

hearse. A car or carriage for carrying dead bodies in funeral processions.

heart. 1. The organ of the body which acts as a pump to drive the blood through the body. 2. The heart of anything is the centre or middle, as the heart of a cabbage. 3. A person is said to have a good heart when he is kind. 4. To learn by heart is to learn something word for word.

heart-broken *(heart'-bro-ken)*. A person is heart-broken when he is very sorrowful or greatly disappointed.

hearth. The floor of a fireplace, which may extend a short distance into the room.

heartless *(heart'-less)*. Said of a person who is unkind.

hearty *(heart'-y)*. 1. A hearty person is one who is always cheerful and good-natured. 2. A hearty meal is a good, full meal.

heat. Warmth.

heath. A rough piece of flat land covered with shrubs and small plants.

heathen *(hea'-then)*. A person who does not believe in God.

heather *(heath'-er)*. A low-growing shrub bearing small purple or white flowers.

heave. 1. To lift up with a jerk. 2. When a ship heaves to, it stops.

heaven *(heav'-en)*. 1. The sky. 2. The kingdom of God.

heavy *(heav'-y)*. 1. A thing which has great weight is heavy. 2. When you sleep deeply you are in a heavy sleep. 3. When your eyes are heavy you are sleepy.

hectic *(hec'-tic)*. 1. A hectic time is a confusing, feverish time. 2. A hectic colour or complexion is one that is flushed.

hedge. A line of thick bushes, shrubs, etc., to serve as an edge to a field, garden, etc.

heed. Pay attention to.

heedless *(heed'-less)*. Paying no attention to; careless.

heel. 1. The back of the foot behind the ankle. 2. A ship heels when it tilts.

heifer *(heif'-er)*. A young cow.

height. 1. When you measure from the ceiling of a room to the floor, you measure the height of the room. 2. Something which is very high is said to be a height, as "He stood on a height of land to see the country".

heir. The person who is allowed by law to take over a person's property and his title, if he has one, when he dies.

heiress *(heir'-ess)*. A woman who lawfully takes over a person's property when he dies.

heirloom *(heir'-loom)*. A piece of personal property that has been handed down from one generation to another.

helicopter *(hel'-i-cop-ter)*. A type of aircraft which is lifted off the ground by large blades or propellers fastened to the top of the body.

helm. 1. The wheel by which the rudder of a ship is turned. 2. A place of control and guidance. 3. A helmet.

helmet *(hel'-met)*. A protective cover for the head.

helpful *(help'-ful)*. Being of help or assistance.

hem. 1. The edge of something made by sewing where the material is turned to cover a raw edge. 2. Things are hemmed in when they are surrounded on all sides.

hemisphere *(hem'-i-sphere)*. Half the earth or globe. England is in the Northern Hemisphere.

hemp. A plant having fibrous stems. They are dried and made into string, rope, etc.

hen. A female chicken or bird.

henceforth *(hence'-forth)*. From now on.

herald *(her'-ald)*. 1. In olden times, a man who carried messages from one ruler to another, or read messages from the ruler to the people. 2. One who proclaims or announces. 3. To proclaim; to announce; to announce the coming of.

herb. 1. A plant with a soft stalk, such as grass. 2. Plants used for seasoning foods, as mint and sage, or for medicinal purposes.

herbage *(herb'-age)*. Grass and other low-growing plants.

herd. 1. Many cattle thought of as one group. 2. To herd people or things together is to push them into a small space.

hermit *(her'-mit)*. A person who lives entirely by himself.

hero *(he'-ro)*. A brave man or boy. The chief character in a story. A brave woman or girl is a **heroine** *(her'-o-ine)*. Heroes and heroines do **heroic** *(he-ro'-ic)* things.

heron *(her'-on)*. A wading bird with a long beak and long legs.

herring *(her'-ring)*. A small fish found in the North Atlantic and used for food.

hesitate *(hes'-i-tate)*. To stop and pause while doing something; to be in doubt.

hew. To chop down such things as trees. The Bible speaks of "hewers of wood and drawers of water".

hexagon *(hex'-a-gon)*. A figure having six equal sides and six equal angles.

hibernate *(hi'-ber-nate)*. To sleep throughout the winter, as many animals do.

hickory *(hick'-o-ry)*. A tree with hard wood and edible nuts.

hidden *(hid'-den)*. Put out of sight; put where it will not be found; concealed or kept secret.

hide. 1. The skin of animals. 2. To put a thing where it cannot be found.

hideous *(hid'-e-ous)*. Frightfully ugly.

high. Being a long way up.

highlands *(high'-lands)*. A hilly or mountainous district. The people living in such parts are called **highlanders.**

highway *(high'-way)*. A main road.

hike. A long walk or tramp.

hilarious *(hi-lar'-i-ous)*. Noisily happy.

hillock *(hill'-ock)*. A small hill.

hilt. The handle of a sword, etc.

hind. 1. A female deer. 2. Back, or rear, as in "a dog's hind legs".

hinder *(hin'-der)*. To get in the way of; to restrain or keep back, as "The trees and bushes hindered us on our march through the woods".

hinge. A metal joint which allows a door or lid to open and close.

hint. 1. To suggest something, without actually saying it. 2. A bit of information, as "Hints on Cooking" in women's magazines.

hip. The joint that stands out on either side of the body just below the waist.

hippopotamus *(hip-po-pot'-a-mus)*. A large, hairless, thick-skinned animal which lives in Africa.

hire. 1. To obtain the use of something in return for payment. If you ride in a taxi, you hire it for the time being and at the end of the run you pay for the use of it. 2. To obtain the services of a person for wages.

hiss. To make a noise as by blowing through the teeth.

history *(his'-to-ry)*. The story of things that have happened in the past.

hit. 1. To strike with a blow. 2. A blow.

hitch. 1. To move by jerking. 2. To fasten. 3. A fault that causes something to go wrong.

hitherto *(hith-er-to')*. Up till now.

hive. 1. A place where bees live. 2. To put bees into a hive.

hoar. White or grey. Hoar-frost is a white frost.

hoard. To store up and hide.

hoarse. When you have a rough or husky voice, you are hoarse and have difficulty speaking.

hoax. 1. A trick played on somebody for a joke. 2. A deception.

hobble *(hob'-ble)*. To walk with a limp.

hobby *(hob'-by)*. A pastime in which a person engages for pleasure and interest.

hockey *(hock'-ey)*. An outdoor game played by two teams, each of eleven players. The ball is small and hard and is hit by a stick curved at one end. The players have the same positions as in Association Football, and the object is to hit the ball into the opponents' goal. **ice-hockey** is similar but is played by skaters on ice. A rubber disk, called a puck, is used instead of a ball. There are six players on each side.

hoe. 1. A garden tool with a small blade and a long handle. It is used for loosening the earth and for digging up weeds. 2. To dig with such a tool.

hog. A pig.

hoist. To lift up or to raise.

hold. 1. To grip with the hands. 2. To contain, as "A quart measure holds two pints". 3. To possess, as "He holds a good position at the City Hall". 4. The hold of a ship is where the cargo is stored.

hole. An opening.

holiday *(hol'-i-day)*. A day free from work on which people enjoy themselves.

hollow *(hol'-low)*. 1. Empty in the centre, as a hollow tree. 2. Insincere; false. 3. A dip in the ground or small valley is a hollow.

holly *(hol'-ly)*. A tree or shrub on which grow green prickly leaves and red berries Holly is used for decoration at Christmas.

holy *(ho'-ly)*. Sacred; sinless; saintly; worthy of being worshipped. God is holy.

homage *(hom'-age)*. The respect or reverence which a person has for someone else.

home. The place where you live.

homonym *(hom'-o-nym)*. A word that sounds the same as another word but has a different spelling and meaning, as hare and hair.

hone. 1. A stone used for putting a sharp edge on knives and cutting tools. 2. To sharpen something on such a stone.

honest *(hon'-est)*. An honest person is one who can be trusted because he is truthful and does not steal or cheat. Such a person shows **honesty.**

honey *(hon'-ey)*. The food which bees make from the nectar of flowers. It is sticky, sweet, and delicious with bread and butter.

honeymoon *(hon'-ey-moon)*. The holiday which newly-married couples have directly after the wedding.

honorary *(hon'-or-ar-y)*. A person is said to be doing honorary work or to be an honorary secretary when he does the work for honour and does not receive pay.

honour *(hon'-our)*. 1. To respect; to esteem. 2. Fame; distinguished position. 3. A mark of respect; a prize or title, etc., given to honour someone. 4. A man of honour is a man who has a fine sense of what is right or wrong, and who does what is right because he does not want to disgrace himself. Such a man is **honourable.**

hood. 1. A covering to go over the head, as worn by Little Red Riding Hood. 2. Other coverings such as those on baby carriages are also called hoods.

hoof. The foot of a horse, cow, etc. Horseshoes are nailed to the hoof of a horse.

hook. A piece of metal, wood, etc., which is bent or curved and used to catch or hold something. A fish-hook is used to catch fish.

hoop. A circular band that fits around something. A cask or a wooden barrel is held together by hoops.

hoot. 1. The cry of an owl. 2. To make a loud sound.

hop. 1. To jump or make short leaps on one foot. 2. A climbing vine, the cones of which are used in making beer.

hope. 1. To wish. 2. A hope is a feeling that what you wish will happen.

hopscotch *(hop'-scotch)*. A children's game in which the players jump over lines drawn on the ground.

horde. A gang of people; a tribe.

horizon *(ho-ri'-zon)*. The line which seems to mark the place where the earth and sky meet.

horizontal *(hor-i-zon'-tal)*. A line is horizontal when it is level or parallel to any horizon which can be seen at sea. A line placed at right angles to a post that stands perfectly upright would be horizontal.

horn. 1. The bony growth on the head of cattle, sheep, etc. 2. A musical instrument. 3. A device which is sounded as a warning, such as the horn on a car or a fog-horn.

hornet *(hor'-net)*. A flying insect of the wasp family.

horrible *(hor'-ri-ble)*. Terrible; dreadful; nasty; frightful. A horrible thing is **horrid** and causes **horror;** it **horrifies.**

horse. 1. A large, four-legged beast with a flowing mane and tail. The horse is ridden by men or used to draw loads. 2. A frame used to hold boards while they are being cut.

horseshoe *(horse'-shoe)*. A metal plate in the shape of a U which is nailed to a horse's hoof to protect it.

horticulture *(hor'-ti-cul-ture)*. The science that deals with the growing of flowers.

hose. 1. Tubing; flexible tube for bringing water to a required place, as a garden-hose and a fire-hose. 2. Hose is a term for stockings and socks. **hosiery** is another term for stockings and socks.

hospitable *(hos'-pi-ta-ble)*. Kind to strangers. Receiving and entertaining guests in a kindly way.

hospital *(hos'-pi-tal)*. A building where sick people are cared for.

hospitality *(hos-pi-tal'-i-ty)*. The kindly treatment of friends or strangers in your home.

host. 1. The master of a house who receives and entertains guests. The mistress of the house is the **hostess.** 2. A great number, as "There was a host of children waiting to ride on the merry-go-round".

hostel *(hos'-tel)*. A place where students live; an inn; a hotel; a place where people may pay to have food and a night's lodgings.

hostile *(hos'-tile)*. Unfriendly; unfavourable.

hotel *(ho-tel')*. A building in which one may rent a room and buy meals.

hothouse *(hot'-house)*. A greenhouse. A place for growing plants out of season.

hound. A dog trained for hunting.

hour. A measure of time equal to sixty minutes. There are twenty-four hours in a day.

house. A building in which people live.

household *(house'-hold)*. 1. The people living in a house. 2. Said of an article supplied for use in a house, as household soap, etc. 3. Domestic, as "Her household affairs are not our business".

hovel *(hov'-el)*. A small, poor, tumble-down house.

hover *(hov'-er)*. 1. Birds hover when they stay in the air in almost the same place. 2. A person hovers about when he does not move far away.

however *(how-ev'-er)*. In whatever way, as "However difficult it may be, you must try".

howl. 1. A mournful cry such as wolves make. 2. When a person laughs loudly he is said to howl with laughter.

hub. The central part of a wheel which fits on to the axle.

hubbub *(hub'-bub)*. An uproar; a tremendous amount of noise.

huddle *(hud'-dle)*. To squeeze close together.

hue. 1. Colour, as "The sun has a golden hue". 2. The words "hue and cry" mean an alarm or outcry calling for the pursuit of a criminal.

huge. Very large.

hulk. The body of an old ship.

hull. The body of a ship without the sails or funnels.

human *(hu'-man)*. Having the qualities of man or mankind.

humane *(hu-mane')*. Kind; anxious for people not to suffer.

humanity *(hu-man'-i-ty)*. 1. The human race. 2. Kindness.

humble *(hum'-ble)*. Lowly; modest; not proud.

humdrum *(hum'-drum)*. Dull; uninteresting.

humid *(hu'-mid)*. Moist; damp, but not actually wet.

humiliate *(hu-mil'-i-ate)*. To make a person lose his self-respect. Such a person suffers **humiliation** *(hu-mil-i-a'-tion)*.

humming-bird *(hum'-ming-bird)*. A small brightly-coloured bird with a long bill.

humour *(hu'-mour)*. 1. Wit; a funny remark. 2. In "Yesterday he was in good humour", humour means frame of mind or temper. 3. In "Why don't you humour him?" humour him means do what he wants.

humorous *(hu'-mor-ous)*. A humorous person is a funny or amusing person.

hump. A lump or bump on the back. A camel has a hump on its back. A person with a hump is a **hunchback.**

hundred *(hun'-dred)*. A number which is ten times ten or ten more than ninety.

hungry *(hun'-gry)*. When you are hungry you want to eat.

hunt. To seek or look for.

hurdle *(hur'-dle)*. 1. An object over which people or horses jump. 2. Anything which is an obstacle.

hurl. To throw away with force.

hurricane *(hur'-ri-cane)*. A violent wind-storm.

hurried *(hur'-ried)*. When you must do something quickly you are hurried.

hurry *(hur'-ry)*. You hurry when you move quickly.

hurt. To injure or cause pain. When something hurts it causes pain. A sunburn will hurt.

husband *(hus'-band)*. The man to whom a woman is married. Your father is your mother's husband.

husbandry *(hus'-band-ry)*. 1. Farming; growing crops. 2. Economy; careful management.

hush. 1. Stillness; quiet. 2. To tell someone to be silent is to hush him.

husk. The outer covering on a grain of corn. Other fruits or seeds also have husks.

husky *(husk'-y)*. 1. A hoarse or dry throat makes your voice sound husky. 2. An Eskimo dog is called a husky. 3. Strong; tough; in good health.

hustle *(hus'-tle)*. To hurry; to push one's way.

hyacinth *(hy'-a-cinth)*. A plant with spikes of bell-shaped flowers.

hybrid *(hy'-brid)*. A plant or animal of mixed parentage. Thus, a mule is a hybrid because it has a donkey for a father and a mare for a mother.

hydrant *(hy'-drant)*. A large, nozzled pipe in the street, which is connected to a water main so that firemen have a supply of water when fighting fire.

hydro-electric *(hy-dro-e-lec'-tric)*. Hydro-electric power is electricity produced by water power.

hydrogen *(hy'-dro-gen)*. An element, usually in the form of a colourless, odourless gas sixteen times lighter than air. Two parts of hydrogen and one of oxygen form water.

hygiene *(hy'-giene)*. The science of looking after our bodies and keeping them healthy.

hymn. A song of praise used in public worship.

hyphen *(hy'-phen)*. A short stroke (-) joining two syllables or words.

hypnotize *(hyp'-no-tize)*. To cause a person to go into a trance in which he follows the directions of the person who caused him to be in the trance. The person who hypnotizes does so by means of **hypnotism** and is called a **hypnotist**.

hypocrite *(hyp'-o-crite)*. A person who pretends to be better than he really is.
hysterics *(hys-ter'-ics)*. A nervous condition in which the sufferer may have attacks of uncontrollable laughing and crying.

I

ice. When water is frozen, it is called ice.
iceberg *(ice'-berg)*. A huge mass of ice floating in the sea.
ice-cream *(ice-cream')*. A frozen, flavoured milk.
icicle *(i'-ci-cle)*. A long strip of hanging ice formed by the freezing of dripping water.
icing *(ic'-ing)*. A coating made from powdered sugar; a mixture used to decorate cakes and puddings.
icy *(i'-cy)*. Like ice; very cold.
idea *(i-de'-a)*. A thought; something that comes to the mind.
ideal *(i-de'-al)*. 1. Perfect. 2. A standard of excellence.
identify *(i-den'-ti-fy)*. To recognize.
idiom *(id'-i-om)*. 1. The language of a country. 2. A phrase, or set of words, with a special meaning, which cannot be understood simply by putting together the usual meanings of the separate words, such as "fed up" and "under the weather".
idiot *(id'-i-ot)*. A person who is unable to learn.
idiotic *(id-i-ot'-ic)*. Stupid; silly.
idle *(i'-dle)*. 1. Vain; lazy; useless. 2. Unemployed.
idler *(i'-dler)*. A person who wastes his time.
idol *(i'-dol)*. 1. A statue, picture, etc., which is worshipped as a god. 2. Something or someone much loved, as "She is the idol of the school", meaning that everybody thinks a great deal of her. **idolatry** *(i-dol'-a-try)* is the worship of idols.
igloo *(ig'-loo)*. A domed hut made of ice or snow by the Eskimos.
ignite *(ig-nite')*. To set on fire.
ignoble *(ig-no'-ble)*. Not noble; without honour.
ignorance *(ig'-no-rance)*. Lack of knowledge.
ignore *(ig-nore')*. To take no notice of.

ill. 1. In "He is ill again", ill means not well. 2. In "It is an ill wind that blows nobody good", ill means bad. 3. In "He can ill afford the money", ill means not very easily.

illness *(ill'-ness)*. A sickness or disease.

illegal *(il-le'-gal)*. Not lawful. When a person does something illegal, he is breaking the law.

illegible *(il-leg'-i-ble)*. Unable to be read.

illiterate *(il-lit'-er-ate)*. Not able to read.

illuminate *(il-lu'-mi-nate)*. To light up.

illustrate *(il'-lus-trate)*. 1. To explain by means of pictures. 2. In "He illustrated his meaning by telling us a story", illustrated means made clear. A person illustrates by means of **illustrations** *(il-lus-tra'-tions)*.

illustrious *(il-lus'-tri-ous)*. Famous or renowned.

image *(im'-age)*. A likeness. If you look in a mirror, you see your image in it.

imaginary *(im-ag'-i-nar-y)*. Not real; existing only in the mind. Imaginary things are those you **imagine.**

imagination *(im-ag-i-na'-tion)*. If I were to describe a place you had never seen, you would form pictures of it in your mind. The ability to form pictures in this way is imagination.

imagine *(im-ag'-ine)*. 1. When you imagine a thing you form a mental picture or an idea of it. 2. When you say "I imagine that he will come", imagine means believe. 3. When you say "I can't imagine what you mean", imagine means think or guess. 4. When a person tells you to imagine you were there, he means you to suppose you were there.

imbecile *(im'-be-cile)*. An idiot; a person with a very weak mind.

imitate *(im'-i-tate)*. To copy or try to make, or be, like.

imitation *(im-i-ta'-tion)*. If one thing is made to be like another, the second thing is an imitation of the first. Children play with imitation guns.

immature *(im-ma-ture')*. Not ripe; not grown up.

immediately *(im-me'-di-ate-ly)*. At once.

immense *(im-mense')*. Very large indeed; huge.

immerse *(im-merse')*. To put into water or other liquid, as "The boy slipped into the pond and was immersed up to his neck".

immigrate *(im'-mi-grate)*. To enter a country not your own and settle down there to live. A person who leaves his own country **emigrates** from his own country and **immigrates** to the new country. He is an **emigrant** as well as an **immigrant**.

immodest *(im-mod'-est)*. 1. Not decent. 2. Boastful; arrogant.

immoral *(im-mor'-al)*. Not moral; wicked; ready to do things that are very wrong.

immortal *(im-mor'-tal)*. Everlasting; never dying.

imp. A naughty child; one who is mischievous.

impact *(im'-pact)*. 1. A collision or hitting. 2. The shock or force of a collision or hitting.

impair *(im-pair')*. To weaken or injure. If you don't have sufficient sleep you will impair your health.

impart *(im-part')*. 1. To give; grant; bestow. 2. Tell.

impartial *(im-par'-tial)*. Just; fair; not favouring one at the expense of another, as "A judge must be impartial".

impatient *(im-pa'-tient)*. Hasty; restless; not ready to put up with delay or opposition.

impede *(im-pede')*. To hinder; to obstruct; to get in the way of.

impenetrable *(im-pen'-e-tra-ble)*. That cannot be entered or **penetrated** *(pen'-e-trat-ed)*, as "After repeated attacks, the enemy realized our fortress was impenetrable".

imperative *(im-per'-a-tive)*. 1. Expressing a command. 2. Urgent.

imperfect *(im-per'-fect)*. Not perfect; having some fault.

imperial *(im-pe'-ri-al)*. Belonging to an empire or an emperor.

imperil *(im-per'-il)*. To endanger. You imperil your life when you do something dangerous.

imperious *(im-pe'-ri-ous)*. Like an emperor; haughty; proud.

impersonate *(im-per'-son-ate)*. To impersonate someone is to pretend you are he.

impertinent *(im-per'-ti-nent)*. Cheeky; impudent; rude.

impetus *(im'-pe-tus)*. The force which makes an object move. Thus if you kick a ball that is lying on the ground, you give it impetus.

implant *(im-plant')*. To put in; plant in; fix in.

implement *(im'-ple-ment)*. 1. A tool. 2. To put into action; to carry out.

implicate *(im'-pli-cate)*. To involve; to bring other people in; to inform about other people.

implicit *(im-pli'-cit)*. 1. Understood though not plainly stated. If your friend tells you that he has just sailed home from Italy, you know that he must have passed the rock of Gibraltar although he did not say so. 2. Complete and unquestioning. If you have implicit faith in a person, you have full or complete faith in him.

implore *(im-plore')*. To beg or entreat; to ask earnestly.

imply *(im-ply')*. To hint at; to suggest; to lead to a conclusion.

impolite *(im-po-lite')*. Rude; showing bad manners.

import *(im-port')*. To bring goods and merchandise into a country. An import *(im'-port)* is something which has been brought into the country.

important *(im-por'-tant)*. Very special; needing immediate attention; having or likely to have great results. A thing that is important has **importance.**

impose *(im-pose')*. 1. To put a tax on or to put a punishment on, as "The government has imposed a tax on motor-cars" and "The magistrate imposed a fine of twelve pounds on the motorist". 2. To impose on others is to force yourself on them or force them to do something for you that you have no right to expect.

imposing *(im-pos'-ing)*. A thing is imposing when it looks very fine and grand.

imposition *(im-po-si'-tion)*. 1. The action of forcing yourself upon another. Thus, "I did not mind his asking me the way to the station, but when he asked me to accompany him there I thought that was an imposition". (See **impose,** No. 2.) 2. A tax. (See **impose,** No. 1.)

impossible *(im-pos'-si-ble)*. Unable to be done, or unable to happen. A thing which is impossible is an **impossibility.**

impostor *(im-pos'-tor)*. A person who pretends he is somebody else and does it to cheat or deceive people.

impotent *(im'-po-tent)*. Without power; weak; helpless.

impound *(im-pound')*. To enclose in a pen, or a pound, or to take in custody, as when the courts impound a car.

impoverish *(im-pov'-er-ish)*. To make poor.

impracticable *(im-prac'-ti-ca-ble)*. Impossible to be done; not wise to do.

impregnable *(im-preg'-na-ble)*. So strong as to to able to stand firm against any amount of force, as "The castle, being impregnable, could not be overcome by the attackers".

impress *(im-press')*. 1. To press upon. 2. To mark by pressure. 3. To fix on the mind. 4. To affect a person strongly.

impression *(im-pres'-sion)*. 1. The marks made by pressing in some way on a thing. (See **impress**.) Thus the printer presses the paper on to inked type and gets an impression. 2. An idea, thus "My impression is that he will not come".

impressive *(im-pres'-sive)*. A thing is impressive when it is able to cause great feeling, excitement or thought. Thus, "The minister gave an impressive sermon" means that the sermon had a great effect on those present, causing them to think deeply.

imprint. 1. *(im'-print)*. Stamp; impression. 2. *(im-print')*. To stamp; to impress.

imprison *(im-pris'-on)*. To place in prison; to lock in.

improbable *(im-prob'-a-ble)*. Not likely to happen.

improve *(im-prove')*. When a thing is made better, it is improved. Thus, if your school-work is better than it was, you have improved it and your work shows **improvement.**

improvident *(im-prov'-i-dent)*. Not caring about the future; thoughtless; failing to provide for the future.

improvise *(im'-pro-vise)*. To do something or make something on the spur of the moment.

impudent *(im'-pu-dent)*. Saucy; insolent; shameless.

impulsive *(im-pul'-sive)*. People are impulsive who do things suddenly and without thinking what the results will be.

impunity *(im-pu'-ni-ty)*. Safety from punishment, danger or loss, as in "None of the animals was dangerous and the children petted them with impunity".

impure *(im-pure')*. Not pure.

impute *(im-pute')*. To blame or charge a person with. Thus if I say that John broke the window, I impute to him the responsibility for the breakage.

in-. A prefix meaning "not". If you are looking for the meaning of a word beginning with **in-** and cannot find it among those listed below, look up the word as it would be without the **in-**. For example, if you wanted to look up "inaccurate" you would not find it listed on this page. Therefore, you should remove the **in-** and look up "accurate". The meaning given is "correct"; "inaccurate", therefore, means "not correct".

inability *(in-a-bil'-i-ty)*. State of being unable; lack of ability; lack of the means to do something.

inaccessible *(in-ac-ces'-si-ble)*. Impossible to reach. Thus if you cannot reach the top of a mountain, it is inaccessible, and if you cannot go into a room because it is locked, it also is inaccessible.

inane *(in-ane')*. Silly; foolish.

inanimate *(in-an'-i-mate)*. Without life.

inattention *(in-at-ten'-tion)*. Lack of attention.

incalculable *(in-cal'-cu-la-ble)*. Not able to be counted or reckoned.

incandescent *(in-can-des'-cent)*. Made to glow through heat. The current in an electric lamp makes the fine wire thread so hot that it glows and is incandescent.

incapacitate *(in-ca-pac'-i-tate)*. To make or render unfit for doing work. Thus, "The wound on the horse's leg incapacitated the animal".

incarcerate *(in-car'-cer-ate)*. To shut up as in a prison.

incendiary *(in-cen'-di-a-ry)*. Causing fire. A bomb that spreads fire is called an incendiary bomb; a person might be an incendiary.

incense *(in'-cense)*. A substance that gives off a pleasant odour while it is burning.

incense *(in-cense')*. To make very angry.

incentive *(in-cen'-tive)*. A reason or a motive that encourages. Thus if I tell John I will dismiss him early if his work is correct, that is an incentive to John to try hard.

incessant *(in-ces'-sant)*. Not stopping; unending; continual.

inch. A measure of length. There are twelve inches in one foot.

incident *(in'-ci-dent)*. A happening; an event.

incision *(in-ci'-sion)*. A cut into. Thus a surgeon makes an incision when doing an operation.

incite *(in-cite')*. To urge on or stir up. Thus "He incited the savages to rebel against the traders".

inclement *(in-clem'-ent)*. Pitiless; unkind; severe. Weather is often said to be inclement when it is cold or stormy.

incline *(in-cline')*. 1. To lean or bend towards. 2. When a person says he is inclined to do something, he means he is thinking he will do it or he is likely to do it. 3. *(in'-cline)*. A slope; sloping ground.

include *(in-clude')*. To contain; to put with. Thus "I included the comic papers in my parcel to the children" means that the papers were put with other things in the parcel.

incoherent *(in-co-her'-ent)*. Not able to be understood; rambling. Incoherent remarks are remarks not made clearly enough to be understood, or remarks that do not make sense.

income *(in'-come)*. The money a person receives from any source.

incompatible *(in-com-pat'-i-ble)*. Things that do not agree or people who cannot get on well together are said to be incompatible.

incompetent *(in-com'-pe-tent)*. Incapable; unfit; not fit to do the work required.

incomprehensible *(in-com-pre-hen'-si-ble)*. Unable to be understood, as "The damage which vandals do to public property is incomprehensible".

inconceivable *(in-con-ceiv'-a-ble)*. Not to be imagined; unthinkable.

inconsistent *(in-con-sist'-ent)*. Not agreeing; not always the same; thus, "He says one thing and does another; that is why I think he is inconsistent".

incorporate *(in-cor'-po-rate)*. To join things together; to make one thing a part of another thing; to unite.

incorrect *(in-cor-rect')*. Wrong; not correct.

incorrigible *(in-cor'-ri-gi-ble)*. Incapable of being corrected. A person is incorrigible when his bad habits are beyond correction.

increase. 1. *(in-crease')*. To become greater; to make greater. 2. *(in'-crease)*. A becoming greater; what has grown; harvest.

incredible *(in-cred'-i-ble)*. Beyond belief; too much to believe.

incriminate *(in-crim'-i-nate)*. To say something that shows another person is guilty. Thus, if I am caught doing something wrong and I say "Well, I am not the only one who has done it. Fred did just the same thing yesterday", I incriminate Fred by telling tales about him.

incubator *(in'-cu-ba-tor)*. 1. An incubator for hatching eggs is a kind of heated box which keeps the eggs warm until they hatch. 2. An incubator for babies is a similar device. Babies that are born smaller than normal are often put in an incubator to be kept warm until they are of normal size.

incur *(in-cur')*. To bring blame or any form of punishment on yourself. Thus, "The motorist drove too fast, and, as a result, incurred a fine of ten pounds".

H

indebted *(in-debt'-ed)*. A person is indebted to another when he owes the other something. It may be money he owes, but it may also be a kindness, a favour, etc.

indecision *(in-de-ci'-sion)*. Hesitation; inability to make up one's mind about a matter.

indeed *(in-deed')*. In fact; really.

indefatigable *(in-de-fat'-i-ga-ble)*. Untiring.

indelible *(in-del'-i-ble)*. Not able to be rubbed or blotted out. Some pencils make marks that cannot be rubbed out; they are called indelible pencils. Anything that is impressed on your mind so strongly that it will never be forgotten is **indelibly** impressed on your mind.

indemnify *(in-dem'-ni-fy)*. To compensate for loss; to give security against loss or damage.

indent *(in-dent')*. To begin writing in from the margin. You should indent the first line of each paragraph of a composition.

independent *(in-de-pend'-ent)*. Neither needing nor wanting help from others. An independent country is one that is free and not ruled by any other country. An independent person looks after himself and does not rely on others.

index *(in'-dex)*. 1. A list at the end of a book showing the contents in alphabetical order. 2. The first finger or the one next to the thumb. 3. Anything that points out something.

Indian *(In'-di-an)*. 1. A native of India. 2. A native of North America before the white man came, or a descendant of such natives.

indicate *(in'-di-cate)*. To point out.

indict *(in-dict')*. To accuse.

indifferent *(in-dif'-fer-ent)*. Not caring what happens.

indigenous *(in-dig'-e-nous)*. Belonging to the country where it is found; native. Thus, kangaroos are indigenous to Australia because they belong there, but they are not indigenous to England.

indigent *(in'-di-gent)*. Poor; needy.

indigestion *(in-di-ges'-tion)*. An uncomfortable and painful condition brought about by the inability of the stomach to dissolve and deal with food.

indignant *(in-dig'-nant)*. Angry because of some mean or wrong thing that has been done. An indignant person is one who shows **indignation** *(in-dig-na'-tion)*.

indigo *(in'-di-go)*. A plant grown in India. It is useful for dyeing materials a blue colour. If you have a blue coat or dress it may have been dyed with indigo.

indiscreet *(in-dis-creet')*. Not wise and careful in the things said or done.

indispensable *(in-dis-pen'-sa-ble)*. A person or thing is indispenable-able when he or it cannot be done without. Thus food, money and clothing are indispensable.

indisposed *(in-dis-posed')*. Not well, as "He was indisposed and did not go to school". His illness is an **indisposition**.

indistinct *(in-dis-tinct')*. Not clear; not easy to see or hear.

individual *(in-di-vid'-u-al)*. 1. A person, as "That man is the individual I saw on the platform". 2. Single, as "That is a very valuable book, but the individual pages are not worth anything".

indolent *(in'-do-lent)*. Lazy.

indoors *(in-doors')*. Inside a house.

induce *(in-duce')*. To persuade; to make a person do a thing.

indulgent *(in-dul'-gent)*. A person who lets others have their own way, or someone who is too kind, is indulgent.

industrious *(in-dus'-tri-ous)*. Hard-working; a person who is always working is industrious.

industry *(in-'dus-try)*. 1. Skill or cleverness in work. 2. Close attention to work. 3. Organised effort, especially in trade or manufacturing. A town with many industries is called an **industrial** town.

inedible *(in-ed'-i-ble)*. Not fit to be eaten, as "Horse-chestnuts are inedible".

inequality *(in-e-qual'-i-ty)*. State of being unequal; lack of equality.

inert *(in-ert')*. Dull; lifeless.

inestimable *(in-es'-ti-ma-ble)*. Worth so much that it is not possible to say how much it is worth.

inevitable *(in-ev'-i-ta-ble)*. Unavoidable. A thing that is bound to happen is inevitable. Day and night inevitably follow each other.

inexpedient *(in-ex-pe'-di-ent)*. Not practical; not advantageous.

inexpensive *(in-ex-pen'-sive)*. Not dear; cheap.

inexplicable *(in-ex'-pli-ca-ble)*. That which cannot be explained is inexplicable.

infallible *(in-fal'-li-ble)*. To be infallible is never to make a mistake. Of course, none of us is infallible.

infamous *(in'-fa-mous)*. Famous in a bad way.

infant *(in'-fant)*. A baby. The period during which one is a baby is called **infancy**.

infantry *(in'-fan-try)*. Foot soldiers.

infect *(in-fect')*. To give disease germs to somebody else. Thus, if a person with measles gives the complaint to another person, he has infected the second person. The **infection** has passed from one to the other.

infer *(in-fer')*. To come to a conclusion; to make up your mind about a thing after taking all the facts into account.

inferior *(in-fe'-ri-or)*. Lower.

infernal *(in-fer'-nal)*. To do with hell. Hell is often called the infernal regions. An infernal machine is one designed to cause destruction.

infest *(in-fest')*. To swarm about; to overrun, said of harmful things, as "The swamp was infested with mosquitoes".

infinite *(in'-fi-nite)*. Without any boundary; endless.

infinitesimal *(in-fin-i-tes'-i-mal)*. Very, very small.

infirmary *(in-fir'-ma-ry)*. A hospital for people who are ill.

infirmity *(in-fir'-mi-ty)*. 1. Feebleness; weakness. 2. Disease.

inflame *(in-flame')*. 1. When a person is inflamed, he is angry and fiery. 2. When a part of a person is inflamed, such as the eyes, a wound, a toe, etc., the part is red, hot and painful.

inflammable *(in-flam'-ma-ble)*. Readily or easily ignited; petrol is very inflammable.

inflammation *(in-flam-ma'-tion)*. When a part of the body is swollen, red, hot and giving pain, there is inflammation present.

inflate *(in-flate')*. To blow up or swell with air. You inflate a balloon by blowing into it.

inflect *(in-flect')*. 1. To change the tone of the voice. A person who does not inflect his voice has a dull voice. 2. To bend or curve.

inflection *(in-flec'-tion)*. 1. A bending. 2. A change made in the tone of the voice when speaking or reading to give the proper meaning. Thus, when you come to a full stop, you drop your voice.

inflict *(in-flict')*. To give a person something painful or unpleasant, as "His next thrust inflicted a slight wound to his enemy's sword-arm".

influence *(in'-flu-ence)*. 1. The power a person has in making others do things, as "He can get the workmen to do anything for him. His influence over them is tremendous". 2. To use this power.

influenza *(in-flu-en'-za)*. A contagious disease which is like a severe cold.

influx *(in'-flux)*. A flowing in, as "When the Queen visited our town, there was a great influx of people to see her".

inform *(in-form')*. To tell or acquaint.

informal *(in-for'-mal)*. Not formal; not done according to set rules. When you talk with your friends your talk is informal; but when a man gets up to speak to a large audience, and begins with "Ladies and Gentlemen", his talk is formal.

information *(in-for-ma'-tion)*. Facts; news, as "A guide gives information to travellers".

infringe *(in-fringe')*. To break; to violate; to trespass. To infringe the law is to do something legally wrong.

infuriate *(in-fu'-ri-ate)*. To make furious; to make very angry.

infuse *(in-fuse')*. 1. To inspire, as "The leader infused courage into his followers". 2. To steep in a liquid; thus dried tea is steeped or infused in hot water.

ingenious *(in-gen'-ious)*. Said of people who think of clever ideas or inventions, and of the things they invent.

ingenuous *(in-gen'-u-ous)*. Frank; innocent.

ingot *(in'-got)*. A bar or brick of gold or silver.

ingrain *(in-grain')*. 1. To fix in one's mind so that it will never be forgotten. 2. To dye materials so that they are the same colour all through, not merely on the surface.

ingratiate *(in-gra'-ti-ate)*. To ingratiate yourself with someone is to win his favour.

inhabit *(in-hab'-it)*. To live in.

inhabitant *(in-hab'-it-ant)*. A person or animal who lives in a place.

inhale *(in-hale')*. To breathe inwards; the opposite to **exhale.**

inherit *(in-her'-it)*. To become the legal owner of money or property on the death of the previous owner.

inhuman *(in-hu'-man)*. Not human. An inhuman person is cruel and brutal.

inimical *(in-im'-i-cal)*. Unfriendly.

inimitable *(in-im'-i-ta-ble)*. Not able to be imitated.

iniquity *(in-iq'-ui-ty)*. Injustice. A wicked action.

initial *(in-i'-tial)*. 1. The first letter of a word; thus the initial of John is J. 2. First, as "Her initial attempt was as good as her last".

initiate *(in-i'-ti-ate)*. 1. To initiate a person into a society is to make him a member of it. 2. To initiate a person in the way of doing something is to show him how to do it. 3. A person who is initiated is sometimes called an initiate.

inject *(in-ject')*. To force into; a doctor uses a syringe or needle to inject serum into a patient's arm.

injudicious *(in-ju-di'-cious)*. Not wise in the things you say or do. A person who says to a lady friend, "Isn't it a pity your hair is going grey so fast", is injudicious in what he says; and a person who offers a tiny stool to a stout lady is injudicious in what he does.

injunction *(in-junc'-tion)*. A command not to do something.

injure *(in'-jure)*. To hurt; harm; damage.

ink. A coloured liquid used with a pen for writing or printing.

inkling *(ink'-ling)*. A hint; anything that gives a person a notion of what is about to happen.

inlaid *(in'-laid* or *in-laid')*. Ornamented or beautified by the inserting of pieces of wood, metal, ivory, etc.

inland *(in'-land)*. 1. Not on the coast; thus Leicester is an inland town. 2. Not foreign; thus there is inland trade and foreign or overseas trade.

inlet *(in'-let)*. 1. A passage by which something is let in. 2. A small bay.

inn. A public house where people may obtain food and lodging; hotel; tavern.

innate *(in-nate')*. Born in (a person); thus we might say that acting is innate in a certain man, if we meant that he is a born actor.

inner *(in'-ner)*. Inside. Thus your inner thoughts are private or secret and you do not tell them to anybody.

innings *(in'-nings)*. The turn of one team to bat in such games as cricket.

innocent *(in'-no-cent)*. Not guilty; not having done any harm.

innocuous *(in-noc'-u-ous)*. Harmless.

innovation *(in-no-va'-tion)*. The introduction of something new or fresh.

innumerable *(in-nu'-mer-a-ble)*. Countless; very many.

inoculate *(in-oc'-u-late)*. To infect or give a disease. To force germs which will give a mild form of a disease into a person's body. The mild form of the disease prevents the person from catching the disease thereafter.

inordinate *(in-or'-di-nate)*. Much more than usual. A person with inordinate strength is tremendously strong.

inquest *(in'-quest)*. An inquiry to find the cause of death, which is conducted by an official known as a coroner.

inquire *(in-quire')*. To ask; to attempt to find out. Also spelled **enquire**. One who inquires makes **inquiries** *(in-quir'-ies)*. Also spelled **enquiries**.

inquisition *(in-qui-si'-tion)*. An inquiry. An inquisition suggests an inquiry of an unpleasant nature.

inquisitive *(in-quis'-i-tive)*. 1. A person who asks many questions is inquisitive. 2. An inquisitive person is also one who wants to know too much about other people's business.

inroad *(in'-road)*. 1. A sudden attack; an invasion. 2. A wearing away; using up.

insane *(in-sane')*. Not sane; mad.

insanity *(in-san'-i-ty)*. Lunacy; madness.

insatiable *(in-sa'-tia-ble)*. Very greedy; never satisfied; never having enough.

inscribe *(in-scribe')*. To write on.

inscription *(in-scrip'-tion)*. Words written or printed on something. You will find an inscription on a coin.

insect *(in'-sect)*. A small creature having six legs and a body divided into three parts—head, thorax and abdomen. A fly is an insect, but a spider, which has eight legs, is not an insect.

insecticide *(in-sec'-ti-cide)*. A powder, fluid, etc., for killing insects.

insecure *(in-se-cure')*. 1. Uncertain. 2. Exposed to danger or loss. 3. Not properly fastened.

insensible *(in-sen'-si-ble)*. 1. Having lost all feeling. 2. Unconscious.

inseparable *(in-sep'-a-ra-ble)*. Not able to be separated. Two friends who are always together are inseparable.

insert *(in-sert')*. To put in; to set in.

inside. 1. *(in'-side)*. The interior, as "The inside of the box is lined with paper". 2. *(in-side')*. Within; on the inside of; on rainy days children play inside the house, and on sunny days they play **outside** *(out'-side)*.

insidious *(in-sid'-i-ous)*. Sly; crafty; underhand.

insight *(in'-sight)*. A person having insight into things is one who has knowledge and understanding of them.

insignia *(in-sig'-ni-a)*. Signs or badges of office, rank or honour. A mayor's chain of office is his insignia.

insignificant *(in-sig-nif'-i-cant)*. Unimportant; trifling.

insinuate *(in-sin'-u-ate)*. 1. To introduce gently. 2. To hint. 3. To creep or flow in. 4. To insinuate yourself is to obtain entry or favour by flattery or stealth.

insipid *(in-sip'-id)*. 1. When said of things eaten or drunk, the meaning is "Not having enough flavour or taste". 2. When said of other things, it means uninteresting.

insist *(in-sist')*. To take a stand on something and refuse to give way; to say firmly that a thing must be done.

insolence *(in'-so-lence)*. Impudence and rudeness.

insolvent *(in-sol'-vent)*. Not having the money to pay one's debts.

inspect *(in-spect')*. To look carefully into.

inspection *(in-spec'-tion)*. When you look carefully into something you give an inspection and a person inspecting is an **inspector.**

inspire *(in-spire')*. 1. To breathe inwards. 2. To influence a person and give him new life and energy.

install *(in-stall')*. 1. To place in office with ceremony, as "The Chairman was installed at a special meeting". 2. To place machinery in position. 3. To place oneself, as "He installed himself at his desk".

instalment *(in-stal'-ment)*. 1. One of several payments, paid at regular intervals, by which a debt is settled. 2. Any one of several parts of a story that is told or published bit by bit.

instance *(in'-stance)*. An example.

instantaneous *(in-stan-ta'-ne-ous)*. Happening in an instant; acting at once.

instantly *(in'-stant-ly)*. At once; immediately.

instead *(in-stead')*. In place of, as "John is going instead of Jim".

instep *(in'-step)*. The arched upper part of the foot, from the toes to the ankle bone.

instigate *(in'-sti-gate)*. To urge on; to bring about by persuasion.

instil *(in-stil')*. To put in little by little, as ideas are instilled into a person's mind. This word is also spelled **instill.**

instinct *(in'-stinct)*. The power to do certain things without ever having learned how to do them. Thus, a baby cries by instinct, but it has to learn how to read and, therefore, reading is not done by instinct. Animals have instincts. Birds build their nests by instinct.

institute *(in'-sti-tute)*. 1. To establish or begin, as "The bank instituted a new plan for savings". 2. A society or group formed for a special purpose, such as a writers' institute.

instruct *(in-struct')*. To teach.

instruction *(in-struc'-tion)*. 1. Pupils receive instruction in arithmetic so they will know how to add, subtract, multiply and divide. 2. The instructions on a medicine bottle are the words written there that tell you how to use the medicine.

instrument *(in'-stru-ment)*. An article by which something is done. Thus a hammer is a carpenter's instrument and a piano is a musical instrument.

insubordination *(in-sub-or-di-na'-tion)*. Disobedience.

insular *(in'-su-lar)*. 1. Anything is insular that has to do with an island. 2. When we say that a person is insular, we mean that he is narrow-minded or dull.

insulate *(in'-su-late)*. To keep one thing apart from another. Electric wires are insulated to prevent damage.

insulin *(in'-su-lin)*. An animal extract used in the treatment of diabetes, discovered by Doctors Banting and Best.

insult 1. *(in-sult')*. To make rude remarks about someone. 2. *(in'-sult)*. A rude remark or action.

insurance *(in-sur'-ance)*. 1. The act of making sure or secure. 2. An agreement by which loss through fire, burglary, etc., will be made good, or a sum of money will be paid, in return for yearly payments called premiums.

insurgent *(in-sur'-gent)*. A rebel; one who revolts.

insurrection *(in-sur-rec'-tion)*. A revolt.

intact *(in-tact')*. Untouched; whole; complete.

integer *(in'-te-ger)*. A whole number, as 9 or 7, but not $\frac{1}{4}$.

intellect *(in'-tel-lect)*. The power of the mind to think, reason, judge or understand. One who has intellect is **intelligent** *(in-tel'-li-gent)*.

intemperate *(in-tem'-per-ate)*. A person who does not do things moderately is intemperate. Often, when we speak of an intemperate person we mean one who drinks too much; but the word may be used for people who smoke too much, eat too much, etc.

intend *(in-tend')*. To mean.

intense *(in-tense')*. Intense cold is extreme cold; intense light is strong light; intense interest is great interest; intense activity is much activity. Thus, intense is used to show a high degree.

intention *(in-ten'-tion)*. Purpose or plan; thus in "What was your intention when you said the boys could go home?" intention means purpose or plan.

inter *(in-ter')*. To bury.

intercede *(in-ter-cede')*. To intervene, usually on behalf of someone.

intercept *(in-ter-cept')*. To seize or stop something while it is going from one place to another; to interrupt; to cut off.

interchangeable *(in-ter-change'-a-ble)*. Things that may be used in place of each other are interchangeable, as the wheels on a car.

interest *(in'-ter-est)*. 1. Money paid for the use of a loan. Banks pay interest on money deposited in savings accounts. 2. A feeling of concern for, as "He takes an interest in the boy's future". 3. To interest someone is to capture his attention or excite his feelings. Thus, if geography interests you, you like learning about it. 4. An interest is something that interests you. Your interests may be camping, football and swimming, or painting, music and reading for example.

interesting *(in'-ter-est-ing)*. Having the power to grip attention.

interfere *(in-ter-fere')*. To meddle with, as "Don't interfere in other people's business".

interim *(in'-ter-im)*. The meantime; the period of time between.

interior *(in-te'-ri-or)*. Inside.

interjection *(in-ter-jec'-tion)*. An exclamation, as "Alas!"

interloper *(in'-ter-lop-er)*. An intruder; someone who should not be present but who finds his way in.

interlude *(in'-ter-lude)*. 1. A short piece of music played between the acts of a stage play. 2. An interval.

intermediate *(in-ter-me'-di-ate)*. Coming between; in the middle.

interminable *(in-ter'-mi-na-ble)*. Endless.

intermingle *(in-ter-min'-gle)*. To mix together.

intermittent *(in-ter-mit'-tent)*. An action that stops and starts over and over again is intermittent.

intern *(in-tern')*. To lock up; confine. When there is a war, the government may intern anyone who may be friendly to the enemy.

internal *(in-ter'-nal)*. Inside.

international *(in-ter-na'-tion-al)*. Having to do with two or more nations. Thus, if athletes of many nations were invited to compete at one place, the competition would be international.

interpose *(in-ter-pose')*. To place between.

interpreter *(in-ter'-pret-er)*. 1. One who can explain the meaning of something. 2. One who can translate meaning from one language to another.

interrogate *(in-ter'-ro-gate)*. To ask questions.

interrupt *(in-ter-rupt')*. To break in between; to stop or hinder, as "A switch is used to interrupt the flow of electricity in a wire". It is impolite to interrupt a conversation.

intersect *(in-ter-sect')*. To cut across. If two roads meet in the shape of an X, they intersect.

interval *(in'-ter-val)*. The time or space between two things; thus the interval between January 1st and February 1st is one month.

intervene *(in-ter-vene')*. To come between.

interview *(in'-ter-view)*. 1. A meeting which is held to discuss a special topic, such as an interview between a teacher and the parents of a pupil. 2. To meet and talk with someone, for a special purpose.

intestines *(in-tes'-tines)*. The long, tube-shaped organ of the body situated in the abdomen. It aids in digesting food and carrying away waste products.

intimation *(in-ti-ma'-tion)*. A hint.

intimidate *(in-tim'-i-date)*. To frighten someone in order to make him do something.

intolerant *(in-tol'-er-ant)*. Not allowing people to have their own opinions; persecuting.

intoxicate *(in-tox'-i-cate)*. 1. To make drunk. 2. To make a person very excited, usually through happiness.

intrepid *(in-trep'-id)*. Fearless.

intricate *(in'-tri-cate)*. A thing is intricate when it is very difficult to do or to understand.

intrigue 1. *(in'-trigue)*. A plot. 2. *(in-trigue')*. To plot. Things that arouse curiosity or interest are said to be **intriguing.**

intrinsic *(in-trin'-sic)*. Of the thing itself. The intrinsic value of a half-crown is about twopence, because that is the real value of the metal in it. Because the metal has been made into a coin of the realm, however, its **extrinsic** value is 2/6d. Gold sovereigns had to be withdrawn because the intrinsic value of the gold came to be worth more than £1.

introduce *(in-tro-duce')*. 1. To bring in, as "Raleigh first introduced potatoes into England". 2. To make one person known to another, as "Let me introduce you to Miss Jones".

intruder *(in-tru'-der)*. A person who comes in without being asked, or without having the right to come in.

intuition *(in-tu-i'-tion)*. The power of the mind to know without having been given any information or without using reason to come to a conclusion. For instance, if you meet someone for the first time and you suddenly know that he is an honest person, although no one has told you that and you have no way of knowing it, you are using intuition. The knowledge that the stranger is honest is an intuition.

inundation *(in-un-da'-tion)*. A flood.

invade *(in-vade')*. To enter a place, using force, for unfriendly reasons. Thus, an army that fights its way into a foreign country invades that country.

invalid. 1. *(in'-va-lid)*. A person who is ill. 2. *(in-val'-id)*. Not valid; not available, or of no use. Thus, a season ticket is invalid after the date upon which it expires or ends.

invaluable *(in-val'-u-able)*. Worth so much that its value cannot be stated; priceless.

invent *(in-vent')*. 1. To make something useful that nobody has ever made before or to think out a new way of doing something. 2. To invent a story, an excuse or other statement is to make up one which is not true, with the idea of gaining an unfair advantage by doing so.

invention *(in-ven'-tion)*. Something new which is made or thought out for the first time. The aeroplane is a wonderful invention.

inventory *(in'-ven-tor-y)*. A list or catalogue of articles that in some way form a kind of collection. Thus, a list of all the furniture in a house is an inventory, and if a stamp collector made a list of all the stamps in his album, that would be an inventory also.

invert *(in-vert')*. To turn upside down.

invertebrate *(in-ver'-te-brate)*. An animal without a backbone, such as a crab or a jelly-fish.

invest *(in-vest')*. 1. To invest money is to buy stocks, shares, or other things, in order to make a profit. 2. To invest someone in office is to install him in a position of authority with solemn ceremony. 3. To besiege.

investigate *(in-ves'-ti-gate)*. To examine very carefully.

inveterate *(in-vet'-er-ate)*. An inveterate smoker is one who has smoked a great deal for many years; an inveterate joker is one who has played jokes for a long time. Thus, an inveterate habit is a habit of long standing.

invidious *(in-vid'-i-ous)*. Giving offence; causing trouble.

invigorating *(in-vig'-or-at-ing)*. Providing vigour or strength; thus, sea air is invigorating.

invincible *(in-vin'-ci-ble)*. Not able to be conquered.

invisible *(in-vis'-i-ble)*. Not able to be seen.

invite *(in-vite')*. To ask a person to do a certain thing; thus, if you invite him to a party, you ask him to come to a party. When you ask him, you give an **invitation** *(in-vi-ta'-tion)*.

invoice *(in'-voice)*. A bill or a list of articles that a customer has bought, with the prices set out for each article, and the total value stated.

invoke *(in-voke')*. 1. To call for help, usually from God. When you say "God help us" you invoke God's help. 2. To summon by a magic spell. When Aladdin was in trouble he invoked the aid of the genie by rubbing the lamp.

involuntary *(in-vol'-un-tar-y)*. Not done by an act of the will; done without intending to do it or without thinking about doing it. Breathing is an involuntary action.

involved *(in-volved')*. Mixed up in; thus if your car is in an accident, it is involved in an accident.

iodine *(i'-o-dine)*. 1. One of the elements (see **element**). It is found in nature in the form of shiny, dark grey crystals. 2. **Tincture of iodine** is a brown liquid antiseptic with a strong odour. It is used to disinfect wounds.

irascible *(i-ras'-ci-ble)*. Said of a person whose temper rises quickly.

ire. Anger.

iris *(i'-ris)*. 1. The plant sometimes called the flag. 2. The ring of colour around the pupil of the eye.

irksome *(irk'-some)*. Tiresome; wearisome.

iron *(i'-ron)*. 1. A common metal from which tools and machinery are made. 2. A device with a flat surface which is heated to press clothing.

ironclad *(i'-ron-clad)*. 1. Anything having iron plates around it as a form of protection. 2. An agreement or regulation which is very difficult to break is said to be ironclad.

irony *(i'-ro-ny)*. Saying the opposite of what you mean in order to be emphatic or funny. If it is raining hard and you say, "What a lovely day!" or if you nickname a boy who is as slow as a snail "Old Lightning", you are using irony.

irrational *(ir-ra'-tion-al)*. Unreasonable.

irregular *(ir-reg'-u-lar)*. Not regular.

irrelevant *(ir-rel'-e-vant)*. Not to do with the matter in hand or the subject under discussion; thus, if we were chatting about our last summer holiday and you asked, "How many pints in a gallon?", your question would be irrelevant.

irreparable *(ir-rep'-a-ra-ble)*. Unable to be repaired or put right.

irrepressible *(ir-re-press'-i-ble)*. Said of a person who cannot be kept in his place or will not be "sat upon".

irrespective *(ir-re-spec'-tive)*. Without regard.

irretrievable *(ir-re-triev'-a-ble)*. Not able to be recovered. Thus, if you threw a penny into the ocean or a lake, it would be irretrievable.

irrigate *(ir'-ri-gate)*. To supply water to fields by cutting trenches or placing pipes across them.

irritate *(ir'-ri-tate)*. To annoy; make angry; vex; to cause to become inflamed.

island *(is'-land)*. A piece of land surrounded by water. An **isle** is usually a small island.

isolate *(i'-so-late)*. To keep apart. When a person has an infectious disease, it is necessary to isolate him, or others may catch the complaint.

issue *(is'-sue)*. 1. To come out, as "Water issued from the tap". 2. The result, as "The issue of the match was a disappointment to the home team". 3. To publish, as *"The Times* is issued every day". 4. A legal term for children, as "He died without issue", meaning that he did not leave any children when he died. 5. Point in question. In "The issue is whether children ought to do home-work", issue means question to be decided. To make an issue out of something means a fuss about it, or make it into a question of great importance.

isthmus *(isth'-mus)*. A narrow strip of land connecting two larger masses of land.

italic *(i-tal'-ic)*. *Italic is a kind of sloping type. The printers have set all this in italics.*

itch. When you want to scratch a place on your body, you want to because there is an itch. A mosquito bite is **itchy.**

item *(i'-tem)*. 1. Each separate thing in a group or list is an item. 2. A news item is a piece of news.

itinerant *(i-tin'-er-ant)*. Wandering; going from one place to another and never staying long anywhere.

itinerary *(i-tin'-er-ar-y)*. A record, route or programme of a journey.

its. In "The dog wagged its tail", its means belonging to it.

it's. It is, as "It's going to turn cold" or it has, as "It's been a hard winter".

ivory *(i'-vo-ry)*. 1. The tusks of elephants and other animals are made of ivory. 2. The light yellow colour of ivory.

ivy *(i'-vy)*. A climbing shrub with green leaves.

J

jab. A thrust with the tip of something, such as a stick.

jack. A tool for lifting heavy articles off the ground. A motorist uses a jack to lift his car in order to change a tyre.

jackal *(jack'-al)*. A carnivorous wild dog of Asia and Africa.

jackdaw *(jack'-daw)*. A black bird resembling a crow.

jacket *(jack'-et)*. A short coat or outer garment.

jackknife *(jack'-knife)*. A knife with a blade which folds into the handle. It is carried in the pocket.

jade. A hard green stone used for ornaments, etc.

jaded *(ja'-ded)*. Tired; worn out by hard work.

jaguar *(jag'-uar)*. A fierce, spotted, leopard-like animal of the American tropical zone.

jail. A prison or place where people are held while awaiting trial or while serving terms. (See **gaol.**)

jam. 1. When you crush or bruise something, you jam it. 2. When logs become heaped in the river, the logs are said to jam the river. 3. When you are unable to lift a window, we say the window is jammed. 4. When fruit is crushed and boiled with sugar, it is called jam.

jamb. One of the two uprights forming the frame of a door or window.

jangle *(jan'-gle)*. 1. An unmusical noise, such as the clanking of a chain. 2. To quarrel.

janitor *(jan'-i-tor)*. A doorkeeper or porter.

January *(Jan'-u-ar-y)*. The first month of the year. It has thirty-one days.

jar. 1. A glass or earthenware container. 2. To shake; to knock; to hit suddenly. 3. To be jarred is to receive a rude shock or an unpleasant surprise, as "The man was jarred by the news that his house was on fire".

jaundice *(jaun'-dice)*. A disease of the liver, which turns the patient's skin a dirty yellow colour.

jaunt. A short walk or hike, taken for pleasure.

jaw. The bones which frame the mouth. The lower jaw opens and closes.

jazz. A kind of popular music, Negro in origin, characterized by a special kind of dance rhythm.

jealous *(jeal'-ous)*. 1. You are jealous of something or someone you want to keep all to yourself. 2. Suspicious. 3. Afraid of losing your advantage. When you are jealous of someone who has succeeded where you have failed, you are annoyed with him because you think he has gained an advantage over you. 4. Envious.

jeep. A small car, usually without a roof, able to travel on rough ground.

jeer. To sneer and make fun of somebody in a coarse way.

jelly *(jel'-ly)*. A soft clear food made of gelatin and flavoured with fruit extracts.

jeopardy *(jeop'-ard-y)*. Danger.

jerk. 1. A sudden pull. 2. To give a sudden pull.

jersey *(jer'-sey)*. 1. A close-fitting sweater which is pulled over the head. 2. A knitted cloth made of wool, silk, etc., 3. A fawn-coloured type of cattle named Jersey because it comes from Jersey in the Channel Islands, near the coast of France.

jest. To say things in fun and not mean them.

jester *(jest'-er)*. A man who makes a habit of joking. In bygone times, jesters were employed in large houses.

Jesus *(Je'-sus)* or Jesus Christ. The Son of God.

jet. 1. A hard, black stone. 2. A jet of water, air, gas, etc., is a stream which shoots out of a narrow opening. 3. A jet plane is an aeroplane which is propelled by a jet engine.

jetsam *(jet'-sam)*. The cargo thrown overboard from a ship which is in distress and which needs to be lightened for its safety.

jetty *(jet'-ty)*. A pier or breakwater running out to sea, used either for the mooring of boats or to break the force of the waves dashing against the land.

jewel *(jew'-el)*. A gem or precious stone.

jewellery *(jew'-elle-ry)*. Ornaments made from gems and precious metals. (Sometimes spelled **jewelry**.)

jib. The three-cornered sail at the front of a yacht.

jingle *(jin'-gle)*. 1. A tinkling sound like that made by small bells. 2. Poetry that rhymes in a simple way.

job. 1. A position; a situation. 2. A piece of work.

jockey *(jock'-ey)*. A man or boy who rides horses in races.

jocular *(joc'-u-lar)*. Joking; given to jesting; merry.

join. 1. A point of junction. 2. To bring together, to unite, as "The girl's mother was able to join the handle to the teapot with glue". 3. To associate yourself with, as "The girl joins the Girl Guides". 4. To come together with, as "The boy ran across the street and joined his friends".

joint. A place where things are joined.

jointly *(joint'-ly)*. Together, as "The boys built the cart jointly".

joist. A thick strip of wood to which the floor-boards of a room are nailed.

joke. A funny story.

jolly *(jol'-ly)*. Merry; happy.

jolt. To shake in jerks.

jostle *(jos'-tle)*. To knock or bump against; to struggle with.

jot. 1. As small a portion as can be had of a thing. 2. To jot down something is to scribble it quickly.

journal *(jour'-nal)*. 1. A newspaper. 2. A book in which an account, or daily record, is kept.

journey *(jour'-ney)*. A going from one place to another; a trip.

jovial *(jo'-vi-al)*. Said of a merry person who is always good-natured.

joyful *(joy'-ful)*. Glad.

jubilant *(ju'-bi-lant)*. Joyful; very happy.

jubilee *(ju'-bi-lee)*. A time of celebration and rejoicing, often to celebrate an anniversary. When a king has reigned 25 years a Silver Jubilee is held.

judge. 1. A person who conducts a court and decides on points of law. 2. When you decide that a thing is right or wrong, you judge it.

judgement *(judge'-ment)*. 1. Opinion or estimate. 2. A decision or sentence in a court of law given by a judge. 3. The power of the mind to judge as "Use your judgement to decide which answer is right". Also spelled **judgment.**

judicious *(ju-di'-cious)*. Careful and sensible.

jug. A receptacle with one handle, used for holding liquids.

juggle *(jug'-gle)*. 1. To perform tricks requiring great nimbleness of the hands. One who performs juggling tricks is a **juggler.** 2. To cheat; to deceive.

juice. The liquid held inside something, usually fruit or vegetables. When you squeeze half an orange, juice comes out.

juicy *(juic'-y)*. Full of juice.

July *(Ju-ly')*. The seventh month of the year. July has 31 days.

jumble *(jum'-ble)*. 1. A muddle, as "All my clothes are in a jumble". 2. To muddle things together, as "I jumbled all the ribbons together and put them in a box".

junction *(junc'-tion)*. A spot where two or more things meet. A railway junction is a place where railway lines meet.

June. The sixth month of the year. June has 30 days.

jungle *(jun'-gle)*. A forest so dense that a man can hardly pass through it. Most jungles are in hot countries.

junior *(jun'-ior)*. 1. Younger. 2. Of lower rank.

junk. 1. A Chinese boat. 2. Things having no value are called junk.

jury *(ju'-ry)*. A certain number of people (usually 12) gathered together in a court of law, who listen to all the facts and then give their opinions on them. The usual question put to a jury is "Is the prisoner guilty or not guilty?" Each person serving on a jury is known as a **juryman** or **juror.**

justice *(jus'-tice)*. 1. Fairness. 2. Use of authority in upholding the law. 3. A judge or magistrate.

justify *(jus'-ti-fy)*. 1. To show that a thing is just or right. 2. To give good reasons for.

jut. To stand out or beyond something else. Your nose juts out from your face.

juvenile *(ju'-ve-nile)*. Youthful; young.

K

kaleidoscope *(ka-lei'-do-scope)*. A tube with an eyepiece, having a number of small pieces of glass of all colours placed between two small disks of glass, and three long mirrors. As the tube is shaken, the pieces of glass form an endless variety of beautiful geometric patterns.

kangaroo *(kan-ga-roo')*. An Australian mammal with powerful hind legs for leaping. The female has a pouch in which to carry her young.

kayak *(kay'-ak)*. An Eskimo canoe made by stretching skins over a frame. A kayak carries one person.

keel. A wooden or metal piece which extends along the length of the bottom of a boat. The keel supports the frame and steadies the boat.

keen. 1. Sharp, as "My knife is keen". 2. Eager, as "He is keen to go fishing".

keep. 1. Retain for your own use, as "You may keep that book". 2. Look after or provide for, as "He keeps his aged mother". 3. Stay, as in "Keep off the grass". 4. The strong central tower of a castle.

keg. A small cask or barrel.

kennel *(ken'-nel)*. A house or place in which dogs are kept.

kerb. The stone edging to the pavement.

kerchief *(ker'-chief)*. A piece of cloth which is worn around the neck or head.

kernel *(ker'-nel)*. 1. The soft material found inside the hard shell of a nut. 2. A grain of wheat or corn.

kerosene *(ker'-o-sene)*. The American name for paraffin oil.

ketch. A sailing boat with two masts.

kettle *(ket'-tle)*. A metal pot used for boiling water and cooking.

key. 1. A tool for working the lock of a door, etc. 2. Each letter on a typewriter or note on the piano is struck by means of a key. 3. The scale in which a piece of music is written. 4. A list of solutions to problems or puzzles.

khaki *(kha'-ki)*. The brownish yellow-green colour of a soldier's field uniform. 2. The cloth of that colour.

kick. To strike with the foot.

kid. 1. A young goat. 2. A kind of very soft leather made from the skin of a kid.

kidnap *(kid'-nap)*. To steal a person.

kidney *(kid'-ney)*. One of the two organs in the back of the middle part of the body which serve to purify the blood and discharge waste products.

kiln. A furnace for drying or baking certain things such as hops, bricks, etc.

kilt. A knee-length, pleated skirt worn by men in the Scottish Highlands.

kimono *(ki-mo'-no)*. 1. A loose outer garment worn by Japanese people. 2. A dressing gown.

kin. Your family or relatives.

kind. 1. Gentle and considerate, as "He is always kind to animals". 2. A class of thing, as "What kind of dog is that?"

kindergarten *(kin'-der-gar-ten)*. A school for very young children.

kindle *(kin'-dle)*. To set on fire.

kindred *(kin'-dred)*. 1. The members of one's family; all one's relations. 2. Things that are alike are said to be kindred things; thus "Music, singing and the kindred arts are the joy of educated people".

kine. Cows.

kingdom *(king'-dom)*. A country ruled by a king or queen. Great Britain is a kingdom.

kingfisher *(king'-fish-er)*. A brightly-coloured, crested bird which eats fish.

kink. A bend, twist or curl in straight hair, rope, piping, etc.

kinsfolk *(kins'-folk)*. Family or relatives.

kit. 1. Equipment that is carried by soldiers or travellers. 2. A set of tools.

kitchen *(kitch'-en)*. The room in a house or building where the food is cooked.

kite. 1. A light frame covered with thin material, launched in the air by the force of the wind, and used as a plaything by children. 2. A bird of prey.

kitten *(kit'-ten)*. A young cat.

knack. Ability to do a thing skilfully and neatly.

knapsack *(knap'-sack)*. A bag for carrying one's belongings on the back.

knave. 1. The Jack in playing cards. 2. A man who is sly, mean and artful.

knead. To mix certain things, such as flour and water or clay and water, using the hands or a machine to squeeze it to an even mass.

knee. The joint between the upper and lower leg.

kneel. To lower the body so that the weight is borne by the knee or knees. Many people kneel in prayer.

knell. The ringing of a bell, with a few seconds' interval between each sound, as at a death or funeral.

knife. A tool with a sharp edge for cutting. **knives** is the plural of knife.

knight. 1. A man who has been honoured with a title that allows him to be called "Sir"; thus Sir John Jones is a knight. At one time a knight was a soldier of a noble lord. 2. One of the pieces used in chess. 3. When a person is knighted, he kneels before the monarch who rests a sword on the person's shoulder. This ceremony is also called the dubbing of a knight.

knit. 1. To form into a knot; to tie. 2. To make garments, such as socks and sweaters, by interweaving loops made on long needles. 3. To contract, as in "His brows were knitted". 4. To grow together, as a broken bone knits.

knob. 1. A rounded bulge; a lump. 2. A knob-like handle or decoration, such as a door-knob, or a knob on a bed-post.

knock. 1. To hit or to rap, as "He knocked on the door". 2. A thumping or rapping noise as that made by banging the knuckles or the top of a cane against a door.

knoll. A small hill, usually covered with grass.

knot. 1. A lump formed by tying two or more pieces of thread, string, rope, etc., together, or by looping and tying a single string, rope, etc. 2. A speed of one nautical mile (6,080$\frac{1}{5}$ feet) per hour. 3. A lump or bump. 4. A knot of people is a little group of people; a knot of flowers is a little bunch of flowers, etc.

know. To be familiar with, acquainted with, or to understand. You may know the capital city of England, but you may not know the capital of Iceland.

knowledge *(knowl'-edge)*. The things that are known; the things that one can learn; information.

knuckle *(knuck'-le)*. A joint of the finger.

L

label *(la'-bel)*. A strip of paper, card, etc., fixed to something to show its contents, its owner, or the address to which it is to be sent.

laboratory *(la-bor'-a-tor-y)*. A room in which scientific experiments are done.

laborious *(la-bo'-ri-ous)*. Involving much hard work.

labour *(la'-bour)*. 1. Work. 2. When you labour at a task, you work at it.

labourer *(la'-bour-er)*. An unskilled worker.

labyrinth *(lab'-y-rinth)*. A place with so many twists and turns that it is difficult to find your way out of it; a maze.

lace. 1. A kind of fancy needlework that is attached to clothing or curtains for ornament. 2. When you lace a shoe, you pull a lace or string-like piece of cloth through the holes to hold the shoe on the foot.

lacerate *(lac'-er-ate)*. To wound by tearing the flesh.

lack. 1. Absence; deficiency; need; as "During a drought there is a lack of water". 2. To lack or be lacking means to be missing; to be absent; to be needed but not at hand. Thus, "When appetite is lacking, no food tastes delicious". 3. To be without; to need and not have, as "I could repair the roof in a moment, but I lack nails", or "The poor, homeless boy lacked food and clothing".

lacquer *(lac'-quer)*. Varnish.

lacrosse *(la-crosse')*. A ball game which is played between two twelve-member teams, each player using a long-handled, webbed racket.

lad. A boy.

ladder *(lad'-der)*. A framework of two parallel side-pieces connected by steps or rungs, on which a person steps as he climbs.

laden *(la'-den)*. Loaded.

ladies *(la'-dies)*. More than one woman. (See **lady**.)

ladle *(la'-dle)*. A long-handled spoon for dipping into soup, etc.

lady *(la'-dy)*. 1. A woman. 2. A title given to the wife of a man holding a title, or to a woman with a title in her own right.

lag. To fall behind.

laggard *(lag'-gard)*. Someone who lags behind; therefore, an idle person.

lagoon *(la-goon')*. A lake-like stretch of water enclosed within a coral atoll.

laid. The past tense of lay. "The hen laid an egg in the nest."

lair. The bed or home of a wild animal.

lake. A stretch of water with land all round it.

lamb. 1. The young of a sheep. 2. The flesh of a young sheep.

lame. Crippled; unable to walk properly.

lament *(la-ment')*. To mourn.

lamentable *(lam'-en-ta-ble)*. 1. Wretched ; fit to awaken mourning, as "The girl has not yet forgotten her father's lamentable death". 2. Disgraceful, as "His shoes are in a lamentable state".

lamp. A device for giving light, such as an oil lamp or an electric lamp.

lance. A long shaft of wood with a spear-head of iron, used by soldiers on horse-back.

land. 1. That part of the world not covered by the sea. 2. A country, such as England. 3. To set foot on shore, as "He landed as soon as the boat was safely tied". 4. To come to rest on land. Thus, "A cat always lands on its feet"; "The aeroplane landed safely". 5. To bring to land, as "The pilot landed the aeroplane in record time", or "My father landed a huge salmon while fishing last summer".

landing *(land'-ing)*. 1. Act of bringing to land or coming to land. 2. A place where a ship is unloaded. 3. A level space at the top of a flight of stairs.

landlocked *(land'-locked)*. 1. Surrounded or nearly surrounded by land. 2. Shut off from the sea, as "landlocked salmon".

landlord *(land'-lord)*. A person who rents houses or land to others. The person to whom the house or land is rented is a **tenant.**

landscape *(land'-scape)*. A country scene or a picture of it.

lane. A narrow road.

language *(lan'-guage)*. The speech, or way of talking, of the people of a particular country. Thus, English is the language spoken in England, Australia and the United States.

languid *(lan'-guid)*. Drooping; without vitality; tired.

languish *(lan'-guish)*. To droop and grow weak.

lantern *(lan'-tern)*. A metal frame with a glass front and a light inside, suitable for carrying about. A portable lamp.

lapel *(la-pel')*. The part of the breast of a coat which laps over and is folded back.

lapse. 1. In "My driving licence has lapsed", lapsed means run out or expired. 2. In "After two years of being honest, the thief lapsed into crime again", lapsed means went back. 3. A failure or careless slip, thus a lapse of the tongue is an error in speaking; a lapse in judgement is an error in judgement.

larceny *(lar'-ce-ny)*. Theft; the crime of stealing.

larch. One of the smaller cone-bearing trees, with needle-like leaves.

lard. The fat of pigs, cooked and purified.

larder *(lard'-er)*. A cupboard or room where food is kept.

large. Big; huge; of great size. Most boys would choose a large apple rather than a small one.

lark. 1. A small song-bird. 2. A piece of fun.

larva *(lar'-va)*. A young insect in its first stage of development, after it hatches out of the egg and before it changes into a pupa.

larynx *(lar'-ynx)*. The upper part of the windpipe.

lass. A girl.

lassitude *(las'-si-tude)*. Lack of energy or strength; faintness; weariness.

lasso *(las'-so)*. A long rope with a running loop at one end, which is thrown over the head or around the leg of a horse or a cow in order to catch the animal. Also called a **lariat** *(lar'-i-at)*.

last. 1. The end one of a number of things, as "December 31 is the last day of the year". 2. To endure or hold out, as "Will the candle last until we have finished?" 3. On the latest occasion, as "When did you see him last?" 4. The wood or metal shape of a foot on which shoes are made or repaired.

latch. The fastening catch on a door.

late. Behind time, as "Because he was late in arriving at the station, he missed the train".

latent *(la'-tent)*. Hidden; undeveloped.

lateral *(lat'-er-al)*. At the side; of the side.

lath. A thin strip of wood. The inside walls and ceilings of a building are sometimes made of laths, on top of which plaster or tile is laid.

lathe. A machine for turning and shaping wood and metal.

lather *(lath'-er)*. Froth made by soap and water.

Latin *(Lat'-in)*. A language spoken and written by the people of ancient Rome. Many words in English come from the Latin language.

latitude *(lat'-i-tude)*. 1. On a map of the world, you will find lines which are parallel to the equator. These are known as lines of latitude. By noting the figures given with the lines, it is possible to find the distance north or south of the equator of any place in the world. 2. Freedom of conduct or action, as "Children are allowed more latitude than they were a century ago".

lattice *(lat'-tice)*. 1. Strips of wood or metal placed across each other to form a network, with open spaces between them. 2. A window made of a network of wood or metal, with glass filling the spaces.

laudable *(laud'-a-ble)*. Worthy of praise.

laugh. When you hear, see, or think of something funny, you laugh by making sounds with the mouth and throat. The sound you make is called **laughter.**

launch. 1. A vessel is launched when it is slid into the water for the first time. 2. A launch is a pleasure boat powered by an engine. 3. To launch something is to start it on a course.

laundry *(laun'-dry)*. 1. The washing of clothes. 2. The place where clothes are washed. 3. Clothes that are to be washed or are being washed.

laurel *(lau'-rel)*. 1. The bay tree, an evergreen with glossy leaves which are used as spice. 2. **laurels** means honours or fame. To rest on your laurels means to be content with the honours you have already won.

lava *(la'-va)*. The melted rock that pours out of an erupting volcano.

lavatory *(lav'-a-to-ry)*. A place where a person may wash and tidy himself.

lavender *(lav'-en-der)*. 1. A small, lilac-flowered, narrow-leaved shrub cultivated for perfume. 2. A pale purple colour.

lavish *(lav'-ish)*. 1. Wasteful; generous. 2. To give generously; to waste.

law. 1. A rule made by the government of a country. 2. The whole body of laws which are in force in a country. 3. The law courts; the whole body of men engaged in enforcing or administering the law. 4. In science, a law is a statement of a never-changing order in things. There is, for example, the law of gravity. 5. A principle; a rule of conduct; a rule which common sense tells us we should keep, such as the laws of health.

lawn. 1. A space covered with grass that is kept trimmed. 2. A thin material, made of linen or cotton.

lawyer *(law'-yer)*. A person trained to give advice about points of law and to act for people in court.

lax. Loose; slack; not strict; careless.

layer *(lay'-er)*. One thickness of anything, as a layer of bricks, a layer of sand, a layer of bed-clothes.

layman *(lay'-man)*. 1. A church term, meaning a person who is not a clergyman. 2. A non-professional man.

lazy *(la'-zy)*. 1. Unwilling to work. 2. Slow.

lead. 1. To guide; to be the first. 2. A soft grey metal. 3. The black core of a lead pencil, which makes the marks.

leader *(lead'-er)*. The chief, as "the leader of the band"; the person who goes first, as "The leader of the column of boys is marching out of step".

leaf. 1. That part of a plant which grows out from the stem or branch and by which the plant breathes. 2. A sheet of paper, each side of which is a page. 3. That portion of the top of a table which can be taken out to make the table smaller.

league. 1. A joining together of people, groups, or nations, for common interests. 2. A distance of three miles.

leak. 1. An unwanted hole in a vessel, pipe, boat, etc., which allows a liquid to enter or escape. 2. To allow liquid to enter or escape through a leak.

leaky *(leak'-y)*. Allowing liquid to enter or escape through a leak or leaks; thus, "As soon as we launched the leaky old boat it filled up with water and sank".

lean. 1. To bend, as "The tree is leaning over". 2. To bend so as to receive support or rest the weight on something, as "The old man was leaning on his cane". 3. Lean meat is meat without fat. 4. Thin; poor. Thus, a lean person is a person who is thin and a lean purse is one with little money in it.

leap. 1. To jump. 2. A large jump.

learn. To gain knowledge, skill or information. Pupils attend school to learn to read, to write and to do arithmetic.

lease. 1. A signed agreement to rent a house, land, etc., for a number of years. 2. To rent.

leash. A strap used for holding or leading animals.

least. Smallest.

leather *(leath'-er)*. A material made from the skins of animals which is used in making shoes, gloves, etc.

leave. 1. To depart, as "You leave home to attend school". 2. To put something down and go away from it, as "Where did you leave my fountain pen?" To go away from a person, as "She left her mother on the railway platform". 3. A holiday, as "When will you get leave?" 4. Permission, as "Give me leave to stay a little longer".

lecture *(lec'-ture)*. 1. An instructive talk on some special subject. 2. To give such a talk. 3. A scolding. 4. To give a scolding.

led. The past tense of lead, as in "The chief led his warriors into battle".

ledge. A narrow shelf, as a window ledge or a mountain ledge.

ledger *(ledg'-er)*. A book in which a person keeps an account of all the money he receives and spends.

leech. 1. A worm that lives in water and sucks the blood of animals for its food. 2. A person who preys on others. (See **prey**.)

leek. A table vegetable belonging to the onion family.

leeward *(lee'-ward)*. The side opposite to windward, that is, the side sheltered from the wind.

left. 1. The past tense of leave, as in "Mr. Jones left yesterday". 2. The side opposite the right.

legacy *(leg'-a-cy)*. Money or property left to someone in a will.

legal *(le'-gal)*. 1. Lawful; in the way required by the laws of the country. 2. Having to do with the law, as "a legal matter".

legend *(leg'-end)*. 1. A story of something that occurred long ago, which may or may not be true. 2. The inscription or motto on a coin, medal, or coat of arms.

leggings *(leg'-gings)*. A covering for the legs, to keep them free from snow, mud, etc.

legible *(leg'-i-ble)*. Able to be read; easy to read. Handwriting, for instance, if well written is legible; but when badly written is often **illegible.**

legion *(le'-gion)*. 1. Originally the name given to a body of Roman soldiers numbering from 3,000 to 6,000. 2. A great number; a multitude.

legislate *(leg'-is-late)*. To make laws.

legislature *(leg'-is-la-ture)*. The body of people who make the laws which govern a country.

legitimate *(le-git'-i-mate)*. Lawful; as the law requires.

leisure *(lei'-sure)*. The time one has which is not taken up by work or sleep; spare time.

leisurely *(lei'-sure-ly)*. Slow; taking plenty of time.

lemon *(lem'-on)*. A sour, yellow citrus fruit which grows on thorny trees in warm climates.

lemonade *(lem-on-ade')*. A drink made by mixing lemon juice, sugar and water.

lend. To give to another person to use temporarily, as "John asked Joe to lend him his book". Banks lend money.

length. The distance from one end to another, as "The length of the room was sixteen feet".

lengthen *(length'-en)*. To make longer.

lenient *(le'-ni-ent)*. Merciful; mild; not strict.

lens. A piece of transparent substance with one or both sides curved for concentrating or dispersing light rays.

lent. 1. The past tense of lend, as "He lent his book to John". 2. **Lent.** The forty days before Easter.

leopard *(leop'-ard)*. An animal much like a tiger, but with spots on its body instead of stripes.

less. 1. Smaller in quantity. 2. Inferior, as "His standing is less than yours". 3. Minus, as "3 less 2 is 1".

lesson *(les'-son)*. Something to be learned.

lest. For fear that.

let. 1. To allow, as "I will let you go if you promise to come back". 2. To rent. "Flat to let" means "flat for rent".

lethal *(le'thal)*. Capable of causing death. Thus, astronauts have to be protected from lethal cosmic rays.

lethargy *(leth'-ar-gy)*. A lack of energy; dullness.

letter *(let'-ter)*. 1. Any of the twenty-six signs of the alphabet, as A or B or C, etc. 2. A message written on note-paper and put in an addressed envelope. 3. In "a man of letters", letters means learning.

lettuce *(let'-tuce)*. A leafy green salad vegetable.

level *(lev'-el)*. A level surface is a flat, even surface.

lever *(lev'-er)*. A long rod or bar used for lifting heavy weights.

levy *(lev'-y)*. To collect or raise money or men for some special use. Thus the government levies money in the form of taxes and it levies men as soldiers when they are needed for fighting.

liable *(li'-a-ble)*. 1. Responsible, as "A man is liable for any damage done by his dog". 2. Likely, as "If you get wet feet you are liable to catch cold".

liar *(li'-ar)*. A person who lies, that is, a person who says things which are untrue.

libel *(li'-bel)*. A statement that injures someone's character. Even if what is said of the person is true, it may still be **libellous.**

liberal *(lib'-er-al)*. 1. Generous, as "He is liberal with his money". 2. Ample or plenty, as "He has a liberal supply of wood to light the fire". 3. The Liberal Party is one of the political parties of England. A Liberal is a member of the Liberal Party.

liberate *(lib'-er-ate)*. To set free.

liberty *(lib'-er-ty)*. Freedom.

librarian *(li-brar'-i-an)*. A person who is trained for work in a library.

library *(li'-brar-y)*. 1. A collection of books. 2. A room or building in which a collection of books is kept.

lice. Small, wingless insects that live in the hair and on the skin of people and animals. Lice is the plural of **louse.**

licence *(li'-cence)*. A written permission to do something; thus before a motor-car may travel on the road, the owner must have a licence. If a man wishes to sell tobacco, he must have a tobacco licence. If you keep a dog, you need a dog licence, etc.

lick. 1. To pass the tongue over. 2. In a report of a fire, it is often said that the flames licked the houses near by.

lid. A covering on or over something, as an eyelid.

lie. 1. A statement which is not true. 2. To lie is to tell a lie. 3. To recline; to place yourself down flat, as you do when you go to bed.

lieutenant *(lieu-ten'-ant)*.   A rank in the armed forces, usually of a junior officer; a man of such a rank.

life.   1. The quality or character which distinguishes an animal or a plant from a dead or inanimate thing, such as a stone or a table.   Because they have life plants and animals are able to eat, grow and reproduce.   2. An individual existence, as "Her life had been full of happiness".

lifebuoy *(life'-buoy)*.   A ring of material that will float, which is used to support a person in water.

lifeguard *(life'-guard)*.   A person who is employed to look after the safety of people swimming at a beach or in a pool.

lift.   1. In "I will lift it up in a moment", lift means raise.   2. In "Give me a lift in your car", lift means help on the way. 3. A machine for raising goods and people to the upper floors of a building.

light.   1. That which shines or is brilliant, usually as a result of burning or great heat; the opposite to darkness.   2. Anything that gives light, as the sun, a lamp, etc.   3. The opposite to dark; yellow, pink and mauve are light colours.   4. Not heavy.   5. Not of great strength.   6. Unimportant; not serious.

lighten *(light'-en)*.   1. To lessen the weight of.   2. To grow light. 3. To make (colour) lighter.

lighter *(light'-er)*.   1. Not so heavy as something else, as "This parcel is lighter than the other".   2. A flat-bottomed boat used for loading and unloading ships that cannot come into dock.

lightning *(light'-ning)*.   A brilliant flash of electricity in the sky, often followed by thunder.

like.   1. A thing is like another when the two look almost or quite the same.   2. A person likes a thing when he is fond of it.

likely *(like'-ly)*.   Probable or probably; almost certain to happen.

likeness *(like'-ness)*.   1. A person's likeness is his portrait. 2. The resemblance of one thing to another.

lilac *(li'lac)*.   A shrub on which small fragant flowers grow in large clusters, usually light purple to dark purple or white in colour.

lily *(lil'-y)*.   A plant with a white, trumpet-shaped flower.

limb. 1. One of the jointed parts of a body, as the arms, legs, wings. 2. A branch of a tree.

lime. 1. The name of a tree. 2. A fruit resembling a lemon, light green in colour, from which lime-juice is obtained. 3. A chalky substance used for making cement, for white-washing, and for treating the soil in gardens to make it sweet.

limestone *(lime'-stone)*. A type of stone used for building and for making lime.

limit *(lim'-it)*. The farthest point to which one can go.

limited *(lim'-it-ed)*. Restricted; confined; not endless.

limp. 1. To walk as though lame. 2. Easily bent or folded; not stiff.

limpet *(lim'-pet)*. A small creature with a tent-shaped shell. It is found clinging to the rocks at the seaside.

limpid *(lim'-pid)*. Clear; transparent.

line. 1. A thread, cord, string or rope, such as a clothes line. 2. A telephone or telegraph wire. 3. In geometry, that which has length but no breadth. 4. In drawing, a long, single stroke. 5. To bring into line is to bring into a straight line. 6. A row of letters or words extending across a page. 7. A boundary or limit. "There I draw the line" means "I will go no further than that". 8. "Drop me a line" means "Write me a letter". 9. A kind of profession or work. "What is your line?" means "What kind of work do you do?" 10. A number of ships or vehicles that regularly go over a certain route. 11. To line something is to put a lining in it.

linear *(lin'-e-ar)*. To do with lines; thus linear measure is the measure of length.

linen *(lin'-en)*. Material or cloth made from the fibre of flax.

liner *(lin'-er)*. A vessel or aircraft belonging to a regular line and used for carrying passengers.

linger *(lin'-ger)*. 1. To stay in the same place or condition. 2. To delay or to be unnecessarily slow in going.

lingerie *(lin-ge-rie')*. Women's underclothes.

linguist *(lin'-guist)*. 1. A person who speaks foreign languages well. 2. A person who studies language.

liniment *(lin'-i-ment)*. A liquid preparation that is rubbed on the skin to cure some ache or pain.

lining *(lin'-ing)*. The inner covering of a thing, such as the lining of a coat.

link. 1. One of the separate parts or loops of a chain. 2. Anything that joins one thing to another.

linoleum *(li-no'-le-um)*. A type of floor covering.

lint. 1. Flax ready for spinning into linen. 2. Fine bits of fluff or thread from cloth. 3. A soft material used for dressing wounds.

lintel *(lin'-tel)*. The top bar in the frame of a door or window.

lion *(li'-on)*. A large, powerful member of the cat family which lives in Africa and Southern Asia.

liquefy *(liq'-ue-fy)*. To dissolve or to make into a liquid.

liqueur *(li-queur')*. A sweet, strong alcoholic drink, taken in small quantities after dinner.

liquid *(liq'-uid)*. 1. A fluid; anything that runs in the way water does. 2. Flowing.

liquidate *(liq'-ui-date)*. To settle one's debts or to pay money that is owing.

liquor *(liq'-uor)*. 1. Any liquid. 2. Any type of alcoholic drink.

liquorice *(li'-quor-ice)*. A black substance obtained from the root of a plant. It is used as a medicine, and also in making sweets.

lisp. To speak incorrectly, pronouncing the sounds s and z as if they were **th**.

list. 1. A list of names is a number of names written down one after the other in columns. 2. To list things is to write down their names in a list. If you listed the things you wanted to do during the summer holidays, you would write down the names of all the activities you had in mind, one under the other. 2. To lean to one side, as "The boat was half full of water and was listing badly".

listen *(lis'-ten)*. To give your attention to hearing, as in "Listen to the waves lapping on the shore".

listless *(list'-less)*. Not having the will or inclination to do anything or to take an interest in anything.

litany *(lit'-a-ny)*. A prayer of supplication in which the clergyman says certain parts and the people say others.

literary *(lit'-er-ar-y)*. Having to do with learning and books.

literature *(lit'-er-a-ture)*. Writing; written productions, such as stories, poems, essays, etc.; the whole body of written works. English literature is all the works that have been written in the English language.

litter *(lit'-ter).* 1. Small pieces of paper, banana skins, orange peel, and other rubbish dropped about on the ground. 2. To drop any of these things on the ground and make the place untidy. 3. The straw bed of animals. 4. A bed or couch arranged on poles in which a sick person may be carried over rough ground. 5. A brood of young animals.

little *(lit'-tle).* 1. Small. 2. Not much, as "He lived in a house in the country and thought little of walking miles through the woods".

live. 1. To be alive is to live, as "We live in the age of rockets". 2. To dwell, as "Some people live in cities and some live on farms". 3. Alive; living; the opposite to dead.

livelihood *(live'-li-hood).* Means of earning a living.

lively *(live'-ly).* Gay; cheerful; the opposite to dull.

liver *(liv'-er).* A large vital organ in man and many other animals, situated between the chest and the intestines. It manufactures bile, a liquid used in the process of digestion, purifies the blood, stores up various food elements, and aids in the making of blood.

livery *(liv'-er-y).* The special dress worn by servants or by a particular group.

live-stock *(live'-stock).* The animals on a farm, such as cattle, horses, sheep, pigs, etc.

livid *(liv'-id).* 1. Deadly pale. 2. The dull, bluish-purple colour of a bruise.

lizard *(liz'-ard).* A type of reptile which has a long tail, four feet and a long body.

llama *(lla'-ma).* A small South American animal similar to a camel but having no hump.

load. 1. To load a cart is to fill it. 2. What the cart carries is its load. 3. To load a gun is to place the bullets in it to make it ready for firing.

loaf. 1. A loaf of bread is a portion of bread dough which has been baked in a tin. The plural of loaf is **loaves.** 2. Anything shaped like a loaf of bread. 3. To loaf is to lounge about; to idle.

loam. A mixture of fertile earth and decayed vegetation.

loan. Something lent, especially a sum of money lent on condition that the borrower repay the sum with interest.

loath. Unwilling.

loathe. To hate very much indeed.

lobby *(lob'-by)*. An entrance-hall or a passage with rooms around it.

lobster *(lob'-ster)*. An edible sea animal with ten feet, the first pair of which form two big claws.

local *(lo'-cal)*. Having to do with a particular place. In your neighbourhood, there may be a local post-office, a local doctor, etc.

location *(lo-ca'-tion)*. A place where something is situated.

lock. 1. A few strands of hair. 2. A fastening operated by a key or a combination. 3. To fasten shut securely with a lock. 4. An enclosure in a river or canal with gates at either end, which is used to raise or lower boats passing from one level to another.

locker *(lock'-er)*. A box, chest or cupboard which locks, and in which one may keep personal things.

locket *(lock'-et)*. A small metal holder which is usually worn about the neck on a necklace, and in which one may keep a picture or a lock of hair.

locomotive *(lo-co-mo'-tive)*. An engine that travels from place to place by its own power; especially, a steam or diesel engine used on a railway.

locust *(lo'-cust)*. 1. A large insect of the grasshopper family. In Asia and Africa migrating swarms often destroy crops. 2. The fruit of the carob-tree. 3. Several different kinds of tree are known as locust-trees.

lodge. 1. A house in the country, occupied only in some special season, such as a hunting lodge. 2. A place where the members of certain societies hold their meetings. 3. To live in a place for a while. 4. To lodge a complaint is to make a complaint. 5. To make something stick in one place. "Lodged", therefore, means stuck.

lodger *(lodg'-er)*. A person who rents a room in somebody's house and lives in it.

loft. A store-room situated at the top of a house; a place where hay is stored over a stable.

lofty *(loft'-y)*. 1. High. 2. Stately. 3. Haughty.

log. 1. A section of a tree. 2. A log cabin is one made from wooden logs. 3. A device which measures the speed of a ship. 4. A book for keeping a record of things that have happened.

logic *(log'-ic)*. 1. The science which teaches how to reason correctly. 2. An orderly way of presenting ideas.

loin. The lower part of the back.

loiter *(loi'-ter)*. To go slowly or to hang about.

loll. 1. To lounge; to lie about. 2. To let the tongue hang out.

lone. Alone; isolated.

lonely *(lone'-ly)*. 1. Sad because of being alone. 2. Solitary.

long. 1. Of very great length in time or space. 2. To wish for.

longevity *(lon-gev'-i-ty)*. Long life.

longing *(long'-ing)*. A great wish for something.

longitude *(lon'-gi-tude)*. On a map of the world, you will find lines which cross the equator at right angles. These are known as lines of longitude. By noting the figures given with the lines, it is possible to find the distance east or west of Greenwich, England, of any place in the world.

loom. 1. A machine which makes cloth by weaving thread. 2. To appear above the horizon; to appear large in darkness or fog.

loop. 1. A ring formed by bending a piece of string or wire, etc. 2. A figure shaped like such a ring. 3. To make such a figure. When a piece of string or wire is looped, it is doubled so that the string crosses itself.

loose. When a thing is not tight or firmly fastened, it is loose.

loot. Plunder; property taken from its owner by force.

lopsided *(lop-sid'-ed)*. Having one side larger or heavier than the other.

loquacious *(lo-qua'-cious)*. Having far too much to say.

lord. 1. One who has power and authority; a master or ruler. 2. A title given in England to noblemen, bishops and judges. 3. Lord, with a capital, is a name given to God or Christ.

lose. When you lose a thing, you are unable to find it.

loss. A losing of something; the absence or disadvantage, etc., caused by losing something, as "The men felt a great loss when their leader died".

lost. The past tense of **lose,** as in "He lost his lunch yesterday, but he will not lose it to-day".

lot. 1. In "Which lot is mine?" lot means share. 2. In "Doesn't he seem to have an unhappy lot!" lot means fate. 3. In

"The auctioneer asked for bids for lot 43", lot means a particular group of things. 4. A small section of land. 5. A token or other small marked object used to decide some question by chance. You and your friends might decide who would be captain of a team by drawing lots. You could put several small pieces of folded paper into a hat. These would be the lots. One of them would be marked on the inside. After shaking them together, each one of you would draw out one without looking at it. Whoever drew the marked one would be declared captain.

lotion *(lo'-tion)*. A liquid for applying to the body in order to heal, soothe or cleanse it.

lottery *(lot'-ter-y)*. 1. A scheme for the distribution of prizes by drawing lots (see **lot**, No. 5). Perhaps one hundred numbered tickets are sold at sixpence each; one hundred numbers are shuffled in a box, three are drawn, and the holders of these numbers are given a first, second and third prize. 2. Anything determined by chance, as "Life is a lottery".

loud. Noisy.

lough. A lake or inlet of the sea in Ireland.

lounge. 1. To be lazy. 2. A room where you can relax.

lout. A silly, clumsy person.

love. Strong affection for someone or something; devotion; very great liking.

lovely *(love'-ly)*. Beautiful. Having qualities that attract love.

low. 1. The opposite to high. 2. Vulgar. 3. To make the noise of a cow; to bellow.

lowland *(low'-land)*. Flat, low-lying country.

lowly *(low'-ly)*. Humble.

loyal *(loy'-al)*. Faithful; true to one's country, school, family, employer, etc.

lozenge *(loz'-enge)*. 1. A diamond-shaped figure. 2. A small tablet of flavoured sugar or medicine to be dissolved in the mouth.

lubricate *(lu'-bri-cate)*. To smear with oil or grease so that there will be no friction or rubbing.

lucid *(lu'-cid)*. Bright; clear; plain.

luck. The good fortune or chance which comes to us without any reason.

lucrative *(lu'-cra-tive)*. Profitable; gainful.

ludicrous *(lu'-di-crous)*. Funny; laughable.

luggage *(lug'-gage)*. The belongings, packed in suitable cases, of a person who is travelling.

lukewarm *luke'-warm')*. 1. When speaking of things, lukewarm means fairly warm though not hot. 2. When speaking of people, it means that they are not particularly keen about whatever is mentioned; they are half-hearted.

lull. 1. In "There was a lull in the storm", lull means a period of calm. 2. In "She began to lull the baby to sleep", lull means to soothe.

lullaby *(lull'-a-by)*. A song sung to send a baby to sleep.

lumber *(lum'-ber)*. 1. Timber or wood in a rough state. 2. Useless things in the house which take up more room than they are worth. 3. To move heavily and noisily.

luminous *(lu'-mi-nous)*. Giving light. The sun is a luminous body and so is a candle. Luminous paint is paint that glows in the dark.

lump. 1. An irregular shaped object such as a lump of coal. 2. A swelling in or on the body.

lunar *(lu'-nar)*. Having to do with the moon.

lunatic *(lu'-na-tic)*. A person who is insane.

lunch. 1. A snack taken between meals, usually in the morning. 2. Short for **luncheon**, the midday meal taken by people who dine in the evening.

lung. One of the two breathing organs in the body.

lurch. 1. A sudden rolling movement. 2. To make a sudden rolling or staggering movement. 3. To leave someone in the lurch means to leave someone in difficulty without staying to help him.

lure. 1. Anything that tempts or attracts, such as the lures used to catch fish. 2. To tempt or attract; to lead on, as "The bandit lured the man into a woods and then attacked and robbed him".

lurid *(lur'-id)*. 1. Of an angry colour like fire. 2. A lurid description of something that has happened is one giving frightful details.

lurk. To lie in wait.

luscious *(lus'-cious)*. Delicious; of a sweet taste.

lust. When a person has a lust for anything, his wish for it is so great that he is ready to do wrong to get it.

lusty *(lust'-y)*. Vigorous; strong; full of life.

luxurious *(lux-u'-ri-ous)*. Providing more comfort than is really necessary. A room which is luxurious is one that is beautifully furnished.

luxury *(lux'-u-ry)*. 1. Something very pleasing to the senses which is costly and difficult to obtain; silks and jewels are luxuries. 2. To live in luxury means to live amid great comfort, in the possession of many costly and pleasing things.

lying *(ly'-ing)*. 1. Not telling the truth. 2. Being in a horizontal position.

lynx. A spotted North American wild cat with a short thick tail and tufted ears.

M

macadam *(mac-ad'-am)*. A kind of road surface made by compressing small hard stones into a firm mass.

macaroni *(mac-a-ro'-ni)*. A paste made from wheat flour, which is rolled into long thin tubes and other shapes and then dried. It is used for food.

mace. 1. A staff carried as a mark of authority. 2. A kind of club used as a weapon. 3. A kind of spice.

machine *(ma-chine')*. Any arrangement of many separate mechanical parts which act together to do a certain kind of work, such as an engine, lathe, etc.

machinery *(ma-chin'-er-y)*. A number of machines.

machinist *(ma-chin'-ist)*. A man who operates a machine.

mackerel *(mack'-er-el)*. An edible fish found in the North Atlantic.

mad. Insane.

madam *(mad'-am)*. Lady. (Used in direct address.)

magazine *(mag-a-zine')*. 1. A publication that appears regularly every week, month, etc. 2. A place for storing explosives. 3. The part of a rifle which stores the cartridges and feeds them one by one into the firing position.

maggot *(mag'-got)*. The grub of a fly or other insect.

magic *(mag'-ic)*. The art of pretending to do things that seem impossible by the use of supernatural powers.

magician *(ma-gi'-cian)*. A person who performs tricks of magic.

magistrate *(mag'-is-trate)*. A person who judges cases in police courts.

magnanimous *(mag-nan'-i-mous)*. Noble-minded and generous.

magnate *(mag'-nate)*. A man who is important and who has a great deal of power.

magnet *(mag'-net)*. 1. A piece of steel or iron that attracts things made of iron or steel to it. 2. Anything that draws other things to it.

magneto *(mag-ne'-to)*. A machine that makes an electric current by the action of magnets.

magnificent *(mag-nif'-i-cent)*. Grand; noble.

magnify *(mag'-ni-fy)*. To make a thing look larger than it is.

magnitude *(mag'-ni-tude)*. Greatness of size or importance.

mahogany *(ma-hog'-a-ny)*. A tree having reddish-brown wood that is much used for furniture.

maid. 1. A young unmarried woman. 2. A woman who acts as a domestic servant.

mail. 1. Letters and parcels which are sent through the post office are known as mail. 2. A suit of armour made of linked rings of iron.

maim. To injure a leg or arm so that it becomes useless.

main. 1. Chief; principal; most important. 2. The principal gas or water pipe. 3. Strength, as in "He worked with all his might and main". 4. The ocean.

mainland *(main'-land)*. A large area of land, such as a continent; an area of land which is not an island.

maintain *(main-tain')*. 1. To keep up, as "He maintains a large house in the country". 2. To uphold, as "He maintained his opinion that he was right".

maize. Indian corn.

majestic *(ma-jes'-tic)*. Noble; grand; stately. When you see mountains topped with snow standing nobly against the sky, you might say they are majestic.

majesty *(maj'-es-ty)*. 1. Great dignity; awe-inspiring splendour. 2. "Your Majesty" is a title used when speaking to a king or queen. "His" or "Her Majesty" is used when referring to a king or queen.

major *(ma'-jor)*. 1. A soldier whose rank is just above that of a captain. 2. Greater, as "The major part of his time was spent in reading".

majority *(ma-jor'-i-ty)*. I. In "The majority of the people went home before dark", majority means the greater part. 2. "He reached his majority last Friday" means that last Friday he became 21 years old.

malady *(mal'-a-dy)*. Disease.

malaria *(ma-lar'-i-a)*. A tropical disease causing the patient to have a very high fever and chills. The germ is carried by a type of mosquito.

malcontent *(mal'-con-tent)*. A person who is never satisfied or happy with things as they are.

male. 1. An animal of the sex that does not bear offspring or lay eggs but enables animals of the female sex to do so by fertilization. 2. A boy or man.

malefactor *(mal'-e-fac-tor)*. A person who does wrong; a felon; a culprit.

malice *(mal'-ice)*. Spite; a desire that someone should come to harm.

malign *(ma-lign')*. 1. To say bad things that are not true about a person. 2. A malign person is one with an evil, spiteful nature.

malignant *(ma-lig'-nant)*. Causing much harm; deadly.

malleable *(mal'-le-a-ble)*. Said of something that is not brittle and, therefore, can be hammered into various shapes without cracking.

mallet *(mal'-let)*. A wooden hammer used by cabinet-makers and carpenters.

malt. Barley left in water until the grains begin to sprout and taste sweet.

maltreat *(mal-treat')*. To treat badly; to injure or hurt.

mammal *(mam'-mal)*. One of the class or group of animals in which the females feed their young with milk from their bodies.

mammoth *(mam'-moth)*. 1. An animal that was like an elephant but is now extinct. 2. Huge, as "London is a mammoth city".

manacles *(man'-a-cles)*. Handcuffs.

manage *(man'-age)*. 1. To look after or plan the arrangements of, as "He managed a baker's shop". 2. To be able to do something, as "He managed to climb to the top of the post". A person who manages is a **manager** and the work is under his **management.**

mane. The long hair on the neck of certain animals, as horses, lions, etc.

manfully *(man'-ful-ly)*. Bravely.

manger *(man'-ger)*. The trough in which the food is placed for horses, cattle, etc.

mangle *(man'-gle)*. 1. A machine for pressing clothes or for squeezing the water out of clothes that have been washed. 2. To spoil or injure by tearing, cutting or hacking repeatedly and roughly, as "The hunter's body was mangled beyond recognition by the lion".

manhood *(man'-hood)*. That part of the male person's life during which he is grown up.

mania *(ma'-ni-a)*. Madness.

maniac *(ma'-ni-ac)*. A mad person.

manicure *(man'-i-cure)*. The care of the hands and finger-nails.

manifest *(man'-i-fest)*. Plain; clear. "He is an absolute scoundrel. Nothing could be more manifest."

manifesto *(man-i-fes'-to)*. A public declaration; something that tells the people about an important government decision.

manipulate *(ma-nip'-u-late)*. 1. To handle a thing with care and skill. 2. To arrange matters cunningly (and often with sly deceit) so as to give yourself some advantage.

mankind *(man-kind')*. The human race; all the people in the world.

manly *(man'-ly)*. 1. Like a man. 2. Brave; upright and honest.

manner *(man'-ner)*. 1. The way in which a person conducts himself. 2. The way in which a thing is done, as "He did his work in a careless manner". 3. **manners** often means politeness.

manor *(man'-or)*. The estate of a lord; an estate with a manor-house, a garden and a farm.

mansion *(man'-sion)*. A large, well-built house.

mantel *(man'-tel)*. A slab of stone, piece of timber or some other material which forms a ledge above the fireplace.

mantle *(man'-tle)*. A cloak with no sleeves, worn over the shoulders.

manual *(man'-u-al)*. 1. Done by hand. 2. A handbook giving information about a subject.

manufacture *(man-u-fac'-ture)*. The making of goods by hand or by machinery. Usually, this word is used when referring to goods produced in large quantities by machines.

manufacturing *(man-u-fac'-tur-ing)*. The process of making things in large numbers.

manure *(ma-nure')*. Animal waste which is applied to the ground as fertilizer.

manuscript *(man'-u-script)*. A book or document written by hand or typed, but not printed.

map. A chart showing land and water areas and the location on the earth's surface of mountains, rivers, cities, etc.

mar. To damage; to injure; to spoil.

marauder *(ma-raud'-er)*. Any person that goes about looking for what can be stolen.

marble *(mar'-ble)*. 1. A hard and beautiful stone, often used for ornamenting buildings. 2. A small ball of stone, glass, clay, etc., used in games.

march. 1. To walk in step in the way soldiers do. 2. A piece of music, timed to suit walking in step.

March. The third month of the year. It has 31 days.

mare. A female horse.

margarine *(mar'-ga-rine)*. A substitute for butter made from vegetable oils.

margin *(mar'-gin)*. 1. The edge around a thing, as "the margin of the pond". 2. In "I have always had a fair margin between what I earn and what I spend", margin means difference. 3. The blank space left at the edge of a printed or written page.

marigold *(mar'-i-gold)*. A small, yellow garden flower.

marine *(ma-rine')*. To do with the sea or its commerce.

mariner *(mar'-i-ner)*. A seaman or sailor.

maritime *(mar'-i-time)*. Found near, or connected with, the sea. The Maritime Provinces of Canada are the provinces that border on the Atlantic Ocean.

mark. 1. Any visible sign, as a stroke, dot, dent, etc. 2. The thing aimed at, as "He reached his mark with one shot". 3. Points gained at school are marks, as "I had ten marks for arithmetic". 4. Pay attention to, as "Mark my words, he will not catch the train". 5. The unit of money used in Germany.

market *(mar'-ket)*. 1. A place where people meet to buy and sell. 2. To sell goods in a market.

marmalade *(mar'-ma-lade)*. A jam made by boiling Seville oranges or lemons with sugar.

maroon *(ma-roon')*. 1. A brownish-red colour. 2. To leave a person stranded in a lonely place such as a desert island.

marquee *(mar-quee')*. A large tent.

marquis *(mar'-quis)*. A nobleman who ranks below a duke.

marriage *(mar'-riage)*. 1. State of being married (see **marry**). 2. A wedding, or the ceremony of marrying.

marrow *(mar'-row)*. 1. A large vegetable. 2. The soft, fatty matter in the hollow centre of bones.

marry *(mar'-ry)*. 1. The act of taking as a partner a husband or a wife. 2. To join two people as husband and wife.

marsh. Swampy, wet ground.

marshmallow *(marsh'-mal-low)*. A kind of soft sweet.

martial *(mar'-tial)*. Warlike.

martin *(mar'-tin)*. Any one of various birds of the swallow family, as the sand martin, the house martin, etc.

martinet *(mar-tin-et')*. A person who is very strict with those placed under him.

martyr *(mar'-tyr)*. 1. A person who is put to death because of his beliefs. 2. A person who has to put up with a great deal of suffering.

marvel *(mar'-vel)*. 1. To wonder. 2. Something wonderful.

marvellous *(mar'-vel-lous)*. Wonderful.

mash. 1. To beat into a mixed mass, as a cook mashes potatoes. 2. A soft mixture.

mask. 1. A piece of paper or cloth which is placed over a person's face to hide his identity. 2. To mask your plans is to hide them.

mason *(ma'-son)*. A man who builds with stone.

masquerade *(mas-quer-ade')*. 1. To wear a mask or disguise. 2. To pretend you are somebody else. 3. A party at which everyone is in disguise.

massacre *(mas'-sa-cre)*. A wholesale murder of people.

massive *(mas'-sive)*. Very heavy and bulky.

mast. The upright pole that carries the sails and the rigging of a ship, a wireless or television aerial, etc.

master *(mas'-ter)*. 1. A person who has others working for him. 2. A title used in addressing an envelope to a boy, as "Master John Smith". 3. A great artist; thus we often speak of "one of the old masters", such as Rembrandt. 4. To master anything is to understand and do it correctly, as "Have you mastered your arithmetic?" 5. In some schools, a male teacher is called a master.

masterpiece *(mas'-ter-piece)*. A piece of work done with marvellous skill.

masticate *(mas'-ti-cate)*. To chew.

match. 1. A stick of wood or cardboard with a tip that catches fire when rubbed. 2. A contest or game, as a football match. 3. To be alike, as "The blue colour of this dress matches the blue colour of the scarf".

matchless *(match'-less)*. Having no equal.

mate. 1. A friend or companion. 2. One of a pair of creatures or things, such as birds, gloves, etc. 3. An officer of a ship, ranking below the captain.

material *(ma-te'-ri-al)*. What a thing is made of. When a dress is made, it is made of dress material, or cloth; a building is made of building material, or boards and blocks, etc.

maternal *(ma-ter'-nal)*. Motherly; of a mother; belonging to a mother.

mathematics *(math-e-mat'-ics)*. The science that has to do with arithmetic, algebra, geometry, trigonometry, etc.

matrimony *(mat'-ri-mo-ny)*. Marriage.

matron *(ma'-tron)*. 1. A motherly woman. 2. The woman who deals with the eating and sleeping arrangements and the health of people who live together in large numbers, as in a boarding school. 3. The head nurse in a hospital.

mattock *(mat'-tock)*. A tool like a pick-axe used for digging or breaking the ground.

mattress *(mat'-tress)*. A soft, thick covering placed over the springs of a bed.

mature *(ma-ture')*. 1. Ripe. 2. Fully developed.

maul. To pull about and injure with the hands or paws, as "The lion mauled the boy".

mausoleum *(mau-so-le'-um)*. A large tomb.

mauve. A light purple colour.

maxim *(max'-im)*. A wise saying, as "A fool and his money are soon parted".

maximum *(max'-i-mum)*. The greatest amount of a thing. If you write an arithmetic examination in which full marks are 100 and you earn 100 marks, you obtain the maximum number of marks. The exact opposite to maximum is **minimum,** which means the least amount of a thing.

May. The fifth month of the year. It has 31 days.

mayonnaise *(may-on-naise')*. A salad dressing made of eggs, oil, vinegar and seasonings.

mayor *(may'-or)*. The head, elected official in a town or city.

maze. A complicated system of paths or passages in which it is difficult to find one's way. A maze, such as the famous maze at Hampton Court, might be built for amusement.

mead. 1. A meadow. 2. A drink made of honey and water.

meadow *(mead'-ow)*. A grassy field.

meagre *(mea'-gre)*. Thin; lean; scanty; poor.

meal. 1. Grain, such as corn, ground into a flour. 2. Breakfast, lunch, dinner and supper are meals.

mean. 1. Stingy or selfish, as "Some people never give to others; they are mean". 2. To intend, as "What do you mean?" 3. Middle or half-way, as "10 is the mean of 5 and 15". 4. Poor, as "He lives in a very mean street".

meander *(me-an'-der)*. To wind about, as a stream does when it has many wide curves.

meaning *(mean'-ing)*. What is meant or what is intended.

measles *(mea'-sles)*. An infectious disease which causes a fever and a rash. Children often catch it.

measure *(mea'-sure)*. 1. To find the size, length, width, etc., of something. 2. Something used to measure with, as a pint measure. 3. Step; suitable action, as "Quarantine is a measure taken to prevent the spread of disease".

meat. 1. The flesh of animals used as food. 2. Food in general, as distinct from drink.

mechanic *(me-chan'-ic)*. A workman who repairs, makes or uses machinery.

mechanism *(mech'-a-nism)*. The parts of a machine that work together.

medal *(med'-al)*. A piece of metal, often in the shape of a coin or a cross, which has been made to celebrate some special event or to be given as a reward for merit. Soldiers are often given medals for doing heroic deeds. Usually, a medal is worn on the breast.

medallion *(me-dal'-lion)*. A medal of large size. A medallion is not usually worn.

meddle *(med'-dle)*. To interfere with things that are not your own business.

mediæval *(me-di-æ'-val)*. Belonging to the Middle Ages (from 500 A.D. to 1450 A.D., approximately). Also spelled **medieval.**

mediate *(me'-di-ate)*. To try to bring together two people who have quarrelled; to act as a go-between.

medical *(med'-i-cal)*. To do with medicine or the work of healing.

medicine *(med'-i-cine)*. 1. The science of the prevention and cure of disease; thus anything a doctor does in his profession has to do with medicine. 2. The preparation which a sick person takes to make him better.

meditation *(med-i-ta'-tion)*. Deep, continued thought.

Mediterranean *(Med-i-ter-ra'-ne-an)*. The sea bounded by Africa, Europe and the Near Eastern countries.

medium *(me'-di-um)*. 1. Middle or half-way, as "Warm is the medium degree of heat between hot and cold". 2. Any substance through which a force acts or through which ideas might be conveyed. Sound reaches your ears through the medium of the air. An artist might use paint as a medium for expressing his ideas.

medley *(med'-ley)*. A mixture.

meek. Mild, gentle and seldom angry. A meek person lets you have your own way; he does not want to force his own wishes on you.

meet. 1. To meet a person is to encounter or join him. 2. To be introduced to a person is to meet him. 3. To pay your bills is to meet your bills. 4. To come together, as "The class will meet for a picnic on Saturday". 5. In "It is meet that we should gather here", meet means fitting or proper.

meeting *(meet'-ing)*. A gathering.

megaphone *(meg'-a-phone)*. A large trumpet open at both ends. By putting the narrow end to the mouth and talking into it, the loudness of the voice is increased, so that what is said can be heard at a greater distance.

melancholy *(mel'-an-chol-y)*. 1. Sad. 2. Sadness or thoughtfulness.

mellow *(mel'-low)*. Soft, sweet or gentle with ripeness or age.

melodious *(me-lo'-di-ous)*. Sweet sounding; musical.

melody *(mel'-o-dy)*. 1. Sweet music. 2. A tune, as "Hum the melody of that song".

melon *(mel'-on)*. A juicy fruit such as water-melon.

melt. To soften or change from solid to liquid, as when ice melts in the spring.

membership *(mem'-ber-ship)*. The state of belonging to some society, club, etc.

membrane *(mem'-brane)*. A thin layer of skin, such as that which covers the inside of the nostrils.

memento *(me-mem'-to)*. An object that serves to remind you of something. You might go to the seaside and bring home a memento or souvenir to remind you of the good time you had.

memorable *(mem'-o-ra-ble)*. Worth remembering.

memorandum *(mem-o-ran'-dum)*. A note made by you to help you to remember something.

memorial *(me-mo'-ri-al)*. Something intended to remind people. Very often, a memorial is a stone monument put in a public place to keep alive the memory of a noted person who has died.

memorize *(mem'-o-rize)*. When you memorize a poem, you commit it to your mind, or remember it.

memory *(mem'-o-ry)*. 1. Your memory is your ability to recall a thing, place, person or idea. 2. A thing, person or event existing no more, as it is remembered.

menace *(men'-ace)*. 1. A threat. 2. To threaten.

menagerie *(me-nag'-er-ie)*. A collection of wild animals.

mend. To repair or improve.

mendicant *(men'-di-cant)*. A beggar.

menial *(me'-ni-al)*. Having to do with domestic servants; low; mean. Menial work is work that is fit to be done by a domestic servant.

mental *(men'-tal)*. To do with the mind. Mental hospitals are for people of unsound mind; mental cases are people who have unsound minds; thus mental is often used in speaking of mad people.

mention *(men'-tion)*. To speak about.

menu *(men'-u)*. Bill of fare; the list of foods served in a restaurant.

mercantile *(mer'-can-tile)*. To do with trade; thus the Mercantile Marine is the name given to all the boats occupied with the carrying of goods across the seas.

mercenary *(mer'-ce-nar-y)*. 1. Working merely for pay; thinking only about the money that is to be made by doing something. 2. A soldier working for pay in the army of a country that is not his own.

merchandise *(mer'-chan-dise)*. Goods to be sold.

merchant *(mer'-chant)*. A man who buys and sells goods.

merciful *(mer'-ci-ful)*. Having mercy; forgiving.

mercury *(mer'-cu-ry)*. 1. A very heavy, silvery, liquid metal, sometimes called quicksilver. 2. **Mercury.** The planet nearest to the sun.

mere. 1. Only this and nothing else; nothing but. 2. A lake or pond.

merely *(mere'-ly)*. Only.

merge. To come together, as when single lanes of traffic merge or are absorbed into three- or four-lane traffic, or when three lanes of traffic come together into one lane.

meridian *(me-rid'-i-an)*. 1. An imaginary circle around the earth passing over both poles and the zenith of any given place. 2. The highest point in the sky reached by the sun, moon or any other heavenly body.

meringue *(me-ringue')*. A mixture of white sugar and egg whites beaten together and baked slowly. A small cake made of this.

merino *(me-ri'-no)*. 1. A kind of sheep that gives wool of high quality. 2. Cloth made from this wool.

merit *(mer'-it)*. 1. Worth; excellence. 2. To deserve. A **meritorious** *(mer-i-to'-ri-ous)* person is one who deserves reward.

mermaid *(mer'-maid)*. In fairy tales, a creature living in the sea who is of female human form above the waist but has a fish's tail.

merry *(mer'-ry)*. Happy; joyful.

mesh. A space between the strands of a net. It is in the meshes of the net that fish are caught.

mess. 1. A dirty, untidy mixture of things, as "Did you make that mess on the table-cloth?" 2. A quantity of food, as the mess of pottage which Esau was given. 3. In the army, navy, etc., a mess is a group of people who regularly eat their meals together, or the place where they eat.

message *(mes'-sage)*. A piece of information sent by one person to another. A person who carries a message is a **messenger.**

Messiah *(Mes-si'-ah)*. The Anointed One, Jesus Christ.

metal *(met'-al)*. Gold, iron, copper, etc., are metals.

metallic *(me-tal'-lic)*. Made of metal.

metaphor *(met'-a-phor)*. A comparison not using "like" or "as"; "The Lord is my shepherd" is a metaphor.

meteor *(me'-te-or)*. A small heavenly body which enters the earth's atmosphere at great speed. Friction with the air causes it to become so hot that it burns and therefore may be seen. Meteors are also called shooting stars. A meteor which reaches the earth before it is entirely burnt up is called a **meteorite**.

meter *(me'-ter)*. A device for measuring, such as a gas meter.

method *(meth'-od)*. 1. A way of doing something, as "I have found a new method of roasting chestnuts". 2. Orderliness; regularity.

methodical *(me-thod'-i-cal)*. Careful and orderly in doing things.

metre. 1. The rhythm in verse and in music. 2. A measure of length equal to 39.37 inches.

metropolis *(me-trop'-o-lis)*. The chief city or town in a country. London is the metropolis of England.

mettle *(met'-tle)*. Pluck; spirit; courage.

microbe *(mi'-crobe)*. A tiny germ.

microphone *(mi'-cro-phone)*. An instrument for picking up sounds and sending them by radio waves or along an electric wire. There is a microphone in the mouthpiece of your telephone which sends your voice along the telephone wires.

microscope *(mi'-cro-scope)*. An instrument containing one or more magnifying lenses, used for making enlarged images of very small objects. Many things which are too small to be seen by the naked eye can be seen when magnified by a microscope.

middle *(mid'-dle)*. 1. Half-way; intermediate. 2. A centre.

midget *(midg'-et)*. A normally formed, but abnormally small, adult person. A human dwarf is a small adult person who has malformed parts.

midshipman *(mid'-ship-man)*. A naval cadet or a young officer in the Navy.

midst. The middle.

mighty *(might'-y)*. Having great power; very strong, as "Samson was a mighty man".

migrate *(mi'-grate)*. To move from one country to another, perhaps with the idea of staying in the new place permanently.

mildew *(mil'-dew)*. A fungus which grows in places that are damp. Each growth is so small that it looks like a speck of dust.

mile. A measure of length equal to 5,280 feet or 1,760 yards.

militant *(mil'-i-tant)*. Ready to fight, or fighting.

military *(mil'-i-tar-y)*. 1. Soldiers. 2. Soldier-like; having to do with fighting, or with the army, navy, etc.

mill. 1. A machine for grinding; thus a flour mill grinds grain to make flour, a coffee mill grinds coffee beans, etc. 2. A factory, as a cotton mill. 3. To mill the edge of a coin is to put grooved lines around the edge, as on a sixpenny piece.

millennium *(mil-len'-ni-um)*. A period of 1,000 years.

miller *(mil'-ler)*. A man who operates a mill.

millinery *(mil'-li-ner-y)*. Women's hats. A millinery shop is one that sells women's hats.

million *(mil'-lion)*. The number 1,000,000, or a thousand thousands.

millionaire *(mil-lion-aire')*. A person who owns at least £1,000,000.

mimic *(mim'-ic)*. To imitate; to copy the peculiar actions which a person has, usually in order to make fun of him.

mince. 1. To cut up into tiny pieces. 2. A person who does not mince matters is one who says exactly what he thinks, whether it hurts others to hear it or not.

mind. 1. The seat of thinking, feeling and willing. 2. When you change your mind, you change your ideas or feelings. 3. When you keep your mind on a task, you give your attention to the task. 4. When you mind your teacher, you obey him. 5. To mind something is to take care of it.

mine. 1. A deep hole made in the earth, with passages dug out at the sides, in order that useful material, such as coal, may be obtained. 2. A place is said to be mined when it has been laid with explosives ready to blow it up at any moment. 3. A mine sometimes means a good store, as "He has a mine of information". 4. Mine may mean belonging to me, as "That book is mine".

miner *(min'-er)*. One who works in a mine.

mineral *(min'-er-al)*. Any substance dug out of the earth, as coal.

mingle *(min'-gle)*. To mix.

miniature *(min'-i-a-ture)*. 1. A small painting or any article made on a small scale. 2. Small or tiny.

minimum *(min'-i-mum)*. The least amount. See also **maximum**.

mining *(min'-ing)*. The act or business of working mines.

minion *(min'-ion)*. A favourite; one who is willing to do all that is asked of him in order to gain favours.

minister *(min'-is-ter)*. 1. A man who holds a high position in the government, as a cabinet minister. 2. A clergyman. 3. To minister to someone is to serve or wait upon him.

mink. An animal which is similar to a weasel and has a soft brown fur worth a great deal of money.

minnow *(min'-now)*. A small freshwater fish.

minor *(mi'-nor)*. 1. A person under twenty-one years of age. 2. Minor also means less or smaller, as "That is of minor importance". 3. In music, there are major and minor keys.

minority *(mi-nor'-i-ty)*. 1. Less than half; thus in "The majority of the people voted for Jones and only a minority for Brown", we are told that Brown had less than half the total votes. "Minority" is the opposite of "majority". 3. The period of life during which you are under age, that is, under 21.

minstrel *(min'-strel)*. 1. In mediæval times, a musical entertainer who accompanied his singing on a harp or lute. 2. Nowadays, one of a troupe of comedians who entertain people by telling jokes and singing popular songs.

mint. 1. A place where metal and paper are made into coins and notes which are used as money. 2. A type of green plant with a refreshing flavour which is used in sauce and flavouring.

minuet *(min-u-et')*. 1. A type of stately dance. 2. The music played for such a dance.

minus *(mi'-nus)*. Less. In subtraction, the word is not written, but indicated by the sign —.

minute. 1. *(min'-ute)*. The sixtieth part of an hour or of a degree of a circle. 2. *(mi-nute')*. Very small indeed.

miraculous *(mi-rac'-u-lous)*. So wonderful as to be unnatural.

mire. A bog; deep mud.

mirror *(mir'-ror)*. A looking-glass.

mirth. Gaiety; hilarity; happy laughter.

misbehaviour *(mis-be-hav'-iour)*. Bad conduct.

miscalculate *(mis-cal'-cu-late)*. To reckon or calculate incorrectly. You may miscalculate a problem in arithmetic and have an incorrect answer as a result, or you may miscalculate the time required to reach school and be late as a result.

miscarry *(mis-car'-ry)*. To go astray or go wrong; thus, "Somehow the letter miscarried and I never received it".

miscellaneous *(mis-cel-la'-ne-ous)*. Mixed; of all sorts; thus "In his pocket, was a miscellaneous assortment of odds and ends".

mischief *(mis'-chief)*. Naughtiness.

mischievous *(mis'-chie-vous)*. 1. Harmful. 2. Given to doing wrong things; naughty.

miscreant *(mis'-cre-ant)*. A vile person; one who does evil things.

miser *(mi'-ser)*. A person who neglects to buy himself proper food, clothes, and to keep his house clean because he is anxious to save money. A miserable person whose only pleasure is in hoarding money.

miserable *(mis'-er-a-ble)*. Unhappy; wretched.

misfortune *(mis-for'-tune)*. Bad luck; ill luck.

misprint. 1. *(mis'-print)*. A mistake in some printed matter, such as a newspaper. 2. *(mis-print')*. To print incorrectly.

miss. 1. To fail to hit, reach or find something. 2. To miss someone when he is away is to be lonely for him. 3. Miss, with a capital, is a title put before the name of an unmarried woman, as "Miss Jane Jones".

missile *(mis'-sile)*. Something thrown, from the hand or from a weapon, with the intention of causing damage or injury. Nowadays, missiles such as rockets are projected by their own power.

mission *(mis'-sion)*. 1. An errand. 2. Persons sent somewhere to do some special work. 3. Their Headquarters.

missionary *(mis'-sion-ar-y)*. A person sent somewhere to teach religion.

mis-spell *(mis-spell')*. To spell a word incorrectly.

mist. A slight fog.

mistake *(mis-take')*. An error.

mistletoe *(mis'-tle-toe)*. A plant with white berries, which is used as a Christmas decoration.

mistress *(mis'-tress)*. 1. A woman who has people working for her. 2. The woman at the head of a household.

misunderstand *(mis-un-der-stand')*. To understand incorrectly.

mite. 1. Anything very small; a very small child. 2. A very small creature something like an insect.

mitigate *(mit'-i-gate)*. 1. To make less severe, as "If you will apologise to Mr. Brown I will mitigate your punishment". 2. To ease the blame, as "You should have been here an hour ago, but if you had a puncture your lateness is mitigated to some extent".

mitre *(mi'-tre)*. 1. A head-dress worn by archbishops and bishops. 2. A corner joint used in woodwork, etc.

mitten *(mit'-ten)*. A type of glove which covers the four fingers together and the thumb separately.

mix. To combine or put together. When a woman makes a cake, she mixes flour, milk, sugar, etc. These things when combined are called a **mixture.**

moan. 1. A long, low-pitched cry of pain. 2. We say that a person is moaning about this or that when we mean he is grumbling.

moat. A ditch, usually filled with water, which in mediæval times was dug around a castle, stronghold, or town to protect it from enemy attack.

mob. A crowd of noisy people.

mobile *(mo'-bile)*. Moving about easily. Mobile police ride about in cars, etc.

mobilize *(mo'-bi-lize)*. To mobilize an army is to assemble troops and prepare them for war.

moccasin *(moc'-ca-sin)*. A type of shoe made of soft leather or deer-skin.

mock. 1. To mimic or imitate with the idea of poking fun. 2. Mock means imitation; thus, in a mock battle the soldiers pretend to fight in order to gain experience. 3. To defy; to express scorn.

mode. 1. Fashion. 2. The way something is done.

model *(mod'-el)*. 1. Something made as an original design to be copied. 2. A copy of something, usually on a smaller scale than the original.

moderate *(mod'-er-ate)*. 1. Not extreme or excessive. A moderate price is neither too high nor too low. 2. To become less extreme, as "The wind moderated".

modern *(mod'-ern)*. Not old-fashioned; recent.

modest *(mod'-est)*. 1. Not boastful; not having a very high opinion of yourself. 2. Simple; unpretentious; the opposite to big and showy, as "He lived in a modest little house in the country".

modify *(mod'-i-fy)*. To change slightly, not greatly.

modulate *(mod'-u-late)*. 1. To alter the tone of the voice while reading aloud or talking. 2. To change from one key to another while singing or playing a musical instrument.

moisten *(mois'-ten)*. To make damp.

moisture *(mois'-ture)*. A slight dampness.

mole. 1. A small animal that tunnels in the ground and throws up tiny hills of earth on the surface. 2. A dark, raised spot on the skin.

molest *(mo-lest')*. To injure or disturb by meddling with.

mollify *(mol'-li-fy)*. To calm down; to soothe away or lessen the anger of. Thus, "My father was very angry when he found that I had not cut the grass as he had asked me to, but he was somewhat mollified when he heard that I had been running errands for my mother".

mollusc *(mol'-lusc)*. A small sea creature with a soft body which, in many cases, is housed in a shell for protection. An oyster and a snail are both molluscs. Also spelled **mollusk.**

molten *(mol'-ten)*. Melted; made of metal that has been melted.

moment *(mo'-ment)*. 1. A length of time too short to measure. 2. Importance, as "Something has happened of considerable moment".

momentous *(mo-ment'-ous)*. Important.

momentum *(mo-ment'-um)*. The force which a moving thing has; thus "Think of the momentum possessed by a train moving at fifty miles an hour".

monarch *(mon'-arch)*. A king; a queen; an emperor, etc.

monarchy *(mon'-arch-y)*. 1. A country ruled by a king or emperor. 2. Rule by a King or Queen.

monastery *(mon'-as-ter-y)*. A building in which monks or nuns live.

Monday *(Mon'-day)*. The second day of the week.

money *(mon'-ey)*. The coins and notes which people exchange for goods when buying and selling.

mongrel *(mon'-grel)*. An animal, usually a dog, whose father is of one breed and whose mother is of another. Thus the animal itself is of mixed breed.

monitor *(mon'-i-tor)*. 1. When a pupil has special duties, he is a monitor. 2. A type of receiving set for radio and television on which programmes are checked.

monk. A man living in a monastery who belongs to a religious order.

monkey *(mon'-key)*. A type of animal which closely resembles man.

monocle *(mon'-o-cle)*. A single eye-glass.

monogram *(mon'-o-gram)*. The initials of a person, looped together to make one design.

monologue *(mon'-o-logue)*. 1. A long speech by one person. 2. A play for one actor.

monoplane *(mon'-o-plane)*. An aeroplane with only one set of wings.

monopolize *(mo-nop'-o-lize)*. To get complete control of something for yourself; thus "The two men monopolized all the seats in their compartment by lying full length on them and promptly going to sleep".

monotone *(mon'-o-tone)*. 1. One single tone or note in music, as "The choir sang the psalm in a monotone". 2. A person is said to speak in a monotone when he says everything in the same tone of voice, without raising or lowering his voice.

monotonous *(mo-not'-o-nous)*. Without variation. Said of something of which one grows tired because it is always the same.

monsoon *(mon-soon')*. A wind that blows regularly at certain times of the year, more particularly in India and neighbouring parts of Asia. During the summer the monsoon blows from the south-west and brings very heavy rain; in winter it blows from the north-east and is dry.

monster *(mon'-ster)*. 1. An unusually large animal or plant, as "We grew a vegetable marrow that was a monster". 2. A person or animal that is misshapen or unnaturally cruel.

month. A calendar month is one of the twelve named months. A lunar month reckoned by the phases of the moon is exactly four weeks.

monument *(mon'-u-ment)*. A building, statue, pillar, etc., erected in memory of the dead.

mood. The state of a person's mind, as "Be careful of John; he is in a bad mood".

moonlight *(moon'-light)*. The light reflected by the moon.

moor. 1. To secure a boat by means of ropes, etc. 2. A large open piece of land with few trees.

moose. A large deer-like animal which lives in Canada.

mop. 1. One or more pieces of cloth, fastened to a long handle and used for cleaning. 2. To clean something by using a mop.

mope. To be dull and gloomy and, usually, to want to be left alone.

moral *(mor'-al)*. 1. A story with a moral is a story that teaches a lesson. 2. A moral person is one who conducts himself properly and virtuously.

morass *(mo-rass')*. Ground that is soft, wet and muddy; a marsh.

moreover *(more-o'-ver)*. Besides.

morning *(morn'-ing)*. The first part of the day, beginning at midnight and ending at noon.

morose *(mo-rose')*. Bad tempered through having a gloomy or sullen nature.

morrow *(mor'-row)*. The next day.

morsel *(mor'-sel)*. A small quantity of food which can be eaten in one bite.

mortal *(mor'-tal)*. 1. Anything that must die some day is mortal; thus, people are mortal. 2. Deadly; fatal; thus, a mortal blow is a blow that kills.

mortar *(mor'-tar)*. Lime and sand mixed with water and used in building. The bricks of a house are held together with mortar.

mortgage *(mort'-gage)*. An agreement by which something will be given up if a loan of money is not paid in due time. A house is **mortgaged** if it is used as security for a loan.

mortification *(mor-ti-fi-ca'-tion)*. Loss of self-respect; shame; humiliation.

mortuary *(mor'-tu-ar-y)*. A place in which dead bodies are kept while awaiting burial.

mosquito *(mos-qui'-to)*. An insect that breeds in swampy places. The female pierces the skins of animals in order to suck their blood. It also spreads malaria.

moss. Small, green, velvety plants which grow over ground, rocks, trees, etc.

mote. A speck of dust.

moth. A four-winged, night-flying insect, related to the butterfly. The clothes-moth lays eggs in woollens, furs, etc., and the larvae eat holes in the material.

mother *(moth'-er)*. 1. A woman who has borne a child. 2. The head of a religious community.

mother-in-law *(moth'-er-in-law)*. The mother of a man's wife or the mother of a woman's husband.

motion *(mo'-tion)*. Movement.

motive *(mo'-tive)*. 1. A thought or feeling that causes a person to do something or act in a certain way. 2. Causing something to move, as "A diesel engine provides the motive power for this train".

motley *(mot'-ley)*. 1. Made of many colours, as the dress of a clown. 2. Mixed or of varied character, as "A motley assembly of people".

motor *(mo'-tor)*. 1. Providing motion. 2. A machine that supplies motive power (see **motive**, No. 2).

mottled *(mot'-tled)*. Streaked or spotted with colours.

motto *(mot'-to)*. 1. A few words inscribed on an object to show the qualities or the resolution of the person who chose them. Mottoes are often put on coats-of-arms. Here is the motto of the Three Musketeers: "All for one, and one for all". 2. A maxim.

mould. 1. Earth as is found in the garden. 2. The shapes used in cooking, etc., for things like jellies; also the shapes used in foundries when casting metal objects. 3. A bluish-green, powdery fungus that forms on damp walls, cheese, etc. Things covered with mould are said to be **mouldy.**

moult. To shed old feathers, skin, etc., when new feathers, skin, etc., have grown in. Birds and snakes moult.

mound. A small hill, or heap of earth or stones.

mount. 1. A mountain; a hill. 2. To climb upwards; to rise to a higher level. 3. To place in position, as "The soldiers mounted their guns on the ramparts". 4. The margin around a picture. 5. An animal you ride. 6. To get on to, as to mount a horse.

mountain *(moun'-tain)*. A natural, raised part of the land, much higher than a hill.

mourn. To grieve; to be sorry for the death of someone.

moustache *(mous-tache')*. Hair grown on the upper lip.

movable *(mov'-a-ble)*. Anything that may be moved is movable.

move. To shift from one place to another.

mow. 1. To cut the crop in a field. 2. In "The infantry mowed down the enemy", mowed down means killed.

Mr. The short form for Mister, used before the name of a man.

Mrs. The short form for Mistress, used before the name of a married woman.

mucilage *(mu'-ci-lage)*. A thick liquid used for sticking things together; glue.

mucus *(mu'-cus)*. A slimy fluid covering the lining of the nose, throat and other inner parts of the body. When you have a cold, the amount of mucus in the nose increases.

mud. Earth mixed with water.

muddle *(mud'-dle)*. 1. Things mixed up and not in their proper places. 2. To mix up.

muddy *(mud'-dy)*. Covered with mud; murky; not clear or bright. Muddy water is water clouded by mud or dirt. Muddy clothes are splashed with mud. Muddy colours are dull brownish or greyish colours.

muff. A piece of fur or cloth, cylindrical in shape, used to keep the hands warm.

muffin *(muf'-fin)*. A kind of small, round cake.

muffle *(muf'-fle)*. 1. To wrap up so as to keep out the cold and wet. 2. To wrap up something in order to deaden the sound; thus if the clapper of a church bell were wrapped in cloth, it would make very little sound; it would be muffled.

mug. A heavy drinking cup used without a saucer.

mulberry *(mul'-ber-ry)*. A kind of bush which bears purplish-red berries.

mule. 1. A strong animal that is the offspring of a horse and a donkey. 2. An obstinate person.

multiple *(mul'-ti-ple)*. 1. A number that is the product of a given number and another number, without a remainder. Thus, 20 is a multiple of 4 and 5. 2. Multiple also means many.

multiplicand *(mul-ti-pli-cand')*. The number to be multiplied by another. When you multiply 5 by 3, 5 is the multiplicand.

multiplier *(mul'-ti-pli-er)*. The number by which another number is multiplied. When you multiply 5 by 3, 3 is the multiplier.

multiply *(mul'-ti ply)*. 1. To increase in number; thus, when you begin with a few plants and by the end of the year have many, the plants have multiplied. 2. In arithmetic, to increase a number a given number of times; to find the product. The act or process of multiplying numbers is called **multiplication** *(mul-ti-pli-ca'-tion)*.

multitude *(mul'-ti-tude)*. 1. A crowd of people. 2. A large number of anything.

mumble *(mum'-ble)*. To speak indistinctly.

mummy *(mum'-my)*. A dead body specially treated to prevent it from decaying. The ancient Egyptians preserved the bodies of some of their dead this way and did it so well that some of their mummies have lasted more than 3,000 years.

mumps. A contagious disease which produces a sore swelling around the lower jaw and neck.

municipal *(mu-nic'-i-pal)*. Having to do with a town, city, etc. A city is governed by a municipal council.

munitions *(mu-ni'-tions)*. Such things as guns, rifles and the shells, etc., needed for them, that are used in war.

mural *(mu'-ral)*. To do with a wall; thus a painting done on a wall is a mural.

murder *(mur'-der)*. To kill someone purposely, unlawfully, and not by accident. A man who kills in this way is a **murderer.**

murky *(murk'-y)*. Dark; gloomy.

murmur *(mur'-mur)*. 1. To speak in a soft voice that cannot be heard clearly. 2. To make soft, indistinct sounds; thus, "The waves murmured as they lapped on the shore".

muscle *(mus'-cle)*. An organ of the body which produces motion. A person with large, powerful muscles is said to be **muscular.**

museum *(mu-se'-um)*. A building in which objects of special value or interest are set out so that the public may see them.

mushroom *(mush'-room)*. 1. Any of a class of umbrella-shaped fungi, all of which are edible. There are poisonous varieties known as toadstools. 2. When something has grown very quickly, it is said to have **mushroomed.**

music *(mu'-sic)*. 1. The art of combining sounds of different pitches in rhythmical patterns to make melodies, harmonies, etc. 2. Sounds having rhythm and melody. 3. Written or printed signs representing music. A person who writes music or performs pieces of music is called a **musician** *(mu-si'-cian)*.

muslin *(mus'-lin)*. A thin material made of cotton, used for clothing, curtains, etc.

mussel *(mus'-sel)*. A sea-creature living in a bluish shell, the shell being made of two parts which are almost alike in size. Many people eat mussels.

muster *(mus'-ter)*. To call together.

musty *(mus'-ty)*. Having a peculiar smell or taste through being kept in a damp place.

mute. Silent; saying nothing. People who cannot speak because of a defect in the organs of speech are called mutes.

mutilate *(mu'-ti-late)*. 1. To injure someone by cutting off parts of his body. 2. To cut off a part of. 3. To damage; to spoil.

mutiny *(mu'-ti-ny)*. The rebelling of people against those in charge of them; refusing to do as you are told.

mutter *(mut'-ter)*. To talk in low, indistinct tones, with little lip movement.

mutton *(mut'-ton)*. The flesh of sheep, used as food.

mutual *(mu'-tu-al)*. If John and Fred both collect stamps they have a mutual interest, that is, they have an interest in common.

muzzle *(muz'-zle)*. 1. The mouth and jaws of an animal. 2. A network or cage put over a dog's mouth to prevent it from biting. 3. To stop a person from talking. 4. The fore-end of a gun, rifle, etc.

myriad *(myr'-i-ad)*. 1. 10,000. 2. A very great number.

mystery *(mys'-ter-y)*. 1. Something that cannot be understood. 2. A secret; secrecy. A thing which puzzles and perhaps frightens you because you cannot understand it is **mysterious** *(mys-te'-ri-ous)*.

myth. A fable; a legend.

N

nag. 1. A small horse or an inferior horse. 2. To scold; to find fault constantly.

nail. 1. A thin piece of metal for fastening wood and other things together. 2. A horny protective covering at the end of the fingers and toes.

naked *(na'-ked)*. Without covering. When the leaves fall, the trees are naked. When you want the naked truth, you want just the facts without any additions.

name. 1. A word by which a person, place, or thing is known. 2. To identify; to give a name to; to call by name.

namely *(name'-ly)*. That is to say.

namesake *(name'-sake)*. A person having the same name as another person; thus if your father has a great friend called William Henry and when you were born he gave you the name of William Henry, you would be the friend's namesake.

nap. 1. A short sleep. 2. The woolly or fluffy surface of certain kinds of cloth.

nape. The back of the neck where it joins the shoulders.

napkin *(nap'-kin)*. A square cloth, generally used at table for wiping the mouth and hands.

narcissus *(nar-cis'-sus)*. A plant which flowers in the spring. It has slender leaves and yellow or white flowers.

narcotic *(nar-cot'-ic)*. Any drug that, taken in small quantities, produces sleep and lessens pain. Opium is a narcotic.

narrate *(nar-rate')*. To tell a story.

narrative *(nar'-ra-tive)*. 1. Any story that has been narrated (see **narrate**) is a narrative. A person who narrates a narrative is a **narrator** *(nar-ra'-tor)*.

narrow *(nar'-row)*. Not wide. A person is narrow-minded when he is unnecessarily strict and can never see another's point of view.

nasal *(na'-sal)*. To do with the nose.

nasty *(nas'-ty)*. Disagreeable; unpleasant.

natal *(na'-tal)*. To do with birth; thus your natal day is the day you were born. The province of Natal *(Na-tal')* in South Africa was so named because it was discovered on Christmas Day, the birthday of Jesus Christ.

nation *(na'-tion)*. All the people living in a country under the same government.

national *(na'-tion-al)*. Having to do with a nation. Thus, we speak of national feelings, national laws, etc.

native *(na'-tive)*. 1. A person born in a certain place is a native of that place. 2. A plant or animal which originated in a certain place or country is native to that country.

natural *(nat'-u-ral)*. 1. According to what is found in nature. The flowers growing in a garden are natural, but paper flowers are not natural: they are artificial. 2. Without man-made changes. 3. Inborn, as natural ability. 4. A note in music not sharp or flat; said of a white key on a piano.

naturalist *(nat'-u-ral-ist)*. A person who is interested in the plants and animals of the countryside.

naturally *(nat'-u-ral-ly)*. 1. According to nature. 2. Of course.

nature *(na'-ture)*. 1. Plants and animals in the uncultivated or wild state. 2. Character, as in "Tom had a kindly nature". 3. Kind or class, as "of that nature".

naught. Nothing.

naughty *(naugh'-ty)*. Mischievous; disobedient.

nauseating *(nau'-se-at-ing)*. Sickening; likely to make a person feel sick.

nautical *(nau'-ti-cal)*. To do with sailors, ships and vessels.

naval *(na'-val)*. To do with the men and vessels belonging to the Navy.

nave. The large middle space in a church or cathedral, usually separated from the side aisles by a row of pillars.

navigable *(nav'-i-ga-ble)*. When a river, waterway or stretch of sea is suitable for the passage of ships, it is navigable. A ship is navigable when it is in good condition.

navigate *(nav'-i-gate)*. To steer or manage a ship, aircraft, etc., while at sea or in the air.

navigation *(nav-i-ga'-tion)*. The science of plotting the course or position of a ship or an aircraft.

navvy *(nav'-vy)*. A labourer who does heavy manual work, especially in digging roads, canals, etc.

navy *(na'-vy)*. All the warships belonging to a nation, along with all the sailors who work on them.

near. Close; a short distance away.

neat. 1. Tidy, as "The room was neat and clean". 2. Smart and clever, as "The conjuror performed some neat tricks". 3. In "He drank his medicine neat", neat means without water.

necessary *(nec'-es-sar-y)*. A thing is necessary when it is impossible to do without it. It is a **necessity.**

neck. That part of the body which joins the head to the shoulders.

necklace *(neck'-lace)*. A string of jewels, pearls, gold, etc., which is worn around the neck for decoration.

nectar *(nec'-tar)*. 1. The little drops of liquid in many kinds of flowers. 2. Any very pleasant drink.

nectarine *(nec'-tar-ine)*. A fruit like a peach, but having a smooth skin.

need. 1. When you need something you cannot do without it. 2. A need is something that is necessary or required. 3. Need also means poverty.

needful *(need'-ful)*. Anything which is wanted or necessary.

needle *(nee'-dle)*. 1. A long, narrow, sharp-pointed piece of steel with an eye at one end, used for sewing. 2. A longer piece of steel without an eye or sharp point, used for knitting. 3. The steel pointer on such things as the mariner's compass. 4. The leaves or spines which cover pine trees, etc.

needy *(need'-y)*. Poor.

ne'er-do-well *(ne'er'-do-well)*. A good-for-nothing; one who never does any good; a worthless person.

negative *(neg'-a-tive)*. 1. "No" is an answer in the negative. 2. There are two kinds of electricity, positive and negative. 3. A photographic film or plate, when developed, is a negative. The pictures or positives are then printed from the negative.

neglect *(neg-lect')*. 1. Not to look after, as "He neglects his business". 2. To fail to do, as "He neglected to turn off the light before going to bed". A person who neglects things is **neglectful.**

negotiate *(ne-go'-ti-ate)*. 1. To confer for the purpose of making an agreement, as to negotiate a sale or a treaty. 2. To manage to get somewhere under difficulties, as "He negotiated the steep climb without mishap".

Negro *(Ne'-gro)*. A member of a black-skinned African race.

neigh. The sound made by a horse.

neighbour *(neigh'-bour)*. A person who lives next door to or near someone else.

neighbourhood *(neigh'-bour-hood)*. The streets, houses, shops, fields, lanes, etc., which form a district. Thus, your neighbourhood consists of your house, those houses near by, the shops, perhaps a railway station, etc. You may also speak of "the neighbourhood of St. John's Church". Then you would mean all the shops and other things round about the church.

neither *(nei'-ther)*. Not one nor the other.

nephew *(neph'-ew)*. The son of your brother or your sister.

nerve. One of the tiny fibres which connect the spinal cord, eyes, nose, mouth, etc., to the brain, so that what you see, do, smell, taste, etc., registers in the mind.

nervous *(nerv'-ous)*. Having to do with the nerves. A nervous person is one whose nerves are out of order and need medical care, or one who is easily frightened about things.

nest. 1. A structure or house built by a bird, in which it lays its eggs. 2. A set of small boxes or drawers arranged one inside the other is known as a nest.

nestle *(nes'-tle)*. To settle oneself snugly; thus a baby nestles in its mother's arms.

net. 1. A net consists of long threads of string, etc., so tied together that there are regularly shaped holes between the threads. Fishermen use such nets. 2. To net means to catch in a net.

nettle *(net'-tle)*. 1. A plant well known because of its stinging hairs. 2. To nettle a person is to irritate him.

neuter *(neu'-ter)*. Neither masculine nor feminine. Neither male nor female.

neutral *(neu'-tral)*. 1. Belonging to neither side in a quarrel or a war. 2. A neutral person is one who takes neither side in a dispute or a war. 3. A neutral colour is one that is quiet in tone, such as grey or beige.

never *(nev'-er)*. At no time.

new. 1. Having existed for only a short time; the opposite to "old". 2. Just made; not yet used. 3. Different; strange; unfamiliar, as "the new lands". 4. Recently introduced, as "a new friend".

news. A report of recent happenings.

newsagent *(news'-a'-gent)*. A person who sells newspapers.

newsboy *(news'-boy)*. A boy who sells or delivers newspapers.

newspaper *(news'-pa-per)*. Large folded sheets of paper on which are printed news events, advertisements, etc.

newt. A small amphibious animal having four short legs.

next. Nearest; coming immediately before or after.

nib. The part of a pen with which the writing is done and which can be replaced when worn out.

nibble *(nib'-ble)*. To eat with quick, small bites, as a rabbit does.

nicety *(ni'-ce-ty)*. 1. A dainty or elegant thing. 2. Delicacy; exactness.

nick. 1. The place from which a small piece has been broken or cut. 2. To nick something is to cut a small bit out of it.

nickel *(nick'-el)*. A hard, silver-coloured metal.

nickname *(nick'-name)*. A name given instead of a real name, usually as a joke. Thus, a boy named Clarke is often called Nobby. This is his nickname.

niece. The daughter of your brother or your sister is your niece.

niggardly *(nig'-gard-ly)*. Stingy.

nigh. Near.

night. The time of darkness between afternoon and morning.

nightingale *(night'-in-gale)*. A small, brown bird which sings melodiously at night as well as during the day.

nimble *(nim'-ble)*. 1. Very quick in moving, especially in moving the feet, as "The mountaineer must have nimble feet in order to climb among the rocks". 2. Quick-witted; alert.

nip. 1. To pinch; a pinch. 2. To take a small, sharp bite; a small, sharp bite.

nitrogen *(ni'-tro-gen)*. One of the elements (see **element**). It is usually found in the form of a colourless, tasteless, odourless gas.

noble *(no'-ble)*. 1. Possessing excellent qualities; excellent; stately; grand. Thus we speak of a noble animal, a noble tree, a noble house, etc. 2. A person of high rank by birth, such as a duke, count, marquis, etc. 3. Well-known; possessing dignity; eminent.

nobly *(no'-bly)*. In a grand or noble manner or way.

nobody *(no'-bod-y)*. No one.

nocturnal *(noc-tur'-nal)*. To do with the night; thus, the owl is called a nocturnal bird because it comes out to hunt at night.

nod. 1. To rock the head forward and backward slowly and gently. 2. To bend the head forward in answer to a question, usually in agreement.

noise. Loud sounds. When you are in a place where there is a lot of noise, you say it is **noisy.**

nomad *(no'-mad)*. A person who moves about and does not live in one place. A gipsy is a nomad; he is **nomadic** *(no-mad'-ic)*.

nominal *(nom'-i-nal)*. 1. Not real; existing in name only. Thus, "Mr. Jones is the nominal head of the business, but as Mr. Brown does all the work we look upon him as the head". 2. Anything so small that it does not count. You might pay a nominal fee, such as a penny, to join a club.

nominate *(nom'-i-nate)*. To name as a candidate for election to an office or a position, as "Whom shall we nominate for football captain?"

K

nonsense *(non'-sense)*. Something without sense or meaning.

nook. A cosy corner.

noon. Twelve o'clock in the middle of the day.

noose. A loop tied with a slip-knot, so that the loop may be tightened.

normal *(nor'-mal)*. Usual; ordinary, as "A potato weighing 3 lbs. is not normal".

north. The compass point opposite south. The top of a wall map is usually the north.

nosegay *(nose'-gay)*. A neat bunch of flowers.

nostril *(nos'-tril)*. Either of the two openings in the nose.

notch. A V-shaped cut.

note. 1. To take notice of. 2. To set down in writing. 3. A short letter. 4. The sign of a musical sound. 5. Fame; importance, as in "He is a man of note". 6. A bank note is a piece of paper money.

noted *(not'-ed)*. Well-known; famous.

noteworthy *(note'-wor-thy)*. Remarkable; worthy of being noticed.

notice *(no'-tice)*. 1. To observe; to see, as "We noticed a rat running along the wall". 2. To pay attention to, as "Please notice how I do this". 3. A general order, as "Notice— Please keep off the grass". 4. When a worker is given a week's notice, he is told he will not be employed after the end of the week.

notify *(no'-ti-fy)*. To notify someone of something is to make it known to him; to tell or to inform.

notion *(no'-tion)*. 1. A hazy idea. 2. A whim.

notoriety *(no-to-ri'-e-ty)*. Fame, usually unfavourable; bad reputation.

notorious *(no-to'-ri-ous)*. Known far and wide for bad qualities.

noun. A word that names a person, place or thing.

nourish *(nour'-ish)*. To feed.

nourishment *(nour'-ish-ment)*. Food.

novel *(nov'-el)*. 1. New and unusual. 2. A prose narrative long enough to fill one volume. A person who writes such stories is a **novelist.**

novelty *(nov'-el-ty)*. Something new or different.

November *(No-vem'-ber)*. The eleventh month of the year. It has 30 days.

novice *(nov'-ice)*. A person who is new to whatever he is doing; a beginner.

nowhere *(no'-where)*. Not in, at or to any place.

nozzle *(noz'-zle)*. The spout or end of a hose, tap, etc.

nucleus *(nu'-cle-us)*. 1. A central part around which matter is gathered. 2. The beginning of a thing which has grown to something much larger.

nugget *(nug'-get)*. A lump of valuable metal, such as gold.

nuisance *(nui'-sance)*. A thing which annoys or troubles you is a nuisance.

null. Having no force; worthless; not worth taking any notice of.

nullify *(nul'-li-fy)*. To cancel; to make worthless.

numb. Having lost most or all of its feeling, as "My toes are numb from walking in the snow".

number *(num'-ber)*. 1. A figure or word which tells how many there are of something, as 4 apples, 39 dogs. 2. In "The men who were there numbered 50", numbered means amounted to. 3. In "There were numbers of crabs on the shore", numbers of means many.

numeral *(nu'-mer-al)*. A figure or word expressing number. "Seven", or "7", is a numeral.

numerous *(nu'-mer-ous)*. Very many.

nun. A religious woman who lives in a convent.

nurse. 1. A person who looks after invalids or young children. 2. To place on your lap and hold closely to you. 3. To look after with great care.

nursery *(nurs'-er-y)*. 1. A play room or living room for very young children. 2. A place where seeds are sown and young plants are raised. A man who looks after such plants is a **nurseryman.**

nurture *(nur'-ture)*. 1. To rear or bring up. 2. Nourishment.

nutriment *(nu'-tri-ment)*. Nourishing food.

nutritious *(nu-tri'-tious)*. Nourishing; having food elements that will promote growth and health.

nylon *(ny'-lon)*. 1. A strong, man-made fibre. 2. A nylon stocking.

O

oak. A large, strong tree which has deeply-notched leaves and bears nuts which are called acorns.

oaken *(oak'-en)*. Made of oak wood.

oar. A pole with one flat end, known as the blade; oars are used for rowing boats.

oasis *(o-a'-sis)*. A place in a desert where there are trees and other vegetation growing. There is always a supply of water at an oasis and that is why the land around about is fertile.

oat. One of the seeds of a tall, grass-like cereal plant. Oats are ground up to make **oatmeal.**

oath. 1. A solemn promise in which the name of God is mentioned. In law courts, a man takes an oath that he will speak the truth. 2. Curses, or swear-words, are also oaths.

oatmeal *(oat'-meal)*. A coarse flour made by grinding or crushing grains of oats. You probably have oatmeal or crushed oats for breakfast sometimes.

obedient *(o-be'-di-ent)*. To do as you are told is to be obedient. Dogs are trained to be obedient and they are tested at **obedience** trials.

obeisance *(o-bei'-sance)*. A respectful greeting; a bow or curtsy.

obelisk *(ob'-e-lisk)*. A tall stone pillar, four-sided and pointed at the top.

obese *(o-bese')*. Very fat.

obey *(o-bey')*. To do as you are told.

obituary *(o-bit'-u-ar-y)*. A notice in a newspaper telling of the death of someone.

object. 1. *(ob'-ject)*. A thing, as "He pushed over the object on the table". 2. The reason, as "What object had you in mind when you came here?" 3. In grammar a word on which a verb operates is called an object. In "Mary broke the doll", doll is the object of the sentence. 4. *(ob-ject')*. To disapprove of or disagree with, as "I object to his being out so late".

objectionable *(ob-jec'-tion-a-ble)*. Disagreeable; nasty.

objective *(ob-jec'-tive)*. The thing aimed at or desired, as "One objective of education is to teach people to think".

obligation *(ob-li-ga'-tion)*. Duty; that which you ought to do.

obligatory *(ob-lig'-a-to-ry)*. Necessary to do; demanded by duty.

oblige *(o-blige')*. 1. If you do something to oblige a person, you do it as a favour to please him. You are obliging him. 2. If you are obliged to do something, you have got to do it; it is **obligatory.**

oblique *(ob-lique')*. An oblique line is a slanting line.

obliterate *(ob-lit'-er-ate)*. 1. To rub out or cover over, as "He obliterated the paint marks on the wall". 2. To blot out, as "The trees were so close together that they obliterated the sky".

oblivious *(ob-liv'-i-ous)*. 1. Forgetful. 2. Unmindful, as "The pupil was so oblivious of what the teacher was saying that he was unable to answer his question".

oblong *(ob'-long)*. A four-sided figure that is longer than it is wide.

obnoxious *(ob-nox'-ious)*. Offensive; nasty.

oboe *(o'-boe)*. A wooden wind instrument which gives a haunting, nasal sound.

obscene *(ob-scene')*. Disgusting; filthy; not decent.

obscure *(ob-scure')*. Dark; not easy to see.

observant *(ob-ser'-vant)*. A person who is quick to notice things is observant.

observatory *(ob-serv'-a-to-ry)*. A building with apparatus for looking at the stars and other heavenly bodies.

observe *(ob-serve')*. 1. To see, as "He observed a large bird in the tree". 2. In "Please observe the rules", observe means note them and keep them. 3. To remark, as "'I see that there are more people here to-day than there were yesterday,' he observed". A person who observes anything is an **observer.**

obsolete *(ob'-so-lete)*. Out of date; no longer used.

obstacle *(ob'-sta-cle)*. Something that stops your doing what you want to do, because it gets in your way. An obstacle race is a race over a course strewn with objects that are deliberately put in the runners' way.

obstinate *(ob'-sti-nate)*. Pig-headed; wanting to have your own way.

obstruct *(ob-struct')*. To hinder; to get in one's way.

obtain *(ob-tain')*. 1. To acquire or procure; to get. 2. To be in existence, as in "The war is over and peace obtains once more".

obtuse *(ob-tuse')*. 1. Dull or stupid; blunt. 2. In geometry, an obtuse angle is one larger than a right angle.

obviate *(ob'-vi-ate)*. To make unnecessary.

obvious *(ob'-vi-ous)*. Clear; certain; easily understood, as "It is obvious that a boy with measles should not go to school".

occasion *(oc-ca'-sion)*. 1. A particular time, as "On one occasion, I called on Mrs. Jones". 2. In "I had occasion to call on Mrs. Jones", occasion means reason.

Occident *(Oc'-ci-dent)*. The countries in the Western Hemisphere; the West.

occult *(oc-cult')*. Hidden; covered over; secret. The word is usually used in references to magic or knowledge of the supernatural.

occupation *(oc-cu-pa'-tion)*. A person's occupation is the work he or she does. Thus, a teacher's occupation is teaching, a housewife's occupation is housework.

occupy *(oc'-cu-py)*. When you occupy a house you live in it.

occur *(oc-cur')*. To happen.

occurrence *(oc-cur'-rence)*. A happening; anything that has happened.

ocean *(o'-cean)*. 1. A huge body of salt water surrounding the land masses of the earth. 2. One of the sub-divisions of this body of water, such as the Atlantic Ocean.

oceanic *(o-ce-an'-ic)*. To do with an ocean.

o'clock *(o'-clock')*. According to the clock.

octagon *(oc'-ta-gon)*. A shape or figure having eight sides and eight angles. A thing with this shape is **octagonal** *(oc-tag'-o-nal)*.

October *(Oc-to'-ber)*. The tenth month of the year. It has 31 days.

octopus *(oc'-to-pus)*. A sea creature having eight long tentacles by which it seizes its prey.

oculist *(oc'-u-list)*. A doctor who treats diseases of the eye.

odd. 1. Here are some odd numbers—3, 7, 15, 21; thus odd in this case means not even. 2. In "I thought that was odd", odd means strange. 3. Not matching, such as odd socks. 4. In "He does odd jobs", odd jobs means any sort of work. 5. In "We played musical chairs and I was the odd man out", odd means the one left over.

ode. A poem with a noble theme, usually addressed to some person or thing.

odious *(o'-di-ous)*. Objectionable; hateful.

odour *(o'-dour)*. A smell, either pleasant or nasty.

offence *(of-fence')*. 1. Words or actions that cause anger or displeasure. 2. A crime.

offensive *(of-fen'-sive)*. 1. Insulting. 2. Bad-smelling; unpleasant; disagreeable. 3. Soldiers are on the offensive when they make an attack.

offer *(of'-fer)*. 1. To present for acceptance or rejection; to declare that you are prepared to give something. 2. What is offered; a bid.

offering *(of'-fer-ing)*. A thing that is given; a present.

office *(of'-fice)*. 1. A place especially fitted for doing business. 2. A position or job a person holds, as "He fills the office of manager".

officer *(of'-fi-cer)*. 1. A person who has a commission in the armed forces, that is, the navy, army or air force. 2. The name given to certain people who perform public services, such as police officers, medical officers, etc. 3. The officers of a club or any other organization are the president, the vice-president, the secretary, the treasurer, etc.

official *(of-fi'-cial)*. 1. An officer. 2. A person holding a position to do with public work, as in the post office, or a person who holds a position in the management of a company. 3. A thing is official when it is agreed to by those in authority.

officious *(of-fi'-cious)*. A person is officious who is too ready to tell you what you have to do or how you ought to do it. He is meddlesome and thinks himself much better than others.

offshoot *(off'-shoot)*. That which branches out of the main part. A young plant is an offshoot.

offspring *(off'-spring)*. A child or children. Parents sometimes speak of their offspring, meaning their children.

often *(of'-ten)*. Frequently; many times.

ogle *(o'-gle)*. To make eyes at.

ogre *(o'-gre)*. An ugly monster existing only in fairy tales.

oil. A greasy liquid. There are three kinds of oil: animal, vegetable and mineral oil. Mineral oil is found by drilling deeply into the ground. It is used as fuel for cars and furnaces.

oilcloth *(oil'-cloth)*. A coated canvas used for covering tables, floors, etc.

oilskin *(oil'-skin)*. A cloth treated with oil to make it water-proof. A garment made from such cloth.

ointment *(oint'-ment)*. A greasy substance which is placed on a wound to heal it.

olive *(ol'-ive)*. 1. A tree growing in warm climates. It has silvery, dull-green leaves. 2. The fruit of the olive tree, which is edible. It is black when ripe, but it is sometimes eaten green.

omelet *(om'-e-let)*. Whipped or beaten eggs, fried and folded, often flavoured with herbs, cheese, etc.

omen *(o'-men)*. An object or a happening which is supposed to foretell good or evil or to be a sign of some future event.

ominous *(om'-i-nous)*. Suggesting that trouble or harm is likely to overtake you; that is, foretelling disaster.

omission *(o-mis'-sion)*. Something left out.

omit *(o-mit')*. To leave out.

omnipotent *(om-nip'-o-tent)*. All-powerful; almighty.

once. One time, as "You can die only once".

onerous *(on'-er-ous)*. Burdensome; heavy; oppressive, as "The regulations have long been severe, but lately they have become really onerous".

onion *(on'-ion)*. A plant which has a white bulb below ground and tapering stems above ground. The onion is used to season food and has a very strong odour.

only *(on'-ly)*. 1. Single of its kind. 2. Merely.

onset *(on'-set)*. 1. An attack; an assault. 2. The beginning.

onslaught *(on'-slaught)*. A fierce attack.

onus *(o'-nus)*. Obligation; responsibility. If an accident happens to a ship, the onus of proving that the trouble was not caused by any neglect rests with the captain.

onward *(on'-ward)*. Forward.

ooze. 1. To flow out or be squeezed out slowly. 2. Anything that oozes. 3. A kind of mud on the bottom of a sea, river or pond.

opal *(o'-pal)*. A precious stone, found in several colours, but most frequently a milky white, though light shades of yellow, brown, red and green are not uncommon.

opaque *(o-paque')*. 1. Not letting light through. 2. Not reflecting light.

open *(o'-pen)*. 1. Not shut or covered over. 2. An open field is one without any barrier around it. 3. In an open season hunters may kill animals. 4. An open position is one which has not been filled. 5. An open mind is a mind that is not prejudiced but is ready to accept new ideas or suggestions. 6. To open something is to take off the covering, the lid, etc., or to make a hole in it. 7. To open a door, window, gate, etc., is to move it from its closed position.

opera *(op'-er-a)*. A musical play in which the dialogue is sung and not spoken.

operate *(op'-er-ate)*. 1. To work or to act. 2. If a surgeon operates, he uses a knife to open the body of a patient. 3. If a radio expert operates his set he sends out or receives a message over the air. 4. If an army operates against the enemy, it fights the enemy. A person who operates is an **operator** and when a surgeon operates he performs an **operation** *(op-er-a'-tion)*.

operetta *(op-er-et'-ta)*. An opera which is light and amusing.

opiate *(o'-pi-ate)*. A medicine which contains opium and which helps a person to sleep or deadens pain.

opinion *(o-pin'-ion)*. What a person thinks about a thing. What I think of you is my opinion of you. If you think it is going to rain, you have the opinion that it will rain.

opponent *(op-po'-nent)*. A person who is on the other side. If you and somebody else play in a tennis match, the other person is your opponent.

opportune *(op-por-tune')*. Appropriate and timely. Thus, if you were on a lake in a sinking boat and another boat came by, its arrival would be opportune.

opportunity *(op-por-tu'-ni-ty)*. A favourable time; a good chance, as "When the captain of the team was ill, Tom had an opportunity to show his powers of leadership".

oppose *(op-pose')*. To be against.

opposite *(op'-po-site)*. 1. If you sit on one side of a table and your friend sits on the other side, he is opposite you. 2. Kindness is the opposite of cruelty; black is the opposite of white; tall is the opposite of short. Opposite, in these cases, means contrary.

oppress *(op-press')*. 1. To treat cruelly continually. 2. To weigh down. 3. To crush.

optic *(op'-tic)*. To do with the eye. Thus, the optic nerve is the nerve connecting the eye to the brain. The science that deals with the behaviour of light is called **optics.**

optical *(op'-ti-cal)*. Having to do with the sense of sight. An optical illusion is something that looks different from what it really is.

optician *(op-ti'-cian)*. A person who makes or sells spectacles.

optimist *(op'-ti-mist)*. A person who always looks on the bright side of things. (See **pessimist**.)

option *(op'-tion)*. Choice.

opulent *(op'-u-lent)*. Wealthy; rich.

oral *(o'-ral)*. Spoken, not written.

orange *(or'-ange)*. A round citrus fruit which grows on trees in warm climates and is reddish-golden in colour. 2. The reddish-golden colour.

orangeade *(or-ange-ade')*. A drink made with orange juice, sugar and water.

orator *(or'-a-tor)*. A person who makes speeches.

orb. A globe or sphere, such as, a ball, moon, etc.

orbit *(or'-bit)*. A path; usually when speaking of the path of one planet around the sun, or the path of a rocket satellite around the earth.

orchard *(or'-chard)*. A place where fruit trees grow.

orchestra *(or'-ches-tra)*. 1. A group of musicians playing together. 2. The instruments of such a group. 3. The part of a theatre in which the musicians sit.

orchid *(or'-chid)*. One of a family of plants having a great variety of flowers. Most of the flowers are of unusual shapes and colours.

ordeal *(or'-deal)*. A difficult, painful experience.

order *(or'-der)*. 1. Arrangement; the way in which one thing follows another, as "He wrote the names in alphabetical order". 2. Tidiness, as "To put his room in order, he picked up all the loose papers, books and clothes and put them in their proper places". 3. A list of things to be supplied, as "Here is my grocery order". 4. To order things is to ask that they be supplied. 5. To command, as "The captain ordered his men to march on". 6. A command, as "He gave the order 'About turn'". 7. A rank; a society, as "He wears the badge of the Order of the Bath".

ordinal *(or'-di-nal)*. Numbers are either cardinal or ordinal. 1st, 6th, 18th and 23rd are ordinal numbers, and 1, 6, 18, 23 are cardinal numbers.

ordinary *(or'-di-nar-y)*. Usual; common.

ore. Any metal in its natural state before it has been separated from the rock, etc., found with it. Thus we speak of iron ore, which is iron and rock together.

organ *(or'-gan)*. 1. A musical instrument, such as a church organ, a mouth organ, a barrel organ, etc. 2. A part of the body, as "The ear is the organ of hearing". 3. A means of conveying information such as a newspaper or a magazine.

organization *(or-gan-i-za'-tion)*. Anything which is made up of parts; thus some people belong to church organizations, etc.

organize *(or'-gan-ize)*. 1. To put in order, as "You will find your work much easier if you organize your tasks". 2. To plan, as "Our teacher organized the picnic". 3. To gather together and prepare to do something, as "The police organized a search party".

orgy *(or'-gy)*. An activity, especially a party, in which people give way to excesses.

Orient *(O'-ri-ent)*. The direction from which the sun rises; therefore, the east. A person or thing coming from the East or the Orient is **oriental.** China is an oriental country. (See **Occident.**)

origin *(or'-i-gin)*. Beginning.

original *(o-rig'-i-nal)*. 1. First; to do with the beginning. 2. Inventive; clever at thinking out new ideas, as "Newton was a most original man". 3. Unusual; fresh; not copied, as "She has many original ideas for designing stage scenery".

ornament *(or'-na-ment)*. A thing that serves no useful purpose, but is valued because it decorates or beautifies.

ornate *(or-nate')*. Very much ornamented.

ornithology *(or-ni-thol'-ogy)*. The science that deals with the study of birds.

orphan *(or'-phan)*. A child who has no father or mother.

orphanage *(or'-phan-age)*. A place where orphans are given a home.

oscillate *(os'-cil-late)*. To swing from side to side, as the pendulum of a clock.

osprey *(os'-prey)*. A kind of hawk which eats fish.

ostensible *(os-ten'-si-ble)*. Pretended; for show; done to hide something else. Thus, "He opened a shop for the ostensible purpose of selling cameras and photographers' supplies, but all the time he was watching the movements of the rich miser who lived on the opposite side of the street".

ostentation *(os-ten-ta'-tion)*. Showing off.

osteopath *(os'-te-o-path)*. A person who cures various diseases by massage and working the hands over the parts giving trouble.

ostrich *(os'-trich)*. A large bird which is unable to fly. The ostrich lives in Africa and Arabia.

otherwise *(oth'-er-wise)*. In a different way; differently, as "You thought that was right, but we thought otherwise".

otter *(ot'-ter)*. A furry, fish-eating animal which is a strong swimmer and has webbed feet.

ought. Should; must.

ounce. A measure of weight. There are 16 ounces in 1 pound.

oust. To push out; drive out.

out-and-out *(out'-and-out')*. 1. Thorough; complete. 2. Absolutely; completely.

outcast *(out'-cast)*. A person who has been driven out of home, society, or country; a degraded person; a vagabond.

outdo *(out-do')*. To be better than; to go one better than.

outfit *(out'-fit)*. All the things necessary for doing something; thus a photographic outfit would include not only a camera but the necessaries for developing.

outlaw *(out'-law)*. A person or thing which is outside the protection of the law. Thus a criminal is an outlaw.

outlay *(out'-lay)*. The amount spent on something.

outline *(out'-line)*. 1. A drawing of something showing only its shape and none of the details. 2. A written account of something, giving the chief points briefly.

outrage *(out'-rage)*. An action that shows no consideration for another person; a dreadful injury done to someone or something purposely or through great neglect; any act of violence.

outright *(out'-right)*. Complete; completely, as "That man is an outright scoundrel", or "He sold his business outright".

outset *(out'-set)*. Beginning.

outside. 1. *(out'-side)*. Exterior, as "My house is painted white on the outside". 2. *(out-side')*. On the outside of, as "Criminals are men outside the law"; out-of-doors, as "When it is sunny, you like to play outside".

outskirts *(out'-skirts)*. The outside edges; the outlying areas.

ovation *(o-va'-tion)*. A loud burst of clapping or a loud cheer.

oval *(o'-val)*. 1. Having the shape of an egg. 2. A figure with rounded sides which is not circular but is longer than it is broad.

oven *(ov'-en)*. The part of a cooker or stove used for baking or roasting.

overawe *(o-ver-awe')*. A person is overawed when he cannot go on doing what he was doing because of fear, reverence, or wonder. Thus, "The small girl was so overawed when the curtain went up and showed Aladdin in his magic cave that she stopped eating sweets".

overbearing *(o-ver-bear'-ing)*. Haughty; fond of telling others what they should do.

overboard *(o'-ver-board)*. Over the side of a boat and into the water. One alarm used on a ship is the cry "Man overboard", which means that a person has fallen into the water.

overcast *(o-ver-cast')*. When the sun is hidden by thick clouds and everything seems dull, the weather is overcast.

overcome *(ov-er-come')*. To get the better of; to conquer.

overflow. 1. *(o-ver-flow')*. To flow over; to flood; to overwhelm. 2. *(o'-ver-flow)*. That which flows over; a pipe for carrying away spare or waste water.

overhaul *(o-ver-haul')*. 1. To examine thoroughly in order to make necessary changes or repairs. 2. To catch up with.

overseer *(o'-ver-se-er)*. One whose duty is to see that others do their work.

oversight *(o'-ver-sight)*. A mistake; an omission; a failure to notice something.

overthrow. 1. *(o-ver-throw')*. To defeat; to conquer; to get rid of by force. 2. *(o'-ver-throw)*. Defeat; collapse; state of being overthrown.

overture *(o'-ver-ture)*. A musical introduction to an opera, a stage play, a concert, etc.

overwhelm *(o-ver-whelm')*. To overpower; to crush.

owe. When you owe a person something, you must repay that person because you are in debt to him.

owl. A bird of prey which has large eyes, a hooked bill and feeds on mice and small birds. It usually hunts at night.

own. You own anything which belongs to you. You may own a bicycle or a doll, etc.

oxygen *(ox'-y-gen)*. One of the elements (see **element**). It is usually found in the form of a tasteless, colourless, odourless gas. It is necessary to life and supports combustion, or burning.

oyster *(oys'-ter)*. An edible mollusc housed in a clam-shaped shell. Some kinds of oyster make pearls.

P

pace. 1. A step made in walking, as "He took a pace forward". 2. The rate of walking, as "He walked at a good pace".

Pacific *(Pa-cif'-ic)*. A large ocean which is bordered by North and South America on one side and by Australia and Asia on the other.

pacify *(pac'-i-fy)*. To calm; to soothe a person so that he becomes more peaceful in mind.

pack. 1. To do up in a parcel, put in a bag, etc., as "Mary packed her things in a suitcase and then awaited the arrival of the taxi". 2. A bundle of things done up ready for carrying, as "The hiker had his pack slung over his shoulders". 3. A number of animals, as "We came upon a pack of wolves". 4. A set of fifty-two playing cards is called a pack. 5. A group of people of bad character, as "a pack of thieves".

package *(pack'-age)*. A **packet** *(pack'-et)*. A bundle of things, tied or in some other way held together.

pad. 1. A small mass of soft material. 2. A number of small sheets of paper fastened at one end.

paddle *(pad'-dle)*. 1. To walk in the water without shoes and socks. 2. To force a boat along with one oar. 3. The wheel of a paddle-boat which turns and drives the boat along.

paddock *(pad'-dock)*. A grass field where horses graze.

padlock *(pad'-lock)*. A type of lock which can be removed. It hangs on a U-shaped bar.

pagan *(pa'-gan)*. A heathen. One who does not worship the true God.

page. 1. One side of a sheet of paper in a book, etc. 2. A boy who runs errands in a hotel, etc.

pageant *(pag'-eant)*. 1. Any grand show or occasion, involving gorgeous costumes and, usually, a stately procession. The coronation of Queen Elizabeth II is an example. 2. A kind of entertainment at which scenes from different periods in history are shown on a stage.

paid. The past tense of **pay.** When you no longer owe a person cash, you have paid him. When you pay for a thing, the clerk writes "paid" on the bill.

pail. A container made of metal, wood or plastic in which things are carried. Usually a pail is used to carry liquids.

pain. When you suffer or ache, you have a pain. A toothache causes much pain.

paint. 1. A coloured substance which is applied in a thin layer to a surface. 2. To apply such a substance, as "paint a wall". 3. To make a picture, using paint.

painter *(paint'-er)*. 1. One who paints. 2. A rope used to fasten a boat.

pair. Two things that in some way go together, as a pair of gloves.

palace *(pal'-ace)*. A castle or a mansion in which royalty or famous people live.

palatable *(pal'-at-a-ble)*. Pleasant to the taste.

palate *(pal'-ate)*. The roof of the mouth.

palatial *(pa-la'-tial)*. Like a palace.

pale. When a thing is pale, it has little colour. Many people appear pale when sick.

palette *(pal'-ette)*. An oval board on which an artist mixes colours.

palisade *(pal-i-sade')*. A fence made by driving pointed stakes or sticks into the ground and joining them with wire, etc.

pall. 1. A black cloth used for placing over a coffin. 2. In "A pall of smoke lay over the town and people had to light their lamps", pall means a black cloud like the black cloth mentioned in No. 1. 3. When things begin to pall on you, you are getting tired of them.

pallid *(pal'-lid)*. Pale.

palm. 1. The inner part of the hand. 2. A measure equal in length to either the breadth or the length of the hand. 3. A tropical, branchless tree with large leaves at the top.

palmistry *(palm'-is-try)*. The art of telling a person's fortune by looking at the lines on the palm of his hand.

palpable *(pal'-pa-ble)*. 1. Able to be felt. 2. Easily seen, heard, smelt, etc. 3. Plain; obvious, as "It was a palpable lie".

palpitate *(pal'-pi-tate)*. When a person's heart beats quickly, it palpitates. Fear, excitement, too much smoking, all make the heart palpitate.

paltry. Mean; having practically no value, as "He gave the poor man a penny—it was a paltry sum".

pamper *(pam'-per)*. To spoil by too much kindness.

pamphlet *(pam'-phlet)*. A short book, containing anywhere from about 5 or 6 to, usually, no more than 40 pages, generally with a paper cover.

pan. A kind of shallow dish.

pancake *(pan'-cake)*. A kind of thin, flat cake cooked in a frying pan.

pane. A piece of glass to fit a window.

panel *(pan'-el)*. 1. A door panel is one of the divisions of a door, surrounded by thicker strips of wood. 2. A panel in a dress is a piece of material let into it lengthwise. 3. A group of people called together to decide or discuss something.

pang. A sharp pain.

panic *(pan'-ic)*. A sudden fear which spreads quickly.

panorama *(pan-o-ra'-ma)*. 1. An unlimited view. 2. A complete survey of a subject.

pansy *(pan'-sy)*. A small plant of the violet family. It has broad, flat, velvety petals in many colours.

pant. To gasp for breath.

panther *(pan'-ther)*. A leopard.

pantomime *(pan'-to-mime)*. A light-hearted play enjoyed by children at Christmas; but really a pantomime is a play in which no words are spoken and the actors show what they mean by their actions.

pantry *(pan'-try)*. A small room set apart for the storing of food.

papal *(pɪ'-pal)*. To do with the Pope.

paper *(pa'-per)*. 1. The material of which the pages of this book are made. 2. A newspaper. 3. An essay, or long composition on a special subject.

papoose *(pa-poose')*. A North American Indian baby.

parable *(par'-a-ble)*. A story that is told in order to make clear some moral lesson.

parachute *(par'-a-chute)*. A large, umbrella like device used to slow down the descent of things falling through the air. Airmen use parachutes in order to descend safely to the ground after escaping from aircraft.

parade *(pa-rade')*. 1. When bands, people, animals, vehicles, etc., march together along the street, they form a parade. 2. When you parade in front of someone, you make a show of, or flaunt, something.

paradise *(par'-a-dise)*. Heaven; a place of great happiness and comfort; a place of great beauty.

paradox *(par'-a-dox)*. A truth that seems untrue. It is a paradox that a man born on the 29th of February may celebrate his sixth birthday when he is twenty-four years old.

paraffin *(par'-af-fin)*. A solid, white, waxy substance used for making candles, sealing jars, waterproofing paper, etc.; but paraffin often means paraffin oil, which is a liquid form used in oil lamps and heaters.

paragraph *(par'-a-graph)*. A passage of writing containing several sentences on the same subject. The first line of every paragraph is indented, or set in from the margin.

parallel *(par'-al-lel)*. Straight lines which never meet, no matter how far they may be extended at either end, are said to be parallel. Railway tracks are parallel.

paralysis *(pa-ral'-y-sis)*. A condition in which certain parts of the body lose their power to move. A person suffering from paralysis is **paralyzed.**

paramount *(par'-a-mount)*. Better than others and, therefore, taking first place.

paraphrase *(par'-a-phrase)*. To set out the meaning of a passage, spoken or written, in different words; thus, a paraphrase of "The small boy began at once" might be "The youngster commenced immediately".

parasite *(par'-a-site)*. A plant or animal that lives on another, from which it takes its food. Lice and fleas are parasites.

parasol *(par'-a-sol)*. An umbrella used to shield a person from the sun.

parcel *(par'-cel)*. 1. To bundle things together is to parcel them. 2. A parcel is a package.

parch. 1. To burn slightly; to scorch. 2. To become very dry.

parchment *(parch'-ment)*. Originally, parchment was the dried skin of a goat or sheep, used as a writing surface. To-day, it is a kind of paper made to look like the dried skin of a goat or sheep.

pardon *(par'-don)*. 1. To forgive. 2. Forgiveness.

pare. To cut or trim off the outer parts; thus you may pare an apple when you peel it, and you may pare your nails when you cut them.

parents *(par'-ents)*. Your father and mother are your parents.

parish *(par'-ish)*. A small district, usually having a church of its own.

park. 1. An area kept in its natural state as public property, such as a National Park. 2. A kind of large public garden in a city, used for recreation or intended as an ornament. 3. To park a car is to stop it and keep it standing for some time at the side of a road, in a garage or in a car park.

parliament *(par'-lia-ment)*. The group of people elected to pass the laws and govern the country.

parlour *(par'-lour)*. 1. A living room; a room in a house intended mainly for the reception of guests. 2. In business, a room intended for the reception of customers, such as a beauty parlour.

parody *(par'-o-dy)*. An imitation of a certain kind of writing or music which makes fun of what it imitates.

parole *(pa-role')*. 1. A word of honour. Sometimes a captured soldier is allowed certain freedom on parole. He gives his word of honour that he will not run away. 2. When a prisoner is released from jail on parole he is released before he has served his entire sentence on condition that he report regularly to the police.

parrot *(par'-rot)*. A colourful bird which can be trained to speak although the bird does not understand what it says.

parse. To give information about the parts of speech in a sentence.

parsnip *(pars'-nip)*. A white, tapered root which is eaten as a vegetable.

parson *(par'-son)*. A minister.

parsonage *(par'-son-age)*. A house in which a parson or clergyman lives.

part. 1. When you eat a piece of pie, you eat a part of the pie. 2. When you do your part, you do your share. 3. When you part your hair, you divide it along a straight line. 4. When you read a part in a play, you read the lines spoken by one person in the play. 5. To part with someone or something is to separate from it; thus, "Jim was happy to be going to camp, but he did not want to part with his dog".

partial *(par'-tial)*. 1. Not complete, but only a part of, as "He made a partial recovery", that is, he recovered somewhat but not enough to be quite well again. 2. Having a liking for, as "I am very partial to walnuts", meaning "I like walnuts".

participate *(par-tic'-i-pate)*. 1. To have a share; to share. 2. To take part.

particle *(par'-ti-cle)*. A very tiny bit or piece.

particular *(par-tic'-u-lar)*. 1. Single; that one and no other, as in "the particular man of whom I am speaking". 2. Noteworthy; special, as "Have you any particular wish to go swimming?" 3. Fussy; attentive to details, as "John is very particular about his shirts: the collars and cuffs must be slightly starched and the rest not starched at all".

partition *(par-ti'-tion)*. 1. The dividing of something into parts, as in "The bandits were quarrelling over the partition of the spoils". 2. A dividing wall. 3. To divide into parts or shares, as "He partitioned his goods among his three sons".

partner *(part'-ner)*. A person who does something with you. A business partner runs a business with you; a tennis partner plays with you on your side; a dancing partner dances with you. If you are someone's partner in grief, joy, fortune, etc., you share their grief, joy, fortune, etc.

partridge *(par'-tridge)*. A bird belonging to the same family as the pheasant.

party *(par'-ty)*. 1. An organized group of citizens who think alike on matters of public interest and therefore try to have their members elected to government office. 2. The gathering together of people to have an evening's fun. 3. In "A party of boys came along the road", party means group.

pass. 1. When you pass a person, you overtake and move beyond him. 2. When you pass something to a group of people, you offer it to those present. 3. When you pass a field, you go by the field. 4. When you pass a test, you are successful in that test. 5. When you pass a football, you kick it to another player. 6. A pass in a mountain is a path or road. 7. When parliament passes a bill, the bill becomes law.

passable *(pass'-a-ble)*. 1. A thing that is just good enough is passable. 2. A road is passable if you can pass along it.

passage *(pas'-sage)*. 1. A place to walk along, with walls on both sides. 2. A piece taken from a book, speech, etc., as "In one passage, the Bible tells of Moses in the bulrushes".

passenger *(pas'-sen-ger)*. A person going on a journey in a bus, train, boat, etc.

passion *(pas'-sion)*. 1. Originally, this word meant suffering. Therefore, the passion of Christ is the suffering of Christ on the cross, etc. 2. Strong feeling or emotion, especially love. 3. A great liking for, as "I have a passion for oysters".

passionate *(pas'-sion-ate)*. Having strong feelings of anger, love, hate, jealousy, etc.

passport *(pass'-port)*. Permission given to someone by the government of his country to travel in foreign countries. The permission is declared in a passport book, a small book which the traveller must carry with him, and which contains his photograph and other information about him.

past. 1. Something which has gone before. 2. Beyond.

paste. 1. A mass of anything made soft by wetting. 2. A substance used for sticking things together. 3. Imitation precious stones are called paste.

pasteurize *(pas'-teur-ize)*. To heat something, such as milk, in order to kill the harmful germs in it. This process is called **pasteurization** *(pas-teur-i-za'-tion)*.

pastime *(pas'-time)*. Any sport or hobby that passes the time.

pastry *(pas'-try)*. A soft dough used for making pies, etc.

pasture *(pas'-ture)*. Grass-land used for feeding cattle.

patch. 1. A piece of material used to cover a hole, wound or tear. 2. A piece of ground, as "a patch of grass". 3. To put together quickly. 4. To mend with a patch.

patent *(pat'-ent)*. 1. When a person invents a thing he often takes out a patent on it. This is a legal document which grants him the right to be the only person to make and sell that thing for a number of years. **Patented,** therefore, means protected by a patent. 2. Clear; plain; obvious, as "John said he had been in bed with a cold but it was a patent lie, as he had a bad sunburn".

paternal *(pa-ter'-nal)*. Fatherly; belonging to a father.

path. 1. A narrow road or way along which people or animals may walk. A path is usually too narrow for vehicles. 2. The course which a thing or person follows, such as the path of the earth around the sun.

pathetic *(pa-thet'-ic)*. Causing pity.

patience *(pa'-tience)*. 1. The quality of being patient (see **patient**). 2. A card game played by one person.

patient *(pa'-tient)*. 1. Able to wait calmly; able to put up with a great deal without getting angry; long-suffering. 2. A person under the care of a doctor.

patriot *(pa'-tri-ot)*. A person who loves his country. Such a person is **patriotic** *(pa-tri-ot'-ic)* and shows **patriotism** *(pa'-tri-ot-ism)*.

patrol *(pa-trol')*. 1. To walk about in order to watch and protect, as a policeman on his beat; to pass around as a sentry. 2. A man or group of men who patrol; a sentry.

patter *(pat'-ter)*. To make a noise by giving a number of rapid taps, as "The rain patters on the window".

pattern *(pat'-tern)*. 1. A model to be imitated, as "He was a pattern of manliness". 2. A drawing, design or some other sort of guide which shows you how to make something. 3. A design, such as the pattern on a dish. Usually, a pattern is repeated over and over, as on wallpaper.

pauper *(pau'-per)*. A very poor person.

pause. 1. A temporary stop. 2. To stop for a while or a moment.

pave. 1. To cover a path or street with flags, concrete or asphalt. The covering is known as **pavement**. 2. When you pave the way for something, you prepare the way for it.

pavilion *(pa-vil'-ion)*. 1. A large tent. 2. An ornamented building, usually not very solidly made, in a park, garden or woods; a changing-room for athletes or sportsmen.

paw. The clawed foot of an animal.

pawn. 1. To hand over an article to a person who has lent you money on the understanding that the article will be returned to you when the money is repaid. A man who makes a business of lending money in the above way is a **pawnbroker**. 2. One of the pieces used in chess.

pay. 1. When you pay a person, you give him what you owe him. 2. When you give a clerk money for something purchased, you pay him. 3. When you pay attention, you give attention. 4. "Hard work pays" means that hard work is worth while.

pea. A vegetable which is an edible, round green seed inside a long green pod.

peace. 1. Quiet. 2. The opposite of war.

peach. A juicy fruit having a fuzzy skin and a large, rough stone inside.

peacock *(pea'-cock)*. A beautiful bird with colourful tail feathers that spread out like a fan.

peak. 1. The top of a mountain, especially if it is pointed. 2. The eye-shade of a cap. 3. The highest point; the busiest point; the most successful moment, etc. "The peak hours in London's traffic", means the time when it is most busy.

peal. 1. A loud sound such as that made by thunder or church bells. 2. A number of bells tuned to each other.

peanut *(pea'-nut)*. A monkey-nut or ground-nut.

pear. A sweet, juicy, yellow or green fruit, rounded, but smaller at one end.

pearl. 1. A gem, round, lustrous and nearly white in colour, found inside some molluscs. 2. The colour of a pearl.

peasant *(peas'-ant)*. 1. A person who lives and works on the land, away from towns and villages. 2. A rough, ignorant person.

peat. Partly decayed plant matter found in swamps or bogs, which is used to grow plants or as fuel.

pebble *(peb'-ble)*. A small stone.

peck. 1. What a bird does when it strikes at something with its beak. 2. A measure equal to eight quarts.

peculiar *(pe-cul'-iar)*. 1. Belonging to, or characteristic of, one person or thing, as "the climate peculiar to England". 2. Unusual; odd, as "He had the peculiar habit of taking baths by candlelight".

pecuniary *(pe-cu'-ni-ar-y)*. Involving money; of money. A pecuniary reward, therefore, is a reward of money.

pedal *(ped'-al)*. A lever to be worked by the foot. Pedals are provided on bicycles, sewing machines, motor-cars, church organs, etc.

pedantic *(pe-dan'-tic)*. Said of a person who pays too much attention to the formal rules of learning.

peddle *(ped'-dle)*. To carry or sell from house to house. A person who does this is a **pedlar.**

pedestrian *(pe-des'-tri-an)*. A person on foot; a walker.

pedigree *(ped'-i-gree)*. A table showing the ancestors and line of descent of a person or animal.

pedlar *(ped'-lar)*. One who goes about carrying small things for sale.

peek. To peep; to look at slyly.

peel. 1. The outer part or skin of a fruit such as an apple or an orange, or of a vegetable such as a potato. 2. To strip off the outer skin.

peep. 1. To glance through a narrow opening. 2. A noise made by baby birds.

peer. 1. To look at searchingly. 2. A man or woman with the title of a noble. 3. Peer also means someone equal in rank to you; thus, a pupil in your classroom is your peer.

peevish *(pee'-vish)*. Not exactly bad tempered, but in a mood to complain and be difficult.

peg. 1. A piece of wood, metal, etc., standing out from something else so that articles may be hung on it. 2. A piece of wood, metal, etc., driven into two pieces of material to hold them together.

pellet *(pel'-let)*. A tiny ball about the size of a pill. You can make a pellet by screwing up a small piece of paper. Lead pellets are used in the shot fired at birds and rabbits.

pelt. 1. The skin of an animal before it has been cured or tanned. 2. To pelt a person with snow is to throw many snowballs at him.

penalty *(pen'-al-ty)*. The payment that has to be made when a person does wrong and is caught. Thus, "The penalty for pulling the communication cord in a train is £5".

pencil *(pen'-cil)*. A writing tool made of graphite encased in wood.

pendant *(pen'-dant)*. Something that hangs down. A jewel or locket hanging from a lady's necklace is a pendant, and there are electric light pendants that hang from the ceiling.

pendulum *(pen'-du-lum)*. A weight hung so that it is free to swing to and fro easily. Many clocks have pendulums.

penetrate *(pen'-e-trate)*. To go inside; to get into the middle of; to go through.

penguin *(pen'-guin)*. An Antarctic sea-bird which is black with a white breast, stands erect and has flippers for swimming rather than wings for flying.

peninsula *(pen-in'-su-la)*. Land almost, but not quite, surrounded by water.

penitent *(pen'-i-tent)*. A person is penitent when he is sorry for the wrong he has done.

penmanship *(pen'-man-ship)*. The skill of writing.

pennant *(pen'-nant)*. 1. A type of long, narrow flag used for signalling on ships. 2. A banner.

penny *(pen'-ny)*. A coin, twelve of which are worth a shilling.

pension *(pen'-sion)*. A payment made at regular times to support someone.

pensive *(pen'-sive)*. Thoughtful.

pentagon *(pen'-ta-gon)*. A figure having five equal sides and five equal angles. '

Pentecost *(Pen'-te-cost)*. The seventh Sunday after Easter; Whitsuntide.

penury *(pen'-u-ry)*. Poverty; the state of having little or no money.

peony *(pe'-o-ny)*. A perennial garden plant with large flowers.

people *(peo'-ple)*. When you think or speak of men, women and children all together, you think or speak of people. We speak of the people of Great Britain, the people of France, etc.

pepper *(pep'-per)*. A seasoning which tastes hot and makes you sneeze if you hold it near your nose.

perambulator *(per-am'-bu-la-tor)*. A small carriage, often called a pram, in which a baby is wheeled.

per cent. This word means "out of one hundred". Thus, if you obtained 78 on an arithmetic test for which the total marks were 100, your mark would be 78 per cent. The abbreviation for per cent is %.

perch. 1. A fresh-water fish used as food. 2. A pole, set in a cage, on which a bird may rest. 3. To place in a high position, as "The house was perched on the top of a hill".

percolate *(per'-co-late)*. To drip through small holes.

perennial *(per-en'-ni-al)*. 1. Having a life cycle of more than two years; some garden plants are perennial plants, or perennials 2. Continuing for a long time, as "perennial beauty".

perfect *(per'-fect)*. 1. A thing is perfect when all of it is present and no part is missing. 2. A thing is also perfect when it is so good that it cannot be better. 3. *(per-fect')*. To make a thing as good as it can be, as "I shall try to perfect my spelling before the examination".

perfection *(per-fec'-tion)*. The condition of being faultless.

perfectly *(per'-fect-ly)*. 1. Thoroughly; quite, as "I understand perfectly". 2. Without fault, as "She dresses perfectly".

perforated *(per'-fo-rat-ed)*. Having one or more holes. The line of holes between two unseparated stamps is a perforated line. The holes are **perforations** *(per-fo-ra'-tions)*.

perform *(per-form')*. To do; to act.

performance *(per-form'-ance)*. 1. A deed that is done or is to be done; the doing of something. 2. A play or circus, etc. 3. The act of going through the play.

perfume *(per'-fume)*. 1. A pleasing odour. 2. A manufactured liquid having a pleasing odour.

perhaps *(per-haps')*. Maybe.

peril *(per'-il)*. The chance of danger happening; danger; a source of danger.

perimeter *(per-im'-e-ter)*. The distance around a thing; the boundary.

period *(pe'-ri-od)*. 1. A space of time, as "During the period he was in hospital, I went to see him every day". 2. A complete sentence. 3. A full-stop placed at the end of a sentence.

periodical *(pe-ri-od'-i-cal)*. 1. Any magazine, newspaper, etc., that comes out at regular times. 2. Happening regularly again and again, as "He has periodical fits of temper".

periscope *(per'-i-scope)*. A tube containing mirrors so that a person looking into the eyepiece at one end can see objects reflected by the mirror at the other end. With a periscope, a person can see over the heads of taller people in front of him, and the men in a submarine below the surface can see what is above the surface of the sea.

perish *(per'-ish)*. 1. To die. 2. To decay.

perishable *(per'-ish-a-ble)*. Likely to decay or go bad. Milk and butter are perishable.

perjury *(per'-ju-ry)*. Saying things known to be untrue and swearing in a court of law that they are true.

permanent *(per'-ma-nent)*. 1. Lasting for ever. 2. Lasting a long time, as a permanent wave.

permission *(per-mis'-sion)*. Consent; when your father gives you his permission to do something, he tells you that he will allow you to do it.

permit. 1. *(per'-mit)*. A printed or written note allowing a person to do something or go somewhere. 2. *(per-mit')*. To allow.

pernicious *(per-ni'-cious)*. Harmful; wicked.

perpendicular *(per-pen-dic'-u-lar)*. Standing upright. A line is perpendicular to another line when the angle formed by the two lines is a right angle.

perpetual *(per-pet'-u-al)*. Going on forever. A thing that goes on forever goes on in **perpetuity** *(per-pe-tu'-i-ty)*.

perplex *(per-plex')*. To puzzle; to put a person in such a state of mind that he does not know what to do.

persecute *(per'-se-cute)*. To torment; to oppress; to cause someone to suffer because of his beliefs.

persevere *(per-se-vere')*. To continue doing something difficult; to persist.

persist *(per-sist')*. To refuse to stop; to keep on doing or saying something.

person *(per'-son)*. One human being.

personal *(per'-son-al)*. Private; to do with one person only. In "That is a personal matter", personal means concerning one person only.

personality *(per-son-al'-i-ty)*. Your personality involves the qualities which make you different from all other people.

perspective *(per-spec'-tive)*. 1. The art of drawing objects on a flat surface so as to create the illusion of three dimensions and of distance. 2. A view, especially a view into the far distance.

perspiration *(per-spi-ra'-tion)*. Sweat; the moisture given off by the pores of the skin. To **perspire** is to sweat, or give off perspiration.

persuade *(per-suade')*. To coax a person into doing something; to talk someone into doing something; to convince a person that he ought to do something, think something, etc. In persuading a person you use **persuasion** *(per-sua'-sion)*, not force.

pert. Saucy.

pertain *(per-tain')*. To belong; to be concerned with; to have to do with. Thus, **pertaining to** means having to do with, concerned with, etc.

perturb *(per-turb')*. To disturb or upset a person and make him worried.

pervade *(per-vade')*. To spread all over or all through, as "When she entered, her perfume pervaded the whole room".

perverse *(per-verse')*. Stubborn; obstinate; contrary. A perverse person would rather do what he is told not to do, than what he is told to do.

pessimist *(pes'-si-mist)*. A person who always looks on the dismal side of things and fancies that the worst must happen. He is the opposite of an optimist, who can always see the bright side of things.

pest. A person or thing that gives trouble. A wire-worm is a garden pest; a fly is a house pest.

pester *(pes'-ter)*. To annoy.

pestilence *(pes'-ti-lence)*. A disease that spreads through whole groups of people, attacking great numbers at a time and causing many deaths.

pet. 1. A domesticated animal, usually kept in the house. 2. Favourite.

petal *(pet'-al)*. A part of a flower which is usually coloured. Tulips, roses and peonies have brightly coloured petals.

petition *(pe-ti'-tion)*. 1. A request; something that begs for a thing to be done. Thus, if many people living in a town signed a paper asking the town council to widen the river bridge, the paper with the signatures would be a petition. 2. To request earnestly; to request formally in a written petition.

petrify *(pet'-ri-fy)*. To turn into stone.

petroleum *(pe-tro'-le-um)*. A liquid taken from the earth and refined into petrol, oil, etc.

petticoat *(pet'-ti-coat)*. A woman's underskirt or slip.

petty *(pet'-ty)*. Small; mean; of little worth.

petunia *(pe-tu'-ni-a)*. An annual plant with bright, trumpet-shaped flowers.

pew. A long bench or seat in a church.

pewter *(pew'-ter)*. A metal made of tin and lead.

phantom *(phan'-tom)*. A ghost.

pharmacy *(phar'-ma-cy)*. 1. A chemist's shop. 2. The art or science of preparing medicines.

pheasant *(pheas'-ant)*. A bird with a long tail. The male has bright feathers.

phenomenon *(phe-nom'-e-non)*. 1. Any fact, event or existing thing that can be scientifically explained. The plural is **phenomena.** 2. A remarkable or surprising thing. Such a thing is **phenomenal.**

philanthropist *(phi-lan'-thro-pist)*. This word really means "a lover of mankind". It is usually used to describe a person who gives money to deserving causes in order to benefit his fellow man.

philosopher *(phi-los'-o-pher)*. 1. A lover of wisdom; a very learned man who spends his life seeking for the truth about existence, human nature, science, etc. 2. A person who endures misfortune calmly.

phonetic *(pho-net'-ic)*. 1. Having to do with the sounds of speech. 2. Phonetic spelling is a system of spelling words according to how they sound. In such a system the word "phonetic" might be spelled "fonetik".

phosphorus *(phos'-pho-rus)*. One of the elements (see **element**). It is usually found as a yellow, waxy, crystalline substance. Phosphorus glows in the dark; hence, anything containing phosphorus which glows in the dark is **phosphorescent** *(phos-pho-res'-cent)*.

photograph *(pho'-to-graph)*. A picture taken with a camera.

photographer *(pho-tog'-ra-pher)*. A person who takes photographs.

phrase. A group of words forming part of a sentence, as "in the morning".

physical *(phys'-i-cal)*. Belonging to the body; bodily. Thus, we speak of athletes being in good physical condition.

physician *(phy-si'-cian)*. A person trained to heal the sick by the use of medicines.

piano *(pi-an'-o)*. A musical instrument played by striking keys, which operate hammers, which in turn strike wires.

piccolo *(pic'-co-lo)*. A tube-shaped musical instrument which is played by blowing into a hole. It is a small flute.

pick. 1. To gather, as "I went into the garden to pick apples". 2. To choose or select, as "Come with me to pick my Christmas cards". 3. The best, as "That flower is the pick of the whole exhibition". 4. A tool with a sharp point for making holes, as "The workman began to work with his pick and made a large hole".

pickerel *(pick'-er-el)*. A young pike.

pickle *(pick'-le)*. 1. To preserve vegetables and other edible things in vinegar or brine. 2. A thing preserved in this way.

picnic *(pic'-nic)*. A meal, often consisting of sandwiches, eaten out of doors.

picturesque *(pic-tur-esque')*. Charming; pretty; quaint; suitable to be put in a picture.

pie. Fruit, meat, etc., baked in a pastry.

piebald *(pie'-bald)*. Having spots or patches of two colours; generally said of a black and white horse.

piece. A part of a whole thing; a portion.

pier. 1. A place to walk up and down, built out a little way into the sea. 2. A support for the arch of a bridge.

pierce. 1. To push the tip of a pointed article, like a needle, through something. 2. To force a way into.

piety *(pi'-e-ty)*. Goodness; holiness; a person who is devoutly religious is **pious.**

pig. 1. A hog or swine. 2. An oblong mass of iron.

pigeon *(pi'-geon)*. A bird with a fat body and short legs which may be trained to carry messages or to race.

pigment *(pig'-ment)*. The colouring material in such things as paint.

pike. 1. A kind of lance once used by foot soldiers. 2. A freshwater fish that is a great enemy of other fishes.

pile. 1. A heap of material, such as hay, mud or wool, or of things, such as toys, pieces of clothing, etc. 2. A pillar or a thick piece of wood or metal forced into the ground and standing upright. 3. The pile on a carpet, table-cloth, etc., is a thick plush-like surface or nap that makes it feel soft.

pilfer *(pil'-fer)*. To steal small things or small amounts.

pilgrim *(pil'-grim)*. 1. A traveller. 2. A person who wanders from one sacred place to another, and looks upon his journeys as a religious duty.

pill. A small, round object containing medicine, which is to be swallowed.

pillage *(pil'-lage)*. To plunder or take by force.

pillar *(pil'-lar)*. An upright pole made of wood, stone, cement, brick or metal which supports or ornaments part of a building. We often see pillars supporting a roof near the front of a building.

pillion *(pil-li-on)*. A seat behind the driver on a horse, motor-cycle, etc.

pillory *(pil'-lo-ry)*. A frame in which criminals were put, so that they were held by the head and arms. The frame was set up in a public place where passers-by could jeer at the victims.

pillow *(pil'-low)*. A bed-cushion for the head.

pilot *(pi'-lot)*. 1. A man who steers a ship when it is entering or leaving a port. 2. The person who controls an aircraft. 3. To pilot something is to guide or steer it.

pimple *(pim'-ple)*. A small, inflamed spot in the skin.

pincers *(pin'-cers)*. A tool that opens like a pair of scissors and is used for holding objects tightly.

pinch. To grip hard; to press painfully; to nip; to squeeze the flesh so as to give pain.

pine. 1. A fir tree that has leaves in the form of needles. 2. To pine away is to grow thin because of sorrow.

pineapple *(pine'-ap-ple)*. A large fruit shaped like a pine-cone with a bushy crown of prickly leaves. The inside of the fruit is pale yellow. It grows in tropical climates.

pink. 1. Pale red. 2. A sweet-smelling garden flower.

pinnacle *(pin'-na-cle)*. The peak of something, such as "the pinnacle of his career", or the pointed top of a building or of a mountain.

pint. A measure of liquid. There are two pints in a quart.

pioneer *(pi-o-neer')*. 1. A person who goes to a lonely part of the world to open up the way for others to follow. The Pilgrim Fathers were pioneers. 2. A person who is the first to show others how to do something novel or fresh.

pious *(pi'-ous)*. Religious; devout.

pipe. 1. A tube, usually of metal, through which liquids or gases may flow. 2. A device for smoking tobacco, consisting of a bowl and hollow stem.

piquant *(pi'-quant)*. Sharp to the taste; pleasantly stimulating to the mind.

pique. 1. Spite; anger. 2. To arouse anger.

pirate *(pi'-rate)*. 1. A robber at sea. 2. A person who steals the ideas of other people. 3. To steal the ideas of others.

pistol *(pis'-tol)*. A small gun, held and fired by one hand.

piston *(pis'-ton)*. A circular plate fitting and moving up and down in a hollow cylinder, used in pumps and engines.

pit. 1. A hole dug in the ground, as a sand-pit. 2. A small mark or hollow on the skin, such as those found on a person who is pitted with the marks of smallpox. 3. When a wrestler pits his strength against another he puts all his strength against him in an effort to defeat him.

pitch. 1. A black substance used for surfacing roads, etc. 2. To roll and toss, as when a ship pitches on a rough sea. 3. To throw, as when a person playing cricket pitches the ball to the wicket-keeper. 4. Pitch in music is the highness or lowness of a tone. 5. To set up, as when a tent is pitched. 6. When a person pitches into his work, he starts working with much energy. 7. An area of ground prepared for the playing of a game, as a football pitch.

pitcher *(pitch'-er)*. A large jug usually made of earthenware.

pitchfork *(pitch'-fork)*. A fork used by farmers for lifting hay, etc.

pitiful *(pit'-i-ful)*. 1. Deserving of sorrow and sympathy; in such a sad condition as to make people sorry. 2. Pitiful also has the very different meaning, "fit for scorn". Thus a person may be said to be a pitiful rogue, meaning that he is a rogue to be scorned.

pittance *(pit'-tance)*. A small sum of money; a small allowance of money.

pity *(pit'-y)*. When you pity a person you feel sorry for him.

pivot *(piv'-ot)*. A point upon which a thing turns.

placard *(plac'-ard)*. A poster or sign shown in a public place so that all passers-by may see it. The signs on buses are placards.

placate *(pla-cate')*. To soothe a person who is annoyed.

place. 1. A certain part of space such as a town or building, etc. 2. To put into position.

placid *(pla'-cid)*. Calm; quiet; peaceful.

plague. 1. A disease that spreads quickly and kills very many people. 2. To annoy or cause trouble.

plaid. 1. A long piece of woollen cloth, often with a check or tartan pattern, used as the outer garment in Highland costume. 2. The pattern on such a cloth.

plain. 1. Without any pattern or markings, as a plain piece of paper. 2. Not difficult to understand; clear, as "It is as plain as daylight". 3. Not beautiful, as "She is quite plain". 4. Flat land; a stretch of level country.

plan. 1. When you decide how to do a thing beforehand, you plan. 2. When building a model aeroplane, you follow a plan to understand the method of putting the pieces together.

plane. 1. A flat surface, but not flat ground. (See **plain**.) 2. A tool used by carpenters for smoothing wood. 3. A short way of saying aeroplane.

planet *(plan'-et)*. Any one of the bodies in the sky which move round the sun.

plank. A thick, strong strip of timber, thicker than a board.

plant. 1. A young tree, shrub, flower or vegetable. 2. Any living thing that is not an animal. 3. All the machinery and equipment used in the work of a factory is known as the factory's plant. 4. To put in the earth in order to make grow, as you do a seed. 5. To place or situate, as "The spies were planted in various parts of the country".

plantation *(plan-ta'-tion)*. 1. A place planted with trees and bushes. 2. A huge farm on which sugar, cotton, etc., are grown. A plantation has many hired labourers to do the work.

plaster *(plas'-ter)*. 1. Lime, sand and water mixed to form a type of white cement. The ceilings and walls in your house are probably made of plaster. 2. A preparation that is put on a piece of cloth and then applied to the body to cure some disease or to heal a wound. A mustard plaster is often put on the chest to cure a cough; and corn plasters are put on the feet to cure corns. 3. To plaster is to spread thickly, as "Don't plaster the butter on your bread".

plastic *(plas'-tic)*. 1. Soft; easily squeezed into all sorts of shapes. Putty is plastic. 2. Any soft material which when moulded into a shape retains that shape when cooled. 3. A substance made by man which is light, strong, not easily broken, and can be moulded into any shape. Some drinking glasses are made of clear plastic that looks like glass.

plate. 1. Something flat. 2. A thin piece of metal. 3. A round, flat dish on which a meal is served. 4. Articles that are coated with a layer of silver but are not solid silver are called silver plate. 5. A film-coated sheet of glass used in photography. 6. A photograph or coloured picture in a book. 7. Plate glass is very thick glass.

plateau *(plat-eau')*. A flat piece of land set high above sea-level, sometimes called a table-land.

platform *(plat'-form)*. 1. A raised stage. 2. The place where people get on and off a train.

platinum *(plat'-in-um)*. A valuable metal, more costly than gold. It is white and might be mistaken for silver.

platoon *(pla-toon')*. A number of soldiers of the same company under a lieutenant.

platter *(plat'-ter)*. A large flat dish used for serving meat.

plausible *(plau'-si-ble)*. Appearing to be good; seeming to be reasonable.

play. 1. To take part in a game. To amuse oneself. 2. A performance in which people act the parts of others. 3. To perform on a musical instrument, as to play the piano.

player *(play'-er)*. A person who takes part in a game or a performance.

plea. An excuse; an argument; a request.

plead. 1. To ask earnestly, as when a person pleads for mercy. 2. To answer a charge in court, as when a person pleads guilty or not guilty.

pleasant *(pleas'-ant)*. Pleasing; lovely; attractive.

pleasantry *(pleas'-an-try)*. Joking and making fun in a good-natured way.

pleasure *(pleas'-ure)*. When something gives you pleasure, it makes you happy or pleased.

pledge. 1. A solemn promise. 2. If I borrow some money from you and hand you my watch on condition that you return it when I repay the money, you take the watch as a pledge.

plentiful *(plen'-ti-ful)*. Ample; abundant; existing in large amounts, as "Apples are plentiful in autumn".

plenty *(plen'-ty)*. 1. Abundance; a time of plenty is a time when things are plentiful. 2. All that is needed; sufficient; as "You have plenty of time to catch the train".

pliable *(pli'-a-ble)*. Easily bent without cracking or breaking; thus a piece of copper wire is pliable, but a glass rod is not.

plight. 1. In "He was in a dreadful plight", plight means state. 2. "I plight my word", means "I give my promise".

plod. 1. To go along slowly, steadily and without taking much notice of the things around you. 2. To study or work steadily with little pleasure.

plot. 1. A secret plan to do something. 2. A piece of ground. An allotment is a plot. 3. The chief parts of a story without unnecessary details. 4. If you plot a course on a map, you trace the plan of your journey on it.

plough. 1. A piece of machinery used by farmers to dig up the ground for planting. A different kind of plough is used to remove snow. 2. To dig up the ground with a plough.

ploughshare *(plough'-share)*. The cutting blade of a plough which digs itself into the ground and forces the soil to one side.

pluck. 1. Courage. 2. To pull off feathers from a bird or flowers from a plant. 3. To pull sharply at anything. If you sound a note on a stringed musical instrument by pulling at a string with a fingernail, you are said to have plucked the string.

plug. A block or peg used to stop a hole. A bung; a stopper; a wad of material.

plum. A small, round, green or purple fruit with a stone.

plumage *(plum'-age)*. A bird's coat of feathers.

plumb. 1. When a wall is plumb, it is perfectly vertical or straight up and down. 2. A line with a weight at one end used to measure the straightness of a wall or to test the depth of water.

plumber *(plumb'-er)*. A man who has the training to repair plumbing.

plumbing *(plumb'-ing)*. The plumbing in your house is all the pipes inside the walls that carry water, gas, etc.

plump. 1. Comfortably fat; not too much so. 2. To fall straight down.

plunder *(plun'-der)*. To rob by violent measures, especially during war.

plunge. 1. To go suddenly into water or any liquid. 2. Some forms of diving are called plunges.

plural *(plu'-ral)*. The opposite to singular; said of more than one.

plus. 1. With the addition of. 2. Showing that something is to be added, as "a plus sign" (+).

ply. 1. To work with. 2. To go backwards and forwards. 3. **plywood** is wood glued together in many layers.

pneumonia *(pneu-mo'-ni-a)*. A disease of the lungs, which causes them to become inflamed.

poach. 1. To hunt or fish, without permission, on another person's property. 2. To cook an egg by breaking the shell and dropping the contents into boiling water.

pocket *(pock'-et)*. 1. A kind of bag sewn into clothes. 2. Things meant to be carried in a pocket are given the word "pocket" as an adjective; thus, "pocket handkerchief" and "pocket knife". 3. To put into your pocket. 4. To steal, as "He pocketed the contents of the till and bolted". Note that this does not always mean that he pushed the contents into his pocket; but that he grabbed or took them. 5. An air pocket is an apparent vacuum in the air. When an aircraft enters such a pocket it immediately drops some distance. 6. To be out of pocket is to lose money.

pod. The husk or shell of such things as peas.

poem *(po'-em).* A complete work of poetry.

poet *(po'-et).* One who writes **poetry.** A poet has a gift for saying things well; he must have more than the usual powers of imagination, observation and understanding.

poetry *(po'-et-ry).* A work of art made in words, which may describe something or tell a story, but which always expresses thoughts and feelings. The difference between poetry and prose is that poetry is usually arranged in lines which have a rhythm and often rhyme.

poignant *(poign'-ant).* So sharp as to be painful. Smells, flavours or feelings may be poignant.

point. 1. A sharp tip of anything. 2. In geometry, that which has position but no magnitude or size. 3. Marks to be earned in school are sometimes called points. 4. To aim, as when pointing a gun. 5. To show with the hand, as "It is rude to point". 6. The four points of the compass are N., S., E. and W.

poise. 1. To balance. 2. Balance; the carriage of your head and body.

poison *(poi'-son).* Any substance which injures or seriously impairs the health when swallowed or inhaled. Some poisons are deadly.

poker *(po'-ker).* 1. A thing for stirring the fire. 2. A gambling game of cards.

polar *(po'-lar).* To do with the regions around the poles of the earth.

pole. 1. A long piece of wood usually round, such as telegraph pole. 2. One of the ends of the axis of a sphere, especially of the earth, as the North Pole. 3. One of the ends of a magnet. 4. **Pole.** A native of Poland.

police *(po-lice').* A body of men whose duty is to enforce the laws.

policeman *(po-lice'-man).* A man who belongs to the police force.

policy *(pol'-i-cy)*. 1. A printed note issued by an insurance company which agrees to insure your life or your property. 2. A man's policy is his plan of action; thus his policy may be to treat people a little better than they treat him, or to rise early in the morning. The Government's plan for managing the country is its policy.

polish *(pol'-ish)*. 1. To make a thing bright and shining. 2. The material used for polishing. 3. Polish is often used to mean good manners; thus a man may be said to have polish, meaning that he has good manners. 4. **Polish.** Belonging to Poland.

polite *(po-lite')*. Having good manners; courteous.

political *(po-lit'-i-cal)*. Having to do with the government or public affairs.

politician *(pol-i-ti'-cian)*. One who is a member of Parliament or is interested a great deal in politics.

poll. 1. A list of people who have the right to vote. 2. An election. 3. The place where votes are cast is called the polls. 4. To vote. 5. If a candidate polls 15 votes, 15 votes are cast for him.

pollen *(pol'-len)*. The fine powder found inside flowers.

pollute *(pol-lute')*. To soil; make dirty.

polo *(po'-lo)*. A game played by men on horseback who strike a round wooden ball with long-handled mallets and try to drive it into a goal.

polygamy *(po-lyg'-a-my)*. State of having several wives.

polygon *(pol'-y-gon)*. A figure having many sides or angles.

pomp. Stately display; flourish; grandeur.

pompous *(pomp'-ous)*. Self-important; magnificent; having pomp.

pond. A small lake.

ponder *(pon'-der)*. To think over carefully.

ponderous *(pon'-der-ous)*. Heavy and clumsy.

pontoon *(pon-toon')*. 1. A flat, shallow boat, something like a barge. Several pontoons are tied together to form a bridge when soldiers want to cross a river. 2. The floats or boat-shaped attachments on aeroplanes which land on water.

pony *(po'-ny)*. A small horse.

pool. 1. A small pond. 2. A puddle of water. 3. Open-air or indoor swimming-baths are called swimming-pools. 4. When a group of people pool their money, they put their money into a fund which is then divided equally among them or used for some purpose from which they will all benefit.

poop. The back part of a ship.

poorly *(poor'-ly)*. 1. Used as an adjective, poorly means unwell, in poor health. 2. Used as an adverb, poorly means with no great success.

Pope. The head of the Roman Catholic Church.

poplar *(pop'-lar)*. A kind of tree which has soft wood, grows quickly and is often seen in parks and gardens.

poppy *(pop'-py)*. A plant with bright red, orange or yellow flowers.

popular *(pop'-u-lar)*. 1. Of the people; belonging to the people. Thus a popular decision is a decision that most of the people make together. 2. Well-liked by many people. A thing that is well-liked by many people has **popularity** *(pop-u-lar'-i-ty)*.

population *(pop-u-la'-tion)*. The number of people living in a place; thus the population of Great Britain is over fifty million.

porcelain *(por'-ce-lain)*. Earthenware or china of very high quality.

porch. A doorway with a covered roof set over it; thus anyone waiting at the door in the rain has some shelter.

porcupine *(por'-cu-pine)*. An animal of the rodent family which is covered with spines or quills.

pore. 1. A tiny opening in the skin which allows perspiration to escape from the body. Leaves also have pores, through which they take in air and sunlight. 2. To pore over a thing is to study it very hard; thus, "The professor pored over his manuscript and checked each word carefully".

pork. The flesh of pigs.

porous *(po'-rous)*. Full of pores; absorbent like a sponge.

porpoise *(por'-poise)*. A fish-like sea animal that has a blunt nose and looks like a small whale.

porridge *(por'-ridge)*. A breakfast food made by boiling ground oats, etc., in water or milk.

port. 1. A harbour for ships where cargoes are loaded and unloaded. 2. The left side of a ship, which carries a red light after dark. 3. Various openings in a ship's side are known as **portholes** *(port'-holes)*. 4. A red wine.

portable *(port'-a-ble)*. Easily carried.

portcullis *(port-cul'-lis)*. A sliding door held over the gate of a castle or fortress. On the arrival of an enemy, the portcullis is dropped and the entrance is securely closed.

porter *(por'-ter)*. 1. A man who carries things for other people. 2. A man who stands at a door to open and close it for the people coming in and out.

portfolio *(port-fo'-li-o)*. A kind of brief-case; a case for carrying papers.

portion *(por'-tion)*. A share, as when you receive your portion of food at a meal.

portly *(port'-ly)*. Stout; bulging; large, said only of people.

portrait *(por'-trait)*. A picture of somebody. It may be a photograph, an oil-painting, a pen and ink drawing, etc.

pose. 1. When you take a certain position so that others will notice you, you pose. 2. To pose as means to pretend to be; thus, "He tried to pose as a newspaper reporter to gain entrance to a game". 3. An artist often has a person to pose or sit in a fixed position, so that he can paint a picture of him. 4. When you pose a question, you give or ask the question for the purpose of discussion.

position *(po-si'-tion)*. 1. A job or occupation, as "He has a good position with the insurance company". 2. A place where a thing is, as "His shop is in an excellent position for selling chocolates to the people entering the theatre". 3. A way of placing yourself, as "Sit in a more comfortable position".

positive *(pos'-i-tive)*. Certain beyond doubt, as "He is positive the burglar entered his room."

possess *(pos-sess')*. To own. What is owned is a **possession.**

possible *(pos'-si-ble)*. That can be done, can happen.

post. 1. A long piece of wood stuck into the ground, such as a fence post. 2. A job or occupation, as "He has a high post in the bank". 3. To send off a letter is to post it. 4. A position, as "Every man was at his post".

postage *(post'-age)*. The money paid for a letter or parcel to be carried in the post.

poster *(post'-er)*. A sign.

posterior *(pos-te'-ri-or)*. 1. Coming after. 2. The back or hind part.

posterity *(pos-ter'-i-ty)*. A person's children and their children, and the children following them, and so on without end.

Later generations; descendants. All the people that will live in the world.

postilion *(pos-til'-ion)*. A man who rides on one of the horses drawing a carriage.

postman *(post'-man)*. The man who delivers the letters and parcels to homes.

post mortem *(post mor'-tem)*. After death. It usually refers to an examination of a dead body.

postpone *(post-pone')*. To put off until later.

postscript *(post'-script)*. A note written at the end of a letter, after the signature. It usually begins with P.S. (short for postscript) and then says something like this, "Since writing this letter, I have heard that Aunt Mary cannot come".

posture *(pos'-ture)*. The way of holding the body.

posy *(po'-sy)*. A flower or a neat bunch of flowers.

potato *(po-ta'-to)*. 1. A root which is eaten as a vegetable. It is white beneath a brown skin and unevenly rounded. 2. The plant which bears potatoes.

potent *(po'-tent)*. Powerful.

potentate *(po'-ten-tate)*. A king who has great power and who can do anything he likes.

potential *(po-ten'-tial)*. Having the possibility of power, but not actually having it. Thus, if a stone weighing many pounds is perched on the top of a high wall where it has hardly space to rest, the power of the stone is nothing as long as it remains perched there; but give it a slight push and it comes crashing down, smashing everything beneath it. It had plenty of potential power while up there, as is shown by the damage it did when it fell.

pottage *(pot'-tage)*. A thick soup.

potter *(pot'-ter)*. A man who makes dishes, vases, pots, etc., from clay and heats them to harden them. These articles are called **pottery.**

pouch. A small bag for carrying things, as "The mother kangaroo carries her young in a pouch".

poultice *(poul'-tice)*. A soft mass of bread, linseed, mustard, etc., made with boiling water, spread on cloth and applied to a sore part of the body to relieve pain.

poultry *(poul'-try)*. Birds reared in the farmyard for food or eggs, such as chickens, geese, ducks and turkeys.

pounce. To seize by suddenly jumping on; thus a cat pounces on a sparrow in the garden.

pound. 1. A measure of weight, equal to sixteen ounces. 2. A unit of British money. The abbreviation for it is £. 3. An enclosure in which stray animals are kept. 4. To hit heavily, as in "He pounded on the door". 5. To beat heavily, as in "He was very frightened and could feel his heart pounding".

pour. 1. To flow in a stream, as "The river poured over the falls". 2. To cause to flow in a stream, as "He poured the milk out of the jug".

pout. To push out the lips and look sulky.

poverty *(pov'-er-ty)*. State of being poor and needing money.

powder *(pow'-der)*. A fine dust-like substance.

powerful *(pow'-er-ful)*. Very strong or mighty, as "Hercules was a powerful man".

practicable *(prac'-ti-ca-ble)*. Able to be put into practice or to be used; possible to be done. There is no practicable way of carrying water in a sieve.

practical *(prac'-ti-cal)*. Anything which is practical is useful.

practice *(prac'-tice)*. 1. The doing of a thing over and over again, so as to be able to do it well. 2. The custom or habit; thus "It is his practice to go for a walk before breakfast". 3. The professional work or business of a doctor or a lawyer.

practise *(prac'-tise)*. To do habitually; to do over and over so as to gain skill in doing, as "He practised the piece on the piano for three days, until he could play it well".

prairie *(prai'-rie)*. A vast piece of treeless grassland. Alberta, Saskatchewan and Manitoba are the prairie provinces of Canada.

praise. To say nice things about; to approve of a person's good deeds.

prank. A mischievous trick; a playful trick.

pray. To beg or ask very earnestly, especially to beg God for something.

prayer. 1. An earnest request. 2. The act of praying to God.

preach. To talk on a religious subject; to deliver a sermon in church.

precaution *(pre-cau'-tion)*. Care taken beforehand to prevent a possible disaster.

precede *(pre-cede')*. To go before.

precious *(pre'-cious)*. Of great value.

precipice *(prec'-i-pice)*. A steep place, such as the side of a cliff that has an almost upright face.

précis *(pré'-cis)*. A summary or short account of something.

precise *(pre-cise')*. Exact; definite; accurate, as "The carpenter was so precise in his measurements that the drawer fitted perfectly".

precocious *(pre-co'-cious)*. Flowering or ripening before its proper time. Also used of children who are unnaturally clever and behave like grown-ups.

predecessor *(pred-e-ces'-sor)*. A person who held a position before another held it is the second person's predecessor. George VI was Elizabeth II's predecessor.

predicament *(pre-dic'-a-ment)*. An unpleasant, trying or annoying situation.

predicate *(pred'-i-cate)*. The word or words which tell what is said about the subject of a sentence.

predict *(pre-dict')*. To tell what will happen before it does happen.

preen. To trim the feathers with the beak, as a bird does.

preface *(pref'-ace)*. The introductory note printed at the beginning of a book, pamphlet, etc.

prefer *(pre-fer')*. To like something more than something else; thus "She preferred to go to the picnic rather than to the party".

preference *(pref'-er-ence)*. A liking shown for one thing more than for another.

prefix *(pre'-fix)*. 1. To fasten in front of or before something. "Let me prefix my main speech with a story" means, "Let me tell a story before I start my main speech". 2. A small word attached to the beginning of a word which changes its meaning; when the prefix *dis* is put before *honest* to make *dishonest*, the meaning of *honest* is changed.

prehistoric *(pre-his-tor'-ic)*. Of the period coming before written history; said of something very old.

prejudice *(prej'-u-dice)*. An opinion formed before considering all the facts; an unreasonable liking or disliking for something. A person who has a prejudice is said to be **prejudiced.**

preliminary *(pre-lim'-i-na-ry)*. Coming before the rest, as "His preliminary remarks were about himself; then he spoke of his wife"; introductory.

premature *(pre-ma-ture')*. Happening before it should.

premier *(pre'-mi-er)*. 1. First. 2. The Prime Minister is known as the Premier.

premises *(prem'-i-ses)*. Buildings and the land around which together all belong to one owner.

premium *(pre'-mi-um)*. 1. Something given over and above what has been paid for. 2. The annual payment which has to be made to keep an insurance policy in force.

preparation *(prep-a-ra'-tion)*. 1. When moving from one house to another a great deal of preparation is necessary so that all the household articles are packed and ready when the moving day arrives. 2. A medicine is a preparation because it is made up beforehand for a special purpose.

prepare *(pre-pare')*. To get ready.

preposition *(prep-o-si'-tion)*. One of the parts of speech. A word which shows the relationship between two other words in a sentence. In "The children ran across the field", the word "across" is a preposition showing the relationship between the children and the field.

preposterous *(pre-pos'-ter-ous)*. Absurd; silly; ridiculous.

prescribe *(pre-scribe')*. 1. To recommend, as a thing good to do or take or as a remedy. Doctors prescribe medicines for their patients. 2. To order, as "The law prescribes that shops close on Sunday".

prescription *(pre-scrip'-tion)*. Something prescribed, especially a recipe for medicine written by a doctor and made up by a chemist.

presence *(pres'-ence)*. 1. State of being present. When you are in school the teacher sees you are there and records your presence in the register. 2. The way in which a person carries himself, as "He had a commanding presence".

present *(pres'-ent)*. 1. A gift. 2. In attendance; in a certain place, not absent. "All the children in the class were present; not one was away". 3. The present time is this time; the present is this time; now. 4. *(pre-sent')*. To give. To present yourself is to introduce yourself, or to arrive and make your presence known. Someone who presents himself for election to a certain position, offers himself for the position.

presently *(pres'-ent-ly)*. Soon; in a few moments' time.

preserve *(pre-serve')*. 1. To treat in a way so that it does not go bad. 2. Fruit treated in this way is commonly called preserves. 3. To keep, as "He preserved his temper". 4. A preserve is also a place where wild animals are kept.

preside *(pre-side')*. To rule over, as "The Chairman presided over the meeting". Sometimes a person who presides is called a **president** *(pres'-i-dent)*.

press. 1. To put pressure on. 2. An instrument for squeezing things. 3. A printing machine. 4. A printing business. 5. To push forward. 6. A crowd.

pressure *(pres'-sure)*. 1. Force, as "He put pressure on the lazy boys", i.e. he put force on them and made them work. 2. The force exerted by the weight of a thing, as the pressure exerted by water, etc.

presume *(pre-sume')*. 1. To take for granted, as "I presume you will be out late tonight". 2. To presume on something is to take advantage of it, as "He presumed on the old lady's generosity and asked for £5". 3. To dare or venture, as "I would not presume to tell you that you have made a mistake".

presumptuous *(pre-sump'-tu-ous)*. Daring and rash; likely to presume too much.

pretence *(pre-tence')*. 1. Act of pretending. 2. The thing pretended, as in "You do not fool me with your pretence at sickness".

pretend *(pre-tend')*. 1. To make believe, as "The little girl pretended she was Cinderella". 2. To act as though you were something you are not, or thought something you do not, or did something you are not doing, in order to deceive others. "The thief got into the bank vault by pretending to be the bank manager, and stole £1,000." 3. To pretend to something is to claim it.

pretext *(pre'-text)*. An excuse that is not a real one; it is one that is made up to hide the real reason.

pretty *(pret'-ty)*. Pleasing; good-looking.

prevail *(pre-vail')*. 1. To gain a victory, as "The soldiers prevailed over the enemy". 2. To exist most frequently or most strongly, as "The idea prevails that there is a good time coming". This means that most people have the idea that a good time is coming. 3. To prevail upon is to persuade.

prevailing *(pre-vail'-ing).* 1. Most frequent or strongest, as "The boat was sped on her course by the prevailing winds". 2. Generally accepted, as "The prevailing opinion among mothers is that children should be in bed early during the school term".

prevent *(pre-vent').* To stop a thing happening.

previous *(pre'-vi-ous).* Coming before; thus the day previous to Sunday was Saturday.

prey. 1. An animal's prey are the other animals it catches for food. 2. To prey upon something is to make it your prey. We say, for example, that a fox preys upon rabbits. 3. To prey on someone is to rob him and take advantage of him. 4. An idea that preys on your mind is one that worries you constantly.

price. The cost of an article.

prick. To make a tiny hole with something having a sharp point.

pride. 1. Too high an opinion of oneself. 2. The respect that a person has for himself. The first is not a good quality; but the second, which is very different, helps to make a person do his best and appear his best.

priest. A clergyman.

prig. A person who looks down on others and who prides himself on his good qualities.

prim. Neat and careful about the small details of behaviour.

primary *(pri'-ma-ry).* 1. First; first in importance, as "It is his primary wish to succeed in school". A primary school is the one you go to first. 2. Red, blue and yellow are primary colours, or pure, elementary colours. From these three colours all others may be made. Orange, for instance, is made by mixing red and yellow; green by mixing blue and yellow, etc.

prime. 1. First, as the Prime Minister. 2. In first-rate condition, as prime beef. 3. A prime number is a number that cannot be divided by any other number without leaving a remainder; thus 1, 3, 5, 7 and 11 are prime numbers, but 4, 6, 8, 9 and 10 are not.

primitive *(prim'-i-tive).* 1. Belonging to the earliest times, as in "The cave-dwellers were primitive people". 2. Nowadays, primitive people are people whose way of living is very simple; certain tribes in Africa who wear no clothes,

live in rough houses and live by hunting and fishing are
primitive. 3. Very simple; rough.

primrose *(prim'-rose)*. A plant with a pale yellow flower that
is among the first to bloom in spring.

prince. 1. In England, the son or grandson of a king or queen.
2. In some countries the monarch has the title of prince.
3. Any male member of a royal family.

princess *(prin'-cess)*. The feminine of prince.

principal *(prin'-ci-pal)*. 1. Chief, as "London is one of the
world's principal cities". 2. Heads of schools and colleges
are sometimes called principals.

principle *(prin'-ci-ple)*. 1. A primary law or doctrine. The
principles of chemistry are the basic laws of chemistry, and
the principles of Christianity are the basic teachings of the
Christian religion. 2. A rule of conduct; thus "I always make
it a principle to pay my bills as soon as I get them". A
man of principle is a man who acts according to moral
principles.

print. 1. To make a mark by pressing. 2. A mark made by
pressing. Footprints are marks made by pressing the feet.
If you press a rubber stamp onto an ink pad and then press
it onto a piece of paper you will be printing with it. All the
letters on this page are made by printing; therefore, taken
all together they are called print. 3. To write letters of the
same shape as printed letters. 4. Cloth with a pattern on it
made by printing, not woven into it.

prior *(pri'-or)*. 1. Former; earlier. 2. The chief monk in a
priory.

priory *(pri'-o-ry)*. A monastery or nunnery in the charge of a
prior or prioress.

prison *(pris'-on)*. A jail in which **prisoners** or criminals are held
against their will.

privacy *(pri'-va-cy)*. 1. State of being alone where others cannot
watch you; state of being out of public view. 2. A
place where you can be alone and private; retirement;
seclusion.

private *(pri'-vate)*. 1. For yourself, not for everybody. 2. A
matter is private when it is more or less a secret and not for
everyone to know. 3. A soldier of the lowest rank.

privation *(pri-va'-tion)*. State of being deprived of; having to
go without proper food, shelter and clothing.

privilege *(pri'-vi-lege)*. The right to do something that you want to do, which others are not allowed to do; thus "Mrs. Jones gave her the privilege of coming into her garden whenever she liked to pick strawberries".

prize. 1. A reward for some good action. 2. Anything is prized that is very much valued, as "She prized the watch because it belonged to her grandmother".

probable *(prob'-a-ble)*. Likely.

probation *(pro-ba'-tion)*. A period during which a person is on trial; thus "In his new job George was on probation for a month, before he was really appointed".

probe. 1. To examine carefully and thoroughly; to poke something in order to examine it; to poke about in the hope of finding something. 2. A medical instrument, used for probing 3. A search or investigation.

probity *(prob'-i-ty)*. Honesty; uprightness.

problem *(pro'-blem)*. 1. A question needing an answer that is difficult to provide. 2. A difficulty. 3. Something that you have to do something about, but about which you do not know what to do, as "the problem of juvenile delinquency".

procedure *(pro-ce'-dure)*. The way of doing a thing; thus when you cut the lawn you follow one procedure and when you cut paper you follow a different procedure.

proceed *(pro-ceed')*. To go on again after having stopped.

proceeds *(pro'-ceeds)*. Money obtained from something, as "The proceeds of the school bazaar amounted to £45".

process *(proc'-ess)*. 1. State of going on or being done, as "The building was in the process of construction". 2. The steps necessary to be taken in order to do something, as "What process is followed in making a rocket?"

procession *(pro-ces'-sion)*. A number of people or things following one after the other.

proclaim *(pro-claim')*. To tell something openly in public.

proclamation *(proc-la-ma'-tion)*. A formal announcement, as "The royal proclamation was read at court".

procure *(pro-cure')*. To obtain.

prodigal *(prod'-i-gal)*. Wasteful; said of a person who spends his money and does not have it in his possession for long.

prodigious *(pro-di'-gious)*. Marvellous; wonderful; huge; altogether unusual. A thing which is prodigious is a **prodigy** *(prod'-i-gy)*.

produce *(pro-duce')*. 1. To bring into view, as "The conjurer produced eggs from his hat". 2. To make, as "Butter is produced in Denmark". 3. Things that are produced are known as **produce** *(prod'-uce)*; thus we speak of dairy produce, farm produce, etc. A person who produces is a **producer** *(pro-duc'-er)* and what he produces are **products** *(prod'-ucts)*.

product *(prod'-uct)*. 1. A thing which is produced; something made or grown. 2. The answer when you multiply, as "Eight is the product of 2×4".

profane *(pro-fane')*. Not sacred; not reverent.

profess *(pro-fess')*. 1. To declare or say openly. 2. To pretend, as "He professes to be a French nobleman".

profession *(pro-fes'-sion)*. 1. A declaration made openly that you believe in something, as "a profession of faith". 2. An occupation which does not involve trading, farming or any mechanical work, such as the occupation of a teacher, a doctor or a lawyer. 3. All the people working in one profession, such as "the medical profession".

professor *(pro-fes'-sor)*. A senior teacher in a university.

proffer *(prof'-fer)*. To offer.

proficient *(pro-fi'-cient)*. Skilled or expert enough to be able to do something that needs care.

profile *(pro'-file)*. The side view of a person's head and face; the outline of the face when looked at from the side.

profit *(prof'-it)*. Gain; advantage.

profitable *(prof'-it-a-ble)*. Producing a profit or a gain; thus "Don't waste your time. If you have nothing better to do, the reading of a good book will be profitable".

profound *(pro-found')*. Deep.

profuse *(pro-fuse')*. Plentiful. A thing that is profuse is to be had in **profusion.**

progeny *(prog'-e-ny)*. Children.

programme *(pro'-gramme)*. 1. A list of things which it is proposed to do, as "The teacher has laid out a heavy programme for to-day". A concert programme is a list of pieces which are to be played at a concert. 2. An entertainment or concert. 3. The programme for some performances is also a printed sheet listing the names of the performers, director, etc.

progress. 1. *(pro-gress')*. To move forward. 2. To improve. 3. *(prog'-ress)*. Improvement.

prohibit *(pro-hib'-it)*. To forbid; thus "You are prohibited from walking on the grass".

project. 1. *(proj'-ect)*. A plan, as "He had a project for using the rubber from old tyres". 2. *(pro-ject')*. To throw out, as "The guns project the bullets at a rapid rate". 3. To stick out, as "The corner of the table projects too far and I bumped into it".

prolong *(pro-long')*. To make longer.

promenade *(prom-e-nade')*. 1. A place where people walk. 2. To walk.

prominent *(prom'-i-nent)*. 1. Standing out or conspicuous, as "The lady's large nose was the most prominent feature of her face". 2. Well-known, as "The Pope is a prominent man".

promise *(prom'-ise)*. 1. To give your word; to pledge. 2. That which is promised. 3. A cause for hope, or a cause for expecting success, as "There is a promise of spring in the air".

promontory *(prom'-on-to-ry)*. A high rock or cliff jutting into the sea.

promote *(pro-mote')*. 1. To advance; to raise to a higher rank, as "He was promoted from lieutenant to captain". 2. To help something to grow, spread or prosper, as "Missionaries promote the Christian religion".

prompt. Quick; absolutely on time.

prone. 1. Inclined or likely, as "He is prone to exaggerate". 2. In "He was found prone on the ground", prone means lying with his face down.

pronoun *(pro'-noun)*. A word used instead of a noun to avoid repeating the noun too often. He, she and it are examples of pronouns.

pronounce *(pro-nounce')*. To say; utter; speak.

proof. That which proves anything.

prop. A support.

propaganda *(prop-a-gan'-da)*. Anything that spreads opinions, principles, news and information so that they are accepted or believed.

propagate *(prop'-a-gate)*. To make things increase or spread. If you plant cuttings of a plant, you are propagating that plant, because later you will have many plants instead of one. The Society for the Propagation of Christian Knowledge spreads or increases Christian knowledge.

propel *(pro-pel')*. To drive forwards.

propeller *(pro-pel'-ler)*. The blades which turn very fast on the front of an aircraft engine or an outboard motor. The propeller pulls or pushes the plane or boat through the air or water.

proper *(prop'-er)*. 1. Correct, as "The proper thing for a boy to do is to raise his hat when meeting a lady whom he knows". 2. A proper noun is the name of a special person, place or thing, as Henry, London and the Marble Arch.

property *(prop'-er-ty)*. 1. Things owned by a person are his property. 2. Characteristics of a thing are its properties; thus "Onions have a property which makes your eyes water when you peel them".

prophesy *(proph'-e-sy)*. To predict; to say that something will happen in the future. A man who does this is a **prophet** and what he tells will happen is a **prophecy**. In the Bible, the prophets were men who received the word of God and told it to the people.

propitious *(pro-pi'-tious)*. Favourable.

proportion *(pro-por'-tion)*. 1. The relation of a part to another part, or of a part to the whole. When we say "That building has fine proportions" we mean that the parts are beautifully related to the whole. 2. The relation of one thing to another, as the proportion of the money a man makes to the money he spends. 3. "Each person gave money to the church in proportion to his earnings" means "Each person gave as much money to the church as his earnings would allow". Those who had large earnings gave a large amount; those who had small earnings gave a small amount. "In proportion to" means "related to" or "according to".

proposal *(pro-pos'-al)*. A suggestion made for doing something.

proprietor *(pro-pri'-e-tor)*. Owner.

prosaic *(pro-sa'-ic)*. Dull; ordinary; not very interesting or original.

prose. The ordinary language of speaking and writing. Something written in prose is not written in verse; that is, it is not divided into lines having a definite rhythm or rhyming at the end.

prosecute *(pros'-e-cute)*. 1. To bring into court and charge with some offence. 2. To carry out, as "He prosecuted his duties with real pleasure".

prospectus *(pro-spec'-tus)*. A description of something that the writer wants to advertise.

prosper *(pros'-per)*. To flourish, thrive or be successful. Anyone who prospers is **prosperous** and enjoys **prosperity** *(prosper'-i-ty)*.

prostrate *(pros'-trate)*. Lying flat; completely exhausted; having no energy left at all.

protect *(pro-tect')*. To shelter; to defend.

protein *(pro'-tein)*. A substance which exists in the cells of the body and which is a necessary element in the food of men and animals.

protest *(pro-test')*. 1. To complain about something. 2. *(pro'-test)*. Such a complaint.

protract *(pro-tract')*. To draw out; to make longer.

protrude *(pro-trude')*. To stick out or to put out.

proud. 1. Filled with admiration for something or someone that reflects credit on you, as "I am very proud of you, John. You have worked well". You cannot be proud of something or someone that has no connection with you, although you might admire it or him. 2. Haughty; feeling that you are better than other people.

prove. To show that a certain thing is true or correct.

provender *(prov'-en-der)*. Food; dry food for cattle, sheep and horses, such as hay or corn.

proverb *(prov'-erb)*. A wise saying expressing a deep truth in a few simple words, as "Pride goeth before a fall".

provide *(pro-vide')*. To supply when needed; to make ready beforehand.

provision *(pro-vi'-sion)*. 1. Supply. 2. To supply. 3. Provisions usually means food.

provocation *(prov-o-ca'-tion)*. Anything which rouses a person to anger. When a person is aroused in this way he is **provoked** *(pro-voked')*.

prow. The forward part of a ship.

prowess *(prow'-ess)*. Bravery; exceptional skill.

prowl. To creep about looking for something. To rove in search of food or plunder.

proximity *(prox-im'-i-ty)*. Nearness; closeness.

proxy *(prox'-y)*. 1. A document in which one person authorises another to act on his behalf. Some people authorise others to vote for them at elections. 2. The person who acts on the authority of another is also called a proxy.

prudent *(pru'-dent)*. A person is prudent who acts wisely and plans ahead for the future.

prune. A plum that has been dried and preserved.

pry. 1. To pry into other people's affairs is to be curious about them and ask many questions about them in a way that is impertinent. 2. To loosen an object which is wedged or stuck with the aid of a lever is to pry it loose.

psalm. A sacred song or poem. There is a book of Psalms in the Bible.

psalter. The book of Psalms or a book containing the Psalms used in religious services.

public *(pub'-lic)*. Of the people; to do with matters affecting the people.

publican *(pub'-lic-an)*. The keeper of a public house, inn or tavern.

publication *(pub-li-ca'-tion)*. 1. The making known of something, as the publication of the events of the day. 2. A book, magazine, newspaper, etc., which is put on sale.

pucker *(puck'-er)*. To wrinkle; to gather into folds.

pudding *(pud'-ding)*. A soft sweet food which is cooked and served hot or cold.

puddle *(pud'-dle)*. A small pool of water or liquid.

puerile *(pu'-er-ile)*. 1. Boyish; childish. 2. Silly; foolish; ridiculous.

puff. 1. A short, quick breath of air. 2. A small amount of steam, smoke, etc., sent out in one puff. 3. A round, soft mass of something, as a powder puff. 4. To blow with puffs; to pant from being out of breath. 5. To puff something up is to blow it up or fluff it up.

pugnacious *(pug-na'-cious)*. Always ready to fight or bully others.

pull. To move something towards you by force.

pulley *(pul'-ley)*. A grooved wheel around which a rope is pulled in order to make the raising or moving of a heavy object easier. A farmer uses a pulley in the barn to lift heavy bales of hay and feed.

pulp. 1. The soft inside part of many fruits. 2. Anything made soft to resemble the inside of fruits.

pulpit *(pul'-pit)*. A raised box in a church from which the preacher preaches his sermon.

pulse. 1. Regular beating; throbbing. 2. The beating of the heart, which can be felt along the arteries especially at the wrist.

pulverize *(pul'-ver-ize)*. To grind to powder.

pump. A device for raising water or other liquids to a higher level, or forcing them along pipes.

pumpkin *(pump'-kin)*. A large, round vegetable used for food.

punch. 1. To hit with the fist. 2. A mixed drink. 3. **Punch.** A hump-backed puppet in Punch and Judy shows.

punctual *(punc'-tu-al)*. On time; not late; always ready at the right time.

punctuation *(punc-tu-a'-tion)*. The use of full-stops, commas, colons, etc., where they ought to be in a passage of writing.

puncture *(punc'-ture)*. A hole made with a pointed instrument.

punish *(pun'-ish)*. To inflict a penalty on a person because of a wrong he has committed.

puny *(pu'-ny)*. Weak; sickly; undersized.

pupa *(pu'-pa)*. The middle stage in the life of many insects, between the larva and the adult stages. In their pupal stage many insects are enclosed in a cocoon.

pupil *(pu'-pil)*. 1. A student or learner; one who is taking lessons. 2. The round black opening in the middle of the eye, through which we see.

puppet *(pup'-pet)*. A doll which is made to move in either one of two ways. Strings may be attached to its body and pulled from above, or the puppet may be placed over the hand like a glove and moved with the fingers.

purchase *(pur'-chase)*. To buy.

purify *(pu'-ri-fy)*. To make pure; to get rid of all matter that makes the thing unclean.

Puritan *(Pu-ri'-tan)*. 1. The Puritans were a group of people who objected to the ceremonies used in the Church of England and wanted simpler religious services. They lived about 400 to 300 years ago. 2. A person of strict morals.

purloin *(pur-loin')*. To steal in a sneaking way, as by grabbing when no one is looking.

purple *(pur'-ple)*. A colour made by mixing red and blue.

purpose *(pur'-pose)*. Aim; idea; what you intend to do.

purr. 1. The low, buzzing sound made by a cat when it is happy. 2. To make such a sound.

pursue *(pur-sue')*. To chase; to run after. A person who runs after takes part in the **pursuit** *(pur-suit')*.

push. To move something away from you by force.

put. To place.

putrefy *(pu'-tre-fy)*. To go bad; to become rotten. Anything that putrefies is **putrid.**

putty *(put'-ty)*. A paste of whiting and linseed oil. It is used to help hold the glass in window frames.

puzzle *(puz'-zle)*. 1. To perplex or to make you think very hard. 2. A thing that makes you think very hard.

pygmy *(pyg'-my)*. A very small person, particularly one of the tribe living in Africa, the Pygmies. (Also spelled **pigmy.**)

pyjamas *(py-ja'-mas)*. A kind of clothing resembling a shirt and trousers, which is worn for sleeping.

pyramid *(pyr'-a-mid)*. A solid shape having three or more triangular sides which meet at the top in a point, such as the pyramids of Egypt.

python *(py'-thon)*. A huge snake which may be found in Africa or Asia. It kills its prey by coiling around it and crushing it.

Q

quack. 1. The ordinary noise made by a duck. 2. A name given to a person who pretends he is a doctor of medicine when he has no qualifications in medicine.

quadrant *(quad'-rant)*. 1. A quarter of a circle. 2. An instrument used by soldiers and others for finding the heights of places.

quadrilateral *(quad-ri-lat'-er-al)*. Any shape or figure having four sides. A square is, of course, a quadrilateral.

quadruped *(quad'-ru-ped)*. An animal having four feet. A lion is, therefore, a quadruped, and so is a mouse.

quaff. To drink; to drink large draughts.

quagmire *(quag'-mire)*. A piece of boggy ground that cannot be crossed.

quail. 1. A bird belonging to the same family as the partridge. 2. To tremble with fear, as "The small boy quailed before the big, angry man".

quaint. Pretty and old-fashioned.

quake. To shake, as "He quaked in his shoes". Earthquake means a shaking of the earth.

qualification *(qual-i-fi-ca'-tion)*. 1. A thing which fits you for something, as "The doctor's qualifications were the certificates showing his training". 2. Anything which limits, as "The girl's mother said they might go on the picnic but with the qualification that they be home not later than seven o'clock."

qualify *(qual'-i-fy)*. 1. A person who qualifies himself for a certain job makes himself fit and capable of doing it. 2. When you qualify something, such as a remark, you limit it; that is to say you make the remark less vague and more specific. For this reason adjectives are said to qualify nouns.

quality *(qual'-i-ty)*. 1. Attribute; characteristic; property. Thus, if you have a square block, squareness is one of the qualities, or characteristics, of the block. If this block were also red, redness would be another of its qualities. 2. Kind; degree of goodness or badness. 3. Excellence, as in "The horse showed his quality by winning six races".

quandary *(quan'-da-ry)*. A state of doubt; uncertainty.

quantity *(quan'-ti-ty)*. The quantity of a thing is the amount there is of it.

quarantine *(quar'-an-tine)*. A period in which people or animals are kept from contact with others in order to prevent the spread of disease. If a ship is placed in quarantine, it is not allowed to land its passengers or cargo until health officials are sure that there is no danger that they will spread infection.

quarrel *(quar'-rel)*. When two or more people disagree violently about something, they are said to quarrel. A person who often quarrels is **quarrelsome.**

quarry *(quar'-ry)*. 1. A place where stone is dug out of the earth, the stone being used for building and other purposes. 2. An animal that is being chased by huntsmen is said to be the huntsmen's quarry.

quart. A measure of both liquids and dry things. A quart of milk is equal to two pints.

quarter *(quar'-ter)*. 1. One fourth. The figure is $\frac{1}{4}$. 2. A part of a city; a district, as "They drove through the Mexican quarter". 3. Mercy granted to an enemy, as in "The battle was fought fiercely and no quarter was given". 4. **quarters** are lodgings, especially for soldiers.

quartet *(quar-tet')*. Also spelled **quartette**. 1. A group of four people, as "Tom, Dick, Harry and John are a dreadful quartet". 2. A piece of music written for four voices or four instruments. 3. Four singers or four instruments that perform together.

quartz. A hard mineral which is crystalline and usually transparent or semi-transparent. Gold is found in quartz.

quaver *(qua'-ver)*. 1. To tremble, as "His voice quavered when he described the accident". 2. To use trills in singing. 3. A note of a certain length in music.

quay. A landing place for boats.

queen. 1. A female monarch or ruler; the wife of a king. 2. The female of certain insects, such as ants and bees, which lays eggs.

queer. Odd; droll; funny, as "Isn't his house a queer place—full of antiques and musty old books!"

quell. To put down or subdue, as "It did not take long to quell the mob, once the police arrived".

quench. 1. To quench thirst is to satisfy it by drinking. 2. To quench fire is to put it out.

query *(que'-ry)*. 1. A question. 2. To ask.

quest. A search. The Grail was the object of the quest of the Knights of the Round Table.

question *(ques'-tion)*. 1. When a person wants to know something he asks about it. The sentence or words he uses to do the asking is a question. 2. To inquire; ask a question. 3. To doubt. 4. "It is a question of money" means "It has to do with money". "The point in question" is the point being discussed or referred to.

questionable *(ques'-tion-a-ble)*. 1. Doubtful, as "It is questionable whether the weather is good enough for a game of tennis". 2. Of doubtful character.

queue. 1. An orderly line of people, vehicles, etc., waiting their turn at a shop, ticket-office, etc. 2. A pigtail.

quibble *(quib'-ble)*. To try not to come to the point in an argument; to start arguing about little, unimportant points in order to avoid coming to the main point.

quick. 1. Fast; keen. 2. Living, tender flesh, as that below the skin or the fingernails. If you cut your finger to the quick, you cut it deeply. If your feelings are cut to the quick, you are deeply hurt or offended. 3. Living. "The quick and the dead" means "the living and the dead".

quicksand *(quick'-sand)*. A large patch of sand, usually on the shore, which is so soft that anyone walking on it will sink.

quicksilver *(quick'-sil-ver)*. Mercury.

quiet *(qui'-et)*. Free from noise or bustle.

quietude *(qui'-e-tude)*. Stillness.

quill. The large, stout feather of a bird; also the spine of a porcupine.

quilt. A heavy cover used on a bed.

quintuplet *(quin'-tu-plet)*. 1. A collection of five things or beings of one kind. 2. One of five children born at one birth.

quire. Twenty-four sheets of paper.

quit. 1. To conduct yourself, as "Quit you like a man". 2. To leave. 3. To give up.

quite. Completely, as "She was quite right".

quiver *(quiv'-er)*. 1. The case in which arrows are carried. Cupid is usually drawn with a quiver slung on his back. 2. To shake.

quiz. 1. To ask questions. 2. An examination done by quizzing.

quota *(quo'-ta)*. Share; an amount which someone is obliged to produce.

quotation *(quo-ta'-tion)*. 1. Words written or spoken by one person and repeated by another. Thus, if you repeat words spoken by your father, you are **quoting** him, and what you are quoting is a quotation. In writing, words that are quoted have **quotation marks** (" ") put before and after them. 2. If a man asks you the price of some goods you have to sell and you tell him how much they are, you are giving him a quotation for the goods.

quote. (See **quotation**.)

quotient *(quo'-tient)*. If you divide one number by another, the answer is the quotient. Thus, if you divide 12 by 3, 4 is the quotient.

R

rabbi *(rab'-bi)*. The pastor of a Jewish synagogue.

rabbit *(rab'-bit)*. A burrowing animal with long ears, soft fur and powerful hind legs.

rabble *(rab'-ble)*. A mob of noisy people.

rabid *(ra'-bid)*. Mad; raving.

rabies *(ra'-bies)*. An infectious disease that causes inflammation of the brain cells, great excitement, inability to swallow and speedy death. Human beings are usually infected by the bites of dogs suffering from the disease. Rabid dogs wander about and attack everything in their way. They are sometimes called "mad dogs" because they behave as if they were insane.

race. 1. A competition between people, animals, cars, aeroplanes, etc., in which each tries to be the first to cover a certain distance. 2. To run fast, as "He raced down the road to catch the bus". 3. To make a thing run a race or go very fast, as "He raced the engine of his car". 4. A number of people descending from the same ancestors or having the same characteristics, as "the Negro race". Do not confuse *race* with *nation*, which means all the people belonging to a certain country.

rack. 1. A framework on which articles are arranged, as a towel rack. 2. An instrument of torture on which people were stretched. 3. To stretch; to torture; to strain or cause to work very hard, as "He racked his brain for the answer".

racket *(rack'-et)*. 1. An unpleasant and long-continued noise. 2. An illegal business.

racquet *(rac'-quet)*. The bat used in tennis, badminton, etc. Also spelled **racket**.

radar *(ra'-dar)*. An instrument for finding and tracking unseen objects. Radar operates by reflection of radio waves. The word comes from RAdio Detection And Ranging.

radiant *(ra'-di-ant)*. Shining; smiling or beaming.

radiate *(ra'-di-ate)*. 1. To send out rays, as "The sun radiates the heat which warms the earth". 2. To spread out like the spokes of a wheel, as "Seven roads radiate from the Clock Tower".

radiation *(ra-di-a'-tion)*. The sending out of rays. An exploding atomic bomb causes radiation of radio-active rays.

radiator *(ra'-di-a-tor)*. 1. An arrangement of pipes which is connected to a hot water supply to provide warmth in a room. 2. There is a radiator on the front of a car. In this case, its use is to cool the engine.

radio *(ra'-di-o)*. 1. A means of sending and receiving sounds or pictures through the air without using wires. 2. The instrument which picks up the sounds; a wireless set. 3. To radio is to send messages by radio.

radio-active *(ra-di-o-ac'-tive)*. When a substance is radio-active, it sends out invisible rays which can pass through all substances but lead. Exposure to these rays may harm the body and cause death.

radish *(rad'-ish)*. A small, edible root with white or red skin and a sharp hot taste.

radium *(ra'-di-um)*. A radio-active metal used in making atomic bombs and in treating cancer. (See **radiation** and **radio-active**.)

radius *(ra'-di-us)*. The distance from the centre of a circle to its circumference.

raffle *(raf'-fle)*. 1. A kind of lottery. 2. To raffle something off is to sell it by lottery.

raft. Strips of wood fastened together so that they will float and support people and heavy weights.

rafters *(raft'-ers)*. The sloping strips of wood forming the roof of a house, over which long boards and then slates or tiles are nailed.

rag. 1. Worn or tattered cloth. 2. To rag is to tease or play jokes on others.

rage. Violent anger, as "The man was in such a rage that his hands shook, his voice wavered and his eyes blazed". We also speak of a severe storm as a **raging** storm.

ragged *(rag'-ged)*. Torn or worn into tatters.

raid. An enemy attack, as "The air raid, fortunately, did little damage". People taking part in a raid are **raiders.**

rail. A long, narrow strip of wood, iron, steel, etc. There are rails for trains, towels, stairs, fences and thousands of other things.

railway *(rail'-way)*. 1. The two parallel steel rails or tracks on which trains move. 2. To do with a railway.

raiment *(rai'-ment)*. Clothes.

rainbow *(rain'-bow)*. A semi-circle or arch of many colours, which appears in the sky when the sun shines through rain or mist.

raise. 1. To lift a thing is to raise it, as "The pupils were told to raise their hands when they wished to ask a question". 2. When you raise the temperature of a room, you increase the amount of heat which enters the room.

raisin *(rai'-sin)*. A dried grape used in Christmas puddings, etc.

rake. 1. A toothed tool used in the garden for levelling the earth, gathering together the stones on the surface, etc. 2. An unpleasant person who keeps bad company.

rally *(ral'-ly)*. 1. In "The poor old lady rallied before she died", rallied means got better for a short time. 2. In "He rallied his men around him", rallied means gathered together. 3. An enthusiastic gathering in support of something.

ram. 1. A male sheep. 2. To push with great force, as "He rammed the tobacco into his pipe and then it would not light". 3. A weapon used for breaking something by ramming.

ramble *(ram'-ble)*. To roam or wander about.

rampant *(ramp'-ant)*. 1. Growing rapidly, as "The weeds are rampant in my garden". 2. In describing the pictures on a coat of arms or badge, you would use "rampant" instead of "standing on its hind legs". There is a lion rampant on the coat of arms of Scotland.

ranch. A large farm on which cattle are raised, especially in America. A man who owns such a farm is called a **rancher.**

rancid *(ran'-cid)*. Having a taste or smell like stale fat.

rancour *(ran'-cour)*. Spite; ill will.

random *(ran'-dom)*. By chance; not in any set way; thus if there were 50 marbles on the table, and I picked up five of them without looking at them, I should be picking them up at random.

range. 1. A row of hills or mountains. 2. A cooking stove. 3. If you go to a special place to fire a rifle at targets, you go to a rifle range. 4. If a shop has a good range of coloured wools, it has a good selection of them. 5. If you range over the hills, you wander over them.

ranger *(rang'-er)*. A keeper of a forest, etc.

rank. 1. If soldiers are arranged in ranks, they are in rows. 2. If a soldier is in the ranks, he is an ordinary soldier, or a private. 3. If Fred ranks higher in class than Frank, Fred's position is a higher one. 4. If the beans in your garden are growing in a rank way, they are becoming coarse and too tall. 5. If a man is of high rank, he has a high position and he may have a title.

rankle *(ran'-kle)*. When an idea rankles in someone's mind, it makes him very bitter or annoyed and he thinks about it continuously.

ransack *(ran'-sack)*. To search thoroughly; to search by turning everything upside down.

ransom *(ran'-som)*. Money demanded in return for setting someone free.

rap. 1. A smart, quick tap. 2. When people say they do not care a rap, they do not care the least bit.

rapid *(rap'-id)*. Fast moving.

rapids *(rap'-ids)*. A place in a river where the water flows very fast, often over rocks.

rapier *(ra'-pi-er)*. A thin sword with a sharp point.

rapture *(rap'-ture)*. Tremendous joy and delight.

rare. 1. Unusual; not often found; not common. 2. Rare meat is meat that is not well-cooked.

rarely *(rare'-ly)*. Seldom.

rascal *(ras'-cal)*. A ruffian; a scoundrel; a naughty, mischievous child.

rash. 1. Hasty; reckless; too daring; acting or done without thinking what the results will be. 2. A redness of the skin in spots or patches, as that accompanying measles, scarlet fever, etc.

rasp. 1. A coarse file. 2. A harsh, grating sound. 3. To make a harsh, grating sound.

raspberry *(rasp'-ber-ry)*. A small thimble-shaped fruit, usually red, which grows on tall canes.

rat. A type of rodent which has the shape of a mouse but is larger and has a longer tail.

rate. 1. The amount or degree of something which is measured in terms of something else. For example, when we wish to measure speed, we do so in terms of distance and time. Thus, when we say "Forty miles an hour is the rate of speed of this car", we mean that in one hour (time) the car will travel forty miles (distance). Thus, the rate of speed is the amount of speed measured in terms of distance and time. 2. A fixed charge or price, such as railway rates, postal rates, etc. 3. Tax. 4. Class, as in "first-rate", "second-rate", "third-rate", etc. Something which is first-rate is of the first class or highest quality. 5. To place a value on. If you rate yourself highly, you place a high value on yourself; that is, you think yourself a wonderful person.

rather *(rath'-er).* More truly; more exactly; more or less; somewhat. "I would rather go home" means "I prefer to go home".

ratio *(ra'-tio).* The proportion or relation of one number to another.

ration *(ra'-tion).* A fixed allowance, generally of food.

rational *(ra'-tion-al).* Sensible; logical.

rattle *(rat'-tle).* 1. A series of short, sharp, loud sounds. 2. To make these sounds, as in "The old broken car rattled along the street". 3. A baby's toy which rattles when shaken. 4. To rattle something is to shake it in order to make it rattle.

rattlesnake *(rat'-tle-snake).* An American poisonous snake which makes a rattling noise with its tail.

ravage *(rav'-age).* To lay waste; destroy; spoil.

rave. To talk as though mad.

raven *(ra'-ven).* A large black bird.

ravenous *(rav'-en-ous).* Very hungry.

ravine *(ra-vine').* A narrow valley with high, steep sides.

raw. 1. Not cooked. 2. Not manufactured nor made ready for use, as raw materials. 3. Cold and nasty (of weather). 4. A place where the skin has been rubbed off or irritated is said to be a raw spot.

ray. 1. A beam of light or heat. 2. A flat sea-fish.

rayon *(ray'-on).* Artificial silk.

razor *(ra'-zor).* A very sharp cutting tool with which men shave.

reach. 1. In "He reached home at noon", reached means arrived at. 2. In "He reached out his hand and picked up his watch", reached means stretched. 3. In "He tried to reach the top shelf and fell headlong", reach means get up to.

read. 1. When you read a book, you see and understand the words written in it. In this way you come to know about the story contained in it. 2. When you read aloud, you pronounce the words aloud. 3. When you read music, you understand the place and value of the notes.

reader *(read'-er)*. 1. A book which is used in school to teach children to read. 2. One who reads.

ready *(read'-y)*. 1. Prepared to do something. 2. Waiting to be used. 3. Quick; alert, as "a ready answer", "a ready mind".

real *(re'-al)*. 1. Actually existing; not make-believe or imaginary; true; genuine.

realize *(re'-al-ize)*. When you realize something you understand or are aware of it, as "She realized that she had done wrong when her mother explained it to her".

really *(re'-al-ly)*. Actually or truly. We speak of a truly fine person as a really fine person.

realm. A kingdom.

ream. 480 sheets of paper of the same size and quality.

reap. 1. To cut grain, etc., in order to harvest it. 2. To enjoy the benefits of some action, as "He reaped the reward for all his hard work when he was made manager".

rear. 1. The back part. 2. To bring up and care for. You were reared by your parents. A farmer might rear cattle. 3. To raise itself on its hind legs, as a horse does.

reason *(rea'-son)*. 1. The cause, as "The reason for all the trouble was his bad temper". 2. The power of the mind to understand and to make conclusions, as in "We do not think that animals have reason". 3. Sanity. "He has lost his reason" means "He has lost his sanity" or "He has gone mad". 4. To argue, giving reasons for thinking a certain way. 5. To reason something out is to think it out.

reasonable *(rea'-son-a-ble)*. 1. Fair, as "The price is reasonable". 2. Sensible, as "He is a reasonable man".

rebellion *(re-bel'-li-on)*. A revolt against the people who govern. A person who revolts is a **rebel** *(reb'-el);* he **rebels** *(re-bels')* against the government and is **rebellious.**

rebound *(re-bound')*. To spring back; to recoil.

rebuff *(re-buff')*. To repulse; check or stop; defeat.

rebuke *(re-buke')*. To scold.

recapitulate *(re-ca-pit'-u-late)*. To go over or repeat again something that has already been said.

recede *(re-cede')*. To move backwards; to withdraw; to retreat.

receipt *(re-ceipt')*. A written note saying that something, usually money, has been received.

receive *(re-ceive')*. 1. When you receive a thing you accept it. 2. When you receive a visitor into your home, you welcome him.

recent *(re'-cent)*. New; fresh; having taken place not long ago.

reception *(re-cep'-tion)*. 1. When you are given a warm reception, you receive a warm greeting or welcome. 2. A gathering for the special reason of receiving someone, as "A reception was held for the new minister".

recess *(re-cess')*. 1. A space made by setting back a wall; a space set back; a hollow. 2. Time off from regular work, as "Parliament is closed for the summer recess".

recipe *(rec'-i-pe)*. The instructions for making something, as "Your mother uses a recipe when making a cake".

recital *(re-cit'-al)*. A musical entertainment at which one person performs or a group of people perform one at a time.

recite *(re-cite')*. To repeat from memory.

reckless *(reck'-less)*. Rash; not troubling about what could happen.

reckon *(reck'-on)*. 1. To count. 2. To estimate.

reclaim *(re-claim')*. 1. To get back, as "I reclaimed my bag from the lost property office". 2. To bring back to a useful condition, as "Rubber that has deteriorated can be reclaimed".

recline *(re-cline')*. To lean back.

recognize *(rec'-og-nize)*. 1. To know again or identify, as "I should recognize my dog anywhere". 2. To acknowledge, take notice of, as "He recognized Mrs. Jones by raising his hat".

recoil *(re-coil')*. To rebound or spring back; to shrink away from.

recollect *(rec-ol-lect')*. To remember.

recommend *(rec-om-mend')*. 1. To speak well of. 2. To advise.

recompense *(rec'-om-pense)*. 1. To reward a person for things he has done for you. 2. To pay a person for some loss that has come to him through you.

reconcile *(rec'-on-cile)*. 1. To satisfy oneself as to something. "I cannot reconcile myself to living in this small house". 2. To calm someone who has been angry or upset. 3. To restore to friendship two people who have quarrelled.

record. 1. *(re-cord')*. To set down in black and white. To write an account of something. 2. *(rec'-ord)*. A detailed account, as "You ought to keep a record of your spending". 3. Records are kept of sporting performances of all kinds, and if someone does something better than anyone has ever done it before he is said to have broken the record. 4. One of the black disks used on a record player.

recount *(re-count')*. 1. To relate; to tell a story. 2. To count a second time.

recover *(re-cov'-er)*. 1. To get a thing back, as "The wind blew the boy's hat away but he ran after it and recovered it". 2. To get over something such as an illness, as "Though he was terribly ill, he recovered eventually". 3. **re-cover** *(re-cov'-er)*. To put a fresh cover on.

recreation *(rec-re-a'-tion)*. Any form of pastime.

recruit *(re-cruit')*. 1. A newly enlisted soldier, or a new member of any group. 2. To recruit troops is to persuade or force men to join the armed services.

rectangle *(rec'-tan-gle)*. A four-sided figure with all its angles right angles.

rectify *(rec'-ti-fy)*. To put something right that is wrong.

rector *(rec'-tor)*. 1. A clergyman who is in charge of a parish of the Anglican Church. 2. The head of a college.

recumbent *(re-cum'-bent)*. Lying down.

recuperate *(re-cu'-per-ate)*. To regain health and strength, as "The invalid went into the country to recuperate".

recur *(re-cur')*. To happen again.

redeem *(re-deem')*. 1. To buy back, as "He redeemed his pledge" (see **pledge**). 2. To get back by doing something in return, as "He redeemed his good name by saving the child's life".

redress *(re-dress')*. To put right; to make up for some damage done.

reduce *(re-duce')*. To make less, as "They reduced the price of sugar from 10d. per pound to 8d. per pound".

redundant *(re-dun'-dant)*. Repeated unnecessarily. In "He left all his money to his surviving children if any were living when he died", the clause "if any were living when he died" is redundant because the same idea is expressed in the word "surviving".

reed. 1. A plant with long slender leaves and a hollow stalk, which thrives in damp places. 2. The sounding part in wind instruments such as the clarinet, the oboe and the bagpipes.

reef. 1. A ridge of rocks, sand or coral in a body of water which comes just above or just below the surface of the water. 2. To reef a sail is to take it in and roll it up.

reek. To smell unpleasantly.

reel. 1. A reel of thread is a spool with thread wound on it. 2. In "He reeled off one story after another", "reeled off" means "told in rapid succession". 3. In "The old man reeled and nearly fell over", reeled means staggered or tottered as if about to fall. 4. A kind of lively dance.

refectory *(re-fec'-to-ry)*. A dining-hall in a college or monastery.

refer *(re-fer')*. 1. To direct to, or turn to, as "The teacher referred to a dictionary to find the answer". 2. To have to do with; to apply to, as "That law refers to criminal acts". 3. To direct the attention to, as "He referred to something his mother had said that morning"; to mention.

referee *(ref-er-ee')*. A person who decides in disputes between two sides. In sports, a referee is a man who watches the game closely and decides when a point has been scored or a foul committed.

reference *(ref'-er-ence)*. 1. A description of a person's character, as the reference a teacher gives to a boy who is applying for work. 2. Anything to which a person turns for information, as "If this dictionary is often used as a book of reference, your vocabulary will grow greatly".

refined *(re-fined')*. A refined person is one who is free from coarseness and vulgarity.

reflect *(re-flect')*. 1. To throw back light, heat or sound. You can reflect images with a mirror and an echo is the result of a reflected sound. 2. To reflect also means to think, as "He reflected on his past".

reflection *(re-flec'-tion)*. The heat, light or sound which is thrown back. You can see your reflection when you look into a mirror.

reform *(re-form')*. To make a thing better by removing abuses, as "He reformed the laws about children working in coal-mines".

M

reformatory *(re-form'-a-to-ry)*. A place where young law-breakers are sent to be reformed in character.

refrain *(re-frain')*. 1. The chorus of a song, or the part at the end of a verse which is sung over again. 2. To refrain from doing something is not to do it, though you were at first thinking of doing it.

refresh *(re-fresh')*. To make fresh again, as "The rain has refreshed the flowers".

refreshments *(re-fresh'-ments)*. Food or drink.

refrigerator *(re-frig'-er-a-tor)*. A place or container where food is kept cold.

refuge *(ref'-uge)*. A place of shelter where one is free from danger. A person looking for refuge is a **refugee** *(ref-u-gee')*.

refund *(re-fund')*. 1. To pay back, as "The shopkeeper charged 9d. for the sweets, but when he remembered they were only 6d., he refunded 3d. 2. *(re'-fund)*. The thing refunded; the 3d. returned by the shopkeeper was a refund.

refuse. 1. *(re-fuse')*. To say "No!" to what was asked, as "He asked me to climb the tree and steal some apples, but I refused". 2. *(ref'-use)*. Rubbish.

regain *(re-gain')*. 1. To get back, as "After being sick for two months, he regained his health". 2. To get back to, as "He swam back and regained the shore".

regal *(re'-gal)*. Kingly.

regalia *(re-ga'-li-a)*. 1. The crown and all other symbols or signs worn by a king. 2. The signs, symbols or decorations worn by any group.

regard *(re-gard')*. 1. To look at, as "He regarded me as though I were a thief". 2. To consider, believe or think, as "Everybody regards him as the brightest boy in the form". 3. In "with regard to your request", "with regard to" means "referring to". 4. "With kind regards" means with kind thoughts, affection or respect. 5. Respect, as "He had a great regard for his teacher".

regent *(re'-gent)*. A person who rules in place of the real king or queen because the real one is too young, too old or too ill to rule.

regiment *(reg'-i-ment)*. A body of soldiers commanded by a colonel.

region *(re'-gion)*. A part of the world; an area of land; district.

register *(reg'-is-ter)*. A list of names. The names of all the pupils in a class are kept in a book called a register.

registrar *(reg'-is-trar)*. A person who keeps a register. In every area there is a registrar of births, marriages and deaths. He keeps a book in which he enters the names of all those born, married or having died in his area.

regret *(re-gret')*. 1. Sorrow for the loss of something; sorrow for something you have done or have left undone; disappointment; annoyance. 2. To regret something is to be sorry for it.

regular *(reg'-u-lar)*. 1. Usual. 2. Uniform.

regulate *(reg'-u-late)*. To make a thing work as it should, as "He regulated his watch".

rehearse *(re-hearse')*. To practise something. Anything rehearsed is practised at a **rehearsal.**

reign. To rule.

reimburse *(re-im-burse')*. To repay; to pay back someone what he has spent for you, as "When Tom paid for my meal I told him I would reimburse him when I had money".

rein. A long, narrow leather strap attached to one end of a bit, used to guide a horse.

reindeer *(rein'-deer)*. A type of deer found in northern countries.

reinforce *(re-in-force')*. To strengthen; thus reinforced concrete is concrete with steel rods inside to give it added strength.

reiterate *(re-it'-er-ate)*. To say over and over again.

reject *(re-ject')*. To refuse to have; to throw away.

rejoice *(re-joice')*. To be glad.

relapse *(re-lapse')*. To go back or fall back, generally in health or behaviour.

relate *(re-late')*. 1. To tell or describe, as "He related to the policeman how it all happened". 2. To be connected with, as "All your troubles are related to your bad temper".

relation *(re-la'-tion)*. 1. A member of the same family, as "She is a relation of his. I think she is his cousin". 2. Any connection is a relation.

relative *(rel'-a-tive)*. A member of the same family.

relax *(re-lax')*. To slacken; to loosen the muscles.

relay *(re-lay')*. 1. A race run by teams of several people, in which each person on a team carries on from the place where another left off. 2. A number of people who relieve others in carrying on some work. 3. The system of doing anything by relays. 4. A piece of electrical apparatus used to strengthen and send on an electric current. 5. To relay something is to send or pass it on.

release *(re-lease')*. 1. To set free, as "The prisoner was released". 2. To undo, as "Release the hook and the lid will fly up".

relent *(re-lent')*. To be sorry for something you have done; to become less severe.

reliable *(re-li'-a-ble)*. Somebody or something you can trust or depend on is reliable.

relic *(rel'-ic)*. Something still existing from past days; thus Saxon coins or weapons are relics of the past.

relief *(re-lief')*. 1. The removal of pain or distress, as "The medicine gave the patient relief from his pain". 2. Assistance given to poor people. 3. A man who replaces another, as "The bus driver had to wait ten minutes for his relief". 4. A manner of moulding, carving or stamping so that the design stands out from the surrounding surface. Books for the blind are printed in relief so that they may be read by touch.

relieve *(re-lieve')*. To lessen the pain or strain, as "He took medicine to relieve the pain" and "A new regiment of soldiers was sent to relieve the fort".

religion *(re-li'-gion)*. A system of belief in a god or gods and the rules for behaviour which reflect such a belief.

religious *(re-li'-gious)*. 1. Having to do with religion, as "He belonged to a religious group which met on Wednesday". 2. Devoted; conscientious; faithful, as "He looked after his sick mother with religious care" and "He brushed his teeth religiously night and morning".

relinquish *(re-lin'-quish)*. To give up; to abandon.

relish *(rel'-ish)*. 1. To enjoy the taste of. 2. To enjoy, as "He relished his moment of victory". 3. Something eaten with food to make it more enjoyable.

reluctant *(re-luc'-tant)*. Unwilling; not eager.

rely *(re-ly')*. To depend on; to put trust and faith in.

remain *(re-main')*. To stay or to be left; but the **remains** are what is left.

remainder *(re-main'-der)*. The part that is left. When you divide 2 into 7, the remainder is 1.

remark *(re-mark')*. 1. An observation; something said in a casual way. 2. To say; speak; notice.

remarkable *(re-mark'-a-ble)*. Unusual or noticeable, as "That lady's hat is remarkable".

remedy *(rem'-e-dy)*. Anything that cures or banishes ills.

remember *(re-mem'-ber)*. To recall to mind.

remembrance *(re-mem'-brance)*. The act of recalling.

remind *(re-mind')*. To remind someone of something is to make him remember it; thus, "Remind him of his appointment tomorrow".

remiss *(re-miss')*. Neglectful; careless.

remit *(re-mit')*. 1. To send money in payment. 2. To refrain from carrying out punishment is to remit it.

remnant *(rem'-nant)*. A part left over from a much larger part.

remonstrate *(re'-mon-strate)*. To protest or object.

remorse *(re-morse')*. Great sorrow for having done wrong.

remote *(re-mote')*. Far away; distant.

remove *(re-move')*. To take away.

remunerate *(re-mu'-ner-ate)*. To pay; reward. What is paid is **remuneration.**

rend. To tear, split or pull to bits.

render *(rend'-er)*. 1. To make or cause to be, as "He was rendered helpless by the accident". 2. To give, as "He rendered a great service to our club". 3. To pay, as "Render to the conqueror that which is his due". 4. To translate from one language to another. 5. To melt or remove by melting, as "The cook rendered the fat from the roast by placing it in the hot oven".

renegade *(ren'-e-gade)*. One who deserts his friends and joins with the enemy; a traitor; an outlaw.

renounce *(re-nounce')*. To give up; to cast off.

renovate *(ren'-o-vate)*. To make new again, as "Now that the armchair has been renovated it is as good as new".

renown *(re-nown')*. Fame.

rent. 1. A regular payment for the use of property, as "His father pays £2 10s. 0d. per week rent for their house". 2. To rent something is to lend it in return for money. 3. A tear or rip, as "He has a rent in his coat and I can see the lining".

repair *(re-pair')*. 1. To mend or put in working condition, as "The shoemaker repairs shoes". 2. To go to a place, as "Let us repair to the garden".

reparation *(rep-a-ra'-tion)*. Money, etc., given to make up for some injury that has been done.

repast *(re-past')*. A meal.

repay *(re-pay')*. To pay money or service which you owe.

repeal *(re-peal')*. To call back or take back; thus an Act of Parliament may be repealed or cancelled.

repeat *(re-peat')*. To do or say a thing again. If I call out, "Stop, stop, stop", I am repeating the word "stop".

repel *(re-pel')*. 1. To drive or force back. 2. To repulse.

repent *(re-pent')*. To be sorry for something you have done.

repetition *(rep-e-ti'-tion)*. 1. Repeating something; saying or doing something again. 2. Saying something from memory.

replace *(re-place')*. 1. To take the place of, as "Bill will replace Jim in the team". 2. Put in place again, as "You may take the book from the shelf, but please replace it when you have finished".

replenish *(re-plen'-ish)*. To fill again, or to obtain a new supply to make up for what has been used, as "He replenished his petrol tank by buying two more gallons".

replete *(re-plete')*. Full; filled.

reply *(re-ply')*. If someone asks you how old you are and you say "Ten years old", you are replying to his question. What you say is a reply or answer.

report *(re-port')*. 1. An account of something, as a school report, which is an account of a pupil's work. 2. A piece of gossip, as "I heard a report that Mrs. Jones is not nearly as rich as she pretends to be". 3. When someone says "I shall report you", report means tell about you. 4. In "The gun went off with a loud report", report means noise.

reporter *(re-port'-er)*. A man who goes about getting news for a newspaper.

repose *(re-pose')*. 1. To be at rest. 2. A place where one can be at rest; state of being at rest. 3. To put your faith (in), as "He reposed his trust in the mercy of God".

repository *(re-pos'-i-to-ry)*. A place where things are stored.

reprehensible *(rep-re-hen'-si-ble)*. Deserving of blame, as "Tom was very rude to the lady and his conduct was most reprehensible".

represent *(rep-re-sent')*. 1. To stand for, as "The dots on the map represent cities". 2. To act for, as "He represents the

Smith & Jones Company". 3. To bring clearly before the mind; to describe.

representative *(rep-re-sent'-a-tive)*. A person who represents, or acts for, others (see **represent,** No. 2). Members of Parliament are the representatives of the people who elect them.

repress *(re-press')*. To crush; to put down; to put somebody in his place.

reprieve *(re-prieve')*. To put off the time for a punishment; to delay carrying out a sentence.

reprimand *(rep'-ri-mand)*. 1. To scold. 2. A scolding.

reprisal *(re-pris'-al)*. An act of paying back for some wrong done.

reproach *(re-proach')*. To scold; blame; grumble at.

reptile *(rep'-tile)*. A cold-blooded animal that crawls on its belly or on short legs, such as a snake, a lizard, a crocodile, etc.

republic *(re-pub'-lic)*. A country without a monarch, which is governed by representatives elected by the people.

repudiate *(re-pu'-di-ate)*. To refuse to own or refuse to accept. If you repudiate a bill, you refuse to pay it on the ground that you do not owe the money.

repugnant *(re-pug'-nant)*. Disagreeable; nasty; distasteful.

repulse *(re-pulse')*. To repel; drive back.

repulsive *(re-pul'-sive)*. Nasty; hateful.

reputation *(rep-u-ta'-tion)*. What is said or believed about a person or a thing, as "Mary has the reputation of being untidy".

request *(re-quest')*. 1. Something asked; a wish. 2. To ask for.

require *(re-quire')*. 1. To demand, as "I require you to be indoors by 9 o'clock". 2. To need, as "What I require is food. I haven't eaten since yesterday".

requisite *(req'-ui-site)*. 1. Necessary. 2. A necessity; something which is necessary.

rescind *(re-scind')*. To repeal or cancel, as "The new rule about the playing-field being out of bounds has been rescinded".

rescue *(res'-cue)*. To remove from danger; to bring into safety.

research *(re-search')*. 1. A careful search or inquiry. 2. An attempt to find new facts, as "His research enabled the chemist to prepare a new drug".

resemble *(re-sem'-ble)*. To look like; to be like.

resent *(re-sent')*. To be annoyed over something; to object to something, as "The mayor resented the article in the paper which said he wore baggy trousers".

reserve *(re-serve')*. 1. To keep for a special purpose, as "Shall I reserve this seat for you?" 2. The thing kept, as "I have a reserve of logs for use when the cold weather comes". 3. A person of reserve is one who keeps to himself, says little and does not make friends easily.

reserved *(re-served')*. 1. Kept back to be used for a special purpose, as reserved seats in a theatre. 2. A person who is reserved is quiet and slow to make friends.

reservoir *(res'-er-voir)*. A container where a liquid is stored. Reservoirs hold large quantities of water for household use, and a fountain pen has a reservoir for holding the ink.

reside *(re-side')*. To live or dwell. The house in which a person lives is his **residence** *(res'-i-dence)*.

residue *(res'-i-due)*. What is left over; the remainder.

resign *(re-sign')*. 1. To give up your job, as "The man resigned when he heard that he was not going to receive more pay". A person who wishes to resign hands in a **resignation** *(res-ig-na'-tion)*; that is, a letter stating that he wishes to resign. 2. To resign yourself to something is to make up your mind to accept it, although you do not want to. The teacher might say, "The whole class will remain after four; you might as well resign yourselves to it".

resin *(res'-in)*. Sticky, thick sap of most plants, especially of evergreens such as the pine.

resist *(re-sist')*. 1. To fight back; not to give in. 2. To oppose; to do your best to stop something.

resolute *(res'-o-lute)*. Firm; determined. You cannot twist a resolute person around your little finger.

resolution *(res-o-lu'-tion)*. 1. In "He made many resolutions on New Year's Eve but he was unable to keep them", resolutions are the vows he intended to keep. 2. When a resolution is voiced at a meeting, a formal opinion is given about the subject.

resolve *(re-solve')*. 1. To decide; to determine. 2. To separate into parts.

resort *(re-sort')*. 1. A place to which many people go; thus on the coast are many summer resorts. 2. To frequent or to go often. 3. Something to which you look for help or for a refuge.

resource *(re-source')*. 1. A source of supply; a stock than can be drawn on. A person's resources are the money he has and the means he has of getting money. A country's **natural resources** are its supplies of natural products, such as water, minerals, timber, fish, etc. 2. A resource is something you think of to help you out of difficulties.

resourceful *(re-source'-ful)*. Able to do things and make them come right by ways that you yourself have thought of; clever at finding ways out of difficulties.

respect *(re-spect')*. 1. To look up to; to honour, as "He respects his master". 2. The feeling you have towards someone you esteem.

respiration *(res-pi-ra'-tion)*. The act of breathing.

respite *(res'-pite)*. 1. A short period of rest or relaxation from work, worry, battle, etc. 2. To delay or postpone.

resplendent *(re-splend'-ent)*. Splendid; gorgeously dressed; shining.

respond *(re-spond')*. To answer. When a person responds, he gives a **response.**

responsible *(re-spon'-si-ble)*. Answerable. A person is responsible for something when he has to attend to it.

rest. 1. To lie down; to be still and quiet; to relax; to repose oneself; to be dead, as in "May he rest in peace". 2. Repose; leisure; sleep. Thus, "Mother has gone upstairs for a rest", and "He went to the lake for a week's rest". 3. Death, as in "He has gone to rest". 4. The remainder; what is left over, as "I will eat half the apple and you may eat the rest". 5. A rest in music is a period of silence. 6. "That rests with you" means "That is up to you".

restaurant *(res'-tau-rant)*. A place where meals may be bought and eaten.

restitution *(res-ti-tu'-tion)*. Making good; the restoring of something which was lost or taken, as "The thief made restitution by giving back the jewellery he had stolen".

restive *(res'-tive)*. Restless; not able to keep still.

restore *(re-store')*. 1. To bring back, as "She is restored to health". 2. To give back, as "He restored the umbrella he borrowed last Friday".

restrain *(re-strain')*. To hold back; to check; to hinder.

restrict *(re-strict')*. To keep within certain limits; to stop someone doing as much as he wants to.

result *(re-sult')*. That which happens because something has been done.

resume *(re-sume')*. To start again; to begin again on something you have left off doing.

resurrection *(res-ur-rec'-tion)*. The coming to life again.

retail *(re'-tail)*. 1. To sell things in small amounts. 2. To tell over again, as "Mrs. Jones retails all the gossip told her by Mrs. Brown"; to report. 3. To do with the sale of goods in small amounts.

retaliate *(re-tal'-i-ate)*. To pay back an injury with an injury; to give as good as you were given.

retard *(re-tard')*. To hinder; to slow up.

reticent *(ret'-i-cent)*. A person who says very little and does not often speak his mind is reticent.

retire *(re-tire')*. 1. To go back or retreat, as "The handful of soldiers were forced to retire". 2. To give up one's occupation as "He grew old and had to retire". 3. To go to bed, as "It is midnight and we must all retire (to bed)".

retort *(re-tort')*. 1. A sharp reply. An answer that shows the speaker is not pleased with the person who put the question. 2. A container with a long, tube-like arm, used in certain chemical processes.

retreat *(re-treat')*. 1. To go back; to run away. 2. The act of turning back or running away. 3. A place of seclusion.

retrieve *(re-trieve')*. 1. To recover; to regain (something that had been lost or taken away), as "He ran after the thief and retrieved his stolen car-keys". 2. A dog that retrieves goes, finds and brings back game that its master has shot down. A dog trained to do this is called a **retriever.**

return *(re-turn')*. 1. To go or come back. 2. A coming back. 3. To give back, as "Please return that book to the library".

returns *(re-turns')*. Proceeds; profits; reward.

reunion *(re-un'-ion)*. A gathering of people who have not seen each other for some time.

reveal *(re-veal')*. To show or to make known.

revelation *(rev-e-la'-tion)*. Act of making something known or understood; something disclosed, as "The underwater film gave a thrilling revelation of conditions on the ocean floor".

revelry *(rev'-el-ry)*. Merrymaking; boisterous feasting.

revenge *(re-venge')*. 1. Retaliation; the paying back for wrongs done. 2. To revenge a wrong is to take revenge for it. To revenge someone is to take revenge for him, because he has suffered some wrong.

revenue *(rev'-e-nue)*. Income; money received.

reverence *(rev'-er-ence)*. 1. Great respect; awe. If you show reverence you are **reverent**. 2. A respectful bow.

reverie *(rev'-er-ie)*. Vague thoughts of a dreamy kind.

reverse *(re-verse')*. 1. In the sentence "Henry put the car in reverse", the meaning is that Henry changed the gears so that the car would go backwards. 2. In "Things happened just the reverse of what we expected", reverse of means opposite to. 3. The two sides of a coin are known as the obverse (front) and reverse (back). 4. In "The soldiers suffered a reverse", reverse means a set-back. 5. To reverse something is to turn it back to front, or to make it go in the opposite direction. "He reversed his decision" means he took back his decision and made a new one which was just the opposite to the first.

revert *(re-vert')*. To turn back; to return.

review *(re-view')*. 1. A survey of past events. 2. An inspection, as "The soldiers attended a review on the parade ground". 3. An account of a book, play, concert, etc., giving a description and the writer's opinion. Reviews are printed in newspapers and magazines.

revise *(re-vise')*. To alter something; to make corrections in a book, etc., and bring it up to date.

revive *(re-vive')*. 1. To bring back to life; to make conscious again. 2. To come back to life or to come back to good health, as "We thought he was dead, but suddenly he revived and asked for a drink of water". 3. To bring back to good condition, as "A little polish will revive these dirty old shoes".

revolt *(re-volt')*. To rebel against anything.

revolution *(rev-o-lu'-tion)*. 1. A rebellion against the government. 2. A complete turn round a circle.

revolve *(re-volve')*. To turn around in a circle.

reward *(re-ward')*. Something given as a gift because the person who receives the gift has done some action of merit.

rheumatism *(rheu'-ma-tism)*. A disease which causes pain, swelling and stiffness of the joints.

rhinoceros *(rhi-noc'-er-os)*. A large, thick-skinned animal of Africa or Asia with one or two tusks on its snout.

rhubarb *(rhu'-barb)*. An edible garden plant with red stems and large green leaves.

rhyme. The pairing of sounds at the ends of lines of poetry; thus,

> "Old King Cole
> Was a merry old soul."

Here the words *Cole* and *soul* rhyme.

rhythm. The rhythm in music is the regular beat; the rise and fall. People follow the rhythm when dancing. There is rhythm in poetry, in your heart-beat, etc.

rib. 1. A curved bone attached to the breastbone and the spine and enclosing the chest cavity. 2. Something resembling a rib, like the curved pieces of wood in the framework of a boat.

ribbon *(rib'-bon)*. A narrow strip of cloth.

rice. 1. A kind of grass which grows in shallow water and bears small, hard seeds. 2. The seeds of the rice plant, an important food in many countries.

rich. Having a great amount of money, possessions, resources or colour.

rick. A stack of hay, corn, straw, etc.

rid. To free from something unwanted, as in "He tried to rid the barn of rats".

riddle *(rid'-dle)*. 1. A humorous puzzle, as "Why did the jam roll?" Answer: "Because it saw the apple turnover." 2. A coarse-meshed sieve. 3. To riddle with holes is to make many holes in something.

ride. To be carried along on a vehicle, an animal, the waves, etc.

ridge. 1. A horizontal line where two sloping surfaces meet, as the ridge of a roof. 2. A long line of hills.

ridicule *(rid'-i-cule)*. To make fun of somebody or something.

rifle *(ri'-fle)*. 1. A gun. 2. To ransack and steal from.

rigging *(rig'-ging)*. The ropes, etc., of a ship by which the sails are arranged.

right. 1. Correct; not wrong, as "Jane has the right answer". 2. You have two hands, a right hand and a left. The right hand is the hand most people write with. Right and left are directions which mean "to the right-hand side" and "to the left-hand side". 3. What is just or fair. 4. That to which one has a fair claim; a privilege to which one is entitled. 5. To set straight, as "The boat almost upset, but we righted it and sailed on".

righteous *(right'-eous)*. One who does right and is virtuous is said to be righteous.

rigid *(rig'-id)*. 1. Stiff. 2. Strict.

rigorous *(rig'-or-ous)*. Severe.

rim. A raised edge or border; the edge of anything circular.

rind. The peel of fruits and the skin of things like bacon.

ring. 1. A circle or anything in the form of a circle. People may wear rings on their fingers; they may form a ring by joining hands. A ring is also a circular space where performances, games, etc., take place. 2. To sound, as a bell does.

ringlet *(ring'-let)*. A long curl.

rink. A surface used for skating.

riot *(ri'-ot)*. Wild disorder caused by a mob.

rip. To tear or cut clumsily.

ripe. Fully developed. In the case of fruit, etc., ripe means fit to eat.

ripple *(rip'-ple)*. A small wave on the surface of water.

rise. 1. To go up; get up. 2. A place where the land slopes upward.

risk. 1. A chance; danger; hazard. 2. To risk something is to put it in danger, as "A soldier risks his life in battle".

ritual *(rit'-u-al)*. The way the various ceremonies of a religion are performed.

rival *(ri'-val)*. 1. One who competes with another for the same thing. Thus, if you and I ran a race, we would be rivals. 2. To rival someone is to compete with him; to rival also means to be as good as, as "Lilies rival roses in sweetness".

rivalry *(ri'-val-ry)*. Competition; act of competing.

river *(riv'-er)*. A large stream.

rivet *(riv'-et)*. A bolt which is passed through two thicknesses of wood, steel, etc., and then flattened at both ends, so that the two thicknesses are held tightly together. Thus, the two thicknesses are **riveted** together.

rivulet *(riv'-u-let)*. A tiny stream or river.

road. A path along which vehicles travel; a thoroughfare, highway or street.

roam. To ramble about, having no special destination in mind.

roar. 1. A deep, loud noise, as "The roar of the lion frightened the children". 2. To make such a noise.

roast. 1. To cook in an oven. 2. A piece of meat cooked in an oven.

robber *(rob'-ber)*. A thief.

robbery *(rob'-ber-y)*. Stealing.

robe. 1. A flowing dress that does not fit closely, such as a bath robe. 2. A dress that shows its wearer's rank, such as a mayor's robe, or the robes worn by judges, kings, chancellors, etc.

robin *(rob'-in)*. A small song-bird with a red breast.

robust *(ro-bust')*. In good health; strong.

rock. 1. A large stone. 2. To sway gently.

rocket *(rock'-et)*. 1. A self-propelling device or vehicle which is shot through the air by gases that escape from one end. 2. A kind of firework that is shot through the air. 3. To rocket is to fly high and quickly, like a rocket.

rod. 1. A thin metal bar. 2. A long pole used for fishing. 3. A measurement of length equal to $5\frac{1}{2}$ yards or $16\frac{1}{2}$ feet.

rodent *(ro'-dent)*. An animal with front teeth specially suited to gnawing, as a rat or a mouse.

rodeo *(ro-de'-o)*. An exhibition, in N. America, of roping and riding cattle and horses.

roe. 1. Fish eggs, as the roe in herrings. 2. The female of the deer.

rogue. A dishonest person who lives by trickery.

role. 1. A part in a play. 2. The function of someone or something.

roll. 1. To move by turning over and over, or by swaying from side to side. 2. A roll of bread is a small loaf, shaped by rolling over the dough. 3. A roll of paper, etc., is paper that has been rolled up.

romance *(ro-mance')*. 1. A story of knights and beautiful ladies. A story that is very imaginative and fanciful; sometimes a story that is wild, strange and unreal. 2. A love story. 3. A love affair. 4. To invent stories. To make up a story as you go along, perhaps hoping that someone will think it true.

romantic *(ro-man'-tic)*. Connected with romance.

romp. To play in a rough, good-natured way.

rook. 1. A black bird, like a crow. 2. The castle, one of the pieces played with in chess, is also known as a rook.

roost. 1. The pole on which birds perch in order to go to sleep. 2. The action of perching on the pole.

root. 1. The portion of a plant that lives underground and takes food and water from the soil. 2. The cause or beginning of a thing, as "The root of the trouble is his laziness". 3. The root of a word is the old word from which it was made. For example, our word *captain* comes from the Latin word, *caput*, meaning *a head*. Thus, *captain* means the head of a ship, a team, etc.

rope. A strong, thick cord made by twisting smaller strands or cords together.

rose. 1. A fragrant, velvety, red, white, pink or yellow flower which grows on thorny stems. 2. A light-red colour. 3. The past tense of **rise.**

rotary *(ro'-ta-ry)*. Turning round and round like a wheel.

rotation *(ro-ta'-tion)*. 1. The act of turning. (See **rotary.**) 2. In rotation means in turn.

rotten *(rot'-ten)*. Spoiled or decayed.

rotund *(ro-tund')*. Round and fat.

rough. Uneven; not smooth; coarse.

rouse. 1. To awaken. 2. To excite.

rout. 1. To defeat an enemy and drive him away in disorder. 2. A total defeat. 3. A mob or disorderly crowd.

route. A road; a way leading somewhere.

routine *(rou-tine')*. A regular, methodical way of doing one's work.

rove. To wander about without any definite place to go.

rover *(ro'-ver)*. A wanderer; a person who roves.

row. 1. To force a boat along by using oars. 2. A number of things placed in a line. 3. A noisy quarrel.

rowdy *(row'-dy)*. Noisy and boisterous.

rowel *(row'-el)*. A small wheel or disk with sharp points at the end of a horseman's spur.

royal *(roy'-al)*. Anything to do with a monarch can be said to be royal; as "The royal family is the family of the monarch".

rub. To move one thing backwards and forwards on another thing.

rubber *(rub'-ber)*. 1. An elastic, waterproof substance which is made from the juice of some tropical trees. 2. An eraser; a piece of rubber used to remove pencil or ink marks.

rubbish *(rub'-bish)*. Trash; waste matter; nonsense.

ruby *(ru'-by)*. 1. A precious stone, red in colour. 2. A colour like that of a ruby.

rudder *(rud'-der)*. The part of a boat or aeroplane by which the steering is done.

ruddy *(rud'-dy)*. Red. If a person is said to have a ruddy face or complexion, it is usually meant that he has a healthy look.

rude. 1. A rude person is one who is ill-mannered. 2. A thing is said to be rude when it is rough and not carefully finished, as "the rude homes of the ancient Britons".

rudiment *(ru'-di-ment)*. The beginning or early part of a thing. The first simple rules of something. The rudiments of arithmetic are adding and subtracting.

rueful *(rue'-ful)*. Sad and mournful.

ruffian *(ruf'-fi-an)*. A brutal, lawless person.

ruffle *(ruf'-fle)*. 1. To roughen the surface of, as "The wind ruffled the water", and "He ruffled the cat's fur". 2. To annoy or vex. 3. A trimming for a dress, made by gathering a strip of material.

rug. A floor covering.

rugged *(rug'-ged)*. 1. Rough; uneven, as "rugged ground". 2. A rugged cliff is a steep, rocky cliff that is not smooth but full of bumps and cracks. 3. A rugged person is one who is strong and healthy.

ruin *(ru'-in)*. 1. A building in a bad state of repair. 2. To ruin a thing is to destroy or spoil it.

ruler *(rul'-er)*. 1. A person who rules. 2. A piece of wood, metal, etc. used for measuring and for drawing straight lines.

ruminate *(ru'-min-ate)*. 1. To chew the cud as a cow does. 2. To ponder or think about something.

rummage *(rum'-mage)*. 1. To search by turning everything upside down; to ransack. 2. A rummage sale is a sale of odds and ends that people do not want.

rumour *(ru'-mour)*. A story which is repeated by many people, but which may have no basis in truth or fact.

rump. The tail end of something; posterior.

rumple *(rum'-ple)*. To crumple; to crease and make untidy.

run. 1. To move the legs at a faster rate than ordinary walking. 2. To flow, as "The water tap will not turn off and the water is running". 3. To force in, as "He ran a splinter into his hand". 4. To spread, as "I washed my cotton dress and the colour ran".   5. To go, as "This bus runs every five minutes". 6. In "Come for a run in the car", run means ride.   7. In "The play ran for a year", ran means continued.   8. In "He made seven runs at cricket", runs means points scored.

rung.   The step of a ladder.

rupture *(rup'-ture)*.   A break; a breaking.

rural *(ru'-ral)*.   To do with things in the country, as distinct from the city.

ruse.   A trick.

rush.   1. To do something or go somewhere quickly.   2. A rush is also a marsh plant, with long leaves and a thick stem.

russet *(rus'-set)*.   The colour of yellow-brown or red-brown.

rust.   The crust of a dirty red colour which forms on the surface of iron when it is not protected by paint from the air.

rustic *(rus'-tic)*.   Of the country; like the country.

rustle *(rus'-tle)*.   1. A slight crackling or swishing noise, as that made by leaves in the wind.   2. To make such a noise.

rut.   A groove made in the ground like the marks of the wheels of a cart on a soft, muddy country lane.

ruthless *(ruth'-less)*.   Having no pity.

rye.   A kind of grain.

S

Sabbath *(Sab'-bath)*.   Among Jews, the seventh day of the week, which is set apart for rest.   Among Christians, the first day of the week, or Sunday.

sable *(sa'-ble)*.   1. A slender carnivorous animal living in northern countries.   Its fur is thick, brown and very highly prized.   2. The colour black.

sabre *(sa'-bre)*.   A short sword, used by cavalry.

sack.   1. A bag made of rough material.   Sand-bags are sacks filled with sand.   2. To sack a town is to capture and plunder it.   3. A kind of wine.

sacred *(sa'-cred)*.   Holy.

sacrifice *(sac'-ri-fice)*.   1. An offering to God, as mentioned in several places in the Bible.   2. To give up a thing for the sake of something you think more important.

saddle *(sad'-dle)*. 1. A leather seat for a rider, placed on a horse or a bicycle, etc. 2. A ridge between two mountain tops.

safari *(sa-fa'-ri)*. A hunting trip, especially one in Africa.

safe. 1. Secure. A person is safe when he is out of danger. 2. A place for storing valuables, where they will be protected from fire and burglars.

safety *(safe'-ty)*. A state of being safe from danger, as "The lifeguard dived into the sea and brought the boy to safety".

sagacious *(sag-a'-cious)*. Wise.

sage. 1. A plant of the mint family. 2. A wise man.

sail. 1. The piece of cloth attached to the mast of a boat to catch the wind and make the boat move. 2. To sail a boat is to navigate or travel along in any type of boat.

sailor *(sail'-or)*. A person who works on a boat.

saint. A holy person.

salad *(sal'-ad)*. A mixture of uncooked green vegetables, with some kind of dressing or seasoning added. There are also meat, fish, fruit and potato salads.

salary *(sal'-a-ry)*. A regular sum paid as wages for work that is being done.

sale. 1. The selling of things. 2. When a store advertises a "Great Summer Sale" it means a special time of selling when all goods will cost less than usual.

saline *(sa'-line)*. Containing salt.

sallow *(sal'-low)*. A sallow complexion is a sickly yellow complexion.

salmon *(salm'-on)*. 1. A large, edible fish, whose flesh is of a pinkish colour. It is found in sea-water and in fresh-water. 2. A colour, light pinkish-orange.

saloon *(sa-loon')*. A large room fitted for public use.

salt. A fine white substance found in sea-water and below ground. Salt is used to season foods.

salute *(sa-lute')*. To bow; to raise one's hat; to nod, etc., on meeting a person.

salvage *(sal'-vage)*. 1. The saving of property from a fire or from a shipwreck. 2. The property so saved. 3. The payment made by the owner to people who save property.

salvation *(sal-va'-tion)*. 1. A saving from destruction, evil, etc. 2. That which saves. 2. Among Christians the word refers to the saving of a person's soul through faith.

salve. Ointment; a soothing dressing for wounds.

sample *(sam'-ple)*. 1. A small part of something, which is offered in order to show what the whole is like. 2. To sample something means to try or inspect a small part of it in order to find what the whole is like.

sanatorium *(san-a-to'-ri-um)*. A hospital for treating invalids, especially those with tuberculosis.

sanctify *(sanc'-ti-fy)*. To make holy.

sanctimonious *(sanc-ti-mo'-ni-ous)*. Making a great show of being good and holy.

sanction *(sanc'-tion)*. 1. To give permission; to allow. 2. Approval.

sanctuary *(sanc'-tu-ar-y)*. 1. A sacred place, such as the inside of a church. 2. As a person could not be taken captive while in a church, the word "sanctuary" came to mean refuge, and it now means not only refuge in a church but refuge of any kind.

sand. Minute particles of rock found on the beach.

sandal *(san'-dal)*. A shoe consisting of a sole bound to the foot by straps.

sandpiper *(sand'-pi-per)*. A small long-billed bird which lives on sandy shores.

sandstone *(sand'-stone)*. A kind of rock formed of particles of sand packed together.

sandwich *(sand'-wich)*. 1. Two thin slices of bread with meat, cheese, etc., between them. 2. Anything placed between two articles and closely pressed on either side is said to be **sandwiched.**

sane. Reasonable, or of sound mind; sensible.

sanguine *(san'-guine)*. 1. Hopeful. 2. To do with blood.

sanitary *(san'-i-tar-y)*. 1. Free from dirt or germs. 2. Anything that helps to prevent disease is sanitary, so the word may be taken to mean "assisting health".

Santa Claus *(San'-ta Claus')*. Father Christmas.

sap. 1. The watery substance which flows through the veins of plants, carrying food and water to all their parts. 2. To sap someone's strength is to take it away or cause it to be used up.

sapling *(sap'-ling)*. A young tree.

sapphire *(sap'-phire)*. 1. A precious stone, bright or dark blue. 2. Bright or dark blue.

sarcasm *(sar'-casm)*. Words spoken in a sneering way to hurt someone's feelings. A person who uses sarcasm is **sarcastic** *(sar-cas'-tic)*.

sardine *(sar-dine')*. A small fish of the herring family.

sash. 1. A strip of material long and fairly narrow, usually worn round the waist. 2. The frame in which glass is held in a window.

satchel *(satch'-el)*. A small bag for carrying articles such as books.

satellite *(sat'-el-lite)*. 1. A small planet which circles around a larger one. The moon is a satellite of the earth. 2. Objects placed into orbit round the earth by rocket are called artificial satellites.

satiate *(sa'-ti-ate)*. To satisfy with more than enough. If you ate a great quantity of toffee, a time would come when you could eat no more. Then you would be satiated.

satin *(sat'-in)*. A silk or rayon cloth with one smooth, shiny surface.

satire *(sat'-ire)*. A literary composition to ridicule something evil or foolish.

satisfactory *(sat-is-fac'-to-ry)*. Good enough to satisfy. If a pupil's report has the note "satisfactory", it means that his work is good enough.

satisfy *(sat'-is-fy)*. To please or make contented.

saturate *(sat'-u-rate)*. 1. To soak thoroughly. If you are saturated after having been in the rain, you are soaked to the skin. 2. If you have a saturated solution of salt and water, you can dissolve no more salt in the water.

Saturday *(Sat'-ur-day)*. The seventh day of the week between Friday and Sunday.

sauce. A thick or thin liquid served with dinner to improve the taste of meat, fish, etc.

saucer *(sau'-cer)*. A small, round, shallow dish on which a cup is set.

saucy *(sau'-cy)*. Impudent.

saunter *(saun'-ter)*. To walk along at your leisure in a contented frame of mind; to stroll.

sausage *(sau'-sage)*. A tube of seasoned ground beef or pork.

savage *(sav'-age)*. 1. An uncivilized person. 2. Wild, as a savage animal. 3. Cruel, as "He made a savage attack on the woman".

save. 1. To rescue from danger. 2. To store up money and not spend it. 3. Except, as "They all went save Henry", meaning they all went except Henry.

saviour *(sav'-iour)*. One who saves. With a capital, Saviour means Jesus Christ.

saw. 1. A tooth-edged tool used for cutting. 2. Past tense of see. 3. A wise old saying or proverb.

sawdust *(saw'-dust)*. The wood particles produced when sawing wood.

saxophone *(sax'-o-phone)*. A musical instrument used in bands. It is a wind instrument, with a bent metal tube, finger keys and a reed mouthpiece.

scab. 1. The hard matter that forms on a sore while it is healing. 2. A potato disease.

scald. To pour boiling liquid on.

scale. 1. A device for weighing. 2. In music, a series of notes related to one another in a fixed pattern. 3. The scale of a map is the markings in the corner which show the number of miles represented by one inch on the map. 4. Little over-lapping plates on the body of a fish or the wing of a butterfly. 5. A series of things graded from the lowest to the highest. A scale of postal charges is a chart showing the cost of sending letters or parcels of all different weights. 6. To scale a cliff is to climb it.

scalp. The skin under the hair on the head, or the skin and hair.

scamp. A worthless rascal.

scamper *(scam'-per)*. To run suddenly and quickly, like a frightened animal or a playing child.

scandal *(scan'-dal)*. 1. Gossip that injures those who are talked about. 2. Any disgraceful action, as "It is a scandal that the money collected for charity was spent on other things".

scanty *(scant'-y)*. Not enough.

scapegoat *(scape'-goat)*. A person who has to take the blame for the wrong things done by others.

scar. A mark left by a wound that has healed.

scarce. Rare; uncommon.

scare. To frighten.

scarf. A long piece of wool, silk, etc., worn about the neck for warmth or decoration.

scarlet *(scar'-let)*. Bright red.

scatter *(scat'-ter)*. To sprinkle; to throw about.

scavenger *(scav'-en-ger)*. An animal that feeds on filth and decayed things.

scene. 1. A view, as "He looked through the kitchen window and a dreadful scene greeted his eyes". 2. A division of a play. 3. A fuss or row, as "The spoiled child caused a scene when she screamed at her mother and sat on the floor".

scenery *(scen'-er-y)*. 1. The appearance of the land, as "Trees in autumn are beautiful scenery". 2. The fixtures and painted curtains used in a theatre to represent places.

scent. 1. Smell; perfume. 2. To smell, as "The dogs scented a rabbit and were off".

schedule *(sche'-dule)*. A time-table.

scheme. 1. A plan for doing something, as "He had a scheme for selling ice-cream by aeroplane". 2. To make plans in a secretive way.

scholar *(schol'-ar)*. 1. A boy or girl at school. 2. An adult who is very learned.

school. 1. A place where pupils are taught. 2. The followers or imitators of some artist are called his school. 3. A school of fish is a number of fish which swim together.

schooner *(schoon'-er)*. A swift-sailing ship with two masts.

science *(sci'-ence)*. 1. Knowledge. 2. A branch of study concerned with observing and ordering facts, especially facts about nature and the universe. A person who knows a great deal about some particular science is a **scientist**; probably he has had **scientific** *(sci-en-tif'-ic)* training.

scintillate *(scin'-til-late)*. To twinkle or sparkle.

scissors *(scis'-sors)*. A cutting tool formed by two blades which cross and are operated by opening and closing.

scoff. To laugh in a jeering way; to mock.

scold. When your mother scolds you for being naughty, she uses angry words and points out your fault.

scoop. 1. A kind of shovel. 2. To dig or gather, as "She scooped a large hole in the garden", and "Scoop up the sugar you have spilled".

scooter *(scoot'-er)*. A child's two-wheeled vehicle with one wheel at either end of a long narrow foot-board. It is moved by placing one foot on the foot-board and pushing on the ground with the other.

scorch. To burn slightly; to singe.

score. 1. To make marks by cutting, as "He scored his name on the table". 2. An account or record kept of the points won in a game, as "They played darts and Jones kept the score". 3. To make points in a game, as "Have you scored a hundred yet?" 4. Twenty of anything is a score.

scorn. To look down on; to frown upon; to ridicule.

Scotch. To do with Scotland.

scoundrel *(scoun'-drel)*. A rascal; a villain.

scour. 1. To clean a thing with much rubbing. 2. To search, as "They scoured the park, but they did not find him".

scourge. 1. A whip. 2. To whip or punish. 3. Anything that is the cause of much trouble or suffering. A disease that attacks many people at one time is called a scourge.

scout. 1. A soldier whose work it is to go ahead of the others and see how the land lies and to observe the enemy. 2. A boy belonging to the Boy Scouts.

scowl. To frown; to look very angry or sulky; to frown threateningly.

scraggy *(scrag'-gy)*. Skinny and bony.

scramble *(scram'-ble)*. 1. To struggle against others to get something, as "The boys scrambled to get a portion of the pie". 2. To move or clamber on all fours, as "He had but one choice and that was to scramble up the steep cliff". 3. Scrambled eggs are those cooked in milk after the yolks and whites have been beaten together.

scrap. 1. A small piece of a thing. 2. To throw away or to use no more. 3. A fight. 4. To fight.

scrape. 1. To rub with or against something sharp, as "He scraped the dirt from the old coin with a knife". 2. To make a grating sound as when you scrape glass with a knife.

scratch. 1. To scrape with the nails or claws. 2. To rub, tear or mark the surface with something sharp, as "The thorns scratched his arm". 3. A mark or injury made by scratching.

scrawl. To write carelessly or badly.

scream. A harsh, piercing sound made by someone in extreme pain, joy or fear.

screech. To make a harsh, shrill cry.

screen. 1. To protect. 2. To separate, as gravel is screened to separate the dirt. 3. A piece of furniture used for shielding or hiding a person or thing, such as a fire-screen which shields an open fire.

screw. 1. A kind of nail with grooves running around the stem, which is driven in by being turned. 2. To screw something is to fasten it with a screw. 3. A propeller of a boat.

scribble *(scrib'-ble)*. 1. Careless, badly-formed writing. 2. To write quickly and carelessly.

scripture *(scrip'-ture)*. Holy writings, especially the Bible.

scroll. 1. A piece of paper or parchment with writing on it, which can be rolled up. 2. An ornamental design made of curls, loops, flourishes, etc.

scrub. 1. To clean by rubbing with a brush. 2. Stunted vegetation.

scruple *(scru'-ple)*. 1. A measure of weight used by druggists, 1/350th of a pound. 2. A person who has scruples about doing something hesitates to do it because he feels that it may not be right to do it.

scrupulous *(scru'-pu-lous)*. Careful to do what is right, and behave correctly.

scuffle *(scuf'-fle)*. A fight of the rough and tumble kind.

scullery *(scul'-ler-y)*. The room in which there is a sink to do the washing-up.

sculptor *(sculp'-tor)*. A person who shapes stone, wood or metal into statues, etc.

scum. 1. A film of matter that forms on the surface of some liquids. 2. Worthless, low-class people.

scurry *(scur'-ry)*. To hurry with short, quick steps.

scurvy *(scur'-vy)*. A disease caused by a lack of fresh fruits and vegetables in the diet. The gums swell and bleed and the skin is spotted.

scuttle *(scut'-tle)*. 1. An article for carrying coals. 2. To go quickly. 3. To sink a ship purposely by letting in water.

scythe. A long, curved blade attached to a long handle, used for cutting grass and crops with long stalks.

sea. 1. The large body of salt water which covers the greater part of the earth's surface. 2. A particular part of that water having a name, such as the Red Sea.

seafaring *(sea'-far-ing)*. Connected with travelling on the sea.

seal. 1. A sea animal with a pointed nose, flippers and a tail. It is valued for its sleek black fur. 2. To close something tightly, so that air cannot enter. 3. A design which is stamped on documents, etc., to show that they are official and authentic.

seam. 1. When two pieces of cloth are sewn together, the join is called a seam. 2. A vein of coal or ore running through rocks underground.

seaport *(sea'-port)*. A harbour or port which opens onto the sea.

sear. 1. To burn. 2. To dry up and wither; thus leaves become seared in the autumn.

search. To try to find; to explore. A **searchlight** is a powerful light that is used to find something at night.

sea-shore *(sea'-shore)*. The coast along the sea.

season *(sea'-son)*. 1. Spring, summer, autumn and winter are the seasons of the year. 2. Any special time of the year is called a season; thus people speak of the holiday season, the oyster season, etc. 3. To add to the taste of food, by using seasoning such as herbs. 4. Wood is seasoned when it has had time to dry.

seat. 1. A chair or piece of furniture on which one may sit. 2. To place or tell a person where to sit is to seat him.

seaweed *(sea'-weed)*. A plant which grows in the sea.

secluded *(se-clud'-ed)*. Placed apart from other things; a secluded spot is a place where there is quietness and few or no people.

second *(sec'-ond)*. 1. Next to the first; immediately following the first. 2. A very short period of time, equal to 1/60th of a minute. 3. If, at a meeting, someone made a suggestion of which you approved, you might second or support it. 4. One who acts as another's aid in a duel or prize fight.

second-hand *(sec-ond-hand')*. Not new.

secret *(se'-cret)*. 1. Hidden. When you wish to keep a matter secret, you want to keep other people from knowing about it. 2. A secret is a piece of information which is kept from others.

secretary *(sec'-re-ta-ry)*. A person who attends to the letters and other matters of a busy person, a company, a club, etc.

secrete *(se-crete')*. 1. To hide. 2. To give off, as "The pores in the skin secrete perspiration".

section *(sec'-tion)*. 1. A division or part of a complete thing, as a section of a book. 2. If a thing is cut in two, the surface thus made is a section.

secure *(se-cure')*. 1. Safe; out of danger. 2. Firmly fixed.

sedan *(se-dan')*. A sedan chair is a covered chair which two men carry no poles.

sedate *(se-date')*. Calm and composed.

sediment *(sed'-i-ment)*. The material which settles at the bottom of some liquids. Medicines have to be shaken in order to mix any sediment there may be throughout all the liquid.

sedition *(se-di'-tion)*. Saying or doing things to make people rebel against the government.

see. To perceive with the eyes.

seed. The part of a fruit, berry, nut, etc., which grows into a new plant.

seedling *(seed'-ling)*. A young plant that has only recently sprung from a seed.

seek. To look for; to search for.

seem. To appear, as "She seems to be ill", i.e. she appears to be ill.

seemly *(seem'-ly)*. Fitting; in a proper manner, as "Your conduct is seemly".

seer. A wise man; a prophet.

seethe. To boil and bubble.

segment *(seg'-ment)*. 1. If a straight line is drawn across a circle and cuts it into two parts, either of the parts is a segment. 2. A small piece of anything detached from the whole.

segregate *(seg'-re-gate)*. To separate and set apart from the rest.

seize. 1. To grab or catch hold of. 2. To take by force.

seldom *(sel'-dom)*. Not often; rarely.

select *(se-lect')*. 1. To choose, as "Yesterday she selected her Christmas cards". 2. Choice or high class, as "He only goes to select hotels".

selfish *(sel'-fish)*. A selfish person cares only about himself.

sell. To exchange for money.

semi-circle *(sem'-i-cir-cle)*. One half of a circle.

seminary *(sem'-i-nar-y)*. 1. A private school. 2. A college where students are trained to become priests.

senator *(sen'-a-tor)*. A member of the Senate, which is a part of the government in some countries.

send. 1. To tell to go. 2. To make go.

senile *(se'-nile)*. Aged; grown foolish through old age.

senior *(sen'-ior)*. 1. Older than someone else, as "My brother is two years my senior". 2. Higher in position than someone else.

sensation *(sen-sa'-tion)*. 1. A feeling, as "Soft mud oozing between your toes gives a pleasant sensation". 2. Some astonishing or shocking thing that gives everyone a great surprise when it is made known, as "A great sensation was caused when the newspaper reported the murder of the Prime Minister".

sense. 1. Any one of the five faculties by which we perceive the world around us, namely, sight, hearing, smell, taste and feeling. 2. Intelligence, or the power to use one's brains, as "John has quite a lot of sense". 3. Meaning, as "Bear can be used in two senses".

sensible *(sen'-si-ble)*. 1. Being wise, clever; knowing how to do the right thing. 2. Able to be felt by one of the senses.

sensitive *(sen'-si-tive)*. 1. Easily upset or hurt, as "As Mary is very sensitive, do not speak to her about her lameness". 2. A sensitive thing is one that changes quickly when conditions become different; thus a sensitive thermometer is one that registers the slightest difference in temperature.

sentence *(sen'-tence)*. 1. In grammar, a sentence is a complete thought put into words. 2. The order by which a judge imposes a punishment on someone who has broken the law. 3. To sentence a criminal is to order him to undergo a certain punishment.

sentiment *(sen'-ti-ment)*. A feeling or point of view that one has towards a subject. The sentiment of pity is aroused in most people if they see a child who is neglected.

sentry *(sen'-try)*. A person who is on guard.

separate *(sep'-a-rate)*. 1. To disjoin; to put apart, as "I separated the two boys who were fighting". 2. Apart; not joined, as England and Scotland are separate countries".

separator *(sep'-a-ra-tor)*. A machine used to separate, as "A farmer uses a separator to separate the milk from the fat or cream".

September *(Sep-tem'-ber)*. The ninth month of the year. It has 30 days.

sequel *(se'-quel)*. That which happens because of something which has already happened; the result; consequence.

serenade *(ser-e-nade')*. Music played out of doors at night by a lover to his lady. Any music suitable for such occasions.

serene *(se-rene')*. Calm and having a pleasant temper.

sergeant *(ser'-geant)*. 1. A rank in the army, lower than lieutenant and higher than corporal. 2. A man holding the rank of sergeant.

serial *(se'-ri-al)*. 1. Belonging to a series. 2. A story which is published part by part. Most comic strips are serials.

series *(se'-ries)*. 1. A number of similar things occurring in order. 2. In arithmetic, a series of numbers is a succession of numbers which are determined by some fixed law. For example, 1, 3, 5, 7 and 9 form a series. The law of the series here is that each number is greater by two than the one before it.

serious *(se'-ri-ous)*. Grave; causing a lot of trouble.

sermon *(ser'-mon)*. The talk which a clergyman gives from the pulpit.

serpent *(ser'-pent)*. A snake.

serrated *(ser'-rat-ed)*. Having an edge like that of a saw.

serum *(se'-rum)*. A liquid which doctors inject into a person with a needle to prevent disease.

servant *(serv'-ant)*. A person who works for another.

serve. 1. To work for someone is to serve him. 2. To serve food is to bring it to a table and give it to those seated there. 3. To serve in the army means to join the army and work there. 4. "To serve as" means to act as or work as. 5. In tennis and certain other sports, to serve is to put the ball into play. 6. To serve a prison term means to go to prison and stay there for a length of time.

service *(serv'-ice)*. 1. The act of serving, that is, doing work for another. 2. The Civil Service is the body of people who work for the government; the armed services are the army, navy and air force; to be on active service means to be fighting with one of the armed services in a war. 3. "The service is poor at the Grand Hotel" means that the guests are not looked after quickly or in a satisfactory way. 4. A church service is a meeting for worship in a church or chapel. 5. In tennis and various other sports the service is the act of serving the ball, or putting it into play. 6. In such phrases as "train service", "bus service", etc., service means the provision of public transport.

serviceable *(serv'-ice-a-ble)*. Useful; willing to serve.

servile *(ser'-vile)*. Humble; like a slave; without a mind or a will of one's own.

session *(ses'-sion)*. A single assembly meeting.

settee *(set-tee')*. A seat for two or more people.

settle *(set'-tle)*. 1. To settle means to sink to the bottom, as drugs in a medicine bottle sometimes do. 2. To make oneself comfortable, as "We have settled ourselves into the two big chairs by the fire". 3. To make or take up one's dwelling in a certain place, as "The family settled in their new house". 4. To settle up is to pay what is owing. 5. To settle a quarrel is to stop the quarrel and put things right. 6. In "The butterfly settled on the flower", settled means came to rest.

settlement *(set'-tle-ment)*. 1. A place where people have settled and made their homes. 2. A clearing up; a payment. 3. The sinking of land.

settler *(set'-tler)*. A person who settles, usually in a new country.

sever *(sev'-er)*. 1. To cut in two. 2. To break off.

several *(sev'-er-al)*. 1. More than two, but not very many. 2. Distinct; particular; various.

severe *(se-vere')*. 1. A severe person is strict and harsh. 2. A severe illness is one that is serious.

sew. To make stitches with a needle and thread. If your mother sews your torn clothes, she stitches the parts together.

sewage *(sew'-age)*. The waste material that flows into the sewers or drains.

sewer *(sew'-er)*. An underground pipe which carries away waste water and refuse.

sex. The character of being male or female. All males taken together form the male sex and all females taken together form the female sex.

sextant *(sex'-tant)*. An instrument that is used for measuring angles and the height of the sun. Every captain of a ship uses one to find his position at sea.

sexton *(sex'-ton)*. A man who looks after a church building.

shabby *(shab'-by)*. 1. Threadbare and worn; not new-looking; badly and poorly dressed. 2. Paltry; mean.

shack. A crude building or a house in poor repair.

shade. 1. A place where the sun is not shining, though it is shining all round; a place in shadow. 2. A shade of colour refers to the depth of colour, whether light or dark. 3. A covering for an electric light. 4. To shade is to protect from light by covering.

shadow *(shad'-ow)*. The dark patch cast by a form that is placed in the sun or in front of an artificial light. Thus if you stand on the beach when the sun is shining, a rough form of yourself will be cast on the sand, on the side of you away from the sun. That rough, dark form is a shadow.

shady *(shad'-y)*. Situated in the shade.

shaft. 1. One of the wooden poles attached to a cart, wagon, etc., between which a horse is harnessed. 2. A wooden handle is often called a shaft. 3. The passage into a coal mine is a shaft and so is the space up and down which a lift travels. 4. The long, slender body of an arrow. 5. Anything considered as being shot or thrown, such as shafts of sunlight or shafts of ridicule.

shaggy *(shag'-gy)*. Having long hair in need of combing and brushing.

shallow *(shal'-low)*. 1. Of little depth, as "The stream was indeed shallow, for it was only a few inches deep". 2. A person is shallow when he lacks intelligence and character.

sham. 1. False; pretended. 2. Something which is not what it pretends to be; a fake.

shame. The unpleasant feeling you have when you know you have done something wrong or foolish.

shampoo *(sham-poo')*. 1. To wash the head and hair. 2. The soapy liquid used for this purpose.

shamrock *(sham'-rock)*. A kind of three-leafed clover, the national emblem of Ireland.

shank. 1. The part of the leg between the ankle and the knee. 2. The shank of a tool is the part which connects the handle to the working part.

shapely *(shape'-ly)*. Anything is shapely that is well-formed or has a pleasing shape.

share. 1. A part of anything belonging to a person when the other parts belong to other people; thus "Mr. Jones does not own the whole of that business. He owns only a share of it". 2. In "I do wish you would eat only your share of the cake", share means portion. 3. In "He shared his lunch with the poor man", shared means divided. 4. Stocks and shares are certificates which show that the person named on them is the owner of part of the company which issues the certificates.

shark. 1. A large sea-fish which attacks people who come within its reach. 2. A person who tries to get money from others by unfair means.

sharp. 1. Having a cutting edge that is keen and does its work well. 2. Quick to understand or to seize an opportunity. 3. Dishonest. 4. In music, a sharp is a note one-half a tone above the note that is sharpened. 5. A sharp taste is a biting, acid taste, such as pickles have; a sharp wind is a cold, biting wind; to speak sharply is to speak crossly; a sharp turn is an abrupt turn.

shatter *(shat'-ter)*. To smash into tiny pieces.

shave. 1. To remove hair with a razor. 2. A close shave often means a narrow escape.

shaving *(shav'-ing)*. 1. A thin slice or piece. A shaving is often curled, as wood shavings. 2. The act of removing hair with a razor.

shawl. A square of material folded diagonally and worn over the shoulders.

sheaf. A bundle of stalks of grain.

shear. To cut with **shears,** or large scissors. Shear is usually used when referring to the cutting of wool from a sheep.

sheath. A scabbard or a case for holding an instrument with a sharp blade or a sharp point. The sheath, in fact, protects the person who carries the weapon.

shed. 1. To throw off, as "The man shed his coat before jumping into the river". 2. To scatter, as "The sun sheds light and heat". 3. To pour out, as "She shed tears on hearing the news". 4. A lightly-made building of one storey, used for storing things.

sheep. A domestic animal which is reared for meat and wool.

sheepish *(sheep'-ish)*. Timid; meek; embarrassed.

sheer. 1. Steep; straight up and down, as "The cliff was sheer". 2. In "She cried from sheer joy", sheer means unmixed or pure.

sheet. 1. A part of bed-clothing made of linen or cotton. 2. A single piece of paper is a sheet of paper. 3. A flat, broad surface such as a sheet of ice, steel, water, etc.

sheikh. The chief of an Arabian tribe. Also spelled **sheik**.

shelf. A ledge fixed to a wall, etc., so that things may be stood on it.

shell. 1. The hard covering of cockles, snails, oysters, etc. 2. The hard covering of nuts, eggs, etc. 3. The hard case in which explosive material is placed, so that it may be fired from guns.

shellac *(shel-lac')*. A liquid like paint which is applied to wood or metal surfaces to make them shine.

shelter *(shel'-ter)*. 1. A place where one can be safe or protected. 2. To shelter someone means to protect him, or provide him with a shelter.

shelve. To slope. It is dangerous to bathe from a steeply shelving beach because you quickly get out of your depth.

shepherd *(shep'-herd)*. 1. A person who looks after sheep. 2. To gather, guard or herd, as "He shepherded his class of boys across the street".

sheriff *(sher'-iff)*. In England a sheriff is the chief officer of the crown in his county. In Scotland the sheriff is the chief judge of a county.

sherry *(sher'-ry)*. A kind of wine.

shield. 1. Originally, a screen carried on the arm to serve as a protection; to-day it can refer to any protective barrier such as a wind-shield on the front of a car or motor-cycle. 2. To shield a person is to protect him from danger.

shift. 1. To move from one place to another. 2. A period of work or duty, as "The policeman was on night shift".

shifty *(shift'-y)*. Said of a person who cannot be trusted.

shin. The front part of the leg between the knee and the ankle.

shine. 1. To give out a bright light. 2. Gloss; sheen; shininess, as "The shine on his boots showed he had cleaned them well". 3. In "Nora shines in arithmetic", shines means that she does work that is noticeably good.

shingle *(shin'-gle)*. The rounded, water-worn pebbles found on beaches.

shining *(shin'-ing)*. Brilliant; gleaming.

ship. 1. A sailing vessel; a large boat. 2. To ship something is to transport it or cause it to be transported.

shirk. To avoid doing something which you ought to do.

shirt. A piece of clothing worn by men on the upper part of the body.

shiver *(shiv'-er)*. To shake or tremble because of cold or fear.

shoal. 1. A great number, as a shoal of fishes. 2. An area of water which is shallow because of the sandbanks present.

shock. 1. Impact; jarring; a sudden shake. 2. Something causing great surprise and dismay, as "His death came as a great shock". 3. To shock a person is to give him a sudden fright or to cause him to become suddenly very upset. 5. If you touch electric wires you may get an electric shock; that is, a current of electricity may pass through your body, momentarily paralyzing you. Electric shocks can cause death. 7. A bundle of stalks of grain is called a shock. "Mary has a shock of red hair" means that Mary's red hair is untidy and sticks out like a bundle of grain-stalks. 8. Someone who suffers an injury or loses a great amount of blood may suffer from shock. Shock in this case means a state in which the temperature of the body is lowered and all the bodily processes are slowed down. Shock can be fatal.

shod. Wearing shoes.

shoddy *(shod'-dy)*. 1. Cloth made from waste that has some new wool mixed with it. 2. Any poor quality article that is made up to look better than it is.

shoe. 1. The covering, usually made of leather, worn on the foot. 2. A covering attached to the foot of something, as a horseshoe.

shook. The past tense of shake, as "He shook the branch of the apple tree and then gathered the apples that fell".

shoot. 1. A plant shoots when the buds begin to open or when it begins to sprout. 2. A sprout. 3. To fire a gun.

shore. 1. The edge of the land where it touches the sea. 2. A prop or support for the side of a building.

short. Not high; the opposite of tall.

shoulder *(shoul'-der)*. The upper part of the body, to which the arm is attached.

shout. To call or talk in a loud voice.

shove. To push.

shovel *(shov'-el)*. A tool with a broad blade at one end for digging.

show. 1. In "I showed him my stamp collection", showed means let him see or look at. 2. In "The Scouts have a show tonight", show means an exhibition or display. 3. To show off is to make a display of yourself, in order to let everyone know how good you are. 4. In "Harry has left for the show", show means a film, play or other entertainment.

N

shower *(show'-er)*. 1. A fall of rain that does not last very long. 2. To shower someone with presents is to give him many presents. 3. A bath in which water is showered on the person through a nozzle above his head.

shred. 1. A narrow strip of something. 2. To cut or tear into shreds.

shrew. 1. An animal like a mouse with a long nose. 2. A bad-tempered woman.

shrewd. Sharp; keen; quick to see and understand things, as "A good general must be a shrewd man".

shriek. A shrill cry.

shrill. A noise is shrill when it is so sharp and piercing that you find yourself putting up your hands to cover your ears.

shrimp. A small shell-fish used for food.

shrink. 1. To become smaller and take up less room. 2. To draw back with pain or fear.

shrivel *(shriv'-el)*. To wither, dry up and become wrinkled.

shroud. 1. The sheet in which a dead body is wrapped for burial. 2. On a ship, the shrouds are ropes running from the tops of the masts to the decks.

shrub. A bush.

shrubbery *(shrub'-ber-y)*. Bushes.

shrug. To draw up (the shoulders). A person shrugs his shoulders when he raises and then drops them to show that he does not care or that he is not certain.

shudder *(shud'-der)*. To tremble from head to foot, but only for a second or so.

shuffle *(shuf'-fle)*. 1. To scrape the feet along the ground when walking. 2. To mix up and put in a different order, as when a person shuffles a pack of cards.

shun. To avoid.

shunt. 1. To move something out of the way. 2. To move a train, or part of it, from one set of rails to another.

shut. To close an opening in something.

shuttle *(shut'-tle)*. 1. A device which holds thread. There is one in every sewing machine, usually just below the tip of the needle. 2. To move to and fro over a short distance.

shy. Timid; cautious.

sick. 1. To be sick is to vomit or bring up food. 2. Ill; not healthy, as "John is sick with the measles". 3. To be sick of something is to be tired of it or fed up with it.

sickle *(sick'-le)*. A cutter with a curved blade and a short handle for cutting long grass or trimming hedges.

sideboard *(side'-board)*. A kind of table, with drawers below, used for storing china in the dining-room.

siege. The surrounding of a castle, town or fortified place by an army in order to capture it.

sieve. A utensil made of fine mesh which is used to separate solids from liquids.

sift. To pass through a sieve; to separate the fine particles from the coarser lumps. Your mother sifts flour when she bakes a cake.

sigh. To let out a long breath. A sigh usually shows some feeling. It may be sorrow, pain, tiredness or relief.

sight. 1. "Bill has keen sight", means that Bill sees very well. 2. In "I caught sight of her", sight means a glimpse. 3. In "Isn't that a beautiful sight", sight means view.

sign. 1. A notice posted with words such as "Beware of the dog" on it. 2. Dumb people who lack the power to speak use gestures instead of words. These gestures or signs are called sign language. 3. In arithmetic these signs are well known, $\times$ and $\div$. 4. When you write your signature, you sign your name.

signal *(sig'-nal)*. 1. A sign (see No. 1 or 2, above). 2. An arm pivoted at the top of a pole, which is used to warn train-engine drivers that the line ahead is, or is not, clear.

signature *(sig'-na-ture)*. Your name written by yourself in your own special way.

significant *(sig-nif'-i-cant)*. Having a special meaning.

silage *(si'-lage)*. Short for **ensilage** *(en'-si-lage)*. Food for animals that is stored in a silo.

silence *(si'-lence)*. Quietness; complete absence of sound.

silent *(si'-lent)*. Noiseless. It is often used to describe a person who says very little.

silhouette *(sil-hou-ette')*. An outline, generally of a person's head or body, cut from black paper.

silk. Soft, shiny dress material made from the fine strands spun by silk worms when making their cocoons.

sill. A piece of stone or wood built into a house along the lower edge of a window or door.

silly *(sil'-ly)*. Foolish.

silo *(si'-lo)*. An air-tight pit or container used for storing food for animals.

silver *(sil'-ver)*. A precious white, shiny metal used for making coins, dishes, knives, forks, jewellery, etc.

silversmith *(sil'-ver-smith)*. A person who makes or deals in articles made of silver.

silverware *(sil'-ver-ware)*. Things made of silver.

similar *(sim'-i-lar)*. Like; alike; the same.

similarity *(sim-i-lar'-i-ty)*. Likeness.

simile *(sim'-i-le)*. A comparison using the words "like" or "as". Here is a simile: "She is as sharp as a needle".

simmer *(sim'-mer)*. To boil gently.

simper *(sim'-per)*. To smile in a silly, sheepish sort of way.

simple *(sim'-ple)*. 1. Easy, as "This question is simple". 2. A person is simple when he has not much intelligence. 3. Plain and not highly ornamented, as "The pattern on this dish is pleasing because it is so simple". 3. In grammar, a simple sentence is one that has only one clause.

simultaneous *(si-mul-ta'-ne-ous)*. Happening at the same time.

sin. 1. To act contrary to the laws of God. 2. To do wrong. 3. A wrong action.

since. 1. After, as "He has not been here since Friday". 2. Because, as "Since you are tired, you must go to bed".

sincere *(sin-cere')*. Honest; genuine.

singe. To scorch; to burn slightly.

single *(sin'-gle)*. 1. One only, as "I saw a single flash". 2. For one person only, as "He has a single bed". 3. Unmarried, as "She is a single woman".

singular *(sin'-gu-lar)*. 1. In grammar, the form of a word which shows that it refers to only one thing, as "Shelf is the singular of shelves". 2. Marvellous; remarkable; extraordinary, as "A cow standing on top of a roof is a singular sight".

sinister *(sin'-is-ter)*. 1. Threatening; villainous and evil-looking. 2. Having wicked intentions.

sink. 1. To go to the bottom; to go down. 2. A wash-place, with a water tap above and usually with a waste-pipe below for draining off waste water.

sinner *(sin'-ner)*. One who sins.

sinuous *(sin'-u-ous)*. Winding; bending in and out.

sip. 1. To drink a drop or two at a time. 2. The quantity of liquid drunk each time in this way.

siphon *(si'-phon)*. 1. A bent tube used for conveying a liquid from one container to another. 2. To transfer liquid by a siphon. 3. A kind of bottle with a tube in it, used for storing bubbly liquids such as soda water.

sir. 1. A title given to a knight. If John Jones were a knight, he would not be called "Mr. Jones" but "Sir John". 2. A title of respect given to any man.

siren *(si'-ren)*. 1. A loud whistle telling of some emergency. A warning sound. 2. The sirens were legendary sea-maidens who lured sailors onto rocks with their sweet singing.

sirloin *(sir'-loin)*. A joint of beef or steak cut from the back of the animal.

site. 1. Situation; the ground upon which a building, or buildings, stand. 2. Position, as "The site of the camp was near a spring".

situated *(sit'-u-at-ed)*. Placed.

situation *(sit-u-a'-tion)*. 1. Position or location, as "We are living in a beautiful situation". 2. Work; job, as "He has left the motor business for a much better situation". 3. Condition; state of affairs; case, as "The situation now seems to be very bad for the enemy".

size. The amount of room which a thing takes up, or its degree of largeness or smallness.

skate. 1. A large, flat sea-fish. 2. A kind of shoe with a steel blade attached to the sole, which is used for travelling over ice. 3. To move on skates.

skein. A hank of wool, thread, etc.

skeleton *(skel'-e-ton)*. 1. The bony frame of the body. All the bones in the body, taken together, make up the skeleton. 2. A framework or outline. Thus the skeleton of a play is a rough draft or outline of the main events in the play. 3. A skeleton key is a key that will open many doors.

sketch. 1. A rough drawing. 2. To describe something briefly and not fully, as "He sketched his plans for the summer holiday".

skewer *(skew'-er)*. 1. A thin, pointed piece of iron or wood, used to keep roasts of meat in shape. 2. To skewer something is to run a skewer through it.

ski. One of a pair of long, narrow pieces of wood which are fastened to the shoes so that one may slide over snow.

skid. 1. When a car skids, it slides sideways out of control. 2. A piece of strong board on which something heavy will slide.

skiff. A small, light boat.

skill. The ability to do something cleverly.

skim. 1. To take the top layer from a liquid; thus cream is skimmed off milk. 2. To pass lightly over, as "The dancer skimmed lightly over the stage". 3. To read in a hurry and without much care, as "She skimmed through three novels yesterday".

skipper *(skip'-per)*. The captain of a small ship or of a sports team, etc.

skirmish *(skir'-mish)*. An unorganized fight in which only a few people are engaged.

skirt. 1. An article of female clothing worn from the waist down. 2. To go along the edge of.

skull. The bony part of the head.

skunk. A black, white-striped North American animal which emits a strong odour when annoyed.

skylark *(sky'-lark)*. 1. A bird that sings while soaring. 2. To frolic or play rough tricks.

skylight *(sky'-light)*. A window in the roof of a building.

slab. A flat, thick piece of material.

slack. 1. Relaxed, not tight; loose. 2. Inactive; not busy, as "The hotel manager expected a slack tourist season because of the bad weather".

slake. To slake a thirst is to quench it by drinking.

slam. To shut a door, etc., with a violent bang.

slander *(slan'-der)*. Untrue things said about a person with the idea of giving him trouble.

slang. 1. Words commonly used in everyday speech which are considered to be outside the standard language, such as the word "cop", used instead of "policeman". 2. A special kind of talk used by a special group of people, as "We could not understand the soldiers' slang".

slant. A line or thing that has one end lower than the other.

slap. To strike with the palm of the hand.

slash. A long cut, made with a sweeping stroke.

slate. A grey rock which splits into thin layers. Slate is often used on the roofs of houses.

slaughter *(slaugh'-ter)*. 1. To kill. 2. A killing; a massacre.

slave. 1. A person who belongs to another person. Slaves are bought and sold. 2. If you are a slave to a habit, you are unable to break the habit.

slay. To kill.

sledge. A conveyance for travelling over ice or snow. It has smooth runners that take the place of wheels.

sleek. Smooth; glossy.

sleep. 1. A state of complete, unconscious relaxation of the body. 2. To be asleep.

sleet. Rain, partly frozen and mingled with hail and snow.

sleeve. The part of a garment which fits around the arm.

sleigh. (See **sledge**.)

slender *(slen'-der)*. 1. Thin, as "He has a slender body". 2. Small, as "She has a slender income".

slice. A thin, broad piece of something.

slight. 1. Small; of little importance, as "Mary's part in the play was slight; she had one line to say". 2. Thin, or slender, as "She is not big and heavy but slight". 3. To treat with lack of respect, as "He was slighted when the others went off and left him". 4. An insult.

slim. Thin.

slime. 1. Soft, oozy mud. 2. The sticky liquid on the skins of earthworms, snails, etc. 3. Filth.

slipshod *(slip'-shod)*. 1. Wearing shoes down at the heels. 2. Untidy, neglectful.

slit. 1. A long, narrow opening. 2. To cut slits into.

sliver *(sli'-ver)*. 1. A small, pointed piece of wood or other material. 2. To cut into slivers.

slop. 1. Dirty water. 2. To spill.

slope. 1. An incline, as "The slope of the roof is very steep". 2. A hill. 3. To slope is to slant upwards or downwards, as "The mountains slope down to the sea".

sloop. A sailing boat with one mast.

slot. A long, narrow opening, through which something can be pushed, as "Put sixpence in the slot of the parking meter".

sloth. Laziness.

slouch. 1. To droop; to sit or stand with the shoulders hunched; to move in a sloppy, clumsy way. 2. A slouching position.

slough. 1. Soft, wet, muddy ground; a swamp or bog. 2. To cast off; to shed, as a snake does its skin.

slovenly *(slov'-en-ly)*. Untidy.

slow. Not fast; needing a long time to do something.

slug. 1. A garden pest that eats the young leaves of plants. It is something like a snail without a shell. 2. A small piece of metal, usually lead, which is used in a gun as a small bullet.

sluggard *(slug'-gard)*. A lazy person.

sluggish *(slug'-gish)*. Lazy; slow.

sluice. A gate built in a river or canal which can be opened or closed; thus the flow of the water can be regulated.

slum. An area or district in a town where the houses are not kept in good condition, where the people are poor and the streets are dirty.

slumber *(slum'-ber)*. 1. Sleep. 2. To sleep.

slut. A dirty and untidy woman.

sly. Artful; two-faced; doing underhand things.

smack. 1. To slap or hit, as "The mother smacked her boy because he pulled the dog's tail". 2. In "He smacked his lips", smacked his lips means made a noise with his lips while opening them. 3. A smack is a small boat, often a fishing boat.

small. Little; tiny; not large.

smart. 1. In "That bang made my hand smart", smart means hurt. 2. In "Tom is a smart boy", smart means clever and quick in all he does. 3. In "She always wears smart clothes", smart means fashionable.

smash. To break noisily into pieces.

smattering *(smat'-ter-ing)*. A little of a thing. "He has a smattering of French" means that he has a little knowledge of French.

smear. 1. A streak of something dirty, such as grease or paint. 2. To spread, as "The boy had smeared chocolate icing all over his face".

smell. 1. Sense with the nose, as "After he smelled smoke, he saw the fire". 2. Perfume or aroma, as "Don't these flowers have a lovely smell?"

smelt. 1. To melt ore to take the metal from it. 2. A small edible freshwater fish.

smile. 1. To show pleasure by stretching the mouth from side to side and turning it up at the corners. 2. A smile is a facial expression made by turning up the mouth at the corners.

smirch. To make dirty.

smite. To strike a heavy blow.

smith. A man who makes things of metal, as a blacksmith, a goldsmith, etc.

smoke. A cloud of vapour present when anything burns.

smooth. Level; even.

smother *(smo'-ther)*. 1. To kill by cutting off the breath. 2. To put out (a fire) by cutting off the air.

smoulder *(smoul'-der)*. To burn slowly, without flames.

smudge. 1. A dirty mark. 2. To blur; to smear; to make dirty.

smug. A person is said to be smug who is very pleased with himself and who thinks he knows more than others and prides himself on what he knows and does.

smuggle *(smug'-gle)*. To bring goods into the country without paying the duty that should be paid on them. (See **contraband.**)

snack. A light meal, usually eaten in a hurry.

snail. A sea creature, or a garden pest that eats young vegetation. It lives in a shell.

snake. A long, slender reptile which crawls on its belly along the ground.

snap. To break with a cracking sound.

snare. A trap of some sort for catching wild animals. A wire loop is a kind of snare for catching rabbits.

snarl. 1. To growl and show the teeth. 2. To speak in a surly manner.

snatch. To grab hold of a thing quickly.

sneak. 1. A sneak is a person who tries to harm you behind your back. 2. To sneak about is to creep about, hoping not to be seen, and to do wrong. 3. To sneak is to tell tales about a person and injure him.

sneer. To curl up your lip and to say nasty things about a person.

sneeze. An explosive sound made by the mouth and nose when something tickles or irritates the inside of the nose.

sniff. 1. To draw air through the nose in short, noisy breaths. 2. When you try the odour of something, you sniff.

snore. To breathe with hoarse grunts and rattles when sleeping.

snort. Breathing out through the nostrils in such a way that a sharp sound is made.

snout. The part of an animal's head which contains the nose and mouth.

snow. Soft, white flakes which fall to the ground in winter. Snow is made of tiny drops of frozen moisture.

snuffle *(snuf'-fle)*. To make a bubbling noise through the nose while breathing.

snug. A person is snug when he is in some place where he is sheltered from draughts and is comfortable and warm.

soak. 1. A person is soaked when he is wet to the skin. 2. When you put things to soak, you leave them in a liquid for a period of time.

soap. A substance used in washing, usually containing fat.

soar. To fly upwards.

sob. To cry with occasional gasps and heaves of the breast and shoulders.

sober *(so'-ber)*. 1. Not drunk, as "For once in his life, the drunkard came home sober". 2. Serious, as "I don't like Mr. Smith; he is as sober as a judge".

soccer *(soc'-cer)*. An abbreviation of Association Football which is a game played by two teams of eleven men in which the team score goals by kicking or heading a round ball between two upright poles.

sociable *(so'-cia-ble)*. Liking the company of other people.

society *(so-ci'-e-ty)*. 1. A business company or a gathering of people who are interested in some special work, as "The British and Foreign Bible Society". 2. In "She moves in society", society means the class of people who have rank and money. 3. People in a community.

socket *(sock'-et)*. A hollow for something to fit into, as a light-bulb socket.

sod. The ground on which the grass is rooted and grows. A piece of ground with grass attached is known as a sod.

soda *(so'-da)*. An abbreviation of washing soda, sodium carbonate.

sofa *(so'-fa)*. A couch.

soft. Giving easily to pressure; the opposite of hard.

soil. 1. To make dirty, as "He soiled his collar". 2. Earth, as "The soil in the garden is of little use for growing fruit trees".

sojourn *(so'-journ)*. To stay at a place for a while.

solace *(sol'-ace)*. Comfort; cheer.

solar *(so'-lar)*. To do with the sun, as "Because the earth revolves around the sun, it is part of the solar system".

sold. The past tense of **sell**, as "The man wishes that he had not sold his skates now that winter is here".

solder *(sol'-der)*. 1. To join two pieces of metal by using a soft, melted metal as glue. When the soft metal cools and hardens, the two pieces of metal hold together as one. 2. A kind of metal which is melted and used in soldering.

soldier *(sol'-dier)*. A man who serves in the army.

sole. 1. One; only, as "He was his mother's sole support". 2. A flat sea-fish. 3. The under part of a person's foot or shoe, as "He stepped on a nail and hurt the sole of his foot".

solemn *(sol'-emn)*. Sacred; serious; grave and ceremonious.

solicit *(so-lic'-it)*. 1. To beg earnestly. 2. To seek for business, money, votes, etc.

solicitor *(so-lic'-i-tor)*. A kind of lawyer.

solicitude *(so-lic'-i-tude)*. Anxiety; concern.

solid *(sol'-id)*. Everything in the world is a solid, a liquid or a gas; so solid in this respect means neither a liquid nor a gas. 2. A thing is solid when it is full, that is, not hollow. 3. Solid is also used to mean strong, hard and firm.

solitary *(sol'-i-tar-y)*. 1. Alone; only, as "He was the solitary survivor". 2. Lonely, as "He lived a solitary life".

solitude *(sol'-i-tude)*. Quiet; being alone; away from bustle.

solo *(so'-lo)*. 1. A piece of music performed by one person. 2. Any performance given by one person such as a dance, a flight of an aeroplane.

soluble *(sol'-u-ble)*. Anything that can be dissolved is soluble; thus sugar and salt are soluble in water.

solution *(so-lu'-tion)*. 1. A liquid with something dissolved in it. 2. The answer to a sum or a puzzle is a solution.

solve. To find the answer to a sum or problem; to find the reason for a thing that seems a mystery.

sombre *(som'-bre)*. 1. Dull or drab in colour. 2. In a gloomy or melancholy mood.

somersault *(som'-er-sault)*. To turn head over heels.

somnambulist *(som-nam'-bu-list)*. A person who walks in his sleep.

son. A boy in a family is a son of the parents.

sonata *(so-na'-ta)*. A piece of music in three or four movements to be played by one or two musical instruments. The most common form of sonata is for piano solo.

song. A short poem set to music.

sonnet *(son'-net)*. A poem having fourteen lines.

sonorous *(so-no'-rous)*. Having a loud, deep sound.

soot. The black bits which result from burning coal, wood, etc. Soot forms on the inside of chimneys and stove-pipes.

soothe. To calm; to comfort.

soothsayer *(sooth'-say-er)*. A person who says he can tell what is going to happen.

soporific *(sop-or-if'-ic)*. Causing sleep. "In summer, the weather is sometimes soporific and makes you feel sleepy."

soprano *(so-pra'-no)*. A singer who can sing high notes. Women and boys, but not men, may have soprano voices.

sorcerer *(sor'-cer-er)*. A magician. What he practises is **sorcery.**

sordid *(sor'-did)*. Mean; dirty; poorly kept.

sore. 1. Painful. 2. A small wound in the skin.

sorrow *(sor'-row)*. Sadness; grief.

sorry *(sor'-ry)*. 1. To be sorry is to regret something you have done or to sympathize with someone's misfortune. 2. Wretched or miserable, as "The wet kitten was a sorry sight".

sort. 1. In "I must sort my stamps", sort means arrange in their groups or classes. 2. In "What sort of boy is he?" sort means kind or type. 3. In "He is out of sorts", out of sorts means ill or ill-tempered.

sought. The past tense of **seek,** as "He sought everywhere for his pencil.

soul. The spiritual part of man.

sound. 1. That which can be heard, as a noise. 2. Whole; healthy; in good condition. 3. To give forth a sound, as "Let the trumpets sound".

soup. A liquid food which is made by boiling meat or vegetables or both in water until the water becomes flavoured.

sour. 1. A thing is sour when it has a bitter taste. 2. A person is sour when he is often bad-tempered.

source. 1. The beginning of a river; the place where a river rises. 2. The starting point of a thing; thus, "I wonder what was the source of that rumour" means "I wonder how that rumour started".

south. The opposite direction to north.

souvenir *(sou-ve-nir')*. A keepsake; a thing which a person keeps to help him remember something; thus, if you visit the seaside and want to remember the visit, you buy something there that will remind you of it.

sovereign *(so'-ve-reign)*. 1. Chief; supreme. 2. The king or queen of a country. 3. To do with royalty, as "the sovereign power". 4. An obsolete British gold coin.

sow. 1. To put seeds in the ground. 2. A female pig.

spacious *(spa'-cious)*. Having plenty of room or **space.**

spade. A shovel used for digging in gardens, fields, etc.

spaghetti *(spa-ghet'-ti)*. Long, thin strips of macaroni eaten with tomato sauce and cheese.

span. 1. The space between a man's thumb and his little finger when stretched out, usually nine inches. 2. A space of time. 3. To extend across; thus "The bridge spanned the river". 4. The portion of a bridge between supports.

spangles *(span'-gles)*. Tiny pieces of bright metal used for ornaments; as "Her skirt was trimmed with rows of spangles".

spaniel *(span'-iel)*. A kind of dog, used for hunting or kept as a pet, which has long hair and drooping ears.

spanner *(span'-ner)*. A hand tool for tightening or loosening nuts on bolts.

spare. 1. To give away something that is useful to you but is more than you need. 2. To do without, as "Spare the rod and spoil the child". 3. In "I have a spare wheel on my car", spare means extra. 4. In "She is a spare little woman", spare means thin.

spark. 1. A particle of fire. 2. To give off sparks of fire.

sparkle *(spar'-kle)*. To glisten; to glitter; to twinkle.

sparrow *(spar'-row)*. A small bird belonging to the finch family.

spasm. A sudden tightening of the muscles, causing a kind of cramp.

spatter *(spat'-ter)*. To scatter liquid in small drops.

spawn. 1. The eggs of frogs, toads, fish, etc., when laid. 2. To lay eggs, said of frogs, fish, etc.

speak. To utter sounds; to talk.

spear. A weapon with a sharp, pointed head and a long shaft.

special *(spe'-cial)*. Of a kind that is not usual, as "He uses a special kind of toothpaste", or "A special train will run for the Boy Scouts".

specially *(spe'-cial-ly)*. Particularly, as "I specially wanted to see you yesterday".

species *(spe'-cies)*. A kind, sort or group of things; thus, "I have found a species of orchid that I have never seen before", meaning a kind of orchid.

specification *(spec-i-fi-ca'-tion)*. Complete information about the details of a thing; thus the specifications of a house would include information about the number of rooms, their size, where situated, how equipped and so on.

specify *(spec'-i-fy)*. To mention particularly, as "When I bought the horse, I specified that it was wanted for heavy work".

specimen *(spec'-i-men)*. One article or a part of an article used for the purpose of showing what all the others or the rest are like; thus an inspector may look at your composition book to see a specimen of your handwriting. If that were good, he would suppose that all your writing was good.

speck. A tiny spot or piece of a thing, as "He has a speck of dust in his eye".

speckled *(speck'-led)*. Marked with various spots; thus chickens are often speckled and so are many snakes.

spectacle *(spec'-ta-cle)*. A sight; a public show.

spectacles *(spec'-tac-les)*. Eye-glasses.

spectator *(spec-ta'-tor)*. A person who looks at something.

spectre *(spec'-tre)*. A ghost.

speculate *(spec'-u-late)*. 1. To think about a thing and turn it over in your mind. 2. To buy and sell (especially shares) in the hope of making profit.

speech. 1. The power of being able to talk. 2. A talk on a certain subject, such as the speeches made by public men at banquets.

speed. 1. The rate at which something is moving. 2. Quick movement; swiftness.

speedometer *(speed-om'-e-ter)*. A gauge or instrument which tells the speed at which a vehicle moves.

speedway *(speed'-way)*. A road or track for racing, usually for cars and motor-cycles.

spell. 1. To say or write the letters that make up a word. 2. A spell is also a magic charm, as "The fairy wove a spell which put the princess in a delightful sleep". 3. A spell is a length of time, as "I think we are in for a spell of bad weather".

spend. To use up, generally money or time.

spendthrift *(spend'-thrift)*. A person who spends his money as soon as he gets it.

sphere. 1. The globe; the world; any round object like the world; thus a ball is a sphere. 2. The area in which a person lives and works, and the people with whom he mixes, all go to make up his sphere of life.

Sphinx. A large statue in Egypt which has a man's head on the body of a lion.

spice. A sweet-smelling plant which is used to flavour food. Pepper, cloves, ginger and nutmeg are spices.

spider *(spi'-der)*. An insect-like animal with eight legs. Spiders spin webs.

spike. 1. A sharp-pointed part, usually slender. 2. The top part of a piece of corn or grain, that is, the ear. 3. A large nail.

spill. To allow the contents of a vessel to fall out, usually by accident.

spin. 1. To turn a thing around quickly, as "See me spin my top". 2. To turn round and round, as "The record spins at the rate of 45 r.p.m.". 3. To draw out in threads. When wool or cotton is spun, its fibres are twisted together and drawn out in threads. 4. To spin a yarn is to tell a story.

spinach *(spin'-ach)*. A green, leafy plant, the leaves of which are cooked and eaten.

spine. 1. The backbone. 2. Spines are thorny points on such plants as rosebushes or such animals as porcupines.

spiral *(spi'-ral)*. 1. Coiled; turning round and round like a circular staircase that winds upward. 2. A coil; something which is spiral in shape.

spire. The structure that comes to a point above a tower.

spirit *(spir'-it)*. 1. The soul of a person. 2. Beings such as ghosts and fairies are spirits. 3. Distilled liquors as brandy and whisky are spirits. 4. A person is said to have a good spirit when he has a good nature, and he is in good spirits when he is good-tempered.

spiteful *(spite'-ful)*. A person is spiteful who does things purposely to hurt another person. Spiteful people have **spite** or ill-will against those who do not please them.

splash. To dabble about in water; to cause the water or liquid to scatter or fly about.

splendid *(splen'-did)*.   Magnificent; brilliant; glorious.

splendour *(splen'-dour)*.   Great brilliance; pomp.

splice.   To join two ends of a piece of rope by undoing the ends and weaving the separate strands together.

splinter *(splin'-ter)*.   1. A small, sharp piece of wood, metal, glass, ice, etc.   2. To shatter in splinters.   3. A tiny sliver of wood, etc., such as you sometimes discover in your hand or finger and remove with a needle.

split.   1. To divide, as "He split the pack of cards into two portions".   2. To crack or break, as "He split each log into two".

spoil.   1. To damage, as "He spoiled his shoes by kicking with the toes".   2. Spoils are things taken that do not belong to those that take them, as "The thief rammed his spoils into a large pocket and walked away as if nothing had happened".   3. To turn sour or rotten.   4. A spoiled child is one whose character has been ruined by parents who have given him too much and demanded too little.

spokesman *(spokes'-man)*.   A person who speaks not only for himself but for others as well, as "Mr. Jones acted as spokesman for all the people living in our road and went to the Council about the dangerous condition of the pavement".

sponge.   1. The porous tissues of a dried sea creature which easily absorb liquids and are used for household cleaning, etc.   2. Any artificial substance with the same properties.   3. To wipe with a sponge.   4. To live of others.

spontaneously *(spon-ta'-ne-ous-ly)*.   Happening in an unforced way and without plan.   When you do something spontaneously, you do it of your own free will, without being told or made to do it.

spook.   A ghost.

spool.   A cylinder on which materials such as wool and cotton are wound.   A photographic spool has sensitized film wound on it; a spool in a sewing machine carries thread, etc.

spoon.   A ladle-shaped utensil used at table, etc., for raising small quantities of liquid.   A spoon is often used as a measure; we then speak of **spoonfuls** (not spoonsful).

sport.   1. Fun; play; game; amusement.   The word is sometimes used to mean some form of hunting.   2. To make sport of a person is to laugh and make fun of him.

spot. 1. In "She has a spot on her dress", spot means a dirty mark. 2. In "Isn't this a delightful spot", spot means place. 3. In "My tie is black with white spots", spots means marks, probably round marks. 4. In "Have you spotted where he is?" spotted means noticed.

spouse. A husband or a wife.

spout. 1. To spout out liquid is to shoot it out in a stream. 2. The spout of a kettle, etc., is the tube through which the water is poured.

sprain. An injury to a muscle or joint.

sprat. A small sea-fish about the same size as a sardine.

sprawl. 1. To lie or sit down and stretch out the arms and legs in a careless, sloppy way. 2. To spread out ungracefully. Vines and plants may sprawl; your handwriting may sprawl.

spray. 1. A small piece of a plant, such as a stalk bearing one or two flowers and a few leaves. 2. To force a liquid into the air in small drops. 3. Liquid in the air in small drops, such as sea-spray, etc.

spread. To make whatever is spread cover a larger area; thus a small piece of butter may be made to cover a slice of bread by spreading; a tin of paint may be spread over the front of a house by a brush, and a piece of news may be spread by people telling one another.

sprig. A small piece of a branch, as a sprig of holly.

sprightly *(spright'-ly).* Lively; brisk; gay; spirited.

spring. 1. One of the four seasons, the others being summer, autumn and winter. 2. To jump, as "Frogs spring into the air when they hop". 3. An elastic device usually of bent or coiled metal, such as a watch spring or a car spring.

sprinkle *(sprin'-kle).* To scatter in drops or in small pieces.

sprout. 1. To start growing, as "My seeds have begun to sprout in the garden". 2. A bud, as Brussels sprouts.

spruce. 1. An evergreen tree with needle-shaped leaves. 2. Neat.

spur. A sharp, pointed piece of metal worn on the heels of a rider. By digging his spurs into his horse's sides, the rider makes the horse go faster. Thus, a spur has come to mean anything that urges a person on to greater efforts, and to spur on means to urge on or encourage.

spurious *(spu'-ri-ous).* Faked; not genuine.

spurn. To look down on; to scorn; to kick.

spy. 1. To watch secretly; to watch without allowing yourself to be seen. 2. A spy is a person who secretly watches others to see what they are doing and then gives the information to their enemies.

squabble *(squab'-ble)*. To quarrel noisily over something that is not important.

squad. 1. A small company of men drawn up in order for drill or inspection. 2. Any small body of men engaged in some common task, as a police squad or a squad of soldiers.

squalid *(squal'-id)*. Poor and dirty.

squall. 1. A sudden strong wind. 2. To yell in the way a fretful baby does.

squander *(squan'-der)*. To spend in a wasteful way.

square. 1. A shape having four equal sides and four angles that are right angles. 2. An open space in a town, with perhaps houses on all sides. 3. The square of a number is that number multiplied by itself; thus the square of 5 is 25. 4. To square up something is to settle it; thus to square one's debts is to pay them.

squash. To crush a thing flat, as "The fat lady squashed his hat when she sat on it".

squat. To sit on the ground with legs bent and toes under the body.

squaw. A North American Indian woman or wife.

squawk. 1. A harsh cry, as is made by a chicken or a crow. 2. To make such a cry.

squeak. 1. A short, shrill noise. 2. To make such a noise, as an unoiled hinge does.

squeal. To cry out sharply as a pig does.

squeamish *(squeam'-ish)*. Easily shocked by anything which is improper or unpleasant.

squeeze. 1. To apply pressure to; to hug. 2. To obtain by pressing, as to squeeze juice from an orange.

squint. 1. To look with cross-eyes, i.e. both eyes not seeming to be directed to the same spot. 2. To look with the eyes half shut so as to protect them from the sun or wind.

squire. Country gentleman.

squirm. To wriggle; to twist.

squirrel *(squir'-rel)*. A rodent that lives in trees and has a bushy, upturned tail.

squirt. 1. To shoot out liquid in a stream as from a syringe or water-pistol. 2. A short spurt of water.

stab. To make a hole in something by means of a pointed knife, dagger, etc. To wound.

stable *(sta'-ble)*. 1. A place in which horses are kept. 2. A thing is stable when it stands firm.

stack. 1. A carefully built-up pile of hay, straw, etc. 2. A pile of things; thus a chimney stack is a pile of bricks. 3. To stack things is to heap them up in some neat order.

stadium *(sta'-di-um)*. A large oval or U-shaped building with no roof, which faces a field on which games are played. A stadium has rows of seats on which people sit to watch games.

staff. 1. A stick, rod, etc., used for walking. 2. The people who work as a body and who attend to some business or other concern; thus the staff of a school consists of the head teacher and the assistant teachers. 3. In written music, the five lines and the spaces coming between.

stag. The male of the red deer.

stage. 1. A platform, such as that in theatres on which the actors play their parts. 2. In "I dug the garden by easy stages", the idea is that the garden was not dug all at once, but a little at a time.

stagger *(stag'-ger)*. To reel from side to side when walking.

stagnant *(stag'-nant)*. Not flowing or running; therefore, used to describe water which is impure from standing still.

staid. Being of a steady, quiet nature.

stain. 1. A spot of colour which is difficult to remove. 2. When a piece of furniture is stained, a special colour is applied to it. 3. Stained glass is coloured glass.

stairs. A series of steps for moving from one level to another.

stake. 1. A stick driven into the ground. 2. In gambling, the stakes are the money which is bet.

stalactite *(sta'-lac-tite)*. A formation of calcium carbonate that hangs like an icicle from the roof of a cave.

stalagmite *(sta'-lag-mite)*. A formation of calcium carbonate, usually in the shape of a cone, that stands up from the floor of a cave.

stale. Old; not new.

stalk. 1. The stem of a plant; the part that has the flower on it. 2. To approach a wild animal without being seen is to stalk the animal. 3. To walk in a stiff, proud way, as "He stalked down the road without speaking".

stall. 1. A kind of table on which goods are spread out for sale. 2. The place in a stable where a horse is tied.

stallion *(stal'-lion).* A male horse.

stalwart *(stal'-wart).* Tall, strong and brave.

stammer *(stam'-mer).* To talk in a halting way by repeating one syllable before going on to the next.

stamp. 1. To bring the foot down with a bang. 2. A small piece of paper showing that the postage due on a letter or parcel has been paid. 3. To make a mark by printing; to imprint. 4. Something used to print with, as a rubber stamp.

stampede *(stam-pede').* A headlong mad dash of frightened animals; any mad and wild rush of people.

stand. 1. To be erect or upright. 2. A pedestal on which another object rests. 3. When you cannot stand a person. you are unable to tolerate him, and when you have a pain which you cannot stand, you are unable to bear the pain.

standard *(stand'-ard).* 1. A flag. 2. Something by which other things are judged, as a writing standard. 3. Ordinary; regular.

stanza *(stan'-za).* A verse of a poem.

staple *(sta'-ple).* 1. An important or principal article of produce, such as wheat. 2. A paper fastener. 3. A U-shaped piece of metal, sharpened at both ends, used for securing wires or ropes by being driven in like a nail.

star. 1. A sun, that is, a heavenly body that gives off light and heat. 2. A person who has gained great fame on the stage or in films.

starboard *(star'-board).* The right side of a ship, facing forward. Port is the left side.

starch. 1. A material used for stiffening clothes after they have been washed. 2. To starch clothes is to stiffen them with starch. 3. A food element, found in potatoes, bread, beans and many other foods.

stare. To look with a fixed gaze.

stark. 1. Completely, as "The poor fellow was stark mad". 2. Stark also means stiff.

start. 1. To begin to do something, as "She started to brush her hair". 2. A sudden movement, as "The noise was so terrific that I awoke with a start".

starter *(start'-er)*. A device or person which starts something or someone in motion. The starter in a car starts the engine turning.

startle *(star'-tle)*. To frighten a person by doing something unexpected.

starvation *(star-va'-tion)*. Suffering caused by lack of food. A person may die of starvation.

starve. To die through not having enough food.

state. 1. The condition of a person or thing, as "The country is in a state of unrest". 2. Name, tell or give, as "Now you must state why your homework has been neglected again". 3. A body of people within a definite region with a government of its own. Thus France is a state; the United States of America is a combination of states under one government.

statement *(state'-ment)*. When you give an oral or a written report, you make a statement; thus a business firm makes a monthly statement in which it states or gives an account of expenses, earnings and profits.

statesman *(states'-man)*. One who devotes himself to looking after the government of his country.

static *(stat'-ic)*. At rest; still.

station *(sta'-tion)*. 1. In "I met him at the railway station", station means a stopping place for trains. 2. In "He took the man to the police station", station means a building in and from which policemen work. 3. In "His station in life is that of a lord", station means position or rank. 4. To place, as "Three soldiers were stationed at the door".

stationary *(sta'-tion-a-ry)*. Not moving; fixed.

stationer *(sta'-tion-er)*. A man who sells note-paper, writing material, cards, string, etc. What he sells is known as **stationery.**

statistics *(sta-tis'-tics)*. Figures that help to prove things about what is happening in a country; thus the statistics or figures about marriages show whether more people were married last year than the year before.

statue *(stat'-ue)*. A figure or shape made in stone, metal, etc., to represent a person, animal, etc.

stature *(stat'-ure)*. The height of a person.

statute *(stat'-ute)*. A law.

staunch. 1. Strong; firm; loyal. 2. To stop the flow of blood.

stay. 1. Not to move, but to remain. 2. In "Our stay here has been very pleasant", stay refers to the time spent at the place. 3. Any rope fixed to something to prevent it moving is a stay.

steadfast *(stead'-fast)*. Constant; not changing.

steady *(stead'-y)*. 1. Firm; unmoving. 2. Reliable, as "John is a steady worker". 3. Regular; even; not changing much, as "We can now go ahead at a steady pace".

steak. A slice of beef that is fried or broiled.

steal. 1. To take something which doesn't belong to you. 2. To move quietly so that no one will hear, as "She stole into her room".

stealth. Secrecy, as "He obtained the ring by stealth; he took it, in fact, while no one was looking".

stealthy *(stealth'-y)*. Furtive or secret.

steam. Water that has been turned into a gas or vapour by heating.

steamer *(steam'-er)*. A boat that is driven by steam.

steed. A horse.

steel. Iron that has been treated with carbon and thereby toughened and hardened.

steep. 1. Rising sharply, as "The boy climbed the steep mountain-side". 2. To soak, as "She allowed the clothes to steep in the hot water".

steeple *(stee'-ple)*. The high tower on a church which usually has a spire on top of it.

steer. 1. To guide, as "The pilot steered his plane into the hangar". 2. A young ox.

stem. 1. The part of a plant which supports the leaves and flowers. 2. Anything which is long and narrow is a stem, such as the stem of a wine-glass. 3. To stem a stream is to dam it or block the flow.

stench. A very unpleasant, unhealthy smell.

stencil *(sten'-cil)*. A thin sheet of metal, paper, etc., with holes cut in it to form a pattern or words. By placing the sheet on a surface and brushing ink, paint, etc., over it, the pattern or words are easily transferred to the surface.

stepfather *(step'-fa-ther)*. If a person's father dies and his mother marries again, the new husband is the person's step-father; also, the person is the new husband's **stepson**. **Step-mothers** and **stepdaughters** are similarly related. If the person's mother married a second time and the man she married already had a son, the son would be the person's **stepbrother**; if he already had a daughter, she would be the person's **stepsister.**

sterile *(ster'-ile).* 1. Not fertile, as "That tree never has any fruit on it—it is sterile". 2. Free of germs, as "That wound is healing nicely; it will continue to improve if you keep it sterile". A wound and its dressings can be kept sterile if they are **sterilized.**

sterling *(ster'-ling).* 1. English money. 2. Standard of fineness of precious metals, such as silver and gold. 3. In "He is a man of sterling qualities", sterling means honest and fine.

stern. 1. The back part of a boat. 2. Severe and harsh, as "His appearance is stern".

stew. 1. To cook by boiling slowly. 2. Stew is meat, vegetables, etc., boiled slowly.

steward *(stew'-ard).* 1. A servant who looks after his master's property. 2. On a boat or aeroplane, a steward looks after the comfort of the passengers.

stewardess *(stew'-ard-ess).* A female steward who serves the passengers on a ship or aeroplane.

stick. 1. A long, narrow piece of wood. 2. A piece of wood for a special purpose, such as a hockey stick. 3. Anything shaped like a stick of wood, as a stick of wax. 4. When you stick a stamp on a letter, you fasten the stamp by wetting the glue on the back of the stamp. 5. When you stick to a job, you continue working at it.

stickler *(stick'-ler).* A person who is excessively careful over details.

stiff. 1. Not able to be bent, as a stiff leg. A stiff neck, finger or leg is often sore. 2. A stiff person is one who finds it difficult to relax.

stifle *(sti'-fle).* To smother.

stigma *(stig'-ma).* A disgrace or a stain on one's character. If a man were sent to prison, it would be a stigma on him.

stile. The steps fitted in a fence or hedge to allow people to climb over without allowing cattle, etc., to stray from field to field.

still. 1. Without noise or motion; quiet; unmoving. 2. Nevertheless; even so; yet, as "Although he broke his leg, he is still going to ski this winter".

stimulate *(stim'-u-late)*. To excite; to make lively; to rouse.

sting. 1. To cause a sharp pain or smarting feeling, as "The soap stung his eyes", or "The lashing hail stung our faces", or "The bee stung the baby". 2. Bees and wasps, etc., have a small sharp point on the tips of their abdomens with which they can sting their enemies. These little points are called stings. Some plants, such as stinging-nettles, also have stings.

stingy *(stin'-gy)*. Said of a person who does not like to spend his money or give any away. Misers are stingy.

stint. 1. To restrict; to limit the amount, as "The children looked half starved, and we believe it was because their mother stinted the food". 2. A share of work, as "Let us all do our stint and the dishes will soon be done".

stipend *(sti'-pend)*. The salary, wages or payment for regular work which a person earns.

stipulate *(stip'-u-late)*. To demand something as a condition of a bargain. For example, "He stipulated that the house must have a green door" means that he stated that he would not buy the house unless it had a green door.

stir. 1. To move, as "Not a creature was stirring". 2. To mix with a spoon or fork, as when a cook stirs the cáke mixture before baking it. 3. To excite, as "He stirred the feelings of discontent among the crew".

stirrup *(stir'-rup)*. A thin metal, wooden or leather support for the foot of a person on horseback. The stirrups hang from the saddle.

stitch. 1. A stitch is the tiny loop of thread made in material when sewing. 2. To stitch is to make these loops. 3. A stitch in the side is a sharp pain that attacks suddenly.

stoat. A long-bodied animal of the weasel family. In northern areas, its coat turns white in winter, when it is known as the ermine.

stock. 1. The articles which a shop has for sale; thus the contents of a shop are the shopkeeper's stock. 2. Cattle and other animals on a farm are called stock. 3. Stocks and shares are certificates which show that the person named on them has invested money in a business. 4. In "He comes from Irish stock", stock means ancestors. 5. The wood in which the barrel of a rifle is fixed. 6. When you stock your kitchen, you supply it with all the necessary things such as salt, sugar, flour, etc.

stockade *(stock-ade')*. A fence made of strong poles for protection.

stocking *(stock'-ing)*. A close-fitting covering of wool, cotton, silk or nylon for the foot and leg.

stoker *(stok'-er)*. A man who feeds fires for engines on trains or boats.

stole. 1. The long strip of silk worn by clergymen round the neck and over the shoulders. 2. A lady's scarf. 3. The past tense of·**steal.**

stomach *(stom'-ach)*. The part of the body in which food is received and digested.

stone. 1. A piece of rock. 2. A precious gem. 3. The hard seed of certain fruits. 4. A British measure of weight equal to 14 lbs.

stool. A seat having no back to lean against.

stoop. To bend the body forward.

stop. 1. To halt. 2. Not to continue doing something, as "I stopped reading". 3. To close up something, as "He stopped the crack under the door and prevented the draught coming in".

stopper *(stop'-per)*. A plug put in a bottle, barrel, etc., to prevent the contents from escaping.

storage *(stor'-age)*. 1. The putting away of goods. 2. The place where the goods are kept.

store. 1. To put things away for later use. 2. A shop selling a variety of different goods is called a store.

storey *(sto'-rey)*. A floor of a building that has several rooms on it, as "Our flat is on the third storey of a building that has eight storeys".

stork. A large bird with long legs, a long neck and a long bill.

storm. 1. Very bad weather with heavy rain and violent wind. 2. To storm a place is to attack it with great force.

story *(sto'-ry)*. 1. A tale. 2. A falsehood.

stout. 1. A stout person is large and strongly built. 2. A person with a stout heart is brave. 3. A stout club is a solid, firm stick.

stove. An apparatus, usually made of metal, which generates heat for cooking or heating.

straddle *(strad'-dle)*. To sit astride.

straggle *(strag'-gle)*. 1. To spread out in a way that has no order about it. 2. To wander; to stray.

straight. 1. A straight line is a line that follows the shortest route between two points. 2. To go straight to a place is to go there at once. 3. A person is straight when he is honest.

strain. 1. To exert oneself sufficiently to hurt, as "His back was sore because he strained himself when carrying the heavy weight". 2. To separate solids from liquids, as "The cook strained the greens before sending them to the table". 3. To tighten, as "The wind strained the rope". 4. A strain may be a few bars of music.

strait. A narrow passage of water linking two larger bodies of water.

strand. 1. A shore. 2. A roadway running by the edge of water. 3. A single thread among the many that are plaited together to make a length of sewing cotton, string, cord, etc. 4. To be stranded means to be without money or help.

strange. An unknown thing, person or sound is strange.

stranger *(stran'-ger)*. A person who is not known to you.

strangle *(stran'-gle)*. To kill by pressing on the throat, so preventing a person or animal from breathing.

strap. A long narrow strip of leather or cloth.

straw. 1. The dried stem of grain after threshing. 2. Artificial straws for sucking up drinks are made of paper or plastic.

strawberry *(straw'-ber-ry)*. A small, juicy, red fruit.

stray. To wander off.

streak. 1. A long, narrow mark of colour different from its surroundings. 2. To run swiftly.

stream. 1. A small river. 2. A flowing of any liquid, as "Streams of oil rushed out of the ground". 3. To flow; to pour, as "At five o'clock the workers stream out of the factory". 4. "Upstream" means against the current; "downstream" means with the current.

streamer *(stream'-er)*. A flag that is long and narrow.

streamlined *(stream'-lined)*. So shaped that it offers very little resistance to the air. A steam-engine, or car, for instance, with as few parts as possible sticking out from the body, is streamlined.

street. A road in a town or city with buildings on both sides.

strength. The quality of being strong, as "An elephant has great strength".

strenuous *(stren'-u-ous)*. Energetic; vigorous; hard-working; needing great effort.

stretch. 1. If you stretch your arms and legs, you extend them, or reach them out, as far as they will go. 2. If you stretch a sweater you pull it out of shape. If you stretch elastic you pull it to make it longer than it was. 3. To spread out; to extend; to reach, as "The Sahara Desert stretches for hundreds of miles across Africa". 4. A stretch of land is an expanse of land; a stretch of time is an extent of time.

stretcher *(stretch'-er)*. A kind of emergency bed for carrying sick people. It is made by stretching canvas or some other material over a wooden frame.

strew. To scatter.

strict. 1. Severe, as "He is a strict master". 2. Perfect or absolute, as "You must pay strict attention to what you are told".

stride. 1. A long step. 2. To take such steps.

strife. A conflict or struggle.

strike. 1. To hit. 2. To make things by stamping them out of metal, as "At the Mint, they strike new coins". 3. If the workers at some factory were dissatisfied with their wages or the conditions under which they worked, they might strike to obtain higher wages or a change in conditions. Strike here means all stop work together. 4. In "The band will soon strike up", strike up means begin. 5. In "When the clock strikes, it will be time to go", strikes means sounds.

string. Thin cord.

strip. 1. A long, narrow piece of something thin, as a strip of cloth. 2. To take away from; to steal from, as "He was stripped of all he possessed and turned out into the street to beg". 3. To undress.

stripe. A narrow strip which is different from the rest of the surface, as the stripe on the leg of a postman's trousers.

strive. To try.

stroke. 1. In "He killed the snake with one stroke", stroke means blow. 2. In "He made bold strokes with the pen", strokes means marks. 3. In "The old man suffered a stroke", stroke means a sudden attack of illness, usually with paralysis. 4. In "He stroked the cat gently", stroked means that he moved his hand over the cat gently.

stroll. To go for a leisurely walk.

stronghold *(strong'-hold)*. A fortress or castle.

struck. The past tense of **strike,** as "He struck at the ball and missed it".

structure *(struc'-ture)*. 1. A building. 2. The way in which a thing of several parts is composed; thus we speak of the structure of the human body, meaning the way the different organs are arranged.

struggle *(strug'-gle)*. To try very hard; to make a great effort.

stubble *(stub'-ble)*. The dried stalks left sticking out of the ground after grain has been cut.

stubborn *(stub'-born)*. Obstinate and unreasonable.

stucco *(stuc'-co)*. A kind of plaster with fine stones which is used on the outside of buildings.

student *(stu'-dent)*. A person who studies at a university, college, etc. Also, a person who studies a subject because of his interest in it.

studio *(stu'-di-o)*. A room in which an artist paints pictures or in which a radio or television programme or a film is made.

study *(stud'-y)*. 1. To learn by reading over and over again. 2. A room set apart for reading or studying. 3. To examine a thing with care, as "She studied the grocer's bill".

stuff. 1. Material; cloth. 2. To stuff something is to fill it to the utmost, as "Fred stuffed his mouth with sweets".

stuffy *(stuff'-y)*. 1. A room is stuffy when the windows are shut and there is no fresh air in it. 2. Often, a person is said to be stuffy when he is too prim or conventional or when he is behind the times and refuses to catch up with new ideas.

stumble *(stum'-ble)*. To fall or nearly fall by catching the foot in something or stubbing the toe; to trip.

stump. 1. The bottom part of a tree which remains after the tree has been cut down. 2. The part of a leg or arm which remains after an amputation.

stung. The past tense of **sting,** as "The bee stung his arm".

stunt. 1. A daring trick or performance, such as walking along a tight-rope. 2. To slow down or stop the growth of; a dwarf is stunted.

stupid *(stu'-pid)*. Dull; foolish; lacking in intelligence or understanding.

stupor *(stu'-por)*. Dazed condition.

sturdy *(stur'-dy)*. Strong; hardy; fit.

stutter *(stut'-ter)*. To stammer. (See **stammer.**) To talk in a halting way by repeating sounds and syllables.

sty. 1. A place where pigs are housed. 2. A boil or sore on the edge of the eyelid.

style. 1. Fashion, as "She dresses in style". 2. The way a thing is done is the style in which it is done.

stylish *(styl'-ish).* Fashionable.

suave. 1. Polite and pleasing in manner. 2. Gentle and soothing.

subdue *(sub-due').* 1. To overcome; to conquer. 2. To quiet or soften. In "The light was subdued", subdued means toned down, not glaring.

subject *(sub'-ject).* 1. A subject of a state is a member of that state who comes under its government. 2. A branch of learning: "Geometry is a subject taught in school". 3. In grammar, the subject of a sentence is the person or thing about which the sentence tells. 4. The theme of a poem or story. 5. Subject also means liable, as "Mary is subject to headaches". 6. *(sub-ject').* To subdue or bring under someone's rule, as "The Austrians were subjected to German rule".

sublime *(sub-lime').* Majestic; noble; lofty.

submarine *(sub'-ma-rine).* 1. Under the sea. 2. A type of vessel that can travel under the surface of the water.

submerge *(sub-merge').* To cover with water; to go under water.

submit *(sub-mit').* To give in; to yield.

subordinate *(sub-or'-di-nate).* Of lesser rank or importance; dependent.

subscribe *(sub-scribe').* 1. To sign your name to. 2. To agree to. 3. To pay or give something, as subscribing to a newspaper so that it will be sent to you regularly, or subscribing to a charity. The money sent in this way is a **subscription** *(sub-scrip'-tion).*

subsequent *(sub'-se-quent).* Following.

subside *(sub-side').* To sink; to settle down.

subsidy *(sub'-si-dy).* A payment of money by a government to assist an undertaking that is thought to be in the public interest.

subsistence *(sub-sist'-ence).* Anything that helps a person to live, such as food and money.

subsoil *(sub'-soil).* The soil or earth that is found under the top layer of earth; thus if you dug deeply in the garden you would come to the subsoil.

substance *(sub'-stance)*. 1. The basic material of which a thing is made, as "Wood and coal are the same substance". 2. The important or essential part of anything is the substance. 3. A person of substance is a person of wealth.

substantial *(sub-stan'-tial)*. 1. Strong and solid, as "The bridge was built of substantial material". 2. Well off, as "He is a substantial man", meaning that he has plenty of money. 3. Real; thus books and men are substantial things, because they are real; but ghosts are not substantial since they are not real.

substitute *(sub'-sti-tute)*. A thing that replaces another thing; thus some people use margarine as a substitute for butter.

subterfuge *(sub'-ter-fuge)*. A ruse or trick to avoid something. Thus, a miser will wear shabby clothes and pretend to be poor so that he will not be asked to give to charity. His pretence is merely a subterfuge.

subterranean *(sub-ter-ra'-ne-an)*. Under the ground.

subtle *(sub'-tle)*. 1. Crafty; cunning. 2. Elusive; hard to grasp or trace; delicate; refined. Thus, "a subtle flavour", "subtle distinctions".

subtract *(sub-tract')*. To take away.

subtraction *(sub-trac'-tion)*. A taking away; the act of subtracting one number from another.

suburbs *(sub'-urbs)*. The outskirts of a town; the area lying on the edge of a town.

subway *(sub'-way)*. An underground road, usually for pedestrians.

succeed *(suc-ceed')*. 1. To follow after; to come next, as Elizabeth II succeeded George VI. 2. To manage to do something you have tried to do, as "He succeeded in getting to the top of the mountain".

success *(suc-cess')*. A favourable result; prosperity; good fortune.

succour *(suc'-cour)*. 1. Help. 2. To help.

succulent *(suc'-cu-lent)*. Juicy.

succumb *(suc-cumb')*. 1. To give way or yield. 2. To die.

suck. 1. To draw something into the mouth. 2. To put something into the mouth and let it melt slowly. 3. To draw up, as "Plants suck up moisture from the ground".

sudden *(sud'-den)*. Unexpected; abrupt; without warning.

sue. 1. To take a person to the law courts and ask for money from him because of some damage he has done to you. 2. To beg or ask for, as "They sued for peace".

suet *(su'-et)*. The hard white fat around the kidneys of beef and mutton, which is used in cooking.

suffer *(suf'-fer)*. 1. To be in pain or trouble, as "He suffered a great deal with his broken arm". 2. To allow, as "Suffer little children to come unto Me".

suffice *(suf-fice')*. To be enough, as "One lump of sugar will suffice".

sufficient *(suf-fi'-cient)*. Enough; adequate.

suffix *(suf'-fix)*. A syllable added to the end of a word to make a new word. Thus, if you add the suffix -*ness* to the end of *sweet*, you make *sweetness*.

suffocate *(suf'-fo-cate)*. To smother; to choke by stopping the breath.

sugar *(sug'-ar)*. A sweet substance which is extracted from sugar canes and beets.

suggest *(sug-gest')*. To hint; to offer a piece of advice, as "He suggested that I should have the tooth out".

suicide *(su'-i-cide)*. 1. The act of killing oneself on purpose. 2. A person who kills himself.

suit. 1. A coat, waistcoat and trousers, or a coat and skirt. 2. A law case. 3. To go well with, as "The blue dress suits her fair colouring". 4. One of the four sets of cards which together make up a pack. The suits are spades, hearts, diamonds and clubs, and there are thirteen cards in each suit. 5. Wooing, with intention to marry, as "John's suit was successful and soon he and Mary were married".

suitable *(suit'-a-ble)*. Proper or fitting.

suite. The word means a set of things, as a suite of furniture, or a group of people, as the king's suite, meaning his attendants.

sulky *(sulk'-y)*. Sullen.

sullen *(sul'-len)*. In bad humour; morose; gloomy.

sully *(sul'-ly)*. To soil or make dirty.

sulphur *(sul'-phur)*. One of the elements (see **element**). It is found in nature as a yellow powder or yellow crystals. It burns with a blue flame and gives off the suffocating smell of rotten eggs.

sultan *(sul'-tan)*. A ruler of a country where the Mohammedan religion is practised.

sultana *(sul-tan'-a)*. 1. The wife of a sultan. 2. A kind of raisin without seeds.

sultry *(sul'-try)*. Hot and damp; we have sultry weather before a thunderstorm.

sum. 1. An exercise in arithmetic. 2. The total when things are added together is the sum; thus "Find the sum of 5, 8 and 10", means add them together. 3. An amount of money; thus "£2 is a useful sum to have in your pocket". 4. To sum up means to set out all the reasons for and against a thing; a judge sums up the evidence before a jury is asked to give its verdict.

summary *(sum'-ma-ry)*. An account omitting all unnecessary detail; thus if you read an account of a bicycle race and you described the race to a friend in fewer words, yours would be a summary of the race.

summer *(sum'-mer)*. One of the seasons of the year, the others being spring, autumn and winter.

summit *(sum'-mit)*. The summit of a mountain is the top.

summon *(sum'-mon)*. 1. To call, as "He summoned the attendant by pressing the bell". 2. In "The grocer was summoned for selling adulterated sugar", summoned means called to the police court to explain his action to a magistrate. When he was summoned, the police handed him a paper which told him he had to go before a magistrate. The paper was a **summons.** It is quite wrong to say a person is "summonsed". A person receives a summons and is summoned.

sumptuous *(sump'-tu-ous)*. Very fine and giving the impression that much money has been spent on it.

sunbeam *(sun'-beam)*. A ray of sunlight.

sundae *(sun'-dae)*. Ice-cream which is served with nuts, fruit, etc.

Sunday *(Sun'-day)*. The first day of the week.

sunder *(sun'-der)*. To separate; to divide.

sundry *(sun'-dry)*. Various; several.

sunstroke *(sun'-stroke)*. An illness caused by the patient's having stayed too long in the sun.

sup. To eat, generally in the evening.

superb *(su-perb')*. Majestic; grand; splendid.

superfine *(su'-per-fine)*. Extremely fine.

superfluous *(su-per'-flu-ous)*. Extra; not needed because there is already enough.

superintend *(su-per-in-tend')*. To manage; to be in charge of others; to direct the work of others. A person who does this is a **superintendent.**

superior *(su-pe'-ri-or)*. 1. In a higher position. 2. Better or finer than, as "My watch is superior to yours". 3. The head of a religious community is often known as the superior. 4. Haughty, as "She gave him a superior smile and walked from the room".

superlative *(su-per'-la-tive)*. 1. (See **adjective.**) Most adjectives may occur in three forms. The two other forms of "good", for example, are "better" and "best". "Good" is in the *positive* form; "better" in the *comparative*, and "best" in the *superlative*. "Blackest", "most", "darkest" are all superlatives. 2. Supreme; surpassing all others, as "The pianist gave a superlative performance".

supernatural *(su-per-nat'-u-ral)*. Above, or outside, nature or the laws of nature. God is a supernatural being; ghosts, likewise, are supernatural. Supernatural happenings are strange, miraculous occurrences that cannot be explained.

supersede *(su-per-sede')*. To take the place of. "Propeller-driven aircraft have been superseded by jet planes on most of the world's air routes."

supersonic *(su-per-son'-ic)*. Faster than the speed of sound.

superstitious *(su-per-sti'-tious)*. Said of a person who believes in ghosts, lucky and unlucky signs, portents, etc.

supervise *(su'-per-vise)*. To superintend. (See **superintend.**) A person who supervises is a **supervisor** *(su'-per-vi-sor)*.

supper *(sup'-per)*. The evening meal.

supplant *(sup-plant')*. To push someone aside and take his place.

supple *(sup'-ple)*. Pliable; easily bent or twisted, as rubber, leather, etc.

supplement *(sup'-ple-ment)*. 1. To add to something which is already complete. 2. A part added to something which is already complete, as a part added to the end of a book.

supplicate *(sup'-pli-cate)*. To beg in a humble way.

o

supply *(sup-ply')*. 1. To provide or give something, as "He supplies our house with bread". 2. A quantity of a thing, as "I have a supply of pencils".

support *(sup-port')*. 1. To hold up, as "He supported the old lady while she was crossing the icy road". 2. To maintain, as "He supports a wife and two children". 3. Help, as "Give me your support in this business".

suppose *(sup-pose')*. 1. To take for granted, as "I suppose you will come to tea". 2. To pretend, as "I am going to suppose I am Father Christmas".

suppress *(sup-press')*. To stop by force; to do away with; to put down.

supremacy *(su-prem'-a-cy)*. The highest rank; state of being highest or in command. Supremacy belongs to those who are **supreme.**

surcharge. 1. *(sur-charge')*. To make an additional charge. 2. *(sur'-charge)*. An additional charge.

sure. Certain; positive; firm.

surely *(sure'-ly)*. Certainly.

surf. The breaking of waves on the shore, or the foam caused by the breaking of waves.

surface *(sur'-face)*. The outside of a thing.

surfeit *(sur'-feit)*. In "He had a surfeit of rich food and was, consequently, very sick", surfeit means far too much.

surgeon *(sur'-geon)*. A doctor who performs operations.

surgery *(sur'-ger-y)*. 1. The art or science of performing operations on living people or animals. 2. A doctor's room where patients go to be examined.

surly *(sur'-ly)*. Nasty tempered.

surmise *(sur-mise')*. To imagine; to guess.

surmount *(sur-mount')*. To overcome; to conquer; to rise above.

surname *(sur'-name)*. If your name is John Smith, John is your Christian name and Smith is your surname or family name.

surpass *(sur-pass')*. To outdo; to be better than.

surplus *(sur'-plus)*. That which is left over; that which is not needed or cannot be used.

surprise *(sur-prise')*. 1. To take a person unawares; to strike someone with astonishment because unexpected, as "The enemy surprised them in a little mountain pass", or "John was surprised to receive a birthday present from the postman". 2. The feeling you have when you are surprised, as "Imagine

our surprise when a cow walked into the living room".
3. Something which surprises, as "I have a surprise for you
in the car".

surrender *(sur-ren'-der)*. To deliver up; to give up; to yield.

surround *(sur-round')*. To be all round; to close in on all sides.

survey *(sur-vey')*. 1. To look at carefully, as "He surveyed the
scene before him". 2. To inspect or examine. 3. To find the
position of a tract of land and to measure its extent with
certain mathematical instruments. 4. *(sur'-vey)*. An inspection or examination. 5. "He made a survey to find how
many people used Sudso soap" means that he asked many
people what kind of soap they used.

survive *(sur-vive')*. 1. To live after, as "He survived the operation", or "He survived his younger brother by three years".
In the second example, the meaning is that he lived three
years longer than his younger brother. 2. To manage to
live, as "The shipwrecked sailors survived on roots and
berries for three weeks".

suspect. 1. *(sus'-pect)*. A person who may be guilty, as "The
police kept watch on the suspect". 2. *(sus-pect')*. To think
a person may be guilty, as "The police suspected him".
3. To be inclined to think, as "I suspect he has missed the
train".

suspense *(sus-pense')*. Anxiety while waiting to know something,
as "The suspense was terrible until they heard that he was
not one of the victims".

suspicious *(sus-pi'-cious)*. 1. Likely to be guilty. 2. Suspecting.

swagger *(swag'-ger)*. To walk confidently about.

swain. 1. A lover (male). 2. A country fellow.

swallow *(swal'-low)*. 1. To cause food or drink to pass from
your mouth to your stomach by making a tightening movement with your throat. 2. A small, fast-flying bird with a
forked tail.

swamp. 1. A marshy district. 2. To fill with so much water
as to sink.

swan. A large graceful water bird which has a long curving
neck. Adult swans are usually pure white in colour.

sward. Ground covered with turf or grass.

swarm. 1. A large number of things of the same kind, close
together, as "A swarm of people came out of the factory as
12 o'clock was striking". 2. A cloud of bees which are

going off to find a new home. 3. When bees swarm, they collect together in a huge cloud and fly off to find a new home. 4. To move in a crowd, as "The audience swarmed onto the stage". 5. To contain in great numbers, as "The leaves were swarming with butterflies".

swarthy *(swarth'-y)*. Said of a person with a dark complexion.

swathe. To bind or wrap in something.

sway. 1. To swing from side to side. 2. To influence or persuade a person to change his mind, as "We tried to sway him, but his mind was made up".

swear. 1. To take an oath in a law court by which you promise to tell the truth. 2. To use bad language.

sweat. 1. Moisture emitted by the pores in the skin. 2. To emit such moisture; to perspire.

sweater *(sweat'-er)*. A knitted garment, often made of wool, worn on the upper part of the body.

sweep. To clean a floor with a broom is to sweep the floor.

sweet. The opposite of sour. Sugar is sweet and lemons are sour.

swell. To grow larger in size.

swelter *(swel'-ter)*. To feel uncomfortably hot and moist.

swerve. To turn from going straight ahead and go in a curve to one side or the other.

swift. Very quick.

swim. When you propel yourself through the water, you swim in the water. You are said to be **swimming.**

swindle *(swin'-dle)*. 1. To cheat. 2. A fraud.

swine. Pigs; hogs.

swing. 1. To make a thing that is hanging go backwards and forwards; to sway to and fro. The pendulum in a clock swings. 2. An arrangement of ropes and a seat on which a person sits and amuses himself by going backwards and forwards.

switch. 1. To change or to shift. 2. The apparatus fitted to electric wires by which the current may be turned on and off.

swollen *(swol'-len)*. The past participle of **swell,** as "His arm was swollen so much that he could not wear his jacket".

swoon. To faint.

sword. A weapon with a long, sharp blade fitted into a handle.

sycamore *(syc'-a-more)*. A tree common in England.

syllable *(syl'-la-ble)*. A part of a word or a whole word which is said all at once and forms one sound. "Man" is a syllable. "Manufacture", however, contains four syllables: Man-u-fac-ture.

syllabus *(syl'-la-bus)*. A short description of the contents of a book, a speech, a lesson or a series of lessons, etc.

sylvan *(syl'-van)*. To do with woods or forests; thus a sylvan glade is a forest glade.

symbol *(sym'-bol)*. A sign, pattern, shape, etc., that stands for something; thus a rose is a symbol for England, and a thistle is a symbol for Scotland.

sympathetic *(sym-pa-thet'-ic)*. Showing a kindly nature, or feeling for you in your troubles. A person who will do this will **sympathize** *(sym'-pa-thize)* with you and show you **sympathy** *(sym'-pa-thy)*.

symphony *(sym'-pho-ny)*. A musical composition for full orchestra.

symptom *(symp'-tom)*. A sign; thus when you are ill, the doctor examines you for symptoms or signs of the illness from which you are suffering.

synagogue *(syn'-a-gogue)*. A place of worship for Jewish people.

synonym *(syn'-o-nym)*. A word that has the same meaning as another word in the same language; thus "commence" is a synonym for "begin".

syringe *(syr-inge')*. 1. A tubular instrument for sucking up a liquid and then squirting it out in a jet. The needles that doctors use to inject patients are syringes. 2. A rubber bulb connected to a nozzle by a long tube. Liquid put into the bulb is squirted out through the nozzle.

syrup *(syr'-up)*. A sweet liquid.

system *(sys'-tem)*. 1. In "I have a system for growing cabbages rapidly", system means plan or method. 2. In "The railway system is rapidly becoming electrified", system stands for the network of lines. 3. System also means the orderly arrangement of things.

T

tabernacle *(tab'-er-nac-le)*. A place of worship.

table *(ta'-ble)*. 1. An article of furniture with a flat upper surface at which we sit to eat our meals, do homework,

TABLEAU 414 **TAIL**

`etc. 2. A list of things, as a time-table or the multiplication table.

tableau *(tab'-leau)*. A group of persons, usually silent and motionless, representing a scene.

table-cloth *(ta'-ble-cloth)*. A cloth which is used as a cover on a table.

tablet *(tab'-let)*. 1. A tablet of some medicine is a kind of flat pill. 2. A writing tablet is a pile of many sheets, all the same size and bound together along one edge, so that each sheet of paper may be torn off easily. 3. On the walls of churches, etc., tablets are often fixed. These are put up to remind us of some person or event.

tacit *(tac'-it)*. Silent; not spoken.

taciturn *(tac'-i-turn)*. Not fond of talking. Said of a person who does not speak much.

tack. 1. A small nail with a large head. 2. To alter the direction in which a sailing boat is going in order to make full use of the wind.

tackle *(tack'-le)*. 1. Gear, or the things needed for doing certain things; thus, a rod, line, float, hook, etc., are fishing tackle. 2. To tackle something is to make an energetic attempt to do it. Thus, "He tackled his homework and was soon finished".

tact. Ability to do or say the right thing when dealing with other people. A man with tact does not quarrel with somebody in a rage; he talks to him gently and smooths out the troubles.

tactics *(tac'-tics)*. 1. The skilful placing of men and guns in warfare, so that they serve to the best advantage. 2. Any plan of action.

tadpole *(tad'-pole)*. The young frog in the stage before it has lost its tail, when it swims in water and does not go on land.

taffeta *(taf'-fe-ta)*. A kind of cloth (usually silk or rayon) which has a glossy finish. Girls wear taffeta dresses.

tag. 1. A piece of cardboard, etc., on which the price of an article, or an address, or other things, are written. Usually, the tag has a string so that it may be tied to an object. 2. A game played by children. One child tries to touch, or "tag", the others.

tail. 1. The end or hind part of something, such as a bird's tail. 2. The hind part of an aeroplane.

tailor *(tai'-lor)*. A person who makes or repairs clothing.

tainted *(taint'-ed)*. Decayed; spoiled; disgraced.

tale. 1. A story, as a fairy tale. 2. To tell tales has a special meaning; it means getting somebody into trouble by describing things you saw him do.

talent *(tal'-ent)*. 1. Ability; a special gift for doing something well, such as a talent for painting. 2. In ancient times, a measure of weight or money.

talkative *(talk'-a-tive)*. Having the habit of talking too much.

tall. Of a great height.

tallow *(tal'-low)*. Fat that is hard. Candles used to be made of tallow.

talon *(tal'-on)*. A bird's claw.

tambourine *(tam-bou-rine')*. A small, one-sided drum, equipped with small, jingling pieces of metal.

tame. 1. Not wild. 2. Weak.

tamper *(tam'-per)*. To meddle with something that you should leave alone.

tan. 1. When the skin of an animal is tanned, it is treated with a liquid and turned into leather. 2. When you expose your body to the sun for a period of time, your skin turns brown and you are said to have a tan.

tandem *(tan'-dem)*. One behind the other. Thus, the passengers in a canoe, or on a bicycle built to carry two people, are said to ride tandem. Such a bicycle is a tandem bicycle. When two horses are harnessed one behind the other and not side by side, they are said to be harnessed in tandem.

tangent *(tan'-gent)*. 1. A line which touches a curve but does not cut it. 2. When a person goes off at a tangent he suddenly changes from one method or plan he has been following and does something else quite unrelated to the first plan. If Jane stopped doing her homework and began to play with the ball, Jane might be said to have gone off at a tangent when she started to play with the ball.

tangerine *(tan-ge-rine')*. A kind of small orange.

tangible *(tan'-gi-ble)*. Able to be touched or felt.

tangle *(tan'-gle)*. 1. A mass of threads or other things jumbled together in great disorder. 2. To jumble things together in this way.

tank. 1. A large container used to hold water or liquids. There is a tank on a car which contains petrol. 2. A war machine

which is able to travel over rough ground by means of caterpillar wheels.

tankard *(tank'-ard)*. A drinking cup, usually of metal.

tannery *(tan'-ner-y)*. A place where skins and hides are turned
into leather.

tantalize *(tan'-ta-lize)*. To tease a person by showing him what
he wants but keeping it out of reach.

tap. 1. A device for regulating the flow of water or any other
liquid. 2. To hit lightly. 3. A light blow.

tape. A narrow band of paper, cloth, etc.

taper *(ta'-per)*. 1. A thin wax candle. 2. To grow narrower
gradually, as "A triangle tapers from the base upwards and
so does a dunce's cap".

tapestry *(tap'-es-try)*. A woven cloth, having a decorative
design or picture and used as a wall hanging.

tapioca *(tap-i-o'-ca)*. A granular preparation made from a
tropical plant, which is used as food.

tar. 1. A black, sticky substance, used on roads and as a pre-
servative. 2. A sailor.

tardy *(tar'-dy)*. Slow; late.

target *(tar'-get)*. 1. The mark at which a man shoots when
practising on shooting ranges. 2. Anything which is the
mark for somebody's ill-feeling, as "Mary was the target
for the other girls' silly insults".

tariff *(tar'-iff)*. The list of payments which have to be made
in the form of customs or duty on certain goods which are
exported, and more especially on goods which are imported.

tarnish *(tar'-nish)*. 1. To become dull after being bright and
shining, as "The brass candlesticks on my desk have tarnished;
they need cleaning". 2. To harm a person's good name.

tarry *(tar'-ry)*. To stay; to loiter; to wait for.

tart. 1. A small pie. 2. Sour; sharp to the taste.

task. A piece of work which has to be done.

tassel *(tas'-sel)*. An ornament made of a bunch of threads that
hang downwards.

taste. 1. To find out the flavour of, as "He tasted the pie to
see if it was good". 2. The flavour of, as "The pie has the
sweet taste of sugar and nothing else". 3. In "She dresses
in good taste", taste means style. 4. In "It was his first
taste of the stick", taste means experience of. 5. In "Give
me a taste of that jelly", taste means a small amount.

tattoo *(tat-too')*. 1. To make patterns on the skin of the body, by pricking it and rubbing in a coloured substance. 2. A signal given by beating drums.

taught. The past tense of **teach,** as "The old prospector taught the boys many things about rocks".

taunt. To sneer at or jeer at.

tavern *(tav'-ern)*. An inn; a place where drinks are sold.

tawdry *(taw'-dry)*. Cheap and showy, and in bad taste. Cheap, flashy jewellery is tawdry.

tawny *(taw'-ny)*. Brownish-yellow in colour, as "The lion's skin is tawny".

tax. 1. Money paid to the government. 2. To accuse; to charge. 3. To make demands on, as to tax one's strength.

taxi *(tax'-i)*. 1. The short form of **taxicab.** A car with a driver, which one may hire. 2. When an aeroplane moves along the ground it is said to taxi.

tea. 1. A shrub that is grown in India, China and Ceylon. 2. A drink made by steeping dried leaves of the tea plant in water.

teach. To instruct.

teacher *(teach'-er)*. A person who teaches.

tea-cup *(tea'-cup)*. A cup used for holding tea.

teak. A hard wood that comes from the East Indies and Africa.

team. 1. A group of people working together to do a certain thing; thus a football team consists of people working together to beat the rival team. 2. Two or more horses are called a team when they are working together.

tear. 1. To pull to pieces; to make holes in. 2. A tear is a slit, a split or a rent. 3. A drop of water that has come from an eye.

tease. To annoy or worry.

teasel *(tea'-sel)*. A tall, prickly plant with a prickly head. It was once used for "teasing" cotton and wool to straighten the fibres before spinning.

technical *(tech'-ni-cal)*. Having to do with practical methods of doing things. A technical school is one where such things as engineering, carpentry, chemistry, bricklaying and printing are taught.

tedious *(te'-di-ous)*. Tiring; boring.

teem. 1. To be full of; to swarm with. 2. To pour.

teeth. The plural of tooth. The white, bony structures for chewing which are found in the mouths of people and animals.

telegram *(tel'-e-gram)*. A message sent by wire.

telephone *(tel'-e-phone)*. An electronic device for sending sounds, especially the human voice, over long distances by means of wires.

telescope *(tel'-e-scope)*. A tube with lenses which makes things that are far away look as though they are close at hand.

television *(tel'-e-vi-sion)*. A device for transmitting pictures by radio waves or for receiving pictures so sent.

tell 1. To make known by speech or writing. 2. To order, as "Tell John to stop making that dreadful noise".

temerity *(tem-er'-ity)*. Boldness; rashness, as "I don't know how you had the temerity to come and ask for a day off after being away all last week".

temper *(tem'-per)*. 1. Frame of mind, as good temper and bad temper. 2. The temper of a metal is the condition of its hardness. 3. To moderate or soften.

temperament *(tem'-per-a-ment)*. Individual character; mood or frame of mind typical of an individual, as "He was of a fiery temperament", meaning he was quick-tempered and ardent.

temperate *(tem'-per-ate)*. Moderate or mild. A temperate climate is neither too hot nor too cold. A temperate person is one who never goes to extremes. The Temperate Zones of the earth are two areas of the earth's surface: the North Temperate Zone is the area between the Tropic of Cancer and the Arctic Circle: the South Temperate Zone is the area between the Tropic of Capricorn and the Antarctic Circle. England is in the North Temperate Zone.

temperature *(tem'-per-a-ture)*. The amount of heat or cold. The normal body temperature (or heat) is about $98\frac{1}{2}$ degrees as measured by a Fahrenheit thermometer or about 37 degrees Centigrade.

tempest *(tem'-pest)*. A storm.

temple *(tem'-ple)*. A building used for religious worship.

temporary *(tem'-po-rar-y)*. Lasting only for a while; not continuing for ever.

tempt. To lure; to entice; to try to persuade to do wrong; to lead on to do wrong. Food is **tempting** when the sight of it makes you want to eat it.

temptation *(temp-ta'-tion)*. 1. Something offered to a person to encourage him to do wrong. 2. State of being tempted or act of tempting.

tenacious *(ten-a'-cious)*. Inclined to hold on tightly.

tenant *(ten'-ant)*. One who pays rent for the use of another person's house or land.

tend. 1. In "Milk tends to turn sour", tends means is inclined to. 2. In "He tends his little brother", tends means cares for.

tender *(ten'-der)*. 1. Soft and gentle; of a kind and protective nature. 2. Not tough, as "This meat is tender". 3. The rear part of a locomotive that carries the fuel. 4. A tender is also the offer to do work at a certain price. 5. To offer; to hold out, as "He tendered the little girl a stick of rock".

tendril *(ten'-dril)*. A thread-like part of a climbing plant by which it holds on to its support.

tennis *(ten'-nis)*. A game played by two or four people, who use racquets to hit a ball backwards and forwards across a net.

tenor *(ten'-or)*. 1. In "the tenor of his speech", tenor means meaning. 2. A man has a tenor voice when he can sing songs that include high notes. 3. In "The tenor of his life was quiet and peaceful", tenor means course.

tense. 1. Taut; strained, as "The rope was tense when the ship swung around". 2. The tense of a verb is the form of the verb which shows at what time the action it expresses took place. The three main tenses are past, present and future. "I run" is in the present tense, "I ran" is in the past tense, and "I shall run" is in the future tense.

tent. A portable shelter made of canvas and supported by poles.

tentacle *(ten'-ta-cle)*. A feeler or arm on an animal or plant, by which it grasps things or moves itself. The octopus has tentacles which are well developed.

tenth. The last in a group of ten.

tepid *(tep'-id)*. Lukewarm; neither hot nor cold.

term. 1. A length of time; thus, many schools are open three terms in a year, each about thirteen weeks in length. 2. In "He spoke in glowing terms of the boy's work" and "He used a number of scientific terms when describing how the engine works", terms means words. 3. Terms sometimes means charges, as in "What are your terms for a week's stay here?". 4. It also means conditions, as in "The peace terms were reasonable".

terminate *(ter'-mi-nate)*. To end; to put an end to. A thing that terminates comes to its **termination** *(ter-mi-na'-tion)* or ending.

terminus *(ter'-mi-nus)*. The end of such things as a railway line, a bus route, etc. Also written **terminal.**

terrace *(ter'-race)*. A raised level or platform of earth, usually on a hillside and supported by a wall. When a hillside is arranged in terraces, it rises from one level to another, like a set of large steps.

terrestrial *(ter-res'-tri-al)*. To do with the earth or the world. Thus, a terrestrial globe is a globe showing the earth.

terrible *(ter'-ri-ble)*. Dreadful; causing fear. A terrible thing terrifies.

terrier *(ter'-ri-er)*. A breed of dog with short, wiry hair.

terrify *(ter'-ri-fy)*. To frighten very much.

territory *(ter'-ri-to-ry)*. Land.

terror *(ter'-ror)*. A feeling of great fear, as "He was filled with terror when he saw the lightning hit the tree".

terse. Short; to the point.

'test. 1. To put to the proof; to examine. 2. A trial of skill or knowledge.

testament *(tes'-ta-ment)*. 1. One of the two portions of the Bible, the Old and the New Testaments. 2. A testament is also a person's will, which describes how the person's belongings are to be divided after his death.

testator *(tes-ta'-tor)*. A person who makes a will (see **testament**). The feminine of this is **testatrix.**

testify *(tes'-ti-fy)*. To bear witness; to say that such and such a thing was done or said.

testimonial *(tes-ti-mo'-ni-al)*. 1. A written description of a person's character, usually stating the best that can be said about the person. 2. A token of thanks or admiration, presented to a person or established in his memory.

tether *(teth'-er)*. 1. A chain, rope or strap to secure an animal. 2. To fasten an animal with a rope or chain.

text. 1. A short piece taken from the Scriptures that is worth remembering, as "God is Love". 2. The text of a book is the main reading part, not the title page, the index, nor the advertisements at the end. 3. A **text-book** *(text'-book)* is a book of instruction.

textiles *(tex'-tiles)*. Fabrics that are made by weaving. Fibres that can be woven into cloth.

texture *(tex'-ture)*. When we say a thing has a smooth or a rough texture, etc., we are speaking of the feel of its surface.

thankful *(thank'-ful)*. When you feel thankful you feel grateful and want to give thanks.

thatched. Said of a roof of a building when, instead of being covered with slates or tiles, it is provided with a covering of neatly arranged straws or reeds.

thaw. To melt.

theatre *(the-a'-tre)*. A building in which plays are acted. In a hospital, the theatre is the room where the surgeons perform operations.

theft. Robbery; stealing.

their. Belonging to them.

theme. 1. The subject of a speech or composition. 2. A composition on a certain subject. 3. A phrase of music that occurs many times in a piece.

theology *(the-ol'-o-gy)*. The study of God and religion. All clergymen have made a special study of theology.

theorem *(the'-o-rem)*. A rule in mathematics and especially in geometry which you have to prove.

there. In that place.

therefore *(there'-fore)*. In "He left: therefore his place was empty", therefore means as a result.

thermometer *(ther-mom'-e-ter)*. An instrument for measuring temperature, or the degree of heat. (See **Fahrenheit** and **Centigrade**.)

thick. Opposite to thin, as "Syrup is thick and water is thin" or "A sheet of paper is thin and a book is thick".

thicket *(thick'-et)*. A group of trees and bushes growing very close together.

thief. A burglar; one who steals. When you speak of more than one thief you say **thieves.**

thigh. The upper part of the leg between the hip and the knee.

thimble *(thim'-ble)*. A covering for the tip of the finger. It is used to protect the finger when sewing.

thin. Slim. (See **thick**.)

third. The last in a group of three.

thirst. A desire to drink. When you are **thirsty** *(thirst'-y)*, your throat feels dry.

thirteen *(thir-teen')*. The number between twelve and fourteen, which is three more than ten.

thistle *(this'-tle)*. A meadow plant with prickly leaves and stem and a tufted purple flower. It is the emblem of Scotland.

thither *(thith'-er)*. To that place.

thorax *(tho'-rax)*. The chest; the part of the body between the head and the abdomen.

thorn. 1. A plant with thorns on its stems, such as hawthorn, blackthorn, etc. 2. A sharp prickle on a plant.

thorough *(thor'-ough)*. Complete. When you are thorough in doing a job, you do it well and leave nothing undone.

thoroughfare *(thor'-ough-fare)*. A road which leads somewhere. The familiar notice, "No thoroughfare", means that there is no way through.

though. In "You may not go, though you cry·and plead", though means in spite of the fact that.

thought. 1. The act of thinking. 2. An idea, as "That thought cheered him up". 3. The past tense of think.

thousand *(thou'-sand)*. A number which is ten times one hundred.

thrash. 1. To beat or whip a person is to thrash him. 2. To shake fiercely, as "The high wind thrashed the trees". 3. To toss about the legs and arms violently; to toss about violently, as "John was having a nightmare and thrashing about in his bed".

thread. 1. To thread a needle is to pass a length of cotton thread, etc., through its eye. 2. Cotton, silk, etc., in the form of a long twisted yarn, as sold on spools.

threadbare *(thread'-bare)*. 1. Having the surface of the cloth worn smooth. 2. Shabby.

threaten *(threat'-en)*. To tell a person that trouble will come to him unless he does as he is told; thus, "The bully threatened to punch the small boy unless the boy gave him some sweets". We also speak of threatening weather, meaning weather that appears to be about to turn bad.

thresh. To beat grain, usually by machine, so that the seeds are separated from the stalks and husks.

threshold *(thresh'-old)*. 1. The stone or wooden part of a door which is set into the floor; thus, the threshold is the spot where the inside and the outside of the house meet. 2. The beginning; the outset.

threw. The past tense of throw, as "During the clowns' act, one clown threw a pie at another clown's face".

thrice. Three times.

thrift. The art of saving; not wasting anything; being economical.

thrill. 1. In "The boys received a thrill when riding the roller coaster", thrill means an exciting feeling or sensation. 2. To thrill someone is to cause him to feel a thrill.

thrive. To be strong and healthy; to grow healthily; to be successful.

throat. The passage inside the neck which links the mouth and nose to the stomach and lungs.

throb. 1. To beat very quickly. Your heart throbs after you have been running. 2. When we speak of a wound or aching tooth as throbbing, we mean that the pain seems to be felt in beats.

throne. The chair upon which the king or queen sits when taking part in some great state business or ceremony.

throng. A crowd of people.

throttle *(throt'-tle)*. 1. To choke a person by clutching his throat. 2. A device which controls the amount of fuel entering an engine.

through. 1. In "He came through the doorway from the hall into the library", through means by way of. 2. In "He read through the book quickly", through means from the beginning to the end of. 3. In "The heat lasted all through the day", through means during.

throw. To send an object through space with a forceful motion, as in "Please throw the ball over the fence".

thrush. A kind of song-bird.

thrust. To push with force.

thumb. The short, fat finger beside the index finger on a person's hand.

thump. 1. To hit heavily. 2. A low, heavy sound.

thunder *(thun'-der)*. The noise following a flash of lightning.

thunderstruck *(thun'-der-struck)*. Greatly surprised.

Thursday *(Thurs'-day)*. The fifth day of the week, between Wednesday and Friday.

thwart. To oppose successfully, as "He thwarted the burglar".

tick. 1. A blood-sucking insect that lives on animals. 2. The sound made by a clock. 3. A small checking mark made against names or items in a list. 4. The stout cover or case which holds the feathers or other stuffing of a mattress or pillow.

ticket *(tick'-et)*. 1. A label, as "The ticket on the bicycle is marked £19 10*s*. 2. A card which gives the holder some special right; thus, a railway ticket allows him to travel by train, a theatre ticket lets him go into the theatre, etc.

tickle *(tick'-le)*. 1. To touch a person lightly and thereby make him have a curious, shivery feeling. A person who is much affected when tickled is said to be **ticklish.** 2. To amuse, as "The book seemed to tickle him".

tide. 1. The rise and fall of the sea twice in every twenty-four hours. 2. Time; season, as morning-tide, Eastertide.

tidings *(ti'-dings)*. News, as "She has had no tidings from her husband since he went to sea".

tidy *(ti'-dy)*. Neat; having everything in its place.

tie. 1. To fasten, as "He tied his shoe-laces in a neat bow". 2. A tie is a thing that fastens or binds; thus builders use iron ties; men wear neck-ties; and there are such things as family ties, which are the bonds between brothers and sisters, fathers and mothers.

tiger *(ti'-ger)*. A large, fierce animal with yellowish fur striped with black. The tiger is a member of the cat family and lives in Asia.

tight. 1. A tight knot is one which is firmly tied. 2. Tight clothing fits snugly and leaves little room for stretching the body. 3. A tight-rope is a rope which is stretched so that it is very firm.

tile. A thin piece of baked clay which is used around fireplaces, on roofs and floors and, when shaped as a pipe, to drain land.

till. 1. A short form of **until.** 2. To cultivate, as "The farmer tills the ground". 3. A drawer in a shop, etc., in which money is kept.

tilt. To raise one side of an object higher than the other.

timber *(tim'-ber)*. Wood for building.

timepiece *(time'-piece)*. A clock; a watch.

time-table *(time'-ta-ble)*. A list showing when things take place, as the arrival of trains, or classes in school.

timid *(tim'-id)*. Easily frightened.

timorous *(tim'-or-ous)*. Easily frightened.

tin. 1. A white, silver-coloured metal. 2. Cans made of sheet iron are called tins, although they are not made of tin. Tinfoil is tin rolled very thin.

tinder *(tin'-der)*. A dry substance easily set on fire.

tingle *(tin'-gle)*. 1. To have a prickling or stinging feeling, as "When she came in out of the cold she felt her cheeks and ears tingle". 2. The prickling feeling.

tinker *(tink'-er)*. 1. A man who mends kettles, pots, pans, etc. 2. To tinker is to do repair work in a clumsy, unsuccessful way.

tinkle *(tin'-kle)*. To make a musical sound like the clinking of glasses.

tinsel *(tin'-sel)*. Inexpensive glittering or sparkling decorations.

tint. A shade or a particular depth of a colour; thus "She wore a dress of the same blue tint as her eyes".

tiny *(ti'-ny)*. Very small.

tip. 1. The pointed end of a thing, as "The tip of a dog's tail". 2. A gift of money given as a reward for some service or in order to obtain some service, as a tip to the waiter. 3. To tip a thing is to upset or tilt it.

tirade *(ti-rade')*. 1. A scolding that consists of many abusive words. 2. A long, angry speech.

tire. When you tire of work, you are weary.

tiresome *(tire'-some)*. If you listen to a tiresome story, you feel bored, annoyed or tired.

tissue *(tis'-sue)*. 1. Your entire body is made up of tissues, that is, collections of cells joined together and forming a structure. There are several kinds of tissue in the body, such as muscular tissue, nerve tissue, bone tissue, etc. 2. Very thin paper, as tissue paper. 3. A kind of very thin, filmy cloth.

titanic *(ti-tan'-ic)*. Very large.

titbit *(tit'-bit)*. A very tasty mouthful of food, or an interesting scrap of news.

title *(ti'-tle)*. 1. A name given to someone to show his rank, as lord, viscount or duke, etc. 2. The name of a book, play, etc.; thus, "The title of one of Shakespeare's plays is *The Merchant of Venice*". 3. When a house is sold, the seller gives the buyer the title deeds of the house, that is, the papers which will show who is the owner of the house.

titter *(tit'-ter)*. To giggle.

toad. A creature like a frog.

toast. 1. To brown both sides of a slice of bread by placing it before a fire. 2. To drink a person's health at a banquet is to toast him.

tobacco *(to-bac'-co)*. Leaves of a certain plant, which are dried and treated and then smoked or chewed.

toboggan *(to-bog'-gan)*. 1. A large, flat sledge without runners which holds several people. 2. To travel on such a sledge.

to-day *(to-day')*. This day; in the present.

toddle *(tod'-dle)*. To walk unsteadily with short steps, as a baby does.

toe. 1. One of the five small finger-like projections on each human foot. 2. The part of a stocking or shoe which covers these parts of the foot.

together *(to-geth'-er)*. 1. In a group. 2. At the same time.

toil. Hard work that lasts a long time.

toilet *(toi'-let)*. 1. The work of washing, dressing, brushing the hair, etc. 2. A place where these things are done. 3. A bathroom, lavatory or water closet.

token *(to'-ken)*. A sign; something which stands for something else.

tolerable *(tol'-er-a-ble)*. Passable; not too bad, as "I spent a tolerable week-end at my uncle's".

tolerate *(tol'-er-ate)*. To put up with; to permit, as "I cannot tolerate this noise".

toll. 1. To ring a church bell, as for a funeral. 2. A payment for some privilege; thus there are many bridges which allow people to cross only after they have paid a toll.

tomahawk *(tom'-a-hawk)*. An Indian war-axe.

tomato *(to-ma'-to)*. A plant with a soft, red, juicy fruit.

tomb. A burial place. The monument placed over a grave is called a **tombstone.**

tomboy *(tom'-boy)*. A girl who acts more like a boy than a girl.

tome. A volume; a book.

to-morrow *(to-mor'-row)*. The day after to-day; the future.

tone. The character of a sound or colour. 2. Bodily health.

tongs. An instrument used to grip things; thus sugar tongs are used for lifting lumps of sugar, coal tongs for placing lumps of coal on the fire, etc.

tongue. 1. The soft fleshy organ in the mouth which is used for tasting and talking. 2. The tongue of a shoe is the piece of leather under the laces. 3. The English tongue is the English language.

tonic *(ton'-ic)*. Something that gives a person strength; thus iron is a tonic and so is fresh air.

to-night *(to-night')*. This night.

tonsil *(ton'-sil)*. An oval-shaped piece of flesh, of which there are two, at the back of the throat. When they become red and swollen, the patient has **tonsillitis** *(ton-sil-li'-tis)*.

took. The past tense of take, as "Yesterday he took his little brother to the park".

tool. An instrument that helps in doing work. Here are some tools—a hammer, saw, pliers and screwdriver.

tooth. 1. One of the white, hard bony parts of the mouth used for biting and chewing. When speaking of more than one tooth, we use the word **teeth.** 2. The points around the edge of a wheel in a machine are called teeth. So also are the prongs of a rake or the spines of a comb.

toothache *(tooth'-ache)*. A painful aching in one or more of the teeth.

tooth-brush *(tooth'-brush)*. A brush for cleaning the teeth.

toothsome *(tooth'-some)*. Pleasant tasting.

top. 1. The highest part of anything, as the top of a mountain and the top of the class. 2. A toy which children spin.

topaz *(to'-paz)*. A precious stone, yellow in colour.

topic *(top'-ic)*. The thing about which people speak, read or write, as "Most boys are interested in the topic of jet planes".

topography *(to-pog'-ra-phy)*. 1. A description of the surface of the land. 2. The shape or nature of the surface of the land, as "Lakes, rivers, mountains, cities, deserts, etc., form the topography of the land".

topple *(top'-ple)*. 1. To fall over. 2. To tilt something and make it fall as a result.

torch. A light that can be carried from place to place. Many years ago, people used bundles of sticks dipped in oil or fat and set alight; now we have electric torches, or flash-lights.

tore. The past tense of **tear,** as "He tore his shirt while playing, and when he reached home his mother saw it was **torn**".

torment. 1. *(tor'-ment)*. Great pain. 2. *(tor-ment')*. To worry or annoy.

tornado *(tor-na'-do)*. A whirlwind; a very violent wind-storm.

torpedo *(tor-pe'-do)*. An explosive shell, made in the shape of a cigar and used by submarines for sinking enemy ships in war-time.

torpor *(tor'-por)*. A sluggish state or condition.

torrent *(tor'-rent)*. A rushing flow of water.

torrid *(tor'-rid)*. Very hot. That part of the world in which the equator lies is known as the Torrid Zone.

tortoise *(tor'-toise)*. A reptile living on land or in water, the body of which is protected by a hard shell on the top and bottom. At any sign of danger, the tortoise can pull his head, feet and tail into his shell. Another word for tortoise is **turtle.**

torture *(tor'-ture)*. 1. Great pain, as "The torture that poor invalid suffers is terrible". 2. To put someone to extreme pain.

toss. To throw up in the air, as when a boy tosses a coin or a bull tosses a man.

total *(to'-tal)*. 1. Whole; entire. 2. The whole; the sum.

totem pole *(to'-tem pole)*. A pole carved by North American Indians on the Northern Pacific Coast. Many different faces of animals were carved and painted on totem poles.

touch. To place the hand or part of the body on something or someone.

tough. 1. Not easily broken. 2. Strong or hardy, as "The boxer showed he was tough". 3. Stubborn.

tour. A journey from place to place. When you go on a tour, you are a **tourist** and you are **touring.**

tournament *(tour'-na-ment)*. 1. A fight between knights on horseback. 2. A contest in which several people try to defeat one another, as a tennis tournament.

tow. 1. To pull along by means of a rope, as "The horse towed the barge along the canal". 2. The coarse threads of flax and hemp.

towards. In the direction of.

towel *(tow'-el)*. A cloth used for drying, as a face towel, a bath towel, a tea towel, etc.

tower *(tow'-er)*. A lofty structure standing alone or forming part of another, as a church tower.

town. A large group of houses, shops, schools, factories, etc. A place larger than a village.

toy. A thing with which a child plays.

trace. 1. A slight mark, as "There is a trace of ink on the white carpet". 2. To trace is to copy by placing tracing paper over the original and marking the lines as they show through. 3. To follow up, as "The detective traced the thief by his finger-prints". 4. A tiny quantity, as "There were traces of poison in the bottle, even after I had washed it carefully" 5. One of the straps by which a horse is attached to a cart.

track. 1. The marks left by anything, as the track of the cart wheels on a muddy road, or the track of a fox when its footprints show in the snow. 2. A path, as "There is a winding track that leads through the forest". 3. A circular course, such as a race track. 4. To track an animal is to follow its tracks; to track down a man is to hunt him down.

tract. 1. A piece of land. 2. A short, printed account of a portion of the Scriptures, usually ending with a moral.

traction *(trac'-tion).* Pulling or drawing; thus a traction engine is one that pulls a heavy load behind it.

tractor *(trac'-tor).* A machine operated by an engine and used to pull things. A farm tractor pulls a plough or other farm implement.

trade. 1. Buying and selling. 2. A man's trade is the work he does; thus some men follow carpentry as their trade, others plumbing.

trader *(trad'-er).* A person who trades.

trading *(trad'-ing).* Having to do with trade.

tradition *(tra-di'-tion).* When people act, believe or think as their fathers, grandfathers, etc., did, they are following tradition. Such a ceremony as a coronation is traditional because kings and queens have been crowned in the same way for hundreds of years.

traffic *(traf'-fic).* 1. Cars, carts and other moving things going along the road, as well as people passing along the footpath. 2. To traffic is to buy and sell.

tragedy *(trag'-e-dy).* 1. A mournful or dreadful event. 2. A play in which one or more characters die. The events in a tragedy are **tragic.**

trail. 1. To pull or drag along the ground after you. 2. To grow over a wide patch, as "The ivy trailed all over the side of the house". 3. The track or scent left by a person or an animal, as "The hounds followed the fox's trail".

trailer *(trail'-er)*. 1. A carriage, wagon, etc., pulled behind a car or lorry. 2. A short film giving a sample of one that is to come.

train. 1. An engine with several coaches or wagons running on a railway line. 2. To bring up or teach, as "Train a child to do what is right". 3. "Ruin stalked in the train of the storm"; here train means following the storm. 4. The part of a dress or robe which trails behind the wearer.

trainer *(train'-er)*. A coach; one who trains others.

traitor *(trai'-tor)*. A person who betrays someone or something, usually one who betrays his native land.

tramp. 1. To walk heavily. 2. A vagrant; a vagabond. 3. A long walk.

trample *(tram'-ple)*. To step on; to crush under foot.

trance. A person is in a trance when he seems to be asleep but is not. He is in a daze or coma. We also say that someone is in a trance when he is lost in thought or day-dreams.

tranquil *(tran'-quil)*. Quiet.

transcribe *(tran-scribe')*. To make a copy of something by writing it out afresh.

transfer. 1. *(trans-fer')*. To move a thing from one place to another, as "I transferred the money to my savings account". 2. *(trans'-fer)*. A picture that when wetted can be stuck on something else, as "I have stuck the transfer on the back of my hand". 3. A moving, as "The transfer of the business from one building to another took two weeks".

transform *(trans-form')*. To change completely the shape or appearance of something.

transformer *(trans-form'-er)*. An electrical device for changing the power of electricity.

transgressor *(trans-gres'-sor)*. A person who breaks the law; a person who does wrong.

transit *(trans'-it)*. A thing is in transit while it is passing from one place to another.

translate *(trans-late')*. To put words of one language into words that mean the same in another language. Thus, "mon cher monsieur", translated from French into English, is "my dear sir".

translucent *(trans-lu'-cent)*. A thing is translucent when light can be seen through it. Frosted glass is translucent, but not **transparent** *(trans-par'-ent)*.

transmit *(trans-mit')*. To send along; to communicate.

transom *(tran'-som)*. A transom window is a small window over a door; it usually opens on hinges.

transparent *(trans-par'-ent)*. A thing is transparent when people and objects can be seen clearly through it.

transplant *(trans-plant')*. To dig up and plant in a different place. Gardeners transplant seedlings.

transport *(trans-port')*. 1. To carry from one place to another. 2. To be transported means to be carried away, that is, to lose control of yourself because of emotion, as "The child was transported with joy when he saw the Christmas tree".

transportation *(trans-por-ta'-tion)*. The act of moving or carrying something from one place to another.

transpose *(trans-pose')*. 1. To change the position of. 2. In music, to change a piece from one key to another.

trap. 1. A device for catching things, as a mouse-trap. 2. A two-wheeled carriage.

trapeze *(tra-peze')*. A bar hung by two ropes, on which a person can swing; a swing used in gymnastics.

trapper *(trap'-per)*. A person who traps animals and sells their fur.

trash. Rubbish.

travel *(trav'-el)*. To go on a journey.

traverse *(trav'-erse)*. To go across.

trawler *(trawl'-er)*. A fishing boat equipped with a net that drags behind it.

tray. A flat, shallow holder on which light lunches or beverages are served. If you have been in hospital or sick in bed, your meals were probably brought to you on a tray.

treachery *(treach'-er-y)*. A betrayal of trust. If a trusted soldier took information to the enemy he would be said to have committed an act of treachery or **treason** *(treas'-on)*.

treacle *(trea'-cle)*. A thick black syrup produced in the refining of sugar.

tread. 1. When you walk, you tread or step along. 2. When you trample paper into a box, you tread down the paper. 3. When swimming, you tread water by moving your arms and legs so as to keep your head above water.

treadle *(tread'-le)*. A lever worked by the foot to set a machine moving.

treason *(trea'-son)*. The crime of betraying your country; treachery.

treasure *(treas'-ure)*. 1. A thing of great value. 2. To regard something or someone as precious and so to guard it or him carefully.

treasurer *(treas'-ur-er)*. A person belonging to a company, club, society, etc., who looks after the money belonging to the organization.

treat. 1. To treat a person is to pay for something for him, as "He treated me to a ride on the merry-go-round". 2. To act towards somebody, either badly or well, as for example, "The man treated his dog badly". 3. Treat also means deal with, as "He treated that subject in his essay". 4. To care for an ill person in order to make him better, as "They treated him at the hospital".

treaty *(trea'-ty)*. A signed agreement between nations. When nations agree to stop fighting and make peace terms, they sign a peace treaty.

treble *(tre'-ble)*. 1. Threefold; triple. 2. To multiply by three. 3. The highest part in music.

trellis *(trel'-lis)*. A piece of wooden lattice-work. Often roses are grown on trellises.

tremble *(trem'-ble)*. To shake through fear, illness, cold, etc. To shiver.

tremendous *(tre-men'-dous)*. Very great.

trench. A long, narrow and perhaps deep hole dug in the ground.

trespass *(tres'-pass)*. 1. To go on land that you have no right to go on. 2. To commit an offence; to sin.

tresses *(tres'-ses)*. Locks of hair or curls.

trestle *(tres'-tle)*. 1. A kind of strong stool used for supporting things while working on them; thus, a carpenter rests a piece of timber on his trestle when he wants to saw it. 2. A trestle is also the supporting framework of a bridge.

trial *(tri'-al)*. 1. An attempt; a putting to the proof. 2. Anything that gives a great deal of trouble or is a hardship is a trial. 3. A trial of strength is a contest in which each of the contestants tries to prove that he is the strongest. 4. In law, a trial is a formal examination of a matter to find out the truth about it and decide what is to be done. A judge presides at a trial, and after he has heard all the evidence, he pronounces a decision.

triangle *(tri'-an-gle)*. A shape or figure having three sides and therefore three angles.

tribe. People belonging to the same group or race.

tributary *(trib'-u-tar-y)*. 1. Contributing to or adding to. 2. A tributary is a stream that flows into another.

trick. 1. An action done with the idea of deceiving somebody. 2. Mischief, as "Tom is up to more of his tricks". 3. One of the stunts a magician performs.

trickle *(trick'-le)*. To fall in drops or in a small stream.

tricycle *(tri'-cy-cle)*. Tri means three and cycle means wheel; thus a tricycle is a vehicle with three wheels which children use to ride about.

trifle *(tri'-fle)*. 1. Something small and unimportant. 2. To trifle with something is not to treat it seriously. 3. Trifle is a kind of pudding made from custard, cream and sponge cake.

trigger *(trig'-ger)*. The catch on a gun, pistol, etc., that, when pulled, fires the shot.

trigonometry *(trig-o-nom'-e-try)*. A branch of mathematics which has to do with the measuring of the angles and sides of triangles.

trim. 1. Neat; in good order. 2. To trim is to clip, as "Help me to trim the hedge". 3. To trim a ship is to adjust its position in the water by rearranging the cargo, taking in or letting out sails, etc.

trinket *(trin'-ket)*. A small piece of jewellery, or an ornament of little worth.

trip. 1. A journey, as "He went for a trip round the world". 2. To step lightly, as "She came tripping down the stairs". 3. To stumble, as "She tripped over a box".

tripe. 1. Parts of the stomach of sheep and cattle used as food. 2. Rubbish.

triplets *(trip'-lets)*. Just as twins are two people having the same mother and born at the same time, so triplets are three people born at the same time of the same mother.

tripod *(tri'-pod)*. Anything having three legs. When a camera is set up on a three-legged stand, it is on a tripod.

triumph *(tri'-umph)*. A great victory or success.

trivial *(triv'-i-al)*. Of no importance at all.

troll. 1. To fish with a hook drawn along or through the water. 2. An ugly dwarf or giant supposed to live in the mountains of northern Europe.

trombone *(trom-bone')*. A brass musical instrument, sounded by blowing into it. The tube is moved in and out to play different notes.

troop. 1. A company of soldiers or boy scouts. 2. To move or gather in crowds, as "The people trooped into the streets to welcome the airmen". (See also **troupe.**)

trophy *(tro'-phy)*. A thing to remind a person of his success; thus, a runner may win a race and be given a silver cup. The cup is a trophy. A huntsman may bring home the horns of a deer he has shot and have them mounted on a wall as a trophy.

tropics *(trop'-ics)*. An area of the earth's surface lying immediately north and south of the equator, between the Tropic of Cancer in the north and the Tropic of Capricorn in the south. The climate in the tropics is hot. (See **Cancer** and **Capricorn.**)

trot. To run with small steps.

trouble *(trou'-ble)*. Disturbance; difficulty.

trough. 1. A long, narrow receptacle for water or for holding the food of animals. 2. The lowest part of the curve between one wave and the one following it.

troupe. A band or company of actors, singers, etc.

trousers *(trou'-sers)*. A garment with two legs that covers the body from the waist to the knees or the ankles.

trout. A game fish living in fast-running streams.

trowel *(trow'-el)*. 1. The tool used by a bricklayer for spreading mortar. 2. A small, scoop-shaped gardening tool.

truant *(tru'-ant)*. A pupil who stays away from school without permission.

truce. The agreement to stop fighting for a definite length of time, as "In 1914, some English and German soldiers agreed to a truce on Christmas Day".

truck. 1. A large, open railway wagon. 2. A cart used in factories, etc.; to move goods from one place to another.

trudge. To tramp wearily.

true. 1. The events described in a true story actually took place. 2. If you are true to your country, you are a faithful or loyal citizen. 3. A true statement is a correct or accurate statement.

trumpet *(trum'-pet)*. A brass musical instrument which is blown into and produces a loud, clear, blaring sound.

truncheon *(trun'-cheon)*. The short club with which a policeman is armed.

trundle *(trun'-dle)*. To roll, push or drag along.

trunk. 1. The stem of a tree. 2. A case for carrying things while on holiday or when travelling. 3. A person's body, not including the head, arms and legs.

truss. 1. A support for a roof or bridge, etc. 2. A belt worn to support the abdomen. 3. A bundle of hay.

trust. 1. When you trust a friend, you believe him to be honest. 2. When something is left in trust, it is left with a person who manages it or looks after it. 3. When you are given a position of trust, you are expected to be honest and responsible.

trustee *(trus-tee')*. A person who has been given the care of another person's property in order to look after it for the benefit of a third person.

truth. That which is true and not a lie or a fiction.

try. 1. To attempt; experiment; strive; test. 2. An attempt, etc.

tub. A vessel used for the purpose of washing or bathing.

tube. 1. A long pipe, open at both ends. 2. The metal container in which we buy such things as toothpaste, glue, etc.

tuberculosis *(tu-ber-cu-lo'-sis)*. A disease, usually of the lungs.

tuck. 1. To fold. 2. A fold.

Tuesday *(Tues'-day)*. The third day of the week between Monday and Wednesday.

tuft. A bunch or tassel of something such as grass, hair, etc.

tug. 1. To pull sharply. 2. A sudden sharp pull. 3. A small steamboat that pulls or pushes other boats into position.

tuition *(tu-i'-tion)*. Teaching; instruction.

tulip *(tu'-lip)*. A plant that bears shiny, brightly-coloured, bell-shaped flowers in spring.

tumbler *(tum'-bler)*. 1. An acrobat who tumbles or falls about. 2. A large drinking glass, so called because formerly it had a pointed base and could not be put down without falling over. 3. A kind of pigeon.

tumult *(tu'-mult)*. A noisy affair; an uproar.

tune. 1. A song; an air or melody; a piece of music. 2. To tune an instrument is to adjust it so that it will play at the proper pitch. 3. To tune in a radio station means to adjust a radio set so as to receive a station clearly.

tunic *(tu'-nic)*. A short dress or long jacket with a belt, worn by soldiers, etc.

tunnel *(tun'-nel)*. 1. A passage-way cut out of the earth and, therefore, underground. 2. To make a tunnel.

turban *(tur'-ban)*. A long piece of material wound round so as to form the head-dress of oriental men.

turbid *(tur'-bid)*. Muddy, as "The water of the river is turbid".

turbine *(tur'-bine)*. A kind of wheel which is made to revolve by jets of water, steam or hot gases.

turbulent *(tur'-bu-lent)*. Unruly; noisy; violent.

tureen *(tu-reen')*. A large kind of dish, used for bringing soup to the dinner table.

turf. 1. Pieces of grass with earth clinging to the roots. A lawn is covered with turf. 2. Horse racing is called the turf.

turkey *(tur'-key)*. 1. A large wild or domestic fowl, usually black with a red head. It is a favourite for Christmas dinners. 2. **Turkey** is a country between the Mediterranean and the Black Sea.

turmoil *(tur'-moil)*. Trouble; disturbance.

turn. 1. To go round and round, as "Wheels turn". 2. To move round a little, as "I turned to see who was standing behind me". 3. To become, as "When I accused him, he turned very red". 4. A fright, as "Why do you creep in like that? You gave me quite a turn". 5. Your place, chance or time in a line or alternating order, as "Whose turn is it to deal the cards?"

turncoat *(turn'-coat)*. A person who switches his loyalty from one side to the other; usually one who changes his political party.

turnip *(tur'-nip)*. A root plant with yellow flesh which is eaten as a vegetable.

turpentine *(tur'-pen-tine)*. An oily fluid obtained from pine trees; it is used for mixing with paint.

turquoise *(tur'-quoise)*. A gem or precious stone of a beautiful blue-green colour.

turret *(tur'-ret)*. A small tower. (See **tower**.)

turtle *(tur'-tle)*. A kind of sea-tortoise.

tusk. A long tooth that comes out beyond the mouth. Boars and elephants have tusks.

tutor *(tu'-tor)*. A private teacher who looks after one or two pupils at a time.

twang. 1. To sound with a quick, harsh ringing noise, as "The banjo twanged its tune". 2. To speak with a twang is to speak as if you were speaking through your nose.

tweed. A kind of cloth made of wool. It is tough and long-wearing and is often used for coats and suits.

tweezers *(tweez'-ers)*. Tiny pincers used for holding small things. Tweezers may be used to draw a splinter out of your hand.

twice. Two times.

twig. A small branch.

twilight *(twi'-light)*. The half-light after sunset and before sunrise, when it is neither quite light nor quite dark.

twill. A cloth with diagonal ribs showing in it.

twine. 1. String. 2. To twist.

twins. Two children born at the same time of the same mother.

twinkle *(twin'-kle)*. To glitter or sparkle.

twirl. To whirl around.

twist. 1. Something twined in the way strands of thread are twined together. 2. To pull out of shape, as "He twisted his mouth into all sorts of shapes". 3. To wind a thing round and round, as "He twisted a piece of cotton round his finger".

twitter *(twit'-ter)*. A light, sweet sound made by birds.

type. 1. The metal letters which are used by printers. 2. In "He is not a nice type of boy", type means sort or kind.

typewriter *(type'-writ-er)*. A machine which prints the letters of the alphabet when its keys are pressed.

typhoid fever *(ty'-phoid fe'-ver)*. An infectious disease marked by a high fever. It can be caught by drinking unclean water.

typhoon *(ty-phoon')*. A severe wind and rain storm which occurs in the area of the China Seas. A hurricane.

typical *(typ'-i-cal)*. Like most of the others of the same kind.

typist *(typ'-ist)*. A person who operates a typewriter.

tyrant *(ty'-rant)*. A cruel master or ruler. He is **tyrannical** *(ty-ran'-ni-cal)* and **tyrannizes** *(tyr'-an-ni-zes)* over those who serve under him. They have to put up with his **tyranny** *(tyr'-an-ny)*.

tyre. The rubber ring around the wheel of a car, bicycle, etc.

U

udder *(ud'-der)*. That part of a cow from which milk is obtained.

ugly *(ug'-ly)*. Unpleasant to look at.

ulcer *(ul'-cer)*. A sore on the body that gives off a discharge of matter.

ulterior *(ul-te'-ri-or)*. Further; beyond; hidden. In "He has some ulterior reason for taking the books away", ulterior means hidden or beyond what he said was his reason.

ultimate *(ul'-ti-mate)*. Last; final.

ultimatum *(ul-ti-ma'-tum)*. A final offer of conditions, with the suggestion that if they are not accepted, something serious will happen.

umbrella *(um-brel'-la)*. A portable, cloth-covered frame which protects a person from rain, sun or snow.

umpire *(um'-pire)*. A referee; a person who rules on the plays of a game.

un-. A prefix meaning "not", which is placed before many words. If you wish to find the meaning of a word beginning with **un-,** and if you cannot find it among those listed below, find the word as it would be without the prefix **un-.** Then add "not" to the meaning. For example, if you wish to find "unacceptable" you will find that it is not listed on this page; therefore, take away the **un-** and find "acceptable". The meaning given is "worth taking". "Unacceptable", therefore, means "not worth taking".

unable *(un-a'-ble)*. Not able, or unfit.

unanimous *(u-nan'-i-mous)*. All of the same mind; everybody agreeing.

unawares *(un-a-wares')*. Unexpectedly, as "He crept up quietly behind us and came upon us unawares"; without knowing, as "I did not mean to shut the door on the dog's tail; I did it unawares".

uncanny *(un-can'-ny)*. Mysterious or weird.

uncertain *(un-cer'-tain)*. When you are uncertain, you are doubtful.

uncle *(un'-cle)*. The brother of your father or your mother; the husband of your aunt.

uncomfortable *(un-com'-fort-a-ble)*. Uneasy; not comfortable.

unconscious *(un-con'-scious)*. Not conscious; not awake; not knowing what is going on around you. If you were knocked out you would be unconscious for a while.

uncover *(un-cov'-er)*. To take the cover off; to reveal.

undergo *(un-der-go')*. To go through; to suffer, as "I am glad to say he will not have to undergo an operation".

underhand *(un'-der-hand)*. 1. By secret or sly means; dishonest. 2. To hit something underhand is to hit it with the arm swinging up from underneath.

underneath *(un-der-neath')*. Below; beneath.

understand *(un-der-stand')*. 1. To comprehend; to perceive and know the meaning of. When you understand a thing you are not puzzled by it but you know what it is, or how it works, or what it means. 2. To come to a conclusion, as "From what you have just said I understand your reason for remaining here".

understood *(un-der-stood')*. The past tense of understand.

undertake *(un-der-take')*. To agree to do. But an **undertaker** is generally a person who arranges funerals.

underwear *(un'-der-wear)*. Clothes which are worn under the outer clothes.

undo *(un-do')*. Unfasten.

undress *(un-dress')*. To take one's clothes off; to strip.

undulate *(un'-du-late)*. To rise and fall gently. Smooth, rolling land is often said to undulate.

unexpected *(un-ex-pect'-ed)*. Without warning.

unhappy *(un-hap'-py)*. Sad.

unicorn *(u'-ni-corn)*. A fabulous (or unreal) animal with a horse-like body and one horn in the middle of its forehead.

uniform *(u'-ni-form)*. 1. The same, said of many things; alike; not differing, as "These sweets are of uniform size". 2. Clothing of a particular style that is worn by persons that do the same work or belong to the same group, etc. Soldiers, sailors and nurses wear uniforms.

union *(un'-ion)*. 1. A joining together of things; marriage. 2. Trade or labour unions are groups of people engaged in similar kinds of work. 3. The Union Jack is the national flag of the United Kingdom, formed by combining the crosses of St. Patrick, St. Andrew and St. George.

unique *(u-nique')*. A thing is unique when it is the only one of its kind, when there is no other like it.

unit *(u'-nit)*. 1. A certain amount or quantity which is set as a standard of measurement. An inch is a unit of measurement of length; a degree is a unit of measurement of heat; an ounce is a unit of measurement of weight. 2. Anything thought of as single, as "Each classroom is a unit in the school".

unite *(u-nite')*. To bring together, as "When people marry, they are united in wedlock".

universal *(u-ni-ver'-sal)*. Having to do with everybody; for all; belonging to everybody.

university *(u-ni-ver'-si-ty)*. A place of higher learning where degrees may be obtained by the students.

unknown *(un-known')*. Not known; strange.

unless *(un-less')*. Except.

unmerciful *(un-mer'-ci-ful)*. Cruel; hard of heart; pitiless.

until *(un-til')*. In "I shall not leave until you arrive", until means up to the time when you arrive. In "Until then, I had forgotten it", until means before.

unusual *(un-u'-su-al)*. Strange or rare.

upbraid *(up-braid')*. To scold; to find fault with.

uphold *(up-hold')*. To side with; to agree with; to support.

upholsterer *(up-hol'-ster-er)*. A person who pads and covers chairs, couches and other furniture.

upland *(up'-land)*. Higher ground, usually inland.

upon *(up-on')*. On.

upper *(up'-per)*. Being farther up; higher, as "He slept in the upper berth". When we say that someone has the upper hand we mean that he has the advantage or mastery or is in control.

upright *(up'-right)*. 1. Erect. 2. An upright person often means one who is thoroughly honest.

uproar *(up'-roar)*. A dreadful noise.

upset *(up-set')*. 1. When you upset your milk, you overturn the glass and spill it. 2. When you feel upset you feel ill or distressed in mind.

upstairs *(up-stairs')*. Up the stairs; on the upper floor.

upward *(up'-ward)*. In the direction of a higher place.

urban *(ur'-ban)*. To do with towns and cities.

urchin *(ur'-chin)*. A mischievous small boy.

urge. To beg someone to do something.

urgent *(ur'-gent)*. Needing to be seen to at once; very pressing.

urn. 1. A type of vase that stands on a base. 2. A large vessel, usually with a tap, for making large quantities of tea, etc.

usage *(us'-age)*. 1. Treatment, as "The poor dog showed signs of bad usage". 2. Usual action or procedure, as "In China it is common usage to eat with chopsticks instead of with knives and forks".

use. 1. When you use a saw, you put the saw into action. 2. When you use up your energy you spend it. 3. The use of a thing is the purpose to which it may be put.

useful *(use'-ful)*. Something is useful when you can do something with it; it is helpful.

usher *(ush'-er)*. 1. A person who takes you to your seat in a theatre, church, etc. 2. To do this.

usual *(u'-su-al)*. A thing is usual when you expect it or when it is customary. It is usual to take a collection in church; thus a collection is **usually** taken.

utensil *(u-ten'-sil)*. A useful tool, implement or container, such as pots and pans, shears and watering cans, etc.

utmost *(ut'-most)*. The very most, as "Come back with the utmost speed".

utter *(ut'-ter)*. 1. Absolute; complete, as "That boy is an utter donkey". 2. To say or speak, as "He uttered something about his wife and three children".

V

vacant *(va'-cant)*. Empty.

vacate *(va-cate')*. To go from a place and leave it empty.

vacation *(va-ca'-tion)*. A holiday from one's duties.

vaccinate *(vac'-ci-nate)*. To give an injection to someone to prevent him from getting some diseases. A **vaccine** is a preparation made from weakened germs that cause disease.

vacillate *(va'-cil-late)*. To change one's mind constantly.

vacuum *(vac'-u-um)*. An empty space from which most or all the air has been drawn.

P

vagabond *(vag'-a-bond)*. A worthless person; one who wanders about and does no work.

vagrant *(va'-grant)*. A tramp; a wanderer.

vague. Not clear or distinct, as "He gave me some vague instructions as to how I could get there, but I lost my way".

vain. 1. A person who is vain is conceited because of his appearance or his personal achievements. "Vain" has not the same meaning as "proud", however. A person who is vain is conceited about something that is of no true value or importance. 2. Vain also means useless; foolish; of no importance. 3. "In vain" means uselessly, or without result.

valet *(val'-et)*. A man-servant who helps his master to dress.

valiant *(val'-iant)*. Brave; gallant.

valid *(val'-id)*. 1. Sound; accurate; true, as "He gave me a valid reason for his absence", meaning a sound reason. 2. In "His ticket is valid until next Monday", valid means good or effective.

validate *(val-i-date')*. To make valid.

valley *(val'-ley)*. The low land between hills.

valour *(val'-our)*. Bravery; courage.

valuable *(val'-u-a-ble)*. A thing which is expensive or means a great deal to you is valuable. A wrist watch is valuable, as is a close friend.

value *(val'-ue)*. The value of a thing is what it is worth.

valve. A device to regulate the flow through a pipe.

van. 1. A covered vehicle for moving things or delivering goods. Most tradesmen use vans for delivering goods to their customers. 2. The front part of an army.

vandal *(van'-dal)*. A person who damages other people's property purposely. If you cut your name with a pocket-knife in a school desk, you are a vandal.

vane. A weather-vane is a movable metal or wooden device which shows the direction of the wind.

vanilla *(va-nil'-la)*. A flavour added to sweets, ice-cream, etc.

vanish *(van'-ish)*. To disappear.

vanity *(van'-i-ty)*. 1. Empty pride or conceit, usually based on personal appearance. 2. Foolishness; unimportance; worthlessness, as "the vanity of worldly wealth".

vanquish *(van'-quish)*. To conquer.

vapour *(va'-pour)*. When water is heated it boils and steam rises from it. The steam is water vapour, that is, water that has been turned into gas by heat.

variable *(var'-i-a-ble)*. Changeable; not always the same. A thing that is variable shows **variations** *(var-i-a'-tions)*.

variance *(var'-i-ance)*. Varying; difference; disagreement; thus things that are at variance show a difference; they disagree.

variegated *(va'-rie-gated)*. Marked with patches of different colours. Some kinds of holly are variegated, having yellow spots on the leaves.

variety *(va-ri'-e-ty)*. An assortment of different kinds. A variety concert is a concert of different kinds of entertainment.

various *(var'-i-ous)*. Several; many; of different kinds.

varnish *(var'-nish)*. A clear, gummy liquid which dries to form a hard, glossy surface.

vary *(var'-y)*. To differ; to change.

vase. A container for holding flowers or for decoration.

vast. Stretching a long way; immense, widespread.

vat. A large cask or tank.

Vatican *(Vat'-i-can)*. A group of buildings in Rome including the palace of the Pope.

vault. 1. To leap. 2. A roof consisting of arches, as found in some churches. 3. An underground chamber. 4. A tomb.

vaunt. Boast.

veal. The flesh of a calf, used as meat.

veer. To turn round. The wind is said to veer when it changes direction.

vegetable *(veg'-e-ta-ble)*. 1. Of a plant; having to do with plants. Vegetable dye, therefore, is dye made from plants. 2. A plant, especially one eaten as food.

vegetarian *(veg-e-tar'-ian)*. A person who eats vegetables and not meat.

vegetation *(veg-e-ta'-tion)*. Plant life, as "They saw many different kinds of vegetation in travelling from Cairo to the Cape".

vehicle *(ve'-hi-cle)*. Any kind of carriage, truck, car, wagon, cart, bicycle or other conveyance which is used on land.

veil. A thin piece of material worn over or about the face for protection or decoration.

vein. 1. A tube that carries blood to the heart from other parts of the body. 2. The ribs on the leaves of plants.

velocity *(ve-loc'-i-ty)*. Speed; the rate at which something is moving.

velvet *(vel'-vet)*. A kind of cloth, made from silk, which has a soft, furry surface.

veneer *(ve-neer')*. Thin pieces of a beautiful, expensive material, especially wood, which are stuck onto the surface of an object made of cheaper material. Furniture is often covered with mahogany veneer to give it a finer appearance.

venerate *(ven'-er-ate)*. To have a great regard for; to think highly of.

vengeance *(venge'-ance)*. Revenge; paying a person back for the wrong he has done to you.

venison *(ven'-i-son)*. The flesh of deer, used as meat.

venom *(ven'-om)*. 1. The poison of snakes. 2. Spite.

ventilate *(ven'-ti-late)*. To allow fresh air to enter.

ventilator *(ven'-ti-la-tor)*. An opening that allows fresh air to enter a room.

ventriloquism *(ven-tril'-o-quism)*. The art of being able to play tricks with your voice so that it seems to come from a point some feet away from you.

venture *(ven'-ture)*. 1. To venture on something is to take a risk. 2. To venture is also to dare. 3. A venture is sometimes a daring undertaking.

veracity *(ve-rac'-i-ty)*. Truthfulness.

verandah *(ve-ran'-dah)*. A covered porch or passage along the front or side of a house.

verb. The word in a sentence that tells what is done or that mentions the action; thus the verb in "He bought some ice-cream" is "bought". "To be" and "to have" are also verbs. In "I am ill and Mary has measles" the words "am" and "has" are the verbs.

verbal *(ver'-bal)*. Spoken and not written, as "He gave me verbal instructions", meaning he did not write them.

verbatim *(ver-ba'-tim)*. Word for word; thus, if something is told you verbatim, every word of it is told you, as it was first recorded.

verbose *(ver-bose')*. Said of a person who has a lot to say, who is always talking. Very wordy.

verdant *(ver'-dant)*. Green; fresh.

verdict *(ver'-dict)*. 1. The decision of a jury at a trial. Thus, "The verdict was 'Not Guilty'". 2. A decision; a judgement.

verge. 1. The edge, as "He is on the verge of ruin". 2. The grass strip beside a country road is also a verge.

verify *(ver'-i-fy)*. To prove to be right. If you work your sum a second time to make sure it is right, you verify the answer.

vermilion *(ver-mil'-ion)*. The colour bright red.

vermin *(ver'-min)*. Small animals which are considered pests. Mice are vermin and so are fleas.

vernal *(ver'-nal)*. To do with spring. The snowdrop is a vernal flower because it blooms in the spring.

versatile *(ver'-sa-tile.)* Able to do many things well.

verse. 1. A line of poetry. 2. Poetry. 3. A short division of a metrical composition, as the verses in a hymn or in a song.

versus *(ver'-sus)*. Against. This word is often shortened to v. and we see such announcements as "Boxing Match— Tom Jones v. Fred Smith".

vertebrate *(ver'-te-brate)*. Having a backbone. You are a vertebrate and so are a horse and an elephant.

vertical *(ver'-ti cal)*. Up and down; at right angles to the ground. The margins of this page are vertical, but the lines of print are horizontal.

vertigo *(ver'-ti-go)*. Dizziness.

vespers *(ves'-pers)*. Evening service held in church.

vessel *(ves'-sel)*. 1. A ship. 2. Anything that will hold a liquid; thus a cup is a drinking vessel.

vest. 1. A garment worn under a shirt, blouse or dress. 2. To vest authority in someone is to give him authority, as "He vested in his brother authority to sell his property".

vestibule *(ves'-ti-bule)*. A hall or lobby.

vestige *(ves'-tige)*. A trace of something that no longer exists.

veteran *(vet'-er-an)*. 1. An old soldier. 2. Anyone who has done a certain kind of work for very many years.

veterinary *(vet'-er-i-nar-y)*. 1. To do with the medical treatment of animals. 2. A veterinary surgeon is an animal doctor.

veto *(ve'-to)*. To forbid; to vote against and thus cancel, as "The headmaster vetoed the suggestion that children be given a holiday from school".

vex. To upset, worry or distress.

vexation *(vex-a'-tion)*. That which upsets, worries or distresses.

viaduct *(vi'-a-duct)*. A bridge that spans a valley. Often a viaduct has a river running below it.

vibrate *(vi'-brate)*. To move very quickly to and fro; to throb. The sound produced by a violin is due to the **vibration** *(vi-bra'-tion)* of the strings.

vicar *(vic'-ar)*. A clergyman. He lives in a **vicarage.**

vice. 1. Sin; evil; a bad habit. 2. A tool used for holding things tightly. It has two jaws that are tightened by a screw.

vicinity *(vi-cin'-i-ty)*. Neighbourhood; the area near at hand, as "In the vicinity of my house, there is a golf course".

vicious *(vi'-cious)*. 1. Having vices; evil; wicked, as "That man has led a vicious life; he has been a liar and a drunkard". 2. Savage; likely to attack fiercely. A wolf is a vicious animal.

victim *(vic'-tim)*. A person who suffers from something that has happened.

victor *(vic'-tor)*. A conqueror; one who wins something. He gains a **victory** and is **victorious** *(vic-to'-ri-ous)*.

victuals *(vict'-uals)*. Food.

view. 1. To view is to look at. 2. A view is a scene or something to look at. 3. In "In my view, you should not have done that", view means opinion or impression.

vigil *(vig'-il)*. A watch, usually during the night.

vigilance *(vig'-i-lance)*. Watchfulness.

vigorous *(vig'-or-ous)*. Energetic; full of strength.

vigour *(vig'-our)*. Physical strength or energy.

Viking *(Vi'-king)*. One of a race of men who long ago set out from Norway and Denmark on voyages of adventure, war and plunder.

vile. Loathsome; bad.

villa *(vil'-la)*. A house in the country or on the edge of a town, usually standing in its own grounds.

village *(vil'-lage)*. A very small town.

villain *(vil'-lain)*. A bad person. He is **villainous.**

vindicate *(vin'-di-cate)*. To defend or justify, as "He vindicated himself by showing that the crime for which he was arrested was committed while he was out of the country".

vine. A climbing plant. There are several kinds, but the grape vine is the one best known.

vinegar *(vin'-e-gar)*. A sharp, sour liquid which is taken in small quantities with certain foods. Also used for pickling.

viola *(vi-o'-la)*. 1. A musical instrument which looks just like a violin but is larger and has a deeper tone. 2. A family of plants. The violet and the pansy belong to this family.

violate *(vi'-o-late)*. 1. To break a law is to violate it. 2. Violate also means to damage, especially when sacred things are damaged.

violence *(vi'-o-lence)*. Extreme force; injurious treatment.

violet *(vi'-o-let)*. 1. A small, dainty plant which has purple, blue, or white flowers. 2. The colour bluish-purple.

violin *(vi-o-lin')*. A four-stringed musical instrument played with a bow.

violinist *(vi-o-lin'-ist)*. A person who plays the violin.

viper *(vi'-per)*. A poisonous snake; the adder.

virile *(vir'-ile)*. Manly.

virtuous *(vir'-tu-ous)*. Morally good.

virulent *(vir'-u-lent)*. When said of snakes, plants, etc., this means poisonous. When said of a disease it means dangerous or deadly.

visage *(vis'-age)*. The face or features.

visible *(vis'-i-ble)*. Able to be seen; thus "The plane was visible, though it was high in the sky".

vision *(vi'-sion)*. 1. Sight, as "The old man is rapidly losing his vision". 2. A dream, as "While he was asleep he had a vision".

visit *(vis'-it)*. To go to see someone or to pay a call on someone is to visit him. The one who goes is a **visitor.**

vital *(vi'-tal)*. Necessary for life.

vitamin *(vi'-ta-min)*. Any of certain substances in food which help the body to grow and remain in good health. A lack of vitamins causes disease and poor health.

vitiate *(vi'-ti-ate)*. To spoil; injure.

vivacious *(vi-va'-cious)*. Lively; full of gaiety.

vivid *(viv'-id)*. Very bright and clear. A vivid light would be bright and a vivid imagination would imagine things very clearly.

vocabulary *(vo-cab'-u-lar-y)*. 1. The words of a language. 2. Your vocabulary consists of the words you speak, read and write.

vocal *(vo'-cal)*. Having to do with the voice. The vocal chords are folds of flesh deep in the throat which enable us to speak, sing, etc.

vocation *(vo-ca'-tion)*. A person's vocation is the work he does; it is his business, profession, trade, etc.

voice. The sound made in speaking, singing, etc.

void. 1. Empty. 2. Not valid.

volcano *(vol-ca'-no)*. A cone-shaped mountain from whose centre molten rock once flowed. If the volcano is active, it occasionally erupts, or sends out steam, smoke, flames and molten rock.

volley *(vol'-ley)*. A discharge of many bullets, arrows, stones or oaths, as "When the enemy appeared, a volley of bullets greeted them". 2. In tennis a volley is a return of the ball before it touches the ground, and to volley is to hit the ball before it touches the ground.

volt. A measure of electricity.

voluble *(vol'-u-ble)*. Always talking in a noisy way.

volume *(vol'-ume)*. 1. A book, as "I have a volume of the encyclopædia in my desk". 2. Space; thus the volume of a room is the space in the room, found by multiplying the width and length of the floor by the height of the wall. (See **cubic**.)

voluminous *(vo-lu'-mi-nous)*. Bulky; taking up much space.

voluntary *(vol'-un-tar-y)*. Done of your own free will; done because you want to do it, not because you must.

volunteer *(vol-un-teer')*. To offer your services for doing a certain thing; thus, when a war is being fought, many men volunteer to fight.

vomit *(vom'-it)*. To be sick; to bring up food from the stomach.

voracious *(vo-ra'-cious)*. Greedy; gluttonous; able and eager to eat a great deal.

vote. 1. A wish or choice which is written on paper or declared in some other way, as by raising your arm. 2. To vote is to register a vote.

vouch. To guarantee or say you will be responsible for, as "I vouch for the honesty of the boy", meaning that you are so sure he is honest that you are prepared to take the responsibility should it be found he is dishonest.

voucher *(vouch'-er)*. 1. One who vouches (see **vouch**). 2. A written or printed note that vouches or proves payment; a receipt.

vow. 1. A promise. 2. To promise.

vowel *(vow'-el).* The letters a, e, i, o and u are all vowels.

voyage *(voy'-age).* A journey by water or air.

vulgar *(vul'-gar).* In bad taste; offensive; low; coarse; common.

vulgarity *(vul-gar'-i-ty).* Coarseness; commonness; bad taste; offensiveness.

vulnerable *(vul'-ner-a-ble).* Easily injured.

W

wad. A mass of material, such as wool, pressed into a hard lump.

waddle *(wad'-dle).* To walk like a duck, swaying from side to side.

wade. To walk through water.

wading *(wad'-ing).* Walking in the water.

wafer *(wa'-fer).* A thin biscuit, such as is used for making an ice-cream sandwich.

waffle *(waf'-fle).* A small, flat cake like a pancake.

waft. 1. When something is carried along by the breeze or by a current of water it is said to be wafted. 2. A puff of air.

wag. 1. To move from side to side in quick jerks. A dog wags his tail when he is happy. 2. A wag is a funny person who likes playing jokes.

wage. 1. To take part in, as to wage war. 2. A worker's pay is his wage or **wages.**

wager *(wa'-ger).* 1. A bet. 2. To bet.

wagon *(wag'-on).* A four-wheeled cart or truck to carry heavy loads. Also spelled **waggon.**

waif. A person, especially a child, who has no home, no money and no friends.

wail. To moan; to cry because of grief.

waist. The middle of the body. A man wears a belt around his waist.

wait. 1. To stay somewhere until something happens, as "He waited on the platform for the train to come". 2. The time of staying somewhere, as "He had a long wait on the platform for the train". 3. To act as a servant at meal times, as "She waited on her mistress at dinner".

waiter *(wait'-er)*. A man who serves others with meals at table. A woman who does this is a **waitress.**

wake. 1. To end a sleep; to cease sleeping. 2. The wake of a ship or anything moving is the trail that it leaves behind.

wakeful *(wake'-ful)*. Restless and unable to sleep when it is time to sleep.

walk. To move on foot.

wall. The side of a room or a house, etc.

wallet *(wal'-let)*. A pocket-case for money, odd papers, etc., usually carried in a man's breast pocket.

walnut *(wal'-nut)*. 1. A large, round nut. 2. The tree which grows such a nut.

walrus *(wal'-rus)*. A large arctic sea animal, something like a seal but with long tusks. Walrus skin is used for making leather goods.

waltz. 1. A graceful, gliding dance in 3/4 time. 2. The music for such a dance is called a waltz.

wan. Pale; tired-looking.

wand. A long, thin stick. Fairies are often drawn holding a wand

wander *(wan'-der)*. To go off somewhere, having no particular destination. If a person's mind wanders, the person cannot keep his thoughts on one idea.

wane. To grow less in size, strength, success, etc. When the moon wanes it grows thinner and thinner.

want. 1. To need something that you do not have. 2. If a person is in want, it usually means he is poor. 3. To wish for something.

wanton *(wan'-ton)*. A wanton act is one that should not have been done because it causes harm to others. It is a reckless action. A boy who purposely throws a stone through a window does a wanton act.

ward. 1. A room in a hospital which accommodates several patients. 2. A person whose care is the responsibility of a guardian. 3. A division of a large town or city.

warden *(ward'-en)*. 1. A guard. 2. The head of a prison. 3. The head of a school or college. 4. A churchwarden.

warder *(war'-der)*. A prison officer.

wardrobe *(ward'-robe)*. 1. A cupboard in which clothes are hung. 2. All your clothes.

wares. Goods which are made and placed for sale.

warehouse *(ware'-house)*. A building in which goods are stored before they are sold.

warfare *(war'-fare)*. War.

warm. 1. Neither hot nor cold; moderately hot. 2. Warm also means kind or affectionate in such cases as "They gave her a warm welcome".

warmth. 1. In "He felt the warmth of the fire", warmth means heat. 2. In "He spoke with warmth", warmth means eagerness or strong feeling.

warn. To tell of some danger that may happen; to caution. Notices such as "Wet paint" warn you to be careful; they are **warnings.**

warp. 1. To twist out of shape, as "The door has warped and now it will not shut properly". 2. The threads in a piece of cloth, etc., that run the long way of the material. The threads going crossways are the **weft.** 3. A person's mind is said to be warped when his thinking seems to follow a twisted and unnatural course.

warren *(war'-ren)*. 1. A system of burrows made by rabbits. 2. A piece of land kept for the breeding of game.

warrior *(war'-ri-or)*. A soldier fighting in a war, usually one who has done brave deeds.

wart. A small, crusty growth on the skin.

wary *(war'-y)*. Cautious; on guard.

wasp. An insect much like a bee but more slender and less hairy. Its sting is usually more painful.

waste. 1. When you waste money, you spend it on trivial or unimportant things. 2. When you waste food, you do not eat it but throw it away. 3. Waste material is material that is of no use and must be thrown away. 4. A waste or wasteland is a desert or wild, uncultivated place. 5. When you waste away as a result of sickness you become thin and weak.

watch. 1. A small timepiece. 2. To look at.

water *(wa'-ter)*. 1. The commonest liquid. 2. To water the garden is to pour water on it. 3. To water horses is to give them drink. 4. If your eyes water, tears flow. 5. If your mouth waters, you long for a certain thing to eat. 6. Watered silk has wavy markings on it.

waterfall *(wa'-ter-fall)*. A steep drop in a river-bed, over which the stream tumbles.

waterproof *(wa'-ter-proof)*. 1. A material or substance that will not allow water through it is waterproof. 2. To make a material resist water is to waterproof it.

wave. 1. A ridge on the surface of water which rolls towards the shore. 2. A vibration which passes through air, liquids or solids. 3. A signal or movement made by moving the hand and arm to and fro, as when you wave good-bye. 4. The movement of something in the air, as "The flag waved in the breeze".

waver *(wa'-ver)*. To be undecided; to move one way and then the other.

wax. 1. A fat-like yellow substance made by bees. 2. A coloured substance used for sealing letters. 3. To wax is to become larger. The moon waxes and wanes, meaning becomes larger and smaller.

waylay *(way-lay')*. To lie in wait for and stop.

wayside *(way'-side)*. The space at the side of a country road.

wayward *(way'-ward)*. Wilful; disobedient. A wayward person does what he wants to do whether it is right or not.

weak. The opposite to strong. If you have been ill for some time, you feel weak when you begin your activities again.

weal. 1. A ridge or a mark on the body caused by a cane, a whip, etc. 2. Happiness; prosperity; good fortune.

wealth. 1. Riches; large possessions. 2. Many; a great number, as "I have a wealth of ideas for our next holiday".

weapon *(weap'-on)*. Swords, daggers, guns, pistols, etc. are all weapons, or things with which you may cause injury or death.

wear. 1. To wear clothes is to put them on. 2. To wear out clothes is to make them old and shabby with use.

weary *(wea'-ry)*. Tired; feeling worn out.

weasel *(wea'-sel)*. A small carnivorous animal with a long, thin body.

weather *(weath'-er)*. 1. Outdoor conditions produced at a place by heat or cold, clearness or cloudiness, dryness or moisture and wind or calm. Thus we speak of cold weather, wet weather, windy weather, etc. 2. To come safely through, as "Don't worry; you will weather the trouble".

weave. To take a number of threads, etc., and twine them together into a cloth by using some of the threads for the warp and some for the weft. (See **warp**, No. 2.)

web. A thing that has been made by weaving, such as a spider's web.

wedding *(wed'-ding)*. The marriage of a man and a woman. The marriage ceremony and the festivities after.

wedge. A piece of hard material, narrow at one end and wider at the other. A wedge is used for splitting wood, or in a window frame to stop the wind rattling it, etc.

Wednesday *(Wednes'-day)*. The fourth day of the week, between Tuesday and Thursday.

weed. 1. A plant that grows where it is not wanted. 2. To pull up such plants is to weed.

week. A period of time composed of seven days. There are fifty-two weeks in a year.

weep. To cry.

weigh. 1. To find how heavy a thing is, as "Weigh this meat and tell me the cost". 2. To have a certain heaviness, as "That parcel weighs seven pounds". 2. To consider or think about, as "I have weighed in my mind what you have said and I will . . .".

weight. 1. Heaviness or lightness; degree of heaviness or lightness. 2. Some scales are operated by weighing the goods against lumps of metal. The lumps of metal are called weights.

weighty *(weight'-y)*. Serious; important; influential, as "He gave weighty reasons for leaving".

weir. A dam across a stream or river.

weird. Unearthly; mysterious; blood-curdling.

welcome *(wel'-come)*. A friendly reception.

weld. To join hot metal by hammering, or with a molten metal.

welfare *(wel'-fare)*. The well-being of a person or group of people. When parents insist that children go to bed early, they do so for the welfare of the children.

well. 1. Healthy. 2. Satisfactorily; rightly; excellently. 3. A hole in the ground from which water may be had by letting down a bucket on a chain, or by pumping.

wend. To go.

west. The direction opposite to east. The sun sets in the west.

western *(west'-ern)*. 1. In the direction of the west. 2. A play which is set in the early days of western North America.

whack. 1. A heavy blow with a stick or whip. 2. A share.

whale. A huge animal that lives in the sea. Whales are caught for whale oil, etc.

wharf. A landing place for ships, where they load and unload.

wheat. A kind of grass which produces a very useful grain. Bread is made from wheat.

wheel. A round disk which turns on an axle or pin.

wheelbarrow *(wheel'-bar-row)*. A device for carrying loads which has a wheel at one end and two handles at the other.

wheeze. To breathe with a hissing sound because the breathing tubes are partly clogged.

whelk. A shell-fish, similar to a winkle but larger.

whelp. A puppy; a young dog.

whence. From what place.

wherefore *(where'-fore)*. For what or which reason.

wherever *(wher-ev'-er)*. 1. At, to, or in whatever place, as "Wherever you find human beings, you find dogs". 2. No matter where, as "Wherever you go I will follow you".

whet. 1. To sharpen. A **whetstone** is a stone used for sharpening blades. 2. To excite, as "The first bite whetted his appetite".

whether *(wheth'-er)*. 1. This word indicates that there is a choice between alternatives, as in "He did not know whether to turn right or left". 2. In "We wanted to know whether we should leave", whether means if.

whey. The watery part of milk that is left when the milk has curdled. We speak of curds and whey.

whiff. A puff of air; a sniff of something, as "When she passed, I caught a whiff of perfume".

whimper *(whim'-per)*. To cry in a half-hearted way, probably making a small sound.

whine. To cry as a dog does when it is chained up and unhappy.

whinny *(whin'-ny)*. The low neigh of a horse.

whip. 1. To hit with a whip. 2. A whip is a stick with a cord or a lash tied to it. 3. To beat eggs, etc., into a froth. 4. To do something quickly, as "He whipped out a revolver and pointed it at the burglar".

whirl. Move rapidly round and round in a circle.

whirlpool *(whirl'-pool)*. Water moving round and round in a circle.

whirlwind *(whirl'-wind)*. Wind moving round and round in a circle violently.

whisk. 1. To brush lightly. 2. A small hand brush for brushing the clothes. 3. An instrument for beating eggs, mixing food, etc.

whiskers *(whisk'-ers)*. The beard or hairs on a man's face.

whisper *(whis'-per)*. To speak with the breath only.

whistle *(whis'-tle)*. 1. A shrill sound made by puckering the lips and blowing. 2. To make such a sound. 3. A device into which you blow to make a shrill sound.

white. A colour. Snow is white.

whither *(whith'-er)*. To what or which place.

whiting *(whit'-ing)*. 1. A sea-fish of the cod family. 2. Ground chalk used for making white-wash, etc.

whitlow *(whit'-low)*. A painful swelling on the finger at the side of the nail.

whittle *(whit'-tle)*. To cut down, shape or sharpen to a point with a knife.

whole. 1. If you eat a whole pie, you eat all of it. Anything with all its parts is a whole. 2. 9 is a whole number and $\frac{1}{2}$ is a fraction.

wholesale *(whole'-sale)*. The sale of goods in large quantities. Your grocer, who does not sell in large quantities, sells **retail** *(re'-tail)*; he buys in large quantities from a **wholesaler**.

wholesome *(whole'-some)*. Good for the health; thus bread and butter is wholesome.

whoop. To shout loudly.

wick. The cotton thread in candles and the cotton braid in lamps.

wicked *(wick'-ed)*. Evil; bad; immoral; mischievous.

wicker *(wick'-er)*. Woven from twigs like basketwork.

wide. Broad; a good distance from one side to the other.

widow *(wid'-ow)*. A woman whose husband has died. A man whose wife has died is a **widower**.

width. The distance across.

wield. To handle or use, as "The giant wielded his sword with terrific force".

wife. A married woman is the wife of her husband.

wig. An artificial covering of hair for the head.

wigwam *(wig'-wam)*. A tent made of poles and skins and used by Red Indians; a tepee.

wild. 1. Not tame, as "Lions are wild animals". 2. Not culti-vated, as "Buttercups are wild flowers". 3. Angry, as "When I came home late, father was wild". 4. Uncontrolled, as

"When the doors of the shop opened, people outside made a wild rush to be first at the counters".

wilderness *(wild'-er-ness)*. A wild, uncultivated place.

wilful *(wil'-ful)*. A wilful person is one who has made up his · mind to do as he likes, whether it is bad or good.

will. 1. Wish, desire or purpose. 2. A written account of a person's property and how he wants it shared among his relatives and friends after his death.

willing *(wil'-ling)*. Ready to do whatever is asked.

willow *(wil'-low)*. A tree with branches that can be bent without snapping; the branches are used for making wickerwork.

wily *(wil'-y)*. Tricky; crafty.

win. To be victorious; to beat one's rivals.

wince. To shrink or draw back as from a blow or from pain, as "The boy winced as the car rushed by, narrowly missing him".

wind. 1. Air moving fast enough to be felt. 2. To twist something around, as "Father winds the stem of his watch every morning".

winding *(wind'-ing)*. 1. In "He was winding his watch", winding means turning the stem. 2. In "We travelled on a winding road", winding means full of curves.

windmill *(wind'-mill)*. A mill which is operated by a bladed wheel that turns as it catches the wind.

window *(win'-dow)*. An opening in a wall or car, etc., which allows light or air to enter and allows a person to see out.

windscreen *(wind'-screen)*. The glass at the front of a car which protects the passengers from the wind.

wing. 1. The limb of a bird or insect with which it flies. 2. A part of a large building in some way separated from the main part. 3. The wings of an army are the right and left divisions, and the wings of a football team are the players to the right and left of the man in the centre.

wink. To open and close one eye quickly.

winner *(win'-ner)*. One who wins.

winsome *(win'-some)*. Charming; pleasing.

winter *(win'-ter)*. The coldest season of the year.

wipe. To clean or dry by rubbing.

wire. 1. A thread of metal. 2. To fasten something with wire; to run a wire through something; to provide a thing with wires, etc. 3. To wire someone is to send him a telegram.

wisdom *(wis'-dom)*. The ability to judge properly; the sense and knowledge to do things the right way.

wise. Sensible; having good judgment; not being a fool.

wish. 1. To long for; to have a desire for. 2. A desire.

wistful *(wist'-ful)*. Thoughtful; longing,

wit. 1. Cleverness; funniness, as "He spoke with wit and grace". 2. Sense, as "You have not the wit to do the right thing". (See **witty**.)

witch. In fairy tales, a woman who possesses supernatural powers to do evil; a woman who deals in black magic.

withdraw *(with-draw')*. To draw back.

wither *(with'-er)*. To fade; to shrink; to become dry.

withhold *(with-hold')*. To keep back.

withstand *(with-stand')*. To stand up against; to resist.

witness *(wit'-ness)*. 1. A person who sees something happen or in some other way knows what happened. 2. To witness something is to see it. 3. To witness the signing of a legal paper means to sign your name to it in order to declare that you have seen someone else sign his name to it.

witty *(wit'-ty)*. Funny; amusing. A witty person is called a **wit,** and his funny remarks are also known as **wit.**

wizard *(wiz'-ard)*. 1. A person who is supposed to have magical powers. 2. A clever or wise man.

woe. Much trouble or grief.

wolf. A very savage wild animal resembling a large dog.

woman *(wom'-an)*. A grown human female. The word for more than one woman is **women**.

wonder *(won'-der)*. 1. Great surprise; astonishment; a feeling of being unable to understand something. 2. Anything that causes wonder is a wonder. 3. To wonder is to be doubtful and curious about something. If you say, "I wonder why he came", you show that you do not know why he came and that you would like to know.

wonderful *(won'-der-ful)*. Full of wonder; remarkable.

wont. 1. Accustomed; in the habit of doing, thus "She was wont to fill her mouth with sweets and then start talking". 2. Custom or habit, thus "It was their wont to eat no meat on Fridays". Note the difference between *wont* and *won't*. The latter is a shortened form of *will not*.

woo. To make love to.

wood. 1. The material taken from trees and used to make chairs, tables, etc.; timber. 2. A place where hundreds of trees are growing close together.

woodbine *(wood'-bine)*. Honeysuckle. A climbing plant growing in hedges, the flowers of which have a delightful perfume.

woodpecker *(wood'-peck-er)*. A bird which pecks holes in trees and other wood to catch insects.

wool. The fleece on a sheep's back that is used for making the woollen garments which we wear. Anything that is **woollen** may be said to be **woolly.**

word. 1. The smallest unit of speech that has meaning by itself. All the lines in this book are made up of words and there are spaces between the words. 2. In "He gave me his word that he would never do such a thing again", word means promise. 3. In "He had a word with me on the matter", word means a short talk.

work. 1. The opposite to "play"; that which you do because you must, not in order to amuse yourself. 2. Job, occupation; employment. 3. Something which requires the use of energy to do it. A person who works is a **worker.** A machine that can be worked is **workable.**

world. The earth on which we live and the people on it.

worm. 1. A small, creeping, crawling animal without legs or with very small legs. 2. To work or go about something by slow and cunning means, as "He wormed the secret out of me".

worry *(wor'-ry)*. 1. To annoy; to trouble. 2. To be troubled about something. 3. Something about which you worry is a worry.

worse. In "The doctor said that the sick man was worse", worse means less well than before. His sickness was more severe.

worship *(wor'-ship)*. 1. To adore; to think a great deal of. 2. To go to church, chapel, etc.

worth. 1. Value expressed in terms of money; a thing is worth what it costs to buy it. 2. Worth often means excellent qualities, as in the sentence "He is a boy of worth". 3. If a man is said to be worth so many thousands, it means that he owns that amount of money.

worthy *(wor'-thy).* Having excellent qualities, as "He is a worthy man".

wound. 1. An injury to the body in which the skin is broken. 2. The past tense of **wind**.

wrangle *(wran'-gle).* To quarrel and argue.

wrap. 1. To put a cover round a thing. 2. A covering used by women to put round their shoulders.

wrath. Great anger or rage.

wreath. A circle made of flowers and leaves.

wreck. 1. The sinking of a ship; the breaking-up of a ship. 2. The shell of a wrecked ship. 3. To destroy or spoil anything completely, as "The strong wind wrecked the tents" and "The illness wrecked his life".

wren. A small brown song-bird.

wrench. 1. To twist and pull at the same time. 2. A sudden twisting, pulling motion. 3. A tool which grasps and turns nuts and bolts.

wrestle *(wres'-tle).* 1. To grip a person round the body and try to throw him to the ground. 2. To struggle with, as "Tom wrestled with the problem but could not solve it".

wretch. 1. A bad person, as "It served him right for he is a wretch". 2. A very sad, miserable person, as "The poor wretch had not a penny with which to bless himself".

wriggle *(wrig'-gle).* To twist and turn. A worm wriggles.

wring. To twist and squeeze out water from. When you have used a face cloth, you wring it out.

wrinkle *(wrin'-kle).* A crease, usually on the face, as "His forehead was a mass of wrinkles".

wrist. The joint between the hand and arm.

write. 1. To make letters, words or figures on paper, etc., with a pen or pencil. 2. To compose a piece of literature, as a **writer** does.

writhe. To twist and turn about because of pain, anger, etc.

wrong. 1. Evil, bad. 2. An evil or unjust deed. 3. Mistaken; incorrect.

wry. Twisted, as "He made a wry face when he tasted the sour apple".

X

X-rays *(X'-rays)*. Invisible rays something like light rays which can penetrate any substance but lead. They can leave a record on a photographic plate and so show us what the inside of something, such as the human body, looks like.

xylophone *(xy'-lo-phone)*. A musical instrument with a series of bars of different lengths, each of which gives a different note when struck. It is played by striking it with small wooden hammers.

Y

yacht. A sailing boat, steamboat or motor boat used for pleasure and racing.

yak. An ox with long hair which lives in Asia.

yard. 1. A measure of three feet. 2. A small piece of ground adjacent to a house, factory, etc.

yarn. 1. Thread that is ready for weaving or knitting. 2. A story.

yawn. To gape; to open the mouth wide without wanting to, through sleepiness.

year. A period of time, usually 365 days. Every four years, however, the year has 366 days and is called leap year.

yearling *(year'-ling)*. An animal between one and two years old.

yearly *(year'-ly)*. Happening every year; once a year; from year to year.

yearn. To have a great longing.

yeast. A substance consisting of a great many small living cells. Yeast causes fermentation and it also causes dough to rise and become light and airy.

yell. 1. To cry or shout with a sharp noise. 2. The noise made by such a cry.

yellow *(yel'-low)*. A colour. Lemons are yellow.

yelp. The bark of a dog, etc.

yesterday *(yes'-ter-day)*. The day before to-day.

yet. 1. Nevertheless, as "That is not bad, yet I think it might be a little better". 2. Up to the present, as "He has not come yet". 3. Still, as "She is here yet".

yew. An evergreen tree.

yield. 1. To give up; to surrender, as "The beaten soldiers yielded to the conquerors". 2. To produce, as "That field has yielded a good crop of oats".

yoke. A wooden frame which holds two animals together for working. 2. A frame placed across the shoulders for carrying pails, baskets, etc.

yolk. The yellow part of an egg.

yonder *(yon'-der)*. Over there.

youth. 1. Young people. 2. A young man; the time of a person's life when he or she is young.

yuletide *(yule'-tide)*. Christmas time.

Z

zeal. Enthusiasm; great interest or devotion; eagerness to do something. A person with zeal is **zealous**.

zebra *(ze'-bra)*. An animal much like a horse, but having bands of black and white on the body.

zenith *(zen'-ith)*. 1. The part of the heavens that is directly overhead. 2. A thing is said to have reached its zenith when it has reached its highest or best position.

zephyr *(zeph'-yr)*. A gentle breeze.

zero *(ze'-ro)*. Nothing; nought.

zest. Relish; great enjoyment, as "He ate his dinner with zest for it was very tasty".

zigzag *(zig'-zag)*. Turning sharply in and out; bent from side to side.

zinc. A soft white metal.

zodiac *(zo'-di-ac)*. An imaginary (not real) circle in the heavens divided into twelve equal parts, called signs of the Zodiac.

zone. A district; an area; a belt on the earth, such as a war zone or the torrid zone.

zoo. A place where wild animals are kept in captivity.

zoology *(zo-ol'-o-gy)*. The study of animals.

Zulu *(Zu'-lu)*. A member of the great Bantu tribe of South Africa.

APPENDIX

ABBREVIATIONS IN COMMON USE

A.B.   Able-bodied Seaman.
A.D.   *Anno Domini* (The year of our Lord).
a.m.   *Ante meridiem* (Before·noon).
B.A.   Bachelor of Arts.
B.Sc.   Bachelor of Science.
B.B.C.   British Broadcasting Corporation.
B.C.   Before Christ.
B.E.A.   British European Airways.
B.E.M.   British Empire Medal.
B.O.A.C.   British Overseas Airways Corporation.
B.S.T.   British Summer Time.
Bt.   Baronet.
B.T.U.   British Thermal Unit.
c.c.   Cubic centimetres.
Ch.B.   Bachelor of Surgery.
C.I.D.   Criminal Investigation Department.
C.O.D.   Cash on delivery.
D.D.   Doctor of Divinity.
D.Sc.   Doctor of Science.
D.V.   *Deo volente* (God willing).
e.g.   *exempli gratia* (for example).
E.R.   *Elizabetha Regina* (Elizabeth the Queen).
G.C.   George Cross.
G.M.T.   Greenwich Mean Time.
G.P.O.   General Post Office.
H.C.F.   Highest Common Factor.
H.M.S.   Her Majesty's Ship.
H.R.H.   His (or Her) Royal Highness.
I.N.R.I.   *Iesus Nazarenus Rex Iudæorum* (Jesus of Nazareth, King of the Jews).
I.O.U.   I owe you.
I.Q.   Intelligence quotient.
J.P.   Justice of the Peace.
Kt.   Knight Bachelor.

L.C.M. Least Common Multiple.
M.A. Master of Arts.
M.B. Bachelor of Medicine.
M.P. Member of Parliament.
M.R.C.P. Member of the Royal College of Physicians.
M.R.C.S. Member of the Royal College of Surgeons.
M.C.C. Marylebone Cricket Club.
m.p.h. Miles per hour.
N.B. *Nota bene* (Note well).
N.C.O. Non-commissioned Officer.
No. *Numero* (Number).
N.S.P.C.C. National Society for the Prevention of Cruelty to Children.
O.B.E. Order of the British Empire.
O.H.M.S. On Her Majesty's Service.
O.M. Order of Merit.
P.C. Privy Councillor.
Ph.D. Doctor of Philosophy.
p.m. *Post meridiem* (after noon).
Q.C. Queen's Counsel.
R.N. Royal Navy.
R.S.P.C.A. Royal Society for the Prevention of Cruelty to Animals.
R.I.P. *Requiescat in Pace* (May he rest in peace).
R.S.V.P. *Répondez s'il vous plait* (Answer, if you please).
T.U.C. Trades Union Congress.
U.K. United Kingdom.
U.N.E.S.C.O. United Nations Educational, Scientific and Cultural Organization.
U.N.O. United Nations Organization.
U.S.S.R. Union of Soviet Socialist Republics.
v. *Versus* (against).
V.C. Victoria Cross.
V.I.P. Very Important Person.
W.H.O. World Health Organization.
W.R.A.C. Women's Royal Army Corps.
W.R.N.S. Women's Royal Naval Service.
W.V.S. Women's Voluntary Services.

COMMON FOREIGN PHRASES

a la carte (Fr.)—According to the Bill of Fare.
a la française (Fr.)—In the French fashion.
a la mode (Fr.)—In the fashion.
a votre santé (Fr.)—Good health.
ad hoc (L.)—For this special purpose.
ad infinitum (L.)—To infinity.
ad interum (L.)—In the meanwhile.
ad libitum *or* **ad lib.** (L.)—At pleasure.
ad nauseam (L.)—To the point of disgust.
adsum (L.)—I am here; present (used at roll-call in some schools).
affaire d'honneur (Fr.)—An affair of honour; a duel.
agent provocateur (Fr.)—A secret agent.
amour-propre (Fr.)—Self esteem.
ante meridiem (L.)—Before noon (usually a.m.).
au pair (Fr.)—On mutual terms; exchange of services.
au revoir (Fr.)—Goodbye, till we meet again.
bon marché (Fr.)—Cheaply; a bargain.
bon vivant (Fr.)—A gourmet; someone who likes good food.
bon voyage (Fr.)—A good journey to you.
carte blanche (Fr.)—Full powers.
casus belli (L.)—Something which involves war.
chemin de fer (Fr.)—Railway.
ci-devant (Fr.)—Former.
comme il faut (Fr.)—as it should be.
concierge (Fr.)—A porter or doorkeeper.
corps de ballet (Fr.)—The dancers in a ballet.
corps diplomatique (Fr.)—The diplomatic corps.
corrigenda (L.)—Things to be corrected.
coup d'état (Fr.)—A stroke of policy.
coup de grâce (Fr.)—A finishing blow.
de facto (L.)—Actually; in fact.
Dei Gratia (L.)—By the grace of God.
de jure (L.)—In law; by right.
de novo (L.)—Anew.

Deo Gratias (L.)—Thanks to God.

de profundis (L.)—Out of the depths.

de rigueur (Fr.)—Necessary.

de trop (Fr.)—Superfluous; not wanted.

Dieu et mon droit (Fr.)—God and my right (the motto of the British crown).

distingué (Fr.)—Of distinguished appearance.

dramatis personae (L.)—The characters in a drama.

en casserole (Fr.)—Cooked in a covered pot with vegetables.

en famille (Fr.)—In the family; informal.

en fête (Fr.)—On holiday; celebrating.

en masse (Fr.)—In a body.

en route (Fr.)—On the way.

entente cordiale (Fr.)—Friendly understanding between nations.

entre nous (Fr.)—Between ourselves.

erratum (L.)—Error.

espirit de corps (Fr.)—Team Spirit.

et cetera (L.)—**(etc.)** And the rest; and so on.

ex officio (L.)—By virtue of his office.

fait accompli (Fr.)—A thing already done.

faux pas (Fr.)—A false step; a mistake.

femme de chambre (Fr.)—A chambermaid.

force majeure (Fr.)—Overwhelming force.

gourmet (Fr.)—(See bon vivant.) One who likes good food.

haute finance (Fr.)—High finance.

haut monde (Fr.)—High society.

hic jacet (L.)—Here lies.

Hoch! (Ger.)—Your health.

hoi polloi (Grk.)—The people.

hors de combat (Fr.)—Out of condition to fight.

ich dien (Ger.)—I serve.

ici on parle français (Fr.)—Here French is spoken.

id est (L.)—**(i.e.)** That is.

in camera (L.)—In secret.

infra dignitatem (L.)—**(infra dig.)** Below one's dignity.

in loco parentis (L.)—In place of a parent.

in situ (L.)—In its original position.

in statu quo (L.)—In the former state.

in toto (L.)—Entirely.

ipso facto (L.)—Obvious from the facts.

laissez faire (F.)—Let alone.

locum tenens (L.)—A deputy or a substitute.

maître d'hotel (Fr.)—Hotel proprietor; sometimes used for head-waiter.

mal de mer (Fr.)—Seasickness.

modus operandi (L.)—Manner of working.

mot juste (Fr.)—The exact word.

multum in parvo (L.)—Much in little.

née (Fr.)—Born; her maiden name being.

ne plus ultra (L.)—Nothing further.

nil desperandum (L.)—Nothing despairing.

noblesse oblige (Fr.)—Nobility imposes obligations.

nom de guerre (Fr.)—An assumed name.

nota bene (L.)—**(N.B.)** Note well.

nouveau riche (Fr.)—One who is newly enriched; an upstart.

nulli secundus (L.)—Second to none.

obit (L.)—He (or she) died.

on dit (Fr.)—They say.

ora pro nobis (L.)—Pray for us.

outré (Fr.)—extravagant; in bad taste.

par excellence (Fr.)—Of very high standard.

par exemple (Fr.)—For example.

parole d'honneur (Fr.)—Word of honour.

per annum (L.)—By the year.

per ardua ad astra (L.)—Through hardship to the stars (motto of the R.A.F.)

per capita (L.)—Per head.

per centum (L.)—**(per cent)** By the hundred.

per diem (L.)—By the day.

per interim (L.)—Meanwhile.

per mensem (L.)—By the month.

persona grata (L.)—An acceptable person.

piéce de résistance (Fr.)—The principal course (at dinner) or scene (at the theatre).

pied-à-terre (Fr.)—Temporary lodging.

post meridiem (L.)—Afternoon (usually p.m.).

poste restante (Fr.)—Post Office department where letters are kept till called for.

post mortem (L.)—After death.

prima ballerina (It.)—The principal dancer.

prima donna (It.)—The principal singer.

pro forma (L.)—As a matter of form.

COMMON FOREIGN PHRASES

pro patria (L.)—For one's country.
pro rata (L.)—In proportion.
quid pro quo (L.)—One thing for another of equal value; tit for tat.
quod erat demonstrandum (L.)—(**Q.E.D.**) Which was to be demonstrated.
quod erat faciendum (L.)—(**Q.E.F.**) Which was to be done.
quod vide (L.)—(**q.v.**) Which see.
raison d'être (Fr.)—Reason for existence.
rara avis (L.)—A rare bird; something prodigious.
reductio ad absurdum (L.)—Reduction of an argument to the absurd.
rendez-vous (Fr.)—A meeting place; an appointment.
répondez s'il vous plait (Fr.)—(R.S.V.P.) Please reply.
résume (Fr.)—A summary.
sang-froid (Fr.)—Cold blood; calmness; coolness.
sauve qui peut (Fr.)—Save himself who can; every man for himself.
savoire faire (Fr.)—Knowing how to do; skill; tact.
sic (L.)—Thus.
sine die (L.)—Without date; indefinitely.
sotto-voce (It.)—In a whisper or in an undertone.
status quo (L.)—As things were.
stet (L.)—Let it stand.
sub judice (L.)—Under consideration.
sub rosa (L.)—Under the rose; secretly.
table d'hote (Fr.)—A set meal.
tempus fugit (L.)—Time flies.
terra firma (L.)—Solid earth.
tête-à-tête (Fr.)—Head to head; a conversation between two people.
tour de force (Fr.)—A feat of strength or skill.
tout ensemble (Fr.)—The whole taken together; the general effect.
versus (L.)—(**v.**) Against.
via (L.)—By way of.
vice versa (L.)—The other way round.
via-a-vis (Fr.)—Face to face; an opposite number.
viva voce (L.)—By the living voice; oral.
vox populi (L.)—The voice of the people.
wagon-lit (Fr.)—A sleeping-coach on a railway.
Note.—Fr.=French; L.=Latin; Ger.=German; Grk.=Greek; It.=Italian.

ETYMOLOGY OF PLACE NAMES

ABAD (Persian)—a dwelling. Hyderabad.
ABER (Celtic)—a confluence. Aberdeen.
ARD (Celtic)—high. Ardrossan.
ATH (Irish)—a ford. Athlone.
AVON (Celtic)—a river. Avon.
BAD (Teutonic)—a bath. Baden.
BALLY (Irish)—a village. Balmoral.
BEDD (Welsh)—a grave. Beddgelert.
BEN (Gaelic)—a mountain. Ben Nevis.
BOROUGH (Anglo-Saxon)—a hill. Ingleborough.
BURGH (Teutonic)—a fortified place. Edinburgh.
BURN (Scotch)—a brook. Bannockburn.
BY (Scandinavian)—a dwelling. Derby, Rugby.
CAM (Celtic)—crooked. Cam (River).
CARRICK (Gaelic)—a rock. Carrick-on-Suir.
CASTER, CHESTER, CESTER (Latin)—a camp. Lancaster.
CHEAP and CHIPPING (A.S.)—a market. Cheapside.
COLN (Latin)—a colony. Lincoln.
COMBE (A.S.)—a hollow between hills. Wycombe.
DAL (Scandinavian)—a dale. Kendal.
DUM, DUN (Gaelic)—a fortress. Dumfries, Dunstable.
ECCLES (Greek)—a church. Eccleston.
ESK (Gaelic)—water. Esk, Exe.
FELL (Norse)—a mountain. Scafell.
FOLK (A.S.)—people. Norfolk.
GATE (Teutonic)—a road. Reigate.
GLEN (Gaelic)—a narrow valley. Glenmore.
GORM (Gaelic)—green. Cairngorm.
HALL (Teutonic)—a stone house. Walsall.
HAM (A.S.)—a home. Buckingham.
HAR (Teutonic)—the army. Harwich.
HITHE (A.S.)—a haven. Greenhithe.
HOLM (Scandinavian)—an island in a lake. Stockholm.
HURST (A.S.)—a wood. Lyndhurst.

471

ETYMOLOGY OF PLACE NAMES

INVER (Gaelic)—mouth of river. Inverness.

KENN (Gaelic)—a head. Kenmore.

KIL (Gaelic)—a hermit's cell. Kilmarnock.

LEA (A.S.)—a meadow. Hadleigh.

LLAN (Welsh)—a church. Llandaff.

LOCH, LOUGH (Gaelic)—a lake.

LOW and LAW (A.S.)—a rising ground. Hounslow.

MARK (Teutonic)—a boundary. Denmark.

MERE, MOOR (A.S.)—a lake, marsh. Mersey, Windermere.

MINSTER (A.S.)—a monastic foundation. Westminster.

MOR (Celtic)—the sea. Glamorgan.

MULL (Gaelic)—a headland. Mull of Cantyre.

NANT (Celtic)—a brook. Nantwich.

NESS or NAZE (Scandinavian)—a nose. Dungeness.

OLD, ELD, ALT (Teutonic)—old. Althorpe.

POLIS (Greek)—a city. Sebastopol.

PONT (Latin)—a bridge. Pontefract.

PORT (Latin)—a harbour. Southport.

ROS, ROSS (Celtic)—a promontory. Kinross.

SCAR (Scandinavian)—a cliff. Scarborough.

SET (A.S.)—a seat. Dorset.

SEX (A.S.)—Saxons. Essex, Sussex.

SIERRA (Latin)—a saw. Sierra Nevada.

STAPLE (A.S.)—a store. Barnstaple.

STEAD (A.S.)—a town. Hampstead.

STOC, STOKE, STOW (A.S.)—a stockaded place. Tavistock.

STRATH (Gaelic)—a broad valley. Strathmore.

TAIN (Gaelic)—a river. Tyne.

TAM (Celtic)—still, smooth. Thames.

THORPE (Norse)—a village. Burnham Thorpe.

TOFT (Danish)—an enclosure. Lowestoft.

TOR (Celtic)—a tower-like rock. Torquay.

TRE (Welsh)—a dwelling. Coventry.

VILLE (Latin)—an abode. Yeovil.

WEALD, WOLD (German)—a wood. Cotswolds.

WORTH (A.S.)—a farm. Worthing.

MADE AND PRINTED IN GREAT BRITAIN BY A. WHEATON AND CO. LTD., EXETER